BOWHUNTER'S ENCYCLOPEDIA

BOWHUNTER'S ENCYCLOPEDIA

Practical, Easy-to-Find Answers to Your Bowhunting Questions

Dwight Schuh

Stackpole Books

Published by
STACKPOLE BOOKS
Cameron and Kelker Streets
P.O. Box 1831
Harrisburg, PA 17105

Printed in the U.S.A.

Library of Congress Cataloging-in-Publication Data

Schuh, Dwight R.
    Bowhunter's encyclopedia.

    Includes index.
    1. Hunting with bow and arrow—Dictionaries. I. Title.
SK36.S37   1987   799.2′15′0321   87-6473
ISBN 0-8117-0258-8

To my wife, Laura, who loves me for better. And for worse.

Many Thanks

My thanks go out to the many equipment makers who've given me time and products for use in conjunction with this book, and also to the many archery experts who've shared their time and knowledge. Throughout the book, I've given credit to them.

My special thanks go to my friend Pat Miller, who has invested many hours in the darkroom and behind a camera for my sake. My thanks also go to my wife, Laura, for her patience and help putting this book together, and to my daughters, Emily and Margie, for their patience with their dad.

A

AIMING METHODS Aiming can be classified in two general ways—without sights (bare bow) or with sights. Neither method is inherently better than the other as long as you aim quickly and spontaneously.

Regardless of method, you should shoot with both eyes open. To do that you must shoot on the side with the dominant eye (see Dominant Eye). Two eyes give you a triangulation effect (the same principle used in a range finder), which is the source of depth perception. If you close one eye, you eliminate depth perception. Also, with one eye closed, you can't judge arrow flight or trajectory. I normally shoot right-handed, but because of shoulder problems I've shot left-handed a little. I can do it all right, but because my right eye is dominant, I have to close it to aim with my left eye. So I have no idea what my arrows are doing from the time they leave the bow until they hit the target.

Aiming without Sights

Instinctive Aiming. Basically, with this method you look at the target, draw your bow, and, when everything "feels" right, you shoot. You don't purposely judge range and use a sight or other reference for aiming. Not consciously, at least.

Many instinctive shooters say they subconsciously picture the trajectory of the arrow to the target, an instinct often compared to throwing a ball. If you're throwing a baseball to home plate from centerfield, for example, you obviously picture a much higher arc on the ball than if you're throwing in from second base. With an arrow, the longer the shot, the higher you instinctively "throw" the arrow. My first half dozen years in archery I shot instinctively, never consciously aiming with any part of my arrow or bow. However, I'm sure that I, and other instinctive shooters, mentally form some kind of sight picture relating the arrow point to the target.

"Instinct" may not accurately describe this shooting method, because the ability must be learned. Arrow trajectory depends on arrow weight, bow weight, draw length, fletching size, and so forth, and you have to shoot a specific bow setup regularly to develop your instincts with it.

Most instinctive-shooting advocates say it eliminates the need for range estimation in the field. If you've shot enough, you automatically aim correctly regardless of distance. It can be much faster than any other aiming method, too. With practice, many instinctive shooters can hit flying targets—and running game—

Instinctive shooting, which involves no sights or other aiming aids, allows a quick draw and release, and many hunters prefer this method over sight shooting. It's most common among recurve and longbow shooters, but some compound bow shooters also shoot instinctively.

consistently. That's virtually impossible with methodical sight-aiming methods.

The spontaneous, natural quality of instinctive shooting is well suited to some bowhunting situations, and many of today's best bowhunters shoot this way. It's not the best method for everybody, however, because you have to shoot regularly from varied distances to keep your ability honed. If you live in town and do 90 percent of your practice at 20 yards in your back yard, you can't really perfect your skill.

And some people may never develop the ability to shoot well this way. Fred Bear, one of the most successful bowhunters of this century, often emphasized that instinctive shooting requires intense concentration at the moment of release. I believe that's true. In my instinctive-shooting days, I practiced for an hour or more every day at various ranges. I almost never missed a paper plate out to 30 yards or so. Yet I missed untold numbers of deer at that range, and an elk or two as well.

Was it because I failed to practice? No, I believe it was because I simply couldn't concentrate well enough under the intense pressure of hunting situations, and that's a problem common to many hunters. In addition, I suspect that some people simply don't have the eye-hand-mind coordination required to become good instinctive shooters. For them—and me—other shooting methods work better.

Gap Aiming. In the gap method, the head of your arrow becomes the front sight. To aim, you judge the distance to the target and hold your arrow point a predetermined amount above or below the target. In essence, it's a crude form of sight shooting. At the same time, it's akin to instinctive shooting because it takes practice—to develop the ability to judge range and to gauge the right gap for various shooting distances. Few shooters use this method any more. They either shoot instinctively, ignoring the arrow point altogether, or they shoot with bowsights.

Point-of-Aim Method. This method was commonly used by target archers before the advent of bowsights. It's like spot bowling, in which you don't look at the bowling pins but rather at a specific board on the alley. If you roll your ball over that board, the ball will hook into the pocket and you'll get a strike. In shooting a bow this way, you don't look at the target at all. Instead you aim at a spot somewhere between yourself and the target or, if the target is beyond your point-on distance, above the target. Years ago this was a common aiming method, but it's rarely used today.

Aiming with Sights

Bowsights have become common in modern bowhunting because they greatly simplify aiming. Some people find it hard to aim when they've got nothing to aim with, which is the case in bare-bow shooting. A bowsight gives you a definite reference point to align with the target. The value of sights can be seen not only in their popularity among bowhunters, but in their efficiency in target archery. Sight shooters and bare-bow shooters are placed in separate classes because bare-bow shooters as a class can't compete with sight shooters.

In one respect, sight shooting can be considered instinctive, because you must develop the instinct to judge range instantly. Many sight shooters, in fact, do not consciously judge range at all. When they draw on an animal, they hold their sights below the target and then slowly raise the bow—or start above and lower the bow—until the sight picture looks right, and then they release. Whichever way it's done, this ability requires much practice in the field at varied ranges.

On the other hand, you can make sight shooting a very mechanical process, by deliberately judging the range and picking the sight pin for that range.

With practice, you can learn to judge distances out to 50 yards or more with amazing accuracy. Any time you're walking along, on a city street or backcountry trail, practice guessing distances to nearby objects and then pacing them off. To develop a quick eye, practice while moving. For even greater accuracy, stop to analyze the distance. Rather than guessing the distance in one lump, segment it, say in five-yard intervals, and you'll become a lot more proficient.

With an accurate range finder, such as the Ranging 80/2, you can measure the precise distance to an animal. Then, if your sights are set correctly and your form is good, you should not miss. Of course, it's not as simple as it sounds. Many animals won't hold still long enough for you to use the range finder, and also a range finder doesn't work well on steep uphill and downhill angles. (For details, see Trajectory.)

Because sight shooting can be more systematic and requires less concentration and hand-mind coordination than instinctive shooting, many shooters find they're more accurate on game, especially under high-pressure situations, with sights. On the other hand, shooting with sights generally is slower and doesn't lend itself to quick, spontaneous situations. (For details, see Bowsights.)

ALABAMA Alabama has an area of 51,609 square miles. Generally, the northern two thirds has a higher human population and

Shooting with sights is a much more deliberate process than shooting bare bow. As Gale Cavallin does here, sight shooters first estimate yardage, and then pick a sight pin and aim carefully.

lower deer densities, and the southern third, roughly south of Montgomery, has fewer people, large land ownerships, and high deer numbers. All private land in Alabama is posted by law, and permission is required to hunt. Some large timber companies allow public hunting for a modest fee, but the trend on private land in Alabama has been toward large-scale hunting leases, and private clubs or commercial hunting operations now control much of the best hunting. More than two dozen state wildlife areas totaling 657,000 acres are open to public hunting, and the U.S. Forest Service and other agencies administer more than 500,000 acres open to the public.

Deer

For the past several years, Alabama has had an average of 200,000 deer hunters, with an estimated 50,000 of them archers. The average annual harvest has been 157,000 deer, and the highest harvest on record, which took place in the 1981–1982 season, was 202,000 deer. No separate figures are available for archery harvest or success rate.

In 1940, Alabama's deer population was estimated at 18,000 animals; by 1950, it had shrunk to 3,000. Following extensive stocking programs and other enhancement efforts in the 1950s, deer numbers built rapidly, and now the population is estimated at 1.3 million. Whitetails are abundant in all counties. Bow seasons are liberal in some counties, running from October through January. The bag limit generally is one buck per day. Alabama has produced only one Boone and Crockett buck, which scored about 175.

Other Game

Turkeys. Alabama is a major turkey state, with the best hunting in the hardwood uplands of the southwest. There are both spring and fall seasons.

Small Game. Squirrels and rabbits are hunted throughout the state, and annual combined harvest runs into the millions of animals.

Contact. Department of Conservation and Natural Resources, Administrative Division, Montgomery, AL 36130-1901.

ALASKA This huge state covers 586,000 square miles. Since most of the land is public, getting permission to hunt isn't the problem — getting *to* a hunting area in the first place is. Bush planes are involved in virtually all big-game hunting in Alaska. River floating also provides access to good game country, although that normally also involves flying to get to a river. Nonresidents must hire a guide to hunt for Dall sheep and grizzly bears. Other species can be hunted unattached, and drop-camp hunts for moose and caribou have become popular with bowhunters. Bowhunting-only seasons and areas are virtually nonexistent in Alaska except for the Pipeline Corridor (Dalton Highway) from the Yukon River north to Prudhoe Bay; only bowhunting is allowed in a ten-mile-wide strip, five miles on each side of the highway.

Simply getting to a hunting area in Alaska can be a challenge. Virtually all Alaskan hunting involves the use of bush planes. *Photo courtesy Jay Massey.*

Big Game

Sitka Deer. The Sitka blacktail is the only species of deer in Alaska. Sitka deer are native to southeastern Alaska, but they have been transplanted and are now well established near Yakutat, on Prince William Sound southeast of Anchorage, and on Kodiak and Afognak islands. Their range generally coincides with coastal spruce and hemlock forests, where big trees keep most of the ground free of snow so that food is available throughout the winter. One exception exists on Kodiak Island, where deer have thrived in the absence of big timber.

Seasons in several units run from August 1 through December 31, and the bag limit is four or five deer per year, depending on the unit. In units where populations are low, either the season is closed or only limited buck hunting is allowed. Most of the harvest comes from Units 2 and 4 (southeastern islands) and Unit 8 (Kodiak and Afognak islands). (For details, see Sitka Deer.)

Caribou. These are probably the most popular animals for visiting bowhunters. The average bull weighs little more than 400 pounds, so hunters can kill and pack caribou reasonable distances, which can't be said for moose, and caribou live in open country where they're visible enough to keep hunting excitement high. Caribou seasons open as early as July 1 on the North Slope and in August in the rest of the state. Most bowhunters hunt in August and September when they find the animals on the open tundra, either north of the tree line on the North Slope or above timberline in timbered country such as the Alaskan Peninsula. (For details, see Caribou.)

Moose. The Alaska-Yukon moose of Alaska are the largest members of the deer family in the world. Many hunters drop-camp hunt for moose, but the huge size of these animals limits how far from the nearest transportation you can kill one. River floating has become a popular approach to moose hunting because rivers flow through some of the best moose habitat—that is, lowlands with lots of willows—and the river offers a way to get the meat out without miles of packing. (An excellent book on this topic is *Bowhunting Alaska's Wild Rivers* by Jay Massey.) Moose seasons open August 1 in some units and early to mid-September in many others. Moose rut from mid-September through October, and calling can be the best way to hunt at that time. (For details, see Moose.)

Bears. Nonresidents can't legally hunt brown and grizzly bears unless accompanied by a guide. These animals can be hunted both spring and fall. The guide requirement doesn't apply to black bears. They thrive throughout most of the state, and seasons are generous. In some units the season is open year-round, and in others it runs from September 1 through the following June. Limit is one to three bears, depending on area.

Dall Sheep. This is the only subspecies of *Ovis* found in Alaska. Nonresidents must hire guides, and the price of sheep hunts is high. The season opens August 10 and runs through September 20 in most areas. (For details, see Sheep.)

Mountain Goat. These cliff dwellers live primarily in the vertical mountains above tidewater in southeastern Alaska. Do-it-yourself bowhunters commonly hire a bush pilot to drop them off on a beach, and then they backpack straight up to alpine goat country. In some places, large bays and inlets send fingers among the mountains, and you can use a small boat to cruise these calm waters and glass for goats from the water and then hike up to the animals. No matter how you do it, goat hunting can be an ordeal. Most goat seasons open August 1 and extend through December. Some hunters say the easier way to hunt goats is to wait until December when deep snow forces the animals to low country near the beaches. (For details, see Mountain Goat.)

Elk. Alaska's hunting reputation hasn't been built around elk, but good populations of Roosevelt elk are hunted on Afognak and Raspberry islands. Seasons open either August 1 or October 1, depending on unit.

Musk Oxen. These animals are hunted on Nunivak and Nelson islands, and a limited number of permits are issued by drawing only.

Bison. Limited hunting is permitted in several units of eastcentral Alaska with a year-round season (July 1 to June 30).

Other Game

In addition to these major big-game species, Alaska offers hunting for wolves, wolverine, and a variety of other predators and small game such as ptarmigan and snowshoe hares.

Contact. Department of Fish and Game, P.O. Box 3-2000, Juneau, AK 99802.

ALBERTA Alberta, with an area of 255,285 square miles, is particularly noted for huge whitetails, elk, and bighorn sheep. It has great potential for trophy animals, and bow seasons are reasonably generous. Nonresidents cannot legally hunt without a guide.

Big Game

Deer. An estimated 6,000 bowhunters kill about 600 deer each year in Alberta. Big-game zones 4, 5, and 6 encompass the backbone of the Rocky Mountains from alpine country at 10,000 feet down to forested foothills. Some whitetails live in the bottomlands, but this is primarily mule deer country. Deer numbers are good but not outstanding throughout the mountain zones. The Boone and Crockett world-record nontypical mule deer, with a score of 355²/₈, was killed near Chip Lake in 1926, but few other huge bucks have showed up since then. However, bowhunters have taken a number of Pope and Young mule deer.

The southeast corner is primarily prairie grasslands and grainfields with deer cover restricted to river bottoms. North of the prairies toward Edmonton, aspen parklands are prevalent. Whitetails predominate throughout eastern Alberta; they're abundant in suitable cover, and they extend as far north as the Peace River. Most of the northern one third of Alberta consists of flat spruce country and muskeg, which isn't good habitat for deer.

The bowhunting-only zones around Edmonton, Calgary, and Banff Park produce some huge whitetails. A bow season of ten days to three weeks precedes the firearms season

throughout the province. Again, nonresidents must be accompanied by a licensed guide.

Elk. Alberta has an estimated 20,000 elk and an annual harvest of about 1,300. Those numbers are small compared to some states, yet Alberta ranks third in trophies entered in Boone and Crockett. In other words, trophy potential is quite high. Many of the best bulls recorded from Alberta have been killed by rifle hunters in late seasons after the elk get snowed out of Banff and Jasper provincial parks. A few huge bulls are killed early in the year, however. The bow zone south of Banff is particularly known for big bulls in the 350 class and higher. The bow season there runs from September through November. In other elk areas, the bow season runs for one to two weeks prior to the general rifle season. It falls in early September, during the rut.

Other Big Game. Alberta has produced many of the largest bighorn sheep ever taken. All the northern and mountain zones offer moose hunting. Black bear hunting is excellent in some areas. In the spring, hunters along the Peace River sometimes spot several dozen bears a day as the bears climb trees to eat buds, and spring float hunts have become very popular. Alberta also has spring and fall grizzly bear seasons, as well as good cougar hunting. The province has limited mountain goat and antelope hunting.

Contact. Energy & Natural Resources, Fish and Wildlife Division, Main Floor, North Tower, Petroleum Plaza, 9945-108 Street, Edmonton, AB, Canada T5K 2G6.

ANCHOR POINT One time a friend of mine complained that he couldn't hit anything with his bow. Sometimes he shot low, sometimes high, sometimes who knows where? He asked for help, so I watched him shoot a few arrows.

"Where's your anchor point?" I asked.

"Anchor point? What's that? I just pull back to my ear and let 'er fly."

Definition of Anchor

An anchor point is the spot at which you hold the bowstring at full draw. You can choose any one of a dozen methods for anchoring. The technique itself doesn't count. What does count is that your anchor position be consistent from one shot to another. If it varies even slightly, your arrows will fly everywhere but where you're aiming—just as my friend's did.

To put it another way, your anchor point is the rear sight of your bowshooting system, and it serves the same purpose as the rear sight on a rifle. You can imagine how inaccurate you'd be if your rifle had a loose rear sight that wobbled to a new position after each shot. You'd spray bullets all over the target.

The same thing happens when your anchor point varies. It must be solid and consistent, and that's true whether you shoot with sights or instinctively. For your "instinct" to work correctly, the relationship of the nock and head end of the arrow must be the same on every shot.

In addition to developing a solid anchor system, some hunters who shoot with bowsights install a peep sight in the bowstring as a secondary rear sight. (For details, see Peep Sight.)

Jim Pickering demonstrates a common anchor point—the tip of the index finger at the corner of the mouth. Pickering also presses the big knuckle of his index finger against his cheekbone, and lays the bowstring lightly against the side of his nose.

Anchoring Methods

Corner of the Mouth. Many bowhunters anchor by placing the tip of the index finger at the corner of the mouth. Some shooters have a sharp tooth they anchor against, and others just place the tip of the finger at the edge of the lips. You have to develop your own system that works best for you.

Many archers also use secondary pressure points to assure that the anchor is solid. For example, famous archer Jim Pickering presses the big knuckle of his index finger up under his cheekbone, and in addition he lays the bowstring lightly against the tip of his nose. That gives him three anchor check points—corner of mouth, cheekbone, nose—to assure perfect string alignment every shot.

Some shooters use the index finger at the corner of the mouth, and then they hook the thumb on that hand around behind their neck. The thumb pulling against the neck gives the string hand solid support.

Instinctive shooters commonly anchor at the corner of the mouth with the middle finger rather than the index finger. That "high anchor," as it's sometimes called, brings the arrow closer to the eye so that the arrow flies closer to the line of sight.

To carry that concept even further, some hunters forego the common Mediterranean draw (two fingers under the arrow, one over) and use an Apache draw (three fingers under the arrow). (For more details, see Apache Draw.) With three fingers under, they then anchor with the index finger at the corner of the mouth, or to carry the concept to the extreme, with the middle finger at the corner of the mouth. That brings the arrow shaft very close to the eye for a "gun barreling" effect. It's a deadly anchor method, especially for close-range, instinctive shooting. The point-on distance, however, is very close, so it's not well suited to shooting at longer distances. (For details, see Point-On).

Under the Chin. Many target archers, as well as bowhunters who shoot with bowsights, use this system. They press the big thumb knuckle

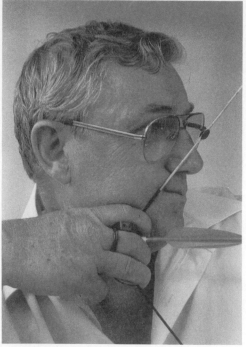

Some sight shooters anchor low, either under the chin or at the back of the jaw.

Release aids offer many anchoring options. Using a rope release, Jim Pickering prefers to hold his hand vertically and to anchor with the knuckles behind his jawbone. It doesn't matter exactly how you anchor, as long as you always do it the same way.

into the soft area just behind the chin bone. To supplement this anchor point, many also use a kisser button on the string (for details, see Kisser), and they may also lay the string lightly against the tip of the nose. That gives three checkpoints for a consistent hold. Because this system places the arrow well below the line of sight, it's not well suited to instinctive shooting, particularly at short range. It's used almost exclusively by sight shooters.

Anchoring with a Release Aid. Mechanical release aids come in so many configurations, it's impossible to prescribe one "right" way to anchor. With wrist-strap models I anchor with the "V" of my thumb and index finger wedged around the back corner of my jaw. With other models you might press your hand under your chin or against a certain spot on your cheek. It doesn't matter so much *where* you anchor as long as you anchor solidly and consistently from one shot to the next. Many release shooters also use a peep sight on the string as a

secondary checkpoint to assure consistent anchoring.

ANTELOPE *(Antilocapra americana)*. These animals more correctly should be called pronghorns since they're not actually members of the antelope family but a totally separate family, *Antilocapridae*, that includes only one species, the pronghorn. But since most hunters call pronghorns "antelope," I'll follow that convention here.

The Nature of Antelope

Compared to massive animals like elk or big deer, antelope look somewhat elfish. The average pronghorn buck stands about 3 feet high at the shoulder and weighs 100 to 125 pounds on the hoof. Both sexes of antelope have horns, but on females, they are very small. The average buck has 10- to 12-inch horns, and really good bucks have horns 14 inches or longer with pronounced prongs.

Power and Grace. What antelope lack in size, they make up for in beauty and grace. When an antelope walks it doesn't lope or lumber, it tiptoes, like a waiter carrying a trayful of drinks. When it runs, its body appears to be suspended, drifting along on a cushion of air. I've often thought you could put a glass of water on an antelope's back and he could run 30 miles an hour without spilling a drop.

All this grace belies the incredible power underneath. When an antelope turns on the afterburners, energy seems to ripple from the center of the body outward through the shoulders and hips and through the tiny legs right to the hooves, pulsing through the muscles like waves of electricity. I've often been skeptical about reports of antelope running 60 miles an hour, but I don't question whether they're far faster than any other animal in North America.

One time I was driving along a rutted road through the sagebrush when a buck antelope appeared nearby and loped parallel with the road. I speeded up, the buck kept pace. Soon I was hitting 35 miles an hour, about three times faster than I should have been going on that road, and the antelope cruised alongside as if warming up. Suddenly his body rippled with a surge of power and he shot past my truck. From far outside the roadside ditch he uncoiled, hit the middle of the road with an explosion of dust, and with his next contact hit far outside the ditch on the other side. He had to have covered nearly 100 feet with two bounds.

Antelope seem to do nothing slowly. They'll be feeding along placidly, and suddenly they'll sprint away as if shot from a gun. Then they'll stop just as suddenly and start feeding again. Their movements are unpredictable and insectlike, and their markings—delicate and intricate, tan and white with black on the muzzle and horns—heighten the insect image.

Tough to Hunt. Antelope have taken a back seat to other animals in popularity among bowhunters. For the novice archer viewing his first prairie pronghorn as a tan speck shimmering in the heat waves two miles from any cover, the possibility of getting within bow range seems remote at best. I talked to one newcomer after the second day of Oregon's antelope bow season. "I don't know why I applied for this tag," the man grumbled. "This is crazy. There's no way anybody's going to get within range of an antelope. Look at 'em out there," he said, gesturing toward a small herd grazing halfway across a sagebrush prairie. "I'm going home. This is impossible."

Another deterrent to all-out serious hunting has been difficulty in getting tags, generally limited in number. However, most western states—the Dakotas, Nebraska, Montana, Wyoming, Colorado, New Mexico, Nevada, Utah, Arizona, California, Oregon, and Idaho—hold special bow seasons, and the odds for drawing a tag are comparatively good. Some states—among them Montana, Colorado, and Idaho—have offered unlimited bow licenses for antelope.

Growing Success. With special seasons, bowhunters are taking new interest in antelope, and success is rising. In some areas, bowhunters have a 25 percent success rate, and some take antelope virtually every year. Judd Cooney, an outfitter in Colorado who specializes in antelope, has guided his clients to a solid 80 percent success, and many of his hunters who haven't filled their tags have missed close shots. Cooney's first 51 antelope-hunting clients killed 41 bucks, 37 of which made the Pope and Young record book. Obviously, bowhunters can get within range of those tan dots out on the flats—if they just know how.

Stand Hunting for Antelope

Without question, waterhole stands offer the best chance. Antelope must come to water every day, and since they're daytime animals, they generally won't sneak in to water at night as deer might do. The need to water during the day presents the weakest link in an antelope's chain of survival.

Blind Sites. The most common waterholes are stock tanks scooped into open prairie or desert flats. Most are simply catchbasins for

Judd Cooney killed this huge buck antelope while hunting from a waterhole stand. Cooney wears complete camouflage and blackens his face, and he digs deep blinds where he's hidden in shadows and has plenty of room to shoot. *Photo courtesy Judd Cooney.*

rain and snowmelt, although some could be fed by springs. Windmills that feed stock tanks also present good places for blinds. Some hunters actually climb the windmill towers and wait on small platforms up there, and others build a brush blind at the base of the windmill. In some country you'll find enough trees, most commonly juniper, to place a tree stand near a waterhole.

Unlike deer, which normally jump over fences, antelope commonly crawl under, and they use traditional fence crossings. You can find these by watching animals, or you can walk fencelines to find the worn places where they've gone under. A ground blind can be productive there, and I know hunters who've taken several antelope by hunting from stands placed in juniper trees near fence crossings.

You can check waterholes for tracks, but because antelope are highly visible, you can scout

best with your eyes simply by looking for animals. Watch early in the morning to see where antelope herds go and when they go there.

Optics for Scouting. You've undoubtedly heard or read dozens of stories about the fantastic eyesight of antelope. To really grasp an antelope's seeing power, take the most exaggerated stories you've heard and double them and you're close. Lots of writers say an antelope's eyes are equal to 8x binoculars, but I'd say 10x is more like it. And they not only spot moving objects at a distance, but they'll pick out stationery objects at a half mile. To put yourself on any kind of equal footing with those eyes, you must have high-quality optics. Most serious antelope hunters carry 10x binoculars and supplement that with a 20x spotting scope. I'd count good optical equipment as the most important gear for antelope hunting. (For details, see Optics and Spotting.)

Build a Blind. When you've located a likely waterhole or two, build a blind there. Some hunters like to place their blinds on trails leading to and from the water, but others—Cooney among them—prefer to blind in within shooting range of the water itself.

A good blind is the real secret to collecting an antelope. Not only can antelope see a long way, but they can spot the tiniest movement at close range. You have to be able to draw and shoot without being seen—which is no easy task.

I vividly recall the first antelope I shot at. I was in a shallow blind near a seeping spring in the sagebrush. A lone buck first came into view 2 miles away, and he walked steadily my way for an hour until he stood drinking 25 yards from my blind. Slowly I raised my bow and started to draw. Without even looking up, the buck shot away as if flung from a catapult. By the time I released an arrow, he was 50 yards away and flying. My arrow hit a good 20 feet behind him.

"You can always tell a beginner's blind because he has to raise up to shoot over it," Judd Cooney said. "If you don't have cover behind you, they'll see you every time.

"On the other hand, an antelope looking

from bright sunlight into shadows can't see very well, so I always try to build my blinds so that antelope coming in are looking toward the sun and the hunter is in the shadows. I dig deep pits and dig a seat right into the bank so the hunter is comfortable, and I make the pit deep enough so there's plenty of leg room and bow clearance."

Cooney builds up the back of the blind heavily with grass or sage so the hunter sits in shadows and is not silhouetted, but he leaves the front fairly open for clear shooting. And he always wears, and insists that his hunters wear, dark camouflage including black face paint, so he blends into the shadows. To check a blind like this, walk out to the waterhole and look into the blind from an antelope's point of view. You'll see the spots that need additional work.

Wait for the Shot. Commonly antelope will come to the edge of a waterhole and start to drink, and then they'll jerk their heads up to look around. To get a good shot, you must wait until an animal is drinking heavily. Cooney said he's seen them drink for as long as three minutes without looking up. "They'll drink and drink. If they're looking at you, there's no way you'll get a shot. One of my hunters missed nine shots one day because she was waiting until the animals finished drinking."

Antelope have reasonably good noses, so you should take wind direction into consideration when placing a blind. Even if antelope smell you, however, they often won't run away. One morning two bucks and a doe came in downwind of my blind, and I could tell they smelled me because the hair stood up on their necks and they walked stiff-legged and continually stared in my direction. Still they circled back and forth three times downwind of my blind within 40 yards, and they didn't leave until I shot at one of the bucks.

Hunt the Morning. Morning presents by far the best time to take a waterhole stand. Under normal conditions, animals will start coming to water about 7:00 A.M., and they may continue to come and go all morning until noon or later. The best approach is to get into your

blind before daylight under cover of darkness and stay there until at least noon. Antelope aren't nearly as active in the evening, although occasionally one will still come in then, particularly if animals have been spooked away in the morning.

Stalking

Stalking antelope isn't the simplest hunting task you'll ever attempt, but it can be done under the right circumstances. Steve Gorr, who outfits bowhunts in Wyoming, said his hunters take 10 to 15 antelope every year by stalking.

The Right Country. For good stalking, the country must be right. In expansive, table-flat terrain with ankle-high grass, stalking within bow range of an antelope is, for all practical purposes, impossible. In contrast, some good antelope areas are broken with many draws and ravines and cliffy hills, and the sage and other shrubs and trees offer reasonably good cover. I've often found lone bucks in August hanging out in seemingly marginal habitat consisting of fairly heavy juniper forests broken by small pockets of open sage. Nearly every little opening has its own single buck antelope, and during the heat of day, the antelope bed in the shade of trees at the edges of openings. Here they can be stalked much like deer.

No matter what the terrain, your chances of stalking within bow range of a herd of antelope border on the impossible. You might successfully stalk two antelope together, but lone bucks are the easiest.

Use Your Eyes. Again, as in scouting waterhole antelope, you must use high-power optics. Find a good vantage point at first light in the morning and look until you see a lone buck. Antelope often will walk a fairly straight course, particularly if they're heading to water, and sometimes you can get ahead and ambush them.

In most cases, though, you'll do best to wait for them to bed down. After going to water and feeding, they'll generally lie down about 9:00 or 10:00 A.M. After one buck lay in the shade of a juniper, I lined up with the tree he was lying behind so he couldn't see me and

Mike Cupell stalked and killed this antelope in Arizona. Stalking in terrain like this takes skill and more than a little patience. This is only an average antelope for Arizona, which may be the best trophy state of all. *Photo courtesy Mike Cupell.*

walked within 30 yards of him. Then I missed the shot.

One precaution: when you've watched a buck bed, never assume he'll be obvious as you approach within range. Take time to mark his position carefully and to identify landmarks that will tell you exactly where he is. If you have to poke your head up above the brush to look for your quarry, he'll spot you right away. When you're going against the eyes of an antelope, you have no margin for error.

Peripheral Vision. Also, remember that an antelope's eyes stick out from his head. If he's looking straight away he can't see you, but if he's looking even slightly to the side, he can. His field of view is about 270 degrees, so he virtually has eyes in the back of his head. You must stay fully out of sight, and move very slowly to keep from being seen, or move only when he's looking straight away. (For more details, see Stalking.)

Flagging

Curiosity. With their great eyes, antelope instantly notice any slight object out of place, and because they're curious they often come on the run to investigate. The trick of flagging has been written about many times and it does work.

One time in Montana I saw a couple of antelope bucks walking by 200 yards out. They weren't stalkable right there, so I hid in the sage and waved my hanky. One of the bucks instantly broke my way and trotted within 35 yards, where he stopped and stared. The only problem was that he was looking right at me, and as soon as I released the arrow, the buck was flying. My arrow hit where he'd been standing, but he was at least 30 feet away by then. Flagging like that works well enough for a rifleman, but for a bowhunter, it leaves something to be desired.

Tip-ups. A bowhunter needs something to draw the antelope's attention away from him. Cal Coziah, an Idaho bowhunter who's taken many antelope, uses the flagging trick, but with a different twist. By scouting he discerns general travel routes where antelope come and go from sage hills to fields to feed. He doesn't hunt the fields but rather the trails leading to the fields.

Early in the morning he blinds in near one of

these routes. He digs a pit just deep enough to get his feet down when he sits on the ground, and then he stands to shoot. Near his blind he rigs a springy rod, much like an ice fisherman's tip-up, with a white flag attached. He says a steel radio antenna works well. He puts one of these on each side of his blind, then runs a fishing line from the tip-ups to his blind. As an antelope walks by, Coziah pulls the line to the flag nearest the animal. The flag flips into view and instantly catches the pronghorn's attention, and Coziah, off to the side, has time to shoot at the distracted animal.

"I've had four and five antelope walk by, and when that thing went up, they stopped so fast they just piled into each other," Coziah said.

He warns not to use too big a flag, just a little ribbon four to five inches long. Too much will scare the antelope rather than stop him. One time as an antelope came near the blind, Coziah released one of his tip-ups and the buck spooked and jumped right over Coziah's blind. Needless to say, the hunter didn't get a shot.

Decoying

I first heard of decoying antelope back in 1974 when a friend of mine tried it. He dug a deep pit blind far out on a prairie and put his decoy, a plywood silhouette with a mounted antelope's head attached, 20 yards away. When I asked how he'd done, he said a nice buck came right to the decoy and stood there 20 yards from his blind. Only trouble was, my friend had fallen asleep and never saw the antelope. His wife, watching from a distance, told him what had happened.

You can make an antelope silhouette out of thin plywood, or you can get fancier and make a full-body styrofoam decoy. Most hunters paint their decoys, matching the markings of an antelope as closely as possible, although I've heard of some hunters who covered their decoys with carpet to give them a hairy appearance.

Rut Hunting. For waterhole hunting and stalking, hunting during the rut offers no great advantage, but for decoy hunting it does. Ante-

lope rut from late August through September; the bucks establish territories and gather and hold as many does there as possible. Most hunters who use decoys observe a herd of antelope and learn the dominant buck's territory. They then place a decoy resembling a buck antelope in that territory to lure the dominant buck in for a confrontation.

Some hunters also use a doe decoy. Early in the rut the dominant bucks will be traveling to gather does into their harems, and they most likely will come to a doe to round her up. It might be tough for a hunter who doesn't know a buck's exact state of mind to decide whether a buck or doe decoy will work better at a given moment, so really serious hunters make both kinds of decoys. If one doesn't work, they try the other.

Bringing Him Down

Antelope are relatively fragile compared to most big game, so a heavy bow isn't needed. Any bow of legal draw weight, in the 40- to 45-pound class in most states, will assure adequate penetration. Shooting accuracy is the main concern. Antelope have a built-in aiming stripe, a white line that runs just along the

This pit-blind view of an antelope shows a good aiming point—the vertical white line up the animal's front leg. This alert antelope doesn't present a good shot, however. Wait until the animal is drinking or is looking the other way.

front leg. Aim for that line about halfway up the chest and you'll be right on the money.

Most antelope country is wide open, so once you've hit an antelope, try to keep him in sight. Run like crazy to the top of the nearest ridge, or do whatever is necessary to keep an eye on him. It's a lot easier to track one visually than to crawl along looking for blood.

Judd Cooney said if an animal is hit in heavy muscle—hindquarter or shoulder—he keeps the animal in sight and pushes him. "One gal hit a buck in the front shoulder and she did just as I'd instructed and jumped out of her blind fast and started following that buck. She kept with him a good three, maybe four miles, and she stalked him several times and finally got him."

Field Care and Trophy Hunting

Commonly during early antelope seasons, the weather will be hot. I've often seen 90-degree temperatures while hunting antelope in August. With weather like that, the need for quick field care should be obvious. Gut and skin an animal quickly, bag it in a lightweight cloth bag to keep the carcass clean, and hang it in the shade to cool. Get it to cold storage within a day. If that's not feasible, take a big ice chest full of ice. Bone out the animal and put the meat on ice in the cooler. A boned-out antelope doesn't take a lot of space. Antelope hides have a goaty smell, so some people think the meat will be rank, but that's not true. Antelope meat, well cared for in the field, is excellent.

Most states are capable of growing Pope and Young–size antelope, but by far the most have come from Wyoming because it has more antelope and antelope hunters than any other state. For truly huge pronghorns, Arizona holds the best potential. A friend of mind who lives in Phoenix measures for several record books, and in 1985 alone, he measured 14 antelope from Arizona that qualified for the Boone and Crockett record book. The minimum B&C score is 82, so you can see those were huge animals. Those were mostly rifle kills, but the fact is, the huge antelope were available and

bowhunters had a chance at them during the archery season.

Horn Length. Trophy quality of an antelope can be deceiving, because to a novice hunter, any horns longer than the ears can look pretty good. You need some experience looking over antelope to learn to distinguish so-so heads from outstanding heads. The first thing most hunters consider is horn length. To make the Boone and Crockett record book, the horns just about have to be 16 inches or longer, but 14 inches or longer will get you into Pope and Young as long as other aspects of the horns are strong. A pronghorn's ears are about 6 inches long, so the horns have to be more than twice as long as the ears.

Prong Length. The prong is another important aspect, and it should protrude from the main beam 3 inches or more. Circumference measurements are a major part of pronghorn measurements, so the horns must be fairly heavy, in the 6-inch class, to score well. To measure that well they must be 2½ inches wide or so across the bases.

APACHE DRAW or RELEASE Drawing a bowstring with three fingers under the arrow is commonly called the Apache draw or release. This method offers a couple of advantages over the more common split-finger or Mediterranean draw.

Gun-Barrel Aiming

Out to 30 yards or so, the Apache release proves very accurate, especially for instinctive shooters, because it raises the arrow close to the eye. That brings trajectory of the arrow and line of sight closer together than they are with traditional anchor methods. Steve Gorr, a very successful bowhunter, strongly advocates shooting with three fingers under.

"This method helped me stop shooting over animals at close range," Gorr said. "You don't try to aim down the arrow or use the arrow point for aiming. You shoot instinctively, but with the arrow held closer to your eye, it just presents an easier sight picture to pick up. It changed my point-on distance from 60 yards with split fingers down to about 40 yards, so it's not as good for longer shots, but most animals are killed at 20 to 30 yards anyway, and this method is ideal for those distances."

Cleaner Release

Shooting with three fingers under helps instinctive aiming, but that may not be the major advantage. Even more important could be reduction of finger pinch on the nock at full draw.

"A person with three fingers under doesn't bend the arrow," Gorr said. "Finger pinch results from digging the fingernail on your index finger into the nock. That's what bends the arrow at full draw. With all your fingers under the arrow, it's easier to get off the string cleanly because you're not pinching the nock. And you get better arrow flight, because the arrow doesn't have to straighten out when it leaves the string. I even recommend this method to sight shooters, not because it helps their aiming but because it cleans up their release."

Not only has Gorr killed numerous game animals this way—many of them high in the Pope and Young records—but he also has won his division in a number of major tournaments.

One problem with this system, as in shooting with a release aid, is that you have nothing to hold the arrow on the rest or on the string, so you need a good snap-on knock to hold the arrow on the string and a rest that will hold the arrow. This method also places great upward pressure on the nock, which could force the nocking point up the string. You should either use two clamp-on nocking points, one tight against the other, or wrap dental floss above the nocking point to keep it from slipping. This shooting method also produces more bow noise than the split-finger release, Gorr said, so you need good string silencers to minimize that problem.

Gorr said he teaches beginners to shoot with the index finger at the corner of the mouth, but he personally shoots with the middle finger at the corner of his mouth. You'll have to experi-

ment to see which works best for you. (See also Anchor Point and Release.)

ARIZONA Arizona covers 113,956 square miles. By far the best hunting for all species takes place on public lands owned by the U.S. Forest Service, the U.S. Bureau of Land Management, or the state of Arizona. Arizona contains several large Indian reservations that provide excellent trophy hunting, but fees are high. Arizona may be the best all-round trophy state, especially for elk, antelope, mule deer, Coues deer, black bears, and desert bighorns.

Big Game

Mule Deer. Arizona has three subspecies of mule deer—Rocky Mountain, desert, and burro. North of the Mogollon Rim, which runs diagonally from Flagstaff southeast to New Mexico, you'll find Rocky Mountain mule deer. The North Kaibab on the north rim of the Grand Canyon produces some of the largest mule deer in North America. Many Boone and Crockett heads have been taken here. The extreme northeast corner of Arizona, adjacent to the North Kaibab, commonly called The Strip, also grows huge bucks, although deer are relatively scarce in this low-elevation country. In terms of antlers, the largest typical mule deer from Arizona scored 208⅜, and the largest nontypical 316⅞, and Arizona has produced good numbers of Boone and Crockett mule deer.

South of the Mogollon Rim, the habitat changes to Sonoran desert, and Rocky Mountain mule deer give way to desert mule deer. These animals live at relatively low elevations, 3,000 to 5,500 feet throughout the southeastern quarter of the state. They're not as large, on the average, as their northern cousins, but many respectable desert mule deer come from southern Arizona.

In the southwestern quarter of Arizona, mule deer are sparsely scattered across the hot lowlands from Phoenix to Yuma. Many biologists classify these as burro deer. In this flat, brushy country, deer are tough to find, and they present a unique hunting challenge.

Coues Deer. Also called Arizona whitetails, these small deer live in the same country as desert mule deer throughout southeastern Arizona, some of the most interesting country in North America. It consists of low, hot Sonoran desert interspersed with rugged mountain islands, such as the Santa Rita, Huachuca, Chiricahua, and Graham mountains. In most ranges, Coues deer generally live above 5,000 feet in oak grasslands and pine forests. The world-record typical Coues deer, taken in Pima County in 1953, scored 143. The world-record nontypical, from Cochise County, scored 151⅛. (For details, see Coues Deer.)

Elk. The Mogollon Rim from Flagstaff to New Mexico has the greatest number of elk, although elk can be found through the pinion-juniper country north to the Grand Canyon. All elk hunting, including archery, is limited entry, so the percentage of mature bulls is high. For this reason, many of the top Pope and Young bulls have come from Arizona. For world-record size animals, Arizona ranks No. 1. Archery season is open during the rut in September.

Antelope. Arizona doesn't have the numbers to compare with Wyoming and other states, but it produces some huge antelope. The archery season is open in September.

Black Bear. Arizona might not seem like great bear country, but many of the mountain ranges have good populations. And true to form, Arizona grows some of the biggest bears in North America.

Cougar. Arizona's reputation for record-book animals doesn't extend to mountain lions. What Arizona lions lack in size, however, they make up for in numbers. Arizona has always been one of the top two lion states (along with Utah) with an annual kill in excess of 200.

Javelina. This animal probably attracts more archers to Arizona than any other animal. That's partly because the javelina season is open in January when little other hunting is available, but it's also because javelina, with their poor eyesight, make ideal animals for close-range stalking. They're abundant throughout Arizona south of the Mogollon Rim. Archery season is open all of January.

Desert Bighorn Sheep. Desert bighorns live in most of the arid mountain ranges from the Colorado River along the west side of the state and south along the Mexican border. Drawing odds for tags are very poor, and for nonresidents, tags are very expensive. At this writing, only one archer had taken a desert sheep in Arizona.

Other Game

Turkeys. Arizona has excellent turkey hunting, primarily for the Merriam's subspecies. The greatest number of turkeys live on the Mogollon Rim and in the high pine forests surrounding the Grand Canyon.

Predators and Small Game. Coyotes, bobcats, and foxes are abundant throughout the state, and calling is a major sport in Arizona. Cottontails and jackrabbits are numerous in many areas, and Abert squirrels are hunted heavily in oak and pine forests in the northern half of the state.

Contact. Arizona Game & Fish Department, 2222 W. Greenway Road, Phoenix, AZ 85023.

ARKANSAS This state has an area of 53,103 square miles. The Ozark Mountains, ranging from 300 to 2,800 feet in elevation, cover the northwestern quarter. Hardwood forests, primarily oak and hickory, blanket 75 percent of this steep, bluffy country. Some backcountry pockets receive little hunting pressure. The Ouachita Mountains in eastcentral Arkansas are similar to the Ozarks, but they aren't as steep, and the forests contain more pine.

The Gulf coastal plain in southcentral Arkansas consists of flat to rolling terrain covered with extensive pine plantations owned by large timber companies. The biggest problem here is an overabundance of deer. The Mississippi Delta area has much farmland and deer are scarce overall, although they're numerous in river bottoms where woody plants provide adequate cover. Most land in the delta is private and posted. Wooded breaks along the Mississippi River have the highest deer densities in the state, but private clubs lease virtually all the land here, so it's not available to the general public.

Arkansas does offer a great deal of public hunting, however. The Ozark and Ouachita National Forests cover more than 2.5 million acres, including some wilderness lands. Several national wildlife refuges and state management areas guarantee additional public hunting. Large timber companies own most of the land in the eastern and southern parts of Arkansas. Some companies lease their lands to clubs, some charge a trespass fee, and others allow hunting by permission.

Big Game

Whitetail Deer. Arkansas has an estimated 400,000 whitetail deer. About 260,000 residents and 10,000 nonresidents hunt deer in Arkansas each year. Bow and firearms licenses are not separated, so there are no accurate figures on the number of bowhunters. Average archery harvest has been about 1,500 deer with a high of 2,500 and an average success rate of about 6 percent. Crossbows can be used legally during bow season, which runs from October through January, and the bag limit has been as high as four deer, although it has been reduced in some regions.

The state record typical whitetail scored 186⅞, and the record nontypical, taken near Boydell in 1959, scored 206⅛. Few big bucks have been taken in recent years, and chances for a Pope and Young buck are not high.

Other Game

Turkeys. Arkansas has an annual harvest upward of 5,000 turkeys. Seasons are held in fall and spring, but the spring season is by far the most popular. The Ouachita and Ozark mountains have some of the best turkey habitat.

Small Game. The extensive hardwood forests of these regions also have excellent hunting for eastern gray and fox squirrels, and good numbers of squirrels live throughout the state wherever woodlots offer food and cover. The fall

Arkansas offers more than 2.5 million acres of public hunting. The White Rock Wildlife Management Area in the Ozark Mountains is only one of many such areas.

season runs from September through January, and there's another season in the spring. The cottontail rabbit season is October through February.

Contact. Arkansas Game and Fish Commission, Game and Fish Building, Number 2 Natural Resources Drive, Little Rock, AR 72205.

ARMGUARD　An armguard might seem like an insignificant accessory, but it plays a major role in successful bowhunting.

Reasons for an Armguard

Prevent Pain. As a beginner, you'll commonly hit the inside of your bow arm with the string when you release. Not only will you get a painful green and purple bruise, which is no fun, but even worse, you could start flinching as you release, knowing you're about to get stung. To prevent these problems, wear a large armguard that covers the entire inside of your arm.

Prevent Anguish. Experienced archers learn to shoot so the string never hits their arms. Nevertheless, they still need armguards. I vividly recall watching a big mule deer buck—larger than anything I've killed—walking slowly at the base of a rim. I was sitting on the rim, ready and waiting, anticipating with great joy taking such a fine animal. I drew my bow well before the buck arrived, and when he stopped broadside at 25 yards, I aimed carefully and released, confident the buck was dead.

To my horror, the arrow twirled anemically from my bow and crashed to the ground about halfway between the buck and me. As the deer raced away, I saw the reason for my miss. Earlier a cold wind had come up, and I'd slipped on a wool shirt. I'd forgot to put my armguard over the shirt, and the baggy sleeve had snagged my bowstring. I won't forget the lesson—always wear an armguard.

Choosing an Armguard

For hunting you don't need anything big or elaborate. Armguards made of dull black plastic work great because they're impervious to weather, and the vented pattern allows your arm to breathe so you don't sweat underneath. You don't need anything fancy, because the only purpose is to hold your shirt sleeve away from your bowstring.

Check an armguard for size and comfort before you buy it. Some are made just large

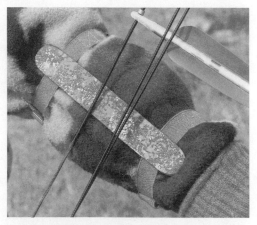

You don't need a big or fancy armguard for hunting. This simple Catguard by Rancho Safari serves the purpose for hunting—holding your shirt or coat sleeve out of the way of the bowstring when you shoot.

enough so they bind up between your elbow and wrist, and that's very annoying. Velcro fasteners are the easiest to use, but they're noisy, and if for some reason you need to take off the armguard as you're hunting, the noise could be bothersome. Metal hooks are quieter and generally last longer than Velcro but they aren't as easy to use.

ARROW BOX   See Arrow Care.

ARROW CARE   One time a friend of mine unknowingly shot a cracked aluminum arrow. When he released the bowstring, the arrow exploded and one piece drove through the thumb on his bow hand. He still has a neat round scar on that thumb as testimony to the need for arrow care.

Damaged Arrows

Cracked Arrows. Always inspect arrows after shooting. Flex wood arrows in all directions and look for splinters or hairline cracks. Never, never shoot a cracked wood arrow, no matter how tiny the crack. Larry Nirk, an authority on wood arrows, said you also should check all shafts to make sure the grain runs the full length of the arrow. If the grain isn't straight enough to run the full length, discard that shaft; it could break when you shoot.

Dents. With aluminum arrows, impact dents are common when arrows hit each other during target practice or bounce off rocks in the field. The dents themselves don't ruin an arrow, but a crack does. Whenever arrows collide, inspect them closely for fine cracks, and throw away cracked arrows. You can't salvage them. If an arrow is only dented you can shoot it again, although precautions should be taken. A dent "work hardens" the aluminum, which makes it brittle and prone to cracking. Easton's Don Rabska suggests holding the dented part of an arrow in a flame (a match will do) for five to six seconds before shooting the arrow again. The heat anneals (softens) the stressed area so it won't crack.

Fiberglass arrows are tough, but they can splinter, and the insert and the point can be

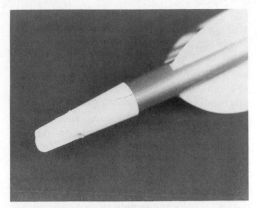

When arrows collide in a target butt, always check nocks on the arrows and replace any like this that are cracked.

and extra fletching, is a good addition to any tackle box. (For details, see Arrow Making.)

Straightening

By Hand. Both aluminum and wood arrows bend fairly easily, but you can straighten and reuse them many times. The procedure is the same for both materials. The simplest way is to lay the bend over the heel of your hand and flex the arrow the opposite direction of the bend. Some bends you can gauge just by sighting down the arrow, but more subtle bends aren't always easy to see. To test an arrow for straightness, lay it over your thumbnail and spin it. A straight arrow will spin smoothly, but a bent arrow will thump up and down at the point of the bend.

Thin-walled aluminum shafts require very little pressure for straightening, but thicker shafts demand some real work. The type of

driven back into the shaft if the arrow hits a rock or other hard surface. Throw away damaged glass shafts.

Check Nocks. Arrow contact in a target butt can crack a nock, and if you shoot that arrow and the nock splits open, the arrow could go about any direction. The result also could be similar to dry-firing, and you could end up with a broken bow.

Inspect nocks regularly, and replace cracked or bent nocks. To remove an old nock, heat it in boiling water or near a flame, and twist it off. Don't cut it off with a knife because you can cut into the shaft and make the taper lopsided, or you might cut off the glue grooves on an aluminum taper so it won't hold a nock securely. Use a taper-cleaning tool or coarse sandpaper to remove old glue and bits of plastic. Then clean the taper with solvent, and glue on a new nock. Your field tackle box should always include nocks and glue. (For details, see Tackle Box.)

Fletching. Fletching can wear out or get shot up. If you shoot holes in vanes, you can just cut off a piece of the vane containing the hole and continue shooting. A little missing vane won't affect your shooting much. If vanes or feathers get totally worn out or torn up, they must be replaced. A simple fletching jig makes this a quick process, and a jig, along with glue

To straighten a wood or aluminum arrow by hand, lay the bend in the arrow over the heel of your hand and bend the opposite direction as the arrow is bent. The thicker the shaft, the more force needed to straighten it.

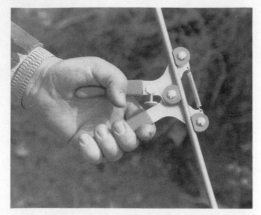

Arrow straighteners like this field model work much like pliers. When you squeeze the handles, the shaft bends over the center block. With practice you can straighten arrows accurately with this method.

alloy makes a difference, too, and tougher alloys such as Easton's XX75, while more durable and less likely to bend in the first place, are harder to straighten when they do bend. Wood arrows generally are easier to straighten than aluminum.

By Machine. You can also use a mechanical arrow straightener. Some field models are made like big pliers. You place the shaft in the jaws of the pliers and squeeze the handles, and the tool bends the shaft back straight.

Precision arrow straighteners have dials to show exactly how much the shaft is bent, and you can control pressure precisely to avoid overbending. If you shoot a lot of arrows — and do a lot of arrow straightening — such a device is worthwhile. If you need to straighten only an occasional arrow, do it by hand or take it to an archery shop.

Bent Inserts and Heads. If you bend the insert in the end of an arrow, remove it and throw it away. That's the beauty of hot-melt glue — you can remove inserts quickly by heating them (for details, see ARROW MAKING). In many cases you can use pliers (another good addition to your tackle box) to straighten bent broadheads well enough for good arrow flight. To check for straightness, set the tip of the broadhead on a hard surface and spin the arrow. If you see any wobble, especially where the head meets the arrow, the head (or shaft, too) is crooked and it won't shoot well. If you can't get it perfectly straight, don't use it for hunting where all your hopes rest on one shot. If you're too cheap to throw it away (as I am), use it for

With a professional arrow straightener, you can detect tiny bends and straighten arrows more precisely than by hand.

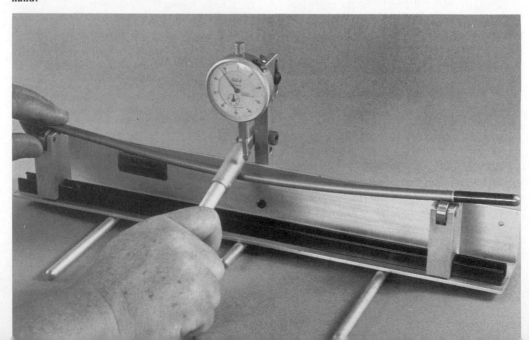

practice. You can finish touching up broadheads with a file and stone. (For more details, see Broadhead and Broadhead Sharpening.)

Protecting Your Arrows

Obviously, most arrow damage occurs during shooting, but you can ruin arrows in other ways. I've fallen on my bow and bent every arrow in the quiver. Back quivers protect your arrows against such disasters. If you prefer a bow quiver, make sure it holds the arrows tight so they're not accidentally jerked out. (For details, see Quiver.)

A good arrow box also protects your arrows during transit in your truck or when packed on a horse. You can buy a fancy arrow box, or you can make one for next to nothing out of PVC pipe. I like four-inch pipe best for all-around use, but you might want a different diameter for special purposes.

To make a box, you need a piece of PVC or similar plastic pipe the length of your arrows, caps for each end, glue for the caps, and foam padding for each end. Glue a cap on one end of the pipe. Cut a piece of foam in a circle the diameter of the pipe and push it into the pipe until it's seated in the sealed end. You could use styrofoam, too. Cut another piece of foam as a plug for the other end.

Put your arrows in the tube so the points stick in the sealed end, push the foam plug in the open end so it seats firmly on the nocks to prevent the arrows from rattling, and cap the open end. You're ready to go. I've found a slip-on cap works well enough on the open end, but if you want to make sure it doesn't come off, use a screw-on cap. A four-inch tube will hold a dozen arrows without binding.

ARROW GRIPPER   See Arrow Puller.

ARROWHEADS   Several types of arrowheads are needed to cover all situations. Some are made for specialized uses, such as fish points (see Bowfishing), but the heads discussed below cover most general bowhunting needs.

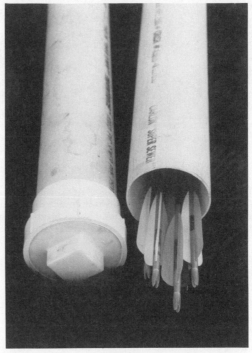

Protect your arrows during transit with an arrow box. These simple cases made out of plastic sewer pipe work well. The arrows are sandwiched between foam at each end to prevent rattling. You can cap the open end with a slip-on cap, or with a screw-on cap like the one on the left.

Styles of Arrowheads

Field Points. These are best suited to target shooting into bales or other target butts because they slip in and out easily without tearing up the butt. They're also the most accurate style of head because they're round and won't plane or throw an arrow out of balance. For that same reason, field points are the only suitable heads for bare-shaft bow tuning. Field points come in various weights from 125 to 180 grains.

Blunts. Blunt heads, bludgeons, and steel blunts are excellent for stump shooting and small-game hunting. Rubber blunts and bludgeons are good for small-game shooting because the wide, flat surface delivers maximum impact to stun small animals instantly, and it

Four general styles of heads (from left to right) cover most bowhunting needs. The field point is best for target practice and bow tuning. The blunt, in this case a Saunders Bludgeon, is suited to stump shooting and small-game hunting. The Zwickey Judo also is ideal for stump shooting and small-game hunting. The broadhead, in this case a Bohning Blazer, is made for big-game hunting.

prevents arrows from passing through small game. They're also effective when coupled with flu-flu arrows for shooting at birds and small game in trees because they won't stick in bark.

Steel blunts aren't as good for small-game hunting, because they pass through small animals, and they make only a small hole without delivering much shock. They're more accurate than rubber blunts, however, so they're good for stump shooting, especially because they're easy to pull from rotten stumps and logs. (For more details, see Small-Game Hunting.)

Judo Heads. These have four spring-loaded arms that catch in leaves and branches to prevent arrows from sliding out of sight. They provide good impact to kill small mammals and birds such as grouse quickly. They're perhaps the best all-around heads for stump shooting and general small-game hunting. (For more details, see Small-Game Hunting.)

Broadheads. Good broadheads for big game must fly accurately and have a sharp cutting edge for quick kills. They also must be durable. (For details, see Broadhead.)

Matching Arrowheads

In choosing arrowheads for various uses, you must match them by weight. A discrepancy of 10 grains or so won't make a lot of difference, but as I've mentioned elsewhere, a variance of 15 grains or more will noticeably affect

dynamic spine of your arrows. Also, each 5 grains of additional weight in an arrow reduces velocity one foot per second, so variations in weight appreciably affect trajectory.

I recall dealing with these very problems before I had sense enough to give arrowhead weight serious thought. I'd sighted my bow in while shooting 125-grain field points, and I regularly shot 125-grain steel blunts for practice in the field. But during a hunt I was shooting Zwickey two-blade broadheads for practice, and they continually shot low and to the right, and my inability to put them on target began to eat at my confidence.

Finally I thought of weighing them and discovered that even though the Zwickeys are 130-grain heads, they weigh—with screw-in adaptors—180 grains. That explains why they shot low and right. Added weight weakened the spine so the arrows flew right, and it slowed them so they dropped low. To get Zwickey heads down near the 125 grains of all my other heads, I had to install them with one-piece adaptors.

Most heads are available in two kinds of mounting systems—screw-in or glue-on. With the screw-in system you first glue an insert into the arrow shaft (assuming you're shooting aluminum or fiberglass), and then you screw either a threaded head or an adaptor into the insert. In the latter case, you then glue a head

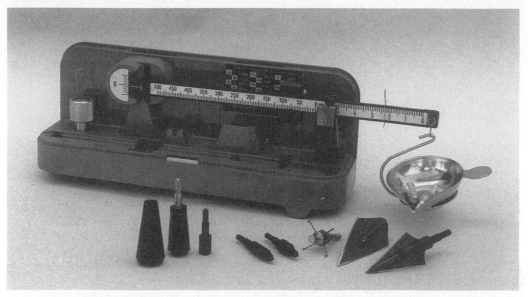

In choosing arrowheads, match them by weight. A discrepancy of 15 grains or more can affect arrow spine and trajectory.

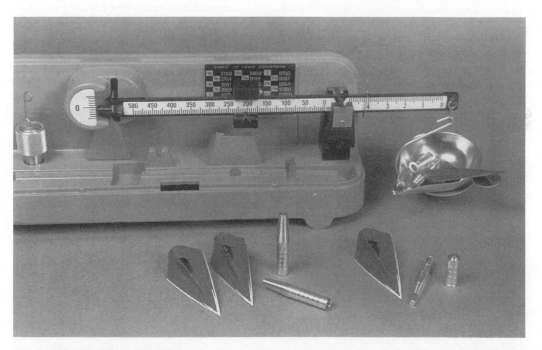

The broadheads mounted with solid, one-piece adaptors (at left) will weigh significantly less than the same broadheads mounted with a shaft insert and a screw-in adaptor. To match arrows, you must weigh the entire adaptor system, not just the head.

onto the adaptor. The screw-in system allows quick changes from one kind of point to another, so it's convenient. Again, however, you must keep weights consistent, and weights can vary considerably, even among heads supposedly of the same weight. (For more details, see Arrow Making.) That's why you can't match point weights by weighing the heads alone. You must weigh the entire insert/adaptor/head assembly to get a meaningful comparison of weights.

Threads in inserts and on adaptors are made of aluminum and they often seize up. To prevent that, lubricate the threads with light oil or paraffin.

ARROW HOLDER This small rubber or plastic arm fits on the side of a bow opposite the arrow rest. It holds an arrow on the rest so you don't have to hold it on with your finger. It's handy for stand hunting or stalking once you've moved within shooting range. It should not be used to hold an arrow as you're hiking. Walking at any time with an arrow nocked is dangerous.

An arrow holder is a useful gadget for stalking or stand hunting when you want to keep an arrow nocked. The rubber hand holds the arrow securely on the rest, but the hand flips out of the way as soon as you start to draw the arrow.

ARROW MAKING Arrow making seems to be the criterion that separates the serious bowhunter from the novice. "You make your own arrows?" beginners often ask incredulously. "You must really be serious about bowhunting!" That implies that making arrows is some kind of mysterious art, reserved for only the most devoted archer. Nothing could be further from the truth. You don't actually "make" arrows. You simply buy the component parts and assemble them. That's why it's so easy.

Why Make Your Own Arrows?

Save Money. You can buy components in bulk, such as nocks and vanes by the 100, to save yourself some money. And you save the cost of labor because you don't pay someone else to assemble them for you. With your own materials, you also can maintain and refurbish your arrows, rather than paying someone to refletch or straighten them for you. (For details, see Arrow Care.)

Customize. Equally important, you can build custom arrows much as a reloader builds custom loads for his rifle or shotgun. From an archery shop, you get standard arrows, all built the same way, and they may not be just right for you. Many shop owners, for example, put $5/16$-inch nocks on certain shaft sizes. What if you shoot a cam bow with an 18-strand string? Most likely the $5/16$-inch nocks will be too tight. If you make your own arrows, you can use nocks made for your string. To fine-tune your tackle, you just about have to make your own arrows. (For more details, see Arrow Shaft Selection, Fletching, and Nock.)

To simplify this discussion of arrow making, I'll assume you'll use aluminum shafts, since these are the most popular today. I'll follow up with tips on making cedar arrows. Many of the suggestions on making aluminum arrows come from Don Rabska, special projects manager for Easton Aluminum, the primary manufacturer of aluminum arrow shafts.

Tools and Materials
• Fletching jig. For home use, a simple jig with one clamp works very well, since you

aren't concerned with turning out great quantities of arrows. The Bitzenburger Dial-O-Fletch has long been a favorite because it allows you to dial in the exact amount of twist or offset you want to give your fletching. The Hoyt Tri-Heli fletcher comes with three fletching clamps, so this tool turns out finished arrows faster than a one-clamp model. Some models have only one clamp per shaft, but they hold six shafts so they'll produce a lot of finished arrows in a hurry.

• Cutoff tool. The only reliable way to cut off aluminum and other tubular shafts is with a rotary cutoff tool. (For details on length, see Arrow Shaft Selection.)

• Arrow shafts. Blank aluminum, wood, or glass shafts of the correct spine weight for your bow. (For details, see Arrow Shaft Selection.)

• Nocks. You can select from any number of nock styles. Buy quality nocks, and buy the same kind for all arrows. (For details, see Nock.)

• Fletching. About the only choices here are feathers or plastic vanes. (For details, see Fletching.)

• Inserts. Tubular shafts require an insert for attachment of the arrowheads. You can use either short inserts that accept screw-in head adaptors or full-length solid insert-adaptors.

• Fletching glue. Bohning's Fletch-Tite, Saunders' N.P.V., and Flex-Fletch Products' Flex-Bond are three good brands of fletching cement.

• Shaft cleaner.

• Hot-melt cement.

• Heat source. A propane torch, small gas stove, or alcohol stove work well.

• Pliers.

Assembling an Arrow

Cut Shafts to Length. You can cut wood shafts with a small saw or sharp knife, but for aluminum and other tubular shafts, use a rotary cutoff tool. The end of the shaft must be absolutely square and you'll never get it that way with a saw. You might be tempted to use a tube cutter, but authorities with Easton, the major aluminum arrow manufacturer, strongly

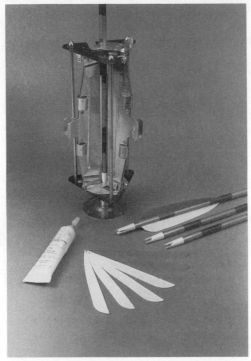

For arrow making you need a fletching jig, in this case a Hoyt Tri-Heli Fletcher, glue, vanes or feathers, arrow shafts, and nocks.

Always use high-quality glue made for fletching arrows. Saunders' N.P.V., Flex-Bond, and Fletch-Tite are all reliable products for putting on nocks and fletching.

To cut tubular shafts to length, always use a rotary cutting tool. It cuts the end absolutely straight and does not crimp the shaft as conventional tube cutters do.

recommend against it. A tube cutter reduces the diameter of the shaft, stresses the brittle aluminum alloy, which could crack it, and leaves a burr you have to ream out, which then thins the wall. Even with a good cutoff tool, you must deburr the shaft, so be careful not to expand the shaft, which can stress and crack it. If you can't afford your own cutoff tool, take

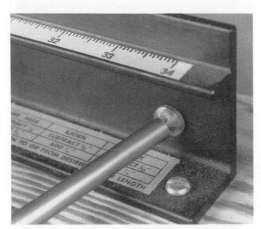

Use very little pressure when deburring the inside of a cut shaft. You want to avoid reducing wall thickness.

your shafts to an archery shop and have them cut to length.

Clean Shafts. Picture yourself ten miles from the nearest road, you've got elk bugling all around, and the vanes are falling off your arrows. Great, huh? To prevent disasters like that, fletchings must be put on right. That calls first for absolutely clean shafts. Many hunters first roughen the shafts slightly with fine sandpaper or steel wool and then wipe them with acetone or other nonoily solvent, or they wash them with Ajax or a similar cleanser to remove all oil or dirt that could prevent a good bond. This method works well.

Bohning Company's Fletch-Lac Metal Conditioner may be even better. To use this you soak the arrow shafts in the conditioner for two minutes; this not only removes oil but etches the shaft so glue will stick. I've had good success with this metal conditioner. Whichever method you use, don't touch the shafts with your fingers — or anything else oily — after you've cleaned them.

Glue on Nocks. You can either glue on nocks now, or you can just slip on a nock during the fletching process and then glue it on later as you tune your bow. You may want to turn your nocks to improve fletching clearance. (For details, see Bow Tuning.)

Regardless of when you glue them on, follow this procedure. Put a small bead of glue on the tapered swage of the arrow. If excess glue gets trapped inside the nock, it can melt the plastic, so don't put too much. Slip the nock onto the end of the arrow, and turn the nock counterclockwise to spread the glue evenly. Now screw the nock on clockwise to seat it firmly. This procedure is recommended because the taper on an aluminum arrow is threaded, and twisting the nock on clockwise literally screws it into place.

A crooked nock virtually assures poor arrow flight, so you must get nocks on straight. Before the glue sets, check each nock for straightness. Roll the shafts along the edge of a smooth table to see if they wobble. Or, if the arrow is already fletched, hold it lightly, blow

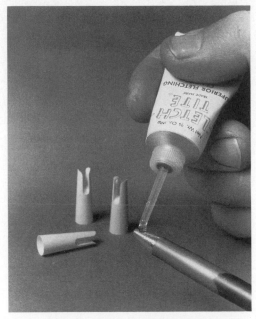

To put on nocks, place a small drop of glue on the nock taper. Don't put more than is needed to coat the taper, because excessive glue may melt the nock.

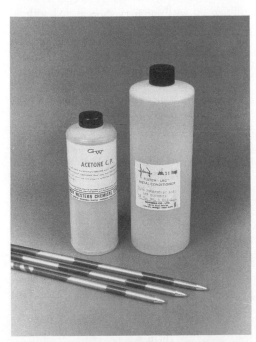

Before fletching, shafts must be clean and oil-free. You can sand the shafts lightly and clean them with acetone or similar cleaners. Or you can clean and etch them chemically with Bohning's Fletch-Lac Metal Conditioner.

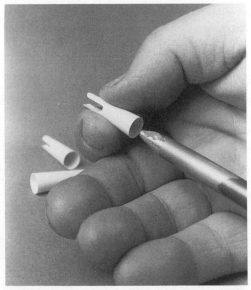

Slip the nock onto the taper, rotate it counterclockwise to spread the glue evenly, and then screw the nock on clockwise to seat it solidly.

Make sure all nocks are straight before the glue sets up. You can spin shafts or roll them along a tabletop to check for wobble, or you can use a nock alignment jig as shown here to check nock straightness.

on the fletching to spin the arrow, and watch the nock for wobble. You can also check nock straightness with a Bjorn Nock Alignment Tool.

Install Inserts. You can do this either before or after you fletch the arrow. Some hunters glue inserts into place with epoxy, but Don Rabska recommends using hot-melt glue, such as Bohning's Ferr-L-Tite. Not only can you change inserts and arrow points easily with the hot-melt glue, but the use of heat on the end of an aluminum shaft anneals the arrow to prevent cracking. With epoxy you don't get this annealing effect, and arrow breakage is more likely.

You can use Ferr-L-Tite glue by peeling back the paper and holding the end of the stick in the flame, but if you're using a torch for heat, it's handier if you melt a stick of glue on the end of a tin can. To use it, direct the flame of your torch onto the glue until it melts. Using pliers, pick up an insert and dip it into the glue to collect a small glob of glue on the insert. Now hold the insert in the flame until the hot-melt glue begins to run. Also, hold the end of the arrow in the flame for five to six seconds to anneal it. Now slip the insert into the end of the arrow and rotate it to spread the glue evenly all the way around and the full length of the insert. Push the end of the arrow against something solid until the glue cools enough to hold the insert in place. You can dip it in cold water to speed cooling.

Glue on Fletching. For simplicity, I'll talk about plastic vanes here, but the same procedure applies to feathers. Place the clean shaft with nock in place into the fletching jig, and

Install inserts with hot-melt glue such as Bohning's Ferr-L-Tite. To make the process easier, melt an entire stick of glue on the top of a can. With a torch, melt the glue and dip an insert into the melted glue. Heat both the insert and the end of the arrow, and slide the insert into the shaft and rotate it to spread the glue evenly. Then hold the insert in place until the glue sets up.

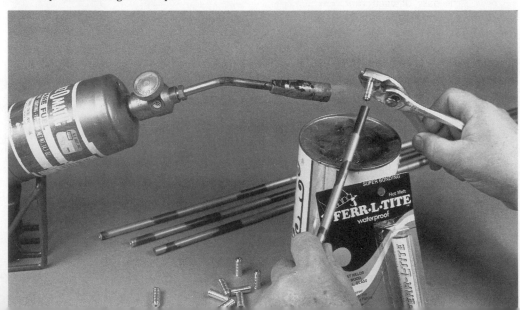

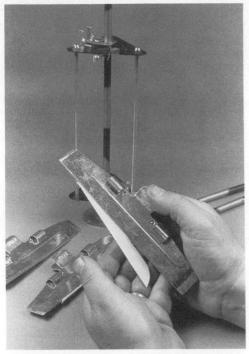

Place a vane or feather in each fletching-jig clamp. Clamps have index marks at the end to serve as a guide for fletching alignment. Make sure each fletching is positioned exactly the same way.

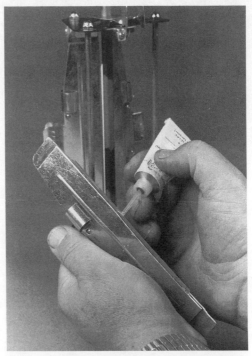

Run a fine bead of glue along the base of the feather or vane. Make sure the entire surface that will contact the arrow is covered. Slip the clamp into the jig solidly so the entire base of the fletching makes solid contact with arrow shaft.

slip a vane into each fletching clamp. Many vanes are coated with a release agent that helps free them from the molds during manufacture. This will prevent glue from sticking solidly, so wipe the base of each vane with acetone, lacquer thinner, or similar solvent to remove the release agent. Now spread a thin layer of Fletch-Tite or similar glue the full length of the base.

Immediately, before the glue starts to dry, slip the clamp into the fletching jig so the base of the vane seats firmly against the shaft. Small beads of glue should squeeze from under the vane, but don't press hard enough to squeeze out all the glue or the vane won't stick well. Place all three vanes on the arrow the same way. Leave them in place for 20 minutes or so until the glue hardens. Then remove the clamps and take the arrow from the jig.

To complete the process, squeeze a small bead of glue onto each end of each fletching to seal the ends and to add strength. Let the glue dry for a few hours, install a field point or broadhead, and you're ready to shoot. You can make arrows as you're doing other projects, and if you keep at it you can easily turn out a dozen arrows a day with a three-clamp jig.

Making Wooden Arrows
The same general principles apply to wood shafts, but there are a couple of differences. Aluminum arrows need no exterior paint or other finish, but wood arrows will hold up much better if they're coated with a durable finish. Larry Nirk, owner of Nirk Archery, a major producer of cedar arrows, recommends lacquer as the best finish. It's durable, it goes

on evenly, and it dries quickly so you can work with the shafts soon after dipping.

Nirk recommends coating the shafts by dipping because that's the best way to get an even coat. You can make your own dip tube out of conduit or similar tubing, or you can buy a commercial dip tube from Bohning and other companies. To coat a shaft, you fill the tube with lacquer and dip the shaft its full length, then stand it up or hang it to dry.

You must taper the ends of wood arrows by hand, and you can buy a simple taper tool for this. The nock end of the arrow requires an 11-degree taper, and the head end requires a 5-degree taper. The taper tool has two cutting units with the appropriate tapers, along with

various guides for different diameter shafts — $5/16$, $11/32$, and so forth.

You must choose glues compatible with the finish on the arrow. You're safe if you use all one company's products. For example, if you coat your shafts with Bohning's Fletch-Lac vinyl plastic finishes, then use Bohning's Fletch-Tite glue. However, this glue doesn't work on regular lacquer. Larry Nirk sells pre-lacquered shafts, and for these he recommends either Duco Cement or Ever-Fast Liquid Cement.

To cut a shaft to length, you can saw it. Or you can lay the shaft on a table and roll it under a sharp knife blade until the shaft is scored all the way around, then snap it off.

To install nocks, use the same glue as you do for the fletching. And use hot-melt cement to install heads. You can buy fittings for wood arrows that allow you to use screw-in arrowhead adaptors.

When you shoot a bow, paradox bends the arrow left and right. Nocks on cedar shafts should be aligned so the arrows bend cross-grain. That is, when an arrow is nocked on your bow, the grain of the arrow should be horizontal. In Little League ball the coach always taught you to hold the trademark on your wooden bat up so you hit the ball with the edge

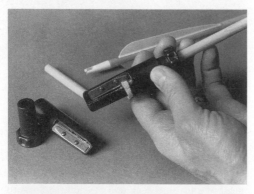

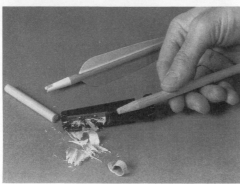

You must taper the ends of wood arrows. There are special tools with an 11-degree taper for the head end and 5 degrees for the nock. Use sharp blades in the tool to ensure a smooth and accurate taper.

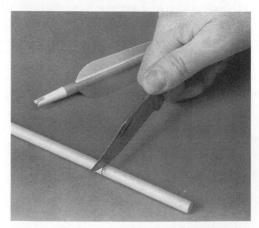

To cut wood arrows, you can use a fine-tooth saw or you can score the arrow with a knife and snap off the end.

of the grain, and the same principle applies to arrows. Some experienced archers say it makes no difference how the grain is turned, especially on super-heavy shafts, and they're probably right. To be safe, though, shoot them cross-grain.

Inspect cedar shafts before shooting them, and throw away any shafts with cracks or other defects. Never shoot a cracked cedar shaft. Also, check the grain to make sure it's reasonably straight. On some low-quality shafts, the grain could be so crooked that individual grain lines might not run the full length of the shaft. Discard these.

ARROW PULLER If you have a hard time pulling arrows from tight bales or dense foam targets, use an arrow puller made of closed-cell foam. This device wraps around the shaft to give you a secure, nonslip grip.

An even bigger problem can be extracting broadheads from logs or trees. You can't jerk the arrow out, at least not without destroying your arrow—and probably your shoulders. Here again, an arrow puller can help. To use a puller, you screw the arrow shaft off the broadhead and screw the puller onto the head. Now you've got a handle you can hold on to. Some stabilizers, like the Jones Ez-It-Out, are built to double as broadhead pullers. With these you can use a block of wood as a fulcrum and the stabilizer as a lever to pry out your broadhead.

ARROW REST The arrow rest may affect arrow flight more than any other part of your equipment, because it's the last point of contact for an arrow. But many hunters virtually ignore this vital piece of gear. If you want good arrow flight, select your arrow rest with care.

Shooting Off the Shelf

Most longbowmen shoot off the shelf, and a number of recurve-bow shooters shoot this way, too. G. Fred Asbell, a custom recurve bowmaker and very successful hunter, strongly advocates this method, and he builds his bows with a curved shelf to accommodate this style. Major benefits are simplicity, speed, and de-

To use this stabilizer as a broadhead puller, you first screw the arrow off the head. Then you remove the stabilizer from your bow and screw the end onto the broadhead. Using the shaft of the stabilizer as a lever, you pry the broadhead loose. A block under the lever gives you better leverage.

pendability. You don't have to worry about your arrow rest breaking, you can nock and shoot an arrow quickly without looking down at the bow, and chances are your arrow will never fall off the rest. Most hunters carpet the shelf with soft material to ensure quietness.

Shooting off the shelf has limitations. For one thing, your arrows must be fletched with feathers. Plastic vanes will bounce off the shelf to give erratic arrow flight. Also, you can't fine-tune a bow as you would with other setups. You can change nocking-point height, vary

Many longbow and recurve archers shoot directly off the bow shelf. For this kind of shooting, you must use feather fletching.

spine weight of your arrows, try different fletching methods, and change brace height of your bow (by shortening or lengthening the string), but that's about it. With well-matched arrows, you can get acceptable arrow flight, and, as many bowhunters do, you may feel the advantages outweigh the disadvantages.

One-Piece, Elevated Rests

Most compound bows these days come equipped with solid rubber or plastic rests.

A solid plastic or rubber rest like this is durable and trouble-free. On the debit side, it can't be finely tuned, and you may have fletching clearance problems. Notice the black streaks on this arrow's vanes where they've been hitting the rest.

Some hunters swear by these, and others swear at them.

Again, strong points are simplicity and dependability. A solid chunk of plastic or rubber can't find many ways to go wrong. I shot the same Jennings rubber rest on my bow for three years and never had any problems, and I shot Hoyt Pro Rests on my recurve bows for years without one malfunction. Steve Gorr, a highly successful bowhunter, shoots a recurve bow, and he swears by the old Bear rest that looks like a little brush sticking out the side of the bow. "I've shot the same rest on three different bows over the past seven years," Gorr said. "I just tear it off the old bow and glue it on the new one. I've never had any trouble with it."

For best arrow flight, a solid rest should be mounted on an adjustable plate so it can be moved in and out for the proper amount of center shot. (For details, see Bow Tuning.) This adjustability is one advantage over shooting off the shelf. You might get away with sticking it directly to the side of the bow, but chances are you'll get poor arrow flight. That's particularly true if you plan to shoot plastic vanes on your arrows, because they probably won't clear the side of the bow. If they're hitting, you'll see a buildup of plastic on the bow handle, and you'll see streaks on plastic vanes where the

40

rubber rest is hitting. If you insist on mounting a solid rest directly on the bow handle, you'll get best flight with feathers.

Also, if you plan to shoot plastic vanes, you should mount a solid rest—or any other rest setup, for that matter—high enough (at least ⅝ inch) so that vanes will clear the shelf.

Solid rests have drawbacks. They have no side play, so when the arrow is shot it's deflected against an immovable object. Most experienced archers agree you can potentially achieve better arrow flight with a springy side plate like the cushion plunger that gives when the arrow deflects off it. Also, solid rubber rests create more drag than more advanced styles discussed below, and they can reduce arrow speed two to three feet per second.

The Flipper Rest II used in conjunction with a cushion plunger offers potential for good arrow flight.

Spring-Loaded Arrow Rests

Cushion Plunger and Flipper. This rest setup consists of a movable arm that supports the arrow and a spring-loaded cushion plunger (or pressure button) at the side that gives when the arrow bends past it. Many serious archers prefer this setup over any other. I personally have found it to be forgiving and easy to tune. New Archery Product's Flipper Rest has long been the standard for flipper-type rests, and I've used these successfully on a number of bows. Cavalier Equipment Company's ST-300, with a looped-wire arm coated with Teflon, has also proven dependable and accurate. A number of companies such as Saunders and Cavalier make excellent plungers.

This flipper-plunger combination yields near-perfect arrow flight with either feathers or vanes because the arm supporting the arrow flips out of the way as the arrow slides past, and the spring-loaded plunger absorbs much of the side pressure as the arrow bends around the bow. With the flipper-plunger, you can adjust both the amount of center shot precisely, and spring tension in the plunger, which, in essence, changes the spine of the arrow. Thus, you can fine-tune your bow to shoot virtually any combination of shaft, fletching, and point.

Of course, sophistication in arrow rests, as in anything else, has its drawbacks. The wire

flipper arm can get bent, and a cushion plunger can rattle loose and change adjustment, which will affect arrow flight. I've also had a plunger freeze solid during bitter cold weather. In selecting a pressure button, look for one with the plunger encased in a Teflon sleeve that keeps out moisture. The Teflon sleeve also assures smooth movement of the plunger. Along these lines, the Cavalier Master Plunger is one of the best. There should be no side play and the button shouldn't hang up when you push it in and out. Cheap pressure buttons aren't much better than solid rubber rests.

Also, the flipper-plunger may not work well for you if you shoot with a mechanical release aid. When you release with your fingers virtually all the paradox (arrow bend) is horizontal, and the bending force takes place sideways against the cushion plunger. When you shoot with a mechanical release, the string thrusts the nock of the arrow downward more than sideways, so the arrow flexes vertically, and the arrow deflects upward off a rest with no vertical give. For that reason, it's best to use a rest that cushions arrow paradox vertically when shooting with a mechanical release.

Spring Rests. One is the popular "springy," which is little more than a spring attached to the side of the bow. The spring bends to cushion the arrow both vertically and horizontally

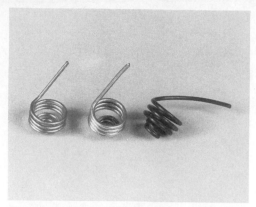

Spring rests have proved popular, particularly with release-aid shooters. Rests come in several hunting weights, such as the 15-, 20-, and 25-ounce springs shown here.

Shoot-Through and Launcher Rests

With all the rests discussed above, the arrow must pass around them. Because of the effects of paradox, especially when shooting with your fingers, the arrow normally bends enough to clear the rest. With shoot-through rests, the cock vane or feather passes through the rest, either between two arms or between a supporting arm and a pressure botton. Many of these feature both vertical and horizontal pressure adjustments so they can be fine-tuned for perfect arrow flight.

With the launcher-type rest, the arrow sits in a notch and the hen vanes or feathers pass on either side. These rests feature vertical pressure adjustments to accommodate vertical paradox created by a mechanical release.

Shoot-through and launcher rests are made primarily with the release-aid shooter in mind,

when you shoot. Target archers, particularly those using a mechanical release aid, have long favored spring rests. To assure complete arrow clearance, they clip the end of the spring so it's just long enough to hold the arrow.

Springy rests can't be ultra-fine-tuned like pressure buttons, but they do come in various weights — 15, 20, and 25 ounces. If one weight doesn't work, then try a heavier or lighter spring.

These rests are simple with no adjustments except in and out for center shot, and they can't freeze up, so they're relatively trouble free. Drawing an arrow shaft across a bare spring produces a scratching sound, but you can eliminate that with a Teflon sleeve slipped onto the spring.

Some hunters swear by spring rests and are pleased with their tuning results. Personally, I've never got hunting-weight arrows to fly well off a spring rest. Shooting with fingers, I've found the flipper-plunger type much easier to tune, and with a release aid I've had better results with the shoot-through rests discussed below. Also, I've talked to hunters who've caught spring rests on brush and ended up with a straight piece of wire sticking out from the bow. That prospect doesn't appeal to me.

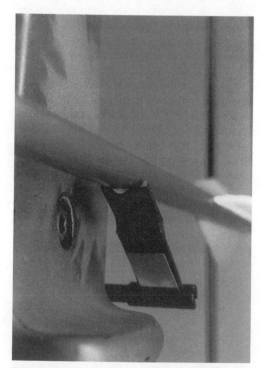

With the launcher rest, the arrow is cradled in a "V" that cushions paradox vertically. The arrow nock must be turned so that fletching will pass on each side of the rest.

although some styles also work very well for shooting with fingers. I've been pleased with my finger-shooting results off a Troncoso TM Hunter rest, which consists of two spring-loaded prongs that support the arrow. Tuning with this rest involves little more than turning the nocks so the cock vane will pass cleanly between the prongs.

Other shoot-through and launcher rests require a little more effort to get vane clearance through or around the rest. And you have to adjust spring tension to match the exact spine of your arrows. And, of course, any equipment that involves springs or moving parts has the potential for failing. If perfect arrow flight is your goal, the Golden Key-Futura and similar rests have a lot to offer.

The Barner Rest, sold by Timeless Archery Products in Mesa, Arizona, is called an "iner-

Golden Key-Futura's Huntmaster 2000 has a metal arm that cushions the arrow vertically and a pressure button that cushions it horizontally. The arrow nock must be turned so the cock vane slides between the arm and the button.

tia rest." It has a spring-loaded arm that holds the arrow. The instant you release the bowstring, the arm drops and your arrow is free-flying. It totally eliminates contact between fletching and arrow rest. You can also get the Barner Rest on a overdraw arm that will fit most bows. The concept behind this rest is sound, because it eliminates virtually all contact between arrow and rest and can be tuned

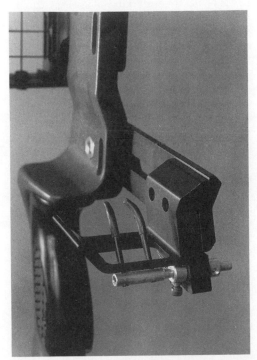

On the TM Hunter rest, the arrow rides on top of two prongs. The cock vane must pass cleanly between the prongs. This rest, particularly ideal for use with a release aid, makes arrow tuning fairly simple.

On the Barner "inertia" rest, the arrow rides in a wire "V." Upon string release, the wire arm drops down and the arrow is free-flying. This type of rest assures complete arrow clearance.

for near-perfect arrow flight. However, you must cock this rest before each shot, and a sharp knock on the bow could release the rest before you're ready to shoot. This rest has good potential for precision shooting. Just be aware of the potential delicacy in rough situations.

ARROW SHAFT SELECTION The two major criteria for selecting arrows are bow weight and draw length. Draw weight is an individual choice that depends on your strength and the kind of game you're hunting. (For details, see Bow Selection.)

Determine Arrow Length

Draw length depends on your size and arm length. To get arrows of the right length, you must first know your draw length, which is defined as the distance from the bowstring at full draw to the pressure point on the bow handle, plus 1¾ inches. You must know that measurement in order to buy a compound bow of the right draw length. (For details, see Bow Selection.)

Assuming you now have a bow set at a comfortable draw length for you, you can determine arrow length. To do that, nock an arrow and pull your bow to full draw and have someone mark your arrow (with a pencil or felt marker) right at the back of the bow (the side away from you). That is roughly your draw length. To that, add ¾ inch to get your arrow length. For example, if your draw length is 30 inches, your arrows should be cut 30¾ inches long. If you shoot an overdraw, arrow length will be the distance from the string at full draw to the arrow rest plus ¾ inch.

The added length assures clearance for the broadhead if you accidentally overdraw. With experience you might decide to reduce arrow length to give yourself only ½ or ¼-inch clearance. That's enough as long as you're sure enough of yourself to know you won't draw too far. Shortening the arrow reduces weight slightly and stiffens the spine of the arrow.

Criteria for Choosing Shafts

Knowing your draw length and draw weight, you're now able to choose shafts for your bow. Arrow shafts must have three characteristics to shoot accurately—they must be straight, consistent in spine, and consistent in weight. These are the qualities that add up to accuracy, and any deviation in any one contributes to inconsistency in your shooting.

Other factors that might influence arrow shaft selection are durability, price, availability, versatility, beauty, and probably others I've overlooked.

Aluminum

Without question, aluminum arrows come closest to meeting the criteria of uniformity in straightness, spine, and weight required for accuracy. They also rate high in durability, versatility, and other factors. Tom Jennings, who has shot nearly every kind of archery equipment ever invented, said bluntly, "There's no use messing with anything but aluminum. No other materials can compare with it."

Choosing Spine. The only trick to using aluminum shafts is choosing the right spine and weight. Spine refers to the amount an arrow bends as it's shot from a bow. The longer the arrow, the heavier the draw weight of your bow, and the heavier the head on the arrow, the more the arrow shaft bends. Spine charts, such as the accompanying chart from Easton Aluminum, serve as a guide for choosing arrows.

Remember that spine charts are only averages, and they're based on arrows equipped with screw-in adaptors and 125-grain heads. If you shoot 150-grain heads, you must compensate with a stiffer arrow. Easton's Don Rabska said a variance in head weight up to 15 grains doesn't significantly affect arrow spine, but more than 15 grains makes a major difference and you must adjust arrow spine accordingly— stiffer for heavier heads, more flexible for lighter heads. If you go 15 grains heavier, say from a 125- to 140-grain head, you must go to a shaft of the next-heavier spine weight, for example from a 2117 to a 2216.

EASTON ALUMINUM HUNTING SHAFT SELECTION CHART

(Most popular size selection is shown in the unshaded area of each box)

ACTUAL BOW WEIGHT (At Your Draw Length)	CORRECT HUNTING ARROW LENGTH (Your Draw Length Plus ½ to ¾ Inch Clearance)																COMPOUND BOW PEAK WEIGHT
	26½-27½ **27"**		27½-28½ **28"**		28½-29½ **29"**		29½-30½ **30"**		30½-31½ **31"**		31½-32½ **32"**		32½-33½ **33"**		33½-34½ **34"**		50% Let-off
	Shaft† Size	Arrow‡ Weight	Shaft† Size	Arrow‡ Weight	Shaft† Size	Arrow‡ Weight	Shaft† Size	Arrow‡ Weight	Shaft† Size	Arrow‡ Weight	Shaft† Size	Arrow‡ Weight	Shaft† Size	Arrow‡ Weight	Shaft† Size	Arrow‡ Weight	
35-39	1913* 1815□ 1816	415 424 440	1913* 1915□ 1916 1818	426 447 471 490	2013* 1916 1917□	451 481 501	2114 2016 8.4M 1917□ 1918	486 507 508 511 537	2114 2016 8.4M 2115□ 1918	496 517 519 524 549	2213* 2115 8.5M 2018	505 530 577 583	2213* 2117 8.5M	514 587 589			42-47
40-44	1913* 1915□ 1916 1818	415 438 461 478	2013* 1916 1917□ 1820**	442 471 490 530	2114 2016 8.4M 1917□ 1918	476 496 497 501 526	2114 2016 8.4M 2115□ 1918	486 507 508 513 537	2213* 2115□ 8.5M 2018	495 519 565 571	2213* 2117 8.5M 2018	505 575 577 583	2117 2216 8.5M	587 587 589			48-53
45-49	2013* 1916 1917□ 1820**	433 461 479 517	2114 2016 8.4M 1917□ 1918	466 486 487 490 514	211 2016 8.4M 2115□ 1920**	476 496 497 502 559	2213* 2115□ 8.5M 2018	485 513 553 558	2213* 2117 8.5M 2018 2020	495 563 565 571 609	2117 2216 8.5M 2020	575 575 577 622	2216 2217□ 8.6M	587 609 640	2413* 2219	544 658	54-59
50-54	2114 2016 8.4M 1917□ 1918	456 475 477 479 503	2114 2016 8.4M 2115□ 1920**	466 486 487 487 546	2213* 2115□ 8.5M 2018 1920**	475 497 541 546 559	2213* 2117 8.5M 2018 2020	485 551 553 558 595	2117 2216 8.5M 2020	563 565 565 609	2216 221□ 8.6M	575 596 626	2413* 2216 2217□ 8.6M 2219	533 587 609 640 644	2413* 2219	544 658	60-65
55-59	2114 2016 8.4M 2115□ 1920**	456 475 477 477 534	2213* 2115□ 8.5M 2018 1920**	465 487 529 534 546	2213* 2117 8.5M 2018 2020	475 539 541 546 582	2117 2216 8.5M 2020	551 551 553 595 598	2216 2217□ 8.6M	563 612	2413* 2217□ 8.6M 2219	523 596 626 631	2413* 2217□ 2219 8.7M	533 609 644 690	2317 2219	641 658	66-71
60-64	2213* 2115□ 8.5M 2018 1920**	455 477 516 522 534	2213* 2117 8.5M 2018 2020	465 527 529 534 568	2117 2216 8.5M 2020	539 539 541 582	2216 2217□ 8.6M	551 571 598	2413* 2216 2217□ 8.6M 2219	512 563 584 612 617	2413* 2217□ 2219 8.7M	523 596 631 675	2317 2219 8.7M	628 644 690	2317	641	72-77
65-69	2213* 2117 2216 8.5M 2018 2020 8.6M	455 515 516 522 555 557	2117 2216 8.5M 2020	527 527 529 568	2216 2217□ 8.6M	558 585	2413* 2216 2217□ 8.6M 2219	502 551 571 598 603	2413* 2216 2217□ 2219 8.7M	512 551 584 617 660	2317 2219 8.7M	614 631 675	2317	628	2317	641	78-83
70-74	2117 2216 8.5M 2020 8.6M	515 515 516 555 557	2216 2217□ 8.6M	527 546 571	2413* 2216 2217□ 8.6M 2219	491 539 558 585 589	2413* 2217□ 2219 8.7M	502 571 603 645	2317 2219 8.7M	588 617 660	2317	614	2317	628	2419	685	84-89
75-79	2216 2217□	515 533	2413* 2216 2217□ 8.6M 2219	481 527 546 571 575	2413* 2217□ 2219 8.7M	491 558 589 629	2317 2219 8.7M	588 603 645	2317	601	2317	614	2419	670	2419	685	
80-84	2413* 2216 2217□ 2219	470 515 533 562	2413* 2217 2219 8.7M	481 546 575 613	2317 2219 8.7M	575 589 629	2317	588	2317	601	2419	655	2419	670	2419	685	
85-89	2413* 2217□ 2219	470 533 562	2317 2219 8.7M	561 575 613	2317	575	2317	601	2419	641	2419	655	2419	670			
90-94	2317 2219	548 562	2317	561	2317	575	2419	627	2419	641	2419	655					

*Available in XX75 only. **Available in GAME GETTER only. □ Indicates Jim Dougherty XX75 "Naturals".

†NOTE: The shaft sizes 1815 through 2419 are contractions of actual physical dimensions of the tubes—example: **2016** has a **20**/64" outside diameter and a .**016**" wall thickness.

‡NOTE: The arrow weight in grains (437.5 grains per ounce) includes a 125 grain broadhead, 30 grain insert and 35 grains (average between plastic vanes and feathers) for nock and fletching. 8.4M 8.5M 8.6M and 8.7M are Bear shaft sizes. The indicated spines are recommended by Bear Archery.

18   The chart indicates that more than one shaft size may shoot well from your bow. The shaft size in the bold type of the box is the most widely used, but you may decide to shoot a lighter shaft for flatter trajectory, or a heavier shaft for greater durability. Also, large variations in bow efficiency, bow design, shooting style, and release may require special bow tuning or a shaft size change to accommodate these variations.

The Easton aluminum arrow shaft selection chart serves as a guide for matching arrows to bows. For cam bows, refer to the left side of the chart under "Actual Bow Weight."

Arrow length affects spine similarly. The longer an arrow of a given shaft size, the weaker the spine; the shorter, the stiffer. For each one-inch increase in length, for example, you must increase spine weight one full shaft size.

Also, arrow charts don't specifically recommend spine weights for cam bows. Rabska said you need 15 to 20 percent greater arrow stiffness for a cam bow than for a round-wheel compound. For example, if your compound bow is set at 60 pounds, the spine chart recommends, for a 30-inch arrow length, a 2117 shaft. For a cam bow at 60 pounds, that arrow isn't stiff enough. To find the right arrow, Rabska said, add 15 percent to the bow weight ($.15 \times 60 = 9 + 60 = 69$ pounds) and use an arrow shaft recommended for a 69-pound compound bow, in this case, a 2216. For a bow with severe cams, add 20 percent, and choose an arrow spined for a 72-pound compound. To simplify shaft selection for cams, I've found that if you just use the "Actual Bow Weight" side of the chart, you come pretty close for cam bows.

Weight and spine of aluminum arrows is designated by two-part numbers. The first two digits indicate shaft size in 64ths of an inch, and the second two digits indicate wall thickness in 1000ths of an inch. For example, the 2016 has a diameter of 20/64 inch, and a wall thickness of .016 inch.

Versatility. Not only does aluminum meet quality standards, but it's more versatile than other materials. Within any given spine weight, you can choose from three to five different shaft sizes with a mass weight range of 100 grains or more. In other words, you can choose a lightweight arrow for speed and relatively flat trajectory, or you can choose a heavier arrow for greater kinetic energy and durability.

Spine and mass weight are functions of arrow diameter and wall thickness. Diameter is measured in 64ths of an inch, and wall thickness in 1000ths of an inch. For example, a 2216 aluminum shaft measures $22/64$-inch outside diameter, and the wall measures .016-inch thick. In general, diameter has a greater effect on stiffness, and wall thickness has a greater effect on weight.

To get the fastest shaft within a given spine range, you want to shoot a shaft with a large diameter and a thin wall. For example, if you shoot a 30-inch arrow from a 60-pound compound, you could use a 2213 shaft that weighs only 485 grains. That would be a fast-flying shaft, but it's not necessarily the best choice, because you pay a price for speed.

First, thin-wall shafts aren't as durable as thicker-walled shafts. The walls of 2213s are so thin (.013 inch) that the arrows will bend if they hit a bale slightly crooked, and any contact with a rock or another arrow will put a serious crease in the shaft. Rabska said the larger diameter, thin-wall shafts are made primarily for bowhunter target shooters and aren't as suitable for hunting. For target shooting he suggested the .013 or .014-inch shafts, but for hunting, he said, most hunters go to arrows with walls of .016 inch or thicker.

Besides lack of durability, lightweight, thin-wall shafts present two other potential problems. One is greater sensitivity to shooting errors. The lighter and faster the arrow, the more it will magnify any problems with form. As bow tester Norb Mullaney said, "It's like comparing the family sedan to a high-speed race car. The race car may be higher performance, but the sedan is easier to control."

Ultralight arrows also could lead to bow

damage. The lighter the arrow, the less energy it absorbs, and the greater the vibration and stress on the bow. Broken strings, cables, and limbs have not been uncommon, especially with high-poundage cam bows, and a lot of the problems stem from shooting ultralight arrows. (For details, see Bow Selection and Bow Efficiency.)

At the other extreme, you could go to the heaviest shafts available at your given draw weight and arrow length. Again using the 60-pound-bow, 30-inch-arrow example, you could shoot 2020 shafts. With a .020-inch wall thickness, 2020s are virtually indestructible, and at 595 grains these shafts deliver significantly more kinetic energy than the 2213s do from the same bow. But the trajectory will be somewhat more curved, which could seriously affect accuracy.

Probably the best choice, at least until you become familiar with your equipment and learn the inherent advantages and disadvantages of weight versus speed, is the middle-of-the-road approach. Going back to the 30-inch arrow for a 60-pound compound, you could choose a 2117 shaft. With a wall thickness of .017 inch, the 2117 is fairly durable, yet at 551 grains it's 44 grains lighter than the 2020, which equates to about 9 feet per second greater arrow speed and a flatter trajectory.

Tom Jennings said, "A good rule of thumb for greatest arrow/bow efficiency is 9 grains of arrow weight per pound of bow weight. Thus if you're shooting 60 pounds, you'd shoot about a 540-grain arrow.

"If you go with an arrow much heavier than that, you get poor trajectory. If you go much lighter, it's hard on the bow. For cam and recurve bows, the ratio is probably a little higher."

Don Rabska had one final word on choosing aluminum shafts (any shafts for that matter): "You get better clearance with a stiffer arrow because in the second mode of paradox, the arrow swings out away from the rest for good clearance. Shooting underspined arrows is the worst thing you can do, because a weak arrow bends around the bow and stays on the rest

longer to create clearance problems. Don't sacrifice stiffness for light weight and speed. A stiffer shaft is a lot more forgiving." (For more details, see Bow Tuning.)

Along the lines of versatility, you can choose among different aluminum alloys. Easton's Game Getter bends slightly easier than the more expensive XX75. At the same time, it's easier to straighten when it does bend. They both come in superb camouflage finishes. If you can afford them, go with XX75s, but if you can't, feel confident you're getting accurate, dependable arrows in the Game Getters.

Aluminum arrows are not only manufactured to precise tolerances and offer a wide spine and weight range, but they're impervious to weather, so you can depend on them under virtually any conditions. They also hold up well. Sure, you can bend aluminum arrows, but you can also straighten them. (For details, see Arrow Care.) You've got to expect to break thin-wall shafts or bend them beyond repair occasionally (one of the prices you pay for speed), but you can bend and straighten the more durable sizes many times. I've shot some of the same shafts for more than ten years.

Wood

If aluminum arrows are so great, why shoot anything else? One reason is economy. You can buy 100 production-grade cedar shafts for less than you'd pay for a dozen XX75 aluminums. With that difference in price, you'll feel a little freer about plinking and stump shooting with them. Many hunters who shoot nothing but aluminum arrows on targets and big game keep a supply of woods on hand for stump shooting and small-game hunting in the rocks. Breaking a few won't put you out of business.

Wood arrows have a strong traditional appeal, too. Saxton Pope and Art Young shot wood arrows, and it makes some modern hunters feel good to shoot similar tackle.

Some hunters would even say wood arrows shoot better. They say wood recovers quicker so is a little more forgiving of shooting errors. Both aluminum and cedar shafts bend, so one is no better than the other in that category, but

PORT ORFORD CEDAR
SHAFT/ARROW SELECTION CHART

Because cedar dampens down immediately after release they can be shot more accurately than aluminum that is not perfectly straight. You'll be able to straighten them easier too.

SELECTION CHART FOR TARGET ARROWS

BOW WEIGHT AT DRAW LENGTH	24	25	26	27	28	29	30	31
20-25#	A	A	A	A	A	B	B	C
25-30#	A	A	A	B	C	D	D	D
30-35#	A	A	A	B	C	D	D	E
35-40#	A	A	B	C	D	E	F	G
40-45#	A	B	C	D	E	F	G	H

SELECTION CHART FOR FIELD & HUNTING ARROWS

BOW WEIGHT AT DRAW LENGTH	24	25	26	27	28	29	30	31
40-45#	B	C	D	E	F	G	H	I
45-50#	C	D	E	F	G	H	I	J
50-55#	D	E	F	G	H	I	J	K
55-60#	E	F	G	H	I	J	K	L
60-65#	F	G	H	I	J	K	L	M
65-70#	G	H	I	J	K	L	M	N
70-75#	H	I	J	K	L	M	N	O
75-80#	I	J	K	L	M	N	O	
80-85#	J	K	L	M	N	O		
85-90#	K	L	M	N	O			

Using the Nirk cedar shaft selection chart, you match draw weight with draw length to arrive at a letter designation. You order shafts by the letter code.

cedar may be a little easier to straighten. (For details, see Arrow Care.) And wood-arrow advocates would say that a crooked cedar arrow will shoot better than a crooked aluminum arrow. Besides all this, cedar smells better.

The major problem with wood is lack of uniformity. Production woods are spined by machine so tolerances aren't real close. Also, they are not weighed, and since the density of wood can vary greatly, the weight of the shafts, even within a given spine range, can vary greatly.

You can overcome that problem to some extent by buying premium-grade cedar shafts. Nirk's Deluxe Shafts, for example, are hand-spined, weighed within a tolerance of plus or minus 10 grains, and are visually checked for grain straightness. With these you know you're buying uniformity. Of course, you pay somewhat more for such hand-selected shafts, so you lose the economy advantage.

Some companies specialize in making custom cedar shafts that are not only carefully matched in weight and spine but are hand painted, too. These are truly works of art and they're as accurate as any arrows made. But for these you'll pay far more than you'd pay for the best aluminum shafts.

Under damp conditions, wood arrows commonly warp, so straightness is always more of a problem with wood than aluminum. Also, wood can crack, and shooting a cracked arrow is a good way to end up with an arm full of splinters. Check wood arrows regularly for any cracks or splits, and throw away damaged arrows. Also, constant shooting breaks down the structure of wood arrows, which eventually weakens the spine. For that reason they're not as long-lived as aluminum.

Shooting wood arrows presents one final problem—you can't get them in long lengths; 31½ inches is the maximum. If you shoot 32-inch arrows or longer, you're out of luck.

Nirk Archery, Potlach, ID 83855, has a unique chart for choosing the right spine weight. You line up draw weight with draw length to get a letter code. If, for example, you shoot a 28-inch arrow at 53 pounds, you want an "H" shaft (see chart).

Acme Wood Products, Myrtle Point, OR 97458, is the largest manufacturer of wood shafts in the world. To save money, you can buy wood shafts in quantities of 100 or greater direct from the company. Acme's spine charts simply list the arrow diameter and spine for given draw weights, say 45–50 pounds, 50–55 pounds, and so forth. These weights are figured for 28½-inch arrows. If your arrows are shorter or longer than 28½ inches, add 2½ pounds for each 1 inch longer, and subtract 2½ pounds for each 1 inch shorter. For example, if you shoot a 55-pound bow at 28½ inches you'll buy arrows spined 55–60 pounds. But if you shoot 55 pounds at 31½ inches you must add

The Penetrator, made by Tink's Safariland Corporation, has a fiberglass shell and a compressed cedar core. Finished arrows weigh 800 grains and more.

5 pounds (2½ pounds per inch) to get 60 pounds, and you should buy cedar shafts spined 60–65 pounds. Regardless of whether you shoot a compound or recurve, buy arrows spined for peak bow weight.

Fiberglass

Several companies have made fiberglass arrows, and some hunters have used them enthusiastically because of the heavy weight and durability. One argument in favor of glass arrows is that they're either straight or broken, so you don't have to worry about bent arrows. That contains a seed of truth, but it's also fallacious because many glass arrows aren't straight to begin with. And they don't offer the wide range of mass weights within a given spine range that aluminum does, so they aren't as versatile. The fact that fiberglass arrows

have not survived the general arrow marketplace probably speaks for the comparative quality of glass and aluminum.

If you really crave the weight and durability of glass, the one fiberglass arrow available at this writing is the Penetrator, sold by Tink's Safariland Corporation. It consists of a compressed cedar core inside a fiberglass shell. It's virtually indestructible and a finished arrow, depending on length, weighs about 800 grains. Such heavy arrows aren't necessary for deer-sized animals, but for oversized game in the elk and moose category, Penetrators could be ideal.

Other Arrow Components

The other parts of a finished arrow are the nocks, fletching, and heads. For details on these, see Arrowhead, Fletching, and Nock.

B

BACKPACK HUNTING Generally, the better the access, the poorer the hunting; the poorer the access, the better the hunting. Certainly there are many exceptions, but for some species, especially those of the West like mule deer, elk, and bear, I think the principle holds. For that reason, I see backcountry hunting as a modern approach to the best big-game hunting.

You can hunt backcountry with an outfitter or on your own. Here I deal strictly with hunting on your own (for details on the outfitted hunt, see Outfitters and Guides), and primarily by backpacking. Some hunters own or rent horses for backcountry hunting, but that's a specialized undertaking beyond the scope of this book. For most of us, backpacking presents a more realistic alternative.

Shelter

It's easy to dream about the fun of backcountry hunting—the sunshine and blue sky, the starlit nights, and bull-elk music in the distance—but that's only a small part of the mountain picture. Along with those come rain and snow and wind and freezing temperatures. If you're prepared, they're little more than inconvenience, but if you're not, they'll wipe out your hunting trip in a hurry. That's why I rate good shelter at the top of the backpacking priority list.

Tents. Good tents cost big bucks, but if I were going to spend big money on any part of a backpack camp, it would be the tent. Even if everything else goes wrong, you're always assured a warm night's sleep if you've got a reliable tent.

Size, shape, and waterproofing methods are the major considerations. Obviously a tent has to be waterproof to be of any value, but it has to shed water in the right way. You might just as well sleep out in the open as to use a fully waterproof tent that doesn't breathe. On one disastrous hunt, I had a small, totally waterproof tent. It didn't leak, but after three days, condensation inside soaked my sleeping bag, until crawling into the tent was like snuggling in with a dog fresh out of the water.

Many tents employ a two-wall system that guarantees dry sleeping. My Gerry, A-frame two-man is a typical example (this tent is no longer made, but dozens of companies make similar tents today). The tent itself is made of ripstop nylon. This nonwaterproof cloth allows moisture from inside to escape so that no condensation forms to dampen your clothes or sleeping bag. A coated, waterproof nylon fly fits over the tent to shed rain and snow. This system probably is the most commonly used today and it rates high in dependability, but tents with rainflies are relatively bulky and heavy for carrying. My Gerry two-man weighs

Generally, the farther you hunt from a road, the better the hunting, and that's especially true for western species like mule deer, elk, and bear. I may look tired here, but the mule deer on my pack makes the effort worthwhile.

6¼ pounds. I have a Coleman two-man dome tent with a rain fly that weighs 7½ pounds.

Many tents are now made with Gore-Tex coated nylon. Gore-Tex forms a vapor barrier that allows moisture to pass one way so that the tent breathes to reduce condensation on the inside, but it's waterproof to keep out rain and snow. A major advantage of Gore-Tex tents is weight. No rain fly is needed, so Gore-Tex tents generally are lighter and less bulky for a given amount of living space than tents with a rain fly. Early Winters' Light Dimension tent, for example, weighs only 3¾ pounds and folds into a compact roll. I've used this tent many times in heavy rain and have found it reliable.

Tents come in dozens of shapes. I can't detail them all here, but I've used three basic designs: A-frame, cylindrical (Quonset), and dome. The A-frame is simple to set up and has a good weight-to-size ratio, but because the walls angle down sharply, elbow room is limited and it may be a little cramped for two hunters. Because of their simple construction, A-frames generally are less expensive than most other shapes.

Cylindrical tents have rectangular floors like A-frames but the roof is rounded like a Quonset hut, so for a given length and width, cylin-

You can hire an outfitter or guide to take you into backcountry, but you can hunt much more economically on your own by backpacking. For today's best hunting, equip yourself with a good packframe to hunt wilderness and other roadless areas.

drical tents offer more elbow room. Early Winters' Light Dimension is a good example. The floor is no larger than my A-frame tent but the round walls provide more air space. If you're looking for a very light tent with adequate elbow room, at generally slightly higher cost than an A-frame, the cylindrical shape is excellent.

The roomiest two-person tents are dome-shaped. With long, narrow tents—A-frame and cylindrical—two sleeping bags side by side take up the entire width of the tent, so you must store excess gear at the foot or head, or outside. With a dome tent you can lay two sleeping bags side by side across the middle, and each person has a generous section of storage space to the side. Rex Thomas and I spent five stormy days sharing a Coleman Omega in Utah, and we had plenty of room to lay out extra clothing and gear inside the tent. We could also dress at the same time without get-

A cylindrical tent like the Early Winters Light Dimension shown here has a rectangular floor like the A-frame tent, but the rounded ceiling provides more air space and elbow room.

The A-frame tent offers good shelter at a reasonable price. The pole system is simple, so the A-frame sets up easily. A vestibule, as shown here, allows you to cook out front as you lie inside out of the weather.

Dome tents like this Coleman Omega provide a lot of elbow room for two hunters. The network of flexible poles makes this tent free-standing, so it doesn't necessarily have to be staked down. That can be a convenient feature, particularly on snow where staking a tent can be a problem.

ting all tangled up with each other. For two hunters on a long-term backpack hunt, a dome may be the best choice. On the minus side, dome tents are relatively bulky to carry, they're heavier than other styles (the Omega weighs 7 pounds, 2 ounces), and they're expensive. They're also slightly complicated and time-consuming to set up.

A vestibule, or front porch, adds immeasurably to the value of a tent. My Gerry A-frame has a floorless vestibule that allows me to sit inside the tent out of the rain and take off my boots without getting mud all over the floor. Better yet, I can cook breakfast in bed, because the roof of the vestibule protects my stove from wind and rain, yet the stove sits on bare ground to reduce fire hazard. Using a stove inside a nylon tent with no vestibule is a good way to cremate yourself.

Some tents are free-standing and others must be staked down. Most dome tents, for example, can stand alone. That's a good feature if you plan to camp regularly on deep snow where staking can be a problem. But you can also stake a regular tent in snow if necessary, so I wouldn't base my decision just on this criterion.

Lean-To Shelter. In addition to a tent, a good backpack camp needs stand-up shelter. Any hunt involves a certain amount of social life such as sitting around the campfire, eating

For traveling light and for quick overnight hunts, a piece of plastic can be used for a simple lean-to shelter. This hunter can sit out of the weather while enjoying the warmth of a fire out front.

and talking. During a downpour, always expectable in mountain hunting, you'll get a bad case of the bends if you have to do all your socializing and cooking inside a tent, and you'll have a bad case of the drips if you do it outside over a fire without protection. Just as important, you need some place to hang soggy clothes to dry, and you'll have trouble with that in a backpack tent.

A 9x12 plastic or waterproof nylon tarp makes a good lean-to. If you build a fire right at the open edge of the lean-to, you can sit out of the rain as you cook over the fire and talk,

With a vestibule, you can sit inside out of the weather and take off your boots on the "front porch" to avoid filling the tent with dirt.

Here's another type of shelter made from a 9 x 12-foot plastic tarp. A simple triangle made of tree limbs holds the tarp solidly.

and you can hang clothes under shelter during the day so they'll be dry when you return at night. For a hunt of a day or two, a lean-to may not be essential, but if you plan to be out for a week or more, you'll find it a welcome addition to your camp.

Here's a cardinal rule for comfortable camping: set up your entire camp *before* you start hunting. Many times I've looked at the sky and decided it couldn't possibly rain or snow and haven't taken time to set up the tent and lean-to as I should. Then I've ended up scurrying to put them up in the rain to protect my already-wet gear.

Sleeping Gear

Sleeping Bags. A good night's rest can make a hunt, so put some thought — and money — into good sleeping gear. First, should you buy a down or synthetic bag? Each has its strong and weak points. For all-around backpacking I like down better because, for a given warmth rating, it compresses smaller than most synthetics. To me that's important on long-term hunts and on overnight bivouacs where space is at a premium. You'll cherish any room you can save with compact gear. Besides, I like the soft, fluffy feel of down better than the springy feel of synthetics.

At one time I was on an ultralight kick and bought a North Face Superlight down bag, which is rated for temperatures down to 5 degrees. In terms of size and weight it was fantastic, but I frequently got cold in it. I've replaced it with a North Face Chamois, which is rated to −5 degrees, and I find it ideal for early to mid-fall hunting. It compresses into a small bag and weighs only 3 pounds, 14 ounces.

Down does have its drawbacks. One is expense. On the average, a down bag costs about twice as much as a comparably warm synthetic bag. Down also absorbs moisture, and if you have any accidents and your bag gets wet, you have a mess.

Synthetics — for example, PolarGuard, Hollofil II, Quallofil — are relatively inexpensive and they don't absorb water, so they dry much quicker than down. Also, synthetic materials

You have to sleep well to hunt well. This hunter's air mattress guarantees comfort throughout the night, and it rolls into a compact ball for packing.

maintain their loft, and thus some warmth, even if they are damp. So for hunting in excessively wet conditions, synthetic bags are more failsafe than down. They're a little hard to stuff into a small sack, and for a given comfort rating, they're slightly heavier and bulkier, so they're not as convenient if space is at a premium.

Mattresses. As a teenager, I always slept directly on the ground, either because I wanted to prove I was tough, or because I actually was tough and could sleep that way. Now one night on hard ground nearly paralyzes me, and a mattress has become just as important to me as a sleeping bag. One of my favorites is made of egg-carton foam. Hospitals use egg-carton mattresses to prevent bed sores on patients. I got a used mattress from a hospital and cut a piece from that. Encased in a nylon cover, it makes an ideal backpack mattress. Some backpack equipment companies sell egg-carton mattresses.

Perhaps an even better choice is an air mattress like the Therm-a-Rest. This durable mattress rolls up tightly, and it inflates itself when you open the valve. It comes in full length (72 inches) or hip length (48 inches). I prefer the shorter mattress because it's lighter and rolls into a smaller package, and I find little need for padding under my legs. At night I spread out my clothes to cushion my legs.

Therm-a-Rest also sells a small pillowcase into which you can stuff a down vest or jacket as a pillow.

Packframes

On my first major backpack trip—two weeks for elk—I had food and clothing hanging all over my pack, because my packframe and bag were too small. On a following trip, I solved that problem by loading up two packs and leapfrogging them nine miles to my destination. Since then I've discovered that a bigger pack might be a better alternative, and that pack selection deserves some thought.

Size. For bivouac and overnight camping, a packbag of 2,500 to 3,000 cubic inches will haul enough gear, and if you plan only to take weekend outings during mild weather, a pack with a capacity of 3,000 to 3,500 cubic inches will serve you well. For all-around backpacking and hunting trips of a week or so, you'll find a pack in the 4,000-cubic-inch class about right, but if you plan to take long trips, say from ten days to two weeks, you need at least 5,000 cubic inches of space to carry the food and clothing required. For long-term, cold-weather

Packframes and bags come in various sizes suited to different purposes. This "family" of Coleman Peak 1 backpacks covers the gamut of sizes. The 790 on the left, with 6,500 cubic inches of space, is built for hunts of a week or longer where you need lots of food and clothing. The 780 in the middle has a capacity of 4,100 cubic inches, and it's ideal for backcountry trips up to a week long. The 635 at right, with its 2,500 cubic inches, is suited to overnight treks and short bivouac hunts.

camping that requires lots of food and added clothing and shelter, consider a pack with 6,000 cubic inches. If you're in doubt about your needs, buy a little large; it's better to have too much space than too little.

Frame Design. Next, do you want an internal or external frame? For general trail hiking, I prefer an external-frame pack. The weight of your gear hangs directly on the frame so it's all supported on your waist and shoulders, and it's held away from your back to provide a cooling air space. In general you can carry a heavier load more comfortably with an external frame than you can with an internal-frame pack.

I've used a Kelty packframe for more than ten years, and it's still as good as new. It's made of welded aluminum tubing, which makes it rugged.

Coleman packframes, made of injection-molded plastic called RAM-FLX II, are rugged and comfortable. The 780 has a 4,100-inch capacity and the 790 has a 6,500-inch capacity. At first I was suspicious of a plastic frame, but after using one, I'm convinced you could drive your car over it without damage—to the packframe, that is. Also, it's flexible, which helps you to move freely, and Coleman's unique "Lash-Tab" system for attaching shoulder pads and hip belts offers an almost infinite degree of adjustability for different body sizes and shapes. The Coleman is very comfortable.

External frames are fairly rigid, so they're not ideal for crosscountry travel where you must bend and twist. Most mountaineers who carry heavy loads, and at the same time clamber up cliffs, use internal-frame packs. These packs employ a hip belt, as all good frame packs do, but they have rigid stays inside the pack rather than an external frame. As a result, they lie close to your body and the weight rides low so it doesn't throw you off balance. Also, most internal-frame packs have a lower profile than external pack frames, so they don't hang up on tree limbs as badly. In general, if your hunting demands a lot of crosscountry hiking, you'll probably find an internal-frame pack best suited to your needs.

On this Vector Woodland internal frame pack, the front-loading feature simplifies packing and unpacking, because you don't have to dig down from the top to pull items from the bottom. Everything is laid out neatly before you.

A padded hip belt is an essential item on any pack. With this belt, you can support up to 80 percent of the pack's weight on your hips. This welded-aluminum Kelty frame is rugged and comfortable.

I've used a Vector Woodland internal frame pack to carry as much as 60 pounds. Several features of the Woodland appeal to me. One is the front-loading main compartment. With top-loading packs I'm forever having to dig to the bottom to find a hidden item, but with the front loader, I simply unzip the one big compartment and everything is laid right out before me. In my opinion, one big, front-loading compartment is the best design for a packbag.

Also the Woodland has handy auxiliary pockets. The top pocket zips off to become a fanny pack, and the front pocket zips off to become a rucksack. These can be used individually, or you can cinch them together to form a roomy daypack combination. That way you don't have to carry a separate hunting pack. Consider handy features like that while you're shopping for packs.

Features that can't be considered options are quality materials, and a good waist belt. Welded aluminum and molded plastic are probably the strongest materials. Avoid cheap drugstore packs that are screwed together, because you could find yourself with a pack of many pieces in the backcountry, especially if you have to pack heavy loads like elk quarters.

Padded hip belts have become so common they're taken for granted, yet some cheap models still come with only a web waist belt,

which is worthless. Don't even consider a pack without a padded, full-circle hip belt. With such a belt, you can support as much as 80 percent of a heavy load on your hips, and that makes all the difference on a long haul. To reduce strain, you can shift the weight back and forth from your hips to your shoulders as you hike.

Clothing

This topic is discussed fully under Clothing, so I'll touch only on points related to backpacking here. The major challenge is to get the most out of each garment you carry. In August when hot weather will be the rule, I wear lightweight cotton camo and carry an extra cotton shirt and pants. Knowing that rain or cool weather could hit anytime in the mountains, I also carry polypropylene longjohns. I wear a

Clothing for backpacking deserves careful thought. This backpacker uses a poncho during a rainstorm to cover both himself and his pack.

lightweight, brimmed hat to keep the sun out of my eyes, but to deal with unseasonal cold, I also include a knit hat, a scarf, and gloves. In addition I take along a down vest on all hunts for warmth around camp. At night it doubles as a pillow.

By September, weather has become unpredictable at best. Temperatures are cooling down, and you can count on rain or snow. So I forsake cotton altogether. Instead I wear either light wool pants or wool knickers for the hike in, and I carry an extra wool or synthetic shirt and pants in my pack. Wool is great, but it does hold a lot of water and takes a long time to dry. For that reason synthetics such as acrylic and polypropylene are handier in a backpack camp because they're easier to dry. Just be extra careful with these around fire.

The polypropylene longjohns, down vest, scarf, and gloves are always included. Instead

of a lightweight Jones-style hat, I usually just wear a warmer hat like Fratzke's knit floppy hat.

For really cold weather, in November and December, I'd take the same gear listed for September, but I'd add another wool shirt or sweater, and in addition to wool gloves I'd throw in a pair of Thinsulate Gore-Tex gloves.

On any trip you'll want at least one change of underwear, and for longer outings you'll want two changes (in addition to those you wear in). That way you'll always have a set washed and drying for future use. Again, stay away from cotton. Go with polypropylene or other synthetics.

On the Hoof. Healthy feet start with socks. Here again, wool and synthetics get the nod. Once cotton socks get damp from sweat, they hold moisture forever and will rub your feet raw. I was wearing cotton socks the only time I've ever gotten serious blisters. The idea in preventing blisters is to wear smooth, snug-fitting socks next to your feet and loose bulky socks over those to absorb shock and moisture. Slippage should take place between the socks, not between the socks and your feet.

I normally wear polished-wool dress socks or polypropylene socks next to my feet and heavy wool socks over those, and with that combination I've never had foot problems. The number of pairs you stuff in your pack depends on the length of your hunt. Always take at least one extra pair so you can have one pair drying every day. For trips of a week or longer, take two changes of socks (in addition to the ones you wear in), so you can wash and rotate your socks every couple of days. On a long hike, take off your boots occasionally to let your feet dry and to straighten out your socks, and you should have no foot problems.

Normally I take two pairs of shoes or boots to match different conditions. In moderate weather I wear leather boots while carrying my pack to protect and support my feet. Heavy boots are terrible for hunting, but if you have to carry a heavy pack—50 pounds or more—over steep, rocky terrain, you'll appreciate the protection of thick Vibram soles and the support of heavy leather uppers. In my pack I carry a pair of lightweight, running-shoe–style hiking shoes for hunting and wearing around camp.

Later in the fall when soggy weather will be the rule and my pack is already overloaded, I might take just one pair of boots. These will be either Gore-Tex hiking boots, or the rubber-and-leather boots like L.L. Bean's Maine Hiking Shoe. Both styles will keep your feet fairly dry, give reasonable support for carrying loads, and allow reasonably stealthy walking. (For more details, see Clothing.)

The Kitchen

I don't rate food as high on the list of back-packing items as I do comfort items — shelter, sleeping gear, clothing — because you can hunt well while feeling a little hungry. But you do need adequate energy, and a good-tasting meal can keep your spirits up, so food selection deserves some thought.

Some hunters might breeze into camp after a long day, chipper as sparrows, eager to prepare a gourmet meal, but I'm normally doing well just to boil a pan of water, so one of my criteria for food selection, next to palatability, is simplicity. That means you boil water and add it to the package. If preparation involves any more thought or effort than that, I won't do it.

Breakfast. In the morning I eat either instant oatmeal — just add hot water — or granola cereal. The granola I prepackage at home in Ziplock plastic bags, one breakfast per bag, and add some powdered milk. Then in the morning I simply pour water, either hot or cold, into the bag and start eating. Simple. Occasionally as a special treat I sleep in and then mix up some pancakes and brew a pot of coffee, but I won't do that on early-morning hunt days.

Lunch. During the day I eat hard rolls and cheese, or tortillas rolled around refried beans. These don't smash or crumble in my hunting pack. Along with a sandwich I carry gorp — a mixture of peanuts, raisins, M&M candies — a couple of candy or granola bars, and several pieces of jerky. Here again, if you're like me,

One criterion for food selection is simplicity. After a long day's hunt, you won't feel like cooking an elaborate meal, so choose foods you can prepare simply by adding boiling water.

you'll find it hard to make lunches after a hard day of hunting, so prepackage lunches at home and seal them in separate bags. Then each day you just grab a bag from your stockpile and you're ready to go.

Dinner. At night I eat freeze-dried dinners. The best I've found are Mountain House and Richmoor. These brands taste reasonably good, and they're simple to prepare. You pour boiling water into the package, wait five minutes, and eat.

One freeze-dried Mountain House dinner doesn't satisfy me, so I carry filler foods to add to them. Dehydrated potatoes are light and you can just dump some into the package before you pour in the hot water. The spuds rehydrate along with the freeze-dried foods. Rice and noodles work, too, but they're not quite as convenient because they require some cooking. I carry a tub of margarine to flavor up the potatoes and rice. In backpack hunting, you need all the energy you can get, and margarine has more calories per unit of weight than any other food, so it pays for itself.

That kind of eating offers simplicity but not a lot of sensual excitement, so you might throw in a treat or two. My friend Gary Nichols, who is built like a fire truck, brings along a bag of apples, cantalope, peaches, and a steak or two, and he shares with me. When I'm with normal people, I throw in instant pudding. It's easy to prepare—just add powdered milk and water—and the rich taste hits the spot after a hard day, and it gives you quick energy. Hot beverages always go well in a backpacking camp, so include plenty of hot chocolate and instant soup mix. The individual packets are convenient.

Stoves. In a backpack stove you want simplicity and speed of operation, dependability, light weight, and small size. I've used three kinds of backpack stoves—gasoline (white gas), liquid gas, and alcohol—and have found strong and weak points with each.

Gasoline stoves produce a hot flame and boil water fast. The smallest ones generate their own pressure. That is, they have no pump, but once they're lit, the heat of the flame creates pressure in the tank. The hotter they get, the greater the pressure and the hotter the flame.

The MSR Firefly shown here connects directly to a gas bottle, and a pump is used to pressurize the bottle.

When one of these stoves really gets going it roars like a miniature jet. Once you've turned one of these stoves off, however, it's hard to relight. You have to let it cool off in order to build up enough pressure to relight it.

For that reason a gasoline stove with a pump is more convenient. The MSR Firefly and WhisperLite stoves are good ones. They're rugged and burn hot. A connecting hose screws directly into a fuel bottle, so you avoid the mess of trying to pour fuel through a little hole into a tank on the stove. Coleman's Peak 1 stove is another dependable gasoline stove with a

Some small gasoline stoves like this generate their own pressure, and the hotter they get, the greater the pressure and the more intense the flame. Such stoves are small and relatively light in weight.

The Coleman Peak 1 stove has a built-in pump, so the gas tank can be pressurized by hand. Pump-up stoves are easier to regulate than self-pressurizing gas stoves.

pump. The fuel tank is built into the stove, so you have to carry extra gas separately. The Peak 1 comes in a two-piece aluminum carrying case that can be used as two pots, and that's an attractive feature. The strong point of pump-up stoves is that you can turn them off and relight them easily, but one drawback is weight. Without gasoline, the WhisperLite weighs 12 ounces, the Firefly 16, and the Peak 1, 28.

Many liquid gas stoves are lighter and more compact than gasoline stoves, and they're convenient because they require no priming or pumping, and you can regulate the heat easily. Hank Roberts, Inc., makes a simple butane stove, and you can remove the self-sealing gas cylinder for convenient packing. Century/Primus makes a liquid propane stove, but it's less convenient because you can't take off the cylinder once it's screwed onto the stove. Unfortunately liquid gas freezes, so these stoves aren't ideal for cold, late-fall hunting. In moderate temperatures they really produce the heat, but in cold weather they produce an anemic flame.

The Ultralight stove burns alcohol and weighs only 10½ ounces, so it's especially suited for superlight packing and overnight bivouacking. When you first touch a match to the alcohol you get a little worried because the clear, blue flame seems rather tame. But when this thing starts vaporizing alcohol and generating heat, watch out because it produces a hot flame and will boil water in a hurry.

Cookware. The best set I've found is called Tyrol cookware, which consists of three nesting pots. I especially like the built-in handles. Maybe I'm just scatterbrained, but any time I use pots with detachable handles, I spend half my camp time looking for the handles. Pots in the Tyrol set have spring-loaded handles that fold over the pots to hold the lids on for packing, and then they spring out for cooking.

Eating Gear. Normally I carry only a fork and spoon to eat with. In place of a plate I carry a large cup, which can double as a plate or for drinking hot chocolate or coffee. I just eat dinners out of the package or directly out of the pot.

Bottled-gas stoves are the easiest to use, but they don't function as well as gas stoves in cold weather.

These pots have built-in handles that can't get lost, and they nest one inside the other to form a compact package. They're convenient for long backpack hunts.

Rounding It Out

This touches only backpacking fundamentals. Other gear—flashlights, lanterns, fire starters, cameras, rain gear, knives—could be discussed ad infinitum. Many of these items become a matter of personal choice, and you must decide how lavish or spare you want to go. Shop around to see what's available. Often the best sources for backcountry gear are not hunting catalogs but backpacking, skiing, and mountaineering catalogs and stores.

Loading Up. The amount of weight you can carry depends on your size and build. The general rule of thumb is one quarter of your body weight, but you'll never get by with that on a long-range trip. For two weeks my pack generally weighs from 60 to 75 pounds, and I'd have a tough time getting it much lighter. I weigh 170 pounds so that's roughly one third of my body weight and I can handle it okay, although I couldn't go much heavier without severe problems.

When you pack, place heavy items close to your back and fairly low to keep your center of gravity over your feet. If you put heavy stuff high or far back, it will throw you off balance and pull excessively on the shoulder straps. Always use the padded hip belt to support most of the weight, but shift the load back and forth from your shoulders to hips periodically to relieve strain.

To hike efficiently, set a steady pace you can maintain. If you charge up the trail and then rest, charge and rest, you'll give out fast. Runners maintain what they call a conversational pace—they run at a pace at which they can talk comfortably. You can use that same general guideline in carrying a heavy pack. If you're breathless and sweating excessively, you're moving too fast. Of course, the heavier your pack or the steeper an uphill grade, the slower your sustained pace will be. But don't force it. You'll get where you're going just as fast with a slow steady pace, and you'll feel a lot better when you get there.

Before you try a tough backpack expedition, get in shape. (For details, see Physical Condition.) Put on your backpack (loaded) and hike for an hour each day. If your area has no hills,

climb stairs. On one deer hunt, a friend and I hiked into a rough desert mountain range. My friend is stout but he hadn't conditioned, and by the time we'd hiked downhill a mile to the bottom of a canyon, his knees and thighs screamed with pain, and he suffered for two days afterward. I'm no he-man, but I'd hiked with a 50-pound pack on my back every day for two weeks before the hunt, and I felt fine after that initial hike in. A little conditioning can go a long way on a hunt, and it's equally important to condition for going downhill as well as up.

List of Backpack Gear

As I've said, final gear selection can involve a lot of personal preference, and it also depends on length of trip, time of year, distance being hiked, and other variables. Nevertheless, some items are fairly standard, and the following list pretty well covers the average backpack hunting trip.

Packframe and packsack
Extra pins and keepers for packframe
Hunting gear
  bow
  ten hunting arrows, three practice arrows
  four extra presharpened broadheads
  finger tab
  armguard
  range finder
  binoculars
  spotting scope (if needed) and tripod
  camouflage face cream
  scents
  appropriate calls (elk, turkey, predator, etc.)
  bowstring wax
  socks for stalking (if needed)
  bow sling
Hiking boots (insoles, if needed)
Hunting shoes or light shoes for camp wear
Socks, three pairs light
Socks, three pairs heavy wool
Two polypropylene T-shirts
Two underwear
Polypropylene longjohns
Lightweight shirt (for warm weather)
Lightweight pants (for warm weather)

Wool pants (for cold or wet weather)
Wool shirt (for cold or wet weather)
Gloves, wool or synthetic
Hunting hat
Sock hat, wool or synthetic
Vest, down or synthetic
Jacket (down or synthetic) for camp use in cold
    weather
Wool scarf
Raingear
Three hankies
Two-man tent, poles, stakes
Nylon or plastic tarp for lean-to shelter
Sleeping bag
Sleeping pad
Rope or twine for camp use
Gasoline stove
One pint extra fuel (or more for longer trips)
Matches or butane lighter for camp use
Cook pots
Fork
Spoon
Cup
Dishcloth
Soap for dishes and hands
Alarm clock (wrist alarm watch)
Assorted plastic bags
Towel and washcloth
Notebook and pen
Toiletry kit
    toothbrush and paste
    toilet paper
    comb
    first-aid items: aspirin, bandages, sterile
      gauze pads, antibiotic ointment, diarrhea
      medicine, moleskin (these supplement
      emergency first-aid kit in hunting pack)
Sweat band
Thermometer (for checking meat temperature)
Flashlight for camp use
Candle lantern and candles for light in tent
Leader and hooks for fishing
Camera, lenses, film
Food
    Breakfasts: either one cup of granola, pre-
      packaged with dry milk, or two packages
      instant oatmeal per breakfast
    Lunches (one per day, prepackaged): hard
      rolls or flour tortillas with cheese, dried

beef, sardines; granola bars or candy bars;
gorp (nuts, raisins, M&M chocolates);
jerky
    Dinners: freeze-dried dinners (Mountain
      House or other brands to which you just
      add hot water); instant potatoes or rice to
      bulk up freeze-dried dinners; instant pud-
      ding and powdered milk for quick-energy
      dessert
Hot chocolate, instant coffee (or tea), instant
    soup packets, orange or lemonade mix
Salt and pepper

Along with the items listed above would go
your standard hunting pack. (For details, see
Hunting Pack and Survival.) To make the
backpacking list complete, I'll list hunting-
pack items here also.

Flashlight
Map
Compass
Fire starters
Knife
Sharpening stone or steel for knife
First-aid kit (Bandaids, sterile 3x3-inch gauze
    pads, adhesive tape, gauze roll, aspirin,
    moleskin, small bar of soap)
50 feet of nylon cord
Whistle for signaling
Signal mirror (could be built into compass)
Fluorescent plastic flagging
Aluminum cup
3 feet of surgical tubing for water siphon
Water-purification tablets
Pen
Snakebite kit (in known snake country)
Sunburn protection (on bright snow)
Sunglasses (on bright snow)
Plastic for emergency shelter
Toilet paper
Needle and thread (to repair disastrous rips)
Lunch and high-energy foods
Warm sweater or shirt
Raingear
Bota bag full of water (if pure water not avail-
    able in field)
Extra bowstring
Spare axle keepers

Spare arrow rest
Allen wrench for limb bolts (or bow stringer)
Spare broadheads
Camera and film
Hunting license and tags
Insect repellent (in buggy country)
Game bags (in warm weather)
Plastic bag for heart and liver
Spare eyeglasses (if you wear glasses)
Folding saw (for off-road where you must saw antlers from head or possibly build emergency shelter)

BACK QUIVER   See Quiver.

BAITING   A method of attracting game by the use of a lure or food. (For details, see Black Bear.)

BARE BOW   Shooting without sights. (For details, see Aiming Methods.)

BEAR   Three varieties of bears are of primary interest to bowhunters—grizzly, brown, and black.

Brown and grizzly bears are classified as the same species, *Ursus arctos*, and they're distinguished only by size and range. Because of their rich salmon diet, brown bears grow considerably larger than interior grizzlies. Brown bears are the largest carnivores in the world (actually that's a tossup between brown bears and polar bears), and a big brown bear will weigh more than 1,500 pounds. In contrast, a huge interior grizzly will weigh little more than 1,000 pounds, and the average is more like 500 to 600. Skull size is equally distinct, as indicated by Boone and Crockett scoring records. The minimum B&C score for grizzlies is 24, for brown bears 28.

Brown bears range the coast of southeast Alaska including the Kenai and Alaska peninsulas and associated islands such as Kodiak and Afognak. The interior grizzly formerly ranged throughout the Great Plains and all the western states, and from central Mexico north through Alaska. Now grizzly bears are restricted primarily to Alaska, the Yukon, Northwest Territories, British Columbia, and Alberta. The only viable grizzly populations in the United States exist in Montana, Wyoming, and Idaho, primarily in Glacier and Yellowstone National Parks and surrounding wilderness lands.

The range of the black bear, *Ursus americanus*, overlaps that of the grizzly throughout Alaska and western Canada, but black bears are still common across all of Canada to the eastern seaboard; in the New England states and south in the Appalachian Mountains to Georgia and Florida; the upper Midwest, particularly in Michigan, Wisconsin, and Minnesota; and throughout the 11 western states except Nevada. (For more details, see Black Bear.)

Distinguishing Grizzly and Black Bears

An average grizzly weighs 300 to 500 pounds, with some up to 800 pounds or more, and grizzlies have a distinct hump on the back above the front shoulders. An average mature black bear, in contrast, weighs 200 to 300 pounds (although really huge blacks will exceed 500 pounds) and has a relatively straight back.

The head of a grizzly bear has a blocky, square appearance, and the dished-in nose is nearly the same color as the rest of the body. The black bear, in contrast, has a more slender face and a straight nose that's often lighter in color than the rest of the body.

Black bears have a wide color range. The most common color phase is black, but in parts of the West, black bears are brown, cinnamon, and even blond. Grizzly bears can vary in color greatly from nearly black to straw-colored, but generally they're dark brown or blackish and the long guard hairs have a silvery appearance, which gives rise to the name silvertip grizzly.

The tracks of a big black bear measure about five inches across, and a grizzly's tracks may be six inches or wider. Size alone isn't a reliable distinction, though, because the track of a huge black bear could be larger than the track of an average grizzly. The grizzly's claws are much longer and may hit the ground two inches in front of the toe pads, and the toe pads fall in nearly a straight line. The black bear's claws are much shorter, and the toe pads form more of an arc.

Encounters with Bears

Black Bears. Occasionally these animals attack human beings but it's very rare, and for all practical purposes, you can forget about black bear attacks as you're hunting.

That doesn't mean black bears don't pose problems. They'll take a meal where they can get it, and that could very well be in your camp. A friend of mine went into the outfitting business, and at first he couldn't figure out why the former outfitter in his area had such a dislike for bears. Six months later, after his first season in the backcountry, he knew. "Those darned bears," he said. "I hate 'em. I can't leave anything in camp but what they're eating it or tearing it up."

To prevent destruction of your camp in bear country, keep things clean. Burn food scraps, and wash your dishes and cooking utensils regularly to keep smells to a minimum. And don't eat in bed. Seal food in plastic bags and hang it over a limb at least ten feet off the ground. Seal perishable foods in coolers. If you must leave a deer or other game you've killed in the field, try to hang it out of a bear's reach. In the backcountry, a small winch can be handy for this purpose.

Grizzly Bears. The same things said about keeping a clean camp in black-bear country apply to grizzly country, but additional precautions are in order. Black bears normally run from people, but that's not always true for grizzlies. Above all you want to avoid surprising a grizzly, so if you suspect the presence of a bear in heavy cover, go around, or make enough noise that the bear knows you're coming and can move away before you get too close.

One of the most dangerous situations for hunters is returning to a kill that has been left in the field. A grizzly that finds your elk all neatly gutted and quartered may very well decide it's *his* elk all neatly butchered. Bear authority Steve Herrero, author of *Bear Attacks—Causes and Deterrents*, said he's documented at least eight cases in which hunters returning to retrieve game in the field have been attacked by grizzlies.

Again, if you must leave game in the field, hang it at least ten feet off the ground. And as you return, assume that a bear has found it and approach noisily. If you find a grizzly bear there, and he hasn't been deterred by your noisy approach, wish him well and leave. Grizzlies won't climb, so if a grizzly actually attacks, you can find safety in a tree, providing you can get up one fast enough and can get out of reach. If that's not possible, your only real hope is to play dead. Curl into a ball to protect your stomach, and lock your hands behind your neck to protect your neck and head. Try not to move until the bear leaves.

Bear Hunting

Brown and grizzly bears are hunted primarily by spotting and stalking in spring and fall. Throughout grizzly range, nonresidents must hire a guide to hunt these animals legally. Montana offers the only exception. There you can hunt grizzlies on your own in the Bob Marshall Wilderness ecosystem. However, it's a tough hunt where bears are hard to find, and the season is closed when 25 bears, regardless of the cause of death—old age, fighting with each other, or whatever—have died.

Black bears, on the other hand, offer extensive hunting potential and are hunted by a variety of methods. (For full details, see Black Bear.)

BELT QUIVER   See Quiver.

BEZ TINE   Also called bay tine. This is the second antler tine, the one just above the brow tine. In North America, the term is most commonly used only with elk antlers. The bez tine curves upward similar to the brow tine, and generally it is longer than the brow tine. It's classified as G-2 on record-book scoring charts.

BLACK BEAR (*Ursus americanus*). Interest in black bears more or less parallels that of the mountain lion. Not too many years ago, these animals were viewed as predators, even vermin, and they generally weren't protected. In the past couple of decades bears and lions have been classified as game animals throughout North America, and interest among hunters, particularly bowhunters, has grown immensely. I can't prove this, but I'd say black bears rank third in popularity among American bowhunters, behind deer and elk.

The name "black bear" can be confusing, because many black bears aren't black. The black phase predominates in the East and Midwest, but in parts of the West, black bears vary in color from coal black to brown to cinnamon to blond. In Wyoming's Bighorn Mountains I shot a cinnamon-colored black bear, and in Montana I've seen them nearly blond.

Opinions—and laws—vary greatly on how and when bears should be hunted. Some states and provinces have spring and fall seasons, others only fall; some have special bow seasons, others only general any-weapons seasons. Some states and provinces allow, in addition to foot hunting, baiting and hunting with hounds. Others permit only hunting with

hounds but no baiting, some allow baiting but no hound hunting, and still others prohibit the use of both hounds and bait, which basically leaves only spotting or still-hunting. You have to study regulations carefully to find a state or province that offers options that interest you most.

Hunting with an Outfitter

Weekend hunting for bears generally doesn't work. The casual approach might be okay for relaxation, but if your goal is to kill a bear, don't get your hopes up. If you're short of time to study bears and their habits, your only realistic hope is to hunt with a guide or outfitter. Some guides spend weeks putting out baits to attract bears, and others have devoted years to training bear dogs. All you have to do as a hunter is show up and sit on a stand a few evenings waiting for a bear to come in, or keep up with the dogs once they find a hot track. That's the way to hunt bears if you can't devote much time and energy to bear hunting. (For more details, see Outfitters and Guides.)

Baiting. Most guides who hunt over baits do not guarantee success. They've spent dozens of hours putting out baits and they can assure you bears are coming in, but they can't be sure you

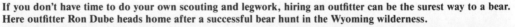

If you don't have time to do your own scouting and legwork, hiring an outfitter can be the surest way to a bear. Here outfitter Ron Dube heads home after a successful bear hunt in the Wyoming wilderness.

can kill a bear when it comes in. For these kind of hunts you pay a flat fee for the outfitter's time and services; if you get a bear, so much the better. Success generally runs pretty high.

Some outfitters work on a "will-call" basis. That is, rather than scheduling you for a specific date, they wait until they have a bear hitting a bait regularly. Then they call you, and you get there as fast as possible to hunt the bear.

Bait hunting with an outfitter can prove fairly relaxing. The outfitter has done all the hard work, so essentially you have little to do but climb a tree and watch for bears. On many of these hunts, you take a stand only in the afternoon, so you can sleep in and spend all morning and early afternoon loafing, fishing, or whatever.

Hunting with Hounds. In contrast, hound hunting can be a rigorous affair. You get out early in the morning, looking for tracks. If you do strike a fresh track, you could be all day running up and down the mountains.

Some houndmen (not all) run guaranteed hunts. They don't necessarily guarantee you a bear, but they guarantee that you won't have to pay unless you do get a bear. Finding and running a bear with hounds is never guaranteed, but once the bear has treed, you're pretty well assured of getting him, so that's why some houndmen feel comfortable in operating that way.

Some people have a jaundiced view of hound hunting because they think it's too easy. Without question, a hunter with good hounds in high-density bear country can catch bears regularly. On the other hand, there's no guarantee you'll find a track hot enough to run. Most houndmen follow the same general procedure. They drive backcountry roads, watching for tracks or other fresh sign. If you think a person can't spot bear tracks while driving along, think again. Most houndmen can spot week-old bear tracks on solid rock. Well, maybe that's exaggerated, but most will instantly notice tracks on soft dirt or dust at the edge of a road.

When they spot a track, they turn out a dog

A big bear track like this one measures about five inches across the pad. Notice that the toe marks in this track form an arc. The toes of a grizzly bear, in contrast, are much straighter across.

or two, and if the track is fresh enough for the dogs to smell, the chase is on. Some hunters also use a "strike" dog, a hound with an especially good nose. They put the dog on a platform either on the hood or bed of a pickup and slowly drive forest roads. When this dog smells a bear or a fresh track, he'll start barking, and he'll often "open" even when the houndman doesn't see the track.

That sounds simple enough, but it's not guaranteed. When conditions are right and bears are concentrated and the weather is right for trailing, catching bears this way is close to a sure thing. When conditions are wrong, it's nearly impossible.

Besides, bears are no respecter of persons, and they'll drag you into some spots you'll wish you'd never seen. Unless you're in reasonably good shape, don't book a hound hunt. But if you think you can handle the grind, it's probably about as sure as any method for collecting a bear rug.

Hunting Bears on Your Own

If you've got time to study bears and you like a challenge, you can successfully hunt bears on your own.

In addition to knowing specialized hunting techniques (explained below), you must recognize bear sign. Tracks are the most obvious sign. You can see the wide, flat tracks of bears coming off road banks in mud or dirt. On dusty roads or trails, you can spot shiny marks left by the pads of a bear's feet. A front track wider than five inches indicates a big bear.

Out in the woods you'll see rocks rolled over by bears looking for insects and grubs, and you'll see logs rolled over and torn up. Big holes dug into rotten logs probably were made by a bear looking for ants. Bears commonly leave their calling cards in the form of scratch marks on trees, and you'll find some trees that have been clawed dozens of times over a period of years. Bears like to eat the tender cambium layer under the heavy bark on trees, and if you see freshly girdled trees, you can bet a bear did the damage. Some timber companies hire professional hunters to kill bears to reduce this kind of damage.

Bear scat looks somewhat like dog scat, but it will vary in color and texture depending on what the bear has been eating. In spring it's green, in fall it might be full of berry pulp and so forth. The bigger the bear, the bigger the pile and the bigger around each stool.

Baiting

If one universal bear-hunting method exists—other than hunting with hounds, a specialized undertaking few of us will pursue on our own—it's baiting. Some persons question the sporting and ethical aspects of baiting, but the fact is, planning an effective bait hunt takes as much or more knowledge as any other kind of hunting, and it's a lot of work. Without question, the person who consistently baits and kills bears works a lot harder for each animal taken than does the average hunter for deer or antelope. Collecting, storing and distributing huge quantities of bait is a task few hunters will stick with long enough to collect a bear. In some localities, baiting presents the only feasible way to hunt bears.

Remember, baiting is illegal in some states, and in others it's restricted. In Wisconsin, for example, it is illegal to "hunt any species of wildlife over any bait other than apples, pastry

or liquid scent," and these must be confined to a hole in the ground measuring no more than two feet square. Other states have similar laws, and some require a baiting permit.

Baiting Materials. The principle is to create a food source that will hold bears in one small area and will pull them into range during daylight. To do that you have to feed them well. A few table scraps thrown out in the woods once a week won't do the job. The bear will eat them up and move on and never come back. Babe Stojonac of Chicago has taken 16 bears over bait in Michigan and Ontario, and he stocks 600 to 700 pounds of bait on each of eight to ten bait stations throughout the season. Every weekend Ray Grenier, who killed eight bears in his first five years of bear hunting—four in Maine, four in New Hampshire—buys 500 pounds of meat scraps (at six cents a pound) from a slaughterhouse to keep four or more bait stations fresh. Oregon bear addict Bill Bechen estimates he hauled 2,400 pounds of apples and meat to his four bait stations one fall.

Meat scraps may be the most common baiting material, but other foods work, too. One guide I hunted with in Idaho used nothing but used cooking grease from restaurants. When Stojonac hunts in Ontario in the spring, he has local trappers save beaver carcasses for him, and he nets spawning suckers from creeks near his hunting area. These baits work spring or fall, but in fall when bears are putting on fat for hibernation, sweets such as apples and other fruits may be even better.

Bob Faufau, who has killed six bears including a whopping 700-pounder in his home state of Wisconsin, swears by pastries. During summer he stores dozens of cases of stale sweet rolls in a walk-in freezer. The use of meat is outlawed in Wisconsin now, but even when it was legal, Faufau found that pastries worked better. "I've seen bears throw meat aside to get to sweet rolls," Faufau said. "In Wisconsin you can hardly make a bear eat fish. I've put carp on a pile and the fish laid there and rotted because bears ate the bread first."

Bechen suggests that any serious bear hunter

should keep a journal and record what happens at the bait pile. After a while you'll see a pattern to the kinds of foods bears prefer in a given area.

Location. Baiting doesn't demand extensive scouting to pinpoint a bear's haunts. That's the purpose of the bait—to pull bears to you. Still, you have to know the general whereabouts of animals and their habits. Grenier begins his scouting at home on topographic maps. In spring he looks for south slopes where the first green grass will attract and hold bears. For fall hunting he prefers draws and canyon bottoms that serve as travel routes for bears. Stojonac also places baits near creek bottoms where thick, dank vegetation makes traveling bears feel comfortable.

Barring drastic habitat changes, the conditions that attract bears to a given area one year will attract bears there another, so don't forget your productive sites. Bechen said he'd been using the same four bait sites for several years, and once he starts baiting in late summer, he consistently has bears on each one all fall. He points out that his baits are a mile or more apart to ensure that he's getting different bears at each site.

Of course, not all bait stations will produce, and these might just as well be abandoned. The same applies if conflicts arise. Rarely is much love lost between bait hunters and houndmen, because hound hunters—sometimes inadvertently, sometimes purposely—will run bears off another hunter's baits.

Bechen said he gave up two bait stations because hound hunters found them and started routinely checking the baits and running bears there. The houndmen killed one large bear Bechen had been watching and trying to kill for several weeks.

Put your baits well away from roads, and if possible, place them at the border of roadless country. Houndmen don't like to run bears near wilderness because they might lose their dogs. In New Hampshire, Grenier often backpacks his baits three fourths of a mile or farther from the nearest road to avoid conflicts with houndmen.

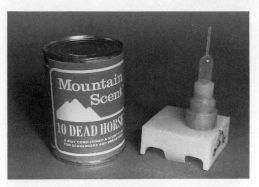

Smelly products like 10 Dead Horse from Mountain Scent and Bugle Manufacturing help draw bears to a bait. The hot-scent station at right intensifies a scent, especially on a cold day.

You can choose bait sites fairly systematically. Grenier said he studies his maps and picks eight or ten "test sites." At each he puts a pile of meat and sprinkles anise oil, a strong licorice-smelling liquid, around on logs and bushes as a powerful attractor scent. After a week or two, he abandons unproductive sites and heavily baits active sites. By the time the season opens he wants four active bait stations going to assure alternatives in case other hunters disturb one or two and to allow hunting under various weather conditions. One might be better with a north wind, another when wind blows from the south.

Getting Their Attention. Attractor scents such as Grenier's anise oil can help pull in bears quicker than clean food alone. Many hunters routinely burn smelly foods such as bacon, honey, or used cooking oil at bait sites to send a plume of attractive smoke throughout the area. Mountain Scent and Bugle Manufacturing of Stevensville, Montana, makes a product called 10 Dead Horse (the name alone ought to attract something) that produces a rotten meat aroma to attract bears, and the same company makes a hot-scent station that emits odors attractive to bears. Nirk's Bear Grenade serves a similar function.

Other companies such as Buck Stop and Tink's Safariland Corporation produce rotten-meat and other attractor scents. Any of these

Several companies make bear baits and other attractors that can be used to enhance the drawing power of a bait station.

can be used not only in establishing new bait stations, but throughout the season to keep bears interested. Dragging rotten meat or other potent scents in a spoke pattern to your bait can help bears find the bait quickly.

Stands. Most bowhunters favor tree stands over ground blinds. From a tree stand you can draw and shoot undetected far more easily than you can on the ground. Even more important, a tree stand gets your scent off the ground so a circling bear won't smell you nearly as easily as if you were on the ground. Just make sure that any blind is downwind of the bait; bears have incredible noses. (For more details, see Stand Hunting.)

Getting the Shot. Setting up a bait and blind doesn't guarantee anything. As Grenier said, "Any fool can haul food into the woods and get a bear to eat it. The trick is to get a good shot at the bear."

That first means getting the animal in during daylight. A suspicious bear will wait until dark to come in, so you want to do everything possible to make him feel comfortable. Your site should be near cover so bears don't have to venture far into the open to feed.

In most cases you should restrict hunting to evenings because bears normally come to a bait in late afternoon and stay nearby until daylight the next morning. If you go to your blind between 2:00 and 3:00 P.M. and stay until dark, you'll be waiting when the bear comes in. But

if you walk to your stand early in the morning, even before daylight, you may spook bears that have been there all night.

When you go in to replenish a bait, always maintain a certain routine, and don't try to sneak in. The bears know you're around so you can't sneak past them anyway, and if you spook one off the bait during daylight, he'll probably start coming in after dark. Bob McGuire, a leading authority on bears and author of the excellent book *Black Bears*, says it's important to establish a consistent routine to avoid surprising bears at the bait. (Incidentally, McGuire's book is the best available on bowhunting for bears and belongs on every serious hunter's bookshelf.)

While maintaining a bait you can't totally prevent leaving some human scent around, but you should do everything possible to prevent bears smelling you when you're on stand. Stands should always be placed downwind of baits, and you should wear clean clothes and bathe before each hunt. It may help to wear rubber boots to keep your scent off the ground, and you should approach your stand from the opposite direction the bears come from to avoid leaving your scent on their trails.

Bait containers vary considerably. Where legal, many hunters put their baits in 50-gallon drums. Others use whole animal carcasses, but these must be wired to a tree or other solid anchor to keep bears from dragging them away. You can also put your bait in a pit.

Whatever method you choose, it's crucial to place the bait so a feeding bear will present a good shot. Bears must be hit perfectly for a quick kill. That's especially true because their thick fat and loose hides can seal an arrow hole, and their long fur soaks up blood, which almost guarantees a skimpy blood trail. Blinds should be close to the bait, anywhere from 20 to 50 feet, and the bait station should be built so the bear must present a good shooting angle, quartering slightly away so the arrow will pass diagonally through both lungs.

Stojonac, among others, goes to great lengths to get that shot. He cuts all bait material into small chunks so a bear can't wander off with big chunks but must stand right there to eat. He points out that if you dump bait in a clearing, a bear can eat facing any direction, but if you pile it against a tree or rock, the bear must turn his back toward you. Stojonac carries that idea further by building a small log crib, which looks like the corner of a split-rail fence. He puts his bait inside the "V" so a bear must put his head right into the crib to eat.

Ambush Hunting

Maybe this could be called "natural" baiting. If you know the habits of bears well enough, you can ambush them in the course of their natural movements. Doug Menzies, a conservation officer with the New Hampshire Fish and Game Department, has perfected this approach.

In northern New Hampshire, Menzies watches abandoned apple orchards or hardwood forests with rich mast crops. Studies show that bears in New Hampshire feed heavily on corn and apples in September and on acorns and beechnuts in October. Menzies scouts promising feed areas, looking for dung piles and scratched-up ground and leaves where bears have pawed for nuts and acorns. When he finds heavy bear sign, he makes a ground blind 50 to 60 yards away on the downwind side and sits on stand the first hour of daylight in the morning and the last two hours in the evening. He shot his first bear this way in an apple orchard in 1975, and he's killed three since—in 1979, 1980, and 1981—by watching oak groves. He rifle-shot these bears, but there's no reason why a bowhunter couldn't apply the same principles.

Spotting and Stalking

This method doesn't work just anywhere. The country has to be steep enough for you to see from one side hill into another and it must be reasonably open. The West offers by far the best spotting potential. In Montana, where baiting and hound hunting are illegal, hunters kill several hundred bears each year, and most are taken by stalking.

As in any visual hunting, binoculars rate as the number one piece of equipment, and a spotting scope is a close second. (For details, see Optics and Spotting.)

Once you have the right equipment and know how to use it, the major step in spotting bears is knowing where they feed. Bears are relatively few and far between compared to most game animals, so you can't look just anywhere. Bears are opportunists when it comes to eating, and they'll travel long distances to chow down a particular delicacy at a given time of year. You have to know where they'll congregate at any given time to see them. On a six-day hunt in Idaho, friends and I spotted 13 bears, and in eight days in Montana we saw 33.

Spring Hunting. Most hunters consider spring the ideal time for spotting. When bears first emerge from hibernation, their stomachs

In many areas, bears can be spotted in the open and then stalked. In central Idaho, I used binoculars to spot this bear across a canyon, and then stalked within 15 yards of the bear. Bears feed on green grass in open meadows in the spring.

aren't ready for a diet of heavy foods such as meat, so they feed heavily on lush green feed. I've watched many bears in spring grazing on green meadow grass just like cattle. In northwestern Montana, the shoulders and borrow pits of many logging roads are seeded with grass, and in April and May a carpet of tender grass sprouting up along the roads attracts lots of bears. In this country, many hunters simply drive the backroads, looking for bears in the borrow ditches. They take a lot of animals this way.

In most areas you'll have to get off the roads to find many bears in the open. Natural openings offer good spring feeding conditions and you'll likely find bears in avalanche chutes eating skunk cabbage or glacier lilies, and you'll see them in meadows eating grass and forbs. Western Montana and central Idaho offer excellent spotting conditions. On the Snake and Salmon rivers and their many tributaries, for example, the canyons are very steep with small meadows interspersed with brush and dense groves of conifers—ideal bear habitat. It's common to sit on one ridge and spot bears feeding on the next ridge over.

In heavily timbered regions, clearcuts serve much the same function as natural meadows in other places. Washington traditionally has had the highest bear harvest in the United States, and in western Washington, a land of heavy rain and junglelike forests, the bears use logged areas in the spring for green feed.

Even in spring, you won't find many bears far out in the open. Bears like concealment, and most likely you'll see them in small green pockets among heavy cover. Watch right along the edges of timber patches, and look into sparse timber. In many cases you'll just see a hint of black occasionally through openings in the forest. In early spring, while they're still on green feed, bears roam small home ranges. If you find sign or see a bear in one place, keep an eye on that spot, because you'll see him there time after time.

Fall Spotting. Most hunters associate spotting with spring hunting, but it can be just as deadly in the fall. Here, though, it's even more important to know the food preferences in a given region. Tim Burton, a wildlife biologist in California, has worked on bear studies for years. Come fall, Burton said, bears may head out suddenly and follow some inexplicable sense as far as 12 miles to the richest food sources. In California that often means acorns or manzanita berries, or if salmon runs are heavy, bears may migrate to coastal streams.

In northwestern Washington, northern Idaho, and northwestern Montana, bears follow ripening huckleberries from lowlands in midsummer to high country in fall, and north-slope huckleberry patches attract bears from miles in all directions in early September. It's not uncommon to see a dozen or more bears feeding in one burn or natural opening where huckleberries are ripe. That's given a normal year. With a hard early freeze, the berry crop might be poor and bears could disperse to look for other foods.

Throughout the Northwest, you'd have a hard time beating the first ten days or so of September for bear spotting. In a period of one hour on September 8 in Oregon's Blue Mountains, I spotted three separate bears feeding on berries. From September 1 through 3 in California's Coast Range, I spotted three bears in three days. They were in the open, eating manzanita berries.

In Arizona, avid bowhunter Jay Elmer said he often finds bears feeding on mast (nuts and acorns) in September and on prickly pears at the edge of the desert in October. He's seen as many as eight bears in an evening gorging themselves on juicy purple "cactus apples."

Take Your Time. If there's any secret to spotting bears, it's patience. Even under ideal conditions bears can be scarce compared to other big game, so spotting bears can take lots of looking. Jay Elmer said he started bear hunting by walking and watching just as he always had for other big game, but that didn't work. Then one year he just sat on a high rim for hours, watching one canyon, and that did work. Even though the oak trees were dense, he found that if he watched patiently, he'd eventually see black hair ghosting among the trees. He also frequently heard bears before he saw them as they rolled rocks and ripped limbs from trees to get acorns.

From 1950 through 1975, Ralph Flowers worked as a professional hunter for the Washington Forest Protection Association, and during that time he killed 1,100 black bears. Granted, those were shot with a rifle, but the techniques Flowers used to spot bears will work for anybody. Hunting from May through August, when bears are in rut and most active, Flowers would sit every morning and evening on one side of a canyon to watch a brushy clearcut on the other side. He concentrated on clearcuts where the brush had grown up enough to make bears feel hidden and comfortable. Eventually he'd see black movement in the brush or would hear a bear smashing logs as it looked for insects.

Stalking. With his rifle, Flowers, of course, could shoot from one side of a canyon to the other, but with a bow you're just starting when you've spotted a bear. And stalking a bear will challenge the best of hunters. Bears make their living primarily with their noses, so it should go without saying they're sharp. On a scale of 1

to 10, I'd give a bear's nose a 15. Unless you've got a good steady wind in your favor, don't try stalking a bear. You'll never get close. Bide your time, and wait until conditions are right.

I think their ears are nearly as good. Not only can a bear hear the tiniest sound, but it can instantly distinguish that sound from natural sounds it's been hearing all along. Again on the scale of 1 to 10, I'd give a bear's ears a 10. Unlike deer or elk, which will peer curiously to identify the source of a sound, bears commonly just take off. Fast. For that reason, you've got to be very proficient and patient to get within bow range of a bear. (For more details, see Stalking.)

Eyesight is probably the most debated of a bear's senses. Some hunters say bears can see well, others say they're blind. Certainly bears will notice movement, but my experience says they have pretty poor eyes. I've walked across an open hillside in plain sight of a bear and have not been detected. Of course, I moved very slowly. Using the 1 to 10 scale again, I'd give bears a 3 for eyesight. And that's where your advantage as a bowhunter comes in. If you have the wind in your favor, and you can move without making a sound, you're almost guaranteed of sneaking within bow range. I've

Calling can be an effective bear hunting technique. Larry Jones, shown here with a bear from Oregon, has called in several bears

stalked within 15 to 20 yards of several bears.

Calling

Probably the least known bear hunting technique is calling, but it can be productive and exciting at times. Reed Peterson, a high school coach in Phoenix, Arizona, has called in 42 bears during a 20-year period. Many of those have been exceptionally large bears.

"You don't have to be a particularly good caller to fool bears," Peterson said. "Calling in a bear is mostly a matter of knowing where the bears are. You can't call up a bear in front of Valley National Bank."

In Arizona Peterson concentrates on the transition country between scrub oak and desert where bears feed on prickly pear cactus in September and October. Then he calls much as he would for coyotes. Using a Circe cottontail call, he squeals and shrieks on the call for a minute, rests 15 seconds, calls another minute, rests 15 seconds, and so on. He gradually shortens the call and blows more quietly.

He does only one thing differently from coyote calling. Rarely does he call from a coyote stand for more than 10 minutes, but he'll stay in one place 30 to 40 minutes for a bear. One time he and a friend were calling when they saw a bear come over a rise a mile away. Peterson called for 45 minutes until the bear finally rambled within range. He said that it's common for bears to take an hour or more coming in.

Peterson believes this kind of calling will work anywhere. "The sound you make with a predator call don't necessarily imitate a dying rabbit," he said. "Those sounds are almost a universal distress call and any predator anywhere will come to investigate."

Peterson is probably right. Rus Willis, a guide out of Heron, Montana, called in three bears one spring in the mountains near his home, using predator calling methods similar to Peterson's. Some hunters vary their calls, too, according to the season, and in Rocky Mountain states, some hunters have used the sounds of deer fawns in the spring to call in bears.

Trophy Bears

To many hunters, bear "trophy" means bear rug, so those hunters look for a high-quality hide. Early spring, when bears first come out of hibernation, probably presents the best time for a good rug; the hair is thick and long. In most areas bears have good hides through May. Then you'll see them in various stages of shedding, although I've talked to outfitters who've taken prime bears through June. The hides again become prime by early to mid-fall. As you study a bear, look for rubbed spots around the head, shoulders, and hips, and pass him up if he's not prime.

Record-book entry is based on two skull measurements—length and width. Without horns or antlers to study, judging trophy quality can be tough. Young bears normally have thin, pointed heads and the ears appear fairly large in relation to the head. As a bear gets older, its head fills out and the head looks broad and round, and the ears are small in relation to the head. Virtually all record-book bears are males, and males normally are solitary. If you see a large bear accompanied by smaller ones, you can assume the bigger one is a sow, and the smaller bears are cubs or yearlings. (For more details, see Trophy Scoring.)

BLACKTAIL DEER (*Odocoileus hemionus columbianus*) Scientists classify 11 subspecies of mule deer, of which the blacktail is one. That would seem to make the blacktail just another variation on the mule deer theme, and indeed similarities do exist.

Blacktails and mule deer both have bifurcated antlers, for example, and physiologically they're closely related. In the Cascade Mountains of Oregon and Washington where their ranges overlap, blacktails and mule deer interbreed to form a cross locally called a "benchleg." These deer generally look like blacktails, but they're larger and they grow larger antlers.

Despite biological similarities, most hunters consider mule deer and blacktails as distinct critters. Blacktails generally live in brushy, temperate climates with dense forests and heavy undergrowth. Although some blacktails do live in the high mountains and migrate long distances between summer and winter ranges, they just as commonly live in tiny woodlots right in the middle of towns and cities and feed on flowers and vegetable gardens at night, and they may live their entire lives within a tiny home range. In this enclosed environment, they tend to hide and peek, acting more like white-tails than like mule deer.

Average weight of blacktails varies considerably from one region to another. In many ranges, 100 pounds would be about the average field-dressed weight for blacktails. In some mountain areas they grow much larger, and some bucks have field dressed heavier than 200 pounds. That would be considered huge, however, and even in the best ranges, a buck that field dresses 150 pounds is bigger than average.

Blacktail antlers are much smaller than those of mule deer. The biggest blacktail antlers ever recorded measure 182²⁄₈. No others come within 10 inches of that. In contrast, the *minimum* Boone and Crockett score for mule deer is 195, and dozens of bucks exceeding that have been killed. Obviously, the hunter who dreams of seeing a huge rack silhouetted on a western horizon has a far better chance in mule deer country, and that's probably one reason blacktails have never gained the popularity of mule deer among western hunters.

Even at that, blacktails have their ardent followers, and for good reason. They are crafty and present a supreme challenge. Anyone who can take big blacktail bucks regularly has to be an exceptional hunter.

Hunters also stand a good chance for killing a blacktail that will make the record books. The minimum Pope and Young score is 90, and any mature three-point buck will score that well. The Boone and Crockett minimum score is 130, and mature four-points that exceed that score are not uncommon. A dedicated bowhunter has good opportunity to put a blacktail not only in the Pope and Young book, but possibly Boone and Crockett.

Blacktail deer range from Los Angeles north along the coast to Prince William Sound in

In some parts of their range, blacktail deer do not grow nearly as large as the average mule deer. Here I'm packing a buck from the California Coast Range, and this buck probably field dresses little more than 100 pounds.

Alaska. Biologists use Smith Sound on the British Columbia coast opposite the northern tip of Vancouver Island as the dividing line between blacktail and Sitka deer, but the Pope and Young record book uses the Alaskan border as the boundary. The record book classifies all deer in Alaska, as well as British Columbia's Queen Charlotte Islands, as Sitka deer, and all coastal deer south of the Alaskan border as blacktails. (For more details, see Sitka Deer.)

California

Central Coast. Most hunters picture blacktails among the ferns and junglelike forests of the Pacific Northwest, but these deer thrive in an extreme of environments. Along the coast of California between San Francisco and Santa Barbara, they live in the Coast Range between the Pacific Ocean and the Central Valley, where summer temperatures commonly exceed 100 degrees and rainfall is scarce. Indeed the brush

Some hunters imagine that blacktail country consists of rain forests and dense brush, but that's not universally true. In parts of California, habitat is open grass-covered hills and scattered oak groves. In this country, you can hunt by spotting.

is thick in places, but it consists of doghair, popcorn-dry chamise chaparral, rather than ferns and old-growth timber.

Much of this southern range also consists of beautiful rolling hills carpeted with wild oats and golden grass, along with scattered oak groves in the draws and north slopes. It's beautiful, open country, a pleasant place to hunt, and deer are quite visible here and can be hunted by spotting, much as mule deer can.

I've hunted this country several times. On

Don Nelson, left, admires his son Steve's first buck, a blacktail from central California. The average mature buck here grows two points to the side. This buck, with a 20-inch-wide rack, is larger than average for this country.

one hunt in the Diablo Range east of San Jose, friends and I hunted exclusively by spotting. The ranch we hunted consisted of open grasslands with oak groves nestled on the north slopes, and scattered patches of dense chamise brush. We still-hunted through some of the oak groves, but more commonly we sat on one ridge and glassed for deer on the opposite ridges. We spotted many bucks this way and then stalked them, just as I've done many times for desert mule deer.

One morning I spotted a buck lying on the very apex of an open peak. I circled around the peak to get the wind in my favor and crawled within 27 yards of that buck, and then shot him when he stood up. It was open-country hunting at its finest, a far cry from the dense brush hunting commonly associated with blacktails.

Unfortunately, most of the land in this region is privately owned so access is poor. Some national forest and military lands offer public hunting, but for the most part, you must know a landowner or be willing to pay to hunt. The average blacktail here grows only two points to the side, and bucks average about 100 pounds field dressed. The buck I killed field dressed about 130 pounds. Its rack had only two points to the side, but it had a 19-inch spread. The ranch owner considered that a very big buck for that region.

This part of California, classified as Zone A in the regulations, offers the earliest bow season in the United States. The season opens in mid-July and closes in early August. Come prepared for hot weather, 100 degrees and up. Traditionally the bag limit has been two bucks, forked horn or larger.

Northern Mountains. North of the Bay Area, in Mendocino, Trinity, Humboldt, and Siskiyou counties, thousands of acres of national forest land offer excellent blacktail hunting. Along the coast, heavy rainfall produces dense vegetation where stand hunting would be most effective. But inland about 50 miles, the interior Coast Range receives much less rainfall, and the high country along the crest of this range presents hunting conditions similar to much mule deer country, with high alpine meadows and steep, sparsely forested canyons. This region contains several wilderness areas — Marble Mountain, Salmon-Trinity Alps, Yolla Bolly — where you can find solitude and big bucks. You also can expect to see black bears here.

I've hunted the higher elevations of the interior Coast Range extensively, where binoculars and a spotting scope are standard gear. Deer

California offers the earliest deer season in the United States with its Zone A deer season, which opens in mid-July. Temperatures near 100 degrees are common, so you must arrange cooling facilities for meat storage.

This young blacktail inhabits typical country along much of California's Coast Range. Wild oat fields and scattered oak trees create a beautiful setting and a pleasant place to hunt.

concentrate in alpine basins where brush and other feed are lush, and I've commonly spotted 20 to 30 bucks in a day, including some big ones. Once I've spotted a good buck, I then stalk him. (For details, see Spotting and Stalking.)

Forests of the higher elevations here consist of fairly open conifers giving way to oak trees and open grasslands in the foothills, and here still-hunting can be effective. (For details, see Still-Hunting.) It's a matter of finding lush feed where deer have concentrated. The Department of Fish and Game has burned thousands of acres in small blocks throughout this region to improve deer habitat, and these small burns attract lots of deer. Northern California has produced more Boone and Crockett entries than any other single region, and you can expect to find good sized three- and four-point bucks here. In the high country, bucks that field dress heavier than 150 pounds aren't uncommon.

Seasons. The season in Northern California generally opens in mid-August and closes in mid-September. The weather is pleasantly warm but not suffocating. Traditionally, the limit has been two bucks, forked horn or larger.

Oregon produces some of the largest blacktails found anywhere. George Shurtleff holds the antlers from the Pope and Young world record blacktail he killed in Oregon's Willamette Valley. He took the other two huge bucks in the same region.

Oregon

Oregon's Coast Range presents extremely dense conditions with heavy underbrush. It's truly a rain forest jungle. Deer are plentiful, but few really large blacktails come from these mountains.

Trophy Bucks. The biggest blacktails come from inland river valleys and the foothills of the Cascade Mountains. The Rogue River valley in Jackson County produces some huge blacktails, but the record-book boundary line has been moved westward to eliminate some of the best territory from classification as blacktail range, so this isn't the best place to hunt if you strictly want a buck for the record book. Nevertheless, the southern Cascades hold some fine blacktail country.

If you're looking for a trophy blacktail, the best region in Oregon, and probably in North America, is the Willamette Valley and the bordering Cascade Mountain foothills. Clackamas, Linn, and Marion counties have produced more than their share of Boone and Crockett entries, and George Shurtleff's Pope and Young world record—172²/₈—came from Marion County. Northern California has produced a greater number of record-book entries, but most of the biggest bucks have come from this part of Oregon.

Here you'll find woodlots of Douglas fir with an undergrowth of blackberry brambles, ferns, alders, and other thick brush, and these plots are intermixed with clearcuts in the foothills and agricultural fields on the valley floor. Many of the best bucks are killed near clearcuts and fields.

Some hunters still-hunt this country with fair success, and others drive the timber pockets to push deer out. However, in the dense cover here, blacktails can see moving hunters and sneak away with little fear of getting shot, so these aren't the best methods.

Stand Hunting. Just as stand hunting has proven most effective for whitetails in thick eastern forests and woodlots, so has it proven best for big blacktail bucks. (For details, see Stand Hunting.) In fact, conditions are very similar, East and West. George Shurtleff has taken three of the biggest blacktails ever killed by archers (or by anybody, for that matter), and he's taken them all while on stand.

Boyd Iverson, a rifle hunter, tried for years to kill a big blacktail by still-hunting. It just didn't work, so he turned to stands and has since killed a buck that scored close to 145, well up in Boone and Crockett, as well as some other enviable bucks. "Stand hunting is about the only way you'll get bucks like that in this heavy brush," Iverson said.

If that's true for a rifle hunter, it's doubly true for archers. The same guidelines that work for whitetails apply to blacktails. In particular, you try to find an intersection of well-used trails, preferably in berry brambles or doghair alders that will funnel deer into one path, and that's where you place your stand.

Other Methods. One other technique has come into its own in Oregon, and that's antler rattling. I know several hunters who've consistently rattled in blacktails. (For details, see Rattling.) Some hunters also have good success calling blacktails with a conventional bleat call. (For details, see Deer Calling.)

Incidentally, blacktails make scrapes although apparently not with the regularity of whitetails. I know of no one who seriously hunts scrapes for blacktails, but I've talked to several hunters who've found scrapes and have proved bucks were using them. Herb Hoppe found what appeared to be a scrape, so he blinded in there and rattled a pair of antlers, and within 20 seconds a wild-eyed buck charged from the brush and ran right up to Hoppe. Jesse Stalcup said he and his friends had found one large scrape and had taken five bucks near it.

Seasons. In Oregon, the general bow season runs from late August through September. Some units open again in November, and this presents the best time to kill a trophy buck, because that's when the deer are in rut. The peak of rut occurs about November 20.

Washington

The Washington coast receives some of the highest rainfall in North America and the vege-

tation grows accordingly, so a hunter here must adapt with brush-country tactics. Overall, Washington hasn't produced as many trophy blacktails as Oregon and California, but some areas have good trophy potential. As in Oregon, the largest bucks do not come from the coastal mountains but farther inland from farmlands and foothills bordering the Cascade Mountains. The Boone and Crockett world record blacktail, with a remarkable score of $182^2/_8$, came from upper Lincoln Creek in Lewis County. A band of counties bordering the Cascades, including Skamania, Lewis, Pierce, and King, have yielded most of Washington's record-book blacktails.

The same hunting tactics that work in Oregon apply to Washington, although seasons generally don't fall during the rut in Washington. Early archery season in western Washington usually runs from early through late September, and many units open again for bowhunting in December.

British Columbia

This province offers an extension of the same brushy conditions found along the Washington coast. Deer are plentiful in British Columbia, but they're hunted mostly by locals. The deer are not large here—very few appear in the record books—and a nonresident hunter must hire a guide, so few hunters go there just to pursue blacktail deer.

BOONE AND CROCKETT CLUB This organization was established in 1887 by Theodore Roosevelt. Although most hunters today equate "Boone and Crockett" with the trophy record book, the club originally was started as a conservation group to stop destruction of wildlife in the West.

The first American record book, called *Records of North American Big Game*, was published in 1932. The measuring system at that time took into account only length and spread, which proved inadequate for many species of deer. In 1949 the Boone and Crockett Club formed a committee to improve the measuring system, and in 1950 the club adopted scoring methods that are basically the same as those used today. In 1952, the Boone and Crockett Club published the first record book based on the current system.

To explain the system for average hunters, Grancel Fitz, a member of the revision committee, wrote a booklet called *How to Measure and Score Big Game Trophies*. Published in 1963, this book became the standard. The Boone and Crockett Club has since published *Measuring and Scoring North American Big Game Trophies*, an excellent and detailed guide on all aspects of measuring.

The Boone and Crockett awards program began in 1947, and since 1970 awards banquets have been held every three years. Top animals entered in each category for the triennium are measured by a panel of judges, and these invited trophies are displayed publicly before and during the banquet. At the awards banquet, the club presents medals or certificates for the largest animals entered during the three-year period. The top three trophies taken by fair chase—that includes rifle, bow and arrow, and other legal hunting methods—receive first, second and third-place awards. Other trophies, such as picked-up heads, are eligible only for certificates of merit. In addition, the Sagamore Hill Award, the highest award given by the Boone and Crockett Club, is presented occasionally for truly outstanding heads.

The Boone and Crockett Club publishes *Records of North American Big Game* (commonly called the Boone and Crockett Book) every six years or when significant changes take place in trophy ranking. Awards books are also published every three years, following the close of the entry period. Entry requirements for each game species for the awards-period books are lower than for the all-time record book.

Entering a trophy head in the Boone and Crockett awards program does not make a hunter eligible for membership in the club. To be considered for membership, a candidate must be referred by four active members, must have an outstanding record in hunting and conservation, and must have taken three adult male animals with a rifle in fair chase. Regular membership is limited to 100. Recently the club has started an associate membership program.

Contact. Boone and Crockett Club, 241 South Fraley Boulevard, Dumfries, VA 22026.

BOW CARE Modern bows are so well made they're virtually maintenance-free. The only problems I've ever had with bows resulted from major accidents. I closed the tip of a recurve bow in a car door, which didn't do it much good, and I fell on a compound bow and broke a limb tip. Friends have told about driving over their bows, which they'd laid on the ground or leaned against their vehicles, or dropping bows from cliffs or trees and breaking them. Aside from such disasters, if you treat a bow with any care at all, it will last for many years.

Preventing Abuse

Bow Case. Undoubtedly some of the worst damage to bows occurs in vehicles on the way to and from hunting, as the bow slides around in the bed of a pickup or rattles in a window rack. A bow case prevents such needless wear and tear.

Bow cases come in two general designs—hard and soft. I find a soft case far more convenient for general use around home, in the car, and at camp. Most soft cases have a heavy canvas or nylon Cordura outer shell and foam padding inside. They have one squared end so

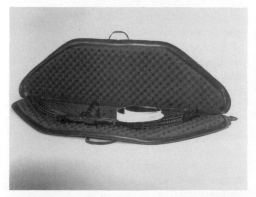

Many soft cases, like PSE's Elite Case, have a nylon or canvas outer shell and thick foam padding inside. They protect a bow well around camp and in a vehicle.

you can put in your bow with the quiver full of arrows. The best ones have several pockets on the outside for spare gear and arrows. My Hoyt/Easton case, for example, has a long pocket that will hold more than a dozen arrows; it has a second pocket big enough for scents, camouflage cream, armguard, stabilizer, and other accessories; and it has a third, smaller pouch for spare broadheads and other small items. I can throw this loaded case into my truck and take off, confident I have all the gear needed for a long hunt.

Hard cases are big and bulky, so they're less than ideal for everyday use. For airplane travel, however, a hard case is a must. Airline workers are well schooled in baggage destruction, and if your bow isn't protected with a tough plastic or aluminum case with a reliable lock, your bow might not make it to the hunt in one piece. A hard case should have strong hinges, or better yet a full-length piano hinge, as well as several strong latches you can lock down. The case should hold your bow, quiver full of arrows, a couple of dozen spare arrows, and spare heads, strings, shooting tab, and other accessories.

Dry Fire. When you shoot a bow, the arrow absorbs a high percentage of the energy released by the limbs. If you dry fire a bow (shoot it with no arrow on the string), the bow itself absorbs all the energy, and the stress of vibration through the limbs, handle, cables, and string can blow things apart. Dry firing is a good way to destroy a bow. Don't do it.

Shooting excessively lightweight arrows can produce similar damage, because light arrows absorb a small percentage of the bow's energy. In essence, shooting ultralight arrows from a heavy poundage bow approaches a dry-fire condition, so it's not recommended. (For more details, see Bow Efficiency and Overdraw.)

Heat. In hot climates, heat ranks as the number one enemy of bows with laminated limbs. I've talked to archery shop owners who can relate dozens of horror stories about bow limbs delaminated by heat. The major culprit is the car-window bow rack. Never hang your bow in a rack in the direct sun, and don't store

Hard cases are bulkier and harder to handle than soft cases, but for use on airlines, they offer much better protection.

a bow in the trunk of your car in hot weather. Keep the bow in a padded case, and store it in the shade, preferably under sleeping bags or other lightweight gear that will help to insulate it. Another choice is to buy a bow with solid-glass limbs. These limbs are made of one solid piece, so there's nothing to come apart, and they're virtually impervious to the effects of heat.

Moisture. I've hunted in endless rain and other soggy conditions and have never had a problem with bow limbs, but bowmakers do warn that moisture can seep between the laminations on limbs and cause them to come apart. Most bows have excellent watertight finishes so you don't need to fret about this problem, but some minor precautions are in order. During heavy rain, wipe your bow dry whenever possible, and at night, store it inside out of the rain. Again, glass limbs also solve the problem. They won't absorb moisture, so they're reliable under the wettest conditions.

Loose Parts. One time on opening day, a friend of mine called a bull elk within good bow range, but when he drew his bow and released, he ended up with cables and string wrapped around his head, and the elk ran away unscathed. An axle keeper, one of those seemingly insignificant little clips snapped on the ends of compound bow axles, had come off. When my friend shot, the axle slipped out of the limb tip, and the wheels, cables, and string came crashing down. Lesson: Check those keepers before each shooting session, and carry some spares in your tackle box and hunting pack.

The same goes for other screws. Recurve and longbow shooters pooh-pooh compounds because of all the screws and bolts and other moving parts. They have a valid point. A compound does present maintenance problems. You have to keep an eye on these parts and check them regularly. My tackle box contains a complete set of Allen wrenches and various screwdrivers, and before each hunt I check all screws and bolts. If sight and quiver screws don't have lock washers, I back the mounting plates with strips of inner-tube rubber. That not only silences the bow, but it acts as a lock washer to keep screws tight.

Rarely will you have problems with cables, but the plastic coating can get stripped off or worn, and then the cables should be replaced. You can buy replacement kits or have an archery pro shop replace the cables. Also, you need to lubricate the axles on a compound bow occasionally. Dry silicone lubricants are best because they don't collect dust and grit, although for wet weather, light oil like WD-40 works well because it keeps out moisture and prevents rust. Spray limb bolts and other steel parts to prevent rust in rainy weather.

Also, wax your bowstring regularly. Waxing helps to reduce wear. If strands are badly frayed or cut, replace the string. (For more details, see Bowstring.)

BOW EFFICIENCY Norb Mullaney, an engineer and possibly the most respected bow technician in the United States, defines bow efficiency as the amount of energy you get out of a bow compared to the amount of energy you put in. Most of the following discussion is based on conversations with Mullaney, and with well-known bow designer Tom Jennings.

Efficiency is expressed in terms of a percentage. That is, most bows are 60 to 80 percent efficient. A bow that's 80 percent efficient, for example, will give back 80 percent of the energy you put into it. For mechanical devices, that's considered very efficient. With an internal combustion engine, in contrast, you may get as little as 10 percent return in the form of movement, and the remaining energy goes into friction, heat, noise, and so forth.

Don't let an initial glance at the figures and charts here scare you. The concept is very simple, and you can figure the efficiency of any bow with very little equipment. You need a bow scale, a grain scale for weighing arrows, graph paper, and a chronograph. If you work on a lot of bows and want to fine-tune them, you might find it worthwhile to buy this gear. If you just want to check the one bow you own, then take it to a local archery shop. Most shops have a scale and chronograph you can use.

Stored Energy

The first aspect of bow efficiency is stored, or potential, energy. At one time this idea boggled my mind. What does "stored energy" mean? To grasp the idea, think of a car battery, a black box full of stored energy (in the form of electricity). The battery will sit there and do nothing until you turn the ignition switch of your car. Then you loose some of the energy to work for you—start the car, play the radio, turn on the headlights, and so forth.

When you pull back the string on a bow, the flexed limbs in essence become storage batteries, only they store mechanical rather than electrical energy. Until you let go of the string, the stored energy does nothing. But when you release that string, you "turn the ignition switch," which releases energy stored in the limbs to work for you, that is, to propel an arrow.

The Force-Draw Curve. You don't have to be

a genius to compute stored energy. You need only a bow scale and graph paper. The horizontal lines on the paper represent bow weight in pounds, and the vertical lines represent draw length in inches. Place your bow on the scale and start pulling it to full draw. At each one-inch interval, note the poundage, and mark that on the graph paper. Continue to pull the bow and mark poundage until you reach maximum draw length. You'll see that the points you've marked on the graph paper form a smooth curve. For a recurve bow the curve will slope gradually upward. For a round-wheel compound, it will slope from zero pounds at brace height up to peak weight at about 24 inches (exact distance depends on draw length), and then it will drop off sharply to the "valley" or minimum holding weight.

A cam bow will produce a graph picture similar to the round-wheel bow, but the front slope of the curve generally will be steeper and the peak will be somewhat broader and flatter. The picture you get on the graph is called a force-draw curve, which is just one way of say-

ing it takes a given amount of force to draw your bow. The curve on the graph paper simply presents a picture of the force required to draw the bow.

Computing Stored Energy. To determine the stored energy for a bow, add the averages of draw weights at each one-inch interval and then add up all the averages. This total gives you the inch-pounds of energy stored in your bow.

Why add the averages rather than the actual weights? As you can see from the curve, you have a triangle at the top of each one-inch increment so you can't get an exact poundage. The best way to even things out, so to speak, is to take an average. That doesn't give you an exact figure, but it's close enough for practical purposes.

As I've said, adding the poundages for each one-inch interval gives you inch-pounds of

Golden Eagle Hunter - @ 55 lbs.

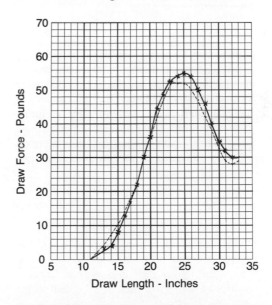

Brackenbury - 53 lbs. @ 28″

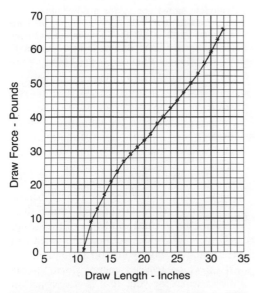

The force-draw curve for a recurve bow slopes gradually upward.

The force-draw curve for a round-wheel compound bow rises fairly sharply, peaks quickly, and slopes fairly gradually to the valley. The higher force-draw curve marked by Xs was made as the bow was drawn. (The lower curve marked by dots was made as the bow was relaxed. The difference between the two is a gauge of friction in the system.)

Browning Hypercam - @ 55 lbs.

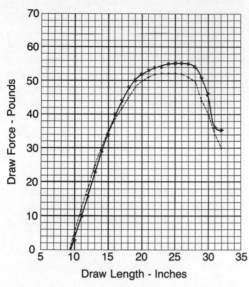

For a cam bow, the force-draw curve rises sharply and maintains peak weight for several inches, then it drops sharply to the valley.

Golden Eagle Hunter @ 55 lbs.

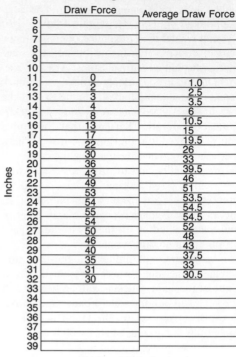

Inches	Draw Force	Average Draw Force
5		
6		
7		
8		
9		
10		
11	0	
12	2	1.0
13	3	2.5
14	4	3.5
15	8	6
16	13	10.5
17	17	15
18	22	19.5
19	30	26
20	36	33
21	43	39.5
22	49	46
23	53	51
24	54	53.5
25	55	54.5
26	54	54.5
27	50	52
28	46	48
29	40	43
30	35	37.5
31	31	33
32	30	30.5
33		
34		
35		
36		
37		
38		
39		

Total = 660 inch pounds

660 inch pounds ÷ 12 = 55 foot pounds

energy, but archers more commonly talk in terms of foot-pounds of energy. To convert inch-pounds to foot-pounds, simply divide the inch-pounds by 12. Thus, from the force-draw curve shown here for the Golden Eagle Hunter set at 55 pounds, you can see that the averages added up 660 inch-pounds, and that figure divided by 12 equals 55 foot-pounds of energy.

To compute stored energy for a bow, add up the average inch-pounds of energy (the column at right) and divide by 12 to get foot-pounds. The Golden Eagle Hunter at 55 pounds and 32-inch draw length stores 660 inch-pounds of energy, or 55 foot-pounds.

Energy-Storing Efficiency

One concern of most hunters would be to obtain the maximum possible stored energy for a given amount of work in pulling the bow, that is, for a given peak draw weight. In other words, most hunters want the highest return possible from their effort.

You can figure this by dividing the total stored energy by the peak draw weight. Thus, for the Golden Eagle Hunter, the figures look like this:

$$\frac{\text{Stored energy}}{\text{Peak draw weight}} = \frac{55}{55} = 1 \text{ foot-pound per pound}$$

In other words, for every pound of draw weight up to maximum poundage, you store one pound of energy. That's about average for a round-wheel compound. To see why some hunters prefer a cam bow to a round wheel, look at the figures for the Browning Hypercam set at 55 pounds. Adding the averaged draw weights at one-inch intervals on the force-draw curve, you get 929.5 inch-pounds of energy, or 77.45 foot-pounds. That means the cam bow stores 27.45 foot-pounds more energy than does the round-wheel bow at an identical draw weight. And it obviously means you store more energy for a given amount of work. Dividing 77.45 by 55 pounds peak weight, you get 1.41 pounds of stored energy for each pound of draw weight.

These figures undoubtedly explain the rising popularity of compound cam bows. As you'll see below, you don't get something for nothing in shooting a cam bow, but still, cam bows do store more energy for a given amount of draw weight than other styles. The average cam bow stores 1.3 to 1.4 pounds of energy per pound of peak draw weight compared to 1 to 1.1 for the round wheel. In other words, the cam bow stores roughly 20 percent more energy.

Efficiency vs. Inefficiency

We've just seen that the cam bow stores energy more efficiently than other styles of bows. However, "efficiency" must be examined closely, because it applies not only to energy storage but also energy delivery, and cam bows deliver energy less efficiently than some other bows. That's because cams place more stress on the bow limbs, bearings, and other moving parts to create more friction, and they flex the arrow more, which takes energy. In other words, they waste more energy than do most round wheel bows.

Some of this energy loss can be measured as hysteresis, the loss of energy to friction. As Norb Mullaney explained, there's no practical way to measure kinetic hysteresis, which occurs when the bow is being shot, but you can measure static hysteresis on a bow scale. If you plot

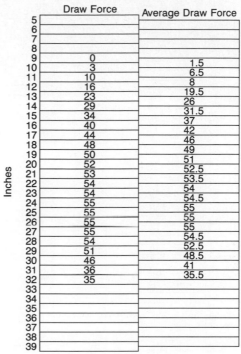

Browning Hypercam @ 55 lbs.

Inches	Draw Force	Average Draw Force
5		
6		
7		
8		
9	0	
10	3	1.5
11	10	6.5
12	16	8
13	23	19.5
14	29	26
15	34	31.5
16	40	37
17	44	42
18	48	46
19	50	49
20	52	51
21	53	52.5
22	54	53.5
23	54	54
24	55	54.5
25	55	55
26	55	55
27	55	55
28	54	54.5
29	51	52.5
30	46	48.5
31	36	41
32	35	35.5
33		
34		
35		
36		
37		
38		
39		

Total = 929.5 inch pounds

929.5 inch pounds ÷ 12 = 77.45 foot pounds

The Browning Hypercam at 55 pounds and 32 inches stores 77.45 foot-pounds of energy.

the force-draw curve as you pull a bow to full draw, and then again plot the curve as you let the bow down, you'll notice that the values at each one-inch interval aren't the same. The curve you plotted as you let the bow down is several pounds lower than the curve plotted as you drew the bow. That difference reflects friction in the bow, or static hysteresis.

That figure may seem to have little practical value, because it really doesn't tell you what happens when the bow is being shot. Nevertheless, it indicates the energy-delivering ability of a bow, and it serves as a way to compare efficiency of different bows. As Norb Mullaney writes in *Archery World* magazine, "It is logical

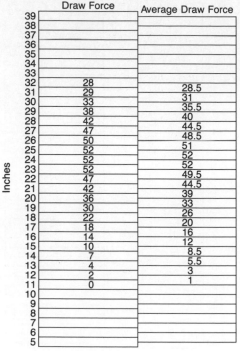

Golden Eagle Hunter @ 55 lbs.

Inches	Draw Force	Average Draw Force
32	28	28.5
31	29	31
30	33	35.5
29	38	40
28	42	44.5
27	47	48.5
26	50	51
25	52	52
24	52	52
23	52	49.5
22	47	44.5
21	42	39
20	36	33
19	30	26
18	22	20
17	18	16
16	14	12
15	10	8.5
14	7	5.5
13	4	3
12	2	1
11	0	

Total = 641 inch pounds

641 inch pounds ÷ 12 = 53.41 foot pounds

This chart shows the force-draw values as the bow was relaxed from full draw to brace height. As you can see, the values are lower than they were as the bow was drawn. That's a measure of static hysteresis, that is, friction and other elements of inefficiency.

Browning Hypercam @ 55 lbs.

Inches	Draw Force	Average Draw Force
32	30	32
31	34	37
30	40	42
29	44	47
28	50	50.5
27	51	51.5
26	52	52
25	52	52
24	52	52
23	52	52
22	52	51.5
21	51	50.5
20	50	49
19	48	46.5
18	45	43.5
17	42	41
16	40	37.5
15	35	32.5
14	30	27.5
13	25	21.5
12	18	15
11	12	8.5
10	5	2.5
9	0	

Total = 895 inch pounds

895 inch pounds ÷ 12 = 74.58 foot pounds

This chart shows the static hysteresis for the Browning Hypercam.

from an engineering standpoint to assume that the bow with the highest static hysteresis will also have the highest kinetic hysteresis and therefore the lowest efficiency, all other conditions being equal."

As you can see from the accompanying graphs, the cam bow weighed here has greater hysteresis than the round-wheel bow. That will hold true generally, so from that you can see that cam bows deliver energy less efficiently than do round-wheel compounds.

That's probably one reason most advocates of round-wheel bows say you gain little advantage from cam bows because you have to work

harder for what you get out of the bow. It's true that cams waste a little more energy through hysteresis, but mathematically you still gain more than you lose. For example, if you gain 20 percent in storage efficiency and lose 5 percent in delivery efficiency, you still have a net gain of 15 percent.

Kinetic Energy

So far I've discussed how to compute the total energy stored in a bow, and energy-storing efficiency. The third element in figuring bow efficiency is the kinetic energy, that is, the amount of energy transferred to the arrow.

Kinetic energy is a function of weight and

speed, so to compute the kinetic energy of your arrow, you must know, first, the weight of the arrow, and second, the speed. This is where the grain scale and the chronograph come in. The standard distance from arrow to chronograph for this kind of testing is three feet.

Once you know the weight and speed, you simply plug the figures into a formula:

$$\frac{(\text{Velocity})^2}{450,240} \times \text{arrow weight (in grains)} = \text{foot-pounds of kinetic energy}$$

Consider this example. Chronograph testing shows that at three feet, the Golden Eagle Hunter shoots 33-inch, 2216 arrows that weigh 605 grains at 181 feet per second. With that knowledge, you can compute the kinetic energy of that setup:

$$\frac{(181)^2}{450,240} \times 605 = \frac{32,761}{450,240} \times 605 = .073 \times 605 = 44.02 \text{ foot-pounds}$$

That's an interesting figure in itself, and it tells you something about the "punching power" of the bow. (For more details, see Penetration.) But that's not the only value in knowing kinetic energy. By comparing the kinetic energy with the stored energy, we can determine the overall efficiency, that is, the percentage of stored energy that is transferred to the arrow. This is the formula:

$$\frac{\text{kinetic energy}}{\text{stored energy}} \times 100 = \text{bow efficiency (expressed as a percentage)}$$

Now we know that Golden Eagle Hunter stores 55 foot-pounds of energy and delivers 44.02 foot-pounds of kinetic energy. Plugging these numbers into the formula, we can determine overall efficiency:

$$\frac{44.02}{55.00} \times 100 = .80 \times 100 = 80 \text{ percent efficiency}$$

That shows not only that the round-wheel bow is relatively efficient, but it gives a base for comparing efficiency of the round wheel with a cam bow. Again, we can use the Browning Hypercam as a basis for comparison. This bow set at 55 pounds shoots the same 605-grain 2216s at 201 fps. Using the above formula, we can compute the kinetic energy of the arrow three feet from the bow:

$$\frac{(201)^2}{450,240} \times 605 = \frac{40,401}{450,240} \times 605 = .09 \times 605 = 54.45 \text{ foot-pounds}$$

We've already seen above that the Hypercam bow stores 77.45 foot-pounds of energy, so we can figure the efficiency:

$$\frac{54.45}{77.45} \times 100 = .70 \times 100 = 70 \text{ percent efficiency}$$

Thus, even though the Browning cam bow stores significantly more energy and imparts more energy to the arrow, it wastes more energy, too. In other words, you get a lower return — 70 percent compared to 80 percent — for the effort expended to draw the bow.

Arrow Weight vs. Efficiency

Obviously, when you shoot a bow at a given draw length and weight, lighter arrows will shoot faster than heavier arrows. That seems good, and it is up to a point, but you'll find that the lighter the arrow weight, the poorer the efficiency. To put it another way, a bow delivers a greater percentage of its stored energy to a heavy arrow than it does to a light arrow.

Here's one example. My PSE Mach Flite 4 set at 55 pounds shoots 28-inch, 2213 aluminum arrows, which weigh 466 grains, at 218 fps (chronographed three feet from the bow). The kinetic-energy formula shows that these arrows deliver 49.19 foot-pounds of energy. Shooting 2117 aluminum arrows, which weigh 530 grains, the average arrow speed from the Mach Flite 4 drops to 207 fps, or 11 fps slower than the 2213s. However, the kinetic-energy formula shows that these slower, heavier arrows pack 50.44 foot-pounds of energy. In other words, the heavier arrows use more of the bow's stored energy than the lighter arrows. That's only one example, but it holds true for all bows at a given draw weight. In other words, the heavier the arrow, the more efficient the bow/arrow combination.

Does this mean you should shoot the heaviest possible arrows your bow will handle? To a certain extent, yes. You will get more energy for better penetration, and your bow will shoot more quietly with less jarring in your hand and less strain on the bow. Radical cams in conjunction with overdraws spit out arrows like lightning bolts, but they're inefficient in the sense that a relatively small percentage of energy stored in the bow is transferred to the arrow. Nobody in his right mind, of course, will dry fire his bow, but in essence, that's virtually the situation when you shoot ultralight arrows from heavy draw-weight bows. The arrow absorbs little of the bow's stored energy, and excess energy vibrates through the limbs, strings, and cables and eventually blows something apart.

On the other hand, you can carry "efficiency" too far and hurt accuracy. Arrows that prove most efficient based on mathematical calculations aren't necessarily the most efficient in a bowhunter's hands. Two components — accuracy and penetration — lead to a clean kill, and one without the other is useless. For that reason, shooting a loglike arrow with a looping trajectory defeats, to some extent, its value. Sure, it packs a wallop and will penetrate deeply, but if it misses the mark, all the energy is wasted.

For that reason, the best solution may be a compromise that settles on a mid-weight arrow. As mentioned in Arrow Shaft Selection, Tom Jennings suggests that 9 grains of arrow weight for each pound of bow weight offers a rule of thumb for maximum efficiency. If you deviate far on the light side, you could severely stress your bow, and if you deviate far on the heavy side, you get a slow-flying arrow and grossly curved trajectory.

BOWFISHING Shooting fish may not be your idea of hunting, but many bowhunters shoot fish just as religiously as they do big game. And for good reason. Seasons, particularly for most of the fish pursued by archers, are long, generally year-round. Few states have bag limits on rough fish, so you can shoot all you want. The hunting is often close to home so you don't need to make major expeditions as you do for many big game species. Bowfishing provides unlimited recreation and shooting practice, with few if any restrictions.

Unquestionably, hunters shoot more carp than any other species. Carp live just about everywhere in the United States and they're prolific, so they're abundant wherever they exist. Carp-shooting tournaments have boomed in Texas and California and now attract nearly as many participants, and pay nearly as much money, as some of the big bass-

Carp are big, tough fish. Monsters like Scott How-ard's 32-pounder can give you a real battle. *Photo courtesy Glenn Helgeland.*

Archers probably shoot more carp than any other species of fish. Carp live throughout the United States and they're prolific. In places where they're thick enough, you might even score a double, as Glenn Helgeland did here. *Photo courtesy Glenn Helgeland.*

fishing tournaments. Carp spawn in the spring and it's common to see them wallowing and splashing raucously in shallow water. That's a good time for shooting. During the summer they cruise shallow water or just below the surface in deeper water, and they can be stalked under these conditions.

Gars live throughout the Mississippi River drainage and west into Texas and Oklahoma. They lie just below the surface in sluggish water where they offer good shots, and they often roll or break to gulp in air. Bowfishermen find shooting at these rolling gars great sport.

In the Plains states, archers shoot a common rough fish called the buffalo. And suckers are popular targets for bowfishermen in some areas, particularly on spring spawning runs

In some regions, suckers are popular targets for bowhunters. Pat Miller took these Lost River suckers in Oregon on their spring spawning run.

when masses of fish congregate in shallow water.

Equipment for Bowfishing

Bows. Compound bows have replaced recurves in the hands of many big-game hunters, but in the bowfishing ranks, the recurve still seems to reign supreme. The recurve is physically lighter, and its simplicity reduces the potential for major tangles between fishing line and cables and wheels. Perhaps most significant, you can draw and shoot a recurve quickly, which can be important for fast shots at rolling gar or cruising carp. On close shots, many bowfishermen draw, touch anchor, and release in one smooth motion, and they believe that's important for success.

Another school—pardon the pun—of bowfishing thought says the compound is superior because you can draw and hold until a fish presents just the right shot. Most bowfishermen who shoot compounds shoot them at fairly low weights—40 to 50 pounds—so they can hold at full draw without strain. I wouldn't say one kind of bow is better than another. It depends on your shooting style and the kind of fishing you're doing.

Reels. Conventional bowfishing reels consist of a large round drum that you shoot through or past. You wrap the line around this drum, and when you shoot, the arrow pulls the line off, spinning-reel fashion. Old styles were taped to the bow, but most of the newer ones screw onto the side of the riser or into the stabilizer bushing on the back of the bow. One drawback is that you must rewrap the line by hand after each shot, which takes some time. Reels like this should have a clip or rubber finger to hold the line in place until you're

Many archers still prefer recurve bows over compounds for bowfishing. The recurve offers a faster draw and release. With this style of reel, the arrow passes through the center of the reel. *Photo courtesy Glenn Helgeland.*

Other fishermen go with relatively light compounds, because they like to be able to hold at full draw for some time, waiting for fish to move into range.

Conventional bowfishing reels consist of a large drum around which you wrap the fishing line. The reel on this archer's bow screws into the stabilizer bushing. Reels like this are relatively slow because you must rewind the line by hand after each shot.

cause it doesn't have the memory of monofilament and is less likely to hang up and tangle. For carp and fish of similar size, 30- to 50-pound line is suitable, but for huge fish like gar, many bowfishermen use line of 60- to 80-pound test. You don't want line much lighter than 30 because you'll lose a lot of arrows. The heavier line allows you to pull arrows free from stumps and similar arrow grabbers, and it helps you land unusually big and scrappy fish.

Arrows. Fish arrows must be heavy so they'll penetrate deeply into the water. Most are made of solid aluminum or fiberglass. Many serious bowfishermen prefer solid glass shafts, because they're more durable. Aluminum arrows will bend if you're shooting into a hard bottom or into unusually big fish. On the other hand, aluminum may be better in some cases. Pat Miller shoots suckers in shallow, rocky streams, and he's totally gotten away from fiberglass, because when an arrow hits a rock just right, it will flex and occasionally shoot right back at

ready to shoot. Otherwise big loops of line will fall off the reel.

Many bowfishermen use closed-face spinning reels. You can buy a bracket that screws into the stabilizer bushing on your bow—the reel attaches to this bracket—or you can make a similar bracket out of an old fishing rod. You cut the rod off at the handle and use just the reel seat. Epoxy a short bolt that will screw into the stabilizer bushing to the reel seat, and you've got it. Various models of Zebco closed-face reels are popular among bowfishermen. With a reel setup like this, you can retrieve line and shoot faster than with a conventional bowfishing reel. On a closed-face reel, remember to push the button before you shoot.

On a conventional bowfishing reel, you need braided nylon line. It's limp and won't kink or spring off the reel. Some shooters use monofilament with closed-face reels, but even with these rigs the braided line may be better be-

In shallow, rocky water like this, Pat Miller prefers aluminum arrows to glass because the aluminum won't bounce back at him as solid glass arrows sometimes do.

him. He far prefers aluminum for this kind of bowfishing because it won't ricochet back.

Most fish arrows come equipped with rubber fletching. The arrows are so heavy and shots generally so short that the fletching doesn't do much for arrow flight. You might as well take the fletching off and shoot the arrow without it.

Heads. Fish heads are barbed (a style that's illegal for big game) so they'll go through but not pull back out. That's great for holding fish on the line, but how do you get them back off? Several head designs help solve that problem. One has blades that fold in, so you can pinch them in to get the blade started back through the fish. Another style has reversible wire barbs; you just flip the barbs to point away from the fish and the head slides back through. A third style comes in two pieces. The base is glued to the shaft, but the tip holding the barbs screws off so you can pull the shaft back through with no barbs on the arrow at all.

Fish heads are barbed to hold fish securely, and several methods are used to help in removing fish. The head at left has a tip that screws off so the arrow can be slipped from the fish. The center head has reversible barbs. And the head at right has barbs that fold in so the head will slide back through the fish.

Rigging Arrows. Fish arrows have two holes—one through the head end, another just in front of the nock. You can use these holes to rig arrows several ways. You can tie the line through the head hole only, or you can tie it through the nock hole only. The second method is used by many fishermen, especially for gar because these fish have armorlike scales that will cut fishing line quickly. If you tie line only to the trailing end of the arrow, the line often doesn't touch the fish. If you use this method, glue your heads on doubly well, because if they break loose, they'll fall off in the water.

A third choice is to thread the line through the nock hole, pull it along the shaft, thread it through the head hole, and tie it securely. Pull the line fairly tight to take out slack along the shaft, and tie a half-hitch around the arrow just below the nock to hold the line tight along the shaft. With line tied through the hole in the head, you won't lose the head if it breaks off.

With a fourth method you use heavy line or steel leader wire and wire clamps, along with a barrel swivel. You slip the wire through the hole at the head end of the arrow and clamp it tight. Then you slide the barrel swivel onto the wire, and clamp the free end of the wire through the hole near the nock (you can do the same by tying heavy line through the holes in each end of the arrow). The wire should be fairly snug so it lies close to the arrow. This setup gives you a wire track with a slide (the swivel) that runs freely the length of your arrow. Now tie a snap swivel to the end of your fishing line. To start fishing, you simply snap the swivel on the line onto the barrel swivel on the arrow. As you draw, the barrel swivel slides along the wire to hold the line out of the way.

Other Gear. Always go equipped with several arrows and heads because you can easily lose arrows to logs, fish, and other obstacles. Include spare nocks, glue, extra line and swivels, and other gear needed for bow or arrow repair.

Also, don't forget your polarized sunglasses. They may be your most important bowfishing gear of all. Polarized glasses eliminate glare off the water, which enables you to see fish clearly

**Polarized glasses add greatly to fishing success be-
cause they reduce surface glare and allow you to see
underwater. Without polarized glasses, you'll overlook many fish.** *Photo courtesy Glenn Helgeland.*

under water. Without glasses you see nothing
but a silvery shine on the water's surface.

Some of the fish shot with a bow are big, and
they won't always be dead when you bring
them in, so include a bonker of some kind. A
length of pipe or a piece of ax handle works
nicely. And don't forget your stringer or fish
box.

Shooting Fish

For early-season carp and other fish spawning or feeding in the shallows, wading may be
the best approach. You can slip along quietly
and stalk them just as you would any other
game. For open water, a stable boat like a John
boat or bass boat is preferred. Some hunters
rig canoes with outriggers especially for bowfishing. They prefer a canoe to a boat because
the canoe will slip through aquatic vegetation
smoothly, allowing a quieter approach.

To shoot fish, you have to learn to shoot
where fish are, not where they appear to be.
The problem is the result of refraction, meaning light bends as it passes from air into water.
That makes a fish appear farther away than it
actually is. To put it another way, you must
aim low to hit a fish under water. The farther
the fish and the deeper it is, the more you must
aim under to hit the fish. There are formulas
for figuring underhold, but you can't measure
the exact distance to the fish, or the fish's exact
depth (and you probably wouldn't take time to
make the needed calculations anyway), so formulas mean little. With some experience—and
it doesn't take much—you'll instinctively learn
how low to aim.

BOW QUIVER   See Quiver.

BOW SADDLE   This is a soft piece of thin
leather with an adhesive backing. It's used to
line a bow handle as insulation in cold weather.
It also provides a better grip when your hand is
sweaty and might slip on a slick handle.

BOW SCALE   A bow scale weighs the draw
force (weight) of a bow. Without a scale you
can only guess the draw weight of your bow.
You might assume the label on a new bow
accurately tells the draw weight, but it doesn't
necessarily. On one of my mail-order bows a
sticker on the limb said the bow was set at
60 pounds, but when I couldn't pull the bow
I weighed it and found the actual weight was
76 pounds. Another "60-pound" bow was set
at 67 pounds.

If you decide to change bow weight by turning the limb bolts, you can't be sure of the
weight you'll end up with, even if you know the
exact starting weight. You commonly read that
one full turn of a limb bolt on a compound
bow equals four pounds in draw weight. On
some bows it does, but on many, a full turn
yields only two pounds difference, and on
others three.

Some adjustments, such as altering string
length or draw length, can change the draw
weight of a compound bow and you need a

You often read that one full turn on the limb bolts changes bow draw weight four pounds, but that's not true with all bows. To measure the exact draw weight when you make adjustments, you must use a bow scale.

the bottom of the board so you can slip a bow with sights or stabilizer onto the hook with the board resting on the floor.

Mount the pulley or winch near the top of the 2x4. I used a small block and tackle, which makes pulling a bow very easy. You can pull the bow by hand, but it's hard work, and you'll have a hard time reading the scale as you pull.

Attach the scale to the pulley, and screw the yardstick onto the board for measuring draw length. To get the yardstick in the right place, put a bow on the hook and attach the yardstick so zero just touches the back of the bow (the side of the bow away from you when you shoot). With the yardstick in place you can measure the exact draw length as you weigh a bow. I've also attached a shelf bracket to the

scale to gauge how much. A scale is also invaluable for fine-tuning a bow, plotting the force-draw curve of a bow, or gauging efficiency. (For more details, see Bow Efficiency and Force-Draw Curve.)

To Make a Bow Scale

Materials. Of course, you can take your bow to the local pro shop for weighing but that's bothersome and time-consuming, and you can make your own scale very easily. At any local feed or hardware store, buy a scale used for weighing hay and other products. Mine is a Hanson scale with a maximum weight of 100 pounds. It's marked in one-pound increments, which allows fairly precise measurement of bow weight.

In addition to the scale, get a yardstick to measure draw length; a hook to hold the bow (I used a hook off an old car-window gun rack); a pulley or winch to pull the bow; and a board on which to mount all these items (I used a six-foot 2 x 4). If portability isn't a concern, you can set up your scale on a wall in your house or shop.

Assembly. Screw the hook onto the 2 x 4 near the bottom. This will be used to hold the bow handle as you weigh a bow. Make sure you leave enough clearance between the hook and

The hook off an old car-window gun rack serves well enough to hold the handle of the bow. I padded this one with cloth to prevent scratching the bow handle. Make sure you leave enough clearance between the hook and the bottom of the board for a bow with a quiver, sights, or stabilizer.

This finished bow scale has a pulley at the top to help in drawing the bow. You can read draw weight on the scale, and draw length on the yardstick.

Bow preferences vary greatly by region. In some parts of the West, hunters like this prefer the relatively flat trajectory of cam bows equipped with overdraw units, but elsewhere other kinds of bow setups are preferred.

back of the 2x4 so I can clamp it in a vise at home, or using a C clamp, can clamp it to a tree limb, fence, or whatever in the field.

To weigh a bow, slip the handle onto the hook at the bottom of the board and attach the scale's hook onto the bowstring. Now pull on the winch until the bow reaches full draw.

BOW SELECTION Any discussion on bow selection is suspect from the beginning, because bow selection and shooting styles are very personal. As Tom Jennings said, "Your bow is as personal as your toothbrush and jockstrap." Opinions—not all based on fact— run stronger in archery than perhaps any other sport.

Tackle preferences vary not only by individual but by region. A shop owner in San Diego said he could scarcely give away a recurve bow, yet another in Ohio sells many recurves. In some regions one brand of bow predominates, and other brands sell better in other regions. One shop owner in California told me he'd sold more than 600 overdraw bows because he believes in them, whereas a shop owner 200 miles away in Oregon said he scarcely stocked overdraws because he doesn't believe in them.

Every region has its share of great archers, regardless of tackle, so the tackle itself isn't what makes a good bowhunter, but the way a person uses it. Any quality tackle will do the job if you believe in it. Nevertheless, some specific guidelines might help in selecting a bow. This discussion assumes you're a novice starting from scratch, so if you've got some experience, you might want to skip over the basics discussed first.

Basics for Bow Selection

The three most basic considerations for choosing a bow are right- or left-handedness, draw length, and draw weight. These fundamentals apply to all bows, regardless of design or brand.

Right- or Left-Handed? A friend of mine, shooting bare bow, couldn't hit the target. I explained how to sight down the arrow but he couldn't get the hang of it. "I'm looking at the side of the arrow," he said.

That got me to thinking, so we tested him for eye dominance, and even though he was right-handed, his left eye was dominant. (For details, see Dominant Eye.) In most cases if you're right-handed your right eye will dominate, and if you're left-handed your left eye will. If that's the case, you've got no problem. You just buy a bow according to muscle dominance, and aiming will come naturally.

But obviously, as with my friend, that's not always true, and having a dominant eye opposite to the dominant hand can cause aiming problems. My friend chose to switch to a left-handed bow, which took some getting used to, but soon he could handle it well and was pleased to find out how easy aiming really could be. Glenn Helgeland, a well-known archery writer, is another who did this. To shoot instinctively — without sights — that's the better choice, because your perspective is much better with both eyes open.

If you don't want to switch hands, you can get by with closing your dominant eye and aiming with your weaker eye, and if you plan to shoot with sights, you can do that. Just make sure you practice enough to make that process second nature.

Draw Length. First distinguish between "draw length" and "arrow length." Arrows might be cut longer than the rated draw length to assure broadhead clearance, or they could be cut much shorter in the case of overdraw bows. (For details, see Arrow Shaft Selection.) Here the discussion centers strictly on bow selection, so draw length, not arrow length, is the major concern.

More specifically, it focuses on compound bow selection. With recurve and longbows, draw length is virtually unlimited, and bows aren't rated according to draw length. Your concern with these bows isn't so much determining draw length as it is arrow length. But compound bows are rated not only according to poundage but according to draw length. That's why you must know your draw length to select any compound bow.

Manufacturers have agreed upon a standard measure for draw length: the distance from the bowstring at full draw (the "valley") to the pressure point of the handle, plus 1¾ inches. (For details, see Draw Length.) On virtually all bows made today, the hole drilled for the arrow rest sits directly above the pressure point on the handle, so to simplify arrow measurement, I'll use the arrow rest hole rather than the pressure point of the handle.

You can best determine draw length by actually pulling a bow and having someone measure your draw. Unless you've been shooting to build your strength, do this with a lightweight bow so you can keep your shoulder and arm fully extended as you will when you shoot. (For details on extension, see Shooting Basics.) It's also important to use the same anchor point and release system you'll use for shooting, because draw length can vary depending on whether you anchor under your chin or at the corner of your mouth, or whether you use a release aid or shoot with your fingers.

Nock an arrow and pull the bow several times until you're loose and comfortable and then hold it at full draw and have someone mark the arrow at the arrow rest hole. Now let up and measure from the string groove in the nock to the mark on the arrow, and add 1¾ inches. That gives you your draw length.

For example, let's say you measure 29¼ inches from the string groove in the nock to the arrow rest hole. To determine your draw length, you add 1¾ inches to get 31 inches. So you would buy a compound bow with a draw-length rating of 31 inches. If you measure 30 inches from the nock to the arrow rest hole, then your draw length comes out to 31¾ inches, and you should buy a bow with a 32-inch draw length.

Many compound bows come with a variable draw length, generally in one-inch increments, but many have additional adjusters on the cables so you can vary draw length by half-inch increments for fine-tuning. If you're just starting in archery, your draw probably will lengthen as you build strength, so buy a bow at the short end of the range to allow room for expansion. That is, if your draw length measures 31 inches, buy a bow with a draw-length range of 31 to 33 inches so you can increase the draw length if necessary.

That may offer another advantage. Everything else being equal, draw length on a compound bow is determined by the size of the wheels, because the larger the wheels the more cable that can be wrapped around them to accommodate a long draw. Thus, longer draw-length bows of a given model will have bigger wheels. Bowyer Tom Jennings said, "Buy the biggest wheels that will give you the right draw length. You don't get quite as much letoff, but the bow stores more energy because the bigger wheels stress the limbs more than smaller wheels do."

If you've been shooting a recurve bow and know your draw length for it, don't assume your draw length will be the same for a compound bow. The compound is easier to hold at full draw, and chances are your draw length could be an inch or more longer with the compound bow.

Bow Weight. This is where the subject of bow selection really gets personal. Right- or left-hand selection, and draw length, are fairly cut and dried. But poundage? That depends on your size and strength, and often to a greater extent on opinions about penetration, arrow speed, self-image, and other subjective details. There are no absolute answers concerning bow weight, so I can only give my opinions.

Standard advice in the past has been to "shoot the heaviest bow you can shoot comfortably." In the longbow era, that advice may

have been valid, because only the heavier bows could cast an arrow fast enough to assure good penetration on oversized animals. For stick-bow shooters today, that advice may still have some validity, although the average 60-pound recurve will shoot a 500- to 600-grain arrow fast enough to kill any game in North America. Unfortunately some hunters take the advice mentioned above to mean "shoot the heaviest bow you can draw." They ignore the "comfortably" part and go to extremes in poundage.

The question is, why shoot high poundage? Faster arrows with flattened trajectory is one reason, and up to a certain point that's a valid reason. If you miscalculate range on an animal by a couple of yards, you have a better chance of scoring a solid hit with faster, flatter-flying arrow.

At some point, however, the value of additional bow weight diminishes. Above 70 pounds draw weight, you generally have to shoot heavy, stiff arrows to get good arrow flight, so you gain little in trajectory past that point. The primary way to increase arrow speed then is to go to an overdraw setup that shoots shorter, lighter arrows. Again, that's great up to a point, but at ultrahigh bow weights you face problems of arrow instability and possible bow breakage. (For details, see Bow Efficiency and Overdraw.)

Penetration is another reason given for heavyweight bows, but here again, how much weight do you need? Virtually any modern compound bow set at 60 pounds will shoot a 550-grain arrow at 200 fps to generate 48.86 foot-pounds of kinetic energy, which most experts agree is more than enough to slay most animals in North America. For moose and grizzly bears you might want a little more pizzazz, but most bows set at 70 pounds will shoot through a moose. Past a certain point, you gain nothing. Complete penetration is complete penetration, whether it comes from a 70-pound or a 100-pound bow. (For more details, see Penetration.)

Now, you might ask, why not shoot high

poundage—70 pounds and up—if you've got the muscle to do it? There are several possible reasons. You've probably heard the term "target panic," a problem that plagues many archers. Most authorities agree that shooting ultraheavy bow weights is one major cause of target panic. (For details, see Target Panic.)

Breakage also attends some heavyweight bows. Cam bows in particular have been notorious for breakage, and this has occurred most commonly with very heavy bows shooting light arrows. Limbs, cables, and strings can break when a small percentage of the bow's stored energy is transferred to the arrow, and that's what happens when you couple a high-poundage bow to a lightweight arrow. (For details, see Bow Efficiency.)

Heavy bows can also yield some physical problems. My shoulders have given me problems for many years, primarily because I shot too-heavy bows when I first started, and I've talked to many other archers with similar problems. Why risk injury when you can drop down in bow weight and kill animals just as cleanly with much less risk of injury? (For details on preventing problems, see Physical Condition.)

My point isn't to discount the value of arrow speed and penetration, both products of bow weight. The point is that if you're a beginner, don't think you have to shoot an elephant bow to kill deer and elk. Sixty pounds will do the job, and high poundage is no substitute for accuracy.

If you're starting out, I'd recommend a bow in the 45 to 60-pound draw weight range. You can draw and shoot that bow without strain at 45 pounds to develop good form, and then you can crank up the poundage. If you find that weight too Mickey Mouse for you, then buy a heavier bow, in the 70- to 80-pound class if you're comfortable with that. Just shoot a bow you can shoot comfortably, or you'll lose more than you gain.

Stick Bows

Recurves and longbows still have their ardent followers, and rightly so. Stick bows are

Some hunters still prefer the simplicity and traditional appeal of the longbow.

simple and beautiful. They have no moving parts but the limbs, so they eliminate all the gadgetry attendant to compound bows. Traditionally we've pictured the beginner as starting out with a cheap recurve and then graduating to the compound, but nowadays, it's usually the other way around. Most hunters start with a compound and graduate to a recurve. I know several bowhunters who've gone from compound bows to recurves because they've got tired of all the wheels, cables, and screws. Few beginners shoot longbows or recurves any more; most stick-bow shooters today rank among the most experienced and successful bowhunters.

Stick bows are relatively light in weight, and they have a smoothly increasing draw weight rather than the herky-jerky motion of the compound bow. For that reason they're generally preferred by hunters who shoot quickly and instinctively, as opposed to the methodical, sight-aided style of most compound-bow shooters.

Some large manufacturers, such as Bear and Hoyt/Easton, still offer recurve bows, but smaller bowyers have taken over much of this market. Many of these bowmakers shun the compound market and concentrate solely on quality recurves and longbows. As custom bowyers they build bows to your specifications with a wide range of draw lengths, draw weights, handle designs, and take-down features, so you can buy recurve bows to your exact specifications, just as some rifle hunters buy guns with stocks built to precise personal dimensions.

Recurves and longbows inherently shoot as accurately as compound bows, but you work harder for what you get, and generally arrow speeds are limited by the amount of weight you can pull and hold. The average longbow in the 60-pound class will shoot an arrow about 170 to 180 feet per second, and a good recurve will shoot an appropriately spined arrow 190 to 200 feet per second. It's simply a matter of physics that stick bows of a given weight can't store as much energy as compound bows at the same weight (for details, see Bow Efficiency), and so compound bows, particularly those with cam wheels, shoot faster for a given weight.

That has led to the idea that compound bows are much faster than recurve bows. To some extent that's true, but that ignores the real difference between stick bows and compounds, namely that you probably can comfortably shoot a compound bow with a much heavier peak weight than you can a recurve or long bow, and yet you hold much less weight at full draw. The fact that you must hold peak weight at full draw with a recurve or longbow is the major limitation with these bows. As I've mentioned, holding heavy poundage can lead to problems such as target panic and shoulder injuries.

Recurves and longbows generally can't be as finely tuned as compound bows. Most have wood handles, which are not cut much past center, and the bow weight is not adjustable.

A few years back, beginners started with recurve bows and graduated to compounds, but today the trend has reversed. Now most beginners start with compound bows, and some of the finest hunters "graduate" to recurves.

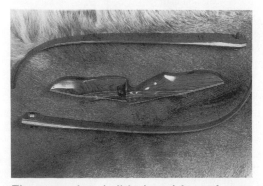

The recurve bow is light in weight, and many models, such as this Brackenbury Legend, can be broken down for compact packing. Many hunters prefer the simple lines and wood-grain beauty over the more complicated and metallic nature of the compound bow.

These facts limit the amount of fine-tuning you can do with any longbow or recurve. (For details, see Bow Tuning.) If you'll accept nothing less than perfect arrow flight, that's a drawback. If you just want to shoot and don't want to fiddle with adjusting limb bolts and arrow rests and all that, it's a strong point.

Compound Bow
Round-Wheel Compounds. Many hunters still ask whether they should shoot a round-wheel compound or a cam bow. On the line at most archery tournaments, you'll see far more round-wheel bows than cams. Tournament archers aren't necessarily looking for arrow speed but for stability, and most agree that the round-wheel bow, which casts an arrow slower at a given draw weight, offers a little more stability and consistency.

Round-wheel bows of a given draw weight pull a little easier than most cams, and I've also found round-wheel bows generally easier to tune than cam bows, probably because the arrow starts out with less thrust and is easier to

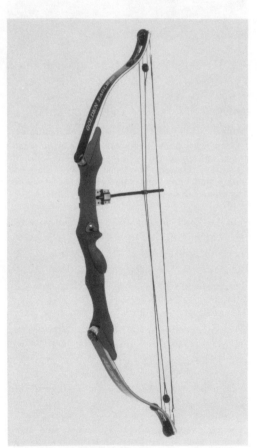

The Golden Eagle Hunter is one example of a dependable round-wheel bow. The recurve limbs produce a smooth draw and beauty, but they don't increase speed or performance.

The Hoyt-Easton Pro Hunter has "Energy Wheels." These have the smooth draw and letoff of round wheels, but an oval lobe on one side stores slightly more energy than a perfectly round wheel.

The egg-shaped cam wheel at left will store more energy than the round, eccentric wheel at right. For a given peak weight, then, the cam will shoot an arrow of a given weight at greater velocity.

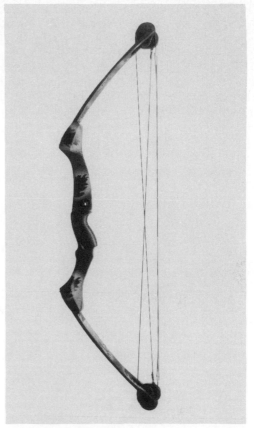

The Browning Wolverine has nylon cam wheels that slide the cables to the side so no cable guard is needed.

control. Round-wheel bows also are more efficient — that is, they deliver a greater percentage of their energy to the arrow than do most cam bows — so they're quieter and smoother to shoot, and they're less subject to breakage.

Because they're accurate, comfortable to shoot, relatively easy to tune, and ruggedly dependable, round-wheel compounds remain popular. In target archery and in hunting situations where close shots are the rule, round-wheel bows will maintain a strong position.

Cam Bows. The cam-wheel compound first hit the market in the early 1980s, and instantly its image was tainted by breakage — split limbs, broken cables, broken strings. That image has soured some archers on cam bows, but needlessly so. Most new products undergo a period of trial, and the cam bow was no different. Now most bugs have been worked out of the cam system, and these bows have become very dependable.

"Second-generation cam bows are much more dependable, and they're very popular," said York Archery's Don Crowder. "Unfortunately, we're still trying to get over the stigma established by first-generation cam bows."

To build more dependable bows, some manufacturers have eliminated the radical cams of the early years for more conservative designs. In addition, they've beefed up cables, and they've gone largely to solid glass limbs, which

in general can take more abuse than laminated wood and glass limbs.

Overstress has been the major reason for breakage with cam bows because they store more energy than round wheels. That's why hunters like them. For a given peak weight, they shoot faster than other kinds of bows.

But that great amount of stored energy can lead to problems. When a bow is shot, the arrow absorbs a certain percentage of the energy released by the bow, and an arrow of a given weight will absorb a smaller percentage of the energy produced by a cam bow. The excess energy has to go somewhere, so it goes into the limbs, cables, string, and other parts of the

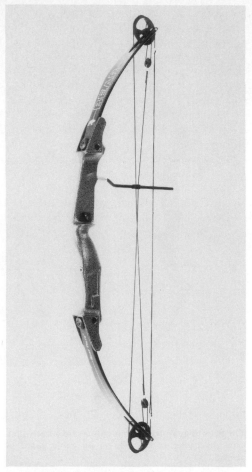

The Bear Flare is another style of cam bow. Today's cam bows, with slightly tamer wheels and beefed-up cables and strings, are far more dependable than first-generation cams of the early 1980s.

terproductive. To some extent that's true. As you can see from a force-draw curve (see Bow Efficiency), the weight builds up quickly on a cam bow and is held for several inches. I've found that cam bows that maintain peak weight for some distance and then drop off radically into the valley seem hard to pull. However, the force-draw curve varies from one cam style to another, and some cam bows, like the PSE Mach Flite 4, feel little different from some round-wheel bows.

Besides, comparing bows of equal poundage is like comparing apples to oranges. To assess the comparative pull of a cam and round wheel, you more realistically should compare bows with comparable stored energy. For example, the average round-wheel bow will store 65 foot-pounds of energy at 60 pounds peak weight, but the average cam bow will store more in the neighborhood of 70 foot-pounds of energy at 50 pounds peak weight. In other words, at a peak weight of 10 pounds *less*, the cam bow stores 5 foot-pounds *more* energy.

What does that mean to you? It means you can shoot a cam bow of much lighter draw weight and get comparable arrow velocity and energy. Maybe a cam bow of equal peak weight is tougher to pull than a round wheel, but set 10 pounds lighter, it's definitely easier. The real value of a cam bow, then, isn't necessarily to produce astronomical arrow speeds, but to get adequate speed and energy at relatively light poundage.

On the minus side, cam bows tend to make more noise than round-wheel bows. That's because they store more energy that is not transferred to the arrow. Excess energy vibrates through the bow and its accessories to produce a distinct thud or twang. That's not universal, however, and the amount of noise varies by make and design.

Cam bows also may not be as accurate. Larry Wise, in his book *Tuning Your Compound Bow*, attributes that to the shape of the force-draw curve. Most cam bows have a valley less than an inch long (it's up to two inches on some round-wheel bows) so if your draw length varies at all, you end up shooting off the "wall"

bow. All this energy vibrating through the bow can be damaging.

Used correctly, however, cam bows can be an asset. First realize that if you insist on shooting light arrows at a heavy draw weight, you risk breakage. If you shoot heavier arrows, however, you can shoot a cam bow safely and gain an advantage in speed and energy over a round-wheel bow.

Many archers say cam bows pull harder than round-wheel bows, so shooting a cam is counin front of the valley or off the "stops" behind it, and that will cause erratic arrow flight, Wise says.

Norb Mullaney, on the other hand, thinks the way the arrow passes the arrow rest is more critical. Because of the steeper draw-force curve, a cam bow launches an arrow with a greater burst of energy than does a round-wheel bow. The moment that arrow leaves the bow is the critical instant for good flight, Mullaney said, and it leaves faster and with more force off a cam bow, so it is harder to control. This could be like comparing a powerful dragster tearing off the line to the family sedan picking up speed gradually. Obviously the dragster is harder to control.

However, Mullaney and other authorities I've talked to think the difference between

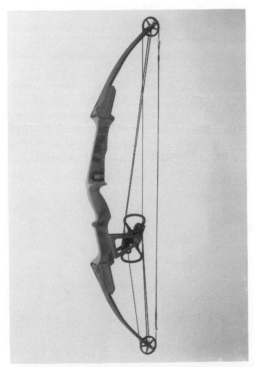

The Jennings Unistar employs a new cam concept. The wheels at the limb tips are concentric, and all cam action takes place in the cam unit attached to the riser.

round-wheel and cam bow accuracy is measured in fourths of an inch—tournament archery accuracy—and is not a serious obstacle for hunting archers. It's up to you to decide whether the greater arrow speed and flatter trajectory of a cam bow make up for the slightly more critical arrow flight. Mullaney himself has opportunity to shoot any style or brand of bow he desires, and he's chosen a cam bow set at 55 pounds.

Overdraws. The overdraw isn't actually a style of bow, only a different way of using any compound bow—or recurve for that matter, although you won't see many overdraw units on recurve bows these days. Overdraws have been around for years, but they've been popularized in recent years.

In essence, the overdraw unit places the arrow rest behind the handle of the bow, which allows you to shoot an arrow much shorter than your actual draw length. Then you not only can cut your arrow shorter, which in itself lightens the arrow, but you can shoot lighter spine-weight arrows to reduce overall arrow weight even more. If your full-length arrows weigh 600 grains, you can reduce that to as little as 400 grains with an overdraw, giving you a much faster arrow. (For details, see Overdraw.)

Other Considerations

Among all compound bows, whether round-wheel or cam, you'll see many variations in construction and quality. Here are some things to consider when buying any compound bow.

Limbs. At one time all quality bows had laminated limbs—strips of wood sandwiched between fiberglass—and only cheap bows had solid glass limbs. Today that's not the case, and for the money, glass limbs are an excellent buy.

In terms of performance they nearly equal composite limbs. My Hoyt/Easton Pro Hunter, for example, has wood-and-glass composite limbs. Set at 60 pounds, the Pro Hunter shoots 33-inch 2216s at 201 fps. I replaced the laminated limbs with solid glass limbs, which in essence makes this a Game Getter, and the same arrows at the same 60-pound bow weight

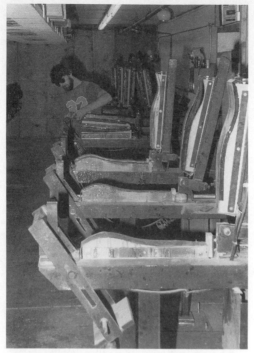

Laminated limbs are more expensive than solid glass because they have many more parts and much labor is required to glue them together.

shoot at 200 fps — one foot per second difference in velocity. That difference is insignificant.

Are glass limbs as accurate? A representative for a large company told me one of the company's target advisors won several major tournaments shooting an inexpensive glass-limbed bow. The company told him to knock it off and to shoot one of the expensive laminated-limb bows because the profit was greater on those. The point is, glass shoots just as accurately as wood and glass.

Bowyer Tom Jennings advocates solid-glass limbs. "Glass has a lot more potential," Jennings said. "You're limited with wood limbs because you can blow them apart. You can get moisture into wood and it starts swelling and will come apart, and it will come apart under heat. Glass is impervious to moisture and heat. It's just a lot more durable."

For that reason, glass limbs are ideal for backcountry hunting in hot or wet weather where you can't carry a spare bow, because you have less fear of ruining a limb. Glass-limb bows are also somewhat less expensive, so you can buy an equally good bow for less money.

On the other hand, glass limbs are heavier. Changing from wood to glass limbs on my Hoyt/Easton Pro Hunter raised the weight a half pound, from 6¼ to 6¾ pounds (that's with eight arrows in the bow quiver). If you're looking for the lightest bow possible, you don't want glass limbs. Of course, that weight could add stability. Tournament archers add weight in the form of stabilizers, and to some degree any mass weight has a similar stabilizing effect. (For more details, see Stabilizer.)

Some archers say that laminated limbs draw more smoothly than glass. I can't feel much difference myself.

Riser Handle. "Wood or metal?" might be your first question. Wood has a traditional appeal, and nothing is prettier than a wood handle with outstanding grain patterns. Some hunters like wood handles because they're not as cold to the touch in cold weather. Also, wood handles must be made thicker for strength, and some hunters like the beefy feel of wood handles, although most experienced archers would say a small grip is more forgiving because it forms a smaller pivot point.

Some hunters prefer the beauty of a wood riser like that of the Browning Hypercam on top here. Others prefer the durability and center-shot qualities of the magnesium riser, in this case on a PSE Mach II.

Lack of strength is generally a shortcoming of wood handles. Wood isn't as strong as metal, so most wood risers are not cut as far past center as metal risers are, and this can lead to tuning problems, particularly arrow clearance. The farther the riser is cut past center, the easier it is to get good clearance. For that reason, metal handles generally are preferable.

Also consider size of the sight window. Many wood handle bows, and some metal ones, too, have small sight windows. If you anchor at the corner of your mouth, or if you shoot without sights, that won't be a problem. However, if you shoot with sights and anchor low, say under your chin, it will be: with a shallow sight window, you can't set short-yardage sight pins. For shooting with sights, the window should be at least six inches high.

If you plan to use a cushion plunger, make sure the plunger hole in the handle is high enough to assure vane clearance. I bought a recurve bow with a plunger hole less than a half inch above the arrow shelf—unknowingly bought, that is—and try as I might, I couldn't get arrows to fly straight off that bow. Finally it dawned on me the vanes were hitting the arrow shelf. My only alternatives were to shoot feather fletching, or to use a solid rest and place it higher above the shelf.

Cost. In many cases, price and performance are not related. PSE's Bob Ragsdale said, "Price has nothing to do with how fast or well a bow will shoot. Price is related to the cost of building the bow and to the accessories—cable guard, arrow rest, finish, paint job. And laminated limbs cost more because they have 28 parts compared to one part for molded glass limbs. Laminated limbs don't shoot any better, they just cost more to make."

Many bows with limb brackets are less expensive than split-limb models, but they shoot just as well. They cost less because they're less expensive to make. As Tom Jennings said, "It's cheaper to build a hanger bow than a split limb, because you don't have to split the limb, and on top of that the hanger is more durable. People equate quality with price, but they're not necessarily synonymous. A hanger bow

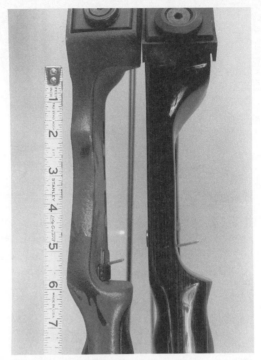

If you plan to shoot with sights, make sure the sight window is large enough to accommodate all your sight pins. It should be at least six inches deep. The sight window at right is too shallow for use with an under-the-chin anchoring system.

is stronger, sturdier, and the wheels roll straighter. The guy who buys a $100 bow is getting a good buy. I'd suggest a guy buy an inexpensive bow to start. It's a good dollar value."

Most inexpensive bows also have nylon wheels, rather than the metal wheels of more expensive bows. That would seem to make the economy bow less durable, but that's not the case, either. Molded nylon wheels are cheaper to make, but they'll hold up under abuse as well as metal wheels.

Adjustability. Versatility has become a standard aspect of the compound-bow market, and it allows you to fine-tune a bow. Most round-wheel bows have "E" or "Tri-Draw" wheels, which have slots in the sides so you can easily adjust draw length over a three-inch range.

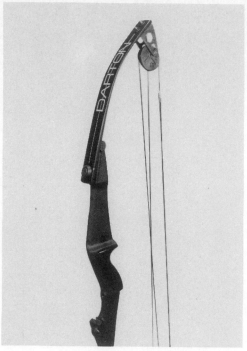

Many economy bows, such as the Darton 20-MX, have solid glass limbs and wheels mounted on hanger brackets. Such bows present a good dollar value.

With some you can adjust the draw length only in one-inch increments, but many bows now have slotted yoke balancers that allow adjustments in half-inch increments. Some cam bows have interchangeable draw-length modules that allow you to change draw length without unstringing the bow or loosening cables. And changing the draw length with this system does not change the draw weight.

Make sure the bow you choose will accept any accessories you'll want to hunt with. Most bows now are equipped with stabilizer bushings, and screw mounting holes for sights, quivers, and so forth. These are fairly standard, but some bows don't offer all features. For example, most bows have a cable-guard mount below the handle, but on others you must mount the cable guard above the handle. I personally prefer it below because there it's

less likely to interfere with nocking an arrow and aiming.

Some bows have removable plastic grips, and you can buy low, medium, or high wrist grips. Try each one to find which grip best suits your shooting style.

Bow length also can affect your decision. The trend has been toward short, maneuverable bows, which is great to an extent. If you have a short draw length, or shoot with a mechanical release aid, string pinch may not be a problem with a short bow. But if your draw length is 30 inches or longer, string angle becomes acute with a short bow, in the 40- to 44-inch axle-to-axle range. For longer draw lengths, I'd say 45 inches or longer is a better choice. Longer bows are also more stable because they resist torquing just as a long stabilizer does.

This discussion doesn't present any absolutes for bow selection, because, as I've said, that's a personal matter. But with these guidelines, you can sort out the many options available and choose a bow that will suit your needs.

BOWSIGHTS Bowsights have become standard equipment among archers, but many beginners still ask whether they should hunt with or without them.

Reasons for Sights

Learning Aid. Sights offer several advantages. First, they help in learning to shoot. Fred Bear, one of the most famous instinctive shooters of all time, has recommended sights for beginners because sights allow the novice to concentrate more fully on shooting style and less on aiming. Tom Jennings, another famous archer, said he likes to start kids off with sights because the kids will hit the target a lot quicker, which keeps up their interest, and they learn better form using sights. "With a sight you can coach yourself and determine reasons for a miss," Jennings said. "You can tell you've plucked the string, for example. A sight *teaches*. That's the value of the sight."

Harold Boyack, a successful bare-bow shooter, said, "With sights, you don't necessarily need to practice at varied yardages. If your sights are set right, the aiming process is the same regardless of distance. That offers a great advantage if you're confined to practicing at fixed yardages in your back yard or basement. I personally prefer to shoot without sights, but to do it well, I have to shoot at varied yardages every day."

Hunting Aid. I think sights will help you in shooting at game, too. For several years I hunted without sights. On targets and other inanimate objects I shot very well. But I missed dozens of easy shots at deer, primarily because during the heat of action I lost concentration and didn't aim. My shooting instincts failed me.

With sights, my percentage of hits on game has been much higher because sight pins give a positive reference point for aiming. They more or less force you to aim, even during intense, close-range encounters. It's hard to forget those sights totally and to draw and release blindly (as you might do without sights). Many bowhunters have told me sights enhance their game-shooting ability because the sights force them to pick a spot on an animal.

Choosing a Sight

Durability. To be of value a sight must be durable. I prefer sights made of one solid metal plate. Some sights have moving parts and various pieces that must be screwed together, but really a bowsight need be little more than a simple bracket to hold several pins in place, and the simpler it is, while still serving that function, the better. A one-piece metal sight is as simple as you can get, yet that's all you need.

The simplest ones screw directly to the side of your bow, and for practical purposes they're permanent. If for some reason you want to remove the sight, say to fit your bow into a case, you might prefer a dovetail mounting system. With this system, you screw a bracket with a V-shaped slot to the side of your bow and then slip the sight into this bracket.

Many hunters find they shoot more accurately with sights than without. Both hunters used sight-equipped bows to kill these deer.

Whichever system you choose, make sure all accessories—sight, quiver, cable guard, arrow rest—are compatible. Not all accessories use the same mounting systems.

Beefy Pins. Some hunting sights have tiny pins, much as target shooters would use, with the idea, I suppose, that the finer the pin, the better the accuracy. Actually they can be too small. First, if the pins are too fine they bend and break easily, and in the rough-and-tumble world of hunting, you don't want to be fussing over fragile equipment. Buy a sight with rugged pins, and also consider one with a pin guard, a heavy, wraparound metal bar that protects the pins.

Second, in poor light and the hurried conditions of hunting, you need fairly beefy pins to show up well. I like pins with heads at least $\frac{1}{16}$

Pins should be fairly heavy and rugged. Also, a wraparound pin guard protects your pins in case you fall or bang your bow.

Good sights are easy to adjust. The best ones have independent windage and elevation adjustments so you can change one setting without disturbing the other. Ideally, you can make these adjustments without the use of wrenches or screwdrivers. The simpler and more solid the adjustment system, the more easily you can fine-tune your aiming. Browning's rack-and-pinion sight has little cogs on the pins so you just roll them along a track, and Hoyt-Easton's Time Sight has screw adjustments for both windage and elevation. These are excellent, easy-to-adjust sights.

Pins vs. Crosshair. Pin-type sights have been most common, but the crosshair sight, with one vertical wire and several cross wires, has a good future in hunting because it virtually guarantees accurate horizontal alignment, much like the crosshairs in a rifle scope. I've

inch in diameter. To enhance visibility, the heads should be painted. Many sight pins are made of untreated brass, which is okay on the target range, but in the field, sunlight will reflect off those pins and give you a flare effect that makes aiming nearly impossible. Either buy a sight with painted pins, or dip the heads of your pins in fluorescent paint. Make sure you clean them thoroughly first so the paint will stick. You can also get sight pins with fluorescent plastic heads. These show up very well, but they break fairly easily, so I favor solid metal pins. If you anticipate shooting in low light, you can buy either a lighted sight pin or a small sight light, powered by a hearing-aid battery, that fastens directly to the sight bracket and shines down onto the pins. I've used one of these extensively for shooting practice in my back yard at night.

Good sights are easy to adjust. This Hoyt-Easton Time Sight has independent vertical and horizontal adjustments, and no tools are needed.

used crosshair sights on many hunts and have found them to be accurate and quick to use. Many come with black wires, which are fine in good light, but in low light they don't show up well so you're wise to paint or spray them fluorescent colors. Fine-Line's crosshair sight is built like a tank, and ProLine and PSE also make good aluminum sights with metal crosswires. The Fisher Sight is made of plastic, which scares me a little, but I've banged one around on my bow for more than a year and have never had any trouble with it, and the fluorescent plastic crossbars make for easy aiming in low light.

Aiming Methods. Some hunters aim with the string just inside the pupil of the eye, others aim with it just outside. These methods work well enough with pins, and if you have a good solid anchor point, the string should line up exactly the same way every shot. With a crosshair sight, however, you'll probably have better success with a string peep. Without one the string parallels the vertical wire on the sight and can cover it up, but a peep allows you to look through the center of the string. Even with pins, I've found I aim more consistently with a peep sight. (For details, see Peep Sight.)

Setting Up Your Sight

Inside or Out? Some hunters prefer to mount their sight outside the bow limb, and others prefer to mount it inside, between the limb and the string, where it's more protected. I've generally mounted my sight inside the bow limb because I figure it's less likely to get banged up there, and the sight doesn't hang up on brush and limbs as easily as one protruding from the front of the bow.

However, you can't mount the sight inside on all bows. Here again, all the accessories must be compatible. Cable guards in the high position, above the handle, and some overdraw units prevent mounting a sight inside the bow limb.

Also, some archers would say that for greater accuracy your sight should be mounted in front of the bow, as far from your face as you can get it. One reason a rifle can be aimed

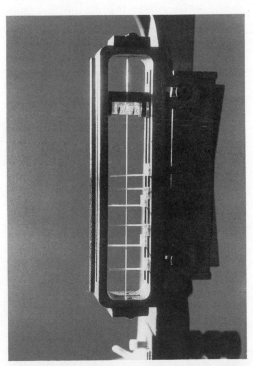

The crosshair sight has become popular among hunters because the vertical wire gives positive alignment while aiming. The Fisher Sight has fluorescent wires that show up well in poor light.

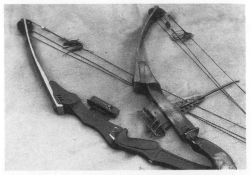

Some hunters prefer to mount their sights inside the bow limb as on the bow at left. With a high cable guard that's not possible, and the sights must be mounted in front of the bow.

more accurately than a pistol is that the sights are farther apart, and the same principle applies to a bow. Most tournament archers mount their sights on brackets extending several inches out front because the greater the distance between the shooter's eye (rear sight) and the sight pin (front sight), the greater the aiming accuracy. However, hunting does not demand the degree of accuracy required in target archery, and a sight protruding out front like a target sight isn't practical. If your sight must be mounted outside the limb, keep it close to the bow.

Pin Settings. Probably the most common sight arrangement consists of four pins spaced at 10-yard intervals: 20, 30, 40, 50. Strictly for tree stand hunting, where distances are known and most shots are close, some hunters prefer a single-pin tree-stand sight set at 15 or 20 yards. And some hunters use single-pin sights or other simple arrangements for all their hunting. Tom Jennings, for example, hunts with one pin set at 35 yards, which will be on a deer anywhere from 0 to 40 yards. To compensate for closer shots he aims at the bottom of the chest, and for longer shots he aims at the back. Some hunters use two pins, say at 20 and 50

The Browning Treestand Sight has only one pin for close-range stand hunting.

yards, and they compensate for various ranges by holding over or under. Some one-pin sights are adjustable. If, for example, you estimate a deer is 23 yards away, you dial in 23 yards on your sight and aim dead on. For some circumstances that might be ideal.

It doesn't matter how you set up a sight as long as you practice with it and feel comfortable with it under pressure. My only caution would be against adding too many sight pins. Some hunters use sights with as many as ten pins set at five-yard increments. If they can make that work, fair enough, but I find that many pins confusing. The simpler your system, the less chance you have for error in the field.

Sighting In

Setting sight pins isn't difficult. Start out with your closest sight pin. Let's say that's 20 yards. Measure off 20 yards accurately. Now aim at the target from that distance and shoot an arrow or two instinctively. As you shoot, mentally note a spot on the sight window of the bow that lines up with the target. In most cases that will be 2½ to 3 inches above the arrow rest, although the distance depends on the shape of your face and your chosen anchoring method (corner of the mouth, under the chin, and so forth). Set one of your sight pins level with the spot you noted on the sight window and shoot a couple of more arrows with the sight dead-center on the target.

Adjusting Pins. Chances are you won't hit right where you aim, so to adjust the sight, move the pin to the point of impact. That is, if the arrow hits left, move the pin to the left; if the arrow hits high, move the sight up; if the arrow hits low and to the right, move the pin down and to the right. Continue to shoot arrows and move the sight until you consistently hit where you aim.

Setting the rest of your pins will be simple. Line them up so they're vertically in line. That should take care of windage. Then accurately measure off 30 yards and go through the same procedure there until you're hitting on; move back to 40, and so forth. With the first two set, you can pretty closely eyeball in the other pins and then confirm them with a few arrows from each position.

Check your pins during additional shooting sessions. If you find that for some reason your groups move slightly, you can move the entire sight bar on some sights so you don't have to alter each individual pin. And with a cushion plunger, you can move your group significantly by turning the plunger in or out (in the direction you want to move your group) a fraction of an inch. Don't move it much or it will alter the tune of your bow. (For details, see Bow Tuning.)

BOW SLING   A bow sling works much like a rifle sling for carrying a bow across your back or over your shoulder. It frees your hands for hiking or glassing. Some slings have clips that screw under the limb bolts. The sling then can be quickly snapped on or off the clips. Others

have snap attachments that go around the bow limbs for quick on and off.

Another style of bow sling is the Spare Arm, a hook on which you hang the bow. The Spare Arm has a strap that goes over your shoulder. When you stop to glass, you can slip the handle of your bow over the hook to free your hands. The Spare Arm Junior is a similar hook that attaches to your belt.

BOW SQUARE   This ruler device is used to measure brace height and nocking-point position. (For more details, see Bow Tuning.)

BOWSTRING   The major consideration in buying a string is getting the right length and strength. All bowstrings for hunting are made of Dacron. For most round-wheel compounds, strings are made with 16 strands of Dacron, and for cam bows they're made with 18

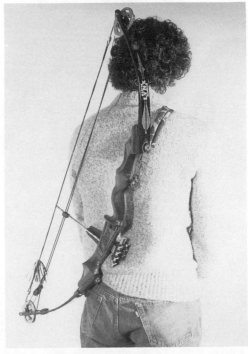

With a bow sling, you can carry a bow over your back or shoulder. It's a handy accessory for hunting, where you want your hands free for glassing and other activity.

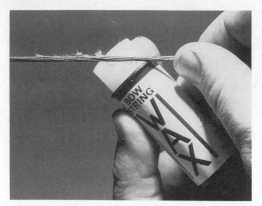

The normal wear and tear of everyday hunting can fray a bowstring. Wax your string regularly to minimize wear.

Always carry an extra string in the field. As this photo shows, I tape an extra string, an Allen wrench that fits the limb bolts, and a spare arrow rest, right to my bow so I'm never caught without these items.

strands. Dacron stretches, which will change your brace height and nocking-point position. Always break in a string by shooting it a day or two before fine-tuning your bow, and break in two or three strings before hunting season so you'll have seasoned strings ready in case you break or cut one while hunting.

String Maintenance

Inspect Your String. Just the normal wear of rubbing against clothes, rocks, and sticks while you're hunting will gradually fray a string. To minimize wear, wax the string regularly during a hunt with beeswax or a commercial bowstring wax.

Also, watch for cut or broken strands. It's a rare hunter who hasn't accidentally touched his string with a broadhead and cut a strand or two. Most strings offer enough leeway in strength that, in a pinch, you can get away with shooting the bow, but you're far better off to change the string immediately. If the string breaks when you draw or shoot, you'll most likely destroy your bow—and maybe yourself. Believe me, it gives you a real thrill.

Extra Strings. In backcountry hunting where you're a long way from the nearest archery shop, always pack at least two or three extra bowstrings with your gear. And keep one in your hunting pack or on your bow so you always have a spare as you actually hunting. I tape a spare string and an Allen wrench that fits the limb bolts right to my bow. That way I'm guaranteed of never getting caught without them. The Allen wrench can be used to relax the limbs to put on a new string in case the old string breaks completely. Of course, you can use a compound bow stringer to do the same thing, and if you prefer that method, make sure you have a stringer with you in the field. (For other string-changing methods, see Bow Stringer.)

Serving a Bowstring

If your nocks fit too tight or loose, you might want to re-serve your bowstring with lighter or heavier serving thread to get proper nock fit. Or possibly the serving on the string will break and unravel. That commonly hap-

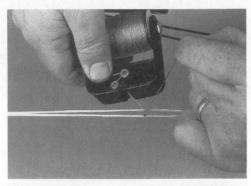

A string bobbin like this makes serving a bowstring easy. First mark the point at which you want to start the serving. Allow plenty of leeway above the arrow rest. Place the end of the serving string through the bowstring at your beginning mark.

Wrap back over the loose end to hold it tight and continue wrapping down the bowstring. You should wrap the serving so that when you draw the bow, your fingers will tighten, not loosen, the serving. That is, if you shoot right-handed, you'll pull the serving in a clockwise direction, so you want to wrap in the same direction.

The wrappings must be tight together. Adjust tension on the bobbin so the serving goes on snug but not too tight. If it's too tight, it could break a strand of the bowstring underneath.

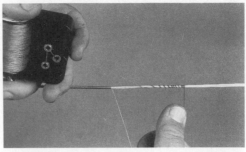

When you get to the end, which will be a point well below the position of the arrow rest, tie off the serving with a whip finish. To do that pull out a large loop of thread, and then wrap inside the loop back toward the main serving. Ten times is enough. The wrap inside the loop must go the opposite direction as the serving. That is, if you've wrapped the serving clockwise, these wraps must be made counterclockwise.

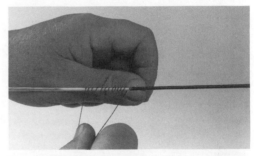

This is another view of the loop with wraps inside. Notice in particular how the thread comes off the far side of the string at the serving but how it crosses the near side at the other end of the loop. That's mandatory so the wraps inside the loop will unwind during the next step.

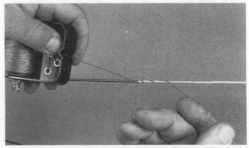

Continue to wind the serving thread around the bowstring, keeping each wrap snug against the serving. As you do this, you're wrapping over the end of the serving thread, and as you wind one side of the loop onto the string, you unwrap the other side.

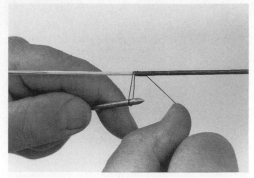

When you've wound all the thread in the loop snug against the serving, hold the final loop tight with a nail or toothpick, and pull on the end of the thread to tighten the last loop.

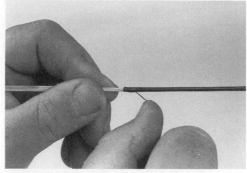

Continue to pull until the loop snugs up against the serving.

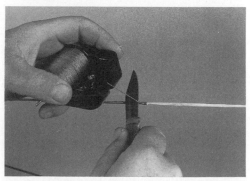

Cut off the thread flush with the serving, wax the serving, install a nock locator, and you're ready to shoot.

pens, particularly with tight nocks on monofilament serving. Knowing how to re-serve your bowstring, or to tie a whip finish to secure the end of a broken serving, can save the day for you on a hunting trip. See the accompanying photo sequence for details on serving a string and tying a whip finish.

String Silencers

A bare string will twang loudly, so silencers are needed to dampen string noise. Silencers come in many forms from little rubber balls to yarn balls to rubber bands. Living rubber like that used on bass plugs has become the most popular form of string silencer in recent years. One common brand is the Catwhisker. To use Catwhisker silencers, you simply tie a little piece of the rubber around the bowstring and

To dampen string twang, install silencers on the string. One way to put on Catwhiskers is to tie a section of rubber on the string, and to pull the rubber tight and cut it slowly with a knife. It will spring into individual strands.

then separate the strands of rubber. If you tie the rubber on and then stretch it tight and cut it slowly with a knife near the end, the strands will separate cleanly and quickly. Move the silencers up and down the string until you find the place where the bow shoots quietest. On most bows two silencers, one near each end of the string, will do the job, but on a noisy bow you might want to add more.

Nocking Point

The nock locator is a critical part of a bowstring because it ensures that the arrow is positioned identically on the string from one shot to the next. You can make a nock locator with serving thread or dental floss by using the same wrapping and whip-finish techniques described above for serving. Or you can use heat-shrink nocks.

The simplest nocks, and the easiest to move during tuning, however, are clamp-on nocks. Using special pliers, you can easily open one of these nocks, move it, and clamp it back into place. Some will come apart with constant moving. The most durable I've found are made by Saunders.

If you shoot with a mechanical release aid, you should stack two nocks together to assure that upward pressure by the release doesn't force the nock out of position. (For details, see Release Aids.)

BOW STRINGER   Many bowhunters string recurves and longbows by bracing the tip of the lower limb against the inside of one foot and then pulling the handle of the bow with one hand and sliding the string onto the upper tip with the other.

Use a Stringer

For Stick Bows. That method takes a lot of strength, and it can be dangerous if the tip slips off your foot. A bow stringer offers a far safer and easier alternative. Most bow stringers are simply long cords with pockets in each end for the bow tips. On some stringers the pockets are fairly large and they totally hide the bow tips so you can't slide the string on. In place of pockets at both ends, some stringers have a flat

This hunter uses the old method for stringing his longbow, by bracing the lower tip against his foot and pulling with his left hand as he slips the string onto the upper tip with his right hand. This method works, but it can be dangerous.

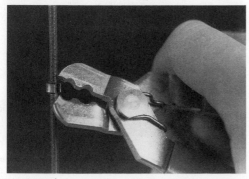

A clamp-on nock locator like this holds the nock securely, but with specially made nock pliers, it can be opened and moved easily.

A simple bow stringer made of cord with pockets at each end simplifies the process. And makes it a lot safer.

cup that sits on the upper limb; this style works better on bows with small tips.

For Compound Bows. Some compound bow stringers are made similarly, except they have hooks on the end in place of leather pockets. To replace the string on a compound bow, however, no stringer is needed. Virtually all compound bows now have cables equipped with teardrop string attachments; to change strings, you simply step on the string that's on the bow and pull up. When the teardrops are close enough together, you slip the new string onto the unoccupied sides of each teardrop and then relax the bow. Now you step on the new string (the one you want left on the bow) and pull up on the handle. When the teardrops are close enough together, you slip off the old bow-

Teardrop string connectors on compound bow cables make string changing simple. You partially draw the bow, slip the new string onto the unoccupied side of the teardrop, and then partially draw the bow with the new string and slip off the old string.

You can fully relax a bow by backing out the limb bolts. Before you do, use a pen or pencil to mark the limb's position in the handle, as shown here. That way you can return the limb to its original position — and thus the same poundage — without the need for a bow scale.

string, and now you're ready to go with a new string.

If the string on your bow breaks, of course, or if you need to relax the bow completely to change draw length or do other work, that method won't work. You can use one of three alternatives. Most archery pro shops use a bow brace, but unless you do a lot of bow work, you probably can't justify owning your own brace. Another choice is to back the limb bolts out on your bow until the limbs are fully relaxed. Before doing this, use a pencil or pen to make a line on each limb where it meets the handle. That way you can return the limbs to the same position, and thus the same poundage, without weighing the draw weight.

The third alternative is to use a long bow-string much as you would a regular bow stringer, except you don't put it on the ends of the bow but on the teardrops at the ends of the cables. To do this you need a string long enough to reach the teardrops on the cable ends even with the bow totally relaxed. To use this method, slip the extra-long string onto the unoccupied sides of the teardrops, stand on that string, and pull up on the bow handle. Slip the string that's already on the bow off the tear-drops and let up on the bow. If the string you're using as a bow stringer is long enough, the limbs will drop to a fully relaxed position. Now you can do whatever work is necessary and then reverse the process to restring the bow.

BOW TERMINOLOGY Probably the most confusing terms relating to a bow are "face" and "back." The back is the side away from you when you shoot; the face is the side facing you. The accompanying illustration shows the general terminology of a compound bow.

BOW TUNING You hear a lot about this subject these days, particularly with the advent of the compound bow, which is more "tune-able" than the recurve bow. Target archers in particular talk about fine-tuning their bows, and when their success rides on shooting accuracy measured in fractions of an inch, the need for fine-tuning is obvious.

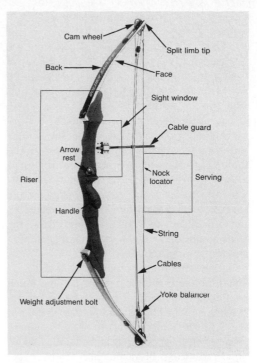

This photo shows common terms applied to modern bows.

But what value does fine-tuning have for bowhunters? A lot. When you get right down to it, tuning may be more critical for bowhunters than target archers. After all, a target archer may be able to redeem himself because he'll get another try, but in hunting, the success or failure of your entire trip may ride on one arrow. You don't want to throw it all away with bad shooting.

Also, broadheads increase the need for fine-tuning. It's relatively simple to get arrows tipped with field points to fly well, but broadheads are another matter. Any slight imperfection in the head sends the arrow planing off course. Poor tuning, which results in wobbly arrow flight, only heightens the planing effect of broadheads. For best flight with broadheads, your bow must be finely tuned. (For more details, see Broadhead.)

What Is Tuning?

To say your tackle is well tuned means your bow, arrows, arrow rest, and string are matched for best performance. The end result is straight-shooting arrows. You should see no wobble in them as they fly, and they should hit where you're aiming.

The most obvious value of tuning is accuracy. When you come down to that one critical shot, you're prepared to put the arrow on the money, not somewhere around the fringes. It also helps penetration. The straighter an arrow hits, the better it will penetrate because the shaft follows directly into the hole created by the broadhead. With a wobbling arrow, the shaft could follow to the side, creating friction and reducing penetration.

Finally, fine-tuning produces confidence. If you doubt your shooting, you can't have much confidence. A friend of mine who shoots instinctively, for example, said his arrows shot to the left of his line of sight, so he just compensated when he shot at a deer by holding right. To say the least, his confidence—and his success rate—are not high. Chuck Adams, a prolific bowhunting writer, is well known for consistency in killing game with a bow. I asked Adams why he does so well. "It starts with fine-tuned equipment," Adams said. "I spend hours tuning my bows and arrows, so when I go hunting there's no doubt that I'll hit what I'm shooting at." That's the kind of confidence you need to kill game consistently.

Equipment for Tuning

Arrows. Tuning starts with matched tackle, and before anything else, your arrows must be the right length, and they must have the correct spine weight for your bow. (For details, see Arrow Shaft Selection.) These should be equipped with field points, and for best tuning, you need at least three normally fletched arrows and three with no fletching, just nock and field point. Field points must weigh the same as the broadheads you plan to shoot. Also, nocks on these arrows should not be glued on because you may want to change nock position later. Easton aluminum arrows have ridges on the nock taper, and you can screw nocks on securely without glue.

Arrow Rest. For best tuning you must use a rest you can move in and out to adjust center shot. The rest also should cushion the arrow vertically and horizontally. That's not to say you can't make a bow shoot decently with a rubber rest stuck directly on the handle, because it will shoot well enough to kill game. But that kind of setup severely limits tuneability, and if you're serious about getting the most from your bow, you'll use a movable rest that cushions your arrow. (For details, see Arrow Rest.)

Nocking Point. In addition you need a nock locator that's easy to move. The best for tuning is the clamp-on nock, because it can be loosened and moved easily. Special pliers, made for opening and clamping down these nocks, make the process easier. (For details, see Bowstring.)

Tools. You need a bow square to measure nock height, tiller, and brace height. To adjust the arrow rest, sights, and bow weight, you need appropriate Allen wrenches.

Spray Powder. Underarm deodorant or foot powder in spray cans can be useful in gauging arrow clearance.

Other Gear. Obviously, you need a target butt and enough room to shoot at least 15 yards. A bow scale is also useful in bow tuning, and if you want to get real fancy, you can evaluate your tackle with a chronograph. Also, for paper tuning (as described below) you need a box or wooden frame that will hold a sheet of paper at least the size of a magazine page.

The Purpose of Tuning

Three potential problems can affect arrow flight, and the goal of tuning is to reduce or eliminate these.

Porpoising is up-and-down wobble in the arrow. It is governed primarily by nocking-point height, although some rests have a vertical-tension adjustment that could influence porpoising. During the tuning process, you always correct this problem first and then proceed with the following two.

Fishtailing is side-to-side wobble of your arrow. It's related to dynamic spine of the arrow and is governed by stiffness of the shaft, draw weight, horizontal position of arrow rest, spring tension of the pressure button, arrowhead weight, fletching size, and possibly other variables.

Fletching contact with the bow also can cause erratic arrow flight and poor groups. It can be corrected by rotating nocks to give better vane clearance, shooting smaller vanes, changing rests, and replacing vanes with feathers.

Getting Started

For simplicity, all directions here relate to right-hand shooters. If you shoot left-handed, do the opposite.

Check Tiller. First, measure the tiller. Compound bows commonly are set so the bottom limb is about 1/8 inch nearer the string than the top limb. (For details, see Tiller.) Most experts say tiller isn't critical on a compound bow, and both limbs can be set the same distance from the string. It doesn't matter, then, as long as the relationship between the top and bottom limbs doesn't change. Changing tiller changes nocking-point height, so tiller measurements must remain constant. Measure and record tiller, and then each time you alter bow weight (by turning the limb bolts), recheck tiller to make sure it's the same as when you started.

Set Nocking Point. Start with the nocking point about one-half inch above 90 degrees. You may move it later, but that's a good average starting position.

Adjust Center Shot. As a starting point for tuning, the arrow must be lined up correctly with the string. To gauge alignment, you must line up the bowstring with the limbs. Limbs on a recurve bow are symmetrical, so the string must center the limbs. Measure limb width just above the handle and make a mark in the exact center of the limb.

On most compounds, the string rides slightly off-center, so "center" of the limb is closer to one side. To align the string on a compound, measure the distance from the string to the side of the bow limb at the tip. Let's say in this case it's 3/4 inch. Now make a mark on the limb just above the handle 3/4 inch from the side of the bow. Most compound bow limbs are square, so the measurement should be the same at the tip as at the handle. If the limbs on your bow are wider at the handle than at the tip, you'll have to compensate. The point is that you want to be able to see the string bisecting the same plane from one end of the bow to the other.

With the bow limb marked, stand the bow down in a corner or resting against a chair, and

Use a bow square to set your nock locator. Start out with the locator about one-half inch above 90 degrees with the arrow rest.

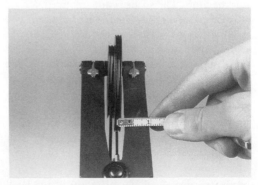

To tune a bow, you must center the arrow with the string. To do that first, measure the distance from the string (or the cable to which the string attaches) to the edge of the bow limb. On this bow the distance is 15/16 inch.

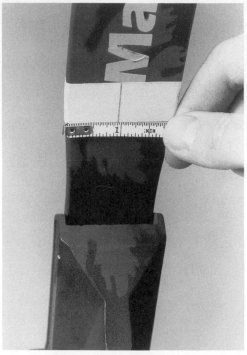

Then mark the upper bow limb just above the riser handle the same distance from the edge of the limb, again 15/16 inch. (This assumes the bow limb is the same width at the wheel and riser.)

Now stand the bow up and nock an arrow. Line up the bowstring with the mark you've made on the limb, which centers the string with the limb, and move the arrow rest or pressure button in or out to bring the arrow into line with the string. For shooting with your fingers, the arrow is properly centered if you can see the head of the arrow just outside the bowstring, as shown here. If you shoot with a release aid, the arrow should be in direct line with the string.

line up the string with the mark you've made on the limb. The string is now centered.

Now place an arrow on the string, and if you plan to shoot with your fingers, adjust your rest or pressure button so the tip of the arrow lies fully visible just to the left (outside) of the string. Dick Tone, a professional bow tuner, pointed out the reason for this. When you release the string, your fingers push the string to the left. It's unavoidable. That forces the nock end of the arrow left, which brings the back of the arrow directly into line with the front, and the arrow is launched straight.

If you start with the arrow tip to the right (inside) of the string—as would be the case with a rest stuck directly to the side of the bow—and your fingers throw the nock to the left, you literally launch the arrow sideways.

You've got wobbly arrow flight the instant the arrow leaves the string.

That alignment applies for finger shooters. A mechanical release aid greatly reduces sideways thrust on the arrow, so if you shoot with a release aid, line up the arrow in direct line with the string, not to the side.

Bare-Shaft Tuning

You can gauge arrow flight many different ways, but I've chosen two that make tuning fairly simple. One is called the "Bare Shaft Planing Test," and I relate it here as described in the Easton Aluminum Target Archery Catalog. In other words, it's not original with me, but I've used it extensively and know it works.

To perform this test, you need two or three fletched arrows and two or three unfletched (that is, bare shafts). Use only field points on these arrows—never shoot broadheads on bare shafts—and make sure all arrows are fletched the same and have the same weight heads. Stand about 15 yards from the target and shoot the fletched arrows. Don't worry whether you hit dead center in the target. Just aim exactly the same way each time so you shoot a tight group.

Now, aiming exactly the same as you did with the fletched arrows, shoot the bare shafts. With good shooting form, you can shoot a tight group with bare shafts at 15 yards. If your bow is properly tuned, the bare shafts will group among, or very close to, the fletched shafts.

If you're working with new equipment you've never shot before, that probably won't be the case. The gear most likely will be out of tune, and the fletched shafts and bare shafts will group several inches or farther apart.

If the bare shafts group above or below the fletched shafts, it indicates porpoising. As I've said, this is the problem you want to solve first, and you do that by moving the nocking point toward the point of impact—up if the bare shafts group high, down if they group low. After moving your nock locator, again shoot the three fletched shafts and then the bare shafts. If necessary move the nocking point some more, and continue this process until the bare shafts and fletched shafts group at the same level.

Now work on fishtailing. That's indicated by the horizontal relationship of the fletched and bare shaft groups. If the bare shafts group right of the fletched shafts, the arrows are too weakly spined. If the bare shafts group left, they're too stiffly spined.

You can make several adjustments to bring these together. Let's say your bare shafts group to the right, that is, they're weakly spined (if bare shafts group left, of course, you make opposite adjustments). First, increase spring

If your arrows are improperly spined for your bow and rest setup, bare shafts will plane to one side of fletched shafts. In this case the bare shafts planed low and right. That means, first, the nocking point must be moved down. It also means the arrows are too weakly spined so the cushion plunger must be stiffened, bow weight must be reduced, or one of several other alternatives must be taken.

tension on your pressure button. If your arrows and bow weight are closely matched, you should be able to bring the groups together by changing spring tension alone.

If you're not using a pressure button, you can move the arrow rest out to the left slightly (most authorities, however, say they like to keep the arrow lined up fairly closely with the bowstring as described above). If these don't bring the groups into line, decrease draw weight of your bow, or shoot a lighter arrowhead (these are summarized in the Tuning Chart, which begins on page 125).

If, after going to extremes of adjustment, you can't bring the groups within four inches or less of each other, your arrows simply aren't matched to your bow. You either have to change bow draw weight drastically (assuming you're shooting an adjustable compound bow) or you have to get arrows of a different spine.

Most authorities say they like the bare shafts grouping slightly left of the fletched shafts (remember, this applies to right-hand shooters), which means the arrows are spined on the stiff side. They say that because stiff shafts assure better arrow clearance past the bow and are more forgiving of shooting errors.

I agree that arrows should be on the stiff side, but I don't totally agree that left-grouping bare shafts indicate perfect bow tune. I say that because bare-shaft tuning is based on the flight characteristics of bare shafts, and fletching on the shafts changes those characteristics. Technically it might be incorrect to say fletching stiffens the spine of an arrow, but, in essence,

that's what happens. The heavier and larger the fletching, the more drag it creates and the "stiffer" the arrow acts.

To get perfect flight with fletched shafts, the bare shafts, in my opinion, should be grouping two to four inches to the right of the fletched shafts. That means the bare shafts are a little weak, but fletching will stiffen the spine and make the arrows fly close to perfect. You can arrive at near-perfect flight for fletched arrows another way. If the bare shafts group dead center with the fletched shafts or to the left, you can then increase the draw weight of your bow three to four pounds, and your fletched arrows will fly near perfect.

I've arrived at those conclusions from shooting through paper (a tuning process described below). I've found that if, during bare-shaft tuning, the bare shafts group slightly right, then fletched shafts shot through paper will fly virtually straight, meaning the fletching has stiffened them enough to bring them into tune. If, on the other hand, bare shafts group left of fletched shafts during bare-shaft tuning, then fletched arrows shot through paper from that same bow/arrow combination will fly tail right, meaning they're too stiff. To make them fly straight, draw weight must be increased three to four pounds.

Paper Tuning

The fallacy behind bare-shaft tuning is that you don't shoot bare shafts on game, and as I've pointed out, fletching in essence changes the spine of the arrow. For that reason, you can only infer what effects fletching might have on an arrow. You can only assume effects on broadheads, too, since you can't shoot broadheads on bare shafts.

With paper tuning, on the other hand, you can shoot fletched shafts, which means you can fine-tune with broadheads if you want to. (I'd suggest you start with field points for initial tuning.) Also, with the paper-tuning method, you don't need much space. It's something akin to bore-sighting a rifle, and you can tune your bow right in your apartment if need be.

Gale Cavallin, a champion archer and sales manager for Golden Eagle Archery, showed me

If your bow is properly tuned, bare shafts should strike at the same level as fletched arrows, and they should be grouped very close to the fletched shafts or slightly right (for a right-hand shooter).

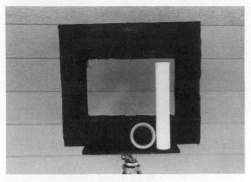

For tuning by shooting through paper, you need only a frame (in this case a cardboard box with a rectangular hole cut out of the bottom), paper to cover the hole, and tape to hold the paper in place. Of course, you need a butt behind the frame to stop your arrows.

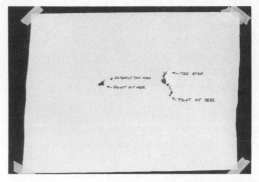

The arrow on the right here flew tail high, which means the nocking point was too high. I moved the nock locator down about ¼ inch, and shot the second arrow. As you can see, it went nearly straight through the paper. This is how the hole from a well-tuned bow should look. These arrows were shot about ten feet from the paper.

this method. Many target archers tune their bows by shooting through paper. It might sound esoteric, but it's very simple. You can make a frame by cutting a square window in the side of a cardboard box, and you can use pages from old magazines for shooting paper.

To use this technique, set up the frame in front of your target butt, and tape a piece of paper tightly over the window. Now stand about ten feet away and shoot a fletched arrow through the paper. If your bow is perfectly tuned, you'll see nothing but a round hole with cuts made by the fletching around it.

An improperly tuned arrow will tear a long hole as it flies through the paper sideways. If the tear is vertical, then your arrow is porpoising and you must move your nocking point to straighten it out. If it flies tail high, move the nock locator down (a tail-high arrow would plane low in the bare-shaft test, so the results are exactly the same in either test). If the shaft flies tail low, move the nocking point up. You can easily "read" the tear, because the head of the arrow makes a rounded impression and the tail leaves fletching cuts.

When your arrows are flying level, work on fishtailing. Here you'll see a horizontal tear, and if the tear is tail left, the arrows are too weakly spined (tail-left arrows will plane right). If the tear is tail right, the arrows are too

stiff. Again, you make exactly the same adjustments as you'd make in bare-shaft testing to straighten out the arrows. (Refer to the Tuning Chart, which begins on page 125, for quick reference.)

When the arrows are flying so you see virtually nothing but a round hole surrounded by fletching cuts, your bow is well tuned. Move back to 10 and 15 yards and shoot through the paper to check flight of your arrows at those

On the upper arrow hole that's marked, you can see that the tail of the arrow hit well to the left of the point (and slightly high), which means it's spined too weak. To straighten this arrow out, I tightened the spring in the cushion plunger to "stiffen" the arrow's spine. Reducing the draw weight of the bow would be another way to straighten out a tail-left arrow.

distances. Continue to adjust your arrow rest and bow weight until you've achieved the best possible flight. Again, if you simply can't get the arrows to fly straight, you've probably got mismatched arrows and bow, and you'll have to change bow weight drastically or buy arrows of a different spine.

Before buying all new arrows, however, try different arrow rests. Some rests simply don't work well with certain combinations of arrows and release methods. For example, using a spring rest and releasing with my fingers, I can't get arrows to fly straight. I've changed from 15- to 20- to 25-ounce springs and have varied the center-shot position as much as one-half inch. The arrows all fly grossly tail left. But if I replace the springy rest with a cushion plunger and flipper-type rest, I can get the same arrows at the same bow draw weight to fly perfectly.

Getting Clearance

To fly well, your arrows must clear your bow fully, particularly if you're shooting plastic vanes. If erratic arrow flight has been a problem for you in the past, inspect your tackle. Chances are good you'll see streaks on the bow window where your vanes have been hitting, or

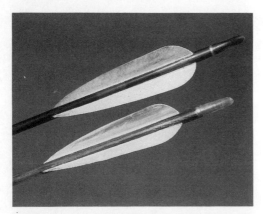

Fletching contact with the bow or arrow rest could be another cause of poor arrow flight. The black streaks on these vanes show that the arrows have been hitting the arrow rest. If you see marks like this on your bow, you've got bad arrow-contact problems.

on the vanes where the vanes have dragged across the rest. Any such contact will cause poor arrow flight, and now is the time to eliminate that.

To judge clearance, spray the side of your bow around the arrow rest with dry spray powder deodorant or foot powder. Don't use sprinkle-on powder like baby powder, because it's loose and blows around when the vanes pass by, and you can't tell much from it. Also spray the vanes on your arrow.

Now shoot an arrow and inspect the side of your bow and the vanes on your arrow. If there's any contact, you'll clearly see marks in the powder on the bow or on the vanes.

To get clearance you must turn your nocks to allow more space between the vanes and the side of the bow and rest. That's why you should dry-nock arrows for tuning rather than gluing on the nocks. Nock an arrow on the string and sight down the arrow to see where the vanes lie closest to the side of the bow. Turn the nock on the arrow to provide better clearance, respray the arrow and bow, and shoot again.

If your bow and arrows are well matched and tuned, you should be able to achieve total clearance just by turning the nocks. Once you've found the right nock position, glue on all your nocks the same way.

If that doesn't do the job, then you can turn out the pressure button or arrow rest to move the arrow farther from the bow. Of course, that will change the tune of the bow, so you'll have to go through the tuning process again. Shooting a stiffer-spined arrow also will improve clearance. If, after all this, you can't get good clearance (which could be the case with some wood-handle bows with little center-shot clearance) you may have to use feather fletching. Feathers will hit the bow or rest, too, but they compress and won't throw your arrow into erratic flight.

Sighting In

With your bow in tune, you're now ready to sight in your bow. Start at 20 yards, or your closest chosen yardage, and set that pin and

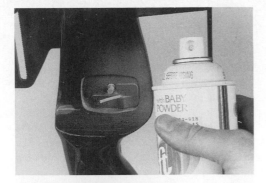

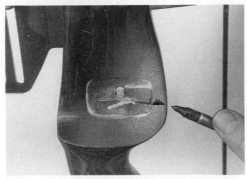

To check for arrow clearance, first spray your bow with a deodorant or foot spray containing powder. Then shoot an arrow and inspect your bow for any indication of contact. As shown here, you can easily see where fletching hits the bow. The nock should be turned on this arrow to bring the bottom vane slightly farther from the bow.

then move back and set the other pins (for details, see Bow Sight).

One problem I've found with movable spring tension rests is that you can artificially change the spine characteristics of an arrow, so that even if arrows are under- or over-spined, you can make them shoot nearly straight off the bow. That's okay to a certain extent, particularly if you shoot with sights, because you can simply screw the pins in or out until the arrows hit on the mark.

If carried too far, however, you'll run out of horizontal adjustment before you can bring the arrows on target. Ideally, the sights should be directly over the arrow shaft, and if they're far off to one side or the other, you can move the

impact point of the arrows into the sight picture by moving the arrow rest in or out or increasing or decreasing spring tension on the cushion plunger. Small adjustments will alter impact point significantly without seriously affecting tune of your bow.

If you shoot instinctively, your arrows must fly where you're looking. You can use the above tuning methods to get good arrow flight, but that doesn't mean the arrows will fly where you're looking. If the bow shoots to one side or the other, you can bring the arrows into line by moving the plunger or arrow rest slightly in the direction you want the arrows to move, or by increasing or decreasing spring tension.

Tuning Chart

Here, in brief chart form, are the basic changes you must make to alter arrow flight. In using the bare-shaft planing test, you judge spine by the direction bare shafts plane away from fletched shafts. In shooting through paper, you judge spine by the direction the tail flies in relation to the point of the arrow. They mean exactly the same, because the arrow planes in the opposite direction of the tail. For example, if an arrow flies tail high, it will plane low. If it flies tail left, it will plane to the right. Incidentally, an arrow that planes right is too weakly spined (too limber) for that bow weight, and an arrow that planes left is too stiff.

Problem	Solution
Tail high (plane low)	Move nock down
Tail low (plane high)	Move nock up
Tail left (plane right)	Increase spring tension
	Move rest to left
	Decrease bow weight
	Use lighter head
	Use stiffer arrows
	Increase fletching
	Shorten arrows (if possible)
	Shoot with mechanical release aid

Tail right (plane left)   Decrease spring
                                       tension
                           Move rest to right
                           Increase bow weight
                           Use heavier head
                           Use weaker spine
                                       arrows
                           Use less fletching
                           Lengthen arrows

Rules of Thumb

- 5 grains in arrow weight equals about 1 foot-per-second difference in velocity.
- 15 grains variance in arrowhead weight equals a significant effect on spine of arrow. Less than 15 grains variance won't make a significant difference in arrow flight.
- A 1-inch variance in arrow length equals roughly 5 pounds difference in spine-weight value.
- 9 grains of arrow weight per pound of bow weight is often used as a rule of thumb for matching arrows to bow for greatest efficiency.

BRACE HEIGHT This term, also called string height, refers to the distance from the handle of a bow to the string when the bow is in a braced position. Brace height can vary from six to ten inches or greater, depending on make of bow. With recurve bows, brace height should be set so the bow shoots smoothly and quietly. Changing brace height is one way to tune a recurve bow. The lower the brace height, the farther the string travels with the arrow and the greater the arrow speed. You want the brace height as low as possible while still maintaining a quiet-shooting bow. If the bow thunks or slaps loudly when you release, the brace height is probably too low. On most recurve bows, only a half-inch or so of the string groove should show from under the string when the bow is in a braced position. You can alter brace height in small amounts by unstringing the bow and twisting the string. If you have to alter it significantly, you should go to a different length string.

On a compound bow, brace height isn't critical as far as arrow speed and quietness go. In another sense, though, it is critical because altering brace height can change draw weight and draw length. Make sure all your strings are the same length so the brace height remains the same when you change strings.

BRITISH COLUMBIA This province covers 366,200 square miles. Nonresidents must be accompanied by a licensed British Columbia guide to hunt any big game in the province.

Big Game

Deer. British Columbia (B.C.) has four subspecies of deer. Mule deer are the most widely distributed, and an estimated 120,000 animals live throughout the southern interior from the border of Alberta west to the Coast Range and north in the Fraser River drainage to Prince George. In some areas these animals inhabit remote country and are lightly hunted, and some very large bucks are taken.

About 30,000 whitetails live in the southeast corner in the thick bottomlands along the Columbia, Kootenay, and Kettle rivers. A few scattered herds live throughout the southern interior, and a separate population lives along the Peace River near the border of Alberta.

An estimated 310,000 blacktail deer live in the dense rain forests along the coast from the U.S. border as far north as Smith Sound and also on Vancouver Island. North of Smith Sound the animals are classified as Sitka blacktails. Sitka deer live on all the islands along the northern coast of British Columbia including the Queen Charlotte Islands. The northwestern quarter and the extreme north end of British Columbia have no deer. Seasons vary greatly by region.

Elk. B.C. doesn't share Alberta's reputation for huge elk, but a high percentage of the elk killed in B.C. are mature bulls, and elk hunting is rated as excellent. Highest elk numbers are found in the Kootenay region of the southeast corner. Seasons are held during the rut in September.

Sheep. Nonresident hunters probably give British Columbia more attention because of sheep than any other big game. The province has four subspecies — Dall, Stone, Rocky Mountain bighorn, and California bighorn — but it's the Stone that gets the most attention. B.C. has a virtual monopoly on these animals and most record-book Stone sheep have come from the northern end of this province.

Mountain Goat. B.C. also has more goats than any other state or province. They're most abundant in the northwest corner in the Coast Range and associated mountains, but they live in many mountain ranges where suitable habitat exists.

Moose. Virtually the entire province has good moose hunting. Many of the largest Canada moose listed in the record books come from B.C.

Caribou. The caribou of B.C. are classified as mountain caribou, and a majority of the record-book animals have come from the mountains at the north end of this province.

Cougar. Hunters kill an average of 300 lions each year, by far the highest harvest of any state or province. Many of the largest lions ever killed have come from B.C.

Bears. B.C. also rates among the best for grizzly and black bears. Grizzly hunting, particularly in the spring, brings a premium price. Black bears are virtually guaranteed in some regions.

Contact. Ministry of Environment, Fish and Wildlife Branch, Parliament Buildings, Victoria, BC, Canada V8V-1X5.

BROADHEAD A broadhead is the business end of a big game arrow. It must have a wide diameter to cut a big hole, and it must be sharp to cut cleanly and penetrate well. Few bowhunters would disagree about what a broadhead should do — fly accurately and kill cleanly. They just disagree on which broadhead designs and brands do that best. I doubt that anyone has an absolute answer because no one head design will do everything best, but a few principles apply to all broadhead selection.

Accuracy

This is the number one concern in broadhead selection. A small broadhead in the lungs will kill a lot neater than a huge broadhead in the guts, so above all you must pick broadheads that will fly well.

Broadheads come in nearly infinite design, size, and weight. Choose heads first for accuracy, then for penetrating qualities and durability.

Broadhead Size. Never take for granted that all broadheads fly straight. Don Rabska, special projects manager for Easton Aluminum, fields hundreds of questions from archers each year. He said the number one question concerns planing of broadheads.

Most bowhunters would say the size of the broadhead, in terms of diameter or total surface area of the blades, affects flight more than any other property, and size probably does have an effect.

"A broadhead in essence gives you a wing out front that wants to steer the arrow," Rabska said. "The larger the surface area of the head the more 'wing' surface it has and the more it wants to control flight of the arrow. That's why you need plenty of fletching with broadheads to stabilize them." (For more details, see Fletching.)

Dick Tone and Tom Fisher have tested broadhead flight extensively. Tone said they could get good flight with most two- and three-blade broadheads by fletching with three five-inch vanes, but with big four-blade heads, they needed four five-inch vanes to shoot tight groups. Fisher added, "Big heads are virtually impossible to steer, so with oversized heads you must go to feathers to get good flight. Some makers recommend that you not use vanes with their heads. Right there they're admitting their broadheads have a deficiency."

Cutouts in the blades, which reduce surface area, help reduce the planing effect of broadheads to some extent. If you want to shoot fairly wide heads, try those that have cutout blades.

Choosing a broadhead, then, comes down to finding one that's wide enough to kill cleanly, yet small enough to shoot well. I would say any blade from 1 to 1¼ inches in diameter is plenty big enough for clean kills. At the same time, heads of that size will shoot well, providing they are well made.

Quality. Andy Simo, an engineer who designed the popular Thunderhead and Razorbak broadheads, said it's not so much the size of the broadhead but precision of construction that determines how well a broadhead will fly.

"If everything is lined up perfectly down the ferrule, then the broadhead will fly straight. Some broadheads are not made precisely, and the blades are warped. The reason wide broadheads plane worse than narrow ones is that they can't be stamped out as precisely as smaller blades, and the slightest warp in a blade acts like the aileron on an airplane's wing and steers the head off course. They must be totally concentric. Any slight eccentricity will throw them off course.

"Given precision manufacturing, it doesn't matter if a head is ⅞ inch or 2 inches across. It will fly straight. That's assuming arrows are properly spined, of course."

Simo also said a well-made three- or four-blade head will fly better than a poorly made two-blade head. "If one blade is off, it doesn't throw the head as far out of balance as a bad blade on a two-blade head does."

How do you choose a good broadhead? "Unless you're an engineer, it's tough because you don't have the equipment to measure minute tolerances," Simo said. "But price offers a reasonable guideline. You can't always gauge quality by price, but generally the more expensive the heads, the better the quality. Bowhunters should never buy cheap broadheads."

Some manufacturers offer heads in various weights and blade configurations. The Thunderhead 125 weighs 125 grains. The Thunderhead 150-grain head has two blades. Both heads, with .027-inch steel blades, are durable and can be shot and resharpened.

Checking Straightness. You also can check broadheads for straightness by spinning them. Install a head on an arrow shaft, set the tip of the head on a hard surface, and spin the arrow like a top. Watch where the head meets the shaft. If you see any wobble, the head is bent. Check several heads of a given brand, and if they don't spin straight, don't buy them.

Also, if you make your own arrows and use glue-on broadheads, always check alignment, and if you see any wobble, work at realigning the head until you get it straight. If you plan to salvage a broadhead after a shot, always check it for straightness. If it's bent, it won't fly well. You can straighten bent heads with pliers and use them for plinking, but for shooting at big game, use new, accurate heads.

Bow Tuning. This can also affect broadhead flight. If your gear is matched so the arrow starts out perfectly straight, then you can get away with a fairly large broadhead. But if your arrow leaves the bow slightly crooked, a planing effect takes place immediately and your arrow never has a chance of flying straight. I would say that if you have to go to four big feathers to stabilize your arrows, then your bow setup needs some work, and you're probably trying to shoot more broadhead than you really need. (For details, see Bow Tuning.)

Broadhead alignment may affect accuracy, too. When you shoot, your arrow bends. That's unavoidable, and the finest tuning can't totally eliminate this paradox. When you shoot with your fingers, most bending motion is side to side. With three-blade and symmetrical four-blade heads, broadhead alignment in relation to paradox doesn't matter because the heads are symmetrical and won't plane one direction worse than another. But heads with one large blade have a wing that will steer them, and you want to align them in a position of least wind resistance—that is, horizontally, with the big blade parallel to the ground.

Shooting with a release aid, that may not be true. Tom Fisher had some interesting thoughts on this. "With a release aid, pressure is down on the corner of the nock, so it pushes the arrow down and spine rotates 90 degrees, and

To shoot accurately, a head must be perfectly concentric. Spin your arrows like this and watch closely, especially where the blade meets the arrow. If you see any wobble, the head is slightly eccentric and will plane to throw your arrow off course.

paradox is off the rest, not the side of the bow," Fisher said. "For that reason, shooting with a release aid you want to align broadheads vertically."

Remember, also, that the faster and lighter the arrow, the more critical the setup and the more a slight imperfection in a broadhead will affect arrow flight. If you go with an ultra-high-speed overdraw setup, you may have to go with low-profile broadheads not much more than one inch in diameter.

Cutting and Penetration

Hitting an animal on the money is the key to clean kills, so first priority goes to accuracy. Never sacrifice accuracy for size. Still, once a broadhead hits an animal, it must cut a maximum of blood vessels and penetrate deeply, so the following criteria must be examined.

Sharpness. Probably the most publicized aspect of bowhunting is sharp broadheads. That's the subject every archery instructor, magazine writer, and shop owner stresses. And rightly so. To penetrate deeply and cut blood vessels, a broadhead must be sharp. That's not a problem with most broadheads with interchangeable blades. If the blades get dull, you can replace them. In most cases these replaceable blades are razor sharp, although I've seen some that weren't. Test the blades before buying a given brand. If you buy one-piece heads, learn to hone them well. (For details, see Broadhead Sharpening.)

Bowhunters often debate whether broadheads should have a smooth, razor-blade edge, or a serrated edge. My opinion is that a broadhead should be as sharp as you can get it, and if the edge is serrated, the head isn't sharp. I think a head should be honed to a razor-sharp, smooth edge. But then, I know bowhunters who've killed a truckload of game with serrated broadheads, so who's to say they're wrong?

Shape of Point. Sharpness isn't the only criterion for judging deadliness. Point shape probably has more effect on penetration. Montana bowhunter Bob Savage has tested penetration extensively. After thousands of arrows shot into different materials, Savage determined that point shape was the single most important influence on penetration. Broadheads sharpened right to the point, which start cutting at the instant of contact, consistently

penetrate better than heads with bullet or pencil-shaped tips. (For more details, see Penetration.)

For that reason I'd recommend sharp-pointed broadheads above all others, especially for oversized or thick-hided game such as elk, moose, and pigs. For lighter-skinned animals, the replaceable-blade broadheads with push-type points will penetrate well enough, but even among them, some will perform better than others. I've found that heads with squared-off tips such as the Thunderheads and Muzzys penetrate better than those with a round tip, probably because flattening the sides reduces surface area and friction.

A flattened ferrule does the same. Andy Simo used to make a 180-grain broadhead, but to reduce weight he shaved off the sides of the ferrule and made it triangular. This reduced weight of the head from 180 to 160 grains, sure enough, but it did something Simo hadn't anticipated — it improved penetration by 15 to 20 percent.

Number of Blades. Number of blades can affect penetration and deadliness of a broadhead. For a given length and diameter, a two-blade head may penetrate better than a three- or four-blade head, simply because it has less surface area (although I question whether that's really true; for more details, see Penetration). That's probably why some hunters still prefer two-blade heads, in addition to the fact that two-blade are easier to sharpen than multi-blade heads.

Many two-blade heads also have larger diameter than three- and four-blade heads, which would seem to increase the cutting potential, but actually it doesn't. If you draw a circle the diameter of a broadhead and draw a line across it to represent a blood vessel, you'll see that you can push a two-blade head through in various ways so it won't touch the vessel. With a multi-blade head you can't do that.

Even though the diameter of a three- or four-blade head might not be as great as for some two-blade heads, the total cutting radius could be greater and it could cause more bleeding. That's because the more blades a head has,

Here are three major broadhead tip designs. At left, the head is sharpened right to the point. This style of broadhead will penetrate best. The center head has a flattened tip, and the head at right has a round tip. Flattened tips seem to penetrate better than conical tips, probably because flattening reduces surface area.

the more capillaries and other tiny blood vessels it will cut, even if it doesn't hit a major artery. For these reasons, I recommend three- or four-blade heads, not two.

Angle of Blades. Cutting tools work by one of two actions—slicing or chopping. The greater the angle of the blade, the more the chopping action replaces slicing. A good broadhead slices, so the flatter the angle, the better the broadhead will slice. This can be gauged roughly by length-to-width ratio. The Howard Hill broadhead, for example, has a ratio of 3:1, three inches long and one inch wide. Some hunters consider that an ideal ratio because it provides a low angle and good slicing action.

However, the longer the blade, the thicker it must be made for strength, which drastically increases weight and thickness. And although the long angle slices well, the length of the broadhead increases surface area drag. Bob Savage said he never got broadheads with a 3:1 ratio to penetrate as well as shorter broadheads. He said he consistently had best results with the Zwickey Eskimo and other blades with a similar 2:1 length-to-width ratio. (For more details, see Penetration.)

With a ratio much less than that, however, you get a chopping action, and penetration will not be as good.

Over the years, heads have been made with spiraled blades, jagged blades, and movable blades that spread out when they hit an animal. Most of these are gimmicks. A friend of mine shot a javelina—a very light, easy-to-kill animal—in the chest with a head with blades that spread on contact, supposedly to make a bigger hole. The head penetrated less than an inch, and my friend trailed that pig for five hours before he finally recovered it. With any regular, dependable broadhead, he'd have found that pig within 50 yards.

Durability. As a rule, solid heads are more durable than replaceable-blade heads, although that depends on the hardness of the steel and construction. You can shoot some welded, one-piece heads dozens of times. If they bend you can straighten them with pliers and resharpen them to hunt again.

The head at left has a 3:1 length-to-width ratio, and the head at right has a 2:1 ratio. Some experts say the 2:1 head will penetrate better, and it's definitely easier to sharpen.

Some multi-piece heads are very durable, and durability depends largely on thickness of the blades. Some manufacturers make blades of steel only .010 or .015 inch thick. These heads won't hold up well, and you can plan to replace the blades after every shot. Such thin blades are also hard to sharpen. The most durable heads have blades made of steel .025 to .030 inch thick. These are nearly as durable as the blades on one-piece heads, and you can shoot and resharpen them many times.

Replaceable-blade broadheads must have a positive locking system that holds the blades in place. I personally don't trust broadheads with blades that slip into slots and can be pulled out. They might come apart before doing any major damage to an animal, and they might leave a loose blade floating around in the meat somewhere, which could promise an unpleasant surprise at dinnertime.

Some heads are made of carbon steel, others of stainless. Because the stainless heads won't rust, they're great on rainy hunts. But the carbon steel blades sharpen up a little better. I'd say the accuracy, design, and weight of a head

Durability is one criterion for choosing broadheads. If heads will come apart after one shot into Styrofoam, they'll probably come apart on contact with an animal. I wouldn't trust these heads for hunting.

are more important than the kind of steel it's made of.

Broadhead Care

To keep heads from rusting in your quiver, coat them with light oil or Vaseline, and to protect spare presharpened broadheads, coat them with oil and push them into a block of Styrofoam. Some hunters make fancy little boxes or cases for storing broadheads.

Broadheads in a quiver will dull gradually from oxidation, dust, and abrasion from pulling them in and out. Don't just put them in at the beginning of the season and leave them there. Check them periodically and touch them up with a hone to keep them sharp. (For details, see Broadhead Sharpening.)

In handling broadheads, always use a broadhead wrench. Screwing them in and out with bare fingers is a good way to lose some flesh.

For safety's sake, always use a broadhead wrench when working with broadheads.

BROADHEAD SHARPENING One thing most bowhunters agree on is the need for sharp broadheads. If a head cuts cleanly, it creates its own channel and assures good penetration. And a sharp edge will cut any blood vessels it hits to promote bleeding, which is the primary purpose of a broadhead.

Differing Opinions

True to form, hunters disagree strongly on how to make a broadhead sharp. Some believe a serrated, rasplike edge proves more effective because, in essence, it has little teeth that rip and tear. One of those teeth, this reasoning says, might catch and tear open a blood vessel that a smooth edge might slide past. Those who believe in the serrated edge sharpen their heads with a file only, because the file produces a coarse edge.

Archers also disagree on point shape. If you use modular heads with a central ferrule and replaceable blades, you're stuck with the kind of point that comes with the head. But if you use solid broadheads that must be sharpened (for more details on this, see Broadhead), you can shape the point any number of ways. And here again, that opens up debate. Some hunters believe the point of a broadhead should be rounded so "it will slide past bone."

I've never talked to anyone who could offer evidence to support that idea. I personally believe a sharp, pointed tip will be more effective in most cases. A sharp point doesn't have to slide past bone; it probably will cut through. And I'd bet the pointed broadhead will penetrate better under most, if not all, circumstances. Besides, the idea is to hit vitals, and if you accidentally hit a shoulder or hip, nothing short of a rifle bullet will help you anyway.

Check for Sharpness

Many things can dull broadheads—shooting them into an animal (or tree, rock, or dirt), corrosion and rust, dust and grit in a quiver. You should check broadheads regularly and re-sharpen any that are even slightly dull.

You can check sharpness the same way you would with a knife, by shaving hair off your arm. If the head shaves your arm cleanly, it's sharp; if it doesn't, it's not. You can also use the rubber band test (a rubber band more or less simulates a blood vessel). Loop a rubber band around the thumb and index finger on one hand and stretch it tight. Now slide a broadhead against the band. Don't apply any pressure other than the weight of the arrow and head. If the broadhead severs the band cleanly, it's acceptably sharp; if it doesn't, it's not.

Sharpening Procedures

Modular Broadheads. You can sharpen any broadhead on a conventional whetstone or steel, but it's awkward with replaceable-blade heads. One slick idea to solve the problem comes from Tim Roberts, inventor of Tru-Angle Hones. Roberts designed small sharpening stones with just the right angle to accommodate either three- or four-blade modular heads. These stones are made of ceramic and don't require oil. You simply slide the broadhead back and forth along the hone. Start with moderate pressure to get the edge started, and then reduce pressure to a very light stroke to take off any wire edge. It's simple because the hone has been built with the proper angle for any given broadhead.

Of course you can forego sharpening and simply replace the blades on your broadheads, but that gets expensive. Using these hones allows you to touch up quiver-dulled heads,

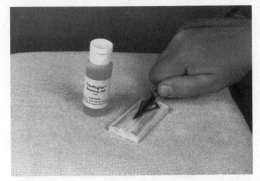

For replaceable-blade broadheads, TruAngle hones offer a slick sharpening system. The hones are beveled to match blade angle of different styles of broadheads. Start out with heavy pressure and then lighten up to produce a smooth, wireless edge.

TruAngle hones also are made for solid broadheads, and they come in coarse and fine grits, as well as the leather strop being used here.

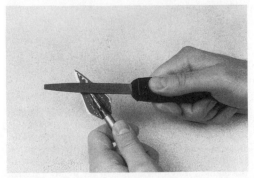

To sharpen a solid broadhead, begin with a file to flatten the bevel of the edges.

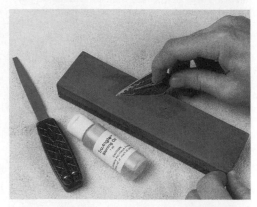

To sharpen a head on a stone, the procedure is much like sharpening a knife. First put oil on the stone. Begin with the back edge of the blade on the stone, and draw the blade toward you as if to slice oil off the stone. As you slice, work from the back end of the blade through the middle to the point. Through this entire stroke, you should see oil being sliced off the stone right at the end of the blade.

and you can even salvage most broadheads you've shot at animals. I've resharpened and used the same Thunderhead 125s to take several animals.

Fixed-Blade Broadheads. Tim Roberts also has made TruAngle hones for fixed-blade heads such as Zwickey Black Diamonds and Bear Razorheads. These hones are made of oilstone and come in coarse and fine grits mounted in oak bases. You also can get a leather strop to go with this set.

If you're starting with new broadheads, file them first to flatten the angle of the edge. Then apply a few drops of oil to each side of the TruAngle hone and slide your broadhead forward as if to slice the oil off the hone. Start with the coarse stone, then use the fine grit, and finish up with the leather.

You can also sharpen solid broadheads as you would a knife (for details, see Knife Sharpening). You can make a handle for broadheads by gluing a screw-in insert into the end of a block of wood. Simply screw a broadhead mounted on an adaptor into the insert. That makes working on the broadhead easier, although I've found I can sharpen a broadhead just as well with the head mounted on an arrow shaft.

To sharpen broadheads this way you need a file, coarse and fine oilstones, honing oil, and ceramic rods (Crock Sticks) or a sharpening steel. First file the edges of the broadhead to flatten out the bevel. Most broadheads come from the factory with much too steep an angle, almost like a chisel blade. Saunders makes a file with a handle that works well for this. You can also use a regular metal file, and Luhr Jensen's fishhook file does a good job. To make filing easier, mount the broadhead in a vise. You can apply more pressure this way to grind the edge down faster. However, always wear leather gloves with this method. One slip will drive a broadhead right through your finger (I speak from experience).

After filing each edge to the proper bevel, begin sharpening on the coarse stone. First oil the stone. Now, holding the broadhead firmly, place the back edge on the stone and draw the

You can sharpen auxiliary blades the same way, although with the small blades shown here, you can make only straight strokes.

Finish up with very light strokes over ceramic Crock Sticks as shown here, or with a sharpening steel or leather strop.

blade into the stone as if to slice the oil off the stone. Work from the back of the blade, through the middle, and to the tip. Flip the blade over and make a similar stroke on the other side. You'll have to alternate from one side of the stone to the other as you work on one edge of the blade.

After a couple of dozen strokes on each side, switch to the fine stone and hone each edge of the blade similarly. When it's sharp enough to dig into a fingernail rather than sliding across the nail, finish the sharpening on ceramic Crock Sticks or a sharpening steel. The purpose of these finishing strokes is to remove the fine wire edge formed by the oilstone. Use virtually no pressure as you draw the edge of the head along the ceramic; the weight of the arrow itself is enough. If the broadhead is sharp, it will shave your arm or cleanly cut a rubber band held between your fingers.

Preserving the Edge

Stainless steel blades present few rust and corrosion problems, but carbon blades will rust, so coat them with Vaseline or a thin layer of oil to preserve the edge. Any blade will dull over time as it's pulled in and out of a quiver or exposed to dust and grit. To keep sharpened blades in good shape, store them in a block of Styrofoam, and wash the rubber in your quiver periodically to get rid of grit.

BROWN BEAR　See Bear.

BROW TINE　This is the antler point nearest the eye on deer and elk. Typically all mature bull elk and buck whitetail deer grow brow tines, but in mule deer, blacktail, and Sitka deer, brow tines may be only short nubs, or they may be absent altogether. Official score charts classify the brow tine as the No. 1 point, or G-1.

BUGLE　During the rut bull elk make a high-pitched sound commonly called a "bugle." The sound could be described more accurately as whistling, screaming, or braying, but somehow it got named bugling, so bugling it is.

Bulls bugle to attract cows, to assert their dominance, to challenge or intimidate other bulls, and probably to do other things no human will ever understand. Throughout the West, bulls start bugling in late August and continue into early October. The peak of breeding takes place the last two weeks in September. During the bugling season hunters call bulls within range by imitating the sounds of bugling, and this has become the most popular and productive form of elk hunting among archers. (For details, see Elk.)

C

CABLE GUARD This rod, which extends from the riser of a compound bow, holds the cables to one side of the string to assure fletching clears the cables during a shot. A cable guard is needed only for thin-wheeled bows on which the cables and string lie nearly in line. On bows with wide wheels, the cables are far enough to the side that a guard isn't needed. Some bows also have a special groove in the wheels that slides the cables to the side at full draw, and a guard isn't needed with these.

On some bows the cable guard is mounted in the high position above the handle, and on others it's mounted low, below the handle. Some bows offer both options. I personally prefer the low position because it gets the cable guard out of my line of sight. A low cable guard also allows you to mount a sight on the inside of the limb, but with most high cable guards, you must mount bowsights outside the limb.

A slide on the cable guard quietens a bow by preventing cable slap, and it reduces cable wear. The simplest cable slide consists of a plastic block held in place on one side of the guard by pressure from the cables. Other slides fit around the cable-guard rod and the cables hang in grooves in the slide. Some of these friction slides squeak and chatter when they're wet, which could be disastrous for hunting. I use a slide during practice, to prevent cable wear, but take it off for hunting. A bow shoots just as well without the slide, and cable wear when hunting without it is minimal. If you do this, readjust your cable guard so cable clearance is the same as it was with the slide.

More elaborate models like the Saunders Roller Cable Guard Slide have little wheels that roll up and down the cable guard. These assure a smooth, chatter-free draw, and they won't squeak. A slide like this could be the answer for all-around use.

CALIFORNIA California extends along the Pacific Coast for nearly 1,000 miles, and covers nearly 159,693 square miles. The habitat is diverse, from rain forests at sea level up to alpine terrain near the highest peak in the Lower 48, Mt. Whitney. California has two major mountain ranges, the Sierra Nevada and the Coast Range, which parallel each other the full length of the state.

Big Game

Mule Deer. These popular animals occupy about 15 percent of the state. Biologists estimate the total mule deer population at 288,000, with several subspecies. The major mule deer counties are Siskiyou, Modoc, Lassen, and Plumas in the northeast corner; in

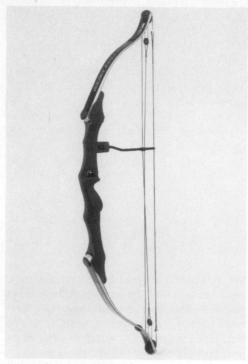

A cable guard holds the cables on a compound bow to one side to assure fletching clearance. On this bow the guard is above the handle, but on others it's below the handle.

The Saunders Roller Cable Guard Slide prevents cable wear, and it doesn't chatter as some friction slides do.

The cable slide at left is held in place by pressure from the cables. The one at right goes around the cable guard rod and the cables hang in slots. These cable slides reduce cable wear, but they chatter and squeak when the cable guard is wet. They can be removed for hunting.

this high, sagebrush desert country are Rocky Mountain mule deer. California mule deer extend down the east side of the Sierras to the Mojave Desert, where the predominant form is the burro deer, a subspecies that exists in very low densities in the blistering deserts along the Colorado River.

In general mule deer are hunted heavily during rifle seasons, and the percentage of bucks is low in many areas. However, to improve the quality of herds, the number of tags has been restricted in some units, such as Zones X5a and X5b in the northeast. Here the hunting success has been high and hunters have taken many trophy bucks. Competition for tags is keen, but if you want to kill a truly good mule deer in California, one of the limited-permit zones is the place to do it.

A nontypical buck taken in Mariposa County in 1972 scored 319⁴/₈, but you have to look hard to find other mule deer from California listed by Boone and Crockett. Some of the limited-entry mule deer zones produce a lot of Pope and Young–type bucks.

Most archery seasons for mule deer take place in August and September.

Blacktail Deer. An estimated 312,000 blacktails live throughout the Coast Range from Los Angeles north to the Oregon border. From Los Angeles to San Francisco, the Coast Range is hot and dry, and the vegetation consists of either open oak forests and grasslands or dense, doghair chaparral. The Los Padres and Angeles National Forests offer some public hunting, but a large percentage of the land is private. You can pay to hunt some of this land, but much of it is leased by private hunting clubs. The deer here are numerous but small.

North of San Francisco, the Coast Range splits into an exterior arm along the coast, and an interior arm about 50 miles inland. The exterior arm has many deer, but virtually all the land is private and leased to hunting clubs.

The interior arm, in contrast, contains vast areas of public land, including three large wilderness areas that offer some of the best blacktail hunting in North America. Unlike much blacktail country, which is dense and hard to hunt, the interior Coast Range consists of fairly open forests and even some alpine country. Heavy chaparral has reduced deer numbers in some places, but prescribed burning has opened up the brush and deer herds have flourished. Hunting pressure during rifle seasons is fairly heavy, but the remote and rugged country provides good sanctuary for deer, and buck-doe ratios are high in some localities. During bow seasons, you can get away from most hunters by hiking into the backcountry.

California grows big blacktails. Nearly 45 percent of the blacktails listed in the eighth edition of *Records of North American Big Game* came from California. The top region is the interior Coast Range in Siskiyou, Trinity, and Mendocino counties.

The archery deer season in Zone A—the central and southern Coast Range—generally opens in mid-July and closes in early August. This is the earliest deer season in the United States. In the northern coastal blacktail zones, the bow season runs from mid-August through early September. The average bow harvest for deer has been 471, with a high in 1977 of 778.

Pigs. Feral hogs are the number two game animal in California. Annual harvest (rifle and bow) exceeds 30,000. The season is open year-round, and the limit is one a day and one in possession. Most hunters go after pigs during fall and winter when the weather is reasonably

cool and pigs are in good shape from eating acorns. Most pigs live in the oak-covered foothills. The upper Sacramento Valley near Redding and Red Bluff has some good pig herds, but the majority of hogs live in the Coast Range from north of the Bay Area south to Santa Barbara. Some national forest and federal military lands offer limited pig hunting, but by far the majority of hogs live on private lands where you must pay to hunt. Popular hunts among bowhunters are the wild pig and feral goat hunts on islands in the Santa Barbara Channel.

Bear. California is one of the top bear states. Baiting is illegal, but hunting with hounds is allowed and that's how most bears are killed. Highest numbers of bears live in the northern Coast Range, although the Sierra Nevada have a good population, too. Bow season for bears is in August and September concurrent with blacktail deer season. Early September is an excellent time to spot a bear feeding in the open. The general hound season runs from September into November.

Antelope. Excellent antelope herds roam the high desert in northeastern California. Bowhunters have done very well, but only residents may apply for the limited number of tags.

Elk. Tule elk are indigenous to California and their numbers are growing, but there is no open season on them. Very limited hunts have been held for Roosevelt elk along the north coast.

Cougar. California may have more cougars than any other state, but the season has been closed for some time.

Sheep. California also has more desert bighorns than any other state, but again there is no open season.

Other Game

Turkeys. California has blossomed into one of the best turkey states in the country. The Sierra foothills bordering the Central Valley, and the Coast Range between San Francisco and Santa Barbara have the most turkeys, but these birds have spread into suitable habitat throughout the state. Unfortunately, virtually

California has blossomed into one of the finest turkey states in the United States.

all the best hunting takes place on private lands, and getting permission to hunt is no simple matter. Many guides run turkey hunts on private land.

Predators. Parts of California are overrun with coyotes. Hunting for bobcats, foxes, and other predators is good, too.

Small Game. Gray squirrel hunting is excellent in most of the northwestern counties, and hunting for cottontails and jackrabbits rates at least good throughout the north end of the state.

Contact. Department of Fish and Game, 1416 Ninth Street, Sacramento, CA 95814.

CAMOUFLAGE My first year of bowhunting I was resting along a forest road when I heard a faint sound and looked up to see a bowhunter right beside me. About all I could see of him were his white teeth shining out from the depths of his camouflage. We chatted briefly, and then he proceeded to tell me everything that was wrong with my camouflage—or lack of camouflage. At the time, I was indignant. After all, I was wearing camouflage coveralls, and I'd painted my beautiful black Wing Thunderbird bow an ugly olive drab. Wasn't that sacrifice enough?

Later, when I really thought about what he said, I knew he was right. My uncovered blond hair looked like a pile of straw moving through the woods, and my silvery aluminum arrows (that was when they still made silver-colored

arrows) were unpainted. Any deer with half an eye would have spotted me from a mile away. No wonder I hadn't been seeing anything.

Value of Camouflage

Since then I've been a nut on the subject, and I fully believe in the value of total camouflage. It does work. On one late hunt in snow, I wore snow camouflage, including a white face mask, as I stalked within 25 yards of a buck and knelt in the snow, ready to shoot. When I whistled the buck rose from his bed and I drew to shoot. But I decided he wasn't big enough and let down. The deer saw the movement and started to trot away. Then he stopped and crept back toward me, peering, trying to see what had moved. Again I drew my bow and the deer started to run. But again he stopped and came back within 20 yards. Not until I stood up and walked toward him did the buck flee for good. My camouflage worked.

Does camouflage work? A big-game animal would have a hard time spotting this hunter.

That's not to say camouflage is a panacea for all bowhunting ills. But I doubt that it will ever hinder your chances, and in many cases it definitely can help, so using camouflage is a no-lose proposition. I figure if camouflage makes a difference one time out of a hundred, it's worth the trouble, because that one time might involve a world-record animal. Besides, I work hard and spend a lot of money for most of my shots, and I'll take no chances.

Sometimes camouflage may not have as much actual value as psychological value. Possibly an animal wouldn't see you even if you weren't camouflaged. But knowing that you've covered every base gives you confidence. So, if for no other reason than the confidence factor, full camouflage works.

Methods of Camouflage

Clothing. Some camouflage doesn't do much, because the differing color blotches are small and have a similar hue; from a distance they appear virtually as one solid color. To the human eye, gray, brown, and green would produce fairly high contrast, but to an animal's eye, which sees in black and white, those three colors would produce almost no contrast. To produce the required effect, the pattern must contain shades of greatly differing light values, from near-black to near-white. And the overall hue must agree with your surroundings. In open sagebrush, camouflage must be fairly light with a small proportion of black. In shadowy conifer forests, the clothes must contain more black with small accents of lighter colors.

I think the actual pattern is the least important part of a camouflage system, and I personally pick clothes first for silence, and then for color pattern. For stationary hunting from a stand, priorities might differ, but for hunting on foot, clothing must, above all else, allow silent, comfortable movement. That means it must be made of wool or equally soft synthetics (for details, see Clothing and Footwear), and you can't always get just the right camouflage pattern in these materials.

That doesn't matter. The overall hue is what counts, and a bold plaid in the right shades is

To be of value, a camouflage pattern must have a boldly contrasting color pattern, and the overall hue must match surrounding vegetation. (No, this hunter didn't get shot in the back. Those arrows are in his hip quiver.)

far better than a camouflage pattern that's too light or dark. In deep woods I often wear olive-green wool pants and a green-and-black plaid wool shirt, and I have complete confidence in the camouflage value of these clothes. No elk or deer will ever distinguish between my drab pants and the trunk of a tree as long as I remain still.

The same that applies to shirts and pants applies to hats. A hat must be quiet, the pattern should be bold, and the general hue should match your hunting conditions. (For details, see Clothing and Footwear.)

Hands, Face, Bow and Arrows. Many hunters wear a camouflage shirt, and do nothing else in the way of camouflage. That makes no sense at all. In many cases as you approach within bow range of animals, your body will be hidden by foliage or terrain and you wouldn't be seen even if you were wearing blaze orange. So in that sense the kind of clothing you wear makes no difference. But to shoot at an animal, three things must always be visible to that animal—your face, hands, and bow. For that reason I think these deserve by far the greatest attention.

When hunting on foot, I like to use face

It makes little sense to wear camouflage clothing and to leave your skin as white as snow. For dark-woods hunting, use lots of black, but for more open country, lighten the camouflage to match the surroundings.

Skin can be the major giveaway in many hunting situations, so use camouflage cream to darken light skin. Cream comes in tubes or in handy boxes like this with a built-in mirror.

paint because a head net makes me sweat and steams up my glasses. In using paint, the principle is the same as in clothing—get good contrast and match the hue to the surroundings. For antelope hunting from pit blinds, Judd Cooney places his hunters so they're always seated in shadows, and he has them totally blacken their faces to blend with the shadows. Similarly dark camouflage would be appropriate in spruce forests or other black timber.

But in open country, especially in sage and other light-color vegetation, too much black is worse than no camouflage at all. A friend of mine believed in using lots of black face paint, which was okay for elk hunting in timber, but out in the desert I could always spot him instantly, even at long range, by his black face. In that kind of country, use mostly light green and brown, accented with small dabs of black. You can wash most face paints off with soap and water. A friend of mine uses treated paper towels such as Wet Ones.

Even when it's covered with camouflage cream, skin shines to some extent, so I think a cloth or netting face mask, which has a softer look like real foliage, actually provides better camouflage. For stand hunting, the face mask can be ideal. To work well, it must fit your face fairly tightly so it doesn't interfere with the bowstring, and it should have eye holes so you can see well. Several companies make head covers that fit your face like skin, and these work very well.

You can't shoot a bow without moving your hands. If anything will catch an animal's eye, it will be that movement, so camouflage on hands can be significant. Camouflage cream might be okay, but I prefer gloves under all conditions. In extremely hot weather, I often wear gloves made of mosquito netting, but for moderate to cool weather I prefer wool Army glove liners. They're tight enough to fit your hands like skin so they don't interfere with shooting. You can get any variety of cotton camouflage gloves, but many are baggy and get in the way of a finger tab (you can cut off the fingers to solve that problem) and they do nothing to keep your hands warm during wet

This hunter's sweater has no camouflage pattern at all, yet it blends well because it has the right greenish hue. Face, hands, and bow are the most important points for camouflage.

For hot weather, Amacker Products' Spando-Flage has good potential. The coarse weave allows good air circulation to your skin, but it provides a good camouflage effect.

and cold weather. (For more details, see Clothing and Footwear.)

Finally, your bow and arrows (assuming you're using a bow quiver) also must be visible when you shoot at an animal, so these must be well concealed. Most factory camouflage jobs these days are adequate, and in buying a new bow that's the way to go. Or you can spray your own. Bohning and other companies make good camouflage kits that will take care of several bows. Dull finish on a bow not only makes the bow blend with vegetation, it also reduces light reflection. In open country, I've spotted hunters nearly a mile away because of the sunlight flashing off their shiny bow limbs.

Some hunters spray paint their arrows, too, but paint can alter the weight and produce a rough finish. Aluminum arrows now come in excellent anodized camouflage patterns, and these are the way to go, in my opinion.

The Way You Move

Camouflage doesn't mean just how you dress and paint your bow. It refers more broadly to remaining unseen, and that involves a lot more than clothes and face paint. It involves how you move. I know some exceptional bowhunters who use no camouflage at all, and they succeed because they know how to move without being seen.

My friend Don Pritchett (who believes in full camouflage, incidentally) one time said his bowhunting success formula was learning how to "flow" with nature, meaning he's learned to move as slow or slower than the animals he's hunting. He figures fast movement means danger to game animals, so he tries to become part of the natural flow of a peaceful woods. No matter how good your camouflage, animals will spot quick movement, so walk slowly, turn your head slowly, raise your bow slowly—do everything in slow motion that won't catch an animal's eye.

It's not just a matter of how you move, but where you move. The human form spells danger to any game animal, and the best camouflage won't eliminate a silhouette. When you're seen on a skyline or against a light background, animals will recognize you as human regardless of your camouflage. Resolve always to move with cover behind and concealment in front. Don't follow the path of least resistance, which can take you across openings and along ridgetops where you're visible for miles; follow the path of least visibility, as any natural predator would do.

Whenever possible, remain absolutely stationary. In most cases animals will never notice you, even when you're wide open. One day I was sitting on an open, grassy hillside, taking pictures, when a doe walked my way. I wasn't camouflaged, so she should have seen me easily. But I sat absolutely motionless, and she kept coming and passed within a few feet of me. Many rifle hunters, dressed in super-bright colors, can relate similar stories about how deer nearly stepped on them simply because

Camouflage clothing can help, but the best camouflage of all may be nonmovement.

they, the hunters, didn't move. Nonmovement may be the best camouflage of all.

CAMPING   As I've said elsewhere (see Hunting Basics), the way you camp and equip yourself in the field has a lot to do with your hunting success. I've talked to many hunters who've had bad trips, and it wasn't because they didn't see game or because they missed easy shots, but because their camping equipment wasn't adequate. When they got wet, cold, and miserable, they had to turn tail and run.

Bad Trip

Here's one experience to make the point. Even though my trip to Colorado had been planned for some time, I'd been busier than normal and didn't prepare well. When the time came to leave, I tossed some basic gear into my

Camouflage isn't just a matter of how you dress but how you move. Stay off the skyline and out of openings where animals will instantly recognize your human form.

truck and took off, figuring if things got bad I'd just gut it out. After all, I wasn't going there for the pleasures of camping, but to hunt.

With easy conditions, I'd have been okay, but conditions weren't easy. Rain started falling the second day, and all my clothes got wet. Then the temperature dropped to zero and all my clothes froze, and on top of that a blizzard dumped a foot of snow. I'd brought a small tent, but it had no stove, so I had no way to dry my clothes and warm up at night. To put it mildly, I was one miserable dude. Finally the pain far outweighed pleasure, and I packed it in. I'd failed.

Failure is failure, regardless of the reason. A good camp contributes as much to a good hunt as a reliable bow or the right tree stand. You can tolerate the rigors of hard hunting if you know the comfort of camp awaits you at night. But to face misery all night as well as all day will break most hunters' resolve. To hunt enthusiastically, you have to be able to warm up at night, dry your clothes, get a good night's sleep, and fill your belly with hot food. Camp is a place of restoration. To make sure it serves its purpose, organize a good outfit and go prepared for the worst.

Camping Alternatives

No one camping method works in every situation. Maybe you have a big motor home or camper and plan to set it in one spot and hunt out of that. Maybe you'd prefer to stay in a motel and drive out to hunt. If so, that's fine, but many bona-fide camping alternatives are cheaper and might serve you better in most situations.

The Mobile Camp. In some cases, you might want to move quickly, and an established camp only slows you down. That's especially true when you're scouting and haven't decided exactly where to hunt. A mobile camp is the answer.

If you have a camper on your pickup, you've got it made because you're self-contained. If you don't, you can still get by. My pickup has only a canopy shell, so I set up a cot in back for a dry place to sleep. If the weather is nice I

When the sun is shining and the living is easy, camping may seem like an insignificant part of hunting. But in weather like this, a secure camp could be the most important part of your hunt.

Regardless of where or how you camp, a hunting camp must provide four essentials — shelter, warmth, rest, and good food. With a cliff overhead to keep them dry, a fire to warm them, and a line to dry clothes, these hunters are prepared for rainy hunting.

cook on the tailgate of the truck, or in bad weather I cook inside the canopy—with all the windows open for ventilation.

If you only have a car, you can set up a backpacking tent for sleeping and a plastic tarp lean-to for cooking shelter in case of rain. The options are endless, but remember, even a mobile camp must provide the necessities— shelter, warmth, rest, and good food—so plan your strategy before the hunt.

Summer Camping. For moderate to warm weather hunting, I have a Coleman American Heritage canvas tent that measures 9 x 11 feet and has 4-foot sidewalls. Many companies make similar tents, both of cotton and nylon, suited to summer and early-fall hunting when you don't need a big stove for heat and protection from severe weather. In hot weather, you'll appreciate the sewn-in floor, screened windows

A simple nylon or canvas tent, like Coleman's American Heritage shown here, makes for good shelter during warm to moderate weather.

and zippered door—standard features on these tents—that keep out flies, mosquitoes, rattlesnakes, and other friendly visitors.

A tent like this serves primarily as a bedroom; it's cramped for cooking and socializing. To increase the effective size, set up a "picnic canopy" in front for shade and for shelter from rain so you can cook and chat outside. Most such canopies are made of reinforced plastic. They have a center pole and four corner poles with guy lines to hold them down. Rounded out with a table, chairs, gasoline cook stove, lantern, and other accessories (see list below), this can be a comfortable hunting camp.

I consider a camp like this semimobile. You can set it up in an hour or less, so you can always pick up and move if you need to. But that's a bother, so you don't plan to move it every day. This kind of camp will also serve in cool to cold weather, but then you must have some kind of stove to heat the tent. A catalytic heater does a reasonable job, and a propane heater will just about drive you out of a tent this size, but you have to keep the windows open for good ventilation.

Backpack Hunting. Backpacking offers another alternative, but that's a subject unto itself. (For complete details, see Backpack Hunting.)

The Permanent Camp

For any cold-weather hunting or situation where you know you'll hunt in one spot, nothing can beat a permanent tent camp. On a hunt in Arizona my friend Pat Miller and I took Pat's 12 x 14 wall tent.

At first we planned to leave the wood stove behind. After all, how could you possibly need heat in Arizona in September? But we found ourselves with extra room, so at the last minute we threw in the stove, just in case. And were we glad! Heavy rain fell nearly every day of our hunt and wind blew incessantly. Even though the air temperature wasn't really cold, we savored every second we spent in that warm tent with the glowing wood stove. And some friends who were hunting the same area out of a skimpy camp gravitated to our wall tent every night.

"This is really nice," they kept saying.

And it was. A comfortable camp with a warm, roomy tent where you can sit around and tell lies, hang up your clothes to dry, and get out of the weather can make a hunt. The variations are endless and what I say here isn't law, but it will give you a good idea of what you need. If you plan to make only a hunt or two on your own, you might save money by motel camping or hiring an outfitter to set up a camp for you, using his equipment. But if you plan to hunt extensively on your own, you won't regret investing in a good camp.

First I'll discuss the principles, and I'll follow up with a list of items needed for a complete camp. You can use this as a checklist to prepare for each hunt. The same list can apply to any camping method, with the needed modifications to account for varied conditions.

Tent. The canvas wall tent has long been the standard for backcountry hunting. Most western outfitters still use wall tents, which seems like a good recommendation. With a wall tent, you can be comfortable under any conditions. In cold weather the big tent, equipped with a wood stove, assures warmth and shelter; in summer, you can lift the sidewalls and use the tent for shade.

Wall tents come in several sizes. A 10 x 12 will serve one or two hunters fairly well, but it's cramped. If you're going to invest in a big tent, you might as well spend a few more bucks and get a 12 x 14, which gives you plenty of room for two people and will handle up to four or five comfortably. If you want lots of room, get a 14 x 16. (Incidentally, if you're big on garage sales, you might pick up a good tent for a song. A friend of mine bought a 12 x 14 canvas tent along with a complete cook box for $25. New, that outfit would have cost more than $500.)

Whatever the outside dimensions, make sure it has four-foot sidewalls. Three-foot walls don't give you much head room. It also should have a sod flap, a strip of canvas around the bottoms of the walls. You can pile dirt or snow on this flap to keep out cold air and hold the

The canvas wall tent has become the standard for backcountry hunting. In winter a wall tent equipped with a wood stove assures a warm, dry place for eating, sleeping, and drying clothes. In summer, the walls can be rolled up and the tent serves as an awning for shade.

tent secure. If the tent doesn't have sod flaps, make sure it at least has loops for pegging down the walls.

Wall tents come in white and olive green. If you plan to use one strictly for sleeping, green is okay, but for all around use, get white. It's much brighter inside. A green tent is like a cave.

Tent Frame. The first time my wife and I ever used a wall tent, we learned an important lesson—put it up right. We stretched a big rope between two trees as a ridgeline. That wasn't real great, because the rope stretched and the tent sagged in the middle like an old horse. That would have been tolerable if it hadn't been for the wind.

The big crash came at 2:00 A.M. First we heard the roar of powerful wind, followed by

A wall tent must have a solid frame. You can cut shear poles (the inverted Vs at the ends of this tent) and a ridge pole from trees in your hunting area, or you can make a similar frame out of steel tubing. Notice how the sides of this tent are staked up for stability.

bang, rip, crash. Suddenly we had tent, table, stove, cook boxes, and who knows what crashing down on us. That was an unforgettable experience. Since then I've seen three other wall tents go down—two from wind, one from heavy snow. Set them up right.

Some hunters cut the needed ridge pole and support poles in the field. Only problem is, you might camp somewhere with no suitable trees, and in some places it could be illegal to cut the trees you need. If you decide to go this route, cut a ridge pole three feet longer than your tent, and then cut four more poles about ten feet long. Make two sets of shear poles—one for the front, one for the back. Spread the bottom ends of the shear poles to form an upside-down V and set the ridge pole at the point of each V. Now stake down the sides.

Making your own frame and taking it with you is easier in the long run. For my 12 x 14 tent, the poles are made of two-inch steel tubing. The ridge pole consists of three sections that slip together. Onto each end of the ridge pole I slide a V-shaped attachment that holds the legs. In place, these legs form an inverted V to give the tent solid footing. To add stability, you can weld a loop onto the bottom of these legs and stake them to the ground. That might seem a bit much, but you won't think so in a

stiff blow. You can make a similar frame out of 2 x 4 lumber.

Your tent will hold up better if you stake up the sidewalls too. For mine I've cut four-foot stakes out of 1 x 2 lumber. I've driven a nail into one end to put through the grommet at the top of the wall and the other end of the stake sits on the sod flap at the bottom. Use stout steel pegs to hold the side ropes and the bottoms of the walls.

Waterproof the Tent. When they get wet, the fibers in cotton canvas swell and become watertight. A new tent needs no treatment. After some use, however, most wall tents start to leak, and you'll have to take special steps to prevent that. You can spread a big, clear plastic tarp over the tent and peg it out tight at the sides so there's some clearance between the tent and the tarp. Or you can treat it with Thompson Water Seal or a similar sealer. Set the tent up on a hot summer day and spray the inside with sealer. A gallon will do a 12 x 14 tent. This will prevent leakage for several seasons.

When you set up the tent, try to find a site on reasonably high ground where you won't get flooded out during heavy rain, and dig a shallow trench around it to channel rain water away.

Obviously, you'll want to find reasonably flat ground for your tent site. At the same time, consider safety. One night my friend Larry Jones and I were lying in bed when we heard a loud pop outside. We rushed out to see what had happened and we found that a stick had fallen off a tree and gone through a tarp outside like a falling sword. It would have skewered one of us if it had hit the tent.

"My uncle got killed just that way," Larry said. "He was asleep when a limb fell off a tree through the tent and speared him."

The lesson ought to be clear enough. Never set up camp under a snag or tree with big dead limbs. Put it in a clearing or among low, bushy trees that won't blow apart in heavy wind.

Also, set the tent up with the rear toward the prevailing wind. Wind blowing into the door will billow the tent out and blow in all kinds of debris. When you're out hunting, tie the door

For larger parties, you can set up a wall tent for cooking and general fellowship, and then put up a smaller tent or two as bedrooms. Avoid placing tents under snags or trees with dead limbs. A falling limb can come right through a tent roof.

shut to prevent billowing. Wind blowing into a big wall tent is like water trickling through a dam—it's the start of a collapse.

After a trip, set up the tent or hang it to dry thoroughly to prevent mildew.

Stove and Other Accessories. A square steel stove will heat a wall tent thoroughly. Some commercial models fold up and slip into a canvas bag, and these are handy if you're horse packing or are short of room in your vehicle. Get a stove with a large flat top so you can heat water or cook on it, and make sure the door is big enough to accommodate fairly large wood.

To put the stove pipe out the roof, you insert a metal sleeve into one of the seams of the tent and slip the stove pipe through that. Make sure this sleeve holds the canvas away from the pipe or you could cremate yourself. The pipe gets hot enough to burn canvas. I know one hunter who has terrible burn scars from a tent fire.

With a two-hunter party, both of you can cook, eat, and sleep in a 12 x 14 tent. For more hunters, you'll probably prefer to set up a separate sleeping tent. With more than two hunters

A good wood stove not only heats a tent but serves for cooking as well.

in camp, I put up my Coleman American Heritage behind the wall tent for sleeping, and use the big tent as a cookhouse and gathering spot. You can put down foam pads and sleep directly on the ground, but you'll get a lot more mileage out of available space if you sleep on cots because you can slip duffel and other gear under the cots.

Here are a couple of final tips to make a hunting camp work. First, always set up camp completely before you start hunting. I vividly recall one night when a couple of friends and I arrived at our camp site after dark. We hardly felt like pitching a tent, so we just threw out our sleeping bags and sacked out. The sky blinked with stars from one end to the other, so what was to worry about? Nothing at all, until 1:00 A.M., when we detected the first splatter of raindrops. Before we could act, the rain was pouring and we were soaked. I could fill half this book with stories about times I've set up camp halfway, assuming the weather would treat me right, only to get blasted.

Second, wherever you go or whatever camping method you choose, go prepared for every contingency. One night my friend Larry Jones and I were lying by a campfire in a bivouac camp somewhere on the dark side of Montana.

"We're really prepared, aren't we?" Larry said. "We could hunt anywhere right now and be comfortable."

At first that seemed like a strange statement. Of course we were prepared. What did he expect? But then I realized what he meant. We could camp out of our car, we could set up a big road camp, or we could backpack into the farthest hinterlands, as we were doing at that moment. In other words, we could do whatever was needed to hunt that country effectively. Indeed, we *were* prepared.

That's the way you should plan your camp. You may expect to set up a big camp, but then you might find game too far from the road to reach by hiking out daily. With a packframe and the needed backpacking items, you can spike out a night or two and live right with the animals (for details, see Backpack Hunting) and that might be the maneuver needed for

success. That's why I include backpack gear and related items in the following camp list.

The Complete Camp

The discussion on camping could go on and on. I've described what I consider the ultimate hunting camp, and provide here a comprehensive list. You can reduce this to whatever level best fits your hunting style. Just remember that a hunting camp must provide shelter and warmth, give you a place to dry your clothes, guarantee a good night's sleep, and promise you a hot meal (food is discussed below).

For ready reference, copy this list — in modified form if that better suits your needs — and use it as checklist to simplify preparation before each hunt.

Equipment Checklist

12 x 14 (or 14 x 16) wall tent, or other suitable tent

Tent pegs for side ropes

4-foot stakes for sidewalls (my tent requires 10)

Frame for tent (mine is made of tubular steel)

Heavy hammer for driving pegs, other odd jobs

Wood stove with stove pipe, legs, side shelf, and oven

Smaller sleep tent

Catalytic heater for sleep tent

Tarps for covering gear outside, covering tent in rain

Table

Chairs or stools

Shelf

Rope for clothesline along ridge pole of tent

Cots and mattresses

Sleeping bags

Pillows

Flashlight for camp use

Gas lanterns

Gas cook stove

Fuel for lanterns and gas cook stove

Cook gear:

    Two frying pans

    Dutch oven

    Three cook pots: small, medium, large

    Dishpan

Wash basin for hands and face
Dishcloth
Pot scrubber
Dish soap
Hand soap
Dish towel
Plates (paper or metal)
Cups (metal or plastic)
Bowls (plastic or metal)
Coffeepot
Table knives
Spoons
Forks
Pancake turner
Potato shredder (for hash browns, fried
   potatoes)
Potato peeler
Can opener
Kitchen knives
Wooden matches
Newspaper for fire starting
Paper towels
Aluminum foil
Plastic sandwich bags (or plastic wrap)
Plastic garbage bags
Toilet paper
Grill for cooking over open fire
Water containers full of water (plastic jugs,
   etc.)
Rope for miscellaneous uses
Nails for miscellaneous uses
Wire for miscellaneous uses
Duct tape for miscellaneous uses
Ax (standard equipment in truck)
Big sharpening stone for knives, ax
Shovel (standard equipment in truck)
Fire extinguisher (standard equipment in
   truck)
First-aid kit (standard equipment in truck)
Hand saw or chain saw (plus oil and gasoline)
Leather gloves for wood cutting, other rough
   chores
Mousetraps
Alarm clock
Ear plugs (to ensure sound night's sleep)
Salt for cape, hide
Snowshoes (in deep snow)
Insect repellent

Thermometer
Money for travel expenses
Full tank of gasoline in vehicle
Spare fuel for vehicle
Fishing gear
Fishing license
Hunting license and tags
Bag for dirty laundry
Clean tarp for wrapping meat during day
Plastic wrap, freezer paper, tape for
   butchering meat
Camera gear (for details, see Photography)
Packframe for packing meat
Backpack gear for bivouac hunting (for
   details, see Backpack Hunting)
Clothes (for details, see Clothing and
   Footwear)
Hunting pack (for details, see Hunting Pack)
Hunting gear: bow, arrows, etc. (for details,
   see Hunting Gear)
Food (see below)

Food

I'm no great cook and don't aspire to become one, so I won't list specific recipes here,
but rather a basic food list that serves as a
foundation for menu planning and shopping.
You can get as fancy as your tastes allow. Obviously, the quantities you buy depend on the
size of your party and the number of days
you'll camp.

**For easy camping, standardize your food and gear so
it's always ready to go. If you plan ahead, you can
get ready quickly, and you'll be assured of having
everything you need for a successful hunt.**

Is a good camp an amenity? Not at all. It's a necessity, and it could be the foundation for good hunting.

The idea, in my opinion, is to standardize your food and gear so it's always ready to go. You can expect mice to get into all your food (not to mention bears, but I think mice are more destructive), so you want to keep all perishable items in sealed containers. For meat, milk, bread, fruits, and vegetables, I normally carry a cooler (or two if needed). In summer, block ice goes into the cooler to keep things cold. In winter the ice isn't needed; in fact, the cooler prevents perishables from freezing.

Seal everything like cereals, cookies, flour, sugar, and hot chocolate in cans or boxes. Old ice chests make excellent dry storage. So do coffee cans with plastic lids. Label them with a felt marking pen so you always know what each contains. Expect anything that will make a sticky mess—jam, sugar, syrup—to spill inside your grub box, and deal with it ahead of time. Seal jelly, jam, and sugar in plastic freezer cartons or coffee cans, and always buy syrup, catsup, mustard, and similar items in plastic squeeze bottles with fail-safe lids.

Staples
Salt and pepper
Flour
Cooking oil or shortening
Milk, soft drinks, etc.
Coffee, tea, hot chocolate

Breakfast
Pancake mix (complete, just add water)
Syrup
Margarine
Eggs
Bacon or ham
Cold cereals
Hot cereals (e.g., instant oatmeal)
Sweet rolls

Lunch
Bread or rolls
Mayonnaise
Ketchup
Peanut butter
Jelly or jam
Cheese
Lunch meat, canned tuna, sardines, etc.
Fresh fruit: apples, oranges, pears, etc.
Soup (dehydrated)
Granola bars
Gorp (raisins, nuts, M&M chocolates)
Jerky

152

Dinner
Meat, frozen or canned
Potatoes
Rice
Canned vegetables
Fresh salad: lettuce, tomatoes, celery, carrots
Macaroni and cheese
Spaghetti mix and noodles
Beans and ham hock
Bisquick for biscuits
Canned fruit
Instant pudding
Cookies

CAPING For head mounts, the antlers (or horns) and the cape are needed. A cape is the hide off the head and neck back to the front shoulder. Some taxidermists prefer to do the caping themselves, so if you're hunting close to town, take the entire head and cape directly to

a taxidermist. If you're in the backcountry where you're forced to keep your animal in the field a few days, you must cape it yourself. It's a simple task if you follow a few easy steps.

Measure First
Before you start caping, measure three areas: (1) from the tip of the nose to the front corner of the eye; (2) from the tip of the nose to the back of the skull; (3) the circumference of the neck. Taxidermists need these measurements to order the right size forms. If you don't have a tape measure along, use the cord you always carry in your survival pack, and tie a knot to mark each measurement.

The Caping Process
The first and worst mistake you could make would be to slit the animal all the way up the belly to the throat, as you would in normal

To cape an animal, first split the hide up the *back* of the neck. Never cut up the throat side.

Slit the hide to a point just forward of the ears.

Cut diagonally from this center cut to the bases of each antler. If done correctly, this will result in a V-shaped flap of skin on top of the deer's head.

field dressing. To gut an animal, cut the hide only to the brisket. And don't slit his throat to bleed him out. That's not necessary.

Then cut the hide around the animal's chest behind the front legs. Most taxidermists say hunters commonly cut capes too short for a good mounting job, so be generous. Cut *behind* the front legs. That way, you're assured of leaving more than enough hide to satisfy the taxidermist.

Now slit the hide up the back of the neck to a point just forward of the ears. As you do this and all further steps in the caping process, always cut from the inside out so you don't cut off any hair.

Cut diagonally from that center cut to the base of each antler. You'll end up with a V-shaped flap of skin right on top of the head. You can now skin out the neck and chest. As

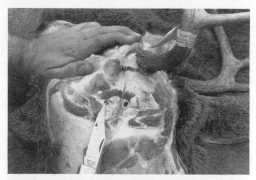

Now skin out the neck and chest. As shown in this photo, cut off the ear flush with the head.

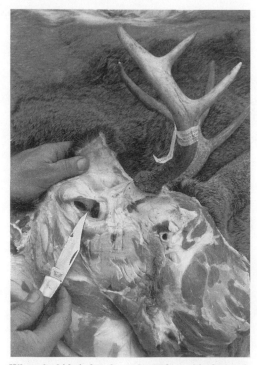

When the hide is free from the antlers, skin forward on the head. Take special care around the eyes to avoid cutting the eyelids.

Work the skin away from the antler bases. The skin is tight here, so be careful not to cut it. You can pry it off with a screwdriver, or if you use a knife, cut from the inside out to avoid cutting hair.

you work your way forward to the head, cut off the ears as close as possible to the head.

Now begin working the skin away from the bases of the antlers. The skin is very tight here, so this requires persistence. Some taxidermists recommend prying the skin away from the antlers with a screwdriver or other blunt object to prevent cutting the hide. With care you can do it with a knife, but again, be sure to cut from the inside out to avoid cutting off hair.

When the hide is free from the antlers, skin out the head. Take special care around the eyes to ensure that you don't cut the eyelids. Taxidermists say the eyes are the easiest places to ruin during the skinning process, and they're the toughest to repair. The corners in particular cling tight to the skull. To get them off cleanly, poke your finger into the eye from the outside and hold the eyelid away from the

skull. Your finger acts as a guide, and you can feel exactly where you're cutting.

Continue skinning forward toward the nose, taking care not to nick the hide. It's important to skin back far enough into the mouth and nose to make sure the entire lips and nose cartilage remain attached to the hide. Again, use your finger as a guide on the nose. Push your finger into each nostril from the outside so you can feel the knife blade working between the hide and the skull. Cut the lips free right at the base of the gum line. A careful job will yield a clean skull and a cape with no nicks or cuts.

Now saw the antlers free from the skull. Be sure to leave plenty of skull bone for the taxidermist to work with. Cut down behind the

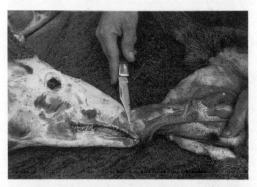

Be sure to cut far enough back into the nostrils and mouth so all the lips and nose cartilage remains attached to the hide.

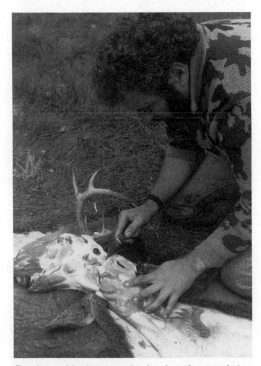

Continue skinning out the head and nose, being careful not to nick the hide.

This is the finished product — a perfect cape and a clean skull.

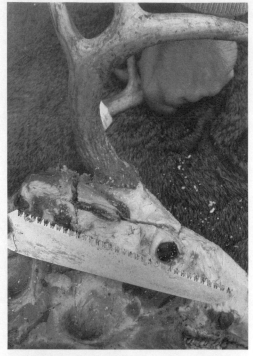

As you cut off the antlers, leave plenty of bone for the taxidermist to work with. Cut down behind the antlers, and meet that cut with another cut back through the forehead.

Deliver the completed cape and antlers to your taxidermist.

antlers and then cut through the skull just above the eyes to meet the first cut. The end results are a cape and antlers ready for the taxidermist.

If the weather is cool, you can stop there. Just handle the cape as you would meat. (For details, see Meat Care.) Hang it open to cool at night, and roll it and store it in the shade during the day. Your taxidermist will put the finishing touches on the cape in his shop.

Preserving a Hide in the Field

If the weather is warm and you must stay in the field for several days, you'll have to salt the cape, but you must complete several more steps before salting.

First, turn the ears. If you salt the cape without turning the ears, the hide will tighten and prevent turning of the ears later. Start skinning at the base of the ear just as you would skin other parts of the animal. When you've skinned about a quarter of the ear, use a blunt object like a table knife, wooden spoon, or pointed stick to separate the skin from the ear cartilage to avoid cutting the delicate skin on the ear. As you do this, gradually turn the ear inside out and pull the cartilage free.

Next split the lips. To do this, hold one hand with the palm up and lay the lips on your hand with the inside of the mouth up, facing you. With your sharp knife, start splitting right where you cut the lip from the gums, sliding your knife flatly between the inside of the lip and the outside, as you would in filleting a fish. Cut until the lip will lay open and flat.

Before you salt the hide, remove as much meat and fat as possible. It's particularly important to remove all fat because salt won't penetrate fat well and the hide could spoil under fatty places. Take special care around the nose, particularly on animals with big noses like moose, to thin down the cartilage there. Salt won't penetrate more than about $1/4$ inch.

When you've completely fleshed the cape, salt it liberally. It's a good idea to keep at least five pounds of noniodized, finely ground salt (not rock salt) in camp for this purpose. A small cape off a deer or antelope will take about three pounds of salt, and the cape off an elk or other large animal will take five pounds or more. Carefully work salt into every little nook and cranny. Then fold the cape with the flesh sides together, roll it and keep it in a cool place out of the sun. It will keep for an indefinite period this way until you can take it to a taxidermist.

CARIBOU *(Rangifer tarandus)*

At one time scientists separated caribou into four separate species, but now they consider all caribou one species. Because of great variation in antler size and conformation from one region to another, however, record-keeping books recognize four categories of caribou. In 1984, the Boone and Crockett Club added a fifth.

Varieties of Caribou

Barren Ground. Except for a few rare animals extending through British Columbia into extreme northern Idaho, caribou are strictly creatures of the far north. Animals at the western end of the range are classified as barren ground caribou (*R. t. granti*). The record books classify any caribou killed in Alaska or in the Yukon Territory north of the Yukon River as barren ground caribou.

Mountain. Traditionally records books considered any caribou taken in British Columbia or Alberta as mountain caribou (*R. t. caribou*), but Boone and Crockett has extended the boundary northward to include the Yukon Territory south of the Yukon River, and the Mackenzie Mountains of the Northwest Territories.

Woodland. The woodland caribou and mountain caribou are considered the same subspecies, and some woodland caribou are scattered across northern Canada. At the eastern end of the range they're consistently smaller than in B.C. and Alberta, so they're placed in a separate scoring category. Virtually all record-book woodland caribou come from Newfoundland.

Quebec-Labrador. As the name implies, the Quebec-Labrador caribou lives in Quebec and Labrador. Most come from the George River region south of Ungava Bay in Quebec.

The Boone and Crockett Club now recognizes a fifth scoring category, the barren ground caribou taken from the Northwest Territories east of the Mackenzie River. Few animals from this region score well enough to compete with barren ground caribou from Alaska and the Yukon.

The Nature of Caribou

Caribou are the only members of the deer family in which both males and females grow antlers. Cows' antlers are much smaller than those of the bulls. Outsized antlers give the impression that caribou are huge animals, but they weigh only from about 150 pounds for cows up to about 400 pounds for the larger bulls. They stand 3½ to 4 feet high at the shoulder. Their hooves are rounded and very large for the size of the animal, well adapted for traveling the muskeg and tundra that carpets much of their range. The hooves make a distinct clicking sound as the animals walk.

Caribou are considered "climax" species, living in regions where plant growth has reached its climax stage. They feed primarily on lichens and low Arctic shrubs. For the most part, caribou summer above tree line. Many barren ground caribou on the North Slope of Alaska and in Arctic Canada live north of the tree line on the vast tundra. In fall, they amass into large herds and migrate south to the tree line, where they winter. Caribou are most commonly pictured in films during these mass migrations.

Throughout the timbered mountains of central and southern Alaska, the Yukon, and British Columbia, they summer on the open tundra above timberline, often in proximity to Dall and Stone sheep, and then they drift downhill into the timber during winter. Mountain caribou don't make the massive, long migrations of barren ground caribou.

Hunting Caribou

Caribou are mobile, restless animals that move around constantly, even when not on

Caribou are animals of the open tundra, and they summer north of the tree line or, in forested regions, above timberline. They're restless animals, constantly on the move. *Photo courtesy Ed Park.*

major migrations. Experienced caribou hunters warn that you'd better do some research or scouting by air before settling into a given spot to hunt. A region could be crawling with animals at one time and devoid another.

Spotting and Stalking. Caribou hunting generally takes two forms, and the most common early in the year is spotting and stalking. As anywhere else, that calls for good optical equipment. (For details, see Optics and Spotting.)

Judd Cooney, who has hunted game all over North America and has specialized in antelope hunting in Colorado, compares caribou hunting to antelope hunting in the sense that it takes place in wide-open country with virtually no cover, and you can spot many animals at long range.

Most hunters agree that caribou have good ears and noses and that you must have the wind in your favor to stalk successfully, but many seem to debate the quality of a caribou's eyes. In his book *The Big Game Animals of North America,* Jack O'Connor said, "Their eyes are very poor, certainly no better than those of a grizzly bear and maybe not as good." Judd Cooney, on the other hand, said caribou have good eyesight, at least comparable to that of deer and elk.

"They'll see you a long way off," Cooney said. "They just don't react the same as most other animals. Their country is wide open and they're not harassed much. If they got shot at like our antelope do, I suspect they'd get spooky, too. But they're used to seeing bears and wolves out in the open, and they just don't panic."

Caribou have a reputation for being goofy. A lot of that comes from their crazy antics during the rut, but it also comes in reaction to insects. On the tundra in summer, mosquitoes and other noxious insects breed incessantly in the vast standing water, and these insects are the bane of caribou. A bull will run a half mile in one direction and then turn around and run right back. To a human he appears daft, but to the caribou, who can't apply Ben's 100 or a head net like the human can, running may seem the only reasonable alternative.

In hunting the North Slope of Alaska, Cooney said he and his companions found the ferocious insects the key to stalking caribou. "In August it got light at 3:00 A.M. and I'd be up ready to go hunting. But we didn't hunt until mid-morning when the bugs got bad, because that's when we had best luck stalking caribou. Sitting around waiting for the bugs about drove me buggy."

As Cooney explained, with swarms of insects attacking, the caribou will move around, and they'll bed in shaded dips and pockets where the bugs aren't quite as bad. That's where they're most stalkable. You can often spot bulls by looking for antlers rising from hidden, shady swales.

Also, a bull will often bury his head in a low shrub, or he'll stand at the edge of a pond and put his nose right next to the water so the bugs won't fly into his nostrils, and he'll close his eyes and just stand there.

"The tundra offers pretty quiet footing, like walking on a waterbed, so noise isn't a problem. I stalked 200 yards in plain sight on an open flat to shoot one bull. He had his head in a bush and never saw me."

Of course, the insects that attack caribou also attack hunters, so a generous supply of repellent and clothing to protect the body must be included on any caribou hunter's equipment list. As one hunter suggested, it also helps to tape your sleeves and cuffs shut to keep out the bugs. The tundra is soggy, so some Alaskan hunters consider hip boots standard equipment, although others prefer conventional footwear and changing socks regularly.

Cooney's experiences might make caribou hunting sound easy, but that isn't necessarily the case. Roger Iveson from Nevada hunted caribou on the Alaska Peninsula in September, and he found them downright tough to stalk. Getting within 100 yards was fairly easy, but from there on it was tough.

"They were always moving so they'd be here one day and gone tomorrow," Iveson said. "We had to relocate a couple of times to keep up with the herds.

"I hunted 19 days to kill a caribou. Like they always do, this bull was moving into the wind and he just kept going, so I got on his trail and decided to stay with him. As soon as he'd go over a rise I'd run to catch up. I chased him a good 12 miles and was within 100 yards of him for the last 5 miles but just couldn't quite get a shot. Finally he got into some willows where I could sneak closer and I nailed him at 50 yards. He scored 376⅞. He was a good one."

Roger Iveson killed this barren ground caribou on the Alaska Peninsula after following the animal for several miles. *Photo courtesy Roger Iveson.*

Ambush Hunting. The other primary hunting method for caribou is taking a stand and waiting near a migration route. That's the most widely practiced method in Quebec. Bowhunting along the George River there has become very popular, and most of the hunting takes place along trails where caribou cross the river during migration. Mississippi bowhunter Billy Ellis hunted there in the early 1980s, and all six members of his party killed Pope and Young bulls. Not all hunters have fared as well, however.

Mississippi bowhunter Billy Ellis killed this Quebec-Labrador caribou on the George River in Quebec. Notice how close the willows grow to the river's edge. Hunters take stands in the willows to ambush animals walking along the river's edge. *Photo courtesy Billy Ellis.*

All six members of Ellis' party killed Pope and Young bulls on the George River in Quebec. *Photo courtesy Billy Ellis.*

"We hit the migration on the nose," Ellis said. "But if you're two weeks early or late, you might miss it. A number of other parties have gone up, and some of them haven't done nearly as well. The timing has to be right."

In this region, caribou migrate down from surrounding high tundra plateaus and swim the river. Ellis and his companions hunted by spotting groups of big bulls coming down trails to cross, and the hunters would position themselves to intercept the animals as they emerged from the river. After the caribou had crossed, they'd walk the beach. Heavy willows line the river, often no more than 20 to 30 yards from the river's edge, so the hunters built blinds in the willows and waited for caribou to walk by. Most shots were no more than 15 to 20 yards.

Even though hunting from a blind, Ellis found binoculars valuable for evaluating the antlers of approaching bulls. He considered this hunt one of the best opportunities for a hunter to take a record-class caribou. Ellis also has hunted caribou in Alaska—the Mulchatna herd near McGrath in early September. Here the caribou are scattered over rolling mountain tundra, and he found, as Iveson did in the same region, that the caribou meander back and forth, making no predictable movements.

They might be one place today, a mile away tomorrow, and back to the original place the next day. Ellis found the Alaskan animals much spookier than those in Quebec, possibly because of the abundant wolves in Alaska, but he also feels that caribou on migration as in Quebec are more single-minded, which makes them more predictable and possibly less sensitive to danger.

The same bow you use for deer and elk will do the job on caribou. In ambush hunting the shots may be close, but in stalking you may be looking at 40- to 50-yard shots, so a reasonably fast bow, which you can shoot accurately at longer ranges, would be best suited there.

Trophy Hunting

Caribou antlers are the most complicated to score, so judging a rack accurately takes a practiced eye. To complicate the matter, many caribou are shot in summer when antlers are still in velvet.

To judge a head in the field, consider these major characteristics. As in scoring deer and elk, main beam length and inside spread are significant measurements. On a really big bull with long beams, the rack appears nearly as high as the animal's body is tall, and looking directly from front or back, the inside spread (not maximum spread) should be somewhat wider than the animal's body.

Brow tines (or shovels, as most hunters call them) are normal formations on caribou antlers, and these should stick out nearly to the tip of the nose. Most caribou have only one, but exceptional heads have double shovels. Bez points grow forward from the main beams just above the shovels, and these should grow out nearly as long as the brow shovels.

The main beams commonly are palmed at the top, and the wider these palms and the longer the points growing from them, the better the animal will score. Total number of points also adds to the score, so the more the better. The actual dimensions vary by category, so study measurements for heads from the region you plan to hunt.

CENTER SHOT The "center of force" of a bow is a line running from the top tip to the bottom tip in line with the string. On a recurve or longbow, vertical center is also the measured center because the bow is built symmetrically, and the string attaches to the exact center of the limb tips. On most compound bows, the center of force is offset to the left (for a right-hand shooter). That's because the string groove in the eccentric wheels is offset to the left.

On traditional longbows and many recurves, the handles were nearly round so that an arrow on the rest sat well outside of center. In essence, the arrow was not pointing where you wanted it to go. To get back to center, it had to flex around the handle, creating a violent paradox.

Most modern bow handles are cut past center so that as you aim, the arrow lies precisely in line with the string and target, or very close to it. These bows are said to be "center shot." Many bows are cut well past center, and to line your arrow up on center, you must turn the arrow rest out from the side of the bow. Having a bow cut past center assures complete fletching clearance as the arrow passes the bow. Most compound bows are cut farther past center than recurve bows. That's because the string

Judging caribou antlers requires a practiced eye. Notice the major formations on the bull's antlers—the brow shovel, bez points growing off the main beams just above the brow shovel, and the palms at the ends of the main beams. Antler width, length of main beams, and length and number of points all figure into the score. Caribou antlers are still covered with velvet during August, so judging antlers then can be doubly tough. *Photo courtesy Ed Park.*

lies to the side of the measured center of the bow to begin with, and if the sight window then is offset, the clearance is even greater. With recurve bows, the center of force and actual center of the bow limbs are the same, so the handle must be cut out more to get a large degree of center shot. Generally that's not possible, particularly with wood handles, because cutting the sight window much past center dangerously weakens the riser. (For more details on finding the center of the limbs, see Bow Tuning.)

CHRONOGRAPH This instrument measures the velocity of an arrow in flight. Chronographs work a couple of different ways. One

The Custom Chronograph 900 is powered by a lantern battery. When the chronograph is in use, the two electric eyes in the foreground are spaced exactly two feet apart, and they measure the elapsed time it takes for an arrow to travel that distance. The speed is projected on a small window in the chronograph.

style has a single screen. An electric eye begins timing your arrow as soon as the point enters the screen and stops when the nock passes. To make this chronograph work, you must record the length of the arrow in the timing device of the machine. The machine computes speed based on the amount of time it takes an arrow of a given length to pass through the screen.

The other kind has two electric eyes spaced a precisely measured distance apart—in the case of my Custom Chronograph 900, exactly two feet. You shoot directly over these eyes. The timing begins when the arrow tip passes the

This photo shows the Custom Chronograph 900 in use. It can be used indoors or out.

first eye and stops when the tip passes the second eye. The chronograph computes arrow speed based on the time required for the arrow to travel two feet. This is a very simple device that operates on batteries and can be used anywhere.

CLICKER This device on a bow clicks as you reach full draw, signaling you to release the string. Some clickers mount on the riser and click when the arrow head passes; others attach to the bowstring so the clicker mechanism is released when the bowstring reaches full draw position. Some clickers also sit on the cable guard of compound bows and click when the cables reach a certain point during the draw. Some silent clickers are designed especially for bowhunting. Clickers are used primarily to prevent or cure target panic. (For details, see Target Panic.)

CLOTHING AND FOOTWEAR To be of value for bowhunting, clothing must be quiet, and it must keep you comfortable, under not only average conditions but at the extremes of weather. It should also help you blend with the surroundings. (For more details, see Camouflage.)

Dressing for Comfort and Silence

Hot Weather. Most discussions of clothing focus on cold-weather hunting and ignore the fact that heat can pose major problems. California's coastal blacktail season opens in July, and I've hunted there when daytime temperatures rose as high as 104 degrees. Many general bow seasons in the West open in August. During one of my hunts for mule deer in Utah, the temperature rose above 95 degrees every day for a week. Weather like that can put you out of commission in a hurry if you're not prepared for it.

Several mechanisms—evaporation, convection, conduction, radiation—contribute to body cooling. Water and wind contribute to all these, so keeping cool in hot weather involves putting moisture and breezes to work for you.

Clothing should be lightweight and porous so air can circulate through it freely. Most camouflage clothing is made of heavy cotton cloth, and it's no good for hot weather hunting because it doesn't breathe. Very little commercial camo clothing is light enough for weather hotter than 70 degrees, so I've had my wife make early-season clothes for me. We found some ideal camouflage at a local fabric store. It's extremely light in weight, and pants and shirts made from it feel like summer pajamas so the breeze blows right through. In these clothes, I've been able to hunt comfortably in the hottest weather. That fabric was also cheap, about $1 a yard, yet it's surprisingly durable.

Some companies make products suitable for hot weather. Camo Clan, for example, makes shirts and pants out of mosquito netting. It's fine enough to serve as good camouflage, but it's porous so a light breeze flows right through. Amacker Products' Spando-Flage is another promising option for hot weather. Arm and head covers are made of stretchy, elastic webbing that slips on skintight like a nylon stocking. The weave is much coarser than mosquito netting so it provides no protection from bugs, but it's tight enough to serve as good camouflage, and the wind blows right through it to keep you cool. For good camouflage on your upper body, you can get by with a lightweight T-shirt and Spando-Flage arm covers.

Cotton T-shirts are no good in cold weather because they soak up sweat and never dry and they'll freeze you to death. But the very quality you don't want in cold weather is what you *do* want in hot, and a cotton T-shirt soaked with sweat can help keep you cool when the mercury soars out of sight.

In hot weather, a cap with a brim or bill keeps your head cool, and the bill shades your eyes so you can look toward the sun without being blinded. Equally important, especially in colder weather, it keeps snow and rain out of your eyes and off your glasses. A bill also casts shadows over eyeglasses to reduce reflections that might catch an animal's eye. The bill on a cap must be relatively short, however, so

In summer, a hat to keep the sun off your head and to shade your eyes is essential, but the brim must be short enough not to interfere with your bowstring at full draw. Here I'm wearing a jacket made of mosquito netting that allows the breeze to blow through for good cooling.

it doesn't interfere with the bowstring when you draw your bow. Camo Clan and Jim Dougherty Archery make good camouflage caps with short bills designed especially for bowhunting.

You might laugh about this, but I've found a sweat band invaluable for hot-weather hunting. I sweat a lot, and I also wear glasses. Sweaty, steamed-up glasses are only one step removed from total blindness, and a sweat band virtually cures the problem. I wouldn't hunt without one.

In hot weather, clothing alone won't keep you comfortable. You need a minimum of one gallon of water a day, so always carry a canteen or bota bag full of water and drink regularly. And take advantage of any spring or other

Laugh if you want, but a sweat band really adds to comfort during hot-weather hunting. That's particularly true if you wear glasses, because it keeps them from getting all steamed up.

For stand hunting and other sedentary types of hunting, a down or synthetic-filled coverall is the answer for warmth.

water source to soak your head and clothes. It will keep you cool, and that's what keeps you going. By using these techniques, I was able to keep hunting during that blistering weather in California and Utah, and killed deer on both hunts.

Cool and Cold Weather. For cool and cold weather the principle is just the opposite. You want to do everything possible to slow down cooling processes so you can preserve body heat. For sedentary hunting, like tree-stand hunting, that's relatively simple because you need primarily bulk to preserve body heat. Down-insulated clothing is ideal, and fully insulated coveralls are well suited to stand hunting in cold weather. The primary concern is to get enough warmth while keeping bulk to a minimum so it doesn't interfere with your shooting.

Clothing for hunting on foot during cold weather demands a little more thought, because you must reconcile the buildup of heat while hiking with the loss of heat while hunting slowly or resting. Since sweating covers you with water, and water, through evaporation and conduction, cools you rapidly, you want to do everything possible to avoid sweating. That's where the age-old layer principle comes in. For example, on your upper body, you might wear a T-shirt, lightweight longjohn top, light wool shirt, and a wool sweater. For extreme cold, you might add a down or fleece vest or a wool jacket. With these layers, you can shed as few or as many garments as necessary to stay cool as you hike. Then when you slow down to hunt, or stop to rest, you can start adding layers to preserve body heat.

To keep you warm, clothing must also be made of the right material. Cotton makes fine dress clothes, and it's okay for hot-weather hunting, but for cool and cold weather, it's anathema. So is denim. These materials absorb water, including sweat, and they take forever to dry. In cool weather they'll freeze you, and they're also very noisy. Even soft cotton swishes loudly when it's wet. Cotton and denim may be okay around camp, but in the field they're terrible.

It's been said so many times I hate to repeat it, but the truth doesn't change: wear wool (actually that truth has changed somewhat, which I'll discuss later). Wool pants are far superior to cotton because they're warm and comfortable under damp conditions, and they're quiet. For really cold hunting, I wear heavy wool pants. They're expensive, but they wear like iron, and they'll save many a cold hunting day for you.

For cool and damp hunting, I wear either light wool pants or knickers. Knickers might draw snickers at a mountain man rendezvous, but they sure beat buckskins in the field. I wore knickers during an entire elk hunt in the Wind River range of Wyoming, where the weather dropped from a very dry 60 degrees to a foggy, dank 12 degrees, and I wore them on a deer hunt in Utah where rain fell steadily for four days. Across those extremes I was comfortable. Best of all, wool knicker pants and heavy wool socks can be soaking wet and yet they don't bind at the knee, and there's no cuff to flap around. After wearing regular pants, you feel jet propelled in knickers. You may look like a pixy, but you'll still be hunting hard while the Marlboro man in his Levis is whimpering by the fire.

As good as wool is, it does have drawbacks.

Hiking during cold weather demands the layering system. As you hike you can shed clothes to prevent sweating, and when you stop to rest you can put on clothes to seal in body heat.

Heavy fog like this and other damp conditions call for special clothing. Wool serves the purpose, but some of the newer synthetics such as knit acrylic and PolarFleece work even better because they absorb very little moisture.

It holds so much water you need reinforced suspenders to hold up wool pants on a rainy day, and it dries very slowly. For that reason synthetic materials are finding their place in the backcountry camp. Pile fabrics made of polyester, nylon, or acrylic provide good insulation, but they don't absorb nearly as much moisture as wool does. Synthetic clothing wicks moisture away from your body, so the clammy feeling that comes with all natural fibers is virtually nonexistent.

Most synthetic clothing also dries rapidly. Bob Fratzke's Winona Camo Systems knits camouflage hunting suits out of acrylic. Fratzke said it takes about 40 minutes to dry a wool garment in one of his commercial dryers, and about 5 minutes to dry similar acrylic clothing. His garments are knit with a special stitch that won't snag, and the knit clothing is very flexible and soft so it doesn't bind at the

knee, even when it's wet. Other excellent outer garments are made of synthetics called bunting and fiberpile.

Another synthetic material shows great promise for bowhunting. Browning calls it PolarFleece and Columbia Sportswear calls it Ninja Cloth. Whatever you call it, this material is soft, quiet, and warm. It could replace wool as the mainstay for backcountry hunting.

Synthetic underwear is also superior to cotton. T-shirts and longjohns made of polypropylene simply don't produce that damp feeling like cotton or cotton-wool blends do. I've worn nothing but polypro T-shirts and longjohns in recent years, and even on the sweatiest and rainiest days, I feel reasonably dry and comfortable. You also can get polypropylene hats, gloves, and socks. Several com-

Columbia Sportswear's Ninja Cloth is soft and quiet, but it's also thick, warm, and tough. It's ideal for cold and wet conditions.

The head and neck are areas of major heat loss, so in cold weather it's vital to wear a hat that protects your head. A scarf, or "Neck Up" as shown here, that protects your neck also goes a long way toward keeping you comfortable on cold days.

panies sell a complete line of polypropylene underwear and synthetic outer garments.

Because the brain demands constant blood flow, the vessels through the neck and into the head are never shunted to decrease circulation under cold conditions as they are in the arms and legs. (For details, see Hypothermia.) Also, blood vessels to the head lie close to the surface of the skin. As a result, the head and neck are the major areas of heat exchange with the air, and controlling heat loss here can be the key to cold-weather comfort — and survival.

For cool and cold weather, knit hats come into their own, but here again, and for the same reasons listed above under hot weather, a cap must have a bill or brim. Some writers consider the sock hat ideal, but I consider it worthless for hunting because it does nothing to protect your eyes. That's particularly a problem if you wear glasses. You need a bill to keep the sun and rain out of your eyes.

The knit acrylic floppy hat made by Fratzke's Winona Mills has become one of my favorites for cool-weather hunting. It will do anything a sock hat will do but it has a brim all the way around to shade my eyes and keep rain off my neck. Winona's Survivor hat is made of the same knit material but it has a small bill sewn in as well as ear flaps, so it's even better for extreme cold. Other companies make insulated Gore-Tex hats with a short bill and knit ear flaps, and these are well suited to cold-weather hunting. I'm not crazy about some of these, however, because they're made "one size fits all," and they squash a big head like mine.

The Jones-style cap with a short bill and turned up ear flaps suits the fancy of many bowhunters, and these offer good protection. But many have a hard finish that's noisy when it rubs a branch or twig, so I'm not real crazy about these and similar hats. I prefer knit material because it's quieter.

In terms of heat regulation, your neck deserves as much concern as your head. Martin Archery sells an acrylic band called a Neck Up that slips over your neck like a scarf, and it can be unrolled to cover most of your face. With some sweaters, like the Fratzke shawl-collar

Rain gear should accompany you on all mountain hunts. For horse hunting, heavy rubberized gear like this is great, but for backpacking and hiking, coated nylon or Gore-Tex rainwear is better.

design, you can zip the collar into a turtleneck position to protect your neck. For hunting in cold weather, I commonly carry a wool scarf because it allows excellent heat regulation. While hiking I open it up to allow air circulation around my neck and prevent sweating, then I wrap it around my neck to preserve body heat when I slow down.

Rain Gear. Rain should be an accepted part of hunting, particularly in some regions of the country, and especially in the high mountains. If you're dressed in good wool or synthetic clothes, you don't need a rain suit for hunting in a light drizzle. But a downpour is something else. You can get soaked to the skin quickly, and a good drenching can end your hunting for the day (or life, if you get hypothermia), so on any backcountry hunt, include reliable rain gear. Coated nylon or Gore-Tex rain gear weighs very little and can be rolled up in a pack. Sure it's noisy, but making a little noise is a lot better than getting soaked to the skin and quitting.

Hand Protection. As mentioned under Camouflage, it's important to camouflage your hands. For virtually all my hunting I wear gloves. Some hunters say gloves interfere with shooting, but I don't find that to be the case if they're the right kind of gloves, which means they must fit your hands snugly. In hot weather, gloves made of mosquito netting are cool and offer good camouflage, although they aren't real rugged. I don't care for cotton camouflage gloves because they don't fit snugly. If you shoot with a release aid that might not matter, and for use with a tab or shooting glove, you can cut off the fingers.

The best all-around gloves I've found are wool Army glove liners. I buy them a size small so they fit my hands like skin. They keep my hands warm in cool to cold weather, and they're ideal for high-mountain mule deer and elk hunting in September. I slip a tab on right over the glove, and the glove in no way interferes with my shooting. A release-aid shooter could wear these gloves without problems.

For late-season hunting when temperatures drop down to zero or below, wool glove liners aren't adequate. In snow or hard wind, I've used Thinsulate gloves with Gore-Tex lining, and these have proved themselves very well. I can shoot with one of these thick gloves on my bow hand, but I have to take off the string-hand glove. With a release aid, taking off the glove may not be necessary.

For extreme cold, heavy mittens are better because your fingers can help keep each other warm like two people in the same sleeping bag, although I personally don't care for mittens because they eliminate all dexterity. I think a preferable alternative for extreme cold is one of the mitt-type handwarmers with a fleece lining. You can put a handwarmer inside one of these to keep your string fingers warm until the moment of truth arrives.

Gaiters. If you wade in deep snow with loose pants cuffs, as will be the case in much late-

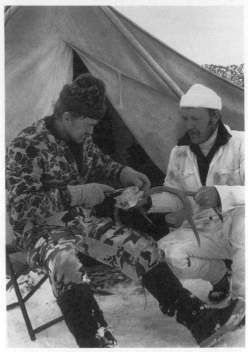

For hunting in snow, gaiters are invaluable. Without them your pants legs will fill up with ten pounds of snow.

season hunting, you'll end up with ten pounds of snow in each pants leg unless you do something to prevent it. You can tie your pants legs tightly shut with a string, which works okay, but a more reliable solution is gaiters. They wrap around your leg from the calf to the ankle to keep snow out of your cuffs and boots.

Footwear

One year my wife, Laura, and I backpacked 6 miles for a go at elk. We forgot the binoculars, and to me hunting without binoculars is like hunting without eyes, so I hurried 12 miles round trip to get them. About halfway through that jaunt I felt hot spots on the bottoms of my feet, but I was in too much of a hurry to worry about it and kept pushing to get back to camp before dark. Back at camp I could hardly walk, and taking my boots off I discovered blisters about two inches across on the balls and heels of both feet. And they were deep, right to the meat underneath. We sat around camp the next four days as I nursed my painful feet, and we finally gave up hunting and headed for home. That hunt was a disaster, to say the least, but it burned into my mind forever the need for foot care in the backcountry.

Socks. Healthy feet start with good socks. Here again, wool and synthetics get the nod. On that disastrous hunt, I was wearing cotton socks that got damp and abrasive as I hiked. The idea in preventing blisters is to wear smooth, snug-fitting socks next to your feet and loose bulky socks over those to absorb shock and moisture. Slippage should take place between the socks, not between the socks and your feet.

I often wear polished-wool dress socks next to my feet. Silk is gentle, but it bunches up and doesn't seem very durable. Early Winters makes an Anti-Blister Sock that actually is two socks in one. Slippage supposedly takes place between the two parts of the sock. I've put a lot of miles on a pair of these and haven't got any blisters, so the system must work. Some hunters also swear by nylon socks.

Over inner socks like these, wear heavy wool or wool blends. On a long hike, occasionally take off your boots to let your feet dry and to straighten out your socks, and you should never have foot problems.

Boots and Shoes. So many new styles of footwear have hit the market recently it would take a book to detail them all. In the past, standard advice has been to buy a good pair of leather boots and break them in before your trip. That's probably still good advice, but today you'll find many alternatives to regular hiking boots, and I think many of them are superior for hunting.

Weight is the primary reason. Leather hiking boots weigh two to three pounds apiece, but many of the new nylon-and-leather hiking shoes weigh a pound or less. A rule of thumb says a pound on the feet equals five pounds on the back, and if that's true then you can see you'll go a lot farther with less effort by shaving a pound off your feet.

Weight also makes a difference in hunting efficiency. A friend once jumped on me for clomping around in heavy leather boots with thick Vibram soles, but I didn't realize how bad those boots sounded until I hunted with another fellow who had equally heavy boots. He sounded like an elephant stomping through the woods. That was the last season I hunted in those clodhoppers.

Heavy boots do have their place in backpacking and carrying heavy loads of meat. If you have to carry a heavy pack, 70 pounds or more, over steep, rocky terrain, you'll appreciate the protection of thick Vibram soles and the support of heavy leather uppers. On excursions where heavy boots seem justified, I also carry a pair of lighter shoes for hunting.

For warm to moderate weather, I often wear lightweight shoes made like running shoes with low tops. They're light in weight, and they have soft soles that help in quiet sneaking. If I plan to hike long distances in steep country, I prefer high-top shoes, but I still like the kind with soft rubber in the soles to absorb some of the pounding of constant walking.

Many hiking shoes and boots these days have Gore-Tex liners, which supposedly makes them waterproof. I've had several different "waterproof" brands, and none could withstand the test of a rainy day. Mind you, I've talked to some hunters who swear their boots

For warm-weather hunting on flat to moderate terrain, low-top shoes like these make for quiet stalking.

Many new hiking shoes are made like running shoes with soft, comfortable soles, yet the high tops give good ankle protection and the lug soles assure traction on steep terrain. The Time Out Hunters and similar shoes by other companies are ideal for warm to cool weather hunting in all kinds of terrain.

For really rough conditions, you need heavy boots like the Brownings at left and the L. L. Beans at right, with Gore-Tex and Thinsulate lining.

are totally waterproof, but I haven't been so fortunate. The only boots I've seen that come close are those with totally seamless Gore-Tex liners, and for wading streams and bogs, they do the job. But I don't expect any miracles from these boots on rainy or snowy days, because all the ones I've had eventually leak. Ad-

Gore-Tex lined boots, like the Rocky Boots at left, and rubber-bottom, leather-upper boots like L. L. Bean's Maine Hiking Shoe, will keep you going in cold and wet weather.

mittedly, I haven't tried every brand. And just as surely, they'll keep your feet a lot drier and more comfortable than plain canvas or leather without the Gore-Tex liner.

For really wet and cold weather, I prefer rubber-bottom, leather-top boots like L. L. Bean's Maine Hiking Shoe. The soles on these boots are soft so you can sneak quietly. Some hunters don't like the traditional chain tread, but I've found that it gives adequate traction until it gets worn down smooth. The soles are fairly thin, so you're wise to add a felt insole to protect the bottoms of your feet from rocks and sticks.

This same style of boot also comes with Thinsulate liners and Gore-Tex waterproofing. For snow and subfreezing temperatures, these are ideal. Some brands have a removable liner, which can be taken out for quick drying. L. L. Bean has one model with the Thinsulate and Gore-Tex liner built right into the boot. It can't be removed, which makes drying a little slower, but these boots are exceptionally comfortable and warm, yet they're not bulky.

For extreme cold, especially where you'll be standing and generating little heat, the ideal is a pac with rubber foot, leather upper, and a thick felt liner. They're bulky, so they're not well suited to long-distance hiking. But they'll keep your feet warm under the most frigid conditions.

COLORADO Colorado, with 104,247 square miles, is without question the most popular western state for nonresident hunters. This state produces the highest elk kill in the United States, and it grows the biggest mule deer. Many large ranches are leased by outfitters, or ranchers themselves charge a trespass fee. Even at that, Colorado has vast amounts of public land, both U.S. Forest Service and BLM, and finding good public hunting is not a major problem. The lowest point in Colorado is about 3,500 feet, and most hunting takes place from 7,000 to 12,000 feet, so Colorado is not the place for a person with heart trouble or altitude-related problems.

Big Game

Deer. On the average about 15,000 residents and 5,000 nonresidents hunt during the deer archery seasons. Average yearly archery harvest has been 1,500 to 2,000, but bowhunters have taken as many as 4,500 deer in one year. Average bowhunting success has been about 15 percent, with a high in 1978 of 25 percent. Timing of seasons has varied greatly, but the general archery season for deer and elk commonly has opened from mid to late August and remained open for a month. (For several years the muzzleloader deer and elk seasons have taken place during the archery season, which isn't ideal for bowhunting.)

The Continental Divide splits Colorado in two. East of Denver, the country consists of farmlands, prairies, and badlands, and whitetails predominate in the bottomlands of three major drainages—the Platte, Republican, and Arkansas rivers. Preseason whitetail population is 5,000 to 8,000. Permits are limited throughout this region so the proportion of old bucks is high. Bowhunters have taken some exceptional whitetails in eastern Colorado. Most of this region is private land, so you must get permission to hunt. The Division of Wildlife owns some public hunting land.

Mule Deer. The mule deer population is estimated at 500,000, although that fluctuates greatly, depending on winter weather. Mule deer are scattered across the uplands of the eastern plains section. Again, rifle harvest is limited so the plains hold lots of mature bucks. The West Slope (mountain terrain from the Continental Divide to the Utah border) contains if not the best at least the most famous mule deer hunting in the United States. The southwest quarter has high numbers of deer and has produced more Boone and Crockett bucks than any other single region in North America. The country around Durango and Cortez, the Dolores River drainage, the Uncompahgre Plateau, Eagle County, Battlement and Grand Mesas—all these areas have high numbers of deer and big bucks.

The northwest quarter often has been described as Colorado's "deer factory." The Piceance Basin near Meeker is reputed to hold the largest single deer herd in North America, at one time as many as 60,000 deer, although the herd is smaller now. This region consists of sagebrush plateaus at modest elevations (for Colorado) of 6,000 to 7,000 feet, and the slopes surrounding these contain dense oak brush and aspen.

The Boone and Crockett world-record typical mule deer, with a score of 225 6/8, came from southwestern Colorado, and the Pope and Young world record, with a score of 203 5/8, came from the White River National Forest. The Pope and Young world-record nontypical also comes from this state. The state record nontypical mule deer scored 306 2/8 (rifle-killed). Colorado has produced 36 percent of the mule deer listed in Boone and Crockett, nearly three times as many as any other state.

Elk. For many years, Colorado has ranked number one for elk with an overall harvest of nearly 30,000 animals. Archers take about 1,500 elk and have a success rate of about 12 percent. The White River Plateau near Meeker has the highest elk densities and has always been the most popular spot with bowhunters, and the Grand Mesa, Battlement Mesa, Roan Plateau, and other "islands" of habitat in the northwest have high concentrations of elk. The Gunnison country, Uncompahgre Plateau, and San Juan Mountains of the southwest quarter have comparable overall numbers of elk, but the animals are spread over more country so the densities aren't as high. Colorado isn't known for huge bulls, but some units have been designated trophy areas with limited permits, and these will produce some big bulls. The archery elk season runs concurrent with the deer season, opening in late August and extending for about a month.

The largest elk ever recorded, with a score of 442⅜, was killed in the Gunnison region, but today, because of heavy hunting pressure, Colorado doesn't produce a lot of huge bulls. Still, bowhunters take several elk scoring between 300 and 350 each year, and with an increased number of trophy units recently (where tags are limited in number), Colorado will produce more outstanding bulls.

Bear. Hunters take roughly 800 bears a year. There is no special bow season. During the spring season, which runs from April through June, you can hunt by baiting or with hounds. Baiting is by far the most popular method used by archers in Colorado. You can also take bears during the deer and elk archery seasons in the fall, but no hounds are allowed.

Antelope. Colorado generally has had liberal bowhunting seasons for antelope. In many units the number of archery licenses is unlimited, and the season extends from August into September. Antelope live along the Wyoming border and throughout the eastern plains. Much of the land is private.

Cougar. The annual harvest for all hunters generally exceeds 100 animals. The season runs from November through April. Lions are taken throughout the mountains of western Colorado, virtually all with the aid of hounds.

Bighorn Sheep. Sheep are thriving in several mountain ranges, and special archery seasons, as well as rifle hunts, are held for these animals. In some units the hunting is tough and few hunters apply, so the odds for drawing a sheep tag are better than in most states. Seasons run from August into September or October, depending on area.

Mountain Goat. Colorado also has special archery goat seasons. Licenses are limited but the odds for drawing an archery tag are reason-

able. The bow season generally runs from August into October.

Contact. Division of Wildlife, 6060 Broadway, Denver, CO 80216.

CONNECTICUT This state has an area of 5,009 square miles. The northwest corner holds the only mountainous country in Connecticut, and northern hardwood forests are extensive here. Much of the land here exceeds 1,200 feet in elevation, and the highest point in Connecticut, 2,380 feet, lies in the extreme northwest corner. The eastern half of the state consists of rolling hills that slope southward into a flat coastal plain. Oak and hickory forests, along with white pine in the northern hills, cover a high percentage of the area, and farm and pasturelands are scattered throughout. The Connecticut River valley and the southwest corner have high human population where antihunting sentiment runs strong, and much land is closed to hunting.

Big Game

Whitetail Deer. An estimated 30,000 whitetails live in Connecticut; bowhunters number about 8,000. Average archery success has been 5.7 percent with a high in 1983 of 7.3 percent and a low in 1975 of 1.5 percent. In recent years the bow season has run from October 1 through mid-November. In many cases the bag limit has been two deer per hunter for each season. By taking part in all seasons (bow, rifle, muzzleloader) a hunter legally could take seven deer in one year. Liberal seasons will continue in some areas to reduce complaints of deer damage, collisions between deer and cars, and other deer-human conflicts.

Connecticut has about two dozen deer management areas totaling more than 130,000 acres. During shotgun and muzzleloader seasons, a limited quota of permits is issued by lottery, but there is no quota during archery season. To hunt legally on private land, a hunter must have written permission on a "consent to hunt" form.

The mountainous northeast corner, an extension of the Berkshire Hills in Massachusetts, has up to 30 deer per square mile, the highest density in the state. Deer numbers aren't as high in the eastern half of the state, but they're moderate and growing as old-growth forests are opened up by logging and firewood cutting.

Contact. Department of Environmental Protection, Wildlife Bureau, 165 Capitol Avenue, Hartford, CT 06106.

COUES DEER *(Odocoileus virginianus couesi)*
To clear the record right off, Coues is pronounced "cows," although many of the locals call them "coos" deer. This deer is also called the Arizona whitetail, and if hunters went by that name, it would eliminate a lot of confusion.

Coues deer are a subspecies of whitetail, but they're much smaller than most other whitetails. The average buck field dresses about 80 pounds, a big one 110 pounds. The antlers are proportionally small. The Boone and Crockett world record Coues deer measures 143 inches, and the B&C minimum score for typical whitetail is 170. Because Coues deer are much smaller than most other races of whitetail, and because they live in a geographic region isolated from other whitetails, records-keeping organizations (Pope and Young, Boone and Crockett) place them in a separate category. Most hunters also consider Coues deer as a different breed from "normal" whitetails, so I'll also treat them as a separate species here.

Distribution
Put simply, the range of Coues deer in the United States takes in southeastern Arizona and southwestern New Mexico. A line drawn north-south through Phoenix would roughly mark the western boundary of Coues deer range, and the Rio Grande River would mark the eastern boundary. The Mogollon Rim, which extends from Flagstaff southeast into New Mexico, forms the northern boundary. The Coues deer range extends several hundred miles south into Mexico.

In brush country bordering the Mogollon Rim, range of the Coues deer is fairly continu-

The Coues deer of Arizona and New Mexico is a miniature version of the whitetail. Mature bucks weigh scarcely more than 100 pounds. This would be considered a large buck. *Photo courtesy Steve Gallizioli.*

ous, but farther south, classic Coues deer country is characterized by low-elevation Sonoran, saguaro-cactus desert interspersed with small, high-elevation mountain ranges. The mountain ranges form "islands" of whitetail habitat. On a ten-mile drive in this fascinating country you can travel from blistering desert at 2,000 feet elevation up through sweeping grasslands to oak woodlands to pine forests to Douglas fir and white fir to spruce forests at 9,000 feet elevation. You climb through a cross section of life zones from desert to subalpine.

Coues deer live at the intermediate level, from about 4,000 to 8,000 feet elevation. Some whitetails inhabit low desert country and some live near cottonwood and mesquite bottomlands amid rolling grasslands. But by far the best whitetail country consists of steep, expansive canyons where scattered oak trees, or oak

This is typical Coues deer country. In this terrain, spotting and stalking is an efficient way to hunt the little whitetails. Many Arizona mountain ranges have extensive backcountry where you'll find little competition.

and pine, provide the predominant cover. This generally falls in the elevation band from 5,000 to 7,000 feet. Many mountain ranges in Arizona—the Santa Catalinas, Galiuros, Pinalenos, Santa Ritas, Baboquivaris, Huachucas, Chiricahuas and dozens more—support thriving whitetail populations. Similar isolated ranges in New Mexico between the Arizona border and the Rio Grande River have good numbers of Coues deer.

On a map these mountains look small, but to a hunter on foot they're big, as tough as any in the West. By far the best Coues deer hunting lies on public land, and most of the mountain ranges hold endless expanses of rugged, roadless country where a bowhunter can wander for days and never see another hunter.

Hunting Methods

Spotting and Stalking. The vertical mountain ranges and relatively sparse vegetation lend themselves to spotting. In some places oak trees and conifers are dense, but even here you can glass from one side of a canyon to the other and spot moving deer. (For details, see Spotting.)

Duwane Adams made his reputation as an outfitter by guiding for trophy Coues deer, and he hunts with his eyes. He finds a vantage overlooking a big rocky canyon with scattered oak trees, sets up his 15x60 Zeiss binoculars on a tripod, sits down behind the glasses, and starts looking. From one spot he'll study the country for several hours, and he commonly spots a dozen or more Coues deer bucks in a day. When he's spotted a buck that really catches his eye, he plans a stalk. He considers stalking the only way to hunt these deer, and he won't hunt terrain where he can't hunt with his eyes and binoculars.

If you're used to looking for mule deer or northern whitetails, you may have to adjust your eyes. At a distance, a Coues deer looks about half the size of the average mule deer, and Coues deer appear somewhat grayer than whitetails I've seen in other regions. I'd describe them as mouse gray.

Dave Snyder, well known for his success as a trophy bowhunter, took Coues deer three years in a row, including the Pope and Young world record nontypical. One important lesson he learned, he said, was that Coues deer remain in very small territories. If you see a large buck but can't get him the first day, look for him right there in the future because he won't be far away. Snyder saw his record buck nine different days in virtually the same spot before he was able to get a killing shot.

You can stalk Coues deer much as you would any other open-country animals. Plan your stalk with the wind in your favor, and in particular look for other nearby deer to avoid spooking them on the way to the buck you want. (For details, see Stalking.)

Some hunters have told me you can't stalk Arizona whitetails because they're too spooky, but I haven't found that so. I've stalked within bow range of several good bucks, and in ways I've found them easier than mule deer. One morning just after sunrise I spotted a buck with about a 15-inch antler spread — huge by Coues deer standards — bedded on a long grassy point. He was a half mile away, so I weaved from one ravine to another to stay out of his sight, and circled around behind him.

That early in the morning a breeze drifted downhill so I came in just below the buck. He lay behind a rock out of my sight, but I knew right where he was bedded. I also could see a spike buck lying in the open 50 yards out front.

As I crawled into shooting position, a doe I hadn't seen spotted me and jumped from her bed and started blowing. She was within 30 yards of the two bucks, and I figured all her commotion would end my hunt. But as she stomped and blew and pranced back and forth for ten minutes, the spike never even looked her way. I don't know what the big buck was doing, but he definitely never stood up to investigate. Finally the doe drifted away, snorting all the while.

I waited for another half hour before either of the bucks stirred. The big buck eventually stood up, 25 yards away. Until then I'd been calm, but the sight of this great trophy so close blew my cool, and I shot over him. He ran and stopped at 40 yards to look back — something mule deer do, but not whitetails — and I shot under him.

Maybe those bucks thought they were hiding when that doe carried on for so long. Most experienced hunters agree that Coues bucks would rather hide than run, and they'll lie tight unless they think they've been detected. That might help during a stalk, because a buck often will lie still, even if he knows you're there, as long as he feels secure.

Arizona traditionally has held two bow seasons for Coues deer, one in September and one in January. The rut for Coues deer begins in late December and runs through January, so that's when the bucks are most active, visible, and vulnerable. That, coupled with the fact that little bowhunting is available elsewhere at that time, has made the January season generally more popular with bowhunters. The weather is also much cooler then, which probably sounds better to most hunters than the blistering heat of September. The fact is, January weather in Arizona's mountains can be bitterly cold and wet, so pack your longjohns, wool clothes, and rain gear along with your camouflage shorts.

January isn't necessarily the best time to stalk these deer. As Dave Snyder pointed out, the bucks can be hard to stalk then because they're fidgety and move constantly. You may be only halfway through your stalk when a buck will run off to chase a doe. In contrast, during September, prior to the rut and when the weather is much warmer, bucks will bed down and stay in the same spot all day long, giving you plenty of time to sneak within range.

Stand Hunting. In any dry country, waterhole stands almost assure game for a patient hunter, and that principle definitely applies to Coues deer. An acquaintance of mine regularly hunts a very brushy mountain range; he can't spot deer at long range, so he stand hunts there. Stock tanks supply the only water in this range, and this man has taken several bucks by watching over one small pond.

For waterhole stands to work, the weather must be dry. The potential is greater in the heat of September than in January, but some winters are very dry in Arizona and deer must continue to use waterholes all winter. Wet weather obviously will decrease your chances on a waterhole. Some mountain ranges have abundant water in the form of springs and creeks, and your chances of catching a buck coming to water there are slim.

Because bucks stick to small territories, you can pattern them and determine good stand locations to intercept them in the course of daily movements. (For more details, see Stand Hunting.)

Trophy Hunting

The limited range, rugged terrain, and relative difficulty of hunting Coues deer has limi-

Harold Boyack shows the record-class Coues deer rack from a buck he killed near Tucson, Arizona. This buck scores about 106, putting it near the top of the Pope and Young records.

ted bowhunters' efforts. As a result, archers have taken few outstanding bucks. In recent years, interest has grown, and new Pope and Young world records have been taken several years in a row. For a hunter who seriously wants to try for a world-record animal, and doesn't care which species it is, I'd say the Coues deer probably offers him the best chance among North American big game.

Coues deer antlers are measured identically to those of northern whitetails, but the dimensions are much smaller. Mike Cupell, who measures for Pope and Young and Boone and Crockett in Arizona, has measured dozens of Coues deer. Cupell said the tip-to-tip ear spread is about 12 inches on a big buck. Distance from the tip of the nose to the antler base

8 to 9 inches, and the chest measures 14 to 16 inches deep. You can use these dimensions as a rough yardstick in the field.

Cupell said most whitetails large enough to make the Boone and Crockett minimum of 110 (which places them in world-record class for Pope and Young) have an inside spread of 13 inches or more. That means the inside of the main beams must be wider than the ear tips. Main beams must be in the 16-inch class. Coues deer typically grow three points on each side (including brow tines), but few 3x3s would score well enough to approach world-record class. A buck just about has to have four points to the side to score high enough. The brow tines must be at least 3½ inches long, nearly as long as an ear, and the second points (G-2) must be 7 to 8 inches long for the buck to score well. Nontypical Coues deer are measured the same as nontypical whitetails.

Bowhunters haven't taken enough really big bucks to indicate the absolute trophy potential of any area. Looking at Boone and Crockett figures, the Santa Rita Mountains have produced by far the most record-book animals, followed by the Canelo Hills and the Chiricahua Mountains. Gila County makes a good showing. That's the country bordering the south side of the Mogollon Rim, including the Mazatzal and Sierra Ancha mountain ranges. Pima County also has more than its share of record-book animals, and many of these probably came from the Santa Catalina Mountains just east of Tucson. Many other mountain ranges have given up a trophy buck or two.

COUGAR See Mountain Lion.

CREEP "Creeping" means your fingers follow the bowstring slightly just before release. In essence, this shortens your draw length a fraction of an inch, which can produce erratic arrow flight and can cause your arrows to hit low. A live, or power, release helps to solve creeping problems. (For more details, see Release and Shooting Basics.)

D

DAGGER POINT The fourth tine on an elk antler (some hunters call it the sword point). The dagger point often is somewhat flattened, and except in abnormal antlers, it's always the longest point. Thus, to quickly count points on an elk's antlers, you can ignore the first three tines and start at the dagger. If the rack has one point past the dagger, the bull is a five-point; if it has two more he's a six-point; and so forth.

DEAD RELEASE See Release.

DEER CALLING Deer seem to be silent animals, but they can produce a wide variety of sounds. Most of their sounds are fairly low in pitch, so hunters rarely hear them, but the fact is they communicate extensively by sound, and you can use vocal communication to fool deer just as you can to fool elk or other vocal animals.

Calling Basics

Wind. The same general principles apply to all kinds of calling. Most important is keeping the wind in your favor. You must hunt into the wind so animals coming to the call don't smell you before they come within range.

The Setup. For each calling sequence, you must have a setup or blind where you can see approaching animals, where you're concealed so you can draw and shoot without being detected, and where you have a clearing or open lanes that allow unobstructed shooting.

Perseverance. Some hunters get the impression that calling doesn't work because they try it once or twice and don't attract any deer. That's like saying hunting from a tree stand doesn't work because you don't kill a buck your first night out. Nothing works all the time, and that includes calling. To call in deer, you have to stick with it long enough to make everything gel.

There are two basic approaches. You can take a stand in good country and stay in that location, calling repeatedly over a long period of time. Or you can set up in one spot, call for 20 to 30 minutes, and if you get no response, move on to a new location and try again.

The Sounds of Deer

Whitetails and other deer make a number of sounds that can be used to your advantage in hunting. Some of these sounds are vocal—that is, they're made by the deer's vocal cords—and others are forced-air sounds, much like you'd make by blowing through your nose forcibly. Some are primarily rut-related and others are made year-round.

Bleat. Two sounds not necessarily related to the rut are the bleat and the alert snort. The bleat is the sound produced by most commercial deer calls, and it imitates a fawn calling for its mother. This call most commonly attracts does, but it will fool bucks, too, and during the rut it could very well attract a doe with a buck close behind. It works for mule deer and blacktails as well as whitetails.

Snort. The alert snort is the characteristic "blowing" you hear from spooky deer. This normally would be associated with alarm and might not seem like a call that would attract deer. However, I've talked to some hunters who've used it effectively to pull deer into the open, possibly because other deer will come to see what the one is blowing about. Even if it's made in alarm, it may not scatter deer instantly.

One time I'd stalked within 20 yards of a whitetail buck and was waiting for him to move to give me a clear shot when a doe just uphill spotted me and started snorting. "Oh, oh," I thought, "the jig's up." At first, however, the buck never even looked up, just kept feeding. The doe blew loudly for five minutes, and finally the buck, curiosity aroused, walked up the hill toward her. He probably would have walked right to her if I hadn't planted an arrow in him. I suspect a hunter making that sound could have attracted the buck, too.

A friend of mine used a Lohman snort call on mule deer and had excellent results. "That thing ought to be banned," he said. "It really made some of those deer look foolish."

Grunt. Other sounds are associated primarily with the rut. The one most commonly heard is the grunt. I'd describe this sound as a cross between a frog's croak and pig's snort. It's a muted *oink, oink* sound. You'll often hear this sound made by bucks trailing does. It's not audible much farther than 50 yards.

With some practice you can make this noise with your own voice. Several instructional tapes include the sounds of live bucks grunting, along with suggestions on how to imitate the sound. You can use the grunt by itself as a general call during the rut, or in combination with rattling. (For more details, see Rattling.)

It can be especially useful when you're in a tree stand and you see a buck going by out of range. A few judicious grunts can turn the buck your way to pull him close enough for a shot.

The snort-wheeze, or grunt-snort-wheeze, are also sounds made by rutting bucks. These are a combination of grunts followed by forced-air sounds through the nose. Bucks produce these sounds during confrontations with each other, and again, these work in combination with rattling. Get some tapes of whitetail deer sounds to learn these calls. (For more on general calling techniques, see Elk and Predator Calling, and for more on attracting deer, see Rattling.)

DELAWARE　Delaware has an area of 2,057 square miles and only three counties: Newcastle, Kent, and Sussex, going north to south. Public lands, state and federal combined, make up 6 to 7 percent of the state. These provide some good hunting, but permits are limited and issued by lottery. Hunting leases on private land are fairly common in Delaware.

Big Game
Whitetail Deer. Delaware has an estimated population of 10,000 deer. An average of 3,300 residents and 154 nonresidents have hunted during archery seasons in recent years. The average kill has been 25 deer (45 to 50 percent bucks), with a high in 1982 of 48 deer. Average bowhunter success has been about 1 percent. Recent seasons have provided as much as 133 total hunting days—113 for archery, 6 for muzzleloader, and 14 for shotgun. Bag limit has been two deer (at least one must be taken during archery or muzzleloader season) of either sex.

In northern Newcastle County, many large estates restrict hunting access, and deer numbers may be above carrying capacity. The tidal marsh area along Delaware Bay and River contains croplands, marshes, and timber, and deer numbers are good throughout this region. The rest of Delaware is fairly flat and consists of mixed woodlands and crop fields, and deer live throughout suitable habitat. Because of the rich food source found in corn and soybean fields, Delaware grows some exceptionally heavy deer.

Other Game

Small Game. Cottontails are popular game animals in Delaware, and they thrive in most brush patches and on abandoned farms. Squirrels are abundant in most stands of hardwoods, and woodchucks live throughout the pasturelands.

Contact. Division of Fish & Wildlife, 89 Kings Highway, P.O. Box 1401, Dover, DE 19903.

DOMINANT EYE With most people, one eye dominates over the other, and that's called the dominant or master eye. You must know your dominant eye to select a bow and to aim accurately. Most commonly, eye dominance and muscle dominance are the same. That is, most right-handed persons are right-eyed; left-handed, left-eyed. If that's your case, you'll have no problem selecting and aiming a bow.

In some cases, however, right-handed persons have dominant left eyes and lefties have dominant right eyes. If you fall into that category, you either have to learn to shoot on the side with the dominant eye, or you have to shoot with one eye closed. Depth perception and perspective are better with both eyes open, so in most cases, particularly if you want to shoot instinctively (without sights), you're wisest to shoot on the side with the dominant eye so you can shoot with both eyes open.

To check eye dominance, point at a distant object so the tip of your index finger lines up with the object. Now, without moving your finger, close first your right eye, then your left. The sight picture won't change when you look with your dominant eye, but when you look with the other eye, your finger will appear to point to the side of the object. (For further discussion, see Bow Selection.)

DRAW LENGTH Traditionally, draw length was measured from the string at full draw to the back of the bow (the side away from the archer) because arrows were cut at roughly that length. The risers on all bows aren't the same width, however, so there was really no standard. One archer could have several different draw lengths, depending on which bow he was shooting.

To standardize the definition of "draw length," the Archery Manufacturers Association measured dozens of bows and found that the average distance from the pressure point on the handles to the backs of the bows was 1¾ inches. So "draw length" is now defined as the distance from the string at full draw to the pressure point on the handle plus 1¾ inches.

Thus, to find your draw length you pull a bow to full draw and measure from the string at your anchor point to the pressure point of the handle, and then add 1¾ inches. For example, let's say you measure 30¼ inches from the string to the pressure point on the handle. You then add 1¾ inches, for a total of 32. You would then buy a bow with a draw-length rating of 32 inches. Recurve and longbows, of course, offer virtually unlimited draw and are not sold according to draw length, so this applies primarily to compound bows. (For additional discussion, see Bow Selection.)

If you've never shot a bow, you could get a distorted reading with this method because the holding weight of the bow could force you to "collapse" a little. You can get a fairly accurate measurement if you assume a shooting stance with your bow arm outstretched and your head turned just as if you were holding a bow at full draw. Then measure from your anchor point (this assumes you know where you'll anchor) to the V formed by your thumb and index finger, and add 1¾ inches. Be cautious about using other methods for determining draw length. You want to be in a shooting stance, because methods in which you face straight ahead and measure only your arms don't take shoulder width or facial features into account.

Draw length should not be confused with arrow length, which can vary greatly from bow to bow even though the draw length remains identical. (For details, see Arrow Shaft Selection.)

Some shooters alter stance or arm extension to reduce draw length, but most authorities I've talked to recommend against that. Theoretically you could shoot most accurately if your eye, bow arm, and bowstring fell in the same plane. Obviously, that can't happen, but the closer you can come to that ideal, the better you'll shoot. You come closest to perfect alignment when you shoot at maximum extension — that is, maximum draw length. (For details, see Shooting Basics.) Underdrawing can cause excessive muscle tension and torque on the string and bow.

DRAW WEIGHT See Bow Scale and Bow Selection.

DRIVING In one of his books, Leonard Rue said you don't really drive deer; all you do is stir them up and they go where they want to go. To a large extent that's true. In 1924, Zane Grey organized possibly the largest deer drive in history to herd overabundant deer from the Kaibab Plateau to less populated ranges across the Colorado River. Despite the abundance of deer and the experienced drivers he hired, no deer were driven from the Kaibab.

Deer aren't cattle, and they can't be driven predictably. Nevertheless, you can devise driving strategies that will produce some good bow-and-arrow shots.

Escape Routes

One year my friend Cliff Dewell and I spotted a tremendous mule deer hanging out on a desert knoll. We tried stalking him, but on the crusty December snow, sneaking within bow range proved impossible. One time when we spooked the buck, however, we watched him exit through a small saddle near the top of the knoll. We also saw other deer go out there, and tracks in the snow indicated this saddle was a common passage for animals.

So one morning I took a stand in the saddle and Cliff came up from below. He didn't move fast or make any noise. We didn't want to create a stampede but only to let the deer know he was there so they'd try to sneak away. It worked to perfection. Not long after Cliff started his drive, I heard crunching footfalls in the snow. A doe and then a buck came by at 10

yards. This wasn't the huge buck we were after, but he was far better than average and I couldn't resist shooting. At the shot, I heard other deer right behind me taking off. When Cliff arrived he had a long face. "I was afraid you'd shoot at that first buck," he said. "The big one was 30 yards away and coming straight at you."

Maybe I'd botched up by not waiting, but the important point is that the drive worked. When you try to stir deer into confusion, you produce fast shots under poor shooting conditions. But if you study animals and analyze what they'll do in reaction to disturbance, you can virtually pick the kind of shot you want.

Posting

Driving is similar to stand hunting in that it involves taking a stand along a trail or similar runway. However, in driving you're not trying to ambush animals between bedding and feeding areas, but along escape routes. To do that, you obviously have to know those routes.

Lazy. In steep country, you can just about pinpoint escape routes simply by studying the terrain. Like people, deer won't put out more effort than necessary. That's why saddles — low points in high ridges — are good points for stands. One time I saw three bucks headed toward a saddle, so I ran ahead and got in that saddle to ambush them. From there, though, I could see them coming and it looked like they were passing on by to cross higher up. That didn't seem logical, and a feeling down deep in my gut said to stay right in the saddle. But I ignored the feeling and ran ahead another 100 yards to get in their path, and then I heard footsteps behind and turned to see the bucks crossing right in the saddle. Deer know the terrain, and in most cases they'll take the path of least resistance. That's where you want to be.

Hidden. Most animals also go out of their way to stay hidden, and they use cover to their best advantage. Wooded stringers, brush patches, or other vegetation or terrain features between openings serve as likely escape routes. One friend of mine calls these "constriction" points, because the nature of the cover constricts moving animals into a very small space. That's where you want to wait for driven animals.

In generally heavy cover, of course, that doesn't apply because constriction points aren't obvious. There you have to look for trails to discern how and where deer move. Keith Monson, a hunter from North Dakota who specializes in driving whitetails, advocates extensive scouting. To drive deer successfully, he says, you have to know where the deer bed—that's where they'll be when you start driving them—and you have to know which trails they'll take to escape. He suggests circling the area, observing all trails coming in and going out. Only with an intimate knowledge of what the deer do there can you know where to place hunters on stand and how to drive the deer.

Blacktail habitat in Oregon is as thick as any whitetail cover, so the same principles apply to both. George Shurtleff, who killed the world-record blacktail, has killed many huge bucks, and he took one of them by scouting for escape routes. He didn't actually organize a drive. Instead he discovered a big camp of bowhunters and, figuring they'd fan out in the morning from camp and move deer ahead of them, he decided to let them be his drivers. With that in mind, he went up the hill above the camp and scouted intensively. He found the confluence of two well-used trails through otherwise impenetrable berry brambles and ferns, a logical escape route for deer coming up from below. He took a ground stand there before dawn the next morning, and before long a buck walked by and Shurtleff brought him down. That buck scored better than 160, a huge blacktail.

Observe. Watch the reactions of deer any time they're pushed. If they react a certain way one time, chances are they'll react similarly the next. That's how Cliff Dewell and I planned the successful drive mentioned above. We saw the big buck exit through a saddle, and we figured he'd do the same again as long as he wasn't disturbed there. And he did.

Whitetails will do the same in heavy cover; they're just not as easy to observe there. Mon-

son terms their habitual reactions "tendencies," and he maintains that observing and learning the tendencies is the secret to productive deer driving. He doesn't say deer will do exactly the same thing every time they're driven, but they will *tend* to react the same way each time, given similar conditions.

At least they will until they find out they're being ambushed. As soon as they run into a human being blocking the trail, or hear an arrow sizzling by, they'll change escape tactics in a hurry. That's why you're wise to rest an area after a drive to avoid forcing deer into new reaction patterns. If you hunt one area regularly, Monson suggests, drive it only every second or third week. Dewell and I saw that principle in action on that big mule deer. We tried the same plan again two days after I'd spooked him, and instead of coming up through the saddle, he ran downhill and exited around the base of the mountain. Deer do have a memory.

Driving

If you simply scare deer out of their wits, they could run about anywhere and you'll have to be purely lucky to put your standers in the right locations. The purpose of driving is to put deer into controlled flight. You want them to know the drivers are present so they'll move out ahead to escape, yet you want them to move slowly in natural escape patterns, the patterns you've already discerned.

For that reason, persons doing the driving should move slowly, deliberately, and quietly, making just enough disturbance so deer know they're coming but moving slowly enough so deer have time to escape gracefully. In most cases, hunters on stand will be downwind of the animals and drivers will be upwind, so the deer between will smell the drivers coming long before they see them, and probably before they hear them.

Monson says the idea is to make deer nervous. The best way to do that is to let deer know the drivers are present—by smell—but not to let them know exactly *where* they are. If deer can't detect the exact locations of the drivers, they'll get nervous and move on out ahead to hunters on stand. On the other hand, if the drivers whistle and talk, or the woods are dry and noisy and the air is calm so the sounds of moving hunters can be heard clearly, deer can pinpoint exact locations of the drivers, and they'll often sneak back through the driving line rather than moving out ahead. Obviously the drivers should be as quiet as possible, but they also can zigzag back and forth to confuse the deer. And, as Monson suggests, under noisy conditions when deer are sure to pinpoint the drivers, the standers can actually take stands behind the drivers to intercept deer doubling back through the driving line.

Taking a stand for a drive is no different from taking any other stand. It should go without saying that standers must get into position quietly without being detected.

How many persons do you need for a drive? Remember, the idea is not to create mass confusion but rather to push a given buck past a person on stand for a close easy shot. Don't try driving huge areas with lots of people. Zane Grey reportedly organized 40 cowboys and 70 Navajo Indians to drive the Kaibab Plateau, and it didn't work. He got mass confusion, and that's what you'll get with big drives. Work on small areas, or small parts of big areas, and use only as many hunters as you can organize and control. Monson suggests no more than three to six, because that's about the maximum number of people who can work together and maintain some semblance of organization.

Even smaller parties can plan excellent mini-drives, and two hunters working together can be very effective. During one of my first years of bowhunting I learned the value of little drives. My friend Don Hummel and I were hunting for mule deer out in the desert. Conditions weren't conducive to stalking so we resorted to small drives in isolated patches of mountain mahogany. These patches were small, no more than 100 feet long and 50 wide, but they offered the only cover so we knew deer had to be there somewhere.

Coming in from downwind, I snuck close to one patch, and then Don approached from upwind, just letting his scent waft into the grove. Slowly a three-point buck tiptoed from the trees on my side, offering a perfect 30-yard shot as he stopped to look back to watch for the smelly guy on the other side. The buck never knew I was there—until I rattled an arrow off the rocks under his belly. Obviously, my shooting needed some work (it probably still does), but that experience proved one point very well: little drives do work for deer.

DROP CAMP   See Outfitters and Guides.

DYNAMIC SPINE   See Spine.

E

ELK *(Cervus elaphus)* Elk of North America formerly were classified as *Cervus canadensis*, but authorities now agree that the elk of North America and the European red deer belong to the same species, so they have the same Latin name.

Varieties of Elk

Taxonomists recognize six subspecies of elk in North America: Rocky Mountain elk *(C. e. nelsoni);* Roosevelt elk *(C. e. roosevelti);* Tule elk *(C. e. nannodes);* Manitoban elk *(C. e. manitobensis);* Eastern elk *(C. e. canadensis);* and Merriam elk *(C. e. merriami).* The Eastern elk historically lived throughout most of the United States east of the Mississippi River, and the Merriam elk lived in Arizona, New Mexico, and south into Mexico. These species are extinct.

Rocky Mountain Elk. These elk have the widest distribution today, from central British Columbia and Alberta south in a virtually continuous range to New Mexico and Arizona, and from eastern Oregon to South Dakota. Small populations have been transplanted to Michigan, Texas, and other regions.

These animals adapt well to varied terrain and vegetation. In northwestern Montana and northern Idaho, they inhabit virtual jungles of spruce, alders, willows, and ferns. In south-western Montana and the Yellowstone country of Wyoming, they live in "classic" elk terrain: alpine meadows and huge parks interspersed with patches of lodgepole pine and black spruce. In Colorado their territory descends from tundra at 12,000 feet, to aspen parks and oak brush tangles, to sagebrush and juniper at low elevations, and in Arizona they're thriving on tablelands as flat as a billiard table in a true desert environment of pinion-juniper and sage-brush. Because of their wide distribution and impressive headgear, Rocky Mountain elk provide by far the greatest elk hunting opportunity, and these are the animals that inspire dreams of backcountry elk hunts into the alpine mountains. Mature Rocky Mountain bulls weigh about 700 pounds on the hoof, and cows weigh about 500 pounds.

Roosevelt Elk. In popularity, Roosevelt elk rank second to Rocky Mountain elk. Their range extends from northern California along the coast of Oregon and Washington and on to Vancouver Island in British Columbia. In Oregon and Washington, Roosevelt elk live from the Pacific Ocean inland to the crest of the Cascade Mountains. A transplanted herd of Roosevelts also thrives on Afognak and Raspberry islands in Alaska.

In terms of body weight, Roosevelts are the largest elk. Mature bulls weigh from 700 to

A pack string heading in the Rocky Mountain high country symbolizes the great American hunting dream, and in most cases that means elk hunting.

1,100 pounds, and cows weigh about 600. Antlers of Roosevelt elk generally don't have the long main beams and wide spread that make Rocky Mountain elk so impressive. Roosevelt antlers generally are shorter and more massive, and commonly they have odd tines growing off the dagger points, ending in multi-branched royals or crowns. Because all these "abnormal" tines become deductions on Rocky Mountain elk scoring charts, official records-keeping

clubs have placed Roosevelt elk in a separate category.

Rocky Mountain elk are often featured as creatures of remote backcountry and lush conifer forests, but they're actually animals of very diverse environments. I killed this bull in the Arizona desert.

Finding Elk

Because elk have such wide range and live in so many different situations, general statements can be misleading. Nevertheless all animals including elk have basic needs, and some general principles apply wherever they live.

Grass and Shrubs. In general, elk are grazers, and they'll feed primarily in open meadows and pastures wherever these are available, so the starting point is to look for lush meadows and grasslands, the same kinds of places that would attract cattle. Some good elk country, however, has virtually no grasslands, and here the animals browse heavily on huckleberries, alder, and other leafy plants. In heavy forestlands with few meadows, clearcuts, or other openings that offer grass feed, look for avalanche chutes, burns, or other natural disturbances where brush has grown up. That's where you'll find elk.

Water. Moisture also characterize elk country. Elk like damp areas where the feed is best and where the moisture cools the air during warm weather. North- and east-facing slopes normally are the coolest and dampest aspects, so, particularly in early seasons, that's where you'll most likely find elk. During the rut, bulls wallow in mud so you'll almost always find these animals around wet meadows or seeping springs in the timber. Arid country, particularly in the Southwest, offers little natural moisture, so here elk must drink from man-made waterholes and trickle tanks, and locating these sources is one of the surest ways of scouting for elk.

Refuge. Elk seek the safety of dense cover and remote drainages. In searching for elk, always look for inaccessible pockets or roadless draws or canyons where the animals can live without disturbance. In the absence of remote refuge areas, look for dense tangles of brush or black timber where the animals can bed in comfort and safety.

Sign. An elk's front hooves are rounded and leave tracks much like small cattle tracks, but the back hooves are narrower and leave impressions more like oversized deer tracks. Tracks of a big bull are about 4 inches long, and those of a cow about 3½ inches. Elk are herd animals, and when they're undisturbed, one herd will hang out in a fairly small area, leaving concentrated sign. Trails here are nearly as obvious as cattle trails, and you'll find other kinds of sign.

If elk are feeding on green grass, their droppings look like small cow pies, but if they're eating browse, the droppings look like huge deer pellets. During the rut, bulls tear up trees and strip off the bark, and in an area with good numbers of bulls, you should find numerous rub trees. You also should find wallows, bathtub-size depressions in meadows or around damp spring areas where bulls have rolled to coat themselves with mud.

Hunting the Rut

Most good elk states now offer archery seasons during the rut. As a result, hunting during the rut, and more specifically hunting by bugling, has become by far the most popular method of bowhunting for elk.

Timing of Your Hunt. Here is the question most often asked about hunting during the rut:

Reading sign is a part of elk hunting. When the animals are eating lush grass, their droppings look somewhat like small cow pies, but when they're eating browse, their droppings look like oversized deer pellets. Droppings from bulls are dimpled on one end.

"When is the best time of year to bugle for elk?"

I'd say you're safe any time in September. In most regions, elk start bugling the last week in August, and they continue until mid-October. Bulls actually start bugling before cows come into heat and breeding starts, so the first two or three weeks, up to about September 10, bulls are roaming to find cows and to gather harems. About September 15, actual breeding starts, and the so-called peak of the rut lasts through about the end of September. Some bugling and mating activity carries on until mid-October. The timing of this pattern applies just about everywhere elk are found, from Alberta to Arizona.

In some states you have little choice about when to hunt, because the season is relatively short, and you'll probably just plan to hunt the whole season. Other states and provinces have much longer seasons and give you wide latitude for hunt timing. As a rule of thumb, I say the earlier in September, the better. At that time bulls are full of vigor as they roam the countryside, looking for cows, and they investigate any and all bugling eagerly.

Possibly more critical, they haven't been hunted hard yet. Hunting early in September, you might be the first person to work on a given bull, and that's your ace in the hole. Thousands of archers can bugle well enough to fool any elk in the woods, so the real secret to killing a bull is being the first one in the woods. Early-season bulls often come in silently but eagerly.

Many hunters routinely plan their hunts for the peak of the rut, the last ten days to two weeks of September. That's okay and you can't really go wrong with that timing. I've taken one bull on September 16 and two on September 22, so obviously I believe in hunting then. You'll generally hear the most bugling at this time and you can experience some great action, but don't think hunting then will necessarily be a snap. By then the bulls have well-established harems and the same bulls have been bugling at each other for some time so they're familiar with each other and they're getting tired. Also, by late September, most bulls will have been harassed by hunters, which only makes them that much harder to fool. They may quit bugling when you get close, and bulls with cows may simply run away from you.

After October 1, I think you'll find bugling toughest of all. That's not to say you can't call in a bull, but by then many of the cows have been bred and the heat of rutting activity has begun to cool. If early October is the only time you can plan a hunt, don't despair, because you'll still be able to locate bulls by calling. But if you have any choice, plan your hunt earlier.

Variables in Rut Hunting. Hunters commonly complain, "The bulls weren't bugling. Hot weather delayed the rut." That's not true. Rut timing is not weather-dependent. In order for calf drop to take place on schedule in the spring, elk must breed on schedule, so the rut is triggered by an annual constant—the length of daylight, or what scientists call photoperiod—rather than whims of seasonal weather. Come early September, elk come into rut, regardless.

Granted, during hot weather (and it's possible to get hot weather any time during September) elk spend more time during the day kegged up in heavy, cool timber, and they're more active at night. So your chances for get-

ting into hot action are poorer during warm spells than during cool weather, but that doesn't mean the elk aren't in rut.

Unseasonable cold or heavy snow or wind can turn off the animals, too. You can plan on getting hit by a blizzard or bitter cold snap any time in September, and when that happens, expect to have a hard time finding elk. Consistently, heavy weather puts an end to the bugling. I don't know if that's because the elk quit bugling, or if they seek shelter and I just can't find them, but I do know hunting can get tough during sudden harsh weather.

Learning to Call. The more you sound like a bull, the better your results. If you persist in blowing an old-fashioned whistle call, you're only robbing yourself of action. Hunting in Arizona, I bugled over a sweeping aspen basin and got an immediate response—from a hunter. How did I know it was a hunter? Because he was blowing an elk whistle, and I instantly recognized the distinct sound. If I could recognize his whistle as phony at a half mile, most elk probably could too.

Many excellent calls are available today. Some have plastic or metal reeds. These sound good, they're simple to blow, and they're durable. For general elk calling, a reed call serves pretty well. The big drawback is that you can't make a variety of sounds with them. The reed makes one kind of sound, and you can't really "personalize" it to add variety to your calling.

Diaphragm calls offer the best of all worlds. Exterior diaphragms have a thin piece of latex stretched over a plastic tube. You place your top lip over the top of the diaphragm and vary the pitch by stretching the diaphragm with your lower lip. These calls produce good volume, and you can make various bugling, grunting, and chirping sounds. The diaphragms are fairly fragile, however, so you're wise to carry replacements.

Mouth diaphragm calls are the most versatile. These fit inside your mouth so you can keep one ready for action all the time. With a mouth diaphragm you can produce any of a hundred sounds to "talk elk" fluently. Also,

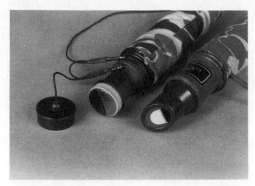

Two popular models of exterior diaphragm calls are the Jones Persuader on the left, and the Carlton Bull Getter. These employ latex diaphragms similar to mouth diaphragm calls, but they are blown outside the mouth.

Diaphragm calls like these have become popular among elk hunters. They fit in the mouth and require no hand movement for operation, and they can produce a variety of sounds.

you can blow the call without moving your hands, which can be significant when you have a bull within close range.

Many hunters use the mouth diaphragm in conjunction with a "grunt tube," a hose or plastic pipe about two inches in diameter that amplifies the volume of the call. A grunt tube may help produce an elky sound, but I'm convinced it's more for the gratification of the hunter than the elk. I just blow the call into my cupped hands and change volume by opening or closing my hands, and this has worked as well for me as a grunt tube. And it eliminates the bulky tube that bangs on branches and gets in the way in the woods.

Voice calling can be very effective, also. Some hunters bugle by expelling all the air from their lungs and then sucking in forcefully to produce a high-pitched squeal. This can be the most realistic method of all, but not all hunters can do it, and after a long day of hunting, you can end up with a raw throat.

Practicing the Sounds. You hear a lot of talk about sounding like a big bull or small bull. I think that's all irrelevant. I've seen small bulls with huge voices, and huge bulls with small voices. Don't worry about sounding small or big. Just try to sound "elky," and learn to produce a variety of elklike sounds.

The most common sound is the high-pitched bugle, which to me sounds more like a squeal, whistle, or scream than a bugle. Learn this call, as well as the various grunts, chuckles, and chirps made by bulls. It's impossible to describe all these sounds on paper, but suffice it to say that your success will be proportionate to the quality of your calling. Get a couple of instructional tapes and practice until you can do as well as the caller on the tape—or better.

Also learn to produce the squealing and mewing sounds made by cows and calves. One writer calls these sounds "cohesion squeals,"

Many hunters use grunt tubes in conjunction with mouth diaphragms. Tapes like this one produced by Golden Eagle help you to learn calling quickly.

because they help animals in a herd stick together. Some hunters refer to it as "herd talk." Many times cow and calf sounds will get a stronger response from a bull than bugling itself will. These are most easily imitated with a mouth diaphragm, and again, you can learn these sounds from tape recordings.

Locating a Bull. Sometimes locating a bull elk can seem simple. In Montana one year my friend Larry Jones and I hiked into a high basin our first morning in a new area, blew our calls, and immediately had five bulls talking around us. Nothing to it, right?

Another time in Oregon, I parked by a little grocery store, hiked up a wooded hill behind the store, and blew my call, 200 yards from a paved road. A bull answered, and a half hour later I called the bull within bow range. Simple, no?

In some cases, yes, but as a rule, locating a bull may be the toughest part of elk hunting. Elk herds can be widely scattered, and as I've said above, weather that's too hot or too cold or too windy can turn things off in a hurry. Then you'd swear every elk in the mountains has grown wings and flown south for the winter.

Keeping the wind in your favor is a major part of elk hunting. Coverup and attractor scents most commonly have been associated with whitetail deer hunting, but they might help in elk hunting, too.

The general scheme for locating elk goes this way: You hike along the top of a ridge, or crosscountry through good elk habitat, bugling as you go. As in all hunting, this presupposes that you're heading into the wind so animals won't smell you coming. The high-pitched bugle works best in these situations, particularly if you're on an open ridge bugling over a basin, but I also grunt and chuckle, because in heavy timber the lower frequencies carry better than high frequencies.

How often should you call? That depends on the country. My rule of thumb says to call often enough so you'll locate a bull by his calling before you accidentally walk into him and spook him. In broken, dense country you might bugle every 100 yards or so, but in open, sweeping country you might call and then walk a half mile before you call again.

Here are a couple of precautions about bugling. One, don't hike across meadows or open hillsides. Elk have tremendous eyes and will see you from a long way off. And don't bugle while you're standing out in the open. A nearby elk could come charging and catch you off guard before you have a chance to hide. Never get careless. Every time you blow that call, expect to have a bull come charging. Be ready.

Bugle several times at each location, and if you don't get an answer, move on and keep moving until you do hear a bull. I commonly hike five to ten miles in a day, up and down ridges, across drainages, around high basins, bugling and listening. If you're not getting answers, or seeing fresh sign, you're wasting your time there. Try somewhere else.

Moving In. Few bulls will travel a long distance to meet you, so once you've heard a bull, you'll probably have to close the gap between you and him. As a general rule I try to get within 200 yards of a bull before trying to call him in. Moving in, I remain quiet to avoid pulling him my way before I'm ready. On the other hand, if I'm not sure just where he is, I'll call again, often several times, to keep track of his location.

At 200 yards or so, I find a place to blind in. A good setup for calling in a bull consists of

Bugling is one of the best ways to locate a bull elk. Sometimes you can blow your call once and get an immediate response, but more commonly you must be patient and work an area carefully.

two crucial elements: open lanes to assure a clear shot, and good concealment.

In most cases, you've got plenty of time, so don't panic and start calling before you're ready. Every experienced elk hunter, including myself, can relate stories about calling a bull within easy range and then not getting a clear shot. In the rain forests of northern Montana, I've been unable to shoot at bulls as close as ten yards. That's because I blinded in hurriedly and didn't take time to find a clearing or opening where I was assured of an open shot. Make sure you have a clear lane on the downwind side. A suspicious bull will circle to get your wind and you want to be able to shoot that way.

Good concealment starts with camouflage (for details, see Camouflage), and it extends to finding a good natural blind. Try to blind in with cover behind you so you're not silhouetted, and also have some cover in front of you. I like to stand behind a small tree and cut out branches to open up shooting lanes in all directions. A bull would have a hard time seeing me hidden this way.

Calling Him In. With this kind of setup, you're ready to call in the bull. Normally I

bugle loudly first. Then with a big stick I rake on a tree and beat the brush to sound like an enraged bull taking out his wrath on the local vegetation. Then I listen to hear what the bull is doing. As a rule, I try to be the aggressor, bugling frequently and sounding as if I'm really getting angry, because this often will make the bull angry and he'll come in recklessly. I continue to bugle and rake and listen. If the bull responds well, I just keep it up, trying to sound more and more heated.

Often it's not long until the bull is coming in. He'll scream louder and louder, and you'll hear the brush rumbling and snapping as he plows toward you. But many elk are furtive, and they'll sneak in on you and just stand out there and holler at you, or they'll head the other way. What do you do then?

If a bull seems reluctant to come in, mix up your calling. Maybe quit bugling, and just grunt and rake on a tree. Or quit sounding like a bull altogether and just talk like a cow elk. Sometimes cow talk will stir up a bull more than bugling will. I don't pretend to know the meaning of all the different utterances, and I can't tell you just what to do to make him come in. But I do know if one thing doesn't work,

In a good bugling setup, you must have heavy cover behind so you're not silhouetted. With good camouflage, you'll blend in well. The idea is to stand motionless, bow raised and ready to shoot, as a bull approaches.

experimentation can pay off, because you often strike a cord that really sets the bull off.

If you call for a half hour or so and he still won't come in, try getting closer to him. Or break off calling altogether and, if conditions permit, stalk him.

If a bull runs away from you, he's probably got cows. Frequently herd bulls will bugle continually as you move in and you think, "Oh boy, I've got a hot one here." But then you get within striking distance, and the next thing you know, that bull is highballing the other direction, two ridges away. What happened? Did you blow it?

Not necessarily. I think herd bulls often would rather run than fight, so when you get threateningly close, they round up their cows and head out. You've got several choices. First,

you can run after the herd and keep harassing the bull, hoping he'll get so worked up he'll abandon all caution and come after you. I've seen this work and have talked to other hunters who've taken bulls this way.

Two, you can keep quiet and circle ahead of the herd to intercept them. This works well if the bull continues to bugle regularly so you know where he is, and if the wind is blowing the right way so the animals don't smell you as you get ahead of them.

Three, you can replace bugling with cow talk. A bull has no reason to run from a cow, and often the sound of a cow calling from the hidden forest will work him into a lather and he'll come right to you.

Four, you can stalk him. In terrain that offers good stalking conditions, this alternative works very well, particularly if you have a partner to help. One of you can stay a long way away and bugle to keep the bull bugling as the other stalks in silently.

Making the Shot. Hunters often ask me, "How long of a shot should I take at an elk?" There's no set answer, of course, because that depends a lot on how good you are with a bow (for details, see Shot Selection), but in general I think you can get very close shots at elk, say 30 yards and closer. All the elk I've shot have been between 8 and 35 yards, never farther. The average has been around 20.

If a bull comes directly toward you, don't panic and start flinging arrows. If you're well blinded—as you should be—the animal won't see you, so stand motionless and wait until he turns broadside. The lungs and heart present the only acceptable target on an elk, and to get that shot you just about have to have the bull broadside or quartering away. With patience you can get that shot.

If you shoot and miss and the bull takes off, immediately bugle loudly. Often you can stop him in his tracks, and just as commonly you can call him right back in. I've called in one bull as many as three times.

Even if you hit the bull, bugle as soon as he runs off. If you don't he could run a quarter mile or farther in frenzied flight. Sudden bu-

With patience, you normally can get shots closer than 30 yards on elk. And with a well-placed arrow, you can put yourself in this picture.

gling often will calm him down, even if he's mortally wounded, and he may stop or slow to a walk and drop within sight.

Stand Hunting

Bugling may be the most popular bowhunting method for elk, but it's not necessarily the best. Under the right circumstances, stand hunting can work just as well. (For details, see Stand Hunting.)

Water can be the key to stand placement. In Arizona and throughout the Southwest, elk live in relatively arid country and waterholes are limited. Elk must come to these to drink, and a patient stand hunter is virtually guaranteed of a shot if he sits at a waterhole long enough. Virtually every waterhole in northern Arizona has either a tree stand or a ground blind on it, and competition among hunters for these prime spots has led to conflicts (physical at times). I'm sure a high percentage of the elk taken by bowhunters in the Southwest are taken from waterhole stands.

In high-mountain country with abundant water, that system isn't reliable because elk aren't forced to use specific waterholes. Stands can still work if you scout thoroughly. As long as they're not disturbed, bulls will use the same wallows over and over, and some hunters have killed bulls by placing tree stands near fresh wallows. The emphasis must be on fresh. If the water has settled clear and tracks around the wallow have aged a few days, don't waste your time there. Bulls aren't using it.

Still-Hunting and Similar Approaches. To still-hunt for elk you must know the country and the habits of the elk. As mentioned above, elk live in herds and a lot of empty woods can separate each herd, so it makes little sense to start sneaking through the woods, hoping to see elk, without solid knowledge of their presence.

Bowhunter Shari Fraker has killed many elk, primarily by still-hunting. As a starting point, she scouts nearly year-round, and when the season arrives, she not only has several herds located, but she knows the habits of these animals and can anticipate their movements. To hunt them she sneaks very slowly, spending all day in one small area. Rather than camouflage, she wears brown clothing the color of an elk.

Still-hunting can work well for elk under the right conditions. But you must spot them before they spot you.

She figures if she gets caught moving, elk might mistake her for another elk.

This kind of hunting works best under specific conditions. During hot, dry weather, elk will spend virtually all day in the cool shade of heavy brush and blowdowns, and sneaking up on them there can be tough. During damp, cool days, they'll move around where they're more visible. I've watched elk feed in the open throughout the afternoon during misty, cold weather, and that presents an ideal situation for sneak hunting. (For details, see Still-Hunting.)

Elk often move deliberately from nighttime feeding grounds to daytime bedding areas, so under the right circumstances you can ambush them. One time, just after daylight, I spotted several cows and a bull feeding along the far side of a canyon. I picked a landmark directly in front of them and took off running. Since I had to go down my side and up the other, it took a half hour to get to the landmark, but I still got there before the elk and ten minutes later they fed by me single file at 25 yards.

Frequently you can head them off that way (as long as the wind favors you, of course). In some country (see description above) you can spot them just as you might deer, but in heavily timbered country, often that's not possible. Even in thick, black timber, though, you can follow elk by their bugling. Some hunters feel their chances for killing bulls are better if they refrain from calling (which gives away their presence and could run off the elk) and try stalking or ambushing the bulls instead. If you hear a bull bugle several times and know for sure he's moving as he calls, stay quiet and hurry to get in front of him and wait quietly for him to walk to you. I know of several large bulls that have been killed this way.

You can stalk elk similarly. Here again, you might locate them by spotting (for details, see Optics and Spotting) or by bugling. Some country with thick brush and blowdown timber doesn't lend itself to stalking, but in suitable places with quiet footing and trails or openings for sneaking, you can stalk elk efficiently. (For details, see Stalking.)

Trophy Hunting

Typical antler formation for mature bulls is six points on each side. Some exceptional five-point bulls will make the Pope and Young record book, but to score really well, a bull just about has to have six points on each side, and seven are better. You can judge the number of points at a glance, because the fourth, or sword, point is normally the longest tine. You just count back from there: and if the rack has two more tines behind the sword, it's a six-point; if three it's a seven-point.

As with deer, symmetry is important, and the weaker side of a rack will dictate the total score. For example, I shot a bull that appeared to have six points on each side, but one brow tine was broken off flush with the main beam. For scoring, that gave him only five points on that side, and in essence he was then measured as a five-by-five. He still scored 291, a pretty decent score for a five-point.

To score well a bull must have long tines. If the brow tines extend out a foot or so and then curve up nearly equal to the end of the nose, they're long. If they're relatively straight and shorter than the nose, they won't score well. The second tines should be equally as long or longer than the brow tines, and the third points also should be as long. Commonly, if a rack has a weakness it will be short third points. The sword points should be at least 16 to 18 inches long. The chest of a mature bull measures about 24 inches across, so you can judge rack dimensions by that. Main beams should be at least 45 to 50 inches long.

You can kill a bull large enough to make the Pope and Young book in virtually any state. It's a matter of hunting fairly remote country where bulls are living through rifle season. For truly huge bulls, Boone and Crockett–type animals, Alberta, Montana, and Arizona have been most consistent, and Wyoming and Idaho have good potential. Colorado, Oregon, New Mexico, and Washington have lots of elk and some fine bulls, but they don't have as high a percentage of truly huge bulls.

ENERGY By dictionary definition, "energy" means "the capacity for doing work and for overcoming inertia. Potential energy is that

To score well a bull must have long tines. Notice that the brow tines on this bull, which scores 419⅝, come well out over the nose, and the second and third tines are as long or longer. Also notice the mass and long main beams. These are the traits of high-scoring antlers.

due to the position of one body relative to another, and kinetic energy is that manifested by bodies in motion."

Potential, or stored, energy then, is the amount of energy a bow stores in its limbs at the full-draw position. Thus, a 60-pound bow held at full draw stores 60 pounds of potential energy. The stored mechanical energy of a bow is similar to the electrical energy stored in a car battery or flashlight cell. It has the potential for doing work, but it must first be released.

Kinetic energy is the amount of energy delivered by a moving object, in this case a free-flying arrow. Kinetic energy is a function of mass and velocity (V), and it can be computed with this equation:

TYPICAL KINETIC ENERGY HUNTING USAGE

Arrow Velocity In Feet Per Second

Arrow Grain Weight	150	155	160	165	170	175	180	185	190	195	200	205	210	215	220	225	230	235	240	245	250	255	260	265	270
	Small Game or Competition							**General Hunting – Big Game With Light Tackle**														**Big Game**		
300	14.99	16.00	17.05	18.14	19.25	20.40	21.58	22.80	24.05	25.33	26.65	28.00	29.38	30.80	32.24	33.73	35.24	36.79	38.37	39.99	41.64	43.32	45.04	46.79	48.57
325	16.24	17.34	18.47	19.65	20.86	22.10	23.38	24.70	26.05	27.44	28.87	30.33	31.83	33.36	34.93	36.54	38.18	39.86	41.57	43.32	45.11	46.93	48.79	50.69	52.62
350	17.49	18.67	19.90	21.16	22.46	23.80	25.18	26.60	28.06	29.55	31.09	32.66	34.28	35.93	37.62	39.35	41.12	42.92	44.77	46.66	48.58	50.54	52.54	54.59	56.66
375	18.73	20.01	21.32	22.67	24.07	25.50	26.98	28.50	30.06	31.67	33.31	35.00	36.73	38.50	40.31	42.16	44.05	45.99	47.97	49.99	52.05	54.15	56.30	58.48	60.71
400	19.98	21.34	22.74	24.18	25.67	27.20	28.78	30.40	32.07	33.78	35.53	37.33	39.17	41.06	42.99	44.97	46.99	49.06	51.17	53.32	55.52	57.76	60.05	62.38	64.76
425	21.23	22.67	24.16	25.69	27.27	28.90	30.58	32.30	34.07	35.89	37.75	39.66	41.62	43.63	45.68	47.78	49.93	52.12	54.37	56.66	58.99	61.37	63.81	66.28	68.81
450	22.48	24.01	25.58	27.21	28.88	30.60	32.38	34.20	36.08	38.00	39.97	42.00	44.07	46.20	48.37	50.59	52.87	55.19	57.56	59.99	62.46	64.99	67.56	70.18	72.86
475	23.73	25.34	27.00	28.72	30.48	32.30	34.18	36.10	38.08	40.11	42.19	44.33	46.52	48.76	51.06	53.40	55.80	58.26	60.76	63.32	65.93	68.60	71.31	74.08	76.90
500	24.98	26.68	28.42	30.23	32.09	34.00	35.98	38.00	40.08	42.22	44.42	46.66	48.97	51.33	53.74	56.22	58.74	61.32	63.96	66.65	69.40	72.21	75.07	77.98	80.95
525	26.23	28.01	29.85	31.74	33.69	35.71	37.77	39.90	42.09	44.33	46.64	49.00	51.42	53.90	56.43	59.03	61.68	64.39	Largest,	Toughest	Game	75.82	78.82	81.88	85.00
550	27.48	29.34	31.27	33.25	35.30	37.41	39.57	41.80	44.09	46.45	48.36	51.33	53.87	56.46	59.12	61.84	64.62	67.46	70.36	73.32	76.34	79.43	82.57	85.78	89.05
575	28.73	30.68	32.69	34.76	36.90	39.11	41.37	43.70	46.10	48.56	51.03	53.66	56.31	59.03	61.81	64.65	67.55	70.52	73.56	76.65	79.81	83.04	86.33	89.68	93.10
600	29.98	32.01	34.11	36.28	38.51	40.81	43.17	45.60	48.10	50.67	53.30	56.00	58.76	61.60	64.49	67.46	70.49	73.59	76.75	79.99	83.28	86.65	90.08	93.58	97.14
625	31.23	33.35	35.53	37.79	40.11	42.51	44.97	47.50	50.11	52.78	55.52	58.33	61.21	64.16	67.18	70.27	73.43	76.66	79.95	83.32	86.75	90.26	93.83	97.48	101.19
650	32.48	34.68	36.95	39.30	41.72	44.21	46.77	49.40	52.11	54.89	57.74	60.67	63.66	66.73	69.87	73.08	76.37	79.72	83.15	86.65	90.22	93.87	97.59	101.38	105.24
675	33.73	36.01	38.37	40.81	43.32	45.91	48.57	51.31	54.12	57.00	59.96	63.00	66.11	69.30	72.56	75.89	79.30	82.79	86.35	89.98	93.69	High	Stress	105.28	109.29
700	34.98	37.35	39.80	42.32	44.93	47.61	50.37	53.21	56.12	59.11	62.18	65.33	68.56	71.86	75.24	78.70	82.24	85.85	89.55	93.32	97.17	101.09	105.09	109.18	113.33
725	36.23	38.68	41.22	43.83	46.53	49.31	52.17	55.11	58.13	61.22	64.41	67.67	71.01	74.43	77.93	81.51	85.18	88.92	92.75	96.65	100.64	104.70	108.85	113.07	117.38
750	37.47	40.02	42.64	45.35	48.14	51.01	53.97	57.01	60.13	63.34	66.60	70.00	73.46	77.00	80.62	84.33	88.11	91.99	95.94	99.98	104.11	108.31	112.60	116.97	121.43
775	38.72	41.35	44.06	46.86	49.74	52.71	55.77	58.91	62.13	65.45	68.85	72.33	75.90	79.56	83.31	87.14	91.05	95.05	99.14	103.32	107.58	111.92	116.36	120.87	125.48
800	39.97	42.68	45.48	48.37	51.35	54.41	57.56	60.81	64.14	67.56	71.07	74.67	78.35	82.13	85.99	89.95	93.99	98.12	102.34	106.65	111.05	115.53	120.11	124.77	129.53

This chart shows computed kinetic energy for arrows of various weights flying at varied speeds. *Chart courtesy Precision Shooting Equipment, Tucson, Arizona.*

$$\frac{V^2}{450,240} \times \text{arrow weight (grains)} = \text{F.P. (foot-pounds of energy)}$$

Let's say your 60-pound bow shoots a 550-grain arrow at 200 feet per second. To figure the kinetic energy you first square the velocity ($200 \times 200 = 40,000$), divide that by 450,240 (40,000 divided by $450,240 = .089$) and multiply that by the arrow weight in grains ($.089 \times 550 = 48.9$). Thus, a 550-grain arrow flying at 200 fps delivers 48.9 foot-pounds of energy.

Knowing how to compute kinetic energy has value in a couple of ways. First, it helps you determine the "hitting power" of your bow. For example, many bowhunters would say bows should deliver at least 40 foot-pounds of energy for hunting deer-size game and 50 foot-pounds or more for elk and other large game. Second, it helps you determine the efficiency of your bow. As you can see, even though the 60-pound bow used in the example above stores 60 pounds of energy, it delivers only 48.9 foot-pounds of kinetic energy, which means the bow is about 80 percent efficient. For mechanical devices, that's very high efficiency. (For more details, see Bow Efficiency and Penetration.)

F

FEATHERS Traditional arrow fletching material. (For details, see Fletching.)

FIELD DRESS See Meat Care.

FINGER TAB Commonly called a tab, the finger tab is a small slab of leather or plastic that protects your string fingers and assures a smooth release. It's held in place by a rubber or plastic ring or a leather thong around the middle finger. Finger tabs comes in various sizes to fit different hands. (For details, see Release Aids.)

FISHTAIL This term describes undesirable side-to-side wobble of an arrow as it is shot from a bow, as opposed to porpoising, which describes up-and-down wobble. Probably the most common cause of fishtailing is shooting arrows of the wrong spine weight, although a sloppy string release, fletching contact with the side of the bow or arrow rest, and other tackle deficiencies can cause an arrow to fishtail. (For solutions, see Bow Tuning.)

FISTMELE This term comes from a medieval word meaning "fist measure," a method for gauging string height. Longbow shooters place the base of the fist on the grip of the bow and extend the thumb. They consider the bow

properly braced if the tip of the thumb just touches the string. For the average man, fistmele would be six to seven inches. Some longbow shooters still use fistmele as a means of gauging proper string height, but more commonly archers today refer to the distance from the string to the low point of the grip as brace height, and they measure this with a specially made bow square. (For more details, see Brace Height.)

FLETCHING This is the guidance system on the back end of an arrow. To be of value, it must steer an arrow on a straight course, maintain good speed, and be quiet and durable.

Vanes versus Feathers

Vanes are plastic fletching. Most are made of urethane, vinyl, or Mylar. Feather fletchings are mostly made from turkey-wing primary feathers.

The subject of vanes versus feathers breeds debate among archers. I've shot both feathers and vanes over a number of years, and I've interviewed any number of experienced archers on this subject, so I can make some comparisons. I've tried to be objective, but many of my conclusions are subjective, based on my personal style of hunting.

Problem Fletching. Strictly from a hunting

197

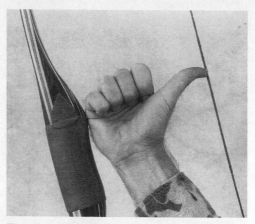

Fistmele is a traditional way to measure the proper distance from the handle of a bow to the string.

viewpoint, I see two problems with feathers. One, they're noisy. If you're hunting from a tree stand where you're not moving, or you use a back quiver that covers the fletchings, that may be irrelevant. But I do a lot of stalking in brush and I use a bow quiver that leaves the fletchings on my arrows exposed, and the scratching of feathers against brush with that setup is unacceptable. All serious bowhunters wear the quietest clothes possible, which is only smart, but one careless move with a feather-fletched arrow can defeat the best clothing system. I'd take vanes to feathers any day if for no other reason than quietness.

Two, feathers aren't nearly as dependable as vanes. Sure, you can spray them with silicone or whatever. I've done that many times, and it may help protect them if you accidentally dunk the feathers in a creek and can shake out the water quickly. But during an all-day, drenching rain, feather treatments are worthless. Feathers mat down and you might just as well shoot bare shafts. A friend of mine swears by feather fletching, but when we're elk hunting he's forever fretting over his feathers, either looking for a plastic bag to cover them or stopping to build a fire to dry them out. And in the car he fumes and fusses over his bow to make sure it's laid just right so his feathers won't get smashed. With good vanes, you can forget all that nonsense.

Along this same line, vanes are much more durable. After a few hundred shots, feather fletching looks like the wings of a moth that got too close to the flame, yet good vanes will last virtually forever. I've shot some vane-fletched arrows thousands of times and have never had to refletch them.

Accuracy. Now comes the bottom line in all bow hunting—accuracy. I doubt that one kind of fletching is more potentially accurate than the other. At least, no bowhunter is good enough to detect the difference. If feathers were inherently more accurate, you'd see nothing but feathers on arrows at major archery tournaments, but that's not the case. Many major competitions have been won with vanes.

Of course, you can't really compare target arrows and heavy hunting arrows tipped with broadheads, and many feather advocates would say feathers are needed to steer a broadhead well. That's probably true for oversized broadheads that try to steer an arrow. The arrow needs some major drag at the back to keep it flying straight. But it seems to me that's more an indictment of the broadhead than a claim for feathers. You don't need huge, heavy broadheads to kill big game. Any sharp broadhead that weighs from 125 to 150 grains and measures wider than one inch will do the job. And vanes will steer that head just as well as feathers.

The idea is to get as near-perfect arrow flight as possible. The fact is, with the right setup and a little time spent tuning, you can get broadhead-tipped arrows to fly as well with vanes as with feathers. (For details, see Bow Tuning.)

Of course, the qualifying phrase there is "the right setup." To shoot vanes well, you have to use an elevated rest on your bow, and you have to shoot a bow that's cut past center to assure vane clearance.

Forgiving Feathers. Many recurve bow shooters like to shoot off the shelf, and validly so: it's a simple, trouble-free way to shoot. To do that you must shoot feathers. They compress as they brush by the shelf to give good arrow flight. Vanes, in contrast, will hit the shelf, bounce off, and send your arrow careening.

Even with an elevated rest, you might have trouble getting clearance with vanes. Wood-handle bows—compound or recurve—typically aren't cut as far past center as metal-handle bows because more wood is needed for strength. As a result, you may not be able to get complete vane clearance, especially if your arrows are a little underspined. One solution is to shoot feathers. Then it doesn't matter if your fletching brushes the bow because the feathers will compress and slide on by.

Some hunters would say feathers are superior for hunting because they're more forgiving of shooting errors. I don't think that's wholly true, because adequate vane fletching will stabilize an arrow and forgive shooting errors, too. Where feathers are more forgiving is in tackle-tuning errors. If you shoot a bow with inadequate clearance or your arrows are spined incorrectly for your given draw and arrowhead weight, then feathers will help compensate and you might get reasonable arrow flight even with poorly matched tackle. If you're happy with that, fair enough. But here again, the fact that feathers perform better for you is not so much a claim for feathers as a critique of your tackle.

Speed. Finally comes the question of arrow speed. Feathers weigh somewhat less than most vanes—on the average about 30 grains less for three five-inch fletchings. As I've pointed out elsewhere, every five grains of variance in arrow weight equals about one foot per second difference in arrow speed. Thus, given identical shafts and heads, arrows fletched with feathers will leave the bow appreciably faster.

But what about down range, where the arrow is hitting the animal? The very point that supposedly makes feathers superior to vanes—more drag—can make them less effective. In essence, feather fletching produces a mild flu-flu effect. The feathers are like small parachutes, and they not only stabilize an arrow well but they slow it down. Bob Ragsdale, a bow designer for PSE, chronograph-tested a number of arrows fletched with vanes and feathers. He shot vane-fletched arrows weighing 540 grains and feather-fletched arrows weighing 506 grains. As you would expect, the feather-fletched arrows took off from the bow somewhat faster. One yard from the bow they flew at 186 feet per second compared to 182 for the vane-fletched arrows.

At 14 yards, however, they were both flying 179 feet per second, and from that point on the heavier-vaned arrow traveled faster. At 60 yards it flew at 167 feet per second compared to 165, and because the arrow with vanes was heavier (and flying faster) it had more kinetic energy—33.45 foot pounds compared to 30.60.

In my opinion, feathers have two things going for them. One is the forgiving nature that allows you to shoot off the shelf. The other is tradition. There's something about doing things the old way that keeps the romantic appeal in bowhunting, and plastic isn't consistent with that romance. On the other hand, virtually all bows made today, including longbows and recurves, have plastic in the limbs to add durability and to improve performance. I can't see much difference between plastic in the bow or on the arrows. It's put there for the same reasons.

Fletching Variables

All fletching must be chosen with two aspects in mind—steerage and clearance. Probably the most important consideration is steerage. It must steer your arrow straight to the target.

Amount of Fletching. Undoubtedly the most common fletching configuration is three five-inch vanes or feathers. These are set on the arrow either with a straight clamp offset two to three degrees, or they're put on with a helical (twisted) clamp. (For details, see Arrow Making.) I've tried a number of combinations, and I usually come back to three five-inch vanes put on the arrow with a moderate helical twist. Shooting Zwickey Eskimo broadheads or Thunderhead 125s, this fletching gives me good arrow flight.

Most of the serious bowhunters I know

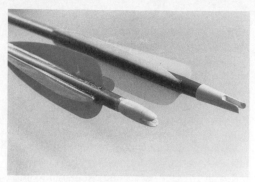

The two most common fletching configurations are four four-inch vanes or feathers, shown at left, and three five-inch vanes or feathers.

fletch their arrows with a fair amount of helical twist. Dick Tone, who has spent his life in bowhunting and tournament archery, has tested fletching and broadhead combinations extensively.

"It's tough to get broadheads to fly well with straight or slight offset," Tone said. "I prefer a tight helical, and with that you can control two and three blade heads with three five-inch vanes. In order to control big four-blade broadheads, though, you may have to use four five-inch vanes or feathers."

Some bowhunters prefer four-inch vanes over five-inch because they're slightly lower profile, which can give better clearance as the arrow passes the bow and rest. Also, with some overdraw setups, the arrow rest and bowstring are so close together that five-inch vanes will ride up on the rest when an arrow is nocked. Four-inch vanes will fit between the string and the rest.

With four-inch vanes, most hunters fletch their arrows with four vanes. A major advantage of four-fletch is that your arrow can be nocked either way. You don't have to worry about turning a cock vane out.

"Four-fletch makes a good setup," Tom Fisher said. "It's lower profile than five-inch so you get better clearance, and you can turn your arrows either way. I'm a firm believer in four-inch, four-fletch, as long as it's put on with helical twist."

Direction of Twist. Some hunters debate which way fletching should be twisted. Convention has always said that a right-handed shooter should fletch his arrows with a right helical twist and lefties should fletch with a left helical twist. I've never found it makes much difference which way vanes are twisted, and most authorities I've talked with agree.

Feathers, on the other hand, must be fletched according to the wing they come from. Feathers off the right wing are twisted to the right, and feathers off the left wing are twisted left. But whether right-hand shooters shoot right-wing feathers, and left-handed, left, doesn't matter. Larry Nirk, a major manufacturer of wood arrows, said, "It makes no difference whether you shoot left or right helical or left or right wing. I've always made up all my arrows with left-wing feathers because turkeys were clipped on the right wing, so left-wing feathers were more plentiful. But it's mostly a matter of personal preference," Nirk said.

Choosing Vanes

Durability. To be of any value, vanes must be durable. That's a major reason for shooting them, and not all vanes qualify. For one thing, they must retain their shape. If they're smashed in your bow case or are pulled through a target,

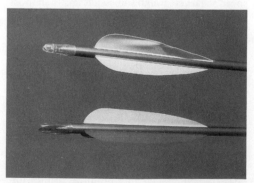

To be of value, vanes must be durable, and they must return to their original shape after abuse. The vinyl vane on top has taken a set and after two weeks, it hasn't straightened out. The urethane vane below was equally crumpled, but it has flattened out.

they must return to normal shape. Vanes made of urethane do this best. Vinyl vanes take a set, and once they're bent they stay bent. Urethane is also strong and you have to work at it to tear it up. PSE Pro Fletch, Flex-Fletch, Bohning Fletch-Tite Vanes, and Plastifletch by Arizona Archery Enterprises are all excellent, durable vanes.

I've found that Dyna Vanes, which have little ridges much like feathers and cutouts in them to reduce wind planing, are very accurate. Dick Tone said he found that Dyna Vanes seem to stabilize broadheads better than standard vanes. The one problem I've found is that they aren't as rugged as regular, solid vanes and a few times through a target butt will tear them up.

Spin Wing vanes, made of Mylar, have proved exceptionally accurate in competitive shooting, and they're available in five-inch lengths for hunting. They're lighter than feathers and give good steerage so they show promise, but the Mylar is rigid so it's noisier in brush than soft urethane. It's also brittle and won't withstand a lot of punishment, so these vanes aren't ideal for rough hunting conditions.

Fletching Repair

As I've said, good plastic vanes will return to normal shape even when they're smashed or pulled through a target. Nevertheless, constant abuse could bend them permanently, but you can restore them fairly well if you steam them and rub them into shape. Feathers will also spring back to their original position by steaming.

Shooting tight groups at the target butt, you'll shoot holes in your vanes. The holes won't seriously affect accuracy, but they'll hiss as the arrow flies. You can eliminate that by cutting the hole out of the vane with scissors or a sharp knife. If feathers or vanes get torn up too badly, you're wise to replace them. (For details, see Arrow Making.)

FLORIDA This state covers 58,560 square miles, and has more than 60 wildlife management areas covering 6 million acres, all open

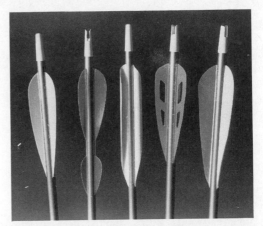

Fletchings come in many styles and sizes. Shown here, left to right, are four-inch conventional vanes, Bi-Delta vanes, Mylar Spin Wings, four-inch Dyna Vanes, and five-inch feathers.

to public hunting. Three national forests are included in this management-area program. Most private land in Florida is leased by clubs or commercial hunting operations, so chances of getting permission to hunt just by asking are slim.

Big Game

Deer. An estimated 650,000 whitetail deer occupy about 70 percent of the state. Florida sells an average of 22,000 archery licenses each year. The average total harvest for a recent ten-year period has been 62,000 deer. Florida doesn't keep separate records for firearms and bowhunters, so no figures are available for archery harvest or success rates.

Archery deer seasons open in late September or early October and remain open for a month. Exact dates vary by region. An additional archery-muzzleloader season has been open for two weeks or more in February. Generally the bag limit is two bucks per day, three in possession, with no season limit. These rules apply generally, but dates and bag limits vary on state wildlife management areas.

For management purposes, the state is broken into five regions. The northwest uplands are covered with pine and oak forests and commercial pine plantations. Deer are numerous, and this is the least human-populated region of Florida so hunting pressure isn't excessive. Northeast Florida has extensive pine flatwoods and agricultural development, so there is less good wildlife habitat than in the northwest. Still, deer numbers are good in some localities and hunting pressure is relatively light.

The central region supports a lot of agriculture and high numbers of people, and deer numbers are generally low on private land, although the Ocala National Forest supports a good herd. South Florida consists primarily of pine flatwoods with a limited deer-carrying capacity. Human population is high, so hunting pressure is heavy on the few public lands.

The Everglades region contains extensive flatwoods as well as thousands of acres of marshland. Fluctuating water levels pose severe management problems, so the total carrying capacity of the Everglades is low, about one deer for every 75 to 100 acres. Hunters must use air boats, half-tracks, or other specialized vehicles to penetrate the marshes, so hunting this region is difficult at best.

Pigs. Florida is the number one wild pig state in the United States with an annual harvest of 70,000 or more. On public lands pigs are considered big game, and there are seasons and bag limits. These vary by area. On private

land pigs aren't classified as game animals, and landowners can set their own regulations.

Bears. Florida offers limited bear hunting in the northeast region. The annual harvest is fewer than 100 animals.

Other Game

Florida has excellent turkey hunting and offers both spring and fall seasons. Squirrel hunting is good.

Contact. Game and Fresh Water Fish Commission, 620 South Meridian Street, Tallahassee, FL 32301.

FLU-FLU ARROW Oversized feather fletching on flu-flu arrows causes them to slow much more quickly than arrows with normal fletching. They're used for shooting into the air at birds or thrown targets, and into trees at small game. They shoot with good speed out to 30 yards or so, and then they slow rapidly and fall to the ground after a flight of less than 100 yards. Flu-flus are much safer than normal arrows for shooting into the air, and they're a lot easier to find.

Making Flu-Flu Arrows

Flu-flu arrows are easy to make with a full-length turkey wing feather. Lay one end of the feather on the shaft and wrap a rubber band around it or hold it down with a wire twist used on plastic bags (you can pin it to a wood shaft).

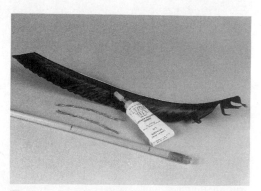

These are the materials needed to make a simple flu-flu arrow: A full-length turkey wing feather, fletching glue, two sandwich bag twist wires, and an arrow shaft.

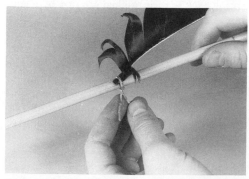

With a wire twist, secure one end of the feather to the arrow.

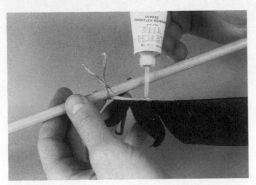

Apply a generous bead of glue the full length of the feather's quill.

Secure the other end of the feather with the other wire twist. Fluff up the barbs on the feather. Wait an hour or so for the glue to harden, remove the wires, and you've got a flu-flu arrow ready to shoot.

Spread a bead of glue the full length of the split quill of the feather. Now spiral the feather around the shaft so the flat side of the quill lies flat against the shaft and the barbs of the feather spread out to form a fan. Spirals should be wide enough so the feather covers four inches or more of the shaft.

When you've wrapped the entire feather around the shaft, rubber band or pin the other end in place. Wait a couple of hours for the glue to dry and take off the rubber bands. Install a head on the arrow and you've got a flu-flu ready for action.

You also can make flu-flus by fletching arrows in a normal fashion with five-inch feathers, except that the feathers should not be burned or cut. They should be left full height.

FOOTWEAR   See Clothing and Footwear.

FORCE-DRAW CURVE   You often see this term in reports on bow efficiency. It may seem like Greek at first, but the principle is simple. A force-draw curve is nothing more than a graphic picture of the force (that is, your effort) required to draw a bow. You can make a force-draw curve for any bow. The only tools required are a bow scale (for details, see Bow Scale), pencil, and graph paper.

The graph paper should be marked with the draw weight in pounds along the left side and

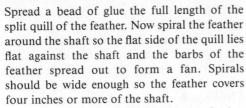

Wrap the feather around the shaft.

These are two popular types of flu-flu arrows. The one at left is fletched with four uncut, five-inch turkey feathers. The other is made from a spiraled turkey feather.

203

Golden Eagle Hunter - @ 55 lbs.

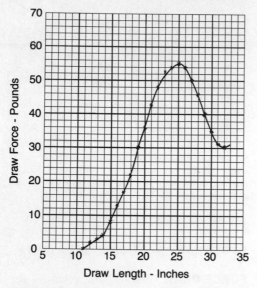

A force-draw curve graphically describes the amount of force (energy) required to pull a bow to full draw.

draw length in inches along the bottom. Put your bow on the scale and slowly start to measure the draw weight. Stop at one-inch increments, note the draw weight, and make a dot on the graph paper in the appropriate spot. Continue to draw the bow and mark the weight at one-inch intervals on the graph paper until you reach full draw.

Now (after you let your bow down from full draw), connect all the dots on the graph paper. You should end up with a smoothly curving line. That line shows how the draw weight of your bow increases and, in the case of a compound bow, decreases. By plotting the force draw for several bows you can compare graphically the comparative amount of work required to draw each one. You also can figure out the amount of stored energy for each bow. The greater the amount of space contained under the curve, the greater the stored energy. (For more details, see Bow Efficiency.)

FREEZING See Target Panic.

G

GAME TRACKER A game tracker, or string tracker as it's commonly called, is a cannisterlike device that screws onto the back of your bow. It contains a spool of fine, tough string several hundred yards long that is attached to the tip of your arrow. When you shoot an animal, the string uncoils from the spool to leave a string trail through the woods.

Some bowhunters have found this device especially valuable in turkey and bear hunting. An arrow-hit turkey, unless its wing is broken, can fly off, and it won't leave a blood trail, so a string tracker offers about the only hope for finding it. Many turkey hunters swear by string trackers.

Bears leave notoriously poor blood trails because their loose hides and fat can seal off an arrow hole and their thick fur can absorb a lot of blood. Some avid bowhunters always use tracking devices to help in recovering wounded bears.

Game trackers aren't foolproof. Obviously, restringing an arrow will take a while after a shot, so for all practical purposes, the tracker is a one-shot device. And string drag on the arrow limits the effective range. Out to about 20 yards, the arrow flies close to normal, but beyond that it's slowed by the string, and it will hit low. The longer the distance, the lower it

will shoot. Before you use one in hunting, practice with it to gauge your trajectory, and limit your shots to ranges at which arrow flight isn't affected.

Limited shooting distance normally poses little problem in hunting bears and turkeys because shots on these animals should be close, but that's not the case with all animals. For that reason, few archers use tracking devices for deer, elk, and other game. Besides, big-game animals with thin hides and short hair normally leave a good blood trail, so a string tracker isn't needed.

GEORGIA With 58,406 square miles, Georgia is the largest state east of the Mississippi. Private-land hunting is fairly restricted for the general public in Georgia. Virtually all good private lands in the Piedmont and southern regions are leased by private clubs. Clubs are not as prevalent in the Blue Ridge and other northern regions. National Forest land provides some public hunting, and the Oconee National Forest east of Atlanta receives heavy pressure. The state maintains about 1 million acres for public hunting on a number of wildlife management areas, and several military bases offer public hunting.

The northern end of Georgia has mountains up to 4,000 feet elevation and forestlands are extensive here. Deer densities range from 15 per square mile in pure hardwood forest areas to 25 per square mile in agricultural areas. The Piedmont region, which runs in a band across the upper one third of the state, is the richest deer area. Densities are 35 to 40 deer per square mile, and 50 percent of the state's annual kill comes from this one region. Pine plantations are prevalent throughout the rolling country here.

Agriculture, primarily in the form of peanuts, cotton, and soybeans, is extensive on the upper coastal plain so deer numbers aren't exceptionally high, but some very large bucks are killed here. The lower coastal plain, which borders Florida and the Atlantic Ocean, contains extensive swamps, pine flatwoods, and palmettos, and deer numbers range from 25 up to 60 per square mile. Deer are relatively small in size here.

The state record typical whitetail scored 184, and the record nontypical 242. The upper coastal plain and Piedmont regions produce the largest bucks.

One example of a game trailing device is Saunders' Trail Tracker. The loose string end attaches to the arrow head. When an animal is hit, it pulls string off the spool to leave a trail of thread through the woods.

Other Game

Turkeys. Spring hunting these birds is a big deal in Georgia, and the annual harvest is about 10,000 (obviously not all bow-killed).

Small Game. Squirrels are abundant throughout the state, and seasons are generous. Pecan farmers are often more than willing to let hunters thin out the squirrels in their orchards. Rabbits live through the state wherever suitable brushy cover exists.

Contact. Department of Natural Resources, 270 Washington Street, S.W., Atlanta, GA 30334.

Big Game

Whitetail Deer. Biologists estimate the deer population at 850,000 animals. Georgia sells about 40,000 archery licenses each year, but no figures are available on bowhunter success. The general gun season opens in mid-October. In the northern zone it closes in early December, and in the southern zone it extends into early January. Archery season opens in mid-September and remains open through the Friday preceding the gun season. Bag limit is three of either sex.

GIARDIASIS This malady has become very common and should be of concern to hunters. It causes acute diarrhea, stomach cramps, and vomiting that can last for days. These are bad enough in themselves, but they also can cause severe dehydration if you're caught in the backcountry for many days. Giardiasis can bring an otherwise good hunting trip to a quick halt.

The infection is caused by a parasite with the Latin name *Giardia lamblia*. These parasites can infest even seemingly pure waters, and drinking even cold water from spring-fed streams doesn't guarantee you won't get it. Giardia are spread through the feces of mammals. It's particularly common among beavers, so many hunters call giardiasis "beaver fever."

Many animals also spread bacteria and other germs through their feces, and these can infect backcountry waters. Some bacteria can cause disorders similar to giardiasis.

Unless you find water bubbling directly from the ground, you're safest to treat all water before drinking. Boiling is one way to purify water. Most authorities recommend boiling for 5 minutes at sea level and adding 1 minute for every 1,000 feet of elevation. Thus, if you're at 10,000 feet, you'd boil water for 15 minutes. You also can purify water chemically with iodine or chlorine. These are available in tablets, and if used according to directions, they'll kill giardia and other germs.

GLOVE   A shooting glove consists of a wrist strap connected to three finger stalls. It's designed to protect a shooter's fingers and to assure a smooth release. (For more details, see Release Aids.)

GRAIN   A unit of measure commonly used in archery to express the weight of an arrow. One ounce equals 437.5 grains. Hunting arrows may weigh anywhere from 400 to 800 grains or heavier. Powder scales used in cartridge reloading as well as some special archery scales are calibrated in grains, and these are handy tools for the serious archer.

GRIZZLY BEAR   See Bear.

GROUSE   Many bowhunters supplement their diets with forest chickens whenever opportunity presents itself. Blue grouse may be the most commonly taken, particularly by Western deer and elk hunters. These big birds live on higher, dry ridges in pine and mixed conifers. Ruffed grouse live across the United States and Canada in dense bottomlands, aspen groves, and willow patches. Spruce grouse are common in damp conifer forests of Canada and states of the Pacific Northwest, and they're commonly taken by elk hunters.

Few archers go out specifically for grouse, but they often shoot these birds incidentally to big-game hunting. All grouse make for excellent eating, whether roasted over an open fire, fried in a pan, or baked in foil. Rubber blunts are the best grouse heads. (For more details, see Small-Game Hunting.)

GUIDED HUNT   See Outfitters and Guides.

H

HARES Hares are members of the genus *Lepus*. Members of this genus live from endless deep-freeze conditions along the Arctic Ocean to endless oven conditions of Southwestern deserts. Best known to bowhunters are the varying hare (or snowshoe rabbit, as it's more commonly called) and the jackrabbits of the West. European hares also have been introduced to some localities of the United States.

Hares Versus Rabbits

Hares and rabbits have different characteristics. Hares have much longer ears and longer legs, and they can run swiftly for long distances. Rabbits such as the cottontail, in contrast, have short ears and legs, and they tend to scamper and hop short distances into cover. Hares live in forms (open nests under bushes) whereas rabbits live in burrows, tree roots, rocks, or similar enclosed shelter. Hares are born with a good coat of hair and with their eyes open, but rabbits are born naked and with their eyes closed.

Hares also undergo drastic population fluctuations. Starting at very low levels, they begin to build until they nearly overrun the land. In southern Idaho, landowners trying to save their crops have been known to herd jackrabbits by the thousands into enclosures and club them to death. Needless to say, that practice has received widespread publicity (not all of it favorable). At other times the same country seems totally devoid of rabbits. Snowshoe hares exhibit similar fluctuations.

Some people think these ups and downs are cyclic, say on a seven-year pattern, but most biologists think they're irregular, periodic eruptions. In regard to jackrabbits, fluctuations don't necessarily cover a broad region. Rabbits can be plentiful in one valley and scarce in the next. If your traditional jackrabbit haunts are down, look around. Other places may have plenty of game.

Snowshoe Hares

These animals range across all of forested Canada and Alaska, and the northern tier of states in the Lower 48, and they're common in the conifer forests of the major mountain ranges of the United States—the Cascades, Rockies, and Appalachians. They weigh two to four pounds.

Snowshoes are brown in summer and turn white in winter, which explains why they're also called varying hares. They're popular game animals in some regions, particularly the upper

The snowshoe, or varying hare, is a popular game animal in the northern conifer forests of North America. In summer these animals are brown, and they turn white in winter.

Midwest and East. In the West, snowshoes are killed most commonly for camp meat in conjunction with elk and deer hunting.

Varieties of Jackrabbit

Because of their large ears, jacks were originally called jackass rabbits. I've read they were also called narrow-gauge mules. Can't you imagine calling up your hunting partner and saying, "Hey, let's go hunt some narrow-gauge mules!"

The blacktail jackrabbit dwells in desert and prairie country from Canada to Mexico and from California to Kansas. These large hares average three to four pounds in weight, but may weigh as much as seven. Their black-tipped ears are six to seven inches long and the top of the tail is black. Blacktails are by far the most common jackrabbits. Whitetail jacks, the largest of North American hares, weigh six to eight pounds. Whitetails live in high-elevation grasslands and mountains throughout the northern Great Plains, Rocky Mountain, and Pacific states. In summer these animals are brownish gray, and as the name implies, the tail

is pure white. In winter, whitetails turn a pale gray or white, much as snowshoe hares do. Antelope jackrabbits, big rangy animals nearly silver in appearance and with huge ears, live in southern Arizona, Texas, and Mexico.

Some states regulate jackrabbit hunting with closed seasons and bag limits, but most states regard jackrabbits as nongame and allow year-round hunting with no bag limit. For that reason, these animals provide nearly unlimited shooting opportunity for archers.

Locating Jackrabbits

Watching for dead rabbits on the highway may be the surest way to scout. Jacks aren't very car wary, and if they're abundant at all, you'll see dead ones on the roads. If you're on dirt roads where few rabbits would get hit, drive around at night to watch for jacks scuttling in the headlights. Jackrabbits are nocturnal, so you may see dozens where they seem nonexistent during the day. Return the next day to hunt where you've seen the most.

Not all desert country promises good hunting. William Clark, who studied jackrabbits in

Utah, said the jack's principal defense is its eyes, so the broken terrain with rock outcroppings preferred by cottontails generally doesn't hold many jacks. These animals prefer open, flat country, and they're particularly abundant on alkali flats dotted only with clumps of greasewood.

In winter, Clark caught animals for his studies in sheltered spots. "Jackrabbits congregate in swales and sagebrush bowls where they're protected from wind and where snow is shallowest," Clark said. "They're also opportunists and will congregate near the best possible feed. Alfalfa fields and seedings of crested wheatgrass attract lots of animals."

In Arizona, Charlie Ash looks for them near the best forage and shelter from heat. "Some Southwestern desert is very sparse and has few rabbits," Ash said. "I look for washes with ironwood, palo verde, creosote bush, and mes-

quite. Finding jacks in the shade there is almost guaranteed."

Hunting Jackrabbits

You'll see by far the most rabbits early and late in the day, out feeding on greenery, so that's the time to spot them and sneak close for a shot.

During the day you can walk around and jump them. They'll usually sprint for a short distance, but unless they're really spooky, they won't go far, and you can watch where they stop and sneak in on them. As long as they feel securely hidden, they'll often hide and you can walk within good range.

One hunter I talked to herds them. He and his friends spread out 50 yards apart and walk parallel with a mesh sheep fence. Rabbits won't cross through the fence unless they're forced to. The hunters push rabbits toward a cross fence

Open alkali flats and endless deserts are the province of the blacktail jackrabbit.

In hot weather, jacks will often sit tight and let you stalk within bow range. Frequently you can spot jackrabbits by looking for pink spots where the sun shines through their ears.

and corner them and shoot as the rabbits run for cover. Shooting with a bow at running rabbits isn't any serious threat to the animals, but it's fun.

In contrast, Charlie Ash in Arizona takes the slow approach. He deliberately hunts jacks in the heat of summer because the animals sit tight then.

"I move a step or two at a time, using binoculars to watch 100 to 200 yards ahead," Ash said. "A rabbit will sit absolutely motionless except for one thing—his twitching ears. That's what I look for. And I watch for pink spots where the sunlight shines through the ears."

Pat Miller used his regular big-game bow and arrows tipped with rubber blunts to take this desert jackrabbit.

Once he's spotted a resting jack, Ash stalks in carefully. "If I can put a bush between us, the rabbit tends to forget I'm around. Then I can move in real slow for a close shot."

Ash points out that summer hunting has drawbacks. Heat is one, and rattlesnakes is another. "In the cool morning I often see rattlers," he said. "One time I shot a rabbit and it flopped right over a big rattler. I almost stepped on the snake as I retrieved the rabbit. I don't sweat snakes bad enough to quit hunting in summer. It just adds spice to rabbit hunting."

Tackle for Hares

Most likely you'll shoot jackrabbits as practice for hunting, and you'll take snowshoes in conjunction with hunting, so you'll shoot your normal hunting bow. To prevent shooting through these animals, use Judo heads, rubber blunts, or stoppers such as Saunder's Roverine behind a field point or a Zwickey Scorpio behind a broadhead. Don't shoot them with straight field points, broadheads, or steel blunts, or your arrows will go on through and you'll just wound the rabbits and probably lose your arrows. (For more details, see Small-Game Hunting.)

Eating Jackrabbits

Somewhere along the line some squeamish individual started a rumor that you can't eat jackrabbits, and the idea just keeps getting passed along. Tain't true. You can and they're good. That rumor probably started because people think all jackrabbits are full of disease. That isn't true either. At least, jackrabbits are no more disease-ridden than cottontail rabbits or any other rodents. Some do carry tularemia, but you can easily avoid those animals. Plague is very rare among solitary animals such as rabbits. There's no good reason for discarding jackrabbits. I've eaten dozens, and find them as good as any other small game. (For more details, see Small-Game Hunting.)

HAWAII Hawaii has a total area of 6,450 square miles.

Big Game

Deer. Hawaii has no native deer. Axis deer, transplanted from India and Ceylon, now number about 10,000 on the island of Lanai. Molokai and Maui also have some axis deer. Blacktail deer were transplanted from Oregon in 1961, and an estimated 500 blacktails live on the island of Kauai.

Archery deer hunters number about 150 residents and 10 nonresidents, and they take an average of four deer each year. These statistics apply to public hunting areas only; they do not include private land. No regulations govern hunting on private lands in Hawaii. Each island that contains deer has large public hunting areas.

The bag limit for blacktails is one buck deer per season per hunter, and hunting is allowed only on the five weekends preceding the last full weekend in October. Hunters are assigned hunting days by public drawing. Hunting for axis deer is allowed only on weekends for nine weeks in March and April. The bag limit is one deer. Hunters are assigned hunting days by public drawing.

Pigs. Bowhunting has become popular in Hawaii because of the wide-open opportunity to hunt pigs, goats, and sheep, which are considered pests in many areas. Pigs were introduced by early settlers and now they're common on all the islands. Seasons are liberal on pigs and much public land is open to pig hunting, although as everywhere else these animals are found, heavily hunted pigs get hard to fool. Several large private ranches offer guided pig hunts, and you'll find easiest pickings here. In some areas the season is open year-round with a daily bag limit of two animals.

Goats. Feral goats also live on all the islands, and these animals can be hunted on both private and public lands under liberal regulations. In some areas the season is open year-round.

Sheep. Hawaii has mouflon sheep, feral sheep, and mouflon-feral hybrids. One form or another is found throughout the islands. Seasons vary by area, but some bow seasons are open year-round.

Contact. Division of Forestry and Wildlife, 1151 Punchbowl Street, Honolulu, HI 96813.

HEAT EXHAUSTION AND HEAT-STROKE These physiological injuries result primarily from hard exertion in hot weather. Inadequate intake of water is a major contributor. Hot-weather problems may seem irrelevant to bowhunters because many hunting seasons take place in cold weather. Some seasons, however, particularly in the West, open in July and August, and heat at this time can pose major concerns.

Heat Exhaustion

Water Needs. If you sweat long hours day after day, and don't replace lost liquids, you gradually dehydrate. Heat exhaustion is the result. Prevention consists of adequate fluid intake. During hard activity, you can't drink enough to replace fluids as fast as they're lost, so you must continue to drink during rest breaks and in the evening around camp. Under normal conditions, you lose as much as two quarts of body fluid a day through sweating, urination, and other normal functions, so you must drink two quarts just to replace that normal loss. During hot weather, with increased sweating, you'll lose more than a gallon of liquid a day, so you must drink that much to keep your body functioning well.

Symptoms. Common signs are weakness and fatigue, irritability, headache, dizziness, and vomiting. A victim's skin will be cool, clammy, and pale, his temperature normal.

First Aid. A victim should lie on his back with feet elevated twelve inches or so. Use wet cloths to keep him cool, and have him sip lightly salted water. If he vomits, don't force him to drink. He should rest and stay out of the hot sun for at least a day after recovery.

Heatstroke

Prevention. Heatstroke (or sunstroke, as it is often called) is much more serious than heat exhaustion. It's caused by a rapid rise in internal body temperature (the opposite of hypothermia, a decrease in body temperature). It can kill you in a hurry. Heatstroke occurs when your body produces heat faster than it can get rid of it, a distinct possibility in warm to hot weather when you're exerting hard.

To prevent heatstroke, rest often to cool down, and drink as much as you can. Never set out in hot weather without adequate water. At the same time, do everything possible to enhance body cooling. Wear light clothing that promotes dissipation of heat, and wear a light hat that prevents sun from beating directly onto your neck and head. Allow breezes to blow through your clothes to evaporate sweat, and take advantage of any water supplies to soak your skin and clothes to enhance cooling.

Symptoms. Heatstroke can strike rapidly, particularly if you're out of shape. At first a victim will sweat heavily and get irritable and tired, and he may have a severe headache and feel dizzy and nauseated. As his body temperature rises to 105 degrees, he will collapse, and his skin will become hot, dry, and red (opposed to the cool, pale, and moist skin produced by heat exhaustion). Dry skin indicates that sweating has stopped, and when that happens, body temperature rises even faster. When internal temperature hits 108 to 110 degrees, the victim dies.

First Aid. This all can happen in a matter of minutes, so don't go for help. Apply first aid immediately, which consists of lowering body temperature quickly. If possible, immerse the victim in ice water. If that's not possible, lay him in the shade, strip off his clothes, and pour water over his body. Then fan him to enhance cooling. Keep pouring on water and fanning until his temperature returns to normal. Take him to a doctor.

HIP QUIVER   See Quiver.

HOUND HUNTING   This is the practice of using dogs to locate game animals. The dogs also chase the game and either bay it on the ground or chase it up a tree until the hunter arrives on the scene. In North America, hound hunting most commonly involves mountain lions or bear, although dogs are used to run wild pigs and deer in some regions. Hounds are also used to run bobcats, raccoons, and various other predators and small-game animals. (For more details, see Black Bear and Mountain Lion.)

HUNTING BASICS   In professional sports, you often hear coaches refer to "getting back to basics," and frequently, teams that stress fundamentals rather than razzle-dazzle are the ones that emerge as perennial winners. I think that hunters who learn the basics, who dwell on fundamentals and master them, most consistently fill their tags. The following list covers what I consider hunting basics, the elements of hunting that you must know and practice to be a well-rounded big-game hunter. Some of these might seem peripheral to you, but if you ignore any one of these steps you only weaken your foundation as a hunter.

Planning

All good hunting starts with location. Ask any really competent hunter why he does well and he'll tell you it's because he's hunting in a good spot. Trophy hunters who quest for only the biggest animals, particularly trophies that will make the record books, place major emphasis on planning. They know they must locate special, small localities with just the right mix of food, cover, and refuge to produce huge animals. Kirt Darner may be the most famous trophy deer hunter of recent times (he hunts with a rifle but the same principles apply to bowhunting) and in his book, *How to Find Giant Bucks*, he devotes two complete chapters to location and hunt planning. Two other chapters on scouting also stress the importance of location in trophy hunting.

We're not all after just huge animals, of course, but the same principles apply to a lesser degree in all hunting. Even if you're happy just killing a forked-horn, you'll stand the best chance for doing that if you plan first to locate a good area. Obviously, if you just want to hunt near home and are willing to accept what you find there, or you desire to hunt with an outfitter and leave the details to him, then planning may play a small role in your hunting scheme. But if you're looking for the best possible hunting and will travel to take advantage of it, and if you want to hunt on your own, then planning must be considered a basic.

Hunt planning involves several predictable steps: extensive reading, map study, talking to local sources, record-book analysis, and study of hunting regulations from several states. Don't take planning lightly. It guarantees great hunting, trip after trip. (For details, see Planning a Hunt.)

Scouting

Scouting becomes the second logical step in making any hunt work. Planning puts you in good territory, but scouting tells you what to do with that territory. Both planning and scouting serve the same function—getting you into game—but scouting takes place on the ground, right where you've planned to hunt. It could be called on-site planning.

Many serious whitetail hunters start scouting the day after the season closes in late fall and they continue on through winter, spring, and summer right up until the opening of next hunting season. They build an intimate knowledge of their country and their quarry, and that's why they take nice bucks every year.

If you plan to hunt far from home—say you'll travel from New York to hunt mule deer in Colorado—you obviously can't do that. Some hunters plan a family summer vacation to their hunting country, and that's ideal. If you can't do that at least try to arrive in your hunting country a couple of days ahead of time to allow for scouting. Even if you arrive during the season, you're wise to forget hunt-ing right away and to scout a day or two before you start hunting seriously. (For details, see Scouting.)

Hunting Methods

Once you've found game, you have to apply hunting methods adapted to the country and game you're hunting, and you must develop skill in whichever methods you choose. It's one thing to have knowledge; you can gain knowledge by reading this and other books. But to develop skill—that is, to make your knowledge work for you—you must practice the following hunting techniques in the field.

Stand Hunting. Without question, stand hunting has become the most popular method among bowhunters, for one good reason—it works. On a stand, you remain motionless, as inert and unnoticed as the trees and rocks themselves, and the game moves to you. To make stand hunting work, you must know your country and habits of the animals, so stand hunting requires a solid background of scouting. You must find trails, runways, bedding or feeding grounds, breeding scrapes, or natural travel routes, such as saddles, as locations for stands. (For details, see Stand Hunting.)

Still-Hunting. With this method, you move slowly along on the ground, trying to spot animals before they spot you. I purposely don't say "walk" along, because walking and still-hunting are far removed. Still-hunting can be deadly under the right conditions. (For details, see Still-Hunting.)

Spotting. To hunt effectively by any method, you must be able to see animals before they see you. That involves using the right optical gear, and it means learning to look in the right places at the right times. Game spotting underlies all good bowhunting. (For details, see Optics and Spotting.)

Stalking. This method works particularly well in open, steep country such as desert or alpine terrain. Common quarries are mule deer, antelope, bears, and bighorn sheep, but stalking works just as well in many cases for whitetails or elk. Spotting is the beginning step because you must first see an animal. Then you sneak within range, undetected. It can be a very efficient method because, as in stand hunting, you almost always spot animals before they spot you, and that gives you the greatest advantage you can have as a bowhunter. (For details, see Stalking.)

Driving. This method is more popular with rifle hunters, because driven animals often move too fast to present a good bow shot. Nevertheless, driving does have its place in bowhunting, and two or more hunters working together can help themselves greatly by pushing animals to each other. (For details, see Driving.)

Calling. Many hunters shun calling because they have no faith that it will work, but in many cases it can be deadly. Antler rattling has accounted for many rutting whitetails, and bugling is no less effective on elk during the rut. Calls that imitate the bleating of fawns are used to call deer within range, and many avid predator hunters imitate the sounds of a hurt rabbit to call in coyotes, bobcats, even bears. And, of course, turkey hunters rely heavily on calling to outsmart wary toms in the spring. Calling works on many game animals, so perfect your calling techniques to round out your basic hunting repertoire. (For details, see Deer Calling, Elk, Predator Calling, Rattling, and Turkey.)

Baiting. Baiting can't be considered a universal hunting method, but it does have its place, particularly in bear hunting. In many regions, baiting has become the predominant method used by archers to take bears. In essence, it involves putting out food, commonly meat scraps or pastries, to attract bears. When a bear starts "hitting" a bait, you put up a stand nearby and wait for the bear to come in. (For details, see Black Bear.)

Hound Hunting. Hound hunting is no more universal than baiting, but it too must be recognized as a legitimate hunting method that fills a niche in the overall hunting picture. Hounds most commonly are used to hunt bears and cats. (For details, see Black Bear and Mountain Lion.)

Tackle

Planning, scouting, and hunting ability help you find game and put you within range, but tackle determines whether you put an animal on the ground. Perfecting your tackle involves more than one-stop shopping at the local discount store. You can buy yourself a bow and some arrows there, and probably even the needed accessories, but that doesn't make you an archer. Tackle must be refined and set up for your specific shooting style, and accessories must be chosen to help you get the most from your physical and mental ability. Tuning your bow, selecting arrows and fletching, choosing the right broadheads, fitting your bow with the best rest—all these and much more go into perfecting your tackle. Getting the most out of your tackle must be considered a basic to good bowhunting. (For details, see Bow Tuning and Tackle Basics.)

Shooting Ability

Fine tackle means nothing if you can't utilize its potential. From my limited observation, I'd say probably the greatest weakness among bowhunters in general is lousy shooting. They don't know the basics of good form. You must have proper stance, hand and arm position, release, and followthrough to shoot well, and that's true regardless of the tackle you shoot or the conditions under which you're hunting. If you want to excel as a bowhunter, learn the basics of shooting before you start hunting. (For details, see Shooting Basics.)

Physical Condition

All right, you say, now he's getting a little far afield. Scouting and hunting method and tackle certainly qualify as basics, but physical condition? What's that have to do with climbing into a tree stand and shooting a deer?

In all honesty, it probably has little to do with stand hunting, but it definitely has much to do with success as a Western hunter for elk, mule deer, and other mountain game. I've asked a number of outfitters why clients fail to collect game, and in most cases they say their hunters simply poop out before they could get a shot.

Western hunting, with its steep mountains, high elevations, and long miles of hiking, demands physical endurance. Unless you've prepared physically, you'll hunt far below your potential. If you work outside at a laborious job year-round, then you may be set to go, but if you have a sedentary job, you'll be in no shape for Western hunting unless you work out regularly to stay in shape. Don't kid yourself into thinking it's enough to know where the animals are and to be a great bow shot. If your legs buckle and your lungs give out before you get to the animal you want, your hours of planning and shooting practice are for naught. (For details, see Physical Condition.)

Camp Gear, Clothing, and Other Gear

Tents and clothes are hunting basics? Absolutely. If you can't endure and persevere under the worst of conditions, you'll find yourself defeated more often than not. One of my most ignominious hunting defeats came not because I couldn't find animals or because I missed easy shots, but because my clothing and camp gear weren't suitable for the conditions.

Clothing. Hunting clothes must fulfill several criteria. They must be quiet to prevent spooking animals; comfortable to allow easy movement; snug so as not to interfere with bow shooting; warm enough for the coldest conditions or cool enough for hot weather; and water-resistant in rain or snow. Similarly, footwear must allow quiet movement while protecting your feet. (For details, see Camouflage and Clothing.)

Camping. If you hunt out of your home, then this may not apply, but if you travel to hunt, you have to know camping basics. Your hunting camp can be simple or elaborate, cheap or expensive; it might consist of a backpack tent, a small canvas tent, an elaborate wall-tent village, or you might live out of the back of your truck. Whatever the method, you have to assure yourself protection from the elements, a place to dry clothing, and warmth. (For details, see Camping.)

Hunting and Survival Gear. Most hunters, particularly in the West where a day's hunt can take you far from camp, carry a hunting pack with necessities such as game bags, knife, saw and rope for hanging meat, spare bowstring, extra broadheads, and so forth.

They also carry survival gear. If you're worried about getting too far from camp or getting lost, then you'll hunt far below your potential. You must assure yourself the ability to make your way in the woods in the dark and to survive if something does go wrong. With this assurance, you can hunt effectively as far from camp as required to kill the game you want. (For details, see Hunting Pack and Survival.)

After the Shot

What does it mean to "get" game? Putting an arrow in an animal? Not at all. I think "getting" an animal means you recover that animal and retrieve it from the woods in edible condition, and that brings up two more important hunting basics.

Trailing. If you've bowhunted at all, you know that animals can travel a long way, even when hit mortally with an arrow. For that reason, trailing plays a significant role in successful bowhunting. You must learn to read blood sign, to follow tracks, to observe hair, broken twigs, smeared mud, or any other clue that will lead you to your downed animal. Perfecting trailing and tracking skills serves as one of the unquestionable basics of bowhunting. (For details, see Trailing.)

Meat Care. Even finding an animal in fresh condition guarantees nothing in terms of edibility. Any butcher who handles game meat can tell dozens of sour-meat horror stories, and in most cases he'll lay blame directly on the hunter. You must know how to gut, skin and butcher game in the field, and you must know how long you can keep it at any given temperature. This knowledge is basic to getting your game. (For details, see Caping and Meat Care.)

The Mind

Most writers dwell heavily on the mechanics of hunting, those basics I've listed above. They ignore possibly the most crucial aspect of all: the hunter's mind. This seems to imply that all hunters continually have a good time in the field and that scoring on game is the only thing on their minds. If you've hunted at all, you know that's not a true picture; you know, in fact, that defeat comes more often from mental breakdown than from lack of gear or hunting ability. Hunters not mentally prepared often just give up when they should be gearing up for a renewed assault. To excel as a hunter, you have to develop realistic expectations, and you must learn to accept defeat.

At home it's easy to dream about the big buck coming under your stand or the bull elk charging to your call and standing broadside at ten yards. Dreams like this make bowhunting the great sport it is, but the reality of hunting doesn't always fulfill those dreams. Reality often includes cold, fatigue, long gameless days, and other traumas that the subconscious mind conveniently leaves out of dreams. To counteract that, you have to consciously dwell on and prepare mentally (as well as physically) for the realities. If you develop realistic expectations before the hunt, you won't be shocked into retreat in the face of hard times.

No bowhunter can always fill his tags with the kinds of animals he wants, so learning to accept defeat also plays a basic role in successful, long-term bowhunting. You'll miss shots, you'll stumble or make noise just when a trophy buck presents the shot of a lifetime, other hunters will blunder on the scene at critical moments — in bowhunting any number of things can go wrong, and you must learn to accept the defeat cheerfully and carry on. If you dwell on failures, on what might have been, you'll defeat yourself as a bowhunter. Developing an attitude of success may be the most important hunting basic of all.

HUNTING GEAR   The following is a generic list of items that go with me on all hunting trips. This could be considered an inclusive list, and not all items apply to all kinds of hunting. Extract those items that apply for you and compile a checklist so that any time you

head to the field, you can just run down the list to quickly assemble your gear.

Bow
Quiver full of arrows (six hunting, two
    practice in eight-arrow quiver)
Finger tab or release aid
Armguard
Range finder
Binoculars
Spotting scope
Calls: elk, turkey, predator, deer, etc.
Rattling antlers
Scents, coverup and attractor
Camouflage face cream
Bowstring wax
Bow sling or spare arm
Tree stand and accessories
Stalking socks
Hunting pack with survival and hunting gear
Camouflage pants, shirt, hat
Longjohns and other undergarments
Boots or hiking shoes
Head hugger to hold glasses snug
Sweat band to keep sweat out of eyes
Tackle box with spare parts and repair
    equipment

HUNTING PACK   In the past a lot of hunters just slipped a knife in one pocket, a candy bar in the other, and away they went. Today it seems like virtually every bowhunter you see in the woods, at least in the West where hunting can take you far from the road, carries a fanny pack, rucksack, special back quiver, or some other kind of pack filled with hunting and survival gear. Hunters today try to equip themselves well, but even at that, it seems most are never satisfied. They're all still searching for the perfect hunting pack.

What you carry and what you carry it in, of course, can vary according to where you hunt. If you just walk 50 yards from your car to a tree stand, you probably won't need ten days' worth of survival gear. But even on simple, close-to-home hunts, how do you know you won't gash your hand and need a first aid kit, or get turned around in fog and need a compass? In Missouri, a pretty civilized state, I got lost in a foggy woodlot and probably would have walked into the next county if I hadn't hit a stream I knew for sure was suddenly running the wrong way. A quick compass check in any country can save you a lot of time and wasted energy.

A hunting pack must hold everything you need to hunt well and to survive any emergency. To be of value, it has to be on hand when you need it, so probably most important are convenience and comfort. If it's too big, heavy, or bothersome, you'll leave it behind occasionally, and that's when you'll learn the First Rule of Survival—you'll need something most when you don't have it. The corollary, of course, is, if you always have it with you, you'll never need it. I'll take the corollary any day.

Criteria for a Pack

Weight. Obviously the lighter a hunting pack the better, so select items carefully. Five pounds would be ideal, but I commonly end up with ten pounds (or more), because I slip in an extra camera, maybe a telephoto lens, a little extra food, and so forth. But I can hunt comfortably with ten pounds in a pack, so I'm willing to carry that much. You have to gauge your own limits.

Comfort. If a pack hurts your shoulders or gives you a stiff neck, you'll dread carrying it and will leave it in camp. For me, comfort means it must be supported at the waist, because even a lightweight rucksack that hangs without support kills my shoulders. If you don't have that problem, you can ignore some of what I say, but one fact is true for everyone: you can carry more weight comfortably if it's supported by your shoulders *and* your hips.

Along the lines of comfort, you have to be able to move without restriction. You can't hunt or shoot effectively if your pack binds every time you bend or twist. It must fit like part of your body.

Convenience. If you have to load your pack every time you head to the field, you'll leave it behind 90 percent of the time. It must be packed, ready to go, all the time, hassle-free. Buy items specifically for the hunting pack and

leave them there. Don't try to get double duty from them around camp or in the car.

Quiet. If the zippers rattle and the cloth shrieks every time you brush a branch, the pack will do more harm than good. On one elk hunt a friend of mine wore a large packframe as a daypack. Calling in a bull, we had to move several times quickly, and every time we set up, my friend had to take off his bulky pack. As he set it down, it scratched and clattered so loud I felt like torching the thing. If a pack makes noise, slows you down, or hampers your stealth in any way, it's no good.

Heavy Loads. Occasionally I carry extra cameras, a tape recorder, a heavy coat, and other items needed in special circumstances. A fanny pack or skimpy rucksack won't handle loads like that.

Even more important is carrying meat. If you're hunting within a quarter mile of a road, this might not be relevant, but if you're far in the backcountry and kill a deer or elk, you want some way to pack out meat. With an inferior pack, you'll have to deadhead to camp for your packframe and then back to the animal just to start packing. With the right pack, you can load up an elk quarter or half a deer right there and carry it out as you go to save yourself a complete round trip.

Pack Styles

Fanny Pack. For near-road, mild-weather, or tree-stand hunting, a small fanny pack or belt pack proves more than adequate. It's small, rides out of the way against your back, and carries plenty of items to serve short-range needs. Some companies even make giant fanny packs that hold everything including the kitchen sink. Only problem is, when you load up one of those freighters, it sags on your rear and bounces up and down when you move fast. A friend of mine made a big leather fanny pack and sewed in all kinds of little compartments and cubbyholes to hold his gear in place. The thing looks like a filing cabinet inside and it will hold more gear than the average hunter would carry. If you're creative, you probably can dream up a similar design.

The fanny pack holds basic hunting and survival gear, and it has become popular with bowhunters.

Rucksacks. Next come rucksacks, small bags supported only by shoulder straps. Manufacturers usually call them daypacks or book bags. They'll do the job and a lot of bowhunters use them, but I personally don't like rucksacks. As I said earlier, weight supported only by shoulder straps hurts my shoulders, especially after a long day of hunting, and unsupported weight on your back can produce a stiff neck. The more weight you carry, the worse the problem gets, so it severely limits the amount of weight you can carry. Besides, a rucksack with any kind of load gets bulky and the nylon (most are made of nylon) scrapes against branches.

As you might guess, I'm not in love with rucksacks. However, I do have a rucksack–fanny pack combination, made by Vector Pack Systems in Lafayette, Colorado, that works quite well. You can strap the two together to form one unit so that the rucksack rides on the fanny pack. That takes some of the weight off your shoulders, and with the two in combination you can carry a bunch of gear.

Frameless Packs. The next step up might be a small frameless or internal-frame pack with a padded hip belt. I've used packs like this made by Coleman and North Face that were big enough to stuff in more gear than you'd want to carry in a day, and with compression straps on the sides you can pull the load tight to reduce bulk and to keep things from shifting. Best of all, these packs have padded hip belts, so you can support most of the weight on your hips, rather than on your shoulders. Most packs like this have a foam pad that rides against your back, which makes the pack comfortable, but it poses a problem common to all frameless or internal-frame packs: you sweat heavily where the pack lies against your back.

Frame Pack. That's where the external packframe comes in. It rides away from your back to allow air circulation so you don't soak your clothes with sweat. Not only that, but with an external frame you can carry a lot heavier load more comfortably. With a small frame you can pack out a quarter of an elk or half a deer, something you'd have a hard time doing in a fanny pack.

Coleman Company makes indestructible

Some hunters like a small rucksack like this because it will hold more gear than a fanny pack. It can be tiring on your shoulders.

One of my favorite hunting-pack systems employs a small Coleman youth-size frame. With the straps attached to the top, the frame rides low so it won't catch on branches, even when I bend. My gear is contained in a small waterproof bag secured with bungee cords.

This is another style of frame made into a hunting pack. This small aluminum frame is out of the way while hunting, and it's comfortable. Yet it's strong and can pack a lot. Pat Miller has carried a quarter of an elk on this small, sturdy frame.

injection-molded polyethylene packframes. These come in two sizes—the full-size frame for bigger men, and the youth model for persons up to about five feet six inches tall. I use the smaller one for a hunting pack. It's shorter and narrower than the full-size model, so when it's on my back it fits snugly. If I can fit through an opening, the pack will slip through without hanging up.

To make it work, I modified the pack a couple of ways. First I took off the nylon pack bag, which is too big and is made of noisy nylon, and replaced it with a small waterproof bag made for river rafting. It holds all my gear with room to spare, so I roll down the top to eliminate all extra space. Then I strap the bag to the frame with rubber bungee cords. This holds everything tight so nothing rattles or sloshes. I can jog with this pack on, and it doesn't bounce or make any noise. To make it even quieter, I slip a wool cover over the waterproof bag.

Most packframes don't work as hunting packs because they stick up above your shoulders; when you bend over to go under limbs, the top of the frame catches. Coleman frames have a unique "lash tab" system that allows infinite adjustment, so I've attached the shoulder straps to the top of the frame instead of the

normal position several inches below the top. Rigged that way, the top of the frame rides below my shoulders, and branches slide off the straps. I've taped all the lash tabs in place so they won't rattle, and I've also wrapped the frame with an elastic band (it's made by Saunders as bow camouflage) to camouflage and silence it. You could wrap it with camo tape.

This isn't the only frame that will work, but whatever kind you choose, consider the benefits of a small frame as a hunting pack. Again, to be valuable a backcountry hunting pack must compact enough so it doesn't increase your "body size"; it must be quiet and comfortable; and it must be stout enough to carry some weight. A small frame, modified to the right specifications, fills the bill.

Gear for the Hunting Pack

Regardless of the pack you choose, it should always contain certain survival and hunting items. Some gear should go with you regardless of conditions, whereas other gear might be contingent. If you don't wear eyeglasses, for example, there's not much reason to carry a spare pair.

Survival gear (for more details, see Survival)
    Flashlight
    Map

Compass
Firestarters
Knife
Sharpening stone or steel for knife
First aid kit (Bandaids, sterile 3 x 3-inch
  gauze pads, adhesive tape, gauze roll,
  aspirin, moleskin, small bar of soap)
50 feet of nylon cord
Whistle for signaling
Signal mirror (could be built into compass)
Fluorescent plastic flagging
Aluminum cup
Three feet of surgical tubing for water
  siphon
Water-purification tablets
Pen
Snakebite kit (in known snake country)
Sunburn protection (on bright snow)
Sunglasses (on bright snow)
Plastic for emergency shelter
Toilet paper
Needle and thread (to repair disastrous rips)
Lunch and high-energy foods
Warm sweater or shirt
Rain gear
Bota bag full of water (if pure water not
  available in field)
Bow-repair equipment
  Extra bowstring
  Spare axle keepers
  Spare arrow rest
  Allen wrench for limb bolts (or bow
    stringer)
  Spare broadheads
Camera and film
Hunting license and tags
Insect repellent (in buggy country)
Game bags (in warm weather)
Plastic bag for heart and liver
Spare eyeglasses (if you wear glasses)
Folding saw (for off-road areas where you
  must saw antlers from head or possibly
  build emergency shelter)

HYPOTHERMIA Exposure is another name for hypothermia. You might question what this has to do with good bowhunting, and the answer is, "Plenty." To hunt well you must feel comfortable and safe, and hypothermia probably poses one of the major threats to your well-being in the field. Hypothermia kills many outdoors people each year, and the insidious nature of this injury probably contributes to the toll. When you see a rattlesnake or bear, you recognize the potential danger and avoid it if possible. With hypothermia, you may not realize you have a problem until it's too late. It sneaks up on you. That's why understanding the nature of hypothermia and constantly taking preventive measures is so important.

Preventing Hypothermia

To function well, your internal body temperature must remain at about 99 degrees. When it drops much below this, bodily functions begin to deteriorate. If internal temperature drops low enough, you lose all control and eventually die.

Studies on hypothermia at the University of Victoria, British Columbia, have shown that a person in 32-degree water will die within about 1½ hours, and in 50-degree water in about 3 hours. The process takes longer in milder conditions, but it can still happen. That's why it's so important for bowhunters to understand this condition, even for early-season hunting. Forty-degree weather seems relatively mild, but when you combine that with a 20-mile-per-hour wind, you get a wind chill equivalent of 20 degrees. Adding moisture accelerates cooling even more, so even relatively mild 40-degree air combined with the chilling forces of wind and water can kill you.

To prevent hypothermia, first of all stay dry. It doesn't matter whether it comes from falling rain, sweat, or any other cause, water is water, and through evaporation and conduction of heat, water chills you quickly. That's why it's so important to dress right. Obviously, you need rain gear to keep you dry during rain or snow, but just as important, you must dress in layers to regulate heat during physical activity. When you're exerting, you shed layers to prevent sweating; when you rest, you add layers to preserve body heat. In particular, protect your head, neck, and trunk of your body. These are areas of major heat loss. In any cool weather, carry a warm hat, scarf, or other neck protection, and a vest or jacket to protect these vital areas. (For more details, see Clothing and Footwear.)

Signs of Hypothermia

Shivering, an involuntary muscular action to generate body heat, is a first sign that you're getting excessively cold. If you're alone and start shivering badly, stop and warm up. Build a fire if necessary, but don't ignore the sign, because if deep-body temperature starts to drop you may not be able to help yourself. If one of your partners begins shivering hard, insist that he stop and warm up before continuing the hunt.

When a person becomes exhausted by shivering, his core body temperature will begin to drop. When it hits 90 degrees, shivering will cease and muscles will stiffen. The victim may become disoriented and move erratically. At 85 degrees, he may become totally irrational, and when body temperature drops to 80 degrees, he'll pass out and die.

First Aid for Hypothermia

First, prevent further heat loss. Get the victim out of the wind, strip off wet clothes, and provide heat. Once core body temperature has dropped below 95 degrees, a person can't generate enough heat to rewarm himself so an external heat source is needed. Again, if someone is just shivering hard, a roaring fire will provide the heat needed for rewarming. Drinking hot liquids helps too because that carries heat right to the core of the body where it's needed most.

For a person who has stopped shivering, further steps may be needed. A warm bath is ideal, but those are scarce in hunting camps, so other action may be necessary. If a person has stopped shivering, you must act fast. Strip him and wrap him in a sleeping bag with other people. The more skin-to-skin contact the better, because it will speed rewarming. Remember, simply stuffing a hypothermic person into a sleeping bag by himself won't do any good because a bag doesn't generate heat, it only preserves it. A person suffering hypothermia is generating little heat; you must provide heat from an external source.

I

IDAHO This Northwestern state with an area of 82,708 square miles can be divided into three general regions. The panhandle consists of very steep mountains blanketed with dense rain forests. Central Idaho, roughly from the Clearwater River south to the Snake River, contains some of the roughest and most remote country in the Lower 48. The Church–River of No Return Wilderness on the Salmon River, and the Selway-Bitterroot Wilderness just to the north, total nearly 4 million acres. The southern one third of the state, south of the Snake River, consists of pure sagebrush desert. Virtually all the best big-game hunting in Idaho takes place on public land, primarily national forest, so getting permission to hunt big game here rarely poses a problem.

Big Game

Deer. About 17,000 archers take an annual average of 800 deer, half bucks and half does, with a high kill of 1,200. Average bowhunting success has been 11 percent. Idaho has such a diversity that seasons vary greatly by region, but bowhunting opportunities are excellent. A general season in some units takes place in September, when you can hunt deer and elk, and both whitetail and trophy mule deer units are open for bowhunting in November and December.

The mule deer population is estimated at 275,000, and these animals live throughout the state. The largest bucks have come from the southeast corner along the Wyoming border and from Adams and Gem counties north of Boise. Idaho is one of the top three states for Boone and Crockett mule deer. The state record typical mule deer scored 214²/₈ and the record nontypical scored 288¹/₈.

North of the Salmon River, whitetail deer predominate. An estimated 50,000 whitetails occupy the northern one quarter of the state. Late bow seasons in some units, where snow concentrates deer at low elevations, offer some of the best whitetail hunting in the country. This region isn't known for huge bucks, but whitetails big enough to make the Pope and Young record book are common. The state record typical whitetail scored 181 and the record nontypical 228⁴/₈.

Elk. Idaho also ranks perennially among the top three or four elk states. Much of the state's reputation for elk has come from wilderness hunting in central Idaho. This huge, roadless region is a land of horseback hunts and wilderness outfitting, but it's not necessarily the best place for bowhunting, because the rifle season opens September 15, and bowhunters must hunt right along with rifle hunters. In northern Idaho, and also in the southeast, a number of

Idaho is a land of nearly infinite wilderness. Backcountry hunting for elk, deer, and bear are major ventures in the Gem State.

units open in September for bowhunting only, and these offer exceptional opportunities for hunting by bugling. The Clearwater River drainage generally has been most popular with bowhunters, and it has some great elk herds. Several units are also open for bowhunting for elk in November and December.

Black Bear. Idaho is one of the best bear states. Hunting is allowed both spring and fall, and you can legally bait and hunt with hounds. The dense north end of the state, from the Salmon River north, has the highest bear numbers. Much of this country, particularly in the Salmon River drainage, has steep canyons with open sidehills, and bears can be hunted by spotting and stalking, particularly in spring when bears feed on green grass in open meadows. Some units have a two-bear bag limit.

Antelope. Antelope archery tags are unlimited in a number of units, so this is one state where you're guaranteed of a chance to hunt antelope. Some depredation hunts around farmlands are held in early August, and general seasons fall in late August and September. Most hunting takes place in the southeast corner.

Cougar. Idaho has outstanding lion hunting. In central Idaho they're hunted in rugged mountains and deep snow, and in southern Idaho they're hunted in desert rimrock country. Virtually all cats are taken with the aid of hounds.

Sheep. Rocky Mountain bighorns live primarily in the remote Salmon River drainage and associated mountain ranges. California bighorns live in the southwest corner in the Owyhee River drainage. Tags are very limited and no more than 10 percent go to nonresidents. Seasons are in September and October.

Mountain Goat. About 50 permits are issued

226

for several units throughout the state. Again, no more than 10 percent go to nonresidents. Seasons run from late August into November.

Moose. Idaho issues about 350 permits for Shiras moose each year, but these are reserved for residents only.

Other Game

Idaho has excellent hunting for coyotes, bobcats, and other predators, as well as small game such as chucks, ground squirrels, cottontail rabbits, jackrabbits, and snowshoe hares. Turkeys are also doing well in some regions, and these birds are hunted on a limited basis.

Contact. Idaho Department of Fish and Game, 600 South Walnut, P.O. Box 25, Boise, ID 83707.

ILLINOIS Illinois has an area of 56,400 square miles. Private land covers most of this intensively farmed state except in the southern end where the Shawnee National Forest provides more than a quarter-million acres of public hunting.

Big Game

Whitetail Deer. Deer inhabit all 102 counties in Illinois, and the population is estimated at 150,000. Illinois sells about 40,000 resident and 100 or so nonresident archery permits each year. In 1983, one of the highest years on record, bowhunters killed 3,500 deer (2,310 bucks and 1,190 does). Archery success runs 10 to 12 percent. The bow season runs from October 1 through December 31 statewide, except that it closes during the firearms seasons (two three-day weekends in November and December) in counties open to firearms hunting.

Highest deer numbers are found in the forests of the northwest corner, south along the Mississippi River where corn and soybean fields are intermixed with woodlands along many creek drainages, and in the oak-hickory forests at the southern tip. With its rich farm crops, Illinois grows some large bucks. The average yearling field dresses 123 pounds, and deer of 4½ years average 185 pounds. The heaviest on record weighed 396 pounds, live weight. Mel Johnson's typical whitetail, killed near Peoria in 1965, measured 204$\frac{4}{8}$ points. It ranks number one in Pope and Young and number three in Boone and Crockett. The state record nontypical scored more than 260 points.

Other Game

Turkeys. These birds are found in several counties, and limited spring hunting is available.

Small Game. Counties in the west and south, wherever hardwoods provide cover and feed, have fair to good hunting for fox and gray squirrels, and rabbit hunting is good throughout the southern third of the state. A number of federal and state forests and state management areas offer some public hunting for these species.

Contact. Department of Conservation, Lincoln Tower Plaza, 524 South Second Street, Springfield, IL 62708-4998.

Mel Johnson's Pope and Young world-record typical whitetail was killed near Peoria, Illinois, in 1965.

IMPERIAL The name some hunters apply to a bull elk with seven antler points to the side. These hunters would call a six-point bull a royal, and an eight-point a monarch. These terms are rarely used among modern hunters.

INDIANA Indiana covers an area of 36,143 square miles. More than 90 percent of the state is privately owned. The Hoosier National Forest assures public access to large tracts of land in the southcentral portion, and some state wildlife management areas provide public hunting throughout the state. Some clubs have leased the hunting rights to private land although the trend hasn't been extensive.

Big Game

Whitetail Deer. An estimated 150,000 whitetails are scattered throughout the state. About 50,000 resident and 500 nonresident archers hunt deer annually in Indiana, and they kill 4,500 to 5,000 deer, about two thirds bucks. Average bowhunting success has been about 8 percent. The archery season opens in early October and closes the day before the gun season opens in mid-November. It then opens again in early December and continues through December 31.

The northern half of the state consists of flat, heavily farmed land. Corn and soybeans are the major crops. Most cover is contained in small woodlots and along brushy stream courses, and deer numbers are fairly high around suitable cover. The southern half of Indiana is generally hilly and wooded with oak-hickory forests. The southcentral section is the most popular for deer hunting, and nearly 40 percent of all the deer killed each year in Indiana come from this region.

The Indiana state record typical whitetail scored 197⅛ and the record nontypical, 254⅛. With abundant farm crops in the northern half, deer grow to heavy size there.

Other Game

Turkeys. These birds are hunted on a limited basis in several counties.

Small Game. Squirrels, cottontail rabbits, foxes, raccoons, and other mammals are plentiful in suitable habitat throughout the state.

Contact. Department of Natural Resources, Division of Fish and Wildlife, 607 State Office Building, Indianapolis, IN 46204.

INSTINCTIVE SHOOTING In a broad sense, this means shooting without bowsights. (For details, see Aiming Methods.)

INTERNATIONAL BOWHUNTING ORGANIZATION (IBO) The IBO was formed in the early 1980s to standardize rules for bowhunter-style archery tournaments. Three major tournaments are held under IBO sanction and rules, and taken collectively these events constitute the Triple Crown of Bowhunting. Hunters can compete in any one tournament or all three. To win the Triple Crown, a shooter has to have the highest aggregate score for all three tournaments, and the Triple Crown winner is recognized as national bowhunting champion. State and local IBO tournaments also are held throughout the country.

IBO shoots are designed to simulate hunting conditions. Most tournaments have 40-target courses, although the number can vary from 30 to 40, and all the targets are nearly life-size three-dimensional animal targets. Shooting distances vary from extremely short yardages out to roughly 60 yards, and they're all unmarked. No strict format dictates how each tournament must be set up, but in general there are two 20-target sides; competitors shoot one side one day, the other side the next day. At Triple Crown events, shooters are given three days to complete the 40-target courses.

Tackle restrictions also keep IBO tournaments within the province of the bowhunter. Everyone (except those in Cub division) must shoot arrows with field points weighing at least 125 grains. Stabilizers and V bars can't extend more than 12 inches beyond the forward part of the bow. Overdraws are allowed in all classes.

To compete in IBO tournaments, you don't have to join any organization. They're for all bowhunters. For more information, contact:

International Bowhunting Organization, P.O. Box 8564, Middletown, OH 45042

IOWA Iowa has an area of 56,000 square miles. Farmland devoted primarily to corn and soybeans covers most of the state, and less than 5 percent is forested. Some 300,000 acres of public lands are open to hunting, but the remainder of the state is private land. At this writing, nonresidents are not allowed to hunt for deer or turkeys.

Big Game

Whitetail Deer. The population is estimated at 100,000 deer. About 20,000 bowhunters (all residents) pursue deer each year in Iowa. The annual bow kill has been about 5,000, roughly two thirds bucks, and the success rate has averaged about 25 percent. The bow season generally runs from early October through November.

During summer, corn "forests" provide good cover and feed for deer, but after harvest animals must retreat into other types of shelter, so deer numbers are limited by the amount of permanent cover. In the northern half of the state, the only permanent cover is found in river bottoms, small woodlots, and marshes, so overall deer numbers are low.

The southern region bordering Missouri has fair amounts of forestland spread over rolling hills, and deer numbers are high, particularly in the southeast corner near the Mississippi River. Deer numbers are also high in the breaks and bluffs north all along the Mississippi River.

With plentiful food in the form of corn and soybeans, Iowa grows some huge bucks. Average live weight of 2½-year-old bucks is 200 pounds, and many mature bucks weigh 250 pounds and heavier (live weight). The heaviest on record weighed 440 pounds. Iowa deer grow equally impressive antlers. The state record typical whitetail scored 199⅝, and the record nontypical scored 282.

Other Game

Turkeys. Like whitetail deer, turkeys have blossomed in Iowa the past two decades. They thrive in country where fields are intermixed with hardwood cover. Here again, nonresidents can't legally hunt these birds.

Small Game. Fox squirrels live throughout the state wherever hardwoods provide food and cover, and gray squirrels are abundant in the eastern part of the state. Cottontail rabbits are also plentiful around suitable brushy cover.

Contact. Iowa Conservation Commission, Wallace State Office Building, Des Moines, IA 50319.

J

JACKRABBIT See Hares.

JAVELINA (*Tayassu tajacu*) Javelinas resemble small pigs with long bristles, but they aren't true pigs. Biologically they differ, and javelinas (also called peccaries) belong to a family of their own. At least three species of peccary live in North and South America, but the only one in the United States, and the one of concern to most bowhunters, is the collared peccary, so named because of the ring of whitish hairs around its neck.

The Nature of Javelina

Range. Javelina, or "pigs" as most hunters call them, range across the southwestern fringe of the United States and south through Mexico into Central and South America.

In Texas, they're numerous south of San Antonio in the famous south Texas brush country. In the flat, brushy terrain here you must sneak around right in the brush to find them. In west Texas, javelina inhabit more open, steep, desert country where you can spot animals from one side of a canyon to the other. Virtually all land in Texas is privately owned, and you either get a special invite from the landowner or you pay to hunt. For that reason javelina hunting alone probably will never attract hunters from far and wide, although package hunts for deer and javelina are catching on. Seasons vary by county from no closed season to seasons that are open only in October, or from November to January. In most counties that have pigs, the limit is two.

In New Mexico, javelina are restricted primarily to the southwest corner in Hidalgo, Grant, Luna, and Catron counties. As in west Texas, they live primarily in rough desert ranges. The javelina season generally runs concurrent with open deer seasons in November, and you must draw for a tag. There has been no special bow season.

Arizona has become the most popular state, because the archery season traditionally opens for the month of January (when nothing else much is going on in other states), bowhunting permits are unlimited, and the best lands are public. At this time the bow season is open for pig, Coues whitetails, and desert mule deer, which are in rut at that time. You can also shoot doves and quail for a memorable mixed-bag hunt. Virtually all of southeast Arizona—south of the Mogollon Rim and east of a line drawn north-south through Phoenix—holds good numbers of javelina. The triangle between Globe, Tucson, and Safford probably holds as many javelina as anywhere. Most pigs

live at elevations of 2,000 to 5,000 feet in steep, rocky desert mountains, although they also live in open, sprawling grasslands and in some of the fertile valleys around agricultural crops.

Size. You hear a lot of discussion about the size of javelina. In any desert range in Arizona, a pig that field dresses 40 pounds must be considered big. No, huge. However, around some croplands, javelina do get bigger. During Doug Walker's annual javelina bowhunt, hunters each year have brought in at least one or two pigs that field dressed heavier than 60 pounds. Most of these big ones have come from agricultural valleys around corn and milo fields.

Ferocity. Stories about the ferocity of javelinas are rife, and there's little doubt they can defend themselves against most of the smaller local predators. They also fight constantly among themselves, which gives them an aura of belligerence. But they're no threat to man, and they do their best to get away. Anyone who's hunted them has certainly had javelina run straight at him, but that's only because the animals have very poor eyesight and run instantly at the hint of danger, and often they just don't see you standing in the way.

A 40-pound javelina like this one I killed near Tucson, Arizona, would be considered large in most areas, although they do grow larger around croplands.

Eyesight is not one of the javelina's strong suits, and if you hunt them enough, you'll sooner or later have one nearly run over you. He's not charging. He just doesn't see you.

Hunting Javelina

One writer suggested if you've never hunted javelina before you're well advised to hire a guide. Actually, if there were ever an animal for which you don't need a guide, it's the javelina. That's the beauty of these animals. They live almost entirely on public land (in Arizona, at least), they're easy to hunt, and you certainly don't need an outfitter with horses to pack out your game.

If any aspect of javelina hunting presents a challenge, it's locating them. Obviously the place to start is getting into good territory. You can learn that by talking to biologists and local hunters before leaving home.

When you arrive in the area, scout for sign. Javelina tracks are round, not pointed like deer tracks, and they're not much bigger than a 50-cent piece. Javelina run in herds so you should find groups of tracks rather than individual tracks. Javelina eat an array of roots, stalks, bulbs, and other vegetation, most of it so tough and spiny that no normal critter would touch it. In particular look for chewed and torn-up prickly pear cactus, Spanish bayonet, or other plants seemingly made of steel and stickers. You can bet javelina did the damage. You'll also find small piles of green droppings.

These wicked-looking teeth have given the javelina a reputation for being vicious, but the teeth are used primarily for eating cactus and other tough plants. In scouting, look for places torn up by javelina.

Once you're convinced you're in good country, start glassing. Much of the best pig country, particularly in Arizona, is rough, broken desert where you can spot from one side of a canyon to the other. Spotting from a distance, much as you would for deer (see Spotting), is the best way to locate pigs, and binoculars may be your most valuable pig-hunting gear. Javelina roam relatively small home territories, probably not much more than two square miles, but all the pigs within that range most likely will be in one herd, so you might have to examine the entire range before you find that one group.

As you look, also keep your ears fine-tuned. Javelina are noisy eaters. You might hear their teeth clacking or hear them tearing apart cactus. They also fight a lot, and you could hear snorting and woofing. Use your nose, too, because they have a distinct musky, skunky smell, and if you're downwind of a herd, you could smell them well before you see them.

Keep in mind that javelina have poor heat-regulating mechanisms, so they constantly seek out the most comfortable temperatures. In summer, when 100-plus temperatures are common, they'll hole up in caves, under rims, or in

Javelina tracks are round, and they're tiny, about the size of a 50-cent piece. These animals roam in herds, so where you find one track, you'll probably find many.

brushy, shaded bottoms during the day and will move in the cool of morning and evening.

In winter, during the bow season, they'll do just the opposite. At night, when temperatures are coolest (even in Arizona the weather can get bitterly cold in January) they'll huddle together in sheltered pockets. They literally pile up at times to keep warm. They won't start moving until the sun comes up to offer them warmth. One year near Safford, a cold wind blew for several days, and some friends and I roamed for miles in search of pigs. We found lots of sign, but we couldn't find an animal. In that cold wind, they just weren't moving. A local told us that during such cold weather, the pigs often crawled inside culverts under the roads to keep warm (although we didn't find any there either, and I couldn't imagine that shooting a pig in a culvert would be very sport-

ing). When the wind finally broke and the weather became warm enough for us to hunt in shirtsleeves, bingo! Pigs appeared everywhere.

Keep in mind that javelina are vulnerable to hunting, and they could be scarce in accessible country, even if the habitat looks ideal. Studies in Arizona have shown that hunting pressure, particularly during the rifle season, can take a heavy toll on javelina. If you're finding old sign but no pigs, hike farther off the road into the foothills and mountains. The studies showed that herds living a mile or more from the nearest roads rarely suffered from overhunting. The average pig will dress no more than 30 to 40 pounds, so packing out your game is no major obstacle.

Once you've located a herd, you've accomplished the hard part. The best way to get a shot is to stalk the animals. Javelina have good

Stalking is the best way to get close to javelina. Their eyesight is poor, so as long as you move slowly, you can get within easy bow range, as this hunter is doing.

You can also call javelina, and this hunter waits at full draw as a javelina comes to his calling.

noses so you must get the wind in your favor, and they have reasonably good ears so you must move fairly slowly and quietly. On the other hand, they have terrible eyes, so you need have little fear of being seen. Taking your time, and assuming the wind is favorable, you should be able to stalk within 10 to 20 yards of any javelina you see. I'd say there's no excuse for ever shooting farther than 20 yards. As in any hunting, camouflage will give you an added margin for error, but it's not mandatory for successful pig hunting.

You also can call javelina within range. Tom Dalrymple has taken javelina with his bow for 16 consecutive seasons, and calling is one of his favorite methods. Often he blows a wounded cottontail predator call the same as you'd use for calling coyotes, but he blows it slightly differently. Rather than starting with a closed hand around the call and then opening it to produce a *to-wah* sound, he starts blowing

with his hand open and then closes it to pinch off the sound. The idea is to sound like a lost pigling, and often this will bring pigs on the run. The closer you are to the pigs, he said, the more likely they are to come in, so Dalrymple commonly spots a herd first and then stalks fairly close before calling. If you're within 60 to 100 yards, your chances of calling them in are good. He said this stirs them up something fierce, and he has literally kicked pigs he's called in and still couldn't drive them off.

Dalrymple said that if pigs are farther than 100 yards away, they're just as likely to run from calling as they are to come in. For that reason, he sometimes uses calling to locate pigs. If he's glassed a canyon or draw diligently and can't spot animals, but he still feels sure they're there, he'll open up with his predator call. This often sends the herd into flight so he can spot them. They won't go far, however, and when they settle down, Dalrymple then goes ahead and stalks them or moves in close for a calling sequence.

He also calls at close range with his mouth. When they're alarmed or angered, javelina make a woofing or chuffing sound. Woof! Woof! Dalrymple often imitates this sound with his mouth, and he's had good success pulling pigs within bow range this way.

As I've said, javelina are small and they're fairly frail, so you don't need your elk bow to kill one. Any legal bow of 40 pounds or so will be more than adequate. Most important is waiting until the animal presents a clear, close-range shot and then putting the arrow in the lungs. As in all hunting, use a sharp broadhead that will kill the animal cleanly and quickly.

How do you pick out a trophy boar? Frankly, it isn't easy. Javelinas are all head and bristles, and even a half-grown sow can look big when it flares its eight-inch guard hairs and bounds through the brush. To pick out a big one, you just about have to have others to compare it with. When you see a herd, study it closely to compare the sizes of animals. Commonly one will stand out clearly as the biggest. You can assume that's a big boar, although distinguishing between males and females is virtually impossible at long range.

One year I spotted about 15 javelina feeding along the bottom of a mesquite wash. One animal was noticeably bigger than the others, so I circled in front of the herd and waited for them to feed to me. That part worked beautifully and soon pigs were snorting and chomping all around, but at close range I couldn't pick out the big one. I'd first start to draw on one animal and then another, but no, they were all the same size. Finally I was sure I'd looked over every pig in the herd and none looked big, when I saw one final animal emerging from

grass to my left. This had to be the one. I drew and aimed and waited as the animal fed my way, and at ten yards I released the arrow. It hit on the money and the pig went right down. My guess turned out right. The boar field dressed 41 pounds, a big javelina in anybody's book.

Javelina get mixed reviews in regard to table quality. They're strictly vegetarian, so their meat has no strong flavor. If anything it's too bland. Barbecued in a pit or over open charcoal with a tangy barbecue sauce, they're quite good in my opinion. Javelina have a musk gland on the back a few inches in front of the tail. Cut this off and discard it before dressing your pig to avoid spreading the skunky-smelling musk on the meat.

I probably wouldn't drive 1,000 miles to Arizona just to hunt javelina, because the end results just aren't that lasting. You're lucky to get 15 pounds of meat off a big pig, and a mounted javelina head can't compare in terms of trophy quality with deer, elk, or other big game. But as part of a mixed bag hunt in the "off season," the javelina offers good excitement. And these animals make ideal bow animals, especially for the hunter who's taken a beating at the hands of more astute big game. With their poor eyesight, javelina are easy to stalk, and any hunter who'll put out a solid effort for two or three days should score on a pig. They're fun to hunt, and they'll do wonders for your bowhunting self-image.

JUMP THE STRING A big-game animal is said to "jump the string" when it reacts fast enough to dodge your arrow. In some cases an animal reacts impulsively to the sound of the bow being shot, and in many cases the animal responds to the sudden movement of the bow limbs. (For details, see Shot Selection.)

K

KANSAS Kansas has an area of 82,264 square miles, with a variety of habitat—hardwood forests in the east, tall-grass prairies and grainfields in the central part of the state, irrigated croplands in the southwest, and short-grass prairie and brushy breaks in the northwest.

Big Game

Deer. An estimated 100,000 whitetails occupy about 75 percent of the state, and 20,000 mule deer live in the western third. All rifle permits are issued by drawing in Kansas, but archery licenses are not limited and the number of archers has increased steadily to about 15,000 bowhunters annually. They've killed an average of 2,186 deer, about two thirds bucks. Overall archery success has been a very respectable 20 percent with a high in 1983 of 29 percent and a low in 1971 of 14 percent. The archery season is open through October and November, and again in late December. Kansas has considered issuing some nonresident permits, but at this writing, nonresidents are not allowed to hunt deer in Kansas.

The eastern edge has about the only extensive woodlands in Kansas, and deer numbers are highest here. Generally central Kansas consists of prairies and grainfields, and cover is restricted to stream bottoms. Whitetails live primarily in these wooded bottoms, and overall numbers are low. However, some very large bucks are taken. The northwest corner has extensive short-grass prairies, rolling hills, and some canyons and breaks. This is the best mule deer country in Kansas, and whitetails also live in the creek bottoms here.

Kansas isn't known for big mule deer, but whitetails are something else. The state record typical whitetail scored 200⅞ and the record nontypical 258⅝, and many bucks large enough to make the Pope and Young minimum are taken each year.

Antelope. A few pronghorns still roam the native prairies of western Kansas. Hunting is very limited and is reserved for residents only.

Other Game

Spring and fall turkey seasons are held for residents only. Turkey flocks are expanding. Prairie dogs, gray squirrels, cottontails, jackrabbits, and other small game offer archers plenty of variety in small game hunting.

Contact. Kansas Fish and Game, Box 54A, Rural Route 2, Pratt, KS 67124.

KENTUCKY Kentucky, with an area of 40,505 square miles, has more than a million acres of public land, including 43 wildlife management areas, four large military reservations

and national forests for public hunting. However, the majority of Kentucky is privately
owned and permission to hunt is required. Traditionally, landowners have granted permission
to polite hunters, but hunting leases have begun to appear, and they undoubtedly will become more prevalent in the future.

Big Game

Whitetail Deer. Deer numbers have increased
steadily through the 1970s and 1980s, and the
population is expected to stabilize at about
400,000 deer. On the average, 50,000 residents
and 800 nonresidents bowhunt for deer in Kentucky each year. Annual harvest has increased
steadily through the 1970s, and reached a high
in 1983 of 4,600. Overall hunting success, including firearms, has been 13 percent. Bow seasons total 85 days, including all of October, the
last two weeks of November, and all of December. The archery limit is one deer of either sex
in most counties. Hunters are allowed one deer
with bow and one with gun, although bag
limits and either-sex hunting may be liberalized
as deer numbers increase.

Topography and vegetation are diverse in
Kentucky from flat farmland to broken,
wooded hills to mountains. Deer numbers are
highest in the western and southcentral portions of the state. Highest harvest per square
mile comes from the Pennyrile region in the
southwest, and the largest bucks killed in Kentucky have come from Pulaski County south
of Lexington in the southcentral region. The
northcentral Blue Grass hills region has several
large cities, so this area is the most heavily
hunted. The Appalachian Mountains extend
into the eastern end of Kentucky, and deer
numbers are low in the relatively infertile hardwood forests here.

The state record typical whitetail, taken in
1982, measured 187⅛, and the record nontypical, also taken in 1982, scored 221⅞.

Other Game

Turkeys. As in many states, turkeys have
been brought back from near extinction to
huntable populations in several parts of the
state.

Small Game. Squirrels, both fox and gray,
are found throughout the state, and rabbits are
abundant around brushy cover in farming regions. Other game such as chucks and foxes
are also available.

Contact. Division of Wildlife, Department
of Fish and Wildlife Resources, #1 Game Farm
Road, Frankfort, KY 40601.

KINETIC ENERGY   See Energy.

KISSER   Also called a kisser button. This is
a small plastic disc tied onto a bowstring to
assure precise anchor position. At full draw,
you "kiss" the button. You can use a kisser only
with an under-the-chin anchor method.

KNIFE SHARPENING   Some hunters think
knife sharpening is a great mystery that takes
some kind of special touch. The fact is, anybody can sharpen any knife in a matter of minutes—yes, even a Buck—with the right technique.

Sharpening Gear

First assemble the needed equipment. I use a
large stone with a coarse side for grinding the
proper bevel onto the blade and a fine side for
putting on a keen edge. Any number of stones
will work, but you must have a coarse and a
fine. You need honing oil to lubricate the stone
and to float away tiny particles of steel, and
you need a steel, ceramic rod, or leather strop
for the finishing touch.

Getting the Edge

Start with the coarse stone. I assume you're
sharpening a new knife or one that's badly
dulled and needs some drastic work. Lubricate
the stone with a few drops of oil. Lay the butt
end of the blade on the upper end of the stone
with the point raised slightly off the stone. Now
draw the blade across the stone as if slicing off
a thin layer of the stone. Finish your slice with
the tip of the blade. As you slice, watch the

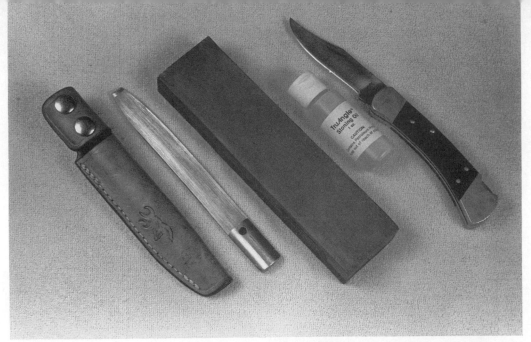

For knife sharpening you need, left to right, a steel (or similar finishing tool such as ceramic Crock Sticks or a leather strop); a stone with coarse and fine sides; honing oil; and a knife.

spot at which the blade edge meets the stone. You should see a small "pile" of oil where the blade shaves the oil off the stone. This is the most important part of sharpening. The edge of the blade must shave the stone through the entire stroke. If it misses even slightly, you'll end up with dull spots.

Some hunters say to maintain a 20-degree angle between the blade and the stone. That sounds great and it's probably about right, but how do you gauge 20 degrees? I don't know. You don't want an acute chisel edge because you can't get it sharp, but you don't want a fine razorblade edge either because it will dull quickly. Somewhere between is about right. The edge on most knives direct from the factory is too acute and must be flattened out a little.

After the first stroke turn the knife over and slice back the other way to grind the other side. Continue to alternate sides. If you're maintaining a consistent stroke with equal pressure going both ways, the edges will appear equally ground on both sides. You must do this systematically, giving an equal number of strokes with equal pressure on both sides. If you just

rub your knife around on the stone, hitting first this spot and then that, you'll never get a good edge.

A number of hunters have said they couldn't sharpen Buck or other hard-bladed knives. That's because they're afraid to apply pressure. When you're using the coarse stone to form a bevel on a blade, bear down. If you hold the knife in your right hand for sharpening, then place the fingers on your left hand on the side

Lubricate the stone with oil.

239

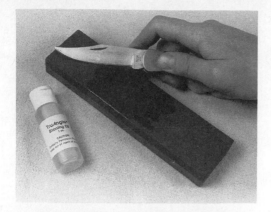

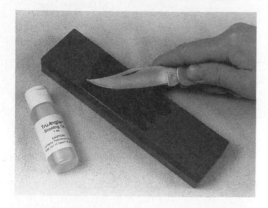

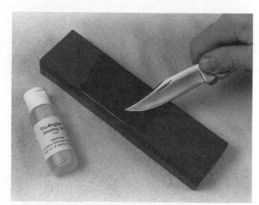

Start with the butt of the blade on the stone, and slowly draw the blade toward you as if slicing oil off the stone. Shift from the butt to the middle to the tip of the blade as you pull the knife across the stone. The blade should "slice" oil evenly throughout the entire stroke.

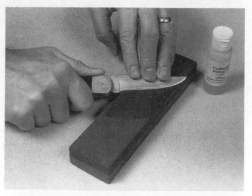

If the blade is new or has been badly nicked, you'll need to apply some real pressure to grind the edge to the appropriate bevel. On blades with hard steel, don't be afraid to bear down.

of the knife blade, and as you make the slicing stroke across the stone, push down hard with your left hand. You can grind any knife into shape in a hurry if you apply enough pressure. Again, keep the strokes consistent to grind the blade evenly from one end to the other.

The Finishing Touch

When you've achieved the desired bevel, switch to the fine-grit stone and continue the same way. Oil the stone and slice off the oil, starting at the butt of the blade and rocking to

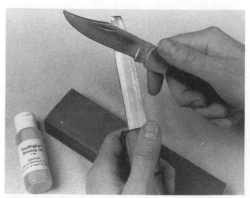

Finish up with a few very light strokes on a sharpening steel.

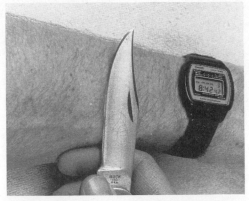

Test for sharpness by shaving your arm. If you've done a good job, the hair should pop off your arm. If you have to saw it off, the blade needs some more work.

Carry Crock Sticks and other sharpening gear in the field with you and touch up your blade regularly.

the tip, keeping the angle the same through the entire stroke. As the edges become smooth and polished, decrease pressure. Finish up with a very light stroke. The weight of the knife alone will apply adequate force. This reduction of pressure is very important, because each time you draw the blade across the stone, a fine wire edge forms on the side of the blade away from the stone. Reducing force on the stone reduces the size of the wire edge.

Apply the finishing touch with a steel (as pictured) or a ceramic rod or strop. The purpose of these is to eliminate any trace of wire edge. To do that you must make very light strokes. Again, the weight of the knife alone will apply enough pressure. If you push harder than that, you'll continue to make a wire edge on the blade, and you'll never get the knife perfectly sharp.

Testing Your Work

If the knife is sharpened well, it will shave hair off your arm. You shouldn't have to saw

the hair off. With each stroke the hair should fairly pop off. If you don't like shaving your arm, drag the blade across your thumbnail. It should bite in. If it slides, the blade has dull spots.

Gutting and skinning a big animal will dull any knife in a hurry, and nothing is worse than trying to skin and cape with a dull knife. You probably won't carry an oilstone in the field with you, but if you include a small steel or ceramic Crock Sticks in your hunting pack, you can touch up the blade as you work. You won't be sorry you did.

L

LABRADOR   See Newfoundland.

LIVE RELEASE   See Release.

LOOSE   This is an old-fashioned word that refers to the process of letting go of a bowstring. Most bowhunters use the term "release" these days. (For details, see Release.)

LOUISIANA   Louisiana has an area of 48,523 square miles. The Department of Wildlife and Fisheries operates 35 wildlife management areas that cover nearly 1 million acres. These are all open to hunting and fishing and are heavily used. Large blocks of land in the western part of the state remain unposted so that public hunting access is good, but better deer lands in the southeast are leased by clubs.

Big Game
Whitetail Deer. Deer numbers are estimated at 450,000. Louisiana sells an average of 20,000 archery licenses each year, primarily to residents. Average kill has been 3,500 deer, about 55 percent bucks. Archery success ranges from 25 to 30 percent. The archery season opens October 1 and runs through January 20 statewide. Either sex of deer may be taken except during gun seasons when all hunters are restricted to bucks only. (Firearms seasons are divided into three parts that run from November into January.) Bag limit is one a day and six per season. The six deer may be taken by any legal means (archery or firearms) during any open season.

The country is diverse in Louisiana. The northwestern quarter of the state and the Florida parishes to the extreme east are forested with pines and hardwoods, and deer are numerous. The Mississippi–Red River Bottomlands that cover the northeastern quarter are heavily farmed, primarily for cotton and soybeans, and deer numbers are low. The Mississippi–Atchafalaya Delta contains 400,000 acres of swamp and timbered bottomland, one of the largest unspoiled swamps in the United States. Deer are abundant but most good lands are leased by clubs. The coastal marshes extend across the entire southern fringe of the state, and deer live throughout the marshes.

Black Bears. The season is open for about a week in mid-October. Use of dogs is allowed. Only the Atchafalaya Floodway near Baton Rouge is open to bear hunting.

Other Game

Turkeys. Louisiana has had a successful restoration program to build a flock exceeding 10,000 birds. Spring seasons range from 16 to 37 days, depending on area. Limit is one per day, three per season.

Small Game. Louisiana has generous seasons and limits on rabbits and squirrels. Pigs also can be taken in some areas.

Contact. Department of Wildlife and Fisheries, P.O. Box 15570, Baton Rouge, LA 70895.

M

MAINE Maine covers 31,885 square miles. Spruce-fir and northern hardwood forests dominate the entire northern and western side, and road access is very limited in some areas. The south end of the state is more heavily settled, and road access is good. Timber companies own large tracts of land in the north, and they allow public hunting. This is one of the few regions in the eastern United States where guided big-game hunting is a common practice. Posting of lands has become more common in the populated southern regions.

Big Game

Whitetail Deer. The deer population is estimated at roughly 200,000 animals. An average of 4,000 resident and 700 nonresident archers hunt deer in Maine each year, and they kill from 100 to 150 deer each year. Average bowhunting success has been 2.5 percent. The statewide archery season generally has opened October 1 and stayed open until late October with a bag limit of one deer, either sex.

Up until the 1930s, the northern half supported nearly 75 percent of the deer in Maine, but since then deer have become far more abundant in the southern half of the state. Throughout the dense conifer and hardwood forests of the northern half, deer densities now range from 3 to 12 per square mile with higher densities around farmlands. Severe winters often take a heavy toll on deer in this northern country.

The central part of the state has less severe winters. Deer grow big in some parts of this region, and densities run from 5 to 15 deer per square mile, with highest numbers and biggest deer around farmlands. Along the coast, winters are mild to moderate so overall survival is better than farther north, and a mix of farmlands, brush country, and timber offers ideal habitat in some regions. Deer numbers are moderate to high, up to 25 per square mile in the better areas.

The state record typical whitetail measured $192^7/_8$ and the record nontypical 259. The Maine Antler and Skull Trophy Club lists dozens of racks that score higher than 150.

Black Bears. Maine has traditionally been the best eastern state for bear hunting, with an annual harvest exceeding 1,000 animals. The general bear season runs from September 1 through November. Baiting and spring hunting were popular practices, but these have been eliminated. Hunting with hounds is still allowed.

Moose. The moose in Maine has become a *cause célèbre* for hunters. Antihunters tried diligently to prevent moose hunting, but biologists and hunters finally prevailed and the first moose season since 1935 was held in 1980. Permits are limited and drawing odds are not good.

Other Game

Snowshoe hares are the most popular small game, and they're abundant throughout the conifer forests. A few cottontails live around farmlands in the south end, and squirrels inhabit central and southern hardwood forests. Predators, such as foxes and bobcats, are also available.

Contact. Department of Inland Fisheries and Wildlife, 284 State Street, Augusta, ME 04333.

MANITOBA Manitoba covers 250,000 square miles. Throughout the northern, central, and southeastern regions, 60 percent of the land is privately owned. In the southwest, 85 percent is private. Nonresident aliens (from outside Canada) must hire a guide to hunt big game legally in Manitoba.

Big Game

Deer. The southern one fourth of the province supports an estimated 150,000 whitetail deer. Mule deer are scarce to nonexistent. Bowhunters number about 2,000, although this figure is growing with increased interest in bowhunting. The average bow kill has been higher than 200 deer each year (bucks and does combined). Average bowhunting success has been 13 percent with a high in 1981 of nearly 17 percent. Archery seasons open in early September and continue into November. In some cases, seasons for nonresidents differ from those for residents.

Most deer live in the agricultural southern one quarter of the province. In the southeast, farms are intermixed with hardwood and coniferous forests and deer are numerous around woody cover. The southwest, consisting of varied country with grasslands, hardwoods, as-

pens, and marshes, as well as farmlands, is the most popular deer region in Manitoba. Farther north, extensive forests of the Riding, Duck, and Porcupine mountains support good numbers of deer. North of there, deer densities are very low. The record typical whitetail, killed in 1980, measured 187⅞. The record nontypical, taken in 1973, measured 256⅝.

Moose. Canada moose are abundant throughout much of northern Manitoba in forested country. To hunt moose legally, nonresidents must buy a complete guided hunting package from one of the local lodges. The seasons are open in September and October.

Bears. The province has good hunting for black bears in many of its forested regions.

Other Game. Manitoba also has woodland caribou and elk, but these are reserved for residents only.

Contact. Department of Natural Resources, Box 22, 1495 St. James Street, Winnipeg, Manitoba R3H-0W9, and Travel Manitoba, Department 3053, Legislative Building, Winnipeg, Manitoba R3C-0V8.

MAP SOURCES Maps can be one of your most valuable aids in hunt planning. Here are major sources for maps. Space doesn't allow listing of every office for public land agencies, so I've listed major offices in each state or region. You can contact them for the addresses and phone numbers of local offices.

Topographic Maps
U.S. Geological Survey
Box 25286
Denver Federal Center
Denver, CO 80225

National Forest Maps
Region 1, Northern
P.O. Box 7669
Missoula, MT 59807

Region 2, Rocky Mountain
11177 West 8th Avenue
Box 25127
Lakewood, CO 80225

Region 3, Southwestern
Federal Building
517 Gold Avenue, S.W.
Albuquerque, NM 87102

Region 4, Intermountain
Federal Office Building
324 25th Street
Ogden, UT 84401

Region 5, California
630 Sansome Street
San Francisco, CA 94111

Region 6, Pacific Northwest
319 S.W. Pine Street
Box 3623
Portland, OR 97208

Region 8, Southern
1720 Peachtree Road, N.W.
Atlanta, GA 30367

Region 9, Eastern
310 West Wisconsin Avenue
Milwaukee, WI 53203

Region 10, Alaska
Federal Office Building
Box 1628
Juneau, AK 99802

U.S. Bureau of Land Management
Alaska State Director
701 C Street
Box 31
Anchorage, AK 99513

Arizona State Director
P.O. Box 16563
Phoenix, AZ 85011

California State Director
Federal Office Building
2800 Cottage Way
Sacramento, CA 95825

Colorado State Director
2020 Arapahoe Street
Denver, CO 80205

Idaho State Director
3380 Americana Terrace
Boise, ID 83706

Montana State Director
222 North 32nd Street
P.O. Box 30157
Billings, MT 59107

Nevada State Director
850 Harvard Way
P.O. Box 12000
Reno, NV 89520

New Mexico State Director
Federal Building
P.O. Box 1449
Santa Fe, NM 87501

Oregon and Washington State Directors
825 N.E. Multnomah
P.O. Box 2965
Portland, OR 97208

Utaho State Director
CFS Building
324 South State Street
Salt Lake City, UT 84111-2303

Wyoming State Director
2515 Warren Avenue
P.O. Box 1828
Cheyenne, WY 82001

Eastern States Office
18th and "C" Streets, N.W.
Room 5600
Washington, D.C. 20240

Some state wildlife agencies also can provide maps or can give you helpful planning information. For addresses, see individual state listings in this book. You also can get aerial photos from some public agencies such as the Soil Conservation Service, and plat maps, available at county courthouses, show much detail such as property boundaries, roads, power lines, streams, and so forth on small blocks of private land.

Another helpful planning guide is the Conservation *Directory*. It lists hundreds of addresses of federal, state, and local agencies, many of whom can supply maps or other useful information. For information contact: National Wildlife Federation, Conservation

This is a typical pose for a yellow-belly marmot: just enough body showing to tempt you to shoot an arrow. Guess where most of your arrows will hit.

Directory, 1412 Sixteenth Street, N.W., Washington, D.C. 20036

MARMOT Marmots of greatest interest to bowhunters are the woodchuck and its Western counterpart, the yellow-belly marmot, or rockchuck as most hunters call it.

Woodchucks are heavy-bodied animals that live throughout the eastern states as far west as the Dakotas and south to Arkansas, Tennessee, Kentucky, and Virginia, and their range extends far north into Canada. Woodchucks measure 20 to 25 inches long, including a 4- to 6-inch tail, and they weigh from 5 to 10 pounds. Woodchucks live primarily in burrows at the edges of green fields where clover and other grasses provide good feed.

Yellow-belly marmots—rockchucks—live throughout the Rocky Mountain and Pacific states at mid-elevations of 4,000 to 8,000 feet. They look similar to woodchucks, with a brown, grizzled coat, but the bellies of adults are bright orange or yellow. Rockchucks also live underground, but most commonly in rock piles rather than in burrows in open fields. Anywhere in the arid West where you see green

pastures or alfalfa fields bordered by rocks or cliffs, you can bet some rockchucks live there.

Throughout Western mountains the hoary marmot takes over elevationally where rockchucks leave off. Hoary marmots live in rocky, open country to the tops of the highest Western mountains, from 6,000 to 14,000 feet. Many a mule deer, elk, or sheep hunter has felt like wiping out every hoary marmot in the West as these animals, just their beady eyes glistening above the tops of boulders, started chirping alarm calls during the critical moments of the hunter's stalk. Hoary marmots are pretty, frosted-looking animals, but it's doubtful many hunters specifically go hoary marmot hunting. The chucks—woodchuck and rockchuck—are of greatest interest to bowhunters.

Chucks start emerging from winter hibernation with the first warm weather of spring, usually in March, but May through early June is the best time to hunt them because the young are just emerging from the burrows. The animals are most numerous then, and they haven't yet wised up to the ways of hunters and other predators. Naive young chucks are fairly easy to hunt, but mature chucks are wily critters, tough to fool, and the most common view of these animals is a pair of eyeballs peeking over a rock or mound of dirt. Anyone who consistently arrows "boss" chucks can consider himself a pretty decent hunter. Mornings and evenings on calm days are the best times to see lots of chucks.

Hunting Chucks

You most commonly hear about hunting chucks with high-power rifles, but anyone can kill them that way. It's shooting them with a bow that offers a challenge and hones hunting skills. My friend Bill Bechen is a serious chuck hunter, and he employs a couple of different methods.

If he's hunting an open rock pile or pasture with little cover, Bechen walks up openly to spook animals underground. Then he sits and waits as motionless as a stump. Usually chucks pop up before long and Bechen gets easy shots. On brushy hillsides next to alfalfa fields and pastures, Bechen still-hunts as carefully as he would for deer, and he frequently sneaks close to sunning chucks. With these two methods he often gets 30 to 40 shots in a day, and he's

killed as many as 9 chucks in one day and 50 in a spring.

Woodchucks commonly live in pastures where soft dirt doesn't take a heavy toll on arrows, but rockchucks, as their name implies, dwell mostly in rocks, and hunting them can be tough on arrows. One shot is the average lifespan of a chuck arrow. To save money, Bechen shoots cedar shafts he fletches himself, and when he breaks an arrow, he pulls off the head and shaves off the fletching to use on new arrows.

Mature chucks are big, tough animals, so a sharp broadhead is the best type of head. A stopper behind the head prevents the arrow from passing on through. With a heavy bow that delivers a good wallop, rubber blunts and Judo heads also do the job.

Safety Precaution

Any discussion of chuck hunting merits a word of caution. Rifle hunters like to blaze away on chucks at long range, and if you're sitting camouflaged in the midst of some burrows or a rock pile waiting for chucks to emerge, you could be in the line of fire of

One way to hunt marmots is to sit patiently, waiting for them to come up from their holes. In the upper left corner a marmot peaks over a rock to see what the hunter is doing. You can see why chuck hunters need lots of inexpensive arrows.

Bill Bechen lines up for a shot on a marmot. He shoots cedar shafts tipped with rubber blunts.

Railroad grades offer good chuck hunting because the animals burrow into the banks to make their dens. Tracks are also a good place for stalking, because the hunter can sneak along one side and pop over for a close-range shot.

unknowing rifle shooters. Chuck hunting gets exciting real fast when bullets start ricocheting past your head. I speak from experience. If you see a car pull up, let the shooters know you're around.

MARYLAND. Maryland has a total area of 10,577 square miles. Thirty-five state wildlife management areas contain about 75,000 acres. The western end of the state is mountainous and forested, and state forests cover nearly 20 percent of Garrett and Allegany counties (the westernmost counties). These forests provide most of the public hunting, and hunting pressure can be high. Otherwise, private lands cover a majority of the state, and clubs have leased most of the better hunting lands.

Big Game
Whitetail Deer. Maryland has an estimated 100,000 animals (that includes about 3,000 Sika deer in Dorchester County and on Assateague Island). In recent years hunters have bought an average of 38,000 bow deer licenses, and average bow harvest has been just under 2,000 with an average success rate of 5 percent.

The archery season runs from mid-September through the first week in January. Firearms season opens the Saturday after Thanksgiving and remains open for seven hunting days (no hunting is allowed on Sunday). A special muzzleloader season is open for seven hunting days in mid-December. The bag limit is one deer during the archery season, one during a firearm season (maximum of two a year). The limit for Sika deer is three during each season, or nine total in one year.

As in most surrounding states, deer numbers reached all-time highs in the 1980s, although urban growth around Washington, D.C., and Baltimore continues to eat away at deer habitat.

Other Game
Turkeys. These birds are expanding their range and are hunted in several counties, primarily in the northwestern end of the state.

Spring season runs for about two weeks in April and May; limited fall hunting is allowed.

Small Game. Squirrels are the most popular small game in Maryland, and numbers are good throughout hardwood forests. Cottontails are abundant around farmlands wherever suitable brush cover is available.

Contact. Department of Natural Resources, Tawes State Office Building, Annapolis, MD 21401.

MASSACHUSETTS This state has an area of 8,000 square miles. More than 15 percent of it is publicly owned, and hunters can hunt any land that isn't posted. As a result, public access is better than average for populous eastern states.

Big Game

Whitetail Deer. Deer numbers are estimated at 30,000 animals. An average of 22,595 hunt deer each year, many with both firearms and bow. Average bow kill has been 379 deer, about two thirds bucks, with a high of 446. Overall average hunting success has been 10 percent. No separate records are kept for firearms and archery hunters. The archery season lasts for about three weeks from early to mid-November. Daily bag limit is one deer, and the season limit is two.

The rolling sand dunes of Nantucket Island and Martha's Vineyard are covered with dense pitch pine and scrub oak, and deer numbers are very high. Nantucket Island produces more deer per square mile than any other part of Massachusetts. These islands offer a fair amount of public hunting. The entire eastern end of the state, with Boston at the center, has exploding development, and deer numbers are suffering. The hilly, forested central region has good deer hunting, although development around Worcester will reduce deer in that area.

The western region, with its Holyoke and Berkshire mountains, has some rugged peaks covered with hardwood and spruce forests that support good deer numbers. This region is the most popular among the state's deer hunters.

Undeveloped land is extensive, and public access is good.

Black Bears. These animals inhabit the Berkshire Mountains, and short bear seasons are held in September and again in November during the archery deer season. Hunting with hounds is allowed in the first season only; a special permit is required.

Other Game

A limited spring season is held in several counties at the western end of the state. Spring season takes place in May. A special permit is required. Seasons are held for rabbits, squirrels and other small game.

Contact. Division of Fisheries and Wildlife, Field Headquarters, Westboro, MA 01581.

MASTER EYE See Bow Selection and Dominant Eye.

MEAT CARE The quality of venison and other wild meat depends on what you do with it in the field. Some hunters complain about "wild" taste, but in many cases they're to blame for that. Do a good job of taking care of your animal in the field, and you'll end up with some good eating.

Field Dress Your Buck

The most fundamental step is what most hunters call field dressing, or "gutting." The accompanying photos and explanations show you how to gut, skin, and pack your animal in the field. The same procedure works on any big game. Big animals just require more effort on your part.

These photos show how to handle an animal on the ground, but if you can find a convenient tree, you can hang the deer and skin it there. Most likely, however, you'll need the help of a companion, or a small winch, to get it up there. If you drag it to the road, you'll probably take the animal back to camp to hang and skin it.

There you can either skin it with a knife, or you can pull the hide off with your vehicle. To

Take your photos now, and then get to work.

do that hang the deer by its antlers, cut the skin around the neck, and skin down the neck far enough to get a loose flap of skin. Also cut off the legs at the "elbows" and slit the hide on the insides of the legs.

Now place a small, hard ball like a golf ball or rock about two inches in diameter on the flap of skin on the neck and tie a rope around this ball. The ball simply keeps the rope from sliding off the slippery hide. Tie the other end of the rope to the bumper of your car and slowly drive away. You can peel the hide off a deer in short order this way.

Washing. Some hunters say you should never put water on meat, and there's some basis for that advice. Water contains bacteria, so washing the carcass can enhance spoilage. If you've made a clean hit and the body cavity is clean,

Your knife should be sharp to start with, but you're smart to carry a steel or other sharpening device to touch up the blade in the field.

Lay the deer on its back and start dressing at the genitals. A partner can hold the deer steady for you, but if you're alone, you'll want to use cord or rope to tie the deer's legs out of the way and to hold him in position while you work.

you can just wipe out any excess blood and moisture with a clean rag and bag up your animal.

On the other hand, if you've gut shot the animal or in some other way contaminated it, you're smart to wash it thoroughly. Water in itself doesn't affect the meat, and the body cavity is already wet. Meat processing plants hang beef and other livestock after butchering and wash them thoroughly, and water won't hurt a deer any more than it will a beef cow. Use lots of water and scrub the animal thoroughly. Then wipe it dry with a clean cloth and bag it to keep it clean.

Always hang animals in the shade and in a

Cut a complete circle around the anus just like you'd cut out the core of an apple. Be sure to keep your knife blade turned out toward the pelvic bone so it doesn't cut the intestine or urine bladder inside the pelvis.

Cut the hide around the testicles and penis, and slit the hide and meat down to the anus. Normally you want to avoid cutting the penis so that urine doesn't leak onto the meat, but on this buck, I tied a cord around the penis to prevent leakage and cut the penis in two so that part of it remained attached to one leg as proof of sex. Some states require proof of sex during buck-only seasons.

Now, starting at the pelvis, slit open the belly skin all the way to the rib cage. To avoid cutting into the stomach or intestines, which is about the worst mistake you can make, cut a small hole in the skin and slide two fingers into the hole, and then cut forward with your knife between the fingers. The two fingers will hold the stomach and intestines away from the blade and serve as a cutting guide.

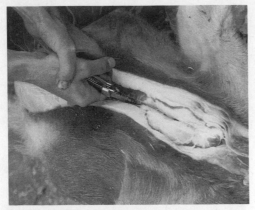

Split the brisket (chest) all the way to the neck. Here I'm using the saw blade on my knife. You can split a deer's brisket using a knife blade, too. Just make sure you cut away from you to avoid stabbing yourself in case the blade slips.

Cut the diaphragm to free the entrails from inside the body cavity. The diaphragm is a tough, thin muscle that separates the paunch area from the chest. As you can see in this photo, it begins right at the back of the rib cage.

Open up the neck and cut off the windpipe and esophagus right at the chin. (If you plan to save the cape for mounting, you'll avoid cuts on throat side of cape. Instead, you'll split the hide down the back of the neck. For details, see Caping.)

place where the air can circulate to dry the meat. Bacteria grow best in moisture, so once you've washed the carcass, dry it completely and then keep it dry. During rain or snow, hang it under cover to keep off moisture.

Handling Big Animals. Under the right circumstances, you can hang and skin elk and other large animals in camp just as you would a deer, but if you're like me, you'll end up by yourself out in the sticks somewhere and you'll have to handle that monster by yourself. The general procedure and the end product, a cleaned and skinned animal, are the same, but a few tips can help you handle outsized game like elk, moose, and big bucks. For simplicity, I'll refer only to elk here.

Unless you've got a winch of some kind (which, incidentally, can be a handy addition

You'll have to reach inside to cut away connective tissue along the back that holds the organs in place.

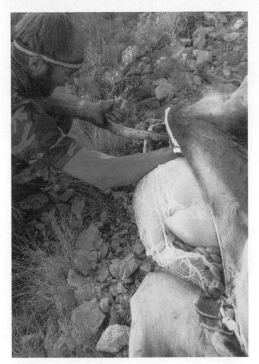

Using the windpipe as a handle, start pulling out the innards.

to your hunting gear), you'll have to skin your elk on the ground. The procedure runs basically the same as for deer. Just make sure when you're elk hunting that you carry at least 50 feet of cord to tie the legs back as you work, or have a buddy along to lend a hand. Trying to hold the legs of an elk out of the way as you gut and skin will leave you battered and bruised.

Quartering. I know hunters who've taken whole elk to lockers for butchering, but that's rare. More commonly, you'll have to cut your elk into pieces to handle him. Most outfitters who pack meat on horses or mules prefer elk cut into quarters. To quarter an elk you need either a saw or an ax.

First cut the animal in half crosswise. To do that, start at the back rib and count forward three ribs and use your knife to cut all the way around the animal between the third and fourth ribs. Then saw or chop the backbone in

As you near the pelvis, take special care with the urine bladder. If you puncture this, you'll fill the body cavity with urine. Cut around inside the pelvis to free the bladder and intestines as they lead to the anus, but be careful to avoid a messy mistake. If you split the pelvis with your saw or knife, you can lift everything out neatly.

Cut off the legs at the "elbows." You can do this with a knife by severing the tendons and breaking the joints, or you can skin back the legs a little and saw them off.

There are variations on the gutting process and no two hunters do it identically, but the end results should be the same: a carcass opened up from stem to stern, with internal organs completely removed. Blood has pooled in the chest of this buck, so the animal should be rolled over to drain. If water is available, wash the body cavity, or at least wipe it clean with a cloth or rag.

Some hunters would stop here and drag their deer to the nearest road. If you plan to drag the animal, you're wise not to split the brisket or the neck. That way it's easier to keep out dirt and debris. Just reach up inside the chest to pull out the lungs, heart, and liver. Then you can split the chest and remove the windpipe and esophagus once you get the animal back to camp or to a cooler.

For long distances, packing is easier than dragging. You can either leave the hide on and cut the animal in half to pack it in two trips, or, as I've done here, you can skin the animal on the spot, bag him, and carry the whole deer at once. To do that, follow these steps:

Roll the deer onto one side and skin the top side all the way to the backbone. Be sure to spread out the hide to keep it clean. It will serve as a drop cloth for the carcass as you skin the other side.

Roll the deer onto the clean hide and skin the other side.

Tie the carcass securely to your packframe. Rubber bungee cords will work, but I like rope better because it keeps the load more stable. Make sure you put at least one loop of rope under the carcass to keep it from slipping down.

Place the skinned carcass in deer bags to keep it clean and to keep off flies. Notice the flies on the bag. In warm weather, you must carry deer bags to protect the meat after field dressing. This entire small buck fit neatly into one large bag. You'll have to split larger deer in two right behind the rib cage and put the front half in one bag, the back half in another. (Or you can bone out larger animals, as described below.)

You're ready to go with an easy pack. Who says the work begins when the animal is down? This is a labor of love.

Big animals are done the same way as the deer, only they require more work. With care you can keep an animal spotless while skinning it right on the ground. In hot weather like this, you must skin large animals quickly to get rid of body heat.

through with the other hatchet. I've never done it this way, but Roger has handled lots of game, so I have faith in what he says.

I recommend quartering only if you plan to have a packer carry out your elk on horses, and only if you've got someone to help you handle the quarters. On one of my bulls, the front quarters weighed 115 pounds apiece, the hind 90. That was an average bull; a big one would weigh 20 pounds more per quarter. Unless you can handle that kind of weight alone, you'll need another method.

Boning. If you're alone you'll find it a lot easier to dissect an elk. To do that it's just as easy to proceed without gutting first, which reduces the mess and helps you keep the meat cleaner. You can take apart an elk with only a knife, although you'll need a saw or ax later to remove the antlers from the skull.

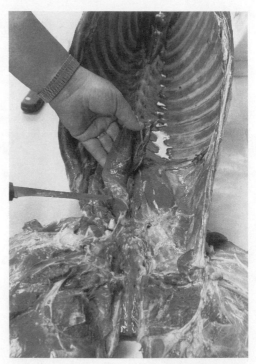

In boning an animal, don't forget to salvage the tenderloins, which lie next to the backbone just in front of the pelvis.

two. Now you've got a front half and a back half.

Now split the halves lengthwise down the center of the backbone. With a small saw you can saw the backbone in half, which is arm-breaking work, or you can use an ax. I've chopped a bull lengthwise with a small ax and found it fairly simple. Start at the back and work forward, and take small controlled strokes with the ax to keep the cut going straight. My friend Roger Iveson says two hatchets make the job easier. You set the edge of one hatchet on the bone and pound it

With the animal lying on its side, start skinning at the belly as described above and skin out the entire top half from the belly to the backbone. If you don't plan to save the hide, or if you'll cape out the animal (for details, see Caping), you can slit the hide down the backbone from the head to the tail and skin from the back to the belly.

Once the top half is skinned, you can take the animal apart in easy-to-handle pieces. Follow the procedure described with the accompanying photos. The pictures show a small deer, but the procedure is identical on an elk or any other animal in the field. This was done at home under clean conditions prior to wrapping the meat for freezing. In the field, always slip boned meat immediately into clean game bags or hang it where it won't get dirty.

Boning, of course, reduces the weight of an animal considerably, and that's the major incentive for boning in the field. As you can see

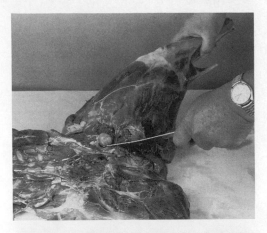

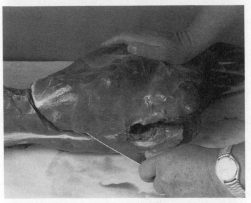

Now cut off the back leg. To do that, lift up the leg and work from the inside of the leg toward the back. Slide your knife right along the pelvic bone so that all the meat comes off with the leg. Be careful not to cut into the body cavity. Soon you'll see the ball-and-socket joint. Push hard on the leg and you can open up this joint to separate the leg bone from the pelvic socket. Then it's just a matter of cutting meat along the top of the pelvis to free the leg from the body.

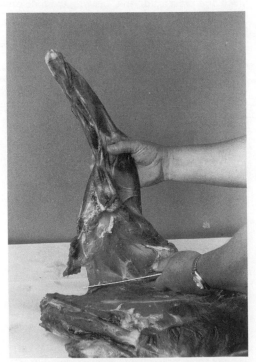

Pull up on the front leg and cut it free from the body.

from just a little experience, a 150-pound buck would weigh 126 pounds field dressed. Packing that on your back would be a tough haul. But by boning it out you can reduce the buck to 72 pounds, which would make one fairly heavy load or two easy loads. A 600-pound elk (whole weight) would weight 498 pounds in the quarters. Boning would reduce that animal to 258 pounds. Any time you have to pack meat

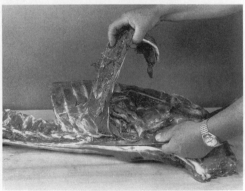

Start at the brisket and fillet meat off the ribs all the way to the backbone. As in the second photo, you might want to work also from the backbone to cut the backstrap out cleanly. Then the rib meat, backstrap, flanks, and neck meat will come off in one big slab.

any distance, boning offers the only reasonable alternative.

Boning also allows meat to cool rapidly. If your animal lies in the field for some time before you find it, boning might save the meat, because boneless meat in small pieces will cool much faster than huge, thick quarters.

Skinning or Not. Hunters often debate whether you should skin an animal in the field. Some say you must skin it immediately to prevent spoilage, and others say you should leave the hide on.

In hot weather (daytime temperatures of 60 or higher, nighttime no lower than 40) you should skin an animal right away to promote cooling. For that reason, during early bow seasons you should carry game bags to keep dirt and flies off the meat. Skinning methods are described above.

In cold weather, when temperatures drop to freezing or lower, skinning isn't necessary for adequate cooling, and the hide keeps meat clean and prevents drying. Leaving the hide on especially helps in horsepacking and other backcountry situations where you must wrestle the meat around and put it in dirty paniers or pack boxes. Leave the hide on until you take the animal to cold storage or to camp where you can skin and bag it under clean conditions.

Small animals like deer and antelope will cool quickly enough with the hide on if you

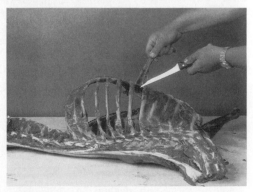

To salvage all meat off this side, cut the strips of meat from between the ribs. It can be ground into hamburger.

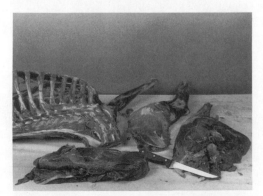

Now you have three slabs of meat—front leg, back leg, and chest meat—and bare bones. Flip the carcass over and repeat the process on the other side.

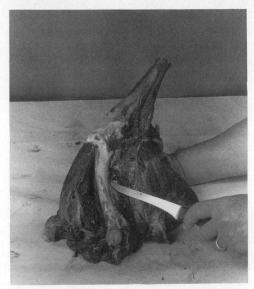

To save additional weight for packing, you may also want to bone out the legs. As in this photo showing the back leg, slide your knife close to the bone to cut off the meat.

simply hang them or lay them over a log and prop open the body cavity to allow good air circulation. On larger animals you have to go a step beyond that. At the least, split big animals lengthwise, and better yet, quarter them as described above. You can quarter an animal as well with the hide on as off. Regardless of how you cut up the carcass, always hang or lay the pieces so air can circulate all the way around to ensure quick cooling.

Even if you skin and quarter an elk or other big animal, you're wise to open up the thickest parts. Bone sour, the result of slow cooling, is particularly common in the hip joints and shoulders. To prevent that, slice down the insides of the back legs to open up the hip joints, and cut under the front legs to open up a space between the legs and the chest.

More Thoughts on Cooling. The first challenge in preserving game meat is getting body heat out of the animal. Meat sours in two ways: from the inside out and from the outside in. When you kill an animal, its body systems, including the cooling system, cease immedi-

ately but the cells continue to work and to produce heat. As a result, when an animal dies its internal body heat actually can rise from a normal 100 degrees to 110 degrees or higher. Unless that heat is dissipated rapidly, the carcass will sour, starting at the bone and spreading into the meat. That's why it's critical to recover animals quickly, and that's why it's important to open up hip joints and shoulders on big animals to promote cooling. Cooling meat to air temperature within 12 hours of the kill virtually eliminates the threat of bone sour.

Meat can still spoil externally, so it's important to chill the meat well and to keep it cold. Ideally, of course, you'll take your animal to cold storage immediately and hang it at 34 degrees for a few days, and then either you or the butcher will cut, wrap, and freeze it.

Unfortunately that's not always possible, and at times you'll have to keep meat in the field for long periods. How much time do you have? Professor Ray Field, an authority on meat care, said, "Life begins at 40." In other words, if you can cool meat to 40 degrees or colder—that's internal temperature—and hold it there, you can keep meat in the field safely for a week or longer. In late seasons that should be no problem, and as long as nights are cold, in the 30s or lower, and daytime temperatures don't rise much above 40, you can

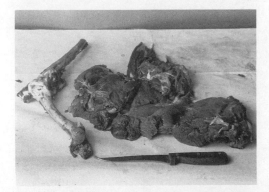

For packing in the field, bag up the boneless meat to keep it clean. You've reduced it in size and weight as much as you can. For butchering at home, separate the muscles into natural groups and cut them into meal-size portions.

just hang your animal in the shade on a meat pole and relax.

In August and September, it might not be that easy. If you're hunting the backcountry where you can't retrieve an animal quickly by yourself, line up a packer to haul the meat. It's irresponsible to hike in several miles and shoot an animal, and then start thinking about how to get it out. I know hunters who have done that and have lost meat, and they have no one to blame but themselves. Always arrange for packing services and cold storage before your hunt. In 65-degree weather, you have only about three days to get that meat into cold storage, and in hotter weather you have less time than that.

If temperatures are warm during the day but are dropping to 40 or lower at night, you can store meat in camp for several days. At night

hang the meat, unbagged, so it will cool to air temperature. Then during the day take it down, bag it, and wrap it in sleeping bags or other good insulation. During the day the internal temperature of the meat will rise no more than two to three degrees. I've kept meat fresh for more than a week with this method.

On the drive home, never lay meat directly on the bed of your pickup. One butcher told me he'd seen a number of animals partially spoiled because of this practice. The exhaust system heats the bed just enough to spoil the meat. Always put down a foam pad or use your clothes bags and packs to insulate the meat underneath. Pile your sleeping bags and other gear over the meat to insulate it from the top and you can keep meat fresh for a two- or three-day drive, as long as it was thoroughly cooled to 40 degrees or lower to begin with.

Wrap each piece of meat in plastic wrap to make the package airtight. Then wrap the meat in coated freezer paper for double protection against freezer burn.

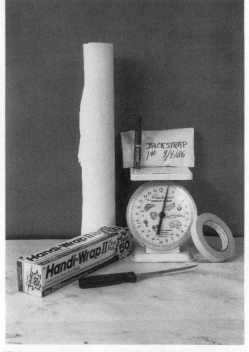

Weigh and label each package of meat with the weight, date, and kind of meat. Needed materials for meat wrapping are plastic wrap, coated freezer paper, knife, scale, tape, and marking pen.

Wrapping and Freezing Meat

You can take your deer or elk to a butcher shop where it will be sawed into cuts similar to those of beef, but you can do a better job yourself. Regardless of how you've handled an animal in the field, I'd suggest you bone it for freezing (follow the procedure shown in the accompanying photos). You'll save freezer space, and you also can trim the meat spotlessly clean, which guarantees good flavor.

Once you've reduced it to the large, boneless pieces shown in the photos, dissect it along natural muscle lines. The hams and front legs come apart in neat muscle groups. Trim off all fat, which can turn rancid even in a freezer, and cut off all bloodshot and tainted pieces that can produce bad flavor.

Cut the meat into meal-size chunks. I generally cut the choice portions into roasts and freeze them in whole pieces, rather than cutting them into steaks. The less surface area exposed, the less drying that will take place. When these roasts are thawed, they can be cooked whole. Or while they're still partially frozen, they can be sliced into steaks. The neck, flanks, and scrap meat are saved for stews, jerky, and hamburger.

Now double wrap each piece of meat, first in plastic wrap, then with coated freezer paper. The plastic ensures an airtight seal, which prevents dehydration. Game meat wrapped this way will stay fresh for a year or longer.

It's important to freeze meat at temperatures at or below zero. Bacteria can still grow at 20 degrees, but at zero, bacterial growth ceases. In addition, ground meat with mixed-in fat, and cured meats with fat and salt, will turn rancid under freezing conditions, so these should be frozen for no more than six months or so.

MEDITERRANEAN DRAW or RELEASE
See Split-Finger Draw.

MICHIGAN
This state covers an area of 57,019 square miles. Public lands are extensive, and the Department of Natural Resources publishes a couple of excellent books as well as detailed maps showing public access and good hunting areas.

Big Game

Whitetail Deer. The deer population is estimated at 1 million animals. Traditionally Michigan has ranked third (behind Texas and Pennsylvania) in total hunting licenses sold, and archery licenses play a big part in those sales. Each year Michigan sells an average of 213,000 resident and 4,200 nonresident archery licenses. Bowhunters kill an average of 26,000 deer, slightly less than 50 percent of them bucks, each year, and bow harvest has approached 40,000 some years. Average bowhunting success has been 10 percent with a high of 17 percent. The bow season runs from October 1 through November 14, and it opens again, following general gun season, for the month of December. The bag limit is one deer.

The Upper Peninsula (U.P.) contains the most wild lands in Michigan. There are some farmlands in the southern and eastern U.P., but otherwise it's all forest, and topography ranges from mountainous to flat. Deer densities are moderate throughout. State and national forests cover a majority of the U.P., and big companies that generally allow hunting own large tracts, so access is virtually unlimited.

The northern Lower Peninsula contains the highest deer numbers and yields the highest harvest in Michigan. Hunters kill an average of five deer per square mile annually from several counties here. Some private lands are leased by clubs, but two national forests and six state forests assure good public access on the northern Lower Peninsula.

The southern Lower Peninsula consists largely of private farmlands, so access is poorest in this region. However, many state game areas do offer public hunting, and the Department of Natural Resources has leased the hunting rights to thousands of acres of private land. Deer numbers are good here.

The overall state record typical whitetail scored 181²/₈ points, and the record nontypical scored 232⁵/₈. In proportion to its high harvest, Michigan doesn't produce a lot of huge bucks.

Black Bears. On the Upper Peninsula, the season is open from mid-September through October. Dogs are allowed. On the northern

Lower Peninsula, the season is much shorter, and a special bow season is held in October. No dogs are allowed during the bow season. Baiting is legal.

Other Game

Michigan holds a spring turkey season. Snowshoe hares and cottontails are abundant throughout the state in suitable habitat, and three kinds of squirrels — fox, gray, and black — offer widespread hunting wherever hardwoods provide suitable feed and cover. Other species of game, such as woodchucks and foxes, are available.

Contact. Department of Natural Resources, Box 30028, Lansing, MI 48909.

MINNESOTA Minnesota covers an area of 84,068 square miles. For management purposes the Department of Natural Resources divides Minnesota into four zones. Zone 1, the northeastern quarter, has heavy forests of hardwoods, aspens, and conifers — spruce, balsam fir, jack pine. Zones 2 and 3, which run diagonally across the state from northwest to southeast, form a transition area between forests to the east and prairie farmlands to the west. This transition zone consists of crop fields interspersed with forested river bottoms and woodlots. It takes in the Mississippi River breaks on the southeast border, which contain virtually the only rough terrain in Minnesota. Historically, Zone 4, which covers the western half of the state, was rolling prairie; now it is covered with corn, soybean, and grain fields. State and national forests assure plenty of public hunting in Minnesota, primarily in the forest and transition zones.

Big Game

Whitetail Deer. The deer population of Minnesota is estimated at 850,000 animals. Just under 40,000 residents and 600 nonresidents buy archery licenses each year. Archery harvest has averaged about 5,500 deer each year, and success rate has been 8 to 10 percent. The statewide bow season runs from mid-September through November, although it's concurrent with the firearms season in November. Bowhunting is allowed in some parts of the state in December too.

Deer densities are fairly high, 20 to 30 deer per square mile, throughout most of the forested zone except in the Boundary Waters Canoe Area in the extreme northeast, where numbers are much lower. The transition zone generally has the highest deer numbers, and some huge bucks come from this region. In the western prairie zone, deer are restricted to wooded river bottoms and wetlands, so overall densities are low.

Minnesota ranks among the top three or four trophy whitetail states. The overall state record typical scored 202, and the record nontypical 268⅝. More than three dozen typicals and two dozen nontypicals — 8 percent of the total in each category — from Minnesota are listed by Boone and Crockett, and dozens of Pope and Young bucks have come from this state.

Black Bears. Hunters kill several hundred bears a year in Minnesota. The season is open for about a month between September and October.

Moose. Moose seasons have been held every other year for many years. Permits are limited and odds are poorer than 20 to 1 for drawing a tag.

Other Game

Turkeys are hunted on a very limited basis. In total, hunters take more than a million squirrels, cottontails, and snowshoe hares each year, and bowhunting for these species can be good in suitable habitat. Hunting for foxes and other predators is major sport in Minnesota, too.

Contact. Minnesota Department of Natural Resources, Division of Fish and Wildlife, 500 Lafayette Road, St. Paul, MN 55146.

MISSISSIPPI Whitetail deer occupy nearly 100 percent of Mississippi's 47,296 square miles. Mississippi contains more than 30 public wildlife management areas, including several national forests that cover more than a million acres. It's possible in some cases to get permission to hunt private land by asking, but the major trend is toward hunting clubs and private leases.

Big Game

Whitetail Deer. An estimated 1.5 to 2 million deer live in Mississippi. During one recent season, 37,000 archers killed 17,400 deer, more than half of them bucks. Average bowhunter success has been about 25 percent, although with Mississippi's liberal bag limits, some bowhunters kill more than one deer per year. The archery season runs from the first Saturday in October through the Friday before Thanksgiving, and this is followed by various firearms seasons, some that allow hunting with dogs and others that don't, and other primitive weapons hunts are held. The bag limit is one antlered buck per day, five per license year, and during legal seasons for taking antlerless deer, one antlerless deer per day, three per license year.

Flat country bordering the Mississippi River is heavily farmed and overall deer numbers are low, except in remaining bottomlands and woodlots. A region called the Loess Bluffs parallels the Mississippi bottomlands, and the wooded breaks in this bluff country support a lot of deer, and the bluffs have a fair amount of public hunting lands.

Deer numbers are good throughout the hilly, wooded northcentral and northeastern parts of Mississippi, and some of the bigger bucks come from the Black Prairie country near Starkville. Southeastern Mississippi is called the Pine Woods region. The low-elevation, flat to rolling country here supports high deer numbers, although animals average smaller in size than in the northern and western regions. Several large blocks of public land assure some access.

The state record typical whitetail measured 183⅝, and the record nontypical 216⅜, but Mississippi isn't noted for huge bucks.

Other Game

Turkeys. Mississippi is a major turkey state with an estimated flock of 100,000 birds.

Hunters take as many as 10,000 gobblers during the spring season, which opens in March and runs through April, and a fall season is held in some regions. Multiple-bird limits are the rule.

Small Game. Squirrels are the most popular game animals in Mississippi, and hunters take more than 3 million in good years. Both fox and eastern gray squirrels are common. Cottontail rabbits are abundant around all suitable brushy edge cover.

Contact. Department of Wildlife Conservation, Southport Mall, P.O. Box 451, Jackson, MS 39205.

MISSOURI Missouri has an area of 68,995 square miles, and a generous amount of that is open to public hunting. The Mark Twain National Forest in the Ozarks contains 1.5 million acres, and the Department of Conservation administers nearly 600,000 acres for public hunting throughout the state. Much of this public land supports good wildlife populations. Still, nearly 90 percent of Missouri is privately owned, and getting permission to hunt can be tough. The idea of leasing hunting rights has become fairly prevalent in Missouri.

Big Game

Whitetail Deer. Missouri has a highly respected deer management program, and the Show Me state produces not only lots of deer but big bucks. An average of 50,000 residents and 2,000 nonresidents hunt deer during Missouri's archery season. In the early 1980s, they killed an average of 4,600 deer annually. Normally the general firearms season runs for nine days in mid-November. The bow season runs from October 1 through the day preceding the rifle season, and it reopens after general firearms season and lasts through December. Hunters can kill one deer during bow season and another during rifle season.

The Missouri River cuts across the middle of the state and roughly divides it in half. The northern half is primarily agricultural, and the southern half contains extensive forests. Missouri has gained a reputation for trophy-class

Northern Missouri in the Green Hill section has many abandoned farms and wooded bottomlands that are loaded with whitetails, turkeys, and small game.

bucks, and most of these have come from the northern half. The northwestern corner, along the Mississippi River and into the Green Hills section, has intermixed farmlands and hardwood forests, and deer numbers are high. Many big bucks come from the Green Hills. The flat country of northwestern Missouri is virtually all farmland with only a scattering of woodland cover in the stream bottoms, and deer numbers are relatively low. Some huge bucks come from private land practically in Kansas City.

The southwestern corner consists of native prairie and croplands, and cover is restricted to creek and river bottoms. Overall deer numbers are moderate, but hunting is very good in some localities. The Ozarks, rugged, forested mountains, cover most of the rest of Missouri. The Ozarks don't grow the huge bucks found north of the Missouri River, but deer numbers are moderate, and the Ozarks provide good hunting.

The number two Boone and Crockett typical whitetail, which scored 205, was taken in Randolph County in 1971, and the former world-record nontypical, with a score of 333⅞, was picked up near St. Louis in 1981. Boone and Crockett lists many other Missouri whitetails, many taken in recent years. Bowhunters have taken their share of huge bucks, including many large enough to make the Pope and Young record book.

Other Game

Turkey. Missouri has fantastic turkey hunting. The more popular region might be the Ozarks of southern Missouri, but the north-central region bordering Iowa also has incredible numbers of birds. During the two-week spring season, all hunters (not just archers) kill more than 20,000 gobblers. Fall seasons are also held, and bowhunters can hunt turkeys throughout the archery deer season.

Small Game. Missouri has excellent squirrel and cottontail hunting in suitable hardwood forest habitat and brushy edge cover.

Contact. Missouri Department of Conservation, P.O. Box 180, Jefferson City, MO 65102.

MONARCH The name some hunters apply to a bull elk with eight antler points to the side. These same hunters would call a six-point bull a royal and a seven-point an imperial. These terms are rarely used among modern hunters.

MONTANA Montana covers 147,139 square miles. This huge state ranks among the best in the United States for variety, quantity, and quality of game. In general, the western one third consists of rugged, heavily timbered mountains, and a majority of the best lands are administered by the U.S. Forest Service, so getting permission to hunt isn't a problem. Getting access to some good country can be, however, because this region contains much wilderness. Many outfitters operate here.

The eastern two thirds consists of rolling farmlands, prairies, breaks, and badlands. National wildlife refuges, such as the C. M. Russell Refuge on the Missouri River, offer thousands of acres of public hunting. In addition, the Bureau of Land Management manages much land here. In general, however, eastern Montana is privately owned, and some of the better game lands are leased by outfitters, although some ranchers will grant permission to hunters who ask.

Big Game

Deer. Mule deer live throughout the state. Sheer numbers are highest in the eastern prairies and badlands, but the biggest bucks come from high mountain ranges of the western half. Whitetails live throughout brushy bottomlands of the eastern half, and their range extends into the river bottoms and forestlands of the northwestern corner all the way to the Idaho border. Montana may have the best whitetail hunting in the United States.

In Montana a license holder can hunt during gun and bow seasons. An estimated 16,000 hunters participate in the archery deer season. During one representative year, bowhunters killed 1,160 mule deer and 631 whitetails, for 13 percent success on mule deer and 9 percent on whitetails.

The bow season runs for six weeks from early September through mid-October, and the rifle season follows from mid-October through November. Other special seasons are held, and frequently multiple licenses are issued for antlerless deer. Some small areas are reserved for bowhunting only. Elk and deer seasons are concurrent, so many archers plan combined hunts.

The overall state record typical mule deer scored 201⁴/₈, and several others are listed in Boone and Crockett. The largest nontypical scored 275¹/₈. Largest bucks come from the western mountains, but Pope and Young–class bucks are common in most regions. The overall state record typical whitetail scored 199³/₈, and the record nontypical 252¹/₈. Flathead, Lake, Missoula, and Lincoln counties produce some of the biggest whitetails, but Pope and Young–class bucks are common wherever whitetails are found.

Elk. Without question, Montana ranks as one of the best elk states, in both quantity and quality. All the mountain ranges of the western end have good elk herds. The biggest bulls generally come from the brushy northwestern corner and from the Yellowstone area in the Madison, Gallatin, and Absoraka ranges, although the Pope and Young world record came from the Big Belt Mountains near Helena. The Missouri River breaks grow some huge bulls, and this open pine country has become popular with bowhunters. The bow season runs concurrent with deer season, from early September until mid-October.

Antelope. Most of eastern Montana has thriving antelope herds, and antelope bow season is generous, running from early September until mid-October. Some years Montana has issued an unlimited number of bowhunting licenses for antelope. Most good antelope country is privately owned, but with some effort you can get permission to hunt.

Black Bears. Montana does not allow baiting or hunting with hounds, yet the annual harvest averages 700 to 800 animals, which attests to the quality of the hunting. Bears live throughout the state, but the northwestern corner, with its thick rain forests, has the highest densities. Spotting in the spring around meadows and in September on huckleberry patches offers the best chances for a bear. No special bow seasons are held, but competition between archers and rifle hunters is little problem during general seasons (you must, however, wear

The forested mountains of western Montana hold some of North America's finest elk hunting.

blaze orange during any gun season, which includes bear season).

Grizzly Bears. Montana holds a grizzly season in October and November. The season is closed immediately when 25 bears have been killed.

Moose. Permits for these animals are issued in more than 50 big-game districts in the western end of the state. Harvest success runs high, but drawing success runs low. Each year nearly 20,000 hunters apply for the 500 to 600 permits. (For more details, see Moose.)

Sheep. Montana has produced a number of record-class Rocky Mountain bighorns. Licenses are limited in the best areas and drawing odds are poor. Montana also offers unlimited licenses in the mountains surrounding the north end of Yellowstone National Park, but this is a tough hunt with very low success. Don't try it unless you're a real go-getter and like punishment. (For more details, see Sheep.)

Mountain Goats. Again, the state has good hunting, but permits are limited and are issued by drawing. (For more details, see Mountain Goat.)

Cougar. Montana has excellent lion hunting. Virtually all lions are taken in the mountains of the western end and with the use of dogs. Most seasons are open from December through February.

Other Game

Turkeys. These birds have done very well in Montana, and the pine and grassland country of the southeast has excellent hunting.

Small Game and Predators. Rabbits—snowshoe hares, cottontails, and jackrabbits—abound in suitable habitat, but they're virtually unhunted. Coyotes, bobcats, and other predators and varmints such as prairie dogs and marmots exist in unlimited numbers, and there are no restrictions on hunting any of them.

Contact. Department of Fish, Wildlife and Parks, 1420 East Sixth Avenue, Helena, MT 59620.

MOOSE (*Alces alces*) North America has three brands of moose: Alaska-Yukon, Canada, and Shiras. The Alaska-Yukon moose, the largest member of the deer family (*Cervidae*) found anywhere in the world, may stand seven feet or taller at the shoulder and may weigh as much as 1,800 pounds on the hoof. Records-keeping organizations classify any moose from Alaska, the Yukon Territory, or Northwest Territories as Alaska-Yukon moose. Canada moose are slightly smaller. The record books classify any moose taken in Canada, excluding the Yukon and Northwest Territories, as well as the moose in Maine and Minnesota, as Canada moose. The largest Canada moose consistently come from northern British Columbia. Shiras moose, or Wyoming moose as they're commonly called, live in the Lower 48. The official records boundary is the Canadian border.

Where to Hunt Moose

Hunting opportunities are virtually unlimited throughout Canada, but nonresident aliens (meaning non-Canadians) must hire a guide to hunt legally in most cases. Alaska still offers the best opportunity to hunt moose unattached. Nonresidents are not required to hire a guide, and many adventuresome souls from the Lower 48 have taken to hunting moose, or moose and caribou in combination, in Alaska on their own. Even at that it's not a cheap operation because virtually all hunting in Alaska requires flying to and from your hunting camp.

Nowhere are tags for Shiras moose unlimited; you must draw for a tag, and the odds aren't good. Montana, for example, issues between 500 and 700 moose permits each year, but nearly 20,000 hunters apply for them. The odds for drawing are about 4 percent.

Wyoming issues a number of moose tags, too, and some bowhunters have excellent suc-

In Alaska, virtually all moose hunting involves flying or floating, or both. *Photos courtesy Jay Massey.*

cess on this hunt, but you must know your country. After eight years of applying, Cliff Dewell, a bowhunter from California, finally drew a moose tag in Wyoming. He was told he could find moose on public lands in his unit, but when the season opened, he searched a full week in the timber and mountains and valleys on public land and never saw a moose, or even any sign. He finally talked to a rancher who would let him hunt some willow bottomlands, and he got into moose right away.

Wyoming holds an archery-only moose hunt in December, but it takes place entirely on private lands, so you'd better be sure of your access before applying. A friend of Dewell's drew one of these tags, and then couldn't get permission to hunt. He finally paid a guide $150 a day to float a river and look for animals, and they never saw a moose. In other units some hunters have found lots of moose on public lands. The

Shiras moose live in the Western states south of the Canadian border. Idaho, Montana, Wyoming, and Utah offer the best hunting for these animals. *Photo courtesy Ed Park.*

important point is to check things out before you apply.

Idaho has good numbers of moose from the panhandle south through the Salmon River country and along the eastern boundary around Yellowstone National Park, but only residents may apply. Utah annually issues several dozen moose tags, but only a half dozen or so are reserved for nonresidents, and they're expensive. Washington also offers occasional moose tags for the Selkirk Mountains near the Canadian border, but permits are few in number.

Hunting for Moose

Biologists would consider moose a successional species. That is, like deer and elk, they thrive primarily where forests have been opened up by fire or other disturbances and woody shrubs abound. That's why moose are most abundant around extensive patches of willow, alder, aspen, and other leafy plants. They also feed heavily on aquatic vegetation,

and much of the best moose country is laced with bogs, marshes, and shallow lakes.

Calling. The rut gives you great advantage in moose hunting just as it does with many other big-game animals. Moose are solitary animals, and before the rut they hang out in dense timber and jungles of willows, where they're tough to locate.

During the rut, bulls start moving to look for cows, and their increased activity, and the fact that they sometimes move into more accessible country, improves your odds considerably. Jay Massey, a successful bowhunting guide in Alaska and author of the excellent book *Bowhunting Alaska's Wild Rivers*, said bulls move down from higher country and become relatively concentrated near rivers during the rut, where they can be hunted more easily by hunters floating the rivers.

Massey said the bulls start acting rutty in Alaska about September 8 and cows come into heat about September 17, and the rut continues on through October. From what I've learned, the same timing applies throughout the moose's range. In Wyoming, friends of mine have had good success hunting rutting moose in late September.

Just as with elk, the bulls and cows both call during the rut. The sound of a moose can best be described as a grunt. The bulls produce a short, guttural grunt, and the cows have a more drawn-out moan. Massey describes the cow moose's call as a "lost heifer" sound.

Both calls will attract bulls. On his Alaskan hunts, Massey said he's found the bull call works better early in the rut when bulls are looking for other bulls with which they spar and fight to establish dominance. Later, when the cows come into heat, bulls will be looking for cows, and Massey said he's found the cow call generally works better then. When one doesn't work he'll try the other, however, and at times he's found that mixing calls does the trick. As is the common practice, he uses only his voice, but he amplifies it with a birch bark megaphone.

Calling works for moose wherever they're found. In Wyoming, Cliff Dewell finally located some moose on private land by glassing down into extensive jungles of willows from nearby ridges. One day he was walking up a river bottom toward a spot where he'd seen some cow moose, when he heard a bull grunt and saw the willows shaking up ahead. Dewell grunted like a moose, and the bull thundered toward him on the run, and he arrowed this bull at 18 yards. He also grunted in another bull for a friend. This hunt took place in late September. A previous year, Dewell had hunted moose in British Columbia in late September, and he found the methods and results to be virtually the same there.

Spotting. Some seasons in Alaska and Canada open before the rut, and if you decide to hunt then, you're handicapped by the fact that you can't call them. At this time, spotting and stalking is by far the most widely practiced method. Climb to any vantage points you can find and glass down into dense brush patches, looking for shadowy, black bodies or the white flash of an antler palm. Through August the antlers will be in velvet, but in early September, when they're freshly rubbed and haven't yet been stained by brush, they will appear nearly white. Bulls are solitary by nature and in late

Jay Massey killed this bull in Alaska. Calling during the rut in September is one of the best ways to lure a bull within range. You don't want to kill a moose far from transportation. The rack alone off an Alaska-Yukon moose could weigh 50 pounds or more. *Photo courtesy Jay Massey.*

summer they hang out by themselves in isolated, brushy pockets and basins, and they can be tough to spot.

They can also be tough to stalk. Moose have excellent noses and ears (Massey rates their hearing as "superb") and they bed and feed in thick cover, so getting close is not guaranteed. You have to stalk as carefully for moose as any other big game. (For details, see Stalking.)

Again, the same methods work throughout moose range, as long as the topography permits. Jim Cox is a well-traveled archer who has taken moose in the Lower 48 as well as Alaska. In Wyoming he hunted the Greys River country. There he found plenty of moose on public lands, and he found all the biggest bulls up high, above 8,000 feet.

He also hunted in September when the animals were in rut, and he grunted in three or four bulls, but he hunted more by spotting.

"We would sit on one side of a canyon and use binoculars to glass the other side, looking for a black spot," Cox said. "When we saw something black, we'd get out the scope to study it and if it looked good, we'd go after it. It was very similar to hunting them in Alaska in early September, where we found them up high in thick willow patches."

In 18 days in Wyoming, Cox passed up chances at 13 bulls, looking for a world-record–class animal. Finally he got in on a bunch of three bulls and two cows that were grunting and carrying on. He'd had a good one picked out, but the animals were in thick willows and when he got in close and shot a bull, it turned out to be the wrong one. Still, it had a 40-inch rack with a record-book score of 137, good enough to make Pope and Young.

"You hear about how easy moose hunting is," Cox said. "But I haven't found that to be the case. This was a tough hunt. But I would go during the September rifle season, not in that late archery season."

As an alternative to spotting the high country, some archers hunt by floating rivers, as Massey and his hunters do in Alaska. In the lake country of eastern Canada, many hunters quietly paddle the shorelines of lakes and ponds, looking for moose, or calling if it's during the rut.

Guided versus Unguided. In Canada, residents hunt moose on their own, but aliens are required by law to hire outfitters, so traveling hunters have no choice there. In Alaska and the Lower 48, any bowhunter can hunt moose on his own if he chooses, but you should give it some careful thought first. Even in Wyoming or Montana, which might seem tame compared to Alaska, you can get a moose down some distance from a road, and you could very well need a packer to get it out. From a big bull you could get 500 to 600 pounds of meat, plus the cumbersome, heavy antlers. The largest Alaska-Yukon moose antlers weigh about 60 pounds, Canada moose about 50, and Shiras moose 30. Break these weights down into individual loads and figure out how far you have to pack it before you shoot your moose.

In Alaska, many bowhunters hunt from drop camps. Virtually all hunting there requires flying into the bush, so hunters hire a pilot to drop them off in good moose country, with arrangements to pick them up later. Then they hunt on their own. That's a good system, but you still have to pack your own meat. Massey advises against shooting a moose farther than two to three miles from the nearest transportation, either a raft on a river or a float plane.

Trophy Hunting

The largest Alaska-Yukon bulls have antler spreads exceeding 75 inches, Canada moose 65 inches, and Shiras moose 55 inches. Those are maximums, and average spreads aren't nearly as large. The greatest spread distance is measured as part of the score, so the wider the rack, the more desirable in terms of making the book.

In scoring the antlers of most deer species, length of the points receives high priority, but in moose only the number of points is counted, and individual point length does not add to the score. The major score measurements are palm length and width, so these are the priorities when judging a rack in the field. Also, for a

To score well, a moose must have wide, long palms, and it should have well-developed brow palms. This bull has only a single brow tine, which will not do much for the score. *Photo courtesy Ed Park.*

moose to score well, it must have a well-developed brow palm, because the brow palm is included in overall length-of-palm measurement, whereas a single brow spike is excluded from this measurement. On really big bulls, the main palms lie flat, but on smaller animals the palms tend to cup upward, which doesn't yield as great a spread credit.

MOUNTAIN GOAT *(Oreamnos americanus)*

Scientists say mountain goats aren't really goats but are more closely related to the antelopes. The mountain goat is one of only three mammals in North America that has a white coat year-round (the others are Dall sheep and polar bear), and mountain goats have no close relatives on this continent.

The Nature of Goats

Goats are probably most famous for their climbing ability. Their hooves are about the same length as those of deer and sheep, but they're more oval-shaped, and they consist of rubbery cushion pads surrounded by a hard shell. The spongy hoof pads give goats traction on the steepest rocks, and they can climb cliffs where no other animal can go.

Size. They're blocky, heavy animals. Average

billies stand 35 to 40 inches at the shoulder and weigh between 150 and 300 pounds. Billies weigh up to 30 percent heavier than nannies. Both sexes have horns from 7 to 12 inches long. Often the horns of females are as long as those of males, but they're more slender. The males use these horns in combat during the rut in November and December, but they fight much differently from their neighbors, the bighorn sheep. Whereas sheep have armor-plated skulls and fight by crashing their heads together, goats have fragile, thin skulls, and they fight by trying to hook each other in the flanks with their needlelike horns.

Range. Goats are more widely distributed in British Columbia than any other province or state. They live the full length of the coastal mountains as well as in the Rockies, and they're also abundant in the Alberta Rockies. Alaska has by far more goats than any other

Mountain goats have spongy hoof pads that provide traction even on near-vertical slick rocks. *Photo courtesy Bill McRae.*

273

state, followed by Washington, Montana, Idaho, Colorado, and South Dakota, in declining order of abundance. Utah, Wyoming, Oregon, and Nevada also have small herds. To hunt legally in British Columbia or Alberta, of course, nonresidents must hire a guide. In other states you can hunt on your own (except in Wyoming, where nonresidents must hire a guide to hunt designated wilderness). Alaska issues unlimited licenses, but in all other states a limited number of licenses are issued by drawing. Washington and Colorado offer the best drawing odds, because these states have special archery-only goat seasons. Idaho also issues a few bow-only goat tags.

Hunting Mountain Goats

Hunting goats isn't so much a matter of how you hunt them as where. Goats live in high, rocky open country, and with their white coats they're relatively easy to spot. Virtually everyone who hunts goats hunts by spotting animals first, looking for one in an accessible position, and then stalking. As in any open-country hunting, quality binoculars and a spotting scope are essential. (For details, see Optics and Spotting.) Few predators dare to tread the near-

Roger Iveson killed this nanny with ten-inch horns in southwestern Alaska. He had a pilot drop him and a friend off on a beach, and then they hiked up several miles through rain-forest jungle to reach goat country. *Photo courtesy Roger Iveson.*

vertical terrain of goat country, so goats aren't overly concerned about danger from above. You want to get above them and stalk down. In most cases, you probably wouldn't have much choice anyway. That being the case, shots could be at sharp downhill angles, so it's important to practice shooting downhill before a goat hunt, or any mountain hunt for that matter. (For details, see Trajectory.)

Roger Iveson from Reno, Nevada, describes what could be considered a fairly typical do-it-yourself goat hunt, in this case in Alaska. He and a friend drove to Haines and then hired a pilot to fly them out and drop them off on a beach between Juneau and Haines. In most places, landing in goat country is out of the question, so you just about have to start your ascent from the beach.

They'd had the pilot fly them over the country to locate goats and to pick out a reasonable route into the mountains. To get up from the beach they had to wade directly up a glacial stream because the devil's club and spruce timber were so thick on the steep, surrounding mountainsides they couldn't force their way through with packs on their backs.

Iveson estimated they'd waded up the stream nearly seven miles before they finally came to a ledge that would allow them to climb to the top of the peaks where the goats live. On top, the country flattened out to some degree, so hiking there and approaching animals wasn't nearly as tough as getting up there in the first place.

They'd scouted by air before heading in so they knew pretty well where to find animals once they'd got to the top, and they had no problem spotting 25 or more goats each day. Iveson saw at least one of world-record class, but he wasn't able to get a shot at it. Still, on the first day he missed one animal and killed one, and his friend shot one with a rifle.

That was the fun part of the hunt, but perhaps not the most memorable. Coming down was the tough part, much harder than going up. Iveson is a gritty individual and was making out okay, carrying his friend's entire goat and gear, but his friend got shaky legs. So they tied a rope around his pack, which contained the cape and boned-out meat of Iveson's goat, and started to let it down easy. But the friend just let go of the rope and gave the pack a shove.

"I couldn't believe that," Iveson said, shaking his head. "That thing flew off into space and it seemed to just hang there in the air for minutes. I tried to grab it but it was doing 80 and I could only do about 5. We tried to come up from the bottom to find it, but there was no way. We lost the whole thing.

"Hunting those goats is a great hunt, but I wouldn't recommend it for anyone who's not in great physical shape. It's rough. I would also suggest they take at least 100 feet of rope to help in climbing those steep places, especially coming down. You can ease yourself and your gear down with the rope."

Iveson also suggested that instead of flying out and landing on a beach, a person could hunt from a small boat in much of southwestern Alaska. "The wind can come up so you have to be careful, but while we were there the bays were glass calm. You could use a small boat to cruise a bay and glass for goats and then climb up when you've got some spotted."

Retrieving an animal can be a major problem. If a wounded goat gets into cliffs, your chances for retrieving him are slim, unless you're an experienced rock climber and have the needed gear along—which isn't a bad idea. Shots predictably could be down onto the back and goats have massive chests, so a heavy bow, something in the class used for elk, is in order. And pick your shots. Don't randomly shoot a goat on the hope you'll be able to retrieve him. Make sure you can get to him before you shoot.

Incidentally, some hunters debate the quality of goat meat. Outdoor writer Ed Park has killed three goats, including one huge billy in Kelly Creek, Idaho, that was so old it had only three teeth. Park said they were all very good eating.

Some goat country might be easier to hunt than other goat country, but none of it is easy. Alaskan hunting is unique because ocean beaches offer the only access to many of the

Judging the trophy quality of a goat requires a practiced eye. Circumference of the horns and curve gives a clue whether a goat is a billy or nanny. The strong sweeping curve and thick bases of this goat's horns indicate it's a billy. An ear is about 4½ inches long, so you can gauge horn length from that. On good trophies, horns are 9 inches or longer. *Photo courtesy Bill McRae.*

best areas. The rest of the details are similar, however, regardless of where you hunt. In Washington, Ed Park said he had to backpack a good full day just to reach good goat country, and the same holds true in Idaho and other states. You just won't find many goats in close-to-road spots. And finding goats isn't always guaranteed. Park said there were plenty of animals in the areas he hunted. Sign—big rounded tracks, droppings similar to deer pellets, white wool on the bushes and rocks— proved that. But on several occasions he's had to look long and hard to find them, and he and a friend killed two goats in Washington in heavy timber.

Trophy Hunting

Most experienced big-game hunters I know agree that goats are the hardest big game to judge in terms of trophy quality. The difference between average and exceptional animals may be no more than fractions of an inch. In fact, distinguishing between billies and nannies isn't necessarily a sure thing. If a mature goat has a kid with it, then obviously it's a nanny. Nannies also tend to be more social and stay in small bands, whereas billies commonly hang out alone, and billies are blockier and more hump-shouldered. Billies' horns normally are heavier at the bases and sweep back in a more gradual curve from butt to tip, whereas nannies' horns may be a little thinner and straighter with a sharper curve toward the tips. A spotting scope is mandatory for making these hair-fine judgments.

If you want a high-scoring goat, it's important to kill a billy because a nanny's horns might not score as well. Of course, to score well the horns must be intact with no broken tips. Mature billies have an average horn length of about 9 inches, but outstanding animals have horns of 10 inches or longer. Average ear length on mature goats is 4½ inches, so good horns will measure more than twice as long as an ear.

In summer, goats shed their long winter hair and take on shorter coats. If you want a prime cape or hide with long hair, wait until October or later to shoot a goat.

MOUNTAIN LION *(Felis concolor)* Many names have been applied to the mountain lion: cougar, panther, painter, puma, catamount. The most commonly used today are cougar and mountain lion. Most avid hunters I know who've spent their lives with the big cats simply call them lions or cougars.

Undoubtedly the biggest misconception about lions is that they're endangered. People assume that because they never see cougars in the wild the cats must be scarce. Nothing could be further from the truth. As of this writing, every Western state has had or has in progress a study of its mountain lions. In all states, lions are classified as big-game animals, which has eliminated the uncontrolled slaughter of bounty hunting, and in many states, harvest is controlled either by a limitation on tag numbers or by a kill quota. Every state reports that lion populations are stable or growing. In Utah

and Arizona, the two highest lion-kill states, hunters have killed more than 200 lions annually for two decades, and harvest has never declined. If numbers were dwindling, kill figures would go down.

The Nature of Lions

The mountain lion has the widest distribution of any mammal in the Western Hemisphere, from northern British Columbia to the southern tip of South America. Historically lions lived in all the Lower 48 states, but now in North America they're restricted to mountainous western Canada, the Western states, and Mexico.

Size. Lions measure anywhere from six to nine feet long from nose to tip of tail, although any cat over seven feet would be considered big. Average weight falls somewhere between 100 and 150 pounds for toms, and 80 to 100 for females. A huge tom might weigh as much as 200 pounds.

I shot a large male in Nevada that weighed 175 pounds and he looked enormous. I'd always pictured cougars as sleek, slender animals with fine lines and ropy muscles, but this cat had a blocky, powerful look with front shoulders and forearms like a Charolais bull. Its meat was light-colored, somewhat like pork, and the carcass was as plump and well filled out as any deer I've ever shot. I boned out most of the carcass and took the meat home to eat. It was excellent and mild-flavored, again somewhat like pork, only it was lean and a little tough. We used slow-cook recipes in the Crockpot or Dutch oven to tenderize it, and it was excellent. If you shoot a cougar, don't waste the meat.

Appearance. Males and females have the same basic coloration of tan or gray on the back, depending on geographic region, shading into pure white on the belly. The tail, which can be as long as 36 inches, has a dark brown or black tip. It can be tough to distinguish a young male from a female cat, but you'll know a mature tom when you see one. The body will be blocky and powerful looking, and compared to the sleek, delicate head of a young tom or female, he'll have a broad face and a big head in relation to the body.

Eating Habits. Some people love cougars, others hate them, and much of the debate revolves around their diet. Most biologists I've talked to agree that lions like their venison and probably average killing one deer a week. That's at least 52 a year, or the equivalent harvest of 200 hunters, given 25 percent success.

My friend Pat Miller watched a lion kill a deer in Utah one August. Pat was looking through his scope at a doe and two fawns when he noticed a fourth animal, a lion. Its belly nearly dragged the ground as it inched toward the deer. At one point it leaped over a low bush, but apparently it timed this move just right so the deer didn't notice. When it was 20 yards from the deer, it lunged forward and after a brief chase caught one of the fawns. It lay down to eat the fawn right there as the doe and other fawn stood nearby, watching.

It's often said that lions take only fawns and weak deer. They might take these first, but they don't stop there. In New Mexico, bighorn-sheep transplanting has been set back at times as lions have killed newly released, healthy sheep. And in an elk study in that state, an 80-pound female lion killed 11 healthy, radio-collared elk.

Lion Hunting

Not only do cougars have a wide geographic range, but they inhabit diverse terrain. In the Northwest they live in the old-growth forests of the high mountains, a land of tall timber and deep snow. In the Great Basin they thrive in desert ranges where the flora consists of sage-brush and a few scattered trees, and where tablelands plunge into huge gashes in the land called canyons. Farther south, many lions live in the dry chaparral hills of central Arizona. No one kind of vegetation or terrain character-izes lion country. Almost universally, though, lion country is rough and remote.

Maybe that's what makes lion hunting great sport. These cats draw you into the toughest places in North America, where you can leave behind any hint of civilization to glimpse a

frontier world. As houndman Steve Harris said, "If I could hunt only one animal, it would be the cougar. He takes you into the roughest country. You won't see any human tracks out there."

Hunting Methods. I have seen places, espe-cially in the Jarbidge country of northern Ne-vada, where a person might expect to spot a lion. A hunter with patience could sit on one side of an open, rimrock canyon and glass the other side, and eventually he'd spot a cat. But could he get a bow shot? Unless you want to dedicate your life to stalking lions, you'd better look to a more reliable method hunting on foot as you would for other game.

Some hunters call lions, just as they do other predators. Arizona hunter Reed Peterson has killed three lions while calling (these were shot with a rifle), and his friend Dr. Elwood Odell has called in nine. Their successes prove it can be done, and as Peterson said, "I wonder how many we call in and never see."

Peterson uses the same calls and techniques he uses for coyotes and bobcats (for details, see Predator Calling), but he emphasizes that it takes infinite patience and time. To kill his first lion he hunted constantly for two full years all over Arizona. "I'd never encourage anybody to take up calling just to kill a lion," Peterson said. "I'd say the odds against it are 10,000 to 1."

Virtually all lions taken by design rather than accident are run by hounds. Even though the average lion could shred a pack of hounds, the cats prefer to run, and with a pack of dogs in pursuit, they normally run up the nearest tree. Then you've got an easy shot, even with bow and arrow.

That might sound unsportingly easy, but don't judge it until you've taken part. Indeed, most houndmen agree that once they've hit a hot track, they're confident they'll tree the cat. Unlike bobcats, which will bound from boul-der to boulder and pull other tricks to evade dogs, cougars normally run full out for a short distance, and then they tree.

But getting a cat isn't guaranteed. For one thing, just getting *to* a mountain lion can be

Virtually all cougars taken by design are taken with the use of dogs. Steve Harris, an avid cat hunter from Oregon, uses redbone hounds.

major work. They live in country that's straight up and down, and you often have to hunt them in deep snow. Finding a track and following the dogs once they start trailing takes good lungs and strong legs.

Conditions play a big part in hunting success. Research biologist Ken Greer said the lion harvest in Montana jumped from a low of 67 in 1981 to a high of 113 in 1982. The lion population certainly hadn't changed that much in one year, but conditions had. In 1981 little snow fell, and lions left inconspicuous tracks on the old crusted snow. In 1982 fresh snow fell every few days, and hunters and dogs were able to pick up new tracks quickly.

In central Arizona and other parts of the Southwest where snow rarely falls, hunters often search for lions on bare ground, using a strike dog to pick up a cat's scent trail, but generally snow is the key to lion hunting. Not

only does snow make the cat tracks visible, but it also concentrates deer, elk, and other prey for lions. You can locate lions by looking for other big game, because the cats will hang out in deep snow, just above concentrations of deer and elk.

In country with lots of back roads, hunters ride snowmobiles to search for fresh tracks, but in steep, roadless country they must hike the ridges on foot. My first lion hunt took place on the Imnaha River, a major tributary of the famous Hells Canyon on the Snake River. Many logging roads penetrate this country, but the roads are snowed in all winter, and snow machines aren't practical in the steep, roadless side canyons. So each day we hiked up from camp on the river bottom to the tops of the ridges and contoured around the hills, just above herds of wintering mule deer, to search for tracks. In knee-deep snow we hiked six to eight miles a day. In eight days we never saw a fresh cat track.

The average home range of a lion covers 30 square miles, and some large males roam a range as large as 250 square miles. Obviously, in that expanse of territory, you have to be lucky to some extent just to see a track. During a study in Oregon's best cat country, researcher David Harcombe averaged 2.7 days of looking for every lion track he found. In 1980, sport hunters in Colorado averaged 19 days of hunting for every lion taken. And in Montana one year, 80 percent of nonresident hunters, even though most hired professional guides with trained hounds, failed to see a cat treed. Obviously, hunting with hounds doesn't guarantee quick success.

Desert Hunting. But then, sometimes it all works out, as it did for me in northern Nevada on my second cougar hunt. Several houndman friends and I had set up camp near the Idaho border there, and we hunted cats far out in the desert where deer, pushed down from nearby mountains by deep snow, spend the winter. In this open sage country we saw many herds of 200 to 300 deer. The cat trap was well baited.

In this open country you can sit on one side of a rimrock canyon and spot tracks on the far

Some mountain-lion country is heavily forested and you must walk to look for tracks, but in Nevada and other desert states, you often can spot lion tracks at long distances across canyons.

side, so rather than walking we glassed with binoculars and scopes. With experience, you can analyze tracks from a mile or more away. My friend Ken Magee pointed out several traits that help distinguish lion tracks from coyote and deer tracks, which are generally common in cat country.

Spotting Tracks. First, the tracks are round, much like those of a house cat, only a lot bigger. The average cougar track measures about four inches across, and a big one will go five inches. In snow, cats pick their feet high and set them straight down so you see distinct pug marks. Coyotes and deer leave drag marks where they slide their feet in and out of the tracks. Coyote tracks fall nearly in a straight line, but cat tracks are slightly more staggered, and on each side the back foot registers directly on the track of the front foot. On coyote or other dog tracks, you can see toenail marks up close, but cats retract their nails and you see no nail marks. Cats tend to jump up onto rocks and to walk logs and ledges, which coyotes and deer rarely do.

Other signs also indicate the presence of cats. You might see tom markings, large scratches in trees. And a group of scavenging birds, such as ravens or magpies, can indicate the presence of a lion kill.

Ken Magee was the first to locate a fresh track on that hunt. Looking down from a rimrock, he'd spotted it in a creek bottom. The rest of us heard the clamor of his hounds in the distance and scrambled to the bottom of a huge canyon to join in the chase. We'd followed

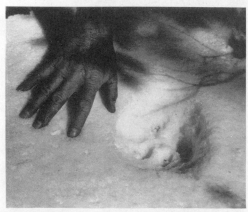

Snow offers a great advantage in cat hunting, because tracks show up clearly. A big lion track is nearly as large as a man's hand.

In lion hunting, the challenge lies in locating tracks and getting to the lion once it's treed. Making the shot should be easy. Notice this big tom's right ear. He apparently lost part of it in a fight.

the tracks for two miles through towering cliffs and boulder slides—not a place for the faint of heart, particularly with ice coating all the rocks—when we jumped the cat from his bed on a rock ledge. He sprinted to the bottom of the canyon, the dogs in hot pursuit, and ran up the biggest juniper he could find.

Viewing that cat up a tree proved to be a thrilling hunting experience, not because I'd accomplished anything as a hunter—after all, the dogs had done the hunting—but because here I viewed a scene I probably never would have seen on my own. Sure, it might be more poetic to stalk a cougar on foot and take him one on one, but for all practical purposes, that's a dream and few of us have the time to make it come true. Using dogs allows the average hunter to encounter one of America's finest big-game animals and to glimpse one of nature's mysteries, and that makes it worthwhile.

Archery Tackle for Lions. Once you've treed a cat, shooting him with a bow should be no tougher than with a rifle. The main thing is to be sure of your shot. One houndman had a jaundiced view of archers because he took an archer hunting, and the bowhunter tried shooting the cat behind the ear. He missed his mark, not far but just enough, and they ended up with a long chase and a mess on their hands.

There's only one place to shoot a lion, and that's in the chest to get the lungs or heart. Slip that arrow in just behind the front leg, slightly below center. Before you shoot, analyze the cat's position and make sure of your target. To shoot that cat in Nevada, I climbed a nearby

These hunters pack a cat to level ground for skinning. Lion hides make great trophies, and the meat makes for fine eating. Don't leave the meat behind.

tree to get a ten-yard shot straight across. Lions have a lot of loose hide, and as this cat lay over a limb the hide bunched up to make his chest look deeper than it was. I shot for the low chest and the arrow hit on the money, but nothing happened. I'd shot through a big fold of skin. I aimed four inches higher the next shot, and when the arrow hit, the cat leaped straight up, flipped over backward, and crashed to the ground dead.

Any bow suited to deer or other big game will do the job. Just use a sharp broadhead and put it in the boiler room.

Where to Hunt Lions

The following list shows each state and the average annual kill there:

British Columbia	300
Arizona	201
Utah	201
Idaho	198
New Mexico	146
Washington	130
Colorado	113
Montana	113
Nevada	46
Oregon	33
Wyoming	20

Alberta also supports a substantial lion harvest each year. California has one of the highest lion populations in the West, but lion hunting there has been banned for many years.

Most cougar seasons take place in winter, although in some states they're open all year. In some states you can buy a tag across the counter, in others tags are issued by drawing. Some states control the harvest by quota. That is, they issue an unlimited number of tags, but once hunters kill a given number of lions, the season is closed. For specifics, contact the individual states.

Trophy Hunting

Record-book listings are based on skull measurements. The score is a combined total of just two measurements: length and width. The following list shows states and their percentage of record-book listings. Record-book

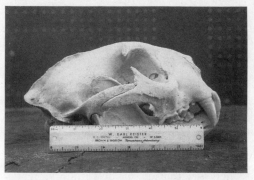

Scoring for the record books involves only two measurements: length and width of skull. Big toms generally have skull measurements totaling more than 14 inches.

analysis should reveal areas that grow the largest animals, and the fact is virtually any region can grow cats with a skull measurement of 13 to 14 inches. That's why, in analyzing Pope and Young listings, I've considered only cats with a score of 14 or higher. That's an arbitrary decision on my part, based on my belief that any cat that measures 14 inches is a big one. The following lists show the percentage of record-book cats taken from each state or province.

Pope and Young lions (score of 14 or more)

Utah	24%
Colorado	20%
Idaho	18%
Montana	11%
Washington	5%
British Columbia	5%
Nevada	5%
New Mexico	4%
Arizona	3%
California	2%
Oregon	1%
Alberta	1%
Wyoming	—

Boone and Crockett lions (B&C minimum is 15 inches)

British Columbia	20%
Idaho	14%
Montana	14%

Utah	11%
Washington	10%
Alberta	10%
Colorado	9%
New Mexico	3%
Wyoming	3%
Arizona	3%
Oregon	2%
California	—

As you can see, the listings don't match up precisely. Pope and Young listings probably reflect distribution of bowhunters, while Boone and Crockett listings tell more about the true potential for taking a huge lion.

MULE DEER *(Odocoileus hemionus)*

Scientists generally recognize eleven subspecies of mule deer and seven or eight of those, depending on which taxonomist you talk to, live north of the Mexican border. These are the Rocky Mountain, desert, southern, Inyo, burro, California mule deer, and the Columbian blacktail and Sitka deer. Most hunters consider the blacktail (*O. h. columbianus*) and Sitka deer (*O. h. sitkensis*) as species unto themselves, and official records-keeping organizations — Pope and Young, Boone and Crock-

Scientists recognize 11 subspecies of mule deer, and these animals provide some of the finest bowhunting opportunities in the West.

ett — also recognize blacktail and Sitka deer as separate entities, so I'll do the same here.

Desert Mule Deer

To simplify this discussion, I'll break mule deer into two types: desert and Rocky Mountain. Desert mule deer and similar subspecies inhabit much of the low-elevation Mohave and Sonoran desert country from southern California across southern Arizona (south of the Mogollon Plateau), southern New Mexico, and west Texas. They range far south into Mexico.

Generally speaking, desert mule deer live at the lower elevations of any given range. In southern Arizona, for example, where many mountain ranges exceed 8,000-feet elevation and support large numbers of whitetails (for details, see Coues Deer), desert mule deer live in the desert and foothills between the mountain ranges at elevations from 1,500 to 4,500 feet. The intense heat and scarcity of water in this environment present some of the harshest conditions for deer found anywhere.

In much of the Southwest desert, densities of mule deer are relatively low. Hunters who pursue burro deer in southwestern Arizona and the southern tip of California along the Colorado River and its tributaries say they might look for days in the flat deserts and dry washes to see one or two deer. In other parts of their range, desert mule deer are fairly plentiful. That's true in parts of the Sonoran desert near Phoenix and Tucson, and in much of west Texas.

Desert bucks generally weigh somewhat less than Rocky Mountain mule deer. Mike Cupell, a Phoenix resident who has bowhunted for desert mule deer seriously for many years, said he knows of desert bucks that have field dressed heavier than 200 pounds, but that's rare. The average mature desert buck, he said, field dresses 20 to 30 pounds lighter than average Rocky Mountain buck from northern Arizona. Most mature desert bucks weigh 130 to 135 pounds field dressed, with exceptional bucks hitting 185 to 200 pounds.

Antlers of desert mule deer generally aren't as large as those of the Rocky Mountain mule

Desert mule deer live throughout low-elevation deserts of the Southwest. This area near Tucson, Arizona, typifies desert mule deer country. Higher country in the background would be home to Coues whitetail deer.

deer, although some fine bucks come from the desert. Cupell, who measures for Pope and Young and Boone and Crockett, found two desert bucks with their antlers locked. One measured about 165 points and the other 175. He said desert bucks scoring in the 170s and 180s aren't uncommon. "There are more good bucks out there in the desert than most people think," Cupell said.

Survival and general well-being of desert mule deer are influenced primarily by seasonal drought, rather than the severe winter weather that periodically devastates Rocky Mountain mule deer. Also, desert mule deer don't migrate in the sense of moving long distances between winter and summer ranges, as Rocky Mountain and other high-elevation mule deer do.

Desert mule deer will shift location, however, to take advantage of the best feed and water at the moment. And bucks will migrate several miles to take part in the rut. For example, does and fawns live year-round in the foothills of the many small mountain ranges of southern Arizona. During most of the year from March through November, however, mature bucks head out into the low-elevation flats

to find solitude and security in dense mesquite and ironwood tangles along dry washes and stream courses, and there they live in virtual isolation.

During the rut, however, bucks leave the flats and move into the foothills in search of does. In the Southwest, first signs of the rut show about December 10, and the rut peaks just after Christmas and lasts until about January 10. Then it tapers off through January, with some secondary rutting activity through February. By March the bucks are moving back onto the inhospitable desert flats by themselves.

Stand Hunting for Desert Mule Deer. During early fall seasons in September, bucks are very difficult to find. The dense, low-elevation flats present poor spotting conditions, and bucks are widely scattered. Water presents the one weak link that might help you find a desert buck then. At this time temperatures soar and water is scarce and bucks must come to water, so a waterhole stand presents the best way to hunt these animals in the early fall.

The same applies during late seasons in December and January, providing the weather remains dry. Precipitation in the Southwest is unpredictable. Some years heavy rains fall all winter, and other years virtually no rain falls. During wet winters, waterhole hunting isn't reliable, but when weather remains dry, deer continue to use waterholes all winter, and stand hunting at a water source can be excellent. Many desert waterholes have no trees big enough to hold a tree stand, so in many cases you'll have to take a ground blind.

Mike Cupell frequently hunts this way for desert bucks. He takes along an ice chest filled with cold water and snacks. He carpets the bottom of the chest so it won't scrape on the ground, and the ice chest doubles as a seat in his blind. Cupell has found that the larger bucks don't always come in to big, obvious waterholes, but often they come to hidden seeps or trickle tanks.

Spotting and Stalking. The rut gives you a major advantage in hunting desert mule deer. Once bucks have moved into the foothills with the does, you can hunt them as you would mule deer in most other places—by spotting. Most of the foothills are slashed by steep, broken, rocky canyons with sparse vegetation—scattered mesquite, a few cactus. That's about it. I've hunted desert mule deer at this time and have seen from 20 to 40 deer a day, including a half dozen bucks or so.

In most cases the deer hang out in groups of

The Rocky Mountain mule deer has a larger range than any other single subspecies of deer in North America, extending from Arizona to northern British Columbia.

five to ten or more, and each group contains one fairly large buck. You'll also see a few good bucks roaming the country alone, looking for receptive does. During my hunt, I stalked deer bedded during the day, but with the rut underway the animals were relatively active, and I had better opportunities for shots by anticipating where the animals would go and trying to intercept them. It wasn't uncommon to hear hooves thundering through a canyon and then to spot a big buck running like a racehorse after a doe. (For details on this kind of hunting, see Spotting and Stalking.)

Rocky Mountain Mule Deer

The range of Rocky Mountain mule deer extends from northern Arizona and New Mexico all the way to northern British Columbia and Alberta. And east to west it reaches from the Cascade Range in Oregon and Washington and the Sierra Nevada in California, eastward into Oklahoma, Kansas, Nebraska, the Dakotas, and Saskatchewan and Manitoba. According to Leonard Lee Rue III in *The Deer of North America*, the Rocky Mountain mule deer has a larger range than any other single subspecies of deer in North America.

Rocky Mountain mule deer also are generally the largest deer in North America. A study in Wyoming showed the average field-dressed weight for yearling bucks was 91 pounds, two-year-old bucks 120 pounds, three- to five-year-old bucks 145 pounds, and six-year-old bucks 175 pounds. In Colorado, nine-year-old bucks had an average field-dressed weight of 212 pounds. Bucks weighing 300 pounds are rare but not unheard of. Rocky Mountain mule deer also have the largest antlers of any North American deer. Virtually all mule deer listed by Boone and Crockett are of the Rocky Mountain subspecies.

Environment of Rocky Mountain Mule Deer

Scientists would scoff at my classification of mule deer habitat, but strictly from a hunter's point of view, I see three major kinds of habitat: high mountain, desert, and prairie. Of

Mule deer live in diverse settings, including spectacular alpine terrain above timberline. Mountain ranges throughout the West hold hunting country like this.

course, there are many gradations between, so I don't present these as hard and fast.

Mountain. The Cascade Range extends from British Columbia southward through central Washington and Oregon, and in essence it continues the full length of California in the form of the Sierra Nevada. To the east, the Rocky Mountains extend from northern Alberta south through Montana, Idaho, Wyoming, Colorado, and New Mexico. Of course these major mountain chains have many tributary ranges and fingers that extend for miles. In many regions, the Rocky Mountains aren't actually a range but a cluster of ranges. Regardless, all high-mountain mule deer ranges have common characteristics.

Generally these major Western ranges are forested at lower elevations, but they also reach above timberline into extensive alpine terrain. In northern regions timberline is much lower than it is farther south. In northwest Montana, for example, it's at 6,000 to 8,000 feet, whereas in Colorado and New Mexico, it's closer to 12,000 feet.

In general, throughout these mountain chains, mule deer summer above timberline in open country. During the fall, as temperatures drop and snow builds up, the deer migrate down through heavy forests, and by late November or December, they're congregated on low-elevation winter ranges.

Desert. The Great Basin and associated desert terrain encompasses a vast region that takes in eastern Oregon, southern Idaho, northeastern California, all of Nevada, and the western half of Utah. This basin and range country has broad expanses of virtually barren, low-elevation desert intermixed with desert mountains, many of which exceed 10,000 feet.

In general, deer live in all the desert above 6,000 feet, although densities are low in the lower elevations during summer. In the desert, high elevation basically equates with water and lush feed, so the greatest numbers of deer summer at the highest elevations. Many of the Great Basin mountain ranges appear barren from a distance (and many of them are virtually treeless) but they're lush above 7,000 to 8,000 feet, and that's where deer concentrate. Just as in the Rocky Mountains, heavy winter snow forces the deer onto low-elevation winter ranges, and they spread out far into the sagebrush deserts.

Prairie/Badlands. The western edge of the

285

Mule deer are also animals of the open plains and sagebrush deserts.

Great Plains—eastern Montana, Wyoming, and Colorado and western North and South Dakota, Nebraska, Kansas, and Oklahoma—offers another kind of mule deer habitat I term generally prairie and badlands. Much of this territory consists of rolling grasslands, the classical antelope range of the West, interspersed with brushy knolls and ridges; badlands and breaks; and meandering rivers and streams bordered by cottonwoods and other riparian cover. Elevations range from 3,000 to 6,000 feet. Mule deer live throughout this region where there are adequate food and cover. This means vegetation in the form of sparse forests or brushland, or terrain in the form of breaks and badlands. Whitetail deer are common in this region too, and generally whitetails live in the riparian bottomlands and mule deer stick to the drier uplands. This region isn't known for the huge mule deer bucks killed in some parts of the Rocky Mountains, but it does produce some big ones and in places deer numbers are very high.

Hunting Methods for Rocky Mountain Mule Deer

Spotting and Stalking. The very nature of mule deer makes these animals ideal subjects for long-distance spotting and stalking. That puts good binoculars and a spotting scope at the top of the hunting-gear list. (For details, see Optics and Spotting.)

In most Western states, general bow seasons open in mid-August or early September. This is a great time of year to hunt, because the weather can be pleasant (it can be terrible, too, especially in the high mountains) and you can hunt high, wild, and lonely places, some of the most spectacular found anywhere. (For details on planning such a hunt, see Backpack Hunting and Outfitters and Guides.)

Early seasons also present ideal spotting conditions, and generally the earlier the better. The most obvious reason is that bucks' antlers are in velvet. The animals don't like banging their tender antlers around on brush and tree limbs, so they stay in the open away from dense cover.

Also, in late summer when bucks are growing antlers and putting on fat for winter, metabolism reaches a peak, and deer feed for longer periods and more frequently than at any other time of the year. At this same time, before early-autumn frosts begin to burn grasses and forbs, the deer find the best feed on open south slopes and in alpine country, right out in

Early seasons present ideal spotting conditions because the bucks' antlers are still in velvet then, and the animals hang out in open country where they're easy to see.

the open. All these things work together to make deer quite visible at this time.

In his seminars and writings, Kirt Darner, a rifle hunter who has taken several Boone and Crockett mule deer, recommends that rifle hunters scout for high-mountain trophy bucks in August and September, prior to general rifle seasons, because that's when the deer are most visible. That may be scouting time for rifle hunters, but for bowhunters it's hunting time, because that's when most Western archery seasons are open.

From late September through October, after their antlers have hardened and frost has burned exposed, open-country feed, deer will drift into timber to browse on shrubs, and they'll drop in elevation as snow accumulates in the high country. At heavily timbered mid-elevations, bucks can be tough to locate and hunt.

By mid-November, the deer are coming into rut, and if heavy snows have fallen the deer will move down on winter ranges. Seasons that fall in late November and December again offer ideal spotting conditions because the bucks are concentrated on relatively open winter range; snow on the ground improves visibility; and bucks are in rut so they're more active than normal. Obviously, late seasons again present a good time to hunt by spotting.

In prairie country of the Great Plains, mule deer don't follow this pattern strictly because they live year-round at lower elevations in

Late seasons in November and December also lead to good hunting, because deep snow in the high country forces deer to lower elevations. They concentrate on open winter ranges where they're relatively easy to see.

During late seasons, bucks also are in rut. When bucks have their minds on does, hunters stand a reasonable chance of scoring.

rough breaks and badlands. Even though the deer don't migrate long distances from summer to winter ranges, the same principles apply to spotting there. I've had excellent success hunting badland bucks in eastern Montana by finding a high vantage and watching the broken canyons and draws. Here you can spot deer this way pretty much all fall, since there's generally little or no heavy timber as in major mountain ranges.

Remember one thing about spotting mule deer: you'll rarely find mature bucks and does in the same spots. As I mentioned, desert mule deer bucks of the arid Southwest fan out into inhospitable, low-elevation, dense mesquite flats for solitude most of the year. Rocky Mountain bucks do the same thing, only in reverse — they gravitate toward the highest, roughest, most open terrain they can find. If you're seeing lots of does, fawns, and yearling bucks, you're most likely looking in the wrong

spots for big bucks, because mature bucks will hang out alone or in bachelor groups. You've probably heard the term "buck pasture," and it accurately describes the situation with mule deer, especially in late summer. Mature bucks live by themselves in select basins and drainages. Where one canyon might attract virtually no bucks, the next one over might hold several dozen. For best mule-deer hunting, look around extensively to find these buck pastures.

The same principle applies during late seasons. During the peak of the rut, of course, bucks and does will be mixed, but otherwise on winter ranges, they'll remain largely segregated. Hunting in Idaho in December, I found hundreds of deer scattered out across the sage and juniper flats. Prospects looked great, but I couldn't find any big bucks there. So I hiked to the tops of the highest ridges, unfriendly places with deep snow and terrible winds, and that's where I found big bucks.

If you can spot a good buck before he spots you, you've won half the bowhunting battle. That's why I emphasize hunting open country during early and late seasons when you can spot bucks most easily. Once you've got a buck in sight, it's a matter of planning your approach and stalking within bow range. Mule deer have average eyes, good ears, and great noses, so you have to stalk with these senses in mind. In most cases, mule-deer country is broken enough that you can stalk within good bow range of nearly any buck. (For details, see Stalking.)

In this kind of hunting you can't expect the same shots you'd get from a tree stand in dense whitetail cover. Shots at mule deer in open country generally fall in the 20- to 50-yard range. It's rare that you can't get within that range. Still, if you're used to shooting whitetails at 20 yards and under, you'll find 50 yards a long distance. Practice shooting at longer distances until you become accurate at 40 to 50 yards, and consider using a range finder. The biggest pitfall in long-range shooting, 30 yards and longer, is range estimation, and with an accurate range finder like the Ranging 80/2, you can eliminate much of the guesswork. A range finder isn't foolproof because you have to stalk well to use it without spooking the buck, but it can help.

Stand Hunting. Tree stands aren't commonly associated with mule-deer hunting, but they can be every bit as deadly for mule deer as they are for whitetails. Jay Verzuh, an outfitter in Colorado, takes many mule-deer hunters each fall. His clients have had 60 to 70 percent success on mule deer, and that includes many repeat clients who've killed small bucks their first year or two and have started holding out for trophy bucks. Some years, 100 percent of Verzuh's hunters have had shots of 30 yards and closer at good-sized bucks. This all compares to an average of 25 percent success for bowhunters statewide.

Verzuh credits the tree stand with his high success rate. "Most guys simply don't know how to move on the ground. And it's not just the guys from back East who hunt from tree stands. A lot of the locals can't stalk successfully either," Verzuh said. "Elimination of tree stands would cut our success rate at least in half."

Verzuh said he and his guides make tree-stand hunting work because they scout extensively, year to year, primarily with binoculars and scopes. Early in the morning they spot deer out feeding, and they watch these animals as the deer filter into daytime bedding grounds. Long-term observation reveals movement patterns, and Verzuh places stands accordingly. He puts some stands in bedding areas, where waiting hunters will ambush bucks returning from early-morning feeding grounds, but more commonly he puts stands on trails between bedding and feeding grounds. He has installed more than 50 permanent tree stands. Given similar conditions, he finds that certain stand locations remain excellent, year after year.

Of course, Verzuh has an advantage over the average hunter, because he hunts the same land each year, but he says anyone can do the same thing if he'll take time to scout. (For details, see Scouting.) As he said, "Most hunters don't find good locations because they think they're wasting precious time by watching deer through

In stalking, a range finder can help you pinpoint distances for clean shots. The range finder guarantees nothing, however, because you have to make a perfect stalk to use it.

binoculars. Nothing could be further from the truth. That's how you find out where to put your stand."

Some observation will give you a general location. If you've got only a week or so to hunt, you'll most likely use a portable tree stand. If, after a couple of days on stand, you find deer bypassing you to one side or the other, try relocating to fine-tune your position.

In mountain country, the best stand locations are trails between bedding and feeding grounds. Water is abundant in most mountain areas, so waterhole stands aren't dependable. In dry country, on the other hand, waterhole stands almost guarantee you a buck. Throughout sagebrush deserts of the Great Basin, stock tanks provide much of the water used not only by cattle but by deer, and if you can find a stock pond or spring that provides the only water for a given area, your chances for ambushing a buck there are good. Here again, the success of the method depends largely on weather. The hotter and drier the conditions, the better your chances. During wet years, it won't work nearly as well.

Still-Hunting. In some regions, mule deer live in timber—pine and fir, aspen, oak brush, pinion-juniper—virtually year-round. Or they may get pushed from preferred open country into timber by numerous hunters. If you find yourself in a place where you can't spot deer

In aspen parks and other timber, still-hunting can be a deadly way to hunt mule deer.

from a long distance, and you don't want to hunt from a stand, you can still-hunt effectively for mule deer. As in stand hunting, success depends largely on scouting. Never waste your time sneaking through the woods just because the place looks good. Cover some ground to find a concentration of sign—tracks, droppings, rubs. As I've said, bucks congregate in specific locations, and the same applies in timber as well as above timberline. Scout first to locate a concentration of deer before you start hunting. (For details, see Scouting and Still-Hunting.)

Driving. Mule deer, like most animals, will adhere to certain escape routes. You can often pick these out just by studying the terrain. A saddle in a ridgetop, a notch in a long rim, a break in a shale slide—these all serve as natural passageways for deer. Much mule-deer country lends itself to driving because the terrain is

steep with impassable cliffs and other obstacles that funnel deer into narrow travel bands.

If you can discern natural passages, driving can be very effective, and it doesn't take a huge gang of noisy drivers. On one hunt a friend and I saw a large buck go through a saddle at the top of a peak, so the next day we returned to see if that was just an accident or if he did it habitually. I climbed up from the back side to stay out of sight of the buck and took a stand in the saddle. When I was in position, my friend walked up from below to push the buck my way. The same big buck trotted up the hill away from my friend right to the saddle and presented me with a ten-yard shot.

Calling. Mule deer will respond to a bleating deer call and does will come in aggressively, but I've never called up big bucks this way, and I don't know any hunters who have. Nor do I know anyone who has consistently rattled in mule deer. It works on occasion, but it's not a method to count on as it is for whitetails.

Trophy Hunting for Mule Deer

Most deer ranges have what it takes to grow bucks large enough to make the Pope and Young record book, so I'd say if that's your goal, then the most important consideration would be finding an area with a high buck-doe ratio. If enough mature bucks escape each hunting season, you'll find bucks that score

Most mule deer hunters only dream of killing bucks like this. Harold Boyack killed this 40-incher in Utah.

higher than 145 (Pope and Young minimum). In general that means hunting some off-road spot that's lightly hunted.

If you're looking for a buck of archery world-record class, or one that would make the Boone and Crockett record book, it's a different matter. Certain localities have produced the majority of such bucks, and you just about have to hunt one of those for even the slightest hope of killing a B&C-type buck. These regions have been well publicized, but that doesn't change the truth that these are the places for huge bucks: southwest Colorado (Montrose, Mesa, Gunnison, Eagle, Delta, Archuleta, La Plata, Garfield, Dolores, and San Miguel counties); northern New Mexico (Rio Arriba County, which has more B&C entries than any other single county; extreme western Wyoming in the Hoback Junction and

Greys River country; and southeastern Idaho along the Wyoming and Utah borders.

Typically, mule deer grow four points off the main beams, and some bucks also grow brow tines. That's considered typical conformation—four points to the side plus brow tines. The record books consider the brow tine a point, and a record-book listing that shows a buck as a five-by-five means the antlers have four points off the main beams plus brow tines. Most Western hunters, however, ignore the brow tine and classify a buck only by the number of points on one side, so they'd call a buck with four points to the side (with or without brow tines) a four-point, or a four-by-four. A buck with three points off the main beam would be called a three-point, or a three-by-three, and so forth. When the point count is uneven, most Western hunters include both

To score well, a mule deer must have wide spread, long tines, and symmetry. Assuming this buck's ears span 20 inches, tip to tip, then he's got at least a 28-inch inside spread. He's also got high antlers and long tines, all the qualities needed to score well. I'd say he's in the 180s.

Mule-deer hunting can push you to the extremes, but it's the kind of hunting that builds lasting memories.

sides — three-by-four, four-by-five, and so forth.

Some three-point bucks will make Pope and Young, but these must be exceptionally large, whereas an average four-point with fairly long tines and a spread of at least 20 to 24 inches will make the Pope and Young record book. Brow tines obviously will help the score, but many four-point bucks without brow tines qualify for Pope and Young.

If you're looking for a world record–type head (or one that would make the Boone and Crockett minimum of 195), you're looking for a different animal. Colorado bowhunter Lee Kline has measured hundreds of mule deer antlers, and he said length of the main beam is most critical. These beams must measure somewhere around 25 inches, and inside spread of the antlers must be about the same. The back tine (G-2 on scoring charts) must be nearly as long as the chest is deep, or about 20 inches, and the other forks must be very deep. The closer the bottom of the fork is to the main beam the better. The rack also must be high. Kline also said brow tines are virtually essential for a buck to make B&C. They can add two to six inches to the score. (For more details, see Trophy Scoring.)

Remember that if you're hunting in August or early September, mule-deer antlers will be in velvet, and the velvet can make them look much bigger than they are. If you're hunting strictly for the record book, study a buck in velvet carefully before you go after him. The velvet must be stripped off before the antlers can be measured.

N

NATIONAL FIELD ARCHERY ASSOCIA-TION (NFAA) This organization was begun in 1939 in response to a demand by bowhunters who wanted competition that closely simulated hunting. Up to that time, the only competition involved target archery sanctioned by the NAA (National Archery Association). Target archery is shot at measured distances, whereas field archery, at least in principle, is shot from unmeasured distances to simulate hunting.

Field archery has developed into another form of target archery, and now all shooting is done from measured distances. The standard field course consists of three rounds: the field, hunter, and animal. Each round has 14 targets, and in the field and hunter rounds, archers shoot four arrows at each target. Targets for the field round are white with black bull's eyes, and hunter-round targets are black with white bulls. In the animal round, you shoot one arrow, and if that arrow hits a scoring zone, you shoot no more. If you miss that first arrow, you shoot a second and third. On-target hits with the second and third arrows count less than on-target hits for the first arrow.

Eight sectional tournaments are held each year to determine qualifiers for the annual national NFAA tournament. Contact NFAA, Route 1, Box 514, Redlands, CA 92373.

NEBRASKA This state has an area of 77,227 square miles, primarily farm and pastureland; in most cases the only major relief occurs in the breaks along rivers and streams. Less than 2 percent of the state has timber cover. Ninety-seven percent of Nebraska is privately owned, but generally farmers will allow courteous hunters on their lands. Some landowners charge a trespass fee.

Big Game
Deer. Nebraska has an estimated 70,000 whitetails scattered across the entire state, and about 40,000 mule deer that live in the western two thirds of the state. Archery harvest has steadily increased from 907 in 1970 to more than 3,000 annually in recent years. Overall bowhunter success has averaged 18 percent with a range from 13 percent to 26 percent. Whitetails make up about 80 percent of the bow harvest. The bow season opens September 15 and closes the day preceding the rifle season (firearms season opens the second Saturday in November and runs for nine days). It then opens after the rifle season and continues through December. Bow licenses are unlimited for both residents and nonresidents.

In the eastern half of the state, whitetails are far more abundant than mule deer. This region consists largely of irrigated farmlands, but numerous tributaries to the Missouri River provide cover in the form of woodlands and broken terrain. Thousands of miles of wooded shelter belts have been planted in this region, and deer frequently use these for protection. Average deer density overall is 1 to 2 deer per square mile, but most wooded stream courses support 10 to 20 deer per square mile, and ideal refuge situations with woods, marshlands, and weedy cover support as many as 100 whitetail deer per square mile.

In the western half, mule deer are more common, and whitetails are limited primarily to bottomlands along drainages. This half of the state has some irrigated crops, but grazing lands are more widespread and drainages with good deer cover are less common than in the eastern half.

The state record typical whitetail scored $196^4/8$, and nearly three dozen typical whitetails taken in Nebraska have been large enough to make the record book. The record nontypical whitetail scored $279^7/8$. This buck, killed by Del Austin, ranks as the Pope and Young world record. Nebraska has produced more than two dozen other nontypical whitetails large enough to make Boone and Crockett. With its limited permit hunting, Nebraska has good trophy whitetail potential. The largest nontypical mule deer scored $256^7/8$, but only one other nontypical mule deer has qualified for Boone and Crockett.

Antelope. Nebraska has pronghorns throughout the western third of the state. At this writing, archery permits were unlimited for residents and nonresidents.

Other Game

Turkeys. Nebraska planted turkeys in the Pine Ridge area in the northwest corner in 1956, and the population exploded from there. Now the state has excellent spring and fall hunting for these birds.

Small Game. Squirrels are abundant wherever there's good woody cover, particularly along stream bottoms. Cottontail rabbits are also plentiful around brushy cover.

Contact. Nebraska Game and Parks Commission, P.O. Box 30370, Lincoln, NE 68503.

NEVADA Nevada covers 110,000 square miles. Much of that is barren, low desert, but there are many high mountain ranges, and all these have good herds of mule deer. The estimated population is 130,000 to 180,000 deer. Since 1975, hunter numbers have been restricted statewide, and herds have built steadily since then. Virtually all good hunting lies on public land—Forest Service or BLM—so access is no problem.

As in many other states, turkey flocks have virtually exploded in Nebraska and now they're hunted extensively.

Mule deer are the major big-game animals in Nevada. Bucks of this size are very common.

Big Game

Mule Deer. The general archery season traditionally opens the second Saturday in August and runs for four weeks. Nonresident bow tags have been limited in number for several years, and they are issued by drawing. The number of available tags fluctuates, depending on deer numbers at the moment, but it has ranged from 250 to 600. Drawing odds are good. Bowhunter success runs about 25 percent.

Nevada consists of classic basin-and-range desert country. Broad, sweeping valleys about 5,000 feet in elevation are interrupted by rugged, isolated mountain ranges, many of which rise to elevations of 11,000 feet and higher. Most mountain ranges higher than 6,000 feet elevation support deer herds, but the largest herds live in the major mountain chains.

Elko County in the northeastern corner consistently produces the most deer. The Jarbidge Mountains near the Idaho border and the Ruby Mountains just south of Elko form the core of highest deer concentrations, but virtually every mountain range in Nevada has good numbers of deer and big bucks. In some places the buck-doe ratio is as high as 40 bucks per 100 does, which indicates excellent trophy potential.

You might picture Nevada as nothing but desert, but many of the mountain ranges are high, remote, and rugged, with elevations from 9,000 to 11,000 feet. Early in the season deer roam high, so you must be in condition for high-elevation hunting. Some deer also live year-round in lower-elevation sagelands wherever adequate water exists in the form of stock tanks or small reservoirs, and some "marginal" country produces the biggest bucks.

The state record (rifle kill) typical mule deer scored $205\frac{2}{8}$, and the record nontypical $299\frac{1}{8}$. Nevada hasn't produced lots of Boone and Crockett bucks, but it may offer a better opportunity to take a mature buck than any other state. The average buck-doe ratio for the entire state is about 25 bucks per 100 does, and in many areas it exceeds 35 per 100, which indicates a very high carryover of bucks each year. In many units, more than half the bucks taken are four-points or larger, and bucks with 30-inch spreads are not uncommon. Bucks large enough to make the Pope and Young record book could be considered a dime a dozen.

Elk. Elk herds have been growing steadily in several mountain ranges in central and southern Nevada. Limited-entry rifle and bow hunts are held and some huge bulls are being taken, but only residents may apply for these hunts.

Antelope. Nevada has a fair number of antelope, with greatest numbers in the northwestern corner. The state has a special archery-only season, but that hunting is reserved for residents only.

Cougar. Find deer in Nevada and you'll find mountain lions. Nevada is one of the best states for cougar hunting, with seasons extending throughout the winter months. Tag numbers are not limited, and nonresidents can hunt lions in Nevada.

Bighorn Sheep. Nevada is the only state with three varieties of sheep—Rocky Mountain, California, and desert. Rocky Mountain bighorns are restricted to the Snake Range on the Utah border, and California bighorns live in the northwestern corner, primarily on the Sheldon Antelope Range. Both varieties are hunted on a very limited basis, and tags are reserved for residents. Desert sheep occupy most arid ranges in the southern end of the state. Nearly 100 tags are issued each year and about 10 of these go to nonresidents. Nevada is one of the best desert sheep states.

Mountain Goat. The Ruby Mountains have a few goats, and occasional tags are issued to nonresidents.

Contact. Department of Wildlife, P.O. Box 10678, Reno, NV 89520.

NEW BRUNSWICK New Brunswick covers 27,985 square miles. To hunt big game in this province, nonresidents are required to hire a local guide.

Big Game

Whitetail Deer. New Brunswick has an estimated 120,000 to 150,000 whitetail deer. Firearms hunters kill about 25,000 deer a year, with an average success of 23 percent. New Brunswick held its first special archery season in 1982, and the following year 1,000 resident and 250 nonresident archers killed 46 deer. The bow season is open for about three weeks in early to mid-October with a bag limit of one deer, either sex. As mentioned above, all nonresidents are required to hunt with a guide.

Other Game. Moose live throughout the province, but nonresidents are not allowed to hunt these animals. Black bears also are common throughout, but they're hunted most heavily by guided nonresidents in northern backcountry areas. Baiting proves most productive. Snowshoe hares are common.

Contact. Department of Natural Resources, Fish and Wildlife Branch, P.O. Box 6000, Fredericton, NB, Canada E3B-5H1.

NEWFOUNDLAND AND LABRADOR Primary big game in these provinces of northeastern Canada are moose, caribou, and black bear. Record books classify caribou in Labrador as the Quebec-Labrador variety. Nonresidents aren't allowed to hunt caribou in Labrador, so virtually all Quebec-Labrador caribou listed by the record books come from Quebec. Caribou in Newfoundland are classified as the woodland variety, and virtually all record-book woodland caribou come from this island off the east coast of Canada. Moose are abundant, but they rarely reach record-book size.

Contact. Wildlife Division, P.O. Box 4750, Pleasantville, St. Johns, Newfoundland A1C-5T7.

NEW HAMPSHIRE New Hampshire has a total area of about 9,000 square miles, nearly 85 percent of it forest. Public access remains good throughout the state. Large blocks of national forestland cover the central part of the state, and timber companies, which own most land in the north end of the state, generally allow hunting on their lands. Lands in the south are in small, private ownership, but true to tradition in New England, hunters can trespass if the land is not posted, and fair amounts of land remain unposted.

Big Game

Whitetail Deer. An estimated 30,000 whitetail deer occupy about 90 percent of the state. About 7,000 residents and 1,400 nonresidents hunt during New Hampshire's archery seasons. Average annual harvest has been about 125 deer (55 percent bucks), and hunting success has averaged less than 2 percent. The archery season opens in mid-September and lasts for about 95 days until mid-December. Bag limit is one deer with bow, one with a firearm, with a maximum of two deer per hunter per season.

Following several mild winters, deer numbers hit all-time highs in the 1960s. Since then hard winters have periodically devastated deer herds. Extensive logging of valuable winter cover has reduced deer numbers in the north end of the state and moose have become predominant there. The White Mountains are rugged, with elevations up to 6,288 feet. Most whitetails live below 2,500-feet elevation, and overall deer numbers are lower here than anywhere else in the state. South of Lake Winnipesaukee white pine and red oak forests cover the rolling hills. Deer densities in this region run from six to ten per square mile, the best in New Hampshire. A bucks-only law, established in 1983, coupled with several mild winters, has helped deer numbers improve generally, but herds will continue to fluctuate in response to winter weather.

Black Bears. New Hampshire has good bear hunting with an annual harvest exceeding 200 animals. The general bear season (there is no special bow season) extends from September 1 to the day before opening of general deer season in early November. Baiting and hound hunting are legal. Most bears come from the White Mountains and Coos County in the north end of the state.

Other Game

New Hampshire has fair turkey hunting in the southern end, and hunting for squirrels, cottontails, and snowshoe rabbits is generally good in suitable habitat.

Contact. Fish and Game Department, 34 Bridge Street, Concord, NH 03301.

NEW JERSEY The Garden State covers an area of 7,836 square miles. Posting and leasing of hunting rights has been the rule on private lands in the northern and agricultural areas, and the trend has spread into southern New Jersey. Now 79 percent of the deer harvest takes place on private land. However, more than 50 public hunting areas on state and federal lands, and in city watersheds provide fairly extensive public access. Hunting pressure on public lands can vary from crowded during regular gun seasons to light during bow seasons. New Jersey prints several guides to public hunting lands.

Big Game

Whitetail Deer. New Jersey has an estimated deer population of 135,000. An average of 41,000 residents and 650 nonresidents hunt with bow and arrow each fall. Many of these also hunt during rifle seasons. Average archery harvest during the early 1980s was 6,885 deer (3,058 bucks and 3,827 does), and average bowhunting success has been about 14 percent. Seasons vary from year to year and by management zone, but they generally follow this pattern: fall bow season, all of October and into November; six-day firearm season, early December; shotgun permit season, one day in December; muzzleloader permit season, several days spread out in December; and winter bow season, about two weeks in January. In total, hunting a combination of all seasons, a hunter could take up to eight deer in one year.

In southern New Jersey, the outer coastal plain has poor, sandy soils and extensive pine forests, swamps, and bottomlands. Deer densities range from 10 to 30 deer per square mile. This region contains extensive public hunting lands. The inner coastal plain bordering the Delaware River is more fertile, and has fields of corn, soybeans, and other crops. Deer that field dress 200 pounds aren't uncommon here, but virtually all land is private and club leases are common. The hilly Piedmont in the center of the state has upward of 50 deer per square mile and large bucks, but most of the land is private and posted. The extreme northwest corner used to be dairy country, but many abandoned farms have grown up into brush and forest and deer numbers are good, ranging from 10 to 50 or more per square mile. Public lands assure some access.

The state record typical whitetail for New Jersey measured 175⅝ points and the record nontypical 214⅜.

Other Game

New Jersey has had a successful turkey transplanting program, and these birds are now fairly abundant and are hunted each year. Squirrel and rabbit hunting are also good in some localities.

Contact. Department of Environmental Protection, Division of Fish, Game and Wildlife, CN 400, Trenton, NJ 08625.

NEW MEXICO New Mexico covers 121,666 square miles. Topography ranges from high, forested mountains to low-elevation desert to farmland. Federal lands are extensive, so finding a place to hunt poses little problem. However, much of the finest hunting, the hunting that has made New Mexico famous, takes place on huge ranches and Indian reservations, where you'll pay dearly to hunt.

Big Game

Mule Deer. New Mexico has an estimated 260,000 mule deer, and they live throughout the state except for large blocks of farmland and prairie in the northwestern corner and along the eastern border. About 3,500 residents and 350 nonresidents hunt during archery seasons each year, and they kill an average of about 400 deer a year, with a high in 1981 of 735. Average archery success on deer has been 7 percent, with a high of 10 percent. General deer and elk archery seasons run for about two weeks in mid-September, and many units are open for deer hunting again in late December and January.

Northcentral New Mexico around Chama has long held the reputation for growing huge mule deer. This country ranges in elevation from 9,000 to 14,000 feet, with a mix of conifer forests, aspens, and alpine terrain. The Carson and Santa Fe National Forests provide exten-

sive public hunting, but much of the best deer country lies on huge ranches that are not open to the general public. The winter bow season here offers good opportunity for a huge buck.

The southeastern corner is considered New Mexico's "deer factory." The Guadalupe and Sacramento mountains and other ranges in this section of the state produce 56 percent of the state's total deer kill. Large blocks of public land assure good access. This region is managed primarily for high numbers of deer, and the buck-doe ratio is low. The Gila National Forest in the southwest grows some good-sized desert mule deer.

The state record typical mule deer scored 212, and the record nontypical 306⅖. More Boone and Crockett mule deer have come from Rio Arriba County near the Colorado border than any other single county in the United States.

Whitetail Deer. Texas whitetails live in the Sacramento Mountains, the Mescalero Sands, and other isolated pockets, but they're not numerous, and few hunters go after them seriously.

Coues whitetails occupy the southwest panhandle, and they're abundant in the Gila National Forest and in the Peloncillo and Animas mountains. Coues deer seem to be spreading here, and some record-class bucks have been taken in recent years. The state record typical Coues deer scored 119. No record-book nontypical Coues deer have been recorded from New Mexico.

Elk. New Mexico has an estimated 15,000 elk. Bowhunting licenses are unlimited, and the archery season takes place for about two weeks during the rut in September. Elk are heavily hunted during rifle seasons, but hunter numbers have been cut back, and bull-cow ratios have improved. Bowhunters have taken some tremendous bulls in recent years. The Gila National Forest in the southwest and the Jemez Mountains and other mountains north to Chama produce the best elk.

Bear. Hounds may be used to run bears, but baiting is illegal. Spring season is open in May and June, and fall season extends from August into December. There is no special bow season for bear.

Antelope. Good numbers of antelope live throughout the eastern half of the state, and some archery-only seasons are held. Licenses are unlimited in some units, and nonresidents can apply.

Cougar. New Mexico has always been among the best lion states. The general season runs from December through February, and bag limit is one. There is no special bow season. Virtually all cats are taken over hounds.

Bighorn Sheep. About ten licenses are issued for Rocky Mountain bighorns in the mountains near Santa Fe. Nonresidents may apply. There is no special bow season. New Mexico also has desert bighorns in southern mountain ranges, but the season has been closed for several years.

Javelina. A general season is held in December; there is no special bow season. Javelina are restricted to the southwestern quarter of the state.

Exotic Big Game. New Mexico has free-roaming herds of oryx, Persian and Siberian ibex, and Barbary sheep, and limited seasons are held for each species. There are no special bow seasons.

Other Game

New Mexico offers some excellent turkey hunting. Small game, in the form of squirrels and rabbits, and predators such as coyotes and bobcats, abound in suitable habitat.

Contact. New Mexico Department of Game and Fish, State Capitol, Villagra Building, Santa Fe, NM 87503.

NEW YORK This state has an area of 47,377 square miles. Very generally, you can divide New York into two sections, north and south. The Adirondack Mountains occupy most of the northern section. This region consists of high mountains up to 5,300 feet near Lake Placid covered with extensive northern hardwood (maple, birch, beech) and spruce-fir forests, and roadless areas are extensive. Throughout the southern section, farmlands are inter-

mixed with woodlands, and most land is privately owned. The Catskill Mountains are steep and heavily forested with peaks rising to 4,000 feet. Statewide, New York offers 4½ million acres of public land open to hunting, about 2½ million in the Adirondacks, and another .25 million in the Catskills.

Big Game

Whitetail Deer. New York has an estimated 600,000 whitetails. An average of 105,000 archers hunt deer each year, and during the early 1980s they killed an average 4,700 deer each year, about 50–50 bucks and does. In 1982 archers had a record high kill of 6,175 deer. Average bowhunter success has been about 5 percent.

In the northern zone, archery season runs from late September through most of October. In the southern zone, archery season opens October 14 and closes just before the regular firearms season in mid-November and then

Bowhunters kill about 5,000 whitetail deer each year in New York.

opens for five days following the firearms season in December.

Overall the Adirondacks have the lowest deer densities in the state, about 15 deer per square mile, but hunting pressure is relatively light, and some big bucks are taken here. The Catskill Mountains offer similar conditions.

The Great Lakes Plain bordering Lake Ontario has fertile soils and extensive agriculture. Only about 20 percent of the area remains wooded, and much of it is hardwood swamps and woodlots. With its rich soils, this region produces some heavy deer and fairly good antler growth. Most land is private, and much of it is posted.

The Appalachian Plateau bordering Pennsylvania has the highest deer densities, but hunting pressure is heavy, and most bucks killed are yearlings. There are many abandoned farms, and vegetation consists of mixed hardwood forests and brushland on rolling hills and steep valleys. Some state parks offer public hunting, and access to private lands is fairly good.

Bear. New York has good numbers of bears. The highest annual kill was over 700 animals (including all seasons, not just archery). The Adirondacks have the most bears, followed by the Catskills and the Allegany region bordering Pennsylvania. Special archery seasons are held in October and November. Season dates vary by region. No hound hunting (during archery seasons) or baiting is allowed.

Other Game

Small Game. Turkeys have expanded their range rapidly the past few years and are now hunted throughout much of the southern zone. Eastern gray squirrels, rabbits, and woodchucks are of interest to archers in southern New York.

Contact. Department of Environmental Conservation, 500 Wolf Road, Albany, NY 12233-0001.

NOCK An arrow nock seems little more than an insignificant piece of plastic, but it's the critical connection between bowstring and arrow.

That connection must be perfect or the arrow doesn't have a chance of flying well.

Nock Straightness

Most critically, nocks must be straight. On some you can see a dye mark inside the string notch. Look to see if it's in the center. If it's off-center, the nock is molded crooked and should be discarded. Then make sure nocks are glued on straight. If you make your own arrows, use a nock-alignment jig, or spin them to make sure they're straight before the glue dries. (For details, see Arrow Making.) If you're buying arrows from an archery shop, check the nocks before you buy. To do that, roll the arrow along a flat table or counter, or hold it loosely in your hands and blow on the fletching to make the arrow spin. As the arrow spins, watch the nock. If it rotates perfectly, it's straight; if it wobbles, it's crooked. Don't buy arrows with crooked nocks.

Nock Fit

Next, nocks must fit the bowstring correctly. If nocks are too tight they essentially affect the spine of your arrows, and if they're too loose an arrow could fall off the string as you're trying to shoot. Nocks should be just tight enough so an arrow will hang on the string when held vertically, but the arrow should fall off when you thump the string. Again, if you make your own arrows, you can buy nocks that fit exactly right. If you buy arrows from a shop, take your bow in and ask the shop owner to try different nocks on the string. Then have him make up your arrows with those nocks.

Nock Size. Two things affect nock tightness: string size and nock size. Many hunters seem to think you should buy nocks to fit a particular arrow shaft—say, a $5/16$-inch nock for a $5/16$-inch shaft—when in fact you should buy nocks to fit your bowstring. Most nocks are of the "snap-on" style these days, and, in general, a $5/16$-inch snap-on nock such as the Bjorn Nock fits just right on a 16-strand bowstring. That nock is much too tight on an 18-strand cam bowstring, however. With the larger string, you should go to an $11/32$-inch nock.

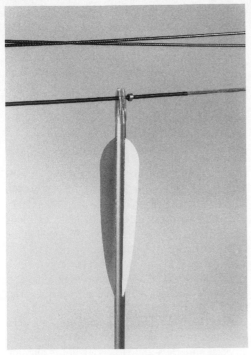

Correct nock fit is vitally important to accuracy. A nock should fit tight enough so an arrow will hang vertically on the bowstring, but the arrow should fall off when you thump the string.

Pro Nocks have flexible sides and a unique shape inside the string groove that ensures good fit on various sizes of string.

That's only a general guideline, because nock dimensions vary greatly among brands. If one brand doesn't work for you, try another. Some brands, such as the Flex-Fletch Pro Nock, are much more flexible than others, and one size of nock will fit well on different sizes of strings. I've found that an $11/32$-inch Pro Nock works very well on both 16- and 18-strand strings.

Serving Size. If for some reason you don't want to change nock size, you can try a couple of other methods to get perfect nock fit. One is to change the serving on your string. Many bowstrings are served with 18-pound monofilament. To reduce size, you can re-serve the string with 15-pound mono, or to increase size you can go to heavier mono or to multifilament serving thread. (For details, see Bowstring.)

If none of those alternatives appeals to you,

try dipping the nocks on your arrows in boiling water (don't touch the nock to the bottom of the pan—it will melt) to soften them slightly. Then, if the nocks are too tight, slip them onto the bowstring until they cool to expand them slightly. If they're too loose, squeeze the ears down slightly to decrease notch size.

Shape. This may be more a matter of personal preference than function. As I've said, virtually all nocks nowadays snap onto the string, and that should be a standard feature. Some have a flared mouth that helps guide the bowstring into the notch for quicker arrow handling, and some have an index mark on one side so you can tell by feel which way to turn

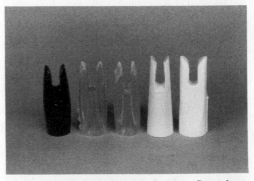

Nocks come in many shapes and colors. Some have index marks, some are thick, some are thin, and so forth. Choosing style and color is a matter of personal preference.

the arrow to get the cock vane in the right position. With four-fletch arrows that's irrelevant because the arrows can be nocked either way.

Nocks come in about any color you could want. I personally like hot pink or chartreuse because these bright nocks show up well. I can see them in flight, and they help me find arrows in the grass. It might seem crazy to have camouflage arrows and vanes (which I do) and to use bright nocks, but I doubt that many animals will spot those nocks. Nocks also come in black or brown, and if you want total camouflage, those are the ones to use.

NOCKING POINT   The point at which an arrow is nocked on a bowstring. The nocking point is marked with a metal or plastic ring around the string or with a thread wrapping. It must be solid so arrow flight is identical from shot to shot. (For details, see Bowstring.)

NOCK LOCATOR   A metal or plastic ring, or a wrapping of thread, on a bowstring that marks the point at which an arrow must be nocked for shooting. (For details, see Bowstring.)

NORTH CAROLINA   This state of 49,317 square miles can be divided into three general regions. The broad, flat coastal plain has large acreages of pine flatwoods and hardwood along the coast and large fields of corn, soybeans, peanuts, cotton, and tobacco inland. The Piedmont consists of rolling hills covered with small crop fields intermixed with small commercial pine plantations and hardwoods along the ridges and bottomlands. The mountain region has some pine plantations and fields at lower elevations, grading into hardwoods at intermediate elevations and spruce and fir forests at the highest elevations. North Carolina's Blue Ridge Mountains, essentially the south end of the Appalachians, contain high, rugged country. Mount Mitchell, elevation 6,684 feet, is the highest point east of the Mississippi.

The Wildlife Resources Commission manages nearly 2 million acres for public hunting. Some areas are heavily hunted, but in some mountain areas, access is poor and hunting pressure is relatively light. Overall, as in most other Southern states, private land is tied up, and much of the better deer lands, particularly in the Piedmont and coastal plain regions, are leased to private hunting clubs.

Big Game
Whitetail Deer. North Carolina has an estimated 400,000 whitetail deer. About 60,000 archery licenses are sold each year, and archery harvest runs about 2,500, half bucks and half does. Seasons vary by region. In general the bow season opens September 10 and runs into October or November. That's followed by a muzzleloader season about one week long, and then general gun season. The gun season varies from 2 weeks to 2½ months, depending on region. Generally, the bag limit is two bucks per day, two in possession, four per season. Special antlerless and either-sex hunts also are held.

In the coastal plain, deer densities vary from extremely high to moderately low. Some places with the highest numbers have poor habitat, so deer quality in terms of body weight and antler size is poor. The northern Piedmont supports high densities of deer, but in the central and southern portions deer herds are below carrying capacity and are expanding, and these areas produce some of North Carolina's heaviest deer and largest antlers. Overall the mountain region isn't as productive as the Piedmont, and deer numbers are relatively low.

Black Bear. Bears live throughout much of the state. No special archery seasons are held, but general seasons are open from mid-October through January 1. Specific dates vary greatly by region.

Pigs. Wild boars are hunted only in the southwestern corner south of Great Smokey Mountains National Park. The season is open in October, November, and December. Hunting with dogs is the most common way of hunting pigs in North Carolina.

Other Game

Turkeys. These birds are abundant, particularly in the northcentral part of the state. Spring season is held in April and May.

Small Game. Gray and fox squirrels are numerous throughout the state wherever hardwoods provide cover and food. Rabbits are most abundant in the Piedmont and coastal plains regions.

Contact. Wildlife Resources Commission, Archdale Building, 512 North Salisbury Street, Raleigh, NC 27611.

NORTH DAKOTA This state covers 70,665 square miles. The eastern fourth, in the Red River, Sheyenne, and James river drainages, is heavily farmed. The Coteau Hills takes in most of central North Dakota east of the Missouri River and north to the Canadian border, and this region contains large grainfields mixed with prairies and marshes. The southwestern quarter of the state has extensive badlands and breaks associated with the Missouri River. The badlands and Missouri River breaks contain fair amounts of public land, and some blocks of state-owned land provide public hunting throughout the state. Otherwise, all of North Dakota is privately owned. However, many landowners will give permission to hunt.

Big Game

Deer. An estimated 135,000 whitetails occupy about 50 percent of the land, and 35,000 mule deer are found in 25 percent of the state. About 8,000 resident and 200 nonresident archers hunt deer each year. The average harvest has been 1,050 whitetails and 200 mule deer. Average bowhunter success has been 14 percent, with a range from 8 percent to 17 percent. The bow season runs from early September until early November, and reopens in late November and remains open through December. The number of bow permits is not limited.

Whitetails predominate throughout the eastern two thirds of the state. In many places they're restricted to brushy bottomlands and wooded stream courses, although they live throughout some farmlands, particularly in sunflower "forests." West of the Missouri River, mule deer are more common, particularly in the uplands, and whitetails are restricted primarily to brushy bottomlands.

The state record typical whitetail scored 187⅝ points, and the record nontypical scored 248⅝. Boone and Crockett lists several other North Dakota whitetails, but few have been taken in recent years. North Dakota isn't known for huge mule deer.

Antelope. These animals live throughout the prairie and grain country of the western one third of the state. Permits are very restricted for rifle hunters, but they're unlimited for both resident and nonresident bowhunters. The antelope bow season is open most of September and October.

Other Game

Gray and fox squirrels are abundant wherever woodlands provide feed and cover, mostly in the eastern part of the state and along the Missouri River. Cottontails are abundant in all brushy cover.

Contact. North Dakota Game and Fish Department, 2121 Lovett Avenue, Bismarck, ND 58505.

NORTHWEST TERRITORIES This huge province covering 1,300,000 square miles is bigger than Alaska and Texas combined. It probably contains more true wilderness than any other region in North America.

Big Game

Moose. Record books classify moose from the Northwest Territories (NWT) as Alaska-Yukon moose. Most of the bigger bulls come from the Mackenzie Mountains at the west end, but moose are hunted throughout the province. In the mountains hunting by horse string remains popular, and in lower areas laced with lakes and rivers, moose are hunted by boat.

Caribou. For the purposes of record-book scoring, NWT has three varieties of caribou.

Animals taken from the Mackenzie Mountains are considered mountain caribou. Any taken north of those mountains are barren ground caribou, but if they're killed east of the Mackenzie River, they're classed as central Canada barren ground, or Peary, caribou.

Dall Sheep. These animals live primarily in the Mackenzie Mountains near the Yukon border. Hunting on horseback and with pack animals has remained common in this area, but some outfitters and hunters backpack for sheep.

Mountain Goats. Some goats live in the south end of the Mackenzie Mountains, but NWT does not have an extensive population of goats.

Bears. Grizzly bears are abundant in the Mackenzie Mountains, and black bears are common throughout subarctic NWT. A few licenses are available for polar-bear hunting on islands north of the mainland.

Muskoxen. These animals are hunted in some of the islands north of the mainland. Snowmobiles are used to locate herds. The number of licenses is very limited.

Other Game. There are few deer in NWT and they're not hunted. Wolves and wolverines are common.

Contact. Government of Northwest Territories, Renewable Resources, Yellowknife, NWT, Canada X1A-2L9. For information on polar bear and muskox hunts, contact Quaiv-vik Limited, Box 1538, Yellowknife, Northwest Territories, Canada X1A-2P5.

NOVA SCOTIA This province, extending into the Atlantic Ocean southeast of Maine, has an area of 21,425 square miles. To hunt big game legally, nonresidents must hire guides.

Big Game

Whitetail Deer. An estimated 150,000 whitetail deer live throughout the province. In recent years, about 80,000 residents and 750 nonresidents hunted deer each year. Average harvest has been about 35,000 deer with an average success rate of 39 percent. No separate bowhunting records have been kept. The general season runs from late October into early December. Bag limit is one deer of either sex. One area on the north peninsula has been set aside for bowhunting-only during the regular season. Nonresidents are required to hire a guide. Some very large bucks are taken, and average field-dressed weight of 2½-year-old deer is 160 pounds.

Other Game. This province has some moose, but only residents can hunt them legally. Black bears are numerous, especially in backcountry areas toward the western end. Seasons are held in spring and fall.

Contact. Department of Lands and Forests, P.O. Box 698, Halifax, NS, Canada B3J-2T9.

O

OHIO Ohio has an area of 40,982 square miles. The Wayne National Forest and several state forests provide public access to roughly 750,000 acres with fairly good hunting in the southeast corner of Ohio. However, the state is 97 percent private land, and permission is required for hunting.

Big Game

Whitetail Deer. The population is estimated at 120,000. An average of 90,000 resident and 1,000 nonresident archers hunt deer in Ohio each year, and they take about 4,000, two-thirds bucks. The bow season runs from October 1 through January 31, except that it's closed during gun seasons. The limit is one deer of either sex. Some special primitive-weapons hunts are also held in restricted areas. Crossbows can be used legally during archery seasons.

The northwest quarter consists primarily of corn and soybean fields and other croplands, and cover for deer is limited to a few scattered stream bottoms, so deer numbers are low here. Rolling hill country with mixed agricultural and forestlands in the southwest quarter support moderate numbers of deer. The northeast corner, with its wooded hills has medium to high deer densities, but Cleveland, Youngstown, and other spreading cities are eating away the good hunting here.

The southeast third of the state contains the best all-around deer country, and an estimated 80 percent of Ohio's deer live in this section. The rolling hills here have extensive hardwood forests intermixed with abandoned farms and brushlands. Deer densities are estimated at 10 to 15 per square mile, the highest in the state. Bucks are generally smaller here than in farming regions.

The state record typical whitetail scored 187 6/8 points, and the record nontypical 342 3/8, which also makes it the Boone and Crockett world record. Boone and Crockett lists many bucks from Ohio, many taken in recent years. Most of the largest bucks come from the northcentral and eastcentral zones where farm crops, such as corn, mixed with woodlots provide ample feed and cover.

Other Game

Turkeys have become well established throughout the timbered southeast quarter of Ohio, and a spring season is held in late April and early May. Much of the better turkey hunting takes place on public lands. Squirrels and cottontail rabbits are abundant throughout the state in suitable habitat.

Contact. Department of Natural Resources, Division of Wildlife, Fountain Square, Columbus, OH 43224.

OKLAHOMA Oklahoma has a total land area of 69,919 square miles.

Big Game
Deer. A total population of 100,000 to 150,000 whitetails live in all 77 of Oklahoma's counties, and an estimated 500 to 1,000 mule deer live in scattered herds in the northwestern and panhandle counties. Archery hunters number about 35,000; only about 100 are non-residents. The average bow harvest for recent years has been about 2,000, and average archery success has been 3 percent with a high slightly over 5 percent. The archery season normally is open for the entire month of October and again for all of December, with gun seasons sandwiched between in November. The bag limit has been two deer (one must be a buck).

The eastern end consists of forested mountains. Deer numbers are good, but hunting pressure is fairly high in this region. Most of central Oklahoma consists of open prairie interspersed with oak woodlands. Deer numbers are fairly good throughout the region.

West of Interstate 35 the country opens up into open short-grass prairies where woody cover is restricted primarily to stream and river bottomlands, and this is where most of the deer are found. Whitetail herds are growing throughout western Oklahoma, and some of the state's largest deer come from this region. The Panhandle contains open sandhills covered with prairie grasses and sage. The area produces a few mule deer along with whitetails that live along the creek bottoms.

Elk. Oklahoma holds very limited elk hunts.

Other Game
Turkeys. A month-long spring season is held in several counties in April and May, with a total bag limit of up to three birds in some counties. Fall seasons are also held at different times in various counties.

Small Game. Throughout oak woodlands, mostly in the eastern half of the state, hunting for fox and gray squirrels is excellent. Rabbits—cottontails statewide, swamp rabbits in the southeast, jackrabbits in the west end—provide excellent hunting.

Contact. Oklahoma Department of Wildlife Conservation, P.O. Box 53465, Oklahoma City, OK 73152.

ONTARIO Ontario covers a total of 412,582 square miles. Probably the major species of interest to nonresidents are moose and black bear, although the province has good deer hunting in some areas.

Big Game
Whitetail Deer. The whitetail deer herd is estimated at 150,000 animals, but only a small portion of the province, primarily the southern edge, supports deer. Roughly 1,000 bowhunters hunt deer each year and they have about 7 percent success. Regulations vary by region, but some units have long bow seasons ranging from October into December. Some units do not allow hunting by nonresidents, and nonresidents are required to hire guides in some areas.

Moose. Hunters harvest an average of 13,000 moose in Ontario each fall, the majority in the central and southern part of the province. During the early part of the season in October, moose are still in rut and calling is a popular hunting method. Later, when snow covers the ground, tracking and still-hunting are more common. Some units are open during September for bowhunting only.

Black Bear. Ontario has high numbers of black bears, and hunting here has long been popular among U.S. hunters from bordering states. Baiting during the two-month spring season from mid-April to mid-June is by far the most popular and productive method.

Other Game
European hares are hunted near the Great Lakes, and snowshoe hares are common throughout forested regions of the province.

Gray squirrels are common near suitable hardwoods in the southern end.

Contact. Ministry of Natural Resources, Toronto, Ontario, Canada M7A-1W3.

OPTICS Regardless of conditions, you do 90 percent of your hunting with your eyes, so you want to get the most from them. That means good optics. (To be precise, *optics* means "the science that treats of the phenomena of light, vision, and sight." However, in popular usage it means optical equipment, so for simplicity I'll use the term to mean binoculars and scopes.)

Game spotting can be broken into two parts—choosing optics best suited to your purpose, and using them to spot game. (For more details, see Spotting.) To choose the right optics, you have to sort out several variables. As you do, remember that optical engineering is an exact science, and you don't get something for nothing. If you gain in one area, you lose in another, so you have to weigh advantages against disadvantages to make the best choice.

It might seem that binoculars and scopes would be suited only for open-country hunting where you can spot animals a mile away or farther, but that's not true. Optics can help just as much in dense forests where visibility is no more than 50 yards. In no situation can you hunt as well without optics as you can with.

Binoculars

You've undoubtedly heard someone say, "You can't kill an animal unless you see it first." That might seem obviously trite, yet many hunters ignore that truth and do nothing to equipment themselves for spotting game. If I had to choose between a cheap bow and expensive binoculars, or cheap binoculars and an expensive bow, I'd put my money on the binoculars every time.

If you hunt seriously under many different circumstances, you might own three or four binoculars, each suited to a different use. If you can't afford that luxury, you must hit a happy medium. Here are some guidelines for choosing binoculars.

Magnification (Power). The most obvious value of binoculars is making objects appear bigger. Seven-power (7X) binoculars magnify objects seven times, so you should be able to see a deer, for example, seven times farther away than you could with your naked eye.

Regardless of circumstances, you do 90 percent of your hunting with your eyes. Many hunters associate high-power optics only with open-country hunting, but they're just as valuable for picking out detail in brush country.

If you wear glasses, you might not be able to hold binoculars perfectly steady, so moderate magnification (6X to 8X) might suit you better than high-power binoculars. You can hold glasses steadier if you hook your thumbs under your cheekbones and brace your fingers against your forehead.

For open-country, long-distance viewing, ultrahigh-power binoculars like the Brunton 12X63 at left is ideal, but for all-around hunting, a smaller glass like the Brunton 7X42 will be more practical.

The question is, how much power do you need? If a little is good, a lot must be better, right? Not necessarily. Here's where the trade-offs come in. With a gain in power, you generally lose field of view, and you lose steadiness. Remember, the glasses magnify not only distant objects but movement too, so if your hands are shaking, your binoculars magnify the movement. Seven-power binoculars magnify it seven times, 10X magnify the movement ten times, so it's harder to hold the higher power steady enough to see well.

It's doubly tough if you wear eyeglasses, because you can't brace the binoculars against your forehead as solidly. So if you wear glasses or are a little shaky, you probably will be happiest with 6X or 7X binoculars, because they don't require as much support for steady viewing. And you'll probably prefer the lower magnification binoculars if you hunt primarily in forests where the view is restricted and dark, because lower power glasses generally have a broader field of view.

On the other hand, if you hunt mostly in desert, prairie, and alpine areas where views are nearly unlimited, and you've got a steady hand, you'll probably prefer glasses of 8X to 10X. Many of the really serious mule-deer hunters I know swear by 10X40s.

Sharpness. Optical engineers generally call this resolution, meaning binoculars will resolve, or make clear, a certain amount of detail at a given distance.

Cheap binoculars with poor resolution will, in essence, degrade your vision. If your eyes are 20-20, you might see the equivalent of 20-30 through poorly made binoculars. Good binoculars, in contrast, will accommodate the sharpest eyes. That's especially important in low light, when resolution diminishes. Good optics maintain a sharp image even in poor light.

Optical engineers judge sharpness on a precise instrument called a lens bench. Unless you work for Bausch & Lomb, you probably won't have access to one, but using a test similar to an optometrist's eye test, you can judge sharpness with reasonable accuracy right in a store. Set up a newspaper or magazine at one end of the

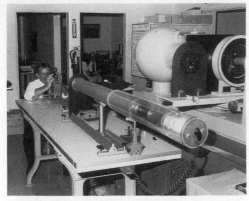

Good binoculars will improve your vision, but cheap binoculars will degrade it. To be of any value, binoculars must be perfectly sharp. Optical engineers use a lens bench, as shown here in Bausch & Lomb's engineering laboratory, to test the sharpness of optical equipment.

store, and then go to the other end and try to read the writing through binoculars. Do this with several pairs. The farther back you can read the print, the sharper the glasses. Change the printed material between each test to avoid memorizing the writing.

Also look at the image around the edges. You'll see some circular distortion with all binoculars, but in good binoculars the image will be sharp out to the very edge. In cheap glasses, the center of the image may appear sharp, but toward the edges it will be blurred.

Brightness. Binoculars not only make an image bigger, but they can make it brighter. It's often said that binoculars "gather" light. Actually, they don't, but high-quality binoculars do an excellent job of transmitting available light, and that coupled with high magnification makes a scene appear brighter than it does to the naked eye.

Two numbers designate the dimensions of binoculars—7X35, 10X40, and so forth. As we've discussed, the first refers to power. The second tells the size of the objective lens in millimeters. Thus, a 7X35 binocular has a 35mm objective lens. For any given power, the larger the objective lens, the brighter the binoculars.

If you hold binoculars about a foot from your face and look into the eyepiece, you'll see a round spot of light. That's the exit pupil. To determine exit pupil size, and thus relative brightness, you divide the objective lens size by the power. For example, 7X35 binoculars have a 5mm exit pupil (35 divided by 7) and 10X40s have a 4mm exit pupil (40 divided by 10).

In general, the larger the exit pupil, the brighter the binoculars. Thus, a 7X35 (5mm exit pupil) will appear much brighter than a 7X24, which has an exit pupil of 3.4 mm. This principle holds up to 5mm; that is, 5mm gives you the maximum brightness. That's one reason the 7X35 binocular has remained so popular.

Now, you ask, what about the 7X50 with its 7.1mm exit pupil (50 divided by 7)? It should be brighter than a 7X35 since it has a bigger exit pupil. Theoretically that's true. However, as Bausch & Lomb's engineering manager, Al Akin, points out, exit pupil size has value only as long as it's no larger than the pupil in your eye. Even in dim light, he said, the pupil in your eye dilates to a maximum of 5mm, so with a 7X50, you've got 2.1mm of exit pupil that for all practical purposes is wasted. That's why he doesn't necessarily recommend so-called night binoculars, such as the 7X50 or 8X56. They're much bigger and heavier than most standard binoculars, but you gain little actual brightness advantage.

The 7X35 like this Bausch & Lomb Classic has always been popular because with an exit pupil of 5mm, it provides the maximum usable brightness.

"Twilight factor" is a term commonly used by German optics makers to express low-light capabilities. To compute the twilight factor, you multiply objective lens diameter by magnification and take the square root. For example, for 7X35s you multiply 35 times 7 and get 245, and the square root is about 15.6. For the 10X40, you multiply 10 times 40 to get 400, which has a square root of 20. Aha! The 7X35 has an exit pupil one full millimeter larger than the 10X40, which means it has better relative brightness, but the 10X40 has a twilight factor 22 percent greater. That's because the twilight factor takes magnification into account, whereas relative brightness measures only the exit pupil size.

The twilight factor means that the 10X40, even with a smaller exit pupil, will reveal more detail in poor light. For that reason, comparing the relative brightness of different power binoculars is like comparing apples to oranges. To compare the dim-light capabilities of binoculars of different powers, use the twilight factor, but to compare the brightness of the same power, use relative brightness.

Two other factors govern brightness: the quality of glass used, and lens coatings. Every uncoated glass surface reflects 5 percent of the light that strikes it. So if the approximately 10 lens and prism surfaces in binoculars were left uncoated, less than 50 percent of the light would reach your eyes. Magnesium fluoride coating reduces light reflection to 1½ or 2 percent, and good binoculars transmit 75 percent or more of the light to your eye. That's why, for maximum brightness, you must buy binoculars with fully coated lenses. And again, that means good binoculars. Buy the best available for maximum brightness.

Field of View. This is the amount of area visible at one time as you look through binoculars. It can be expressed in terms of angle, but more commonly it's expressed in terms of feet at 1,000 yards. For most standard 7X glasses, the field of view is roughly 350 feet at 1,000 yards, but for some wide-angle models it's more than 500 feet. In general, the higher the magnification, the smaller the field of view.

The average field for 10X binoculars is about 275 feet, somewhat narrower than for 7X or 8X binoculars.

It would seem that the wider the field of view, the better, and to some extent that may be true. With wide-angle glasses, you can see more at one glance, and that might give you a slight edge, especially at close range where the view is very restricted. If you hunt primarily in timber where you can't see far, wide-angle binoculars can be valuable.

But they're not really needed for general game spotting. The idea behind spotting is to focus your attention on one small area, and the narrower field of standard binoculars helps you do just that. Most hunters try to look over too much country at once anyway, and when you're in wide-open country, even the relatively restricted view of most 10X binoculars won't be a handicap. I think power, brightness, and resolution are more important considerations than field of view.

One common misconception is that a larger objective lens means larger field of view. That's like saying a 12-gauge shotgun throws a bigger pattern than a 20-gauge because the barrel is bigger around. The size of the barrel has nothing to do with pattern size; internal choke design dictates pattern size. And so it is with binoculars. Objective lens size does not affect field of view; internal eyepiece design governs field.

And that brings up another one of those tradeoffs. If you wear eyeglasses, you must have binoculars with long eye relief (discussed below), and wide-angle binoculars generally have short eye relief. That's because field of view and eye relief are both controlled by design of the eyepiece, and one can be increased only at the expense of the other.

Eye Relief. You read little about this, yet if you wear eyeglasses, eye relief may be the most important factor in choosing binoculars. You'll never do much serious spotting if you have to take off your glasses every time you want to use your binoculars.

In simple terms, eye relief is the shortest distance from your eye to the ocular lens (the binocular lens nearest your eye) at which you can see the full field of view. For example, if your binoculars have an eye relief of 17mm, that means you can see the full field when your eye is 17mm from the ocular lens. If your eye gets closer than that, the image blacks out. That's why binoculars are equipped with eye cups—to hold your eyes the proper distance from the ocular lens.

As your eye gets farther away than 17mm, the field of view narrows, and that's the significant point for eyeglasses wearers. Many binoculars have such short eye relief that you can't, while wearing glasses, get your eyes close enough to the ocular lenses to see the full field.

Two variables affect eye relief. One is magnification. In general, the higher the magnification the shorter the eye relief. However, most quality companies make binoculars up to 10X with adequate eye relief for glasses wearers, so magnification isn't a major concern in terms of eye relief. Just try specific binoculars before you buy them to make sure you can see the full field.

The second variable is field of view, and in general, wide field means short eye relief. You can have one or the other, but not both. Al Akin said, "Wide-angle design poses a terrible handicap to the eyeglasses wearer. If you wear eyeglasses, don't buy wide-angle binoculars."

My Bausch & Lomb Classic 7X35 binoculars have an eye relief of 17mm, and that's more than adequate while I'm wearing glasses. Zeiss offers several models of binoculars with a special "B" designation, and these all have an eye relief of 17.5mm, which makes them ideal for glasses wearers. In contrast, many wide-angle and miniature binoculars have an eye relief of 7mm to 8mm. If you wear glasses, I guarantee you won't be happy with these because you'll have to take off your glasses to use them, and you won't do much spotting that way.

If you wear glasses, one feature you'll want is rubber, roll-down eye cups. But don't be fooled into thinking that roll-down eye cups in themselves affect eye relief. They don't. If binoculars have short eye relief, rolling down the eye cups won't do you a lick of good.

Incidentally, the style of glasses you wear can affect your use of binoculars. I have two pairs of glasses, one with plastic frames and solid nosepieces, one with metal frames and adjustable nose pads. The metal frames sit much closer to my face and allow me to see a far greater field of view in my binoculars than do the plastic frames. For serious hunting, buy glasses that sit close to your face so you can get the most out of your binoculars.

Porro vs. Roof Prism. These are the two basic prism designs used in binoculars. Porro prisms are the traditional "humpback" binoculars, and roof prism binoculars have straight barrels.

For any given magnification and objective lens size, porro prism binoculars will be slightly bulkier and heavier than roof prism binoculars. As a typical example, compare Bausch & Lomb's 7X35 Discover porro prism binoculars (5⅜ inches high, 22 ounces) with the 7X35 Classic roof prism binoculars (5 inches high, 18.6 ounces). Obviously for backcountry hunting, you'd prefer the smaller size and lighter weight. So why even worry about porro prisms? Why not just buy the more compact roof prism binoculars?

Cost. You can get equally sharp porro prism binoculars for a lot less money. As Al Akin pointed out, to get comparable optical quality,

Roof-prism binoculars, like the Bausch & Lomb 7X35 Classic shown here, have straight barrels and are more compact and lighter than comparable porro-prism binoculars. They're also more expensive.

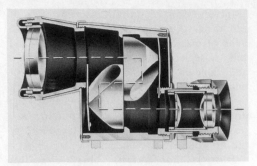

In traditional "humpback" porro-prism binoculars, the light makes two 180-degree turns before reaching your eyes, and the prisms are offset.

roof prism binoculars must be made much more precisely. He said that if you could split the average human hair lengthwise into 500 pieces, one of those pieces would indicate the tolerance level at which the roof prism must be made. A roof prism must be 300 times more accurately made than a porro prism to get equal sharpness. As a result, good roof prisms cost more than good porro prisms, so your choice is strictly one of price versus size and weight.

Mini Binoculars. Miniature binoculars have become a modern rage. The selling point is the small size and weight, but unfortunately, tradeoffs here again enter in. You can't reduce size without giving up something, and in this

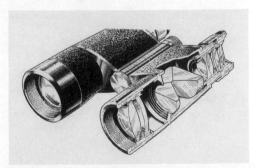

Roof prisms are mounted in straight barrels so the glasses are smaller and more compact. However, roof prisms must be ground and mounted 300 times more precisely than porro prisms, so roof-prism binoculars of comparable quality cost somewhat more.

case it's objective lens size. As you'll see from looking at specification charts, most miniature binoculars have objective lenses of 20mm to 25mm in diameter. The 8X20, then, has an exit pupil of 2.5mm (20 divided by 8), and the 10X25 also has an exit pupil of 2.5mm. An exit pupil that small will not produce a bright image in dim light, and that's an optical reality, no matter how well the glasses are made.

A small exit pupil presents a second problem that I haven't mentioned before, and that's eye alignment. To get the picture, suppose you could view a scene either through a 1-inch pipe or a 12-inch culvert. Obviously you'd have a lot more latitude in eye placement looking through the culvert than through the pipe. And so it is with binoculars. Using compacts with an exit pupil of 2.5mm, your eye must be lined up perfectly to see much of anything, but with a 5mm exit pupil, you can be to one side or the other a little and still see the full field of view. (That's one reason marine binoculars are made with huge objective lenses. The 7X50, for example, has an exit pupil of 7.1mm. That gives you so much latitude in eye placement that even while you're bobbing around on a boat, you can always see the full field of view.)

I think small size and light weight also present a strike against stability. Any serious archer knows that adding a stabilizer for principle applies to binoculars. With super-lightweight binoculars, every little hand tremor will be transmitted to your eyes, but heavier glasses absorb some of that movement.

Compact binoculars might have their place where you need only to check an occasional detail, say from your tree stand, but if you're hunting in a situation for mule deer, antelope, western bear, sheep, or other animals where success depends largely on your eyes, buy full-size, high-performance binoculars. You won't be sorry.

Zoom Binoculars. Variable power would seem to solve a lot of hunters' optics problems, but it doesn't really. For one thing, even the best zoom binoculars can't compare optically—sharpness, brightness, durability—with good fixed-power glasses.

And they don't perform quite the way you might anticipate. It would seem that on low power you would get a very wide-angle view, but the fact is you don't. Instead you feel like you're looking down a tube (which you are). For that reason, zoom glasses aren't as versatile in actual practice as they are in theory, and hunters who buy zoom binoculars are often disappointed.

Rubber Armor and Other Considerations. Many binoculars today are rubber-coated. You can live without rubber armor, but still, if you'll be climbing cliffs, crawling on your belly to stalk game, and generally abusing your binoculars, you'd be wise to get armored binoculars. They weigh slightly more than standard glasses, but the rubber coating can add to their life and make them a little quieter.

If you hunt strictly in rainy country or do a lot of river running or boating, you might want fully waterproof binoculars. Many of these have individual-eye focus, which means you have to focus each eyepiece separately. That's a little slower than the center focusing on standard binoculars, and that could influence your decision. Some companies now make waterproof glasses with center focus. Unless you know you're going to be in extremely wet conditions, waterproofness probably isn't a major concern. All high-quality binoculars are tightly sealed and will not leak or fog up under normal conditions.

Quality. Maybe this is the most important concern of all, and it more or less summarizes everything said above. As a general guideline buy at the top end of any category you're considering. If you decide on porro prism binoculars, buy at the top end of the range; if roof prism, buy the best. If you want 10X, buy at the top end of the 10X price range, and so forth. If you buy top quality, you'll get sharp, bright, and durable binoculars.

One aspect not discussed above is collimation, or alignment, and this must be considered a major reason for buying quality. Just like the barrels on a double-barrel shotgun, the lenses in binoculars must be perfectly aligned to shoot straight. One year, before I learned the

Miniature binoculars and monoculars may be convenient and lightweight, but they can't compare in quality with full-size binoculars. For serious hunting, never sacrifice size for quality.

value of quality optics, I used cheap glasses. I could see fairly well through them, but after an hour of constant glassing, my eyes burned and I got so dizzy I couldn't walk a straight line. That's because they were poorly aligned so that my eyes were actually looking different directions. That's a common problem with cheap glasses. Top-quality binoculars are perfectly aligned so you can look through them for hours with no eye strain.

Good binoculars will last all your life and through the next several generations, so they're a one-time investment. Buy the best. In my opinion, $100 spent on binoculars is money wasted, but $500 is wisely invested.

Spotting Scopes and High-Power Binoculars

Spotting Scopes. You might consider a spotting scope too heavy to be practical, but if you stop to think how many miles of walking it can save you, you'll reconsider its value. On a late-

For any open-country hunting, a spotting scope can save you many miles of fruitless walking.

season mule deer hunt in Idaho, I'd been climbing a high ridge each day, and on my best day I'd seen 8 bucks up there. One morning I got a late start, so rather than climbing, I set up my spotting scope on a road at the bottom and studied the ridge from there. Within two hours I'd spotted 12 bucks, and I watched several of them bed down. By simply looking, I'd seen more bucks than ever before, and I knew right where to hunt them, which saved me a lot of time and energy later. Many of those bucks were more than a mile away, so I would never have seen them without the scope. Not only that, but with the high-power scope, I was able to judge their antlers closely.

In choosing a scope, the "quality" guideline applies just as it does with binoculars. Buy at the top end of the price range and you won't be disappointed.

The primary question might be: What power should I buy? Many scopes come with zoom

lenses with a range of 15–60X. For hunting I think the additional money you pay for a high-power zoom is largely wasted, because you can rarely use the higher powers. Under most conditions, even on snow, heat waves rise off the ground, and haze and other problems can distort your view. Normally 25X is about the maximum useful magnification; anything much higher than that magnifies heat waves so badly you can't see much of anything. Under good viewing conditions, magnifications up around 30X can be useful for sizing up trophy heads. My Bushnell Stalker has a 10–30X zoom lens, and that's a fairly effective range; so is the 12–36X of the Bushnell Trophy.

Often I look through my scope and then zoom in and out until I hit on the best power for a given situation. Consistently that ends up being about 20X. It's never over 25X, and rarely is it as low as 15X. In other words, I've found 20X to be the most versatile power level. I've also used many other scopes, some with fixed-power lenses, and consistently 20X proves to be about the best. For that reason, I think you're as well off to buy a fixed-power scope with a 20X or 25X eyepiece as you are a zoom lens.

Size might influence your choice of scope. If you plan to glass from your vehicle or horseback, then a full-size scope (such as the Bushnell Trophy, an excellent full-size rubber-armored scope) is ideal. On the minus side, it measures 13.6 inches long and weighs 38 ounces, about average for full-size scopes. In contrast, the Bushnell Stalker is 10 inches long and weighs 18 ounces. If you plan to carry a scope as you hike the backcountry, you'll appreciate the smaller size and weight of the Stalker. And optically it's excellent.

Use a Tripod. In some cases, you might be able to lay a scope across a rock or a saddle to take a quick look, but you won't do much prolonged viewing that way. For serious scope use, you need a tripod. Some scopes have a 45-degree eyepiece, and with these you can use a fairly short tripod because you look down into the scope, but if your scope has a straight eyepiece, you need a higher tripod. Sure, you can

With a spotting scope, you can make out small detail and spot deer from long range you'd never see with lesser optics. To hunt efficiently, use your eyes.

lie down to look through a scope on a short tripod, but you'll get tired of that real quick. For prolonged viewing, you must be comfortable, and that requires a tripod tall enough to allow you to sit up straight. Some lightweight tripods, such as the Slik 450G, are very light and compact, yet the legs extend long enough to put the scope at eye level as you're sitting.

Some writers consider scopes specialized equipment that won't interest the average hunter. I can't agree with that. Sure, if you hunt in the Midwest or East where the view is restricted, a scope won't do you much good. But for any Western hunting, I consider a scope invaluable.

Big Binoculars. Ultra-high-power binoculars, such as Zeiss' 15X60, offer an alternative to a spotting scope. Duwane Adams, a hunting guide and trophy hunter in Arizona, swears by his 15X60 binoculars.

"With a scope, you're only using one eye, so you have to squint. While the guy with his spotting scope is rubbing his sore eyes, I'm still spotting deer with these binoculars," Adams said.

I've seen Adams in action and have used similar binoculars myself, and I'm convinced

Ultrahigh-power binoculars serve the same function as a spotting scope—locating game at extra-long ranges. And just like a scope, big binoculars must be used on a tripod to be of value.

315

his system ranks second to none when it comes to spotting game. Adams sits on a small foam pad so he's comfortable, and then he adjusts his tripod to bring his Zeiss 15X60s right to eye level. Looking through these bright, powerful binoculars, rock-steady on a tripod, is like viewing deer through a 15X picture window. With this system, Adams will spot two deer to the average hunter's one. Cost presents the only real drawback. You'll pay $800 or more for binoculars like that, when you can get an optically comparable scope for about $200.

Care of Optics

Obviously if you pay several hundred dollars for equipment, you want it to last. Avoid banging any optics around because it can throw off the alignment. If your binoculars need cleaning or you suspect the alignment is off, never take the glasses apart to repair them yourself. You'll never get them properly realigned. Always return them to the manufacturer.

To clean the lenses, use soft lens-cleaning tissue. In a pinch, you can use a soft T-shirt (never abrasive cloth), but always blow on the lenses first to remove excess dust and to moisten the dust there. Dry dust is gritty like sandpaper, and it can scratch the lens coatings. (For more details on using your eyes, see Spotting.)

OREGON This 97,000-square-mile Pacific state is divided into distinct halves—western and eastern—by the Cascade Range, which runs north and south from Washington to California. Western Oregon comprises low-elevation, very steep mountains where constant rainstorms off the Pacific Ocean during winter produce lush forests and dense, junglelike undergrowth. Eastern Oregon lies in the rain shadow of the Cascade Range, so the eastern two thirds of the state is dry, with an average rainfall of less than 15 inches except in some of the higher mountain ranges. Sagebrush desert covers a good part of eastern Oregon. Federal lands administered by the U.S. Forest Service and BLM are extensive, so access is small problem in most areas.

Big Game

Deer. The statewide early archery season for deer and elk traditionally has been for four weeks in August and September. A late November season on the west side in several units provides good hunting for blacktail deer during the rut. About 20,000 residents and 800 nonresidents buy archery tags each year in Oregon. Bowhunters take about 3,000 deer annually.

Oregon has three varieties of deer—blacktail, whitetail, and mule deer. An estimated 460,000 blacktails live throughout the dense Douglas fir forests and oak-and-grass foothills of western Oregon. The McKenzie and Santiam units, which contain remote country at higher elevations along the Cascade crest as well as private-land sanctuaries in the Willamette Valley, produce the most trophy bucks. This is where George Shurtleff killed the Pope and Young world record, and several of the largest bucks listed by Boone and Crockett come from these units. Jackson County in southern Oregon also produces lots of deer and big blacktail bucks.

Because of the mild climate, abundant feed, and dense escape cover in western Oregon, blacktail numbers remain high, and buck-doe ratios are higher than 25 bucks per 100 does in many units. As a result, blacktail seasons are generous. Most land adjacent to valley floors in western Oregon is private, but you can get permission to hunt in many places. In the foothills and higher into the Coast Range and Cascade Mountains, the Forest Service, Bureau of Land Management, and large timber companies own much of the land, and you'll have no trouble finding a place to hunt.

The state record and Pope and Young world-record scored 172⅖. The top five blacktails listed in the eighth edition of *Records of North American Big Game* came from Oregon. Oregon offers the best chance of any state for a truly huge blacktail.

Arid eastern Oregon has an estimated population of 250,000 mule deer. The greater part of eastern Oregon comprises sagebrush desert and grasslands. Mule deer live throughout the desert at elevations higher than 6,000. They are heavily hunted because many hunters prefer the open vistas of mule-deer country to the enclosed blacktail country. Rifle permits are limited on several desert units such as Steens Mountain and Trout Creek Mountains, but bowhunting is unlimited, and trophy-hunting potential is good. The terrain consists of rim-rocks, plateaus, and deep canyons. Several large mountain ranges—the Wallowas, Blues, and Cascades—have good herds of mule deer, and early-season hunting in alpine country can be good. Deer herds fluctuate drastically with weather extremes in eastern Oregon, and some units have been closed to all hunting recently. Most of the best mule-deer hunting takes place on public lands, so access is little problem.

The Boone and Crockett state record typical mule deer scored 209⁴/₈, and the top nontypical scored 291⁴/₈. However, very few other mule deer from Oregon are listed by Boone and Crockett. Oregon grows plenty of mule deer big enough to make Pope and Young.

Whitetails are hunted only in the extreme northeastern corner in Wallowa, Union, and Umatilla counties. Whitetails aren't numerous, but some large bucks are taken. The Columbian whitetail also lives along the Columbia River between Portland and Astoria, and in the Umpqua Valley near Roseburg, but Columbian whitetails are listed as endangered and are not hunted.

Elk. Oregon ranks among the top elk states and commonly has a total harvest of 20,000 or more, second only to Colorado. Archers take about 1,000 elk each year. The general archery elk season runs concurrent with the deer season in August and September.

Rocky Mountain elk live in all the forested mountains of eastern Oregon, and highest densities are in the northeast corner along the Idaho and Washington borders. Much of this country has road access, but there are several large wilderness areas. Oregon is better known for lots of elk than for big bulls, but every year archers take a bull or two that scores around 350 or better.

In western Oregon, you'll find Roosevelt elk throughout the dense Coast Range and west slope of the Cascades (to be scored as Roosevelts for the record book, they must be taken west of Interstate 5, which eliminates the Cascades). The current world-record Roosevelt bull was killed in northwestern Oregon, and a number of other large bulls have been taken here. In addition to the early general season, a late season is held for Roosevelt elk in December. Permits are limited but drawing odds are good.

Bear. Oregon rates as one of the best bear states. Numbers are very high throughout the Coast Range and in the Snake River country in the northeast, and bears are fairly numerous throughout the Cascade Range and other forested mountains. They can be hunted legally by baiting and with hounds. Oregon has no spring season except along the Snake River, where a limited number of permits are issued. There is no special bow season. The general bear season opens in August and runs through November.

Antelope. General antelope season (rifle) runs for five days in August. Permits are limited and drawing odds are poor. Special archery seasons are held in August and September, and odds for drawing a tag are nearly 100 percent. Archers have killed some good bucks in the Gerber unit.

Cougar. Seasons are open in December and January, and a limited number of permits are issued by drawing. Virtually all lions are taken with the aid of dogs.

Bighorn Sheep. Oregon has established herds of California bighorns in several desert mountain ranges in the southeast, and Rocky Mountain bighorns in the Wallowa Mountains and Snake River canyon in the northeast. Several dozen sheep tags are issued each year, but only residents may apply.

Contact. Oregon Department of Fish and Wildlife, P.O. Box 59, Portland, OR 97207.

OUTFITTERS AND GUIDES If you're just getting started hunting, especially if you want to hunt the Western mountains, you may decide to book with an outfitter. That's particularly true if you're going for species you've never hunted before. Hunting elk, black bears,

Look like a lot of fun? If you plan to hunt on your own, you might end up just like this unless you plan ahead to have an outfitter pack meat for you. If you plan to hunt far off the road, line up meat-packing services well ahead of your hunt.

If you want to hunt the backcountry and enjoy the comforts of home, but you don't want to hunt with a guide, consider a drop camp. An outfitter will set up a comfortable tent for you, and then all you have to do is hunt.

antelope, and mule deer in the wide-open West differs greatly from hunting whitetails in eastern woodlots, and unless you have some woods savvy, experience as a bowhunter, good physical condition, and some inherent grit, you'd be well advised to hunt with an outfitter your first time around.

And, of course, in some cases you're required by law to hire an outfitter. In most Canadian provinces, nonresidents can't hunt legally without hiring a licensed guide or outfitter. In Alaska, nonresidents are required to hire guides for Dall sheep and grizzly bear hunting. In Wyoming, nonresidents must hire an outfitter to hunt designated wilderness.

Services Provided by Outfitters

Meat Packing. If you're a do-it-yourself hunter, you still might hire an outfitter. Let's say you backpack in several miles, find game, and put an arrow in a bull elk. Suddenly you find yourself ten miles from a road with 500 pounds of very dead meat to pack. What to do? If you've got more brawn than brains, you'll start carrying that meat out on your back. If you've got any sense at all, you'll hike out and hire the nearest outfitter to bring his horses to retrieve your elk.

In many areas that's a distinct possibility, but with any kind of outfitted hunting, you must make arrangements before the hunt, not after the services are needed. In some areas you won't find any outfitters, and some outfitters won't pack meat. Talk to outfitters before you go hunting.

And make sure you understand the arrangements. In one case, an outfitter told me he'd pack an elk for $100. So I hunted his area and killed a huge bull elk in a terrible place. Without further ado I notified the outfitter, and he told me the price would be $400. When he'd quote me $100 he meant under one set of circumstances, and I'd killed the bull under another. To avoid surprises, iron out details before your hunt.

Drop Camp. If you want to hunt wilderness country with the luxury of a full camp (opposed to a backpack camp), but you don't want to hunt with a guide, the drop camp might suit you.

Drop camps work a couple of ways. You can have an outfitter pack in all your gear—tents, cook stove, utensils, cots, and so forth—and drop it off at a predetermined spot. Then you hike in (or rent horses from the outfitter and ride in) and set up your own camp.

A more common alternative is to have the outfitter set up a camp for you, using his tents and gear. In some cases the outfitter will even cut and stack wood for you and will supply groceries, too. Obviously, the more services he provides, the more he'll charge. A drop camp like this costs about half what a fully guided hunt would cost.

Of course, to go this route, you have to know hunting. The drop camp is a good choice for experienced hunters who want an unguided backcountry hunt but don't have the pack animals to do it on their own.

As always, hammer out the details before you get to the camp. Make sure you know exactly what services the outfitter will provide. Will he supply cots and mattresses for sleeping? White gas for the lanterns? Food? Will he cut wood? Will he make a meat check to haul

game to cooling facilities? Settle even the slightest details beforehand, and make sure you agree on a price, and you'll be okay. Complaints over drop camps are very common, primarily because of misunderstandings between the outfitter and hunters about services to be provided and price.

Another common complaint concerns quality of hunting. Some hunters accuse outfitters of putting them in second-rate areas. Some such accusations could be true. If an outfitter is guiding hunters at the same time you're hunting from the drop camp, he's not going to put you in his prime spots. He'll take his guided clients there. To safeguard against that, consider doing your own research and selecting your own area. Then find an outfitter who'll take you to the spot you've chosen. That way, if things go wrong you can blame only yourself. Keep in mind, however, that some outfitters won't provide drop camps (they'll take only guided hunters), so always explore the possibilities before establishing plans.

Fully Guided Hunts. If you're new to hunting, or at least to bowhunting, or you have little confidence in your own ability to get around the backcountry, you might be happi-

If you've never hunted Western game such as elk, you may find yourself overwhelmed by the country and the size of the animals. A guided hunt can break you in right. Horses are the foundation for most backcountry hunting.

Many guided elk hunts involve miles of horseback riding just to reach camp. For wilderness hunting, hiring an outfitter might be the smartest move, particularly if you're new to this kind of hunting.

est to book a guided hunt. The same applies if you've never hunted a particular species. Many Eastern hunters are overwhelmed the first time they try hunting elk in Western mountains. They find they're not in good enough shape to hunt well, and if they've never hunted elk before, they're commonly bewildered by their inability to locate animals. Many of these hunters admit they'd have been wise to take at least one guided hunt first, just to get a feel for this brand of hunting.

Guided hunts take many forms. On many mule-deer hunts, you stay in nice cabins or big tents, and you drive out in vehicles each day either to look for deer or to reach a tree stand where you'll sit mornings and evenings. The hunting isn't strenuous, and success runs high. Many antelope hunts, and even some elk hunts, are run similarly.

Many elk hunts, on the other hand, involve long miles of horseback riding just to reach camp. You'll have a warm tent to sleep in and plenty of grub, but the hunting will be tough, with many days of long, hard riding and hiking. Even though you're provided with a horse and guide, such wilderness hunts can wear you down in a hurry. You have to be in good shape.

Some backcountry hunts even involve strenuous backpacking. Decide what you're looking for in a hunt, and understand exactly what services an outfitter provides before committing yourself.

Choosing an Outfitter

Sources. You can get the names of outfitters from many sources: game departments, outfitters and guides associations in each state and province, classified ads in magazines, books and magazine articles about hunting. Incidentally, you can find dozens of articles written about guided hunts. Don't take these as gospel. Many outfitters take writers for free in exchange for potential publicity. That's an ethical and common practice, so there's nothing wrong with that in itself. However, if a writer feels indebted to an outfitter, he may produce a worthy report when, in fact, the hunt was second-rate. So follow up with your own research (as outlined below), no matter how great a writer makes a hunt sound.

Also, consider working through a booking agent. Many agents handle bookings for outfitters, and an agent builds his reputation on happy clients. In most cases, agents screen outfitters carefully, and they won't book for sham outfits. Booking through an agent costs you nothing. The outfitter pays the agent's fee.

Archery Specialists. Once you've got a list of possible outfitters, find out first if they know bowhunting. I've taken a couple of guided hunts on which neither the outfitters nor any of the guides knew the slightest thing about calling elk. Fortunately, before ever going on those hunts I told the outfitters I wanted to bugle for myself and hunt my own way. If their guides wanted to tag along, that was fine with me. The hunts worked out fine. I killed bulls both years, the outfitters learned something about bowhunting for elk, and we all came away happy.

But if I'd been a novice elk hunter, those hunts could have been disasters; the guides didn't know how to get hunters within bow range of elk. Many outfitters, in my opinion, are cowboys moonlighting as hunting guides. They can get by guiding rifle hunters, but they fail miserably with archers. Choose outfitters who themselves are bowhunters, and who specialize in archery hunts. They not only must know how to set up close shots, but they must be patient. Some guides won't tolerate the "ineffectiveness" of archery tackle. They're accustomed to hunters toting .300 Magnums who can blow over elk and deer at 300 yards, and after a couple of blown stalks or missed shots on your part, they may lose patience.

A friend of mine hunted Stone sheep in British Columbia, and when he missed a 40-yard shot at a ram, his guide got so furious he stomped off the mountain to get the horses. As far as the guide was concerned, that ended the hunt. Needless to say, that attitude didn't set well with my friend, who'd paid several thousand dollars for the hunt, so he went the other way by himself and later that afternoon killed that very same ram.

Along this line, listen to how an outfitter talks about previous clients, and beware if he blames his hunters for failure. In many cases it may be the hunter's fault, but if an outfitter makes a habit of blaming clients, remember, you're next. Personally, I hunt to enjoy the mountains and country and the companion-ship of my guide, and personality clashes aren't my idea of pleasure. When I hunted with Ed McCallum in Idaho, I told him I wanted to hunt with a bow and that I might pass up animals and even, heaven forbid, miss a shot or two, which could make him look bad as a guide. "It's your hunt," McCallum said. "Whatever you want to do suits me just fine." He never tried to force me to perform for the sake of his own reputation, and we spent an excellent week together.

Questions to Ask. First, of course, you want to find out the kind of operation an outfitter runs. Will you be horsepacking? Backpacking? Hunting from tree stands? Hiking ten miles a day? Bugling for elk or stalking? Staying in a lodge, tents, or under the stars? How many days will you actually hunt? A ten-day hunt often includes two travel days, so you hunt only eight days.

Find out how many hunters will be hunting with each guide. And find out who'll be guiding you. Some hunters expect the outfitter himself to be the guide, and they're angry when they get stuck with some young buck who, in their opinion, isn't dry behind the ears. Get the guide's name and phone number, and call and chat with him.

Ask about the outfitter's overall success. This figure can be misleading because a lot of things enter in. However, if you get an average success rate for several years, it tells you something about the game available. If an outfitter's success has averaged better than 50 percent over the long term, you know he offers good hunting. If it's been only 20 percent, you might question why it's so low. You stand better odds than that on your own.

Also ask about the quality of game. If you want a six-point bull elk or nothing, you won't want to hunt an area where 80 percent of the elk killed are spikes.

Maybe even more significantly, ask what percentage of repeat clients the outfitter gets. Really successful outfitters rely heavily on repeat bookings. If they have to dig up new clients every year, their operation might be suspect. Also find out how long the outfitter has worked a given area. If he's new there he may not know the country well, and he also may be running a short-lived, shoestring operation. You can just about count on outfitters who've become well established in an area.

References. If you know someone who personally hunted with a certain outfitter, you've got a good informant. If you don't have such a source, ask the outfitter for names and phone numbers of persons who've hunted with him. In particular, get the names of hunters who were unsuccessful. Killing a trophy animal can dull a person's senses to adversity, and anyone who kills a trophy bull or huge buck most likely will give a good report. But what about the guy who didn't kill anything? He'll be totally honest, because he can evaluate the outfitter's operation in a true light unclouded by the sight of giant antlers on his wall. Talk to at least four or five references before drawing conclusions.

Ask your references the same questions you asked the outfitter to see if their stories are similar. Ask about the quality of food, sleeping accommodations, the guide's sensitivity to the hunter's physical limitations, the amount of game seen, and so forth.

Be Honest. Responsibility for a good hunt doesn't rely on the outfitter alone, but on you. Outfitters want good clients just as much as clients want good outfitters. That means you must be honest with yourself and your outfitter. Explain your expectations and goals. Maybe he can fulfill them, maybe he can't. Be honest about your physical condition. If you can run ten miles without breaking into a sweat, you probably can handle about any kind of hunt. But if you consider getting the evening paper from the box hard labor, tell the outfitter that before you arrive. In particular, warn him of any physical problems you may have—bad legs, weak heart, diabetes—so he can plan hunts suited to your ability and meals suited to any specific diet considerations. Don't wait until you arrive in camp to spring surprises on him. That's a good way to get off on bad footing immediately.

OVERDRAW   An overdraw device allows you to shoot short arrows from a bow you draw to normal draw length. For example, if your draw length is 32 inches, an overdraw allows you to shoot arrows much shorter than 32 inches, probably as short as 26 inches. Doing that not only cuts 6 inches off your arrow, which in itself reduces arrow weight significantly, but it allows you to shoot an arrow of much lighter spine weight than you would normally, which reduces weight even more. The result is much higher arrow speed and flatter trajectory than you get with full-length arrows.

Overdraw Styles
Forward Handle. Overdraws come in three basic designs. The forward-handle design, such as the Martin Jaguar, has a handle in front of

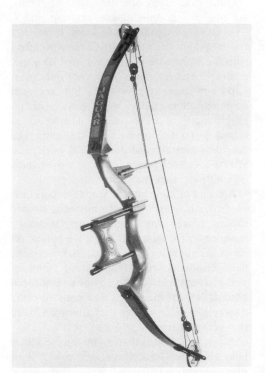

The Martin Jaguar is one example of the forward-handle overdraw system. With this bow, you change draw length by moving the handle forward or backward.

With York's S-T-O (Shoot-Through-Overdraw), the arrow goes directly through the handle. With this bow you can cut your arrow three to four inches shorter than for a normal setup. The shoot-through style may be safer than other overdraw styles, because the arrow can't fall off the rest to shoot you in the hand.

the riser, and you adjust draw length by sliding the handle forward or back. On these bows, the riser itself curves sharply back toward the string and the riser has no handle, so these can be shot only as overdraw units.

Shoot-Through Handle. The York S-T-O (Shoot-Through-Overdraw) is one example (the only one at this writing) of the shoot-through handle. This system looks cumbersome, but it makes sense. All conventional bows torque to some degree because the riser is offset, but the shoot-through design eliminates that problem because it's symmetrical. This bow can be shot either right- or left-handed, and it might be safer than other overdraw

styles. That's because with a standard overdraw, the arrow conceivably could fall off the rest and shoot you in the hand, but that's not as likely with the shoot-through handle.

Overdraw Attachment. Many conventional bows can be converted to shoot shorter than normal arrows with overdraw attachments. Most are simple metal brackets that bolt into the threaded plunger bushing in the sight window of the bow, and they hold an arrow rest midway between the riser and the string. You can put any kind of arrow rest on the bracket.

One shortcoming of this system can be broadhead clearance. With the forward-handle and the shoot-through riser, clearance is not a problem, but with an overdraw bracket on your regular bow, the head of the arrow has to pass the riser. Unless the riser is cut well past center, a big broadhead will not clear. However, some

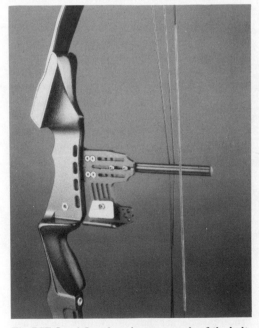

The PSE Omni Overdraw is one example of the bolt-on overdraw attachment. Overdraw brackets like this can be put on any bow. The one problem can be broadhead clearance. Some bows are not cut far enough past center to accommodate an overdraw.

PSE has solved the clearance problem with its Center-Flite handle, which is cut far past center to allow complete clearance for any size or style of arrow head. This handle is made especially with the overdraw attachment in mind.

bows are made specifically to be shot with overdraws. The PSE with the Center-Flite handle is one example. Bows with the C-F handle have an offset riser that allows you to shoot any size broadhead with complete clearance.

In choosing an overdraw, also keep in mind that the rest sits much closer to the string than normal, and it may not give enough room for large fletching. If you insist on shooting five-inch fletching, you'll have to use an overdraw that sits fairly close to the riser. That limits how short you can cut your arrows. If you want the rest closer to the string so you can shoot ultrashort arrows, you'll have to use shorter fletching. Many overdraw shooters go with four, four-inch vanes.

Pros and Cons of Overdraws

Overdraws have been around for years, but they've been popularized in recent years as archers have become more speed-conscious. Popularity varies greatly by region. One archery shop owner I know won't even stock overdraw bows because he doesn't think the average guy can shoot one well.

On the other hand, Cliff Dewell, an archery shop owner in California, believes in overdraws and pushes them. "I shoot better with an overdraw than without," Dewell said. "And I've

started nearly 600 shooters in this area shooting overdraws. It gives them points on the target range, especially at unknown yardages—and that's exactly what hunting is. With an overdraw, I think you gain a lot more than you lose."

Arrow Speed. The gain comes in arrow speed and, as a result, flattened trajectory. By reducing mass weight of your arrow you can increase speed for any bow at a given draw weight by 10 percent or more. With my round-wheel compound set at 60 pounds, for example, my 33-inch 2216 arrows fly at 200 fps. With that same bow, I can shoot 28-inch 2213s at 220 fps. With a cam bow, I can get the same 220 fps at 55 pounds draw weight.

You can see the advantage in sight-pin spacing. On some high-speed bows, the 20- and 60-yard pins are less than 1 inch apart. This kind of spacing gives you somewhat more leeway in range estimation, and a shot that could be a complete miss with a slower bow could produce a killing hit with a high-speed bow.

The advantages show up in some kinds of competitive shooting, particularly at unmarked distances. Over a period of several years, Bob Gentry won many Oregon archery tournaments by shooting a 90-pound Martin Jaguar that spit his arrows out at 280 fps. That's a radical setup. Most tournament shoot-

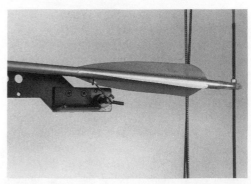

If you equip a bow with an overdraw bracket, make sure you have adequate clearance for vanes. With the setup shown here, the rest either needs to be moved forward, or the arrow must be refletched with four-inch vanes.

ers don't get that extreme, but nevertheless you do see a lot of overdraws in competitive shooting, particularly at unknown distances.

Bow Damage. Of course, the law of diminishing returns applies to arrow speed just as it applies to most good things in life, and when you overdo the light-arrow business, you pay for it. One way could be bow damage. It's no secret that dry firing a bow (drawing the bow and releasing without an arrow on the string) is a good way to destroy a bow. That's because in normal shooting, the arrow absorbs much of the bow's energy, but when you dry fire, all the excess energy surges directly through the limbs, handle, and cables of the bow, and the force can be great enough to blow the bow apart.

Most authorities say there's an ideal ratio of arrow to bow weight—about 9 grains of arrow weight for every pound of bow weight. Thus, for greatest efficiency from a 60-pound bow, you'd shoot a 540-grain arrow (9 grains x 60 pounds = 540 grains). Some deviation isn't critical, but the further you stray from that ideal, the greater the potential for bow damage. When you shoot 400-grain arrows off an 80-pound cam bow, you're virtually dry firing the bow and you're asking for trouble. Also, the lighter the arrow in relation to bow weight, the noisier the setup.

Accuracy. Some shooters also would say you lose more in accuracy than you gain in trajectory. One reason has to do with hand position in relation to the arrow rest. The point at which your hand grips the handle acts as a pivot point, and supposedly the most accurate position for the arrow rest is directly above that pivot point. That's why most bows are made with the arrow rests directly above the handle. Apparently, then, the farther you place the rest from that point the less accurate the setup becomes, because the more the rest will move in response to any torquing or twisting of the bow.

At face value that makes sense, but it may not affect accuracy to the degree that some shooters claim. For one thing, shooting an overdraw reduces the amount of time an arrow stays in contact with the rest, so there's less

time for the rest to affect the arrow. Don Rabska, special projects manager for Easton Aluminum, called it "lock time," a term commonly used in relation to firearms. "With a gun, the shorter the firing pin and the faster the powder, the less time shooter error has to affect flight of a bullet," Rabska said. "With a bow, the same principle applies. The less time that elapses from the instant you release the string until the arrow clears the bow, the less likely you are to throw off the shot. Obviously, a short, quick arrow will clear the bow faster than a long, slow arrow, so it potentially could be more accurate."

It's also possible that placing the arrow rest behind the hand doesn't have the effect that some shooters say it does. Frank Pearson, one of the top tournament archers in the country and a man who lives archery and bow tuning, thinks that idea is totally false. "Your wrist is the pivot point," Pearson said. "For greatest accuracy, then, you want the arrow rest set directly above your wrist, and that's the reason to shoot an overdraw. I don't shoot an overdraw for high arrow speed, but because it's more forgiving than a conventional setup."

Critical Arrow Flight. Some overdraw shooters go for the absolute maximum speed, but others say that high arrow speed alone makes the setup critical and difficult to shoot well. Frank Pearson, for one, believes that. "An overdraw isn't for speed but for forgiveness," Pearson said. "I think you should shoot relatively heavy arrows to hold arrow speed down. I don't like to exceed 220 feet per second. Much faster than that and arrow flight starts getting critical."

Jim Pickering, national sales manager for Hoyt-Easton and also a champion archer and hunter, agrees that too much arrow speed can be counterproductive. "I've talked to most of the top pros, guys who know how to shoot a bow, and most who use overdraws don't shoot arrows much faster than 225 feet per second. The ones with arrow speeds up around 235 to 245 feet per second don't shoot well as consistently as those with more moderate setups. The technicalities of form are just too critical at higher arrow speeds. You don't get away with many mistakes."

To reduce shooting errors, many hunters who shoot ultra-hot bows shoot with release aids. That doesn't mean you must shoot a release aid with an overdraw. With moderate tackle, many hunters shoot overdraw setups very well with their fingers.

Arrow Length. Possibly the greatest influence on accuracy could be arrow length. According to engineer Norb Mullaney, a short arrow has less "moment arm" for fletching control. That is, the distance from the center of gravity to the center of pressure (in this case, the fletching) is shorter. The longer the arrow, the more stable it tends to be.

"That's well proven through tests," Mullaney said. "As you add 2 inches to a crossbow bolt, for example, it becomes much more stable. A 22-inch bolt straightens out much faster and flies more stable than an 18-inch bolt. I would consider 26 inches and shorter to be in the critical range. The shorter the arrow past that point, the less stable it is in flight."

So if you have a naturally short draw, you may be defeating your purpose by going to an overdraw. If you have a 28-inch draw, for example, a 5-inch overdraw would cut your arrow length to 23 inches. It would be lightning fast, all right, but how well will the arrows fly, especially with broadheads on the front?

For the person with a long draw, on the other hand, the overdraw could have valuable application. For example, I have long arms and my arrows are 33 inches long. That severely limits my choice of arrows, and I can't shoot much heavier than 60 pounds draw weight because few shafts are spined stiffly enough to handle higher weights at that arrow length. With an overdraw I can reduce my arrow length to 28 inches, which opens up an entirely new selection of arrows, and I can gain significant arrow speed—20 fps or more—with an insignificant loss in kinetic energy. And at 28 inches and 475 grains (the weight of a 2213 at 28 inches) my arrows are not critically short or light, and at 220 fps, they're not critically fast. Even with my fingers, I shoot this setup very accurately.

P

PARADOX The term *paradox* applies specifically to a statement or idea that appears contradictory or opposed to logic. In archery, it's extended to refer to the action an arrow takes as it is shot from a bow. With older bows, which were not center shot, the arrow pointed to the left of the center of force (for a right-hand shooter). Upon release, when the string moves straight toward the center of the bow, it would seem logical that the arrow would deflect to the left. Paradoxically, however, that doesn't happen. Thus, it's a paradox.

Before the advent of high-speed photography, archers had no way of explaining that, but now we know that the arrow progresses through a series of bends as it flies past a bow, and this bending process brings it onto the intended course. Thus, most bowhunters now refer to the bending process itself as paradox.

The bending phenomenon is controlled primarily by the stiffness, or spine, of an arrow, but it's also affected by release methods. When you're shooting with your fingers, the bowstring slides off your fingertips to the left (for right-hand shooters), which heightens the effects of paradox. When you're shooting with a release aid, the bowstring moves virtually straight toward the bow upon release, and thus the paradox, or bending of the arrow, is slight. As a result, from any bow of a given weight,

you generally can shoot arrows of a lighter spine using a release aid than you can shooting with your fingers.

PECCARY See Javelina.

PEEP SIGHT The peep sight, or string peep, has worked its way from target archery into bowhunting because it does improve accuracy. However, like all gadgets, peep sights have their advocates and their critics.

Pros and Cons of Peeps
String Alignment. If you choose to shoot with a crosshair bowsight, you'll find a peep sight nearly essential. If you simply line up the bowstring with the corner of your eye, as many shooters do with pin sights, the string parallels the vertical wire on the sight and can cover it up, and you'll find yourself peeking around the string to see that vertical wire. A peep allows you to look through the center of the string to see the vertical wire clearly.

With pin-type sights, a peep isn't essential, but it can avert disastrous aiming errors in tight situations. Most hunters who don't use peeps aim with the string aligned along the edge of the pupil of their eye, either just inside or just outside. I used to aim with the string just outside my pupil, and it was an accurate method. But I've missed shots on deer, and missed them badly, because of poor string alignment as a result of awkward shooting angles on steep ground. A string peep can't improve the conditions, but it can force you to line up the string with your eye when you might otherwise just draw and let fire.

Peep Problems. Don't take that as an unqualified sales pitch for peep sights, because they do have their drawbacks. One drop of water during a rainstorm will plug a peep, and in cold weather snow or ice will do the same. You have to check the peep continually to make sure it's clear. Without question, a peep forces you to aim more slowly and deliberately, and in low light you may have trouble seeing through the peep.

There's also the possibility that the peep won't line up quite right and that it will block

Some peep sights employ a length of rubber tubing that connects the peep sight to the bow limb. At full draw the tubing stretches to pull the peep sight into proper alignment with your eye.

your view of the sight pins, which can be more than a little frustrating in the heat of action. However, that shouldn't be a major problem if you've set up your tackle right and have practiced with it regularly. To counter alignment problems, some hunters use self-aligning peeps that have a rubber tube connecting the peep to the face of the bow or the cables. When you draw, the tube pulls the peep sight straight to guarantee proper alignment. These work very well, but they scare me a little because I've had that tube break and slap me in the face, and it could possibly put out an eye. Besides, when you release, the tube makes a slapping sound, which I find bothersome.

Some nocks also are built to line up the string the same way every time you draw. The Posi-Nok has a little blade on it, and the nock of your arrow fits over that blade to prevent the string from twisting as you draw. Some hunters swear by the Posi-Nok.

With other peeps, you just turn the string so that the nock naturally lines up with your eye. If you shoot with your fingers, the peep sight will be turned nearly 180 degrees away from you when the bow is in braced position, and as you draw, the string will roll far enough to rotate the peep into alignment with your eye. If you shoot a release aid, the string rotates little when you draw, and the peep will be in pretty much the same position throughout the draw.

Setting Up a Peep Sight

To place a peep in the string, you simply divide the strands evenly, half on one side of the peep, half on the other, and slip the peep into the string. Don't worry about alignment as you put it into the string.

Peep Height. Now draw the bow and mentally note about where the peep should be to line up with your eye. Slide the peep up or down, and then draw again to check location. Keep moving the peep until it sits directly in front of your eye at full draw. Don't tip or cock your head to see through it. Maintain a natural stance and move the peep until it sits directly in front of your eye.

If you can see through it, you're in business,

but most likely the hole will be to the side, so now twist the string to align the hole. If you need to rotate the peep as much as a half turn, take the string off at the top of the bow, twist it a half turn the appropriate direction, and put it back on. If you need to rotate the peep only slightly, take the string off at the bottom of the bow. The bottom limb is farther from the peep, so each twist of the string affects the peep less. (For details, see Bow Stringer.)

Now draw the bow to see if the peep is right. You must do this with an arrow nocked, and it should have the same nocks you plan to shoot all the time because a variation in nock tightness can affect the amount of string rotation. You may have to twist the string several times to get it just right. When the peep is right, it should come directly in front of your eye with the hole lined up so you can see through it clearly.

Hole Size. The smaller the hole in the peep, the more critical the alignment, and the harder the peep is to see through in low light. For that reason, most hunters prefer peeps with comparatively large holes, 1/16 inch in diameter or larger. If the hole isn't large enough, ream it out with a drill bit until you have a size that works best for you. If it's too large, you can put a drop of black paint in the hole and blow it out. Keep doing this until the hole has decreased to the size you want.

Most string peeps must be served into the string to assure that they won't move. (For details on serving, see Bowstring.) Golden Key-Futura's peep has a movable plate and a set screw that tightens the plate onto the string. It requires no serving, which is a welcome convenience, but don't tighten the screw too much or it will crack the sight.

PENETRATION This is one of the most often debated subjects among bowhunters. Everyone seems to have a pet theory on what constitutes good penetration and how to get it.

Frankly, I think the subject is overworked, and dwelling on penetration diverts attention from a more important aspect of bowhunting—accuracy. During my bowhunting career

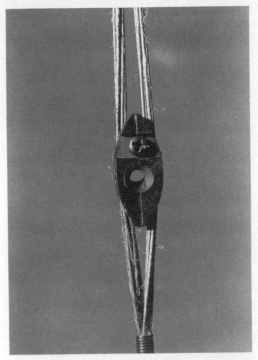

A peep sight is set into the bowstring so you can look through, rather than around, the string at full draw. It serves the same purpose as a rear sight on a rifle. This particular model, made by Golden Key-Futura, has a set screw that can be tightened to hold the peep in position. That eliminates the need for serving the peep in place.

Virtually any legal bowhunting setup will shoot through a broadside deer. On animals like this, the question is not one of penetration but accuracy.

I've hit animals that have not been recovered, and I've talked to dozens of other hunters who've done the same. Rarely has loss of an animal resulted from lack of penetration; it's virtually always from lack of accuracy.

Arrow weight, arrow speed, broadhead design, and broadhead sharpness—major variables affecting penetration—mean nothing if the arrow hits the wrong spot. What good is complete penetration through the guts? Eight inches of penetration into the lungs will kill an animal a lot quicker. I know women who shoot 50-pound bows and relatively light arrows, and they have far better recovery records, including on elk and moose, than most men who shoot much heavier bows. Why? Because they hit animals in vital organs.

Kinetic Energy

Bow Weight. Many writers list charts that say for certain big-game animals, you must shoot a bow with so much draw weight, say 60 pounds for elk-size animals. Actually, bow weight is irrelevant. Certainly there's a correlation between bow weight and penetration, but that's only part of the story. Penetration is a function of an arrow's kinetic energy, and bow weight alone isn't responsible for energy. Kinetic energy is a function of arrow speed and arrow weight in combination. (For details, see Bow Efficiency.)

That points out why bow-weight charts are fallacious. For example, the average recurve bow in the 60-pound class will shoot a 600-grain arrow somewhere around 190 fps. That results in 48.10 foot-pounds of energy, which would be adequate for elk and other comparable game. Some cam bows set at 50 pounds will shoot a 600-grain arrow at about 200 fps, which generates 53.30 foot-pounds of energy. So what's better for elk? The 60-pound recurve or the 50-pound cam bow? The point is that bow weight alone means very little. It's the amount of energy carried by the arrow that counts.

Arrow Weight. Some hunters also stress that a heavy arrow is needed for good penetration. Here again, arrow weight is related to energy,

but arrow weight alone can't take credit. It is true that from any bow at a given draw weight, the heavier the arrow, the greater the energy. But that doesn't mean a heavy arrow always delivers more energy—and thus penetrates better—than lighter arrows, because, as I've said, energy is a function of arrow weight and speed. If a light arrow is traveling fast enough, it will generate more kinetic energy than a slower, heavier arrow, and thus it will penetrate better. As Norb Mullaney, an engineer who has spent his life analyzing bow and arrow performance, said, "All other things being equal, the arrow with the greater kinetic energy will penetrate deeper."

As one example, a 450-grain arrow traveling 220 feet per second produces 48.37 foot-pounds of energy. A 600-grain arrow at 180 fps produces 43.17 foot-pounds of energy. Which will penetrate better? Given the same broadhead and shaft diameter, the lighter arrow will because it delivers greater kinetic energy.

Some hunters have demonstrated excellent penetration with very light arrows. Cliff Dewell, for example, shoots an overdraw bow with 27-inch 2213s that weigh 475 grains and fly 240 fps to generate 60 foot-pounds of energy. Many hunters would consider those arrows too light for big animals, but Dewell has shot completely through several elk. He also shot through (and killed) a Shiras moose with that setup, even though the arrow cut a rib going in and nicked a rib coming out. "I've also shot cleanly through several wild boars," Dewell said. "That's the ultimate test because hogs are tough."

Well-known bow manufacturer Pete Shepley is another advocate of lightweight, fast arrows. He shoots 25½-inch 2114s that weigh 450 grains. From his 85-pound bow these arrows fly 270 feet per second and generate 72 foot-pounds of kinetic energy. Shepley has killed every major animal in North America including moose and grizzly bears. "I play the accuracy game," Shepley said. "That's 95 percent of killing. If you hit them in the right spot, penetration will take care of itself."

This might look like I'm selling high-speed,

lightweight arrows, but that's not the case (I commonly shoot full-length, 600-grain arrows from a 60-pound bow at about 200 feet per second). I only point out that neither arrow weight nor bow weight alone dictates penetration. Kinetic energy is what counts, and it doesn't matter how you get it as long as you've got it.

Energy Suggestions. How much energy is enough? I hesitate to list recommendations at all because many factors (which are discussed below) besides energy affect penetration. Nevertheless, some general guidelines might be valid. For deer and comparable animals, 40 foot-pounds of energy is probably adequate. A bow that delivers a 500-grain arrow at 190 feet per second generates just over 40 foot-pounds, and the average 55-pound recurve or 50-pound round-wheel compound bow will do better than that.

For elk and other big animals, 50 foot-pounds would be a safer minimum. A 450-grain arrow at 225 fps generates 50 foot-pounds of energy, as does a 600-grain arrow at 195 fps. Most recurve bows at 65 pounds, round-wheel compounds at 60, and cam bows at 55 will satisfy those requirements. For moose and brown bears, you might want more than 50 foot-pounds of energy.

Other Influences

Broadheads. Design and sharpness of broadheads could be more significant than bow weight in relation to penetration. Bob Savage, one of the first 25 senior members of the Pope and Young Club and a bowhunter for more than 30 years, has performed extensive penetration tests. He determined that a major influence on penetration was tip shape of a broadhead.

"Most important is that a point cuts on contact," Savage said. "You can take a piece of green deer hide and push different styles of broadheads through the hide to measure the difference. A sharp-tipped head like the Bear Razorhead or the Zwickey Black Diamond will go through with as little as 6 pounds of pressure. It takes 50 pounds of pressure or more to push through some of the round-nosed heads. That hide stretches a lot when a bullet-type point has to push through it. That means the arrow loses much of its energy at the hide and it penetrates poorly. The initial cut through the hide—that's the most important thing."

On big animals like elk, a certain amount of kinetic energy, probably in the 50 foot-pound class, is needed to push an arrow through vital organs. But broadhead design, shaft size, straightness of arrow flight, and other variables influence penetration.

The incision a broadhead makes at the moment of contact greatly affects penetration. The broadhead with a sharp cutting point generally will penetrate better than a head with a conical point.

This isn't to say replaceable-blade broadheads with bullet-type points are no good. You'll probably shoot through most thin-skinned animals like deer regardless of broadhead style. But if you're going after big animals like elk and moose and you shoot a moderate-weight bow, then you must enhance penetration in all possible ways, and shooting cutting-tip broadheads is one way to do it.

"Length of the broadhead also affects penetration," Savage said. "The longer the cutting surface, the more friction and the poorer the penetration. The Howard Hill design has a 3:1 length-to-width ratio, and it doesn't penetrate as well as shorter heads. The Black Diamond has about a 2:1 ratio, and that shape is close to ideal." (See also Broadhead.)

The number of blades and width of a broadhead could affect penetration, too. Norb Mullaney used the term "splash effect," which describes the size and shape of the hole made by a broadhead for the shaft to slide through. The bigger the hole, the less friction on the arrow shaft. Many hunters use two-blade broadheads for maximum penetration, but my guess is (and this *is* a guess because I have no data to back it up) that a three- or four-blade head would give better penetration than a two-blade of the same diameter because the multi-blade head would have a superior splash effect. The hole made by a two-blade head can stretch

tight on an arrow shaft, but three or more blades cut the hide into little flaps that are less likely to stretch tight on the shaft.

Mullaney said a flat-sided ferrule, as on Thunderhead 125, seems to improve penetration, too. Shooting into ethafoam, the Thunderhead 125 had the best penetration of all the broadheads he tested.

Shaft Diameter. This also affects penetration. As Savage said, "The larger the diameter of the shaft, the more drag as it slides through hide and meat. If you have two arrows of identical weight but different diameters, the one with the smaller diameter will penetrate better."

Bow Tuning. A wobbling arrow, in essence, hits an animal sideways, and the shaft must drag along the side of the hole created by the broadhead. A straight-flying shaft follows the broadhead straight through with minimum drag. Dave Snyder, who has killed several world record–class animals, said that moving his nocking point or the position of his arrow rest even a fraction of an inch affected arrow penetration into foam blocks as much as six inches. That's because changing the "tune" of his bow changed the attitude of the arrow in flight, and the arrow must be flying perfectly straight for maximum penetration.

PENNSYLVANIA Pennsylvania contains 45,333 square miles. About 4½ million acres of public land are open to the general public for hunting, and much of it is heavily hunted.

Big Game

Whitetails. The whitetail deer population is estimated at 750,000. Pennsylvania sells about 300,000 archery deer licenses each year, more than any other state. Bow harvest has averaged about 5,000 deer each year, and average bowhunting success has been 3 to 4 percent. The archery season traditionally has run from the first Saturday to the last Saturday in October, and then has opened again for a few days after Christmas. The bag limit is one deer per hunter per license year regardless of hunting method.

The northern region (north of Interstate 80 and west of Scranton) is heavily forested and deer live throughout, but densities aren't high, about 18 per square mile. This region attracts lots of hunters because it has vast public lands. The tradition of deer clubs runs deep here.

The southeast third of the state consists of rich farmlands and orchards interspersed with forested ridges. The hilly country on the north side of this region slopes into flat farmland near Philadelphia. Deer numbers are higher here than in the northern forests, and some of Pennsylvania's largest bucks come from this region. State forest lands assure some public access. In the wooded southwest corner, deer numbers are relatively high, but houses have been built on small acreages throughout the region, so access is poor. A few big bucks are taken in Pennsylvania, but compared to the annual harvest, the odds for a record-book animal are small.

Black Bears. A two-day bear season is held in late November. Chances of arrowing a bear aren't good.

Other Game

Turkeys. Pennsylvania is a major turkey state with a total harvest exceeding 30,000. Both spring and fall seasons are held.

Small Game. The total harvest on gray and fox squirrels may be greater than 2 million, which means a lot of squirrels are available for hunters. Rabbit and other small-game hunting is good in suitable habitat.

Contact. Game Commission, P.O. Box 1567, Harrisburg, PA 17120.

PHOTOGRAPHY Wildlife photography is a subject unto itself, well beyond the scope of a hunting book, but taking pictures of yourself and your friends with trophy game is a big part of any hunting trip. That's why I include this section on photography, and why I concentrate on getting good trophy and camp shots.

It seems incredible, but many hunters who can perform amazing hunting feats can wreak more havoc with a camera on one trip than a hurricane in a paper factory. After association with hundreds of outdoorsmen, I'm convinced that photography is the great American hunting tragedy. Fortunately, bad photography isn't terminal, and with a little thought and practice, any hunter can take pictures he can show with pride.

Getting the Shot

Check Batteries. Photographic disasters fall into two categories: terrible pictures, and no pictures at all. First let's look at the no-picture category. If batteries in your camera are weak, exposures will be off; obviously if the batteries are dead, the camera simply won't work. Most cameras have a battery-check system, so before any hunting trip, test the batteries. And remember it's false economy to try to squeeze every last bit of juice from the batteries. They could go dead right in the middle of a dream hunt, so change the batteries as a matter of course before any major hunt, and always have new replacement batteries among your hunting gear.

Set Film Speed. Next check the ASA setting, which indicates film speed. If the setting on your camera reads 400, and you load up with ASA 64 film, you'll get a batch of black pictures. Incidentally, virtually all professional outdoor photographers shoot Kodachrome 64 (ASA 64) color slide film, because it's sharp and has good color. If you prefer color prints, try Kodacolor 100. The faster the ASA, generally the grainier the photos and the poorer the color. As you can guess, I'm not crazy about superfast color films, but any modern film will produce acceptable pictures. Here's the important point: Pick a film that best suits your needs and stick with it. Film switching is a disaster looking for a place to happen, because sooner or later you'll forget to change ASA. If you must shoot different films, buy separate cameras for each one.

Load Your Camera. Now, make sure your camera is loaded with film. Laugh if you want, but I could cite several examples involving hunters who've taken lots of great shots. With an empty camera. To double check, turn the rewind knob as if you were rewinding the film, until you feel tension. If the knob just keeps turning without resistance, you know there's no film in the camera or you've already rewound it. Either way, you won't get any pictures.

This tip also prevents a more common disaster—film that's not advancing. More than once I've talked to proud hunters who'd got 40 exposures out of a 36-exposure roll, only to discover the film hadn't advanced and they didn't have picture one. In loading your camera, make sure the film-advance sprocket engages the film. Then when you close the camera, pull all slack out of the film by turning the rewind knob. Now when you advance the film, the rewind knob should turn backward. Do this before every photo session and you can rest assured the film is advancing in your camera.

Rewind the Film. When you've finished a roll, rewind it before opening your camera. Sure, any dummy knows that, but I still remember the time I excitedly finished off a roll of great pictures and snapped open my camera to change film and found myself staring at naked film. "Oops, excuse me," I thought as I slammed the camera shut, but it was too late.

Heat ruins film, so store your camera in a cool spot. A friend of mine always carried an Instamatic camera on hunting trips. He shot plenty of film, but he rarely got any photos because he insisted on tossing his camera on the dashboard of his car or into the glove box where it broiled on hot days.

Shoot, Shoot, Shoot. Finally, shoot some film. A camera back in camp won't take many pictures. Always carry your camera, and keep it handy. If you have to dig it from a pack every time you see a good shot, you'll take few photos. I hang my camera around my neck and hold it against my chest with an elastic band around my back. The elastic stretches enough so I can pull the camera up to my eye, but it's tight enough to keep the camera from swinging. If you don't like that idea, carry the camera in a small belt pack. Velcro fasteners are faster and easier to open than a zipper. Whatever method you choose, keep the camera ready for action or you'll miss all the action.

One time I spent a day with Bill McRae, one of the best hunting photographers in the United States. In one afternoon he shot ten rolls of film. He shot every pose from a half dozen angles, and from each angle he shot several different exposures. I suspect that McRae's eye isn't any better than average, but he's a

To get dramatic photos, keep your camera handy. Tired hunters won't have much patience with a partner fumbling around for a camera in his pack. Keep the camera around your neck and shoot the instant you see a picture.

Be ready to snap the action. These are the kinds of moments you don't want to miss. After all, this might be the last time you see that guy alive. You'll never get photos like this with a camera tucked away in your pack.

great photographer because he shoots film until he gets great shots. Obviously casual photographers won't burn film like that, but they should learn from the principle: you've got to shoot 'em to get 'em. As a rule of thumb, shoot at least one 36-exposure roll of film a day, and if a priceless shot comes along—say you with your Pope and Young buck—shoot a couple of rolls on just that one subject. You won't be sorry. The only photos you'll ever regret are the ones you didn't take.

Technical Quality

Here's an aggravating statement: "Your pictures are so sharp and clear. What kind of camera do you use?" To set the record straight, I shoot Konica cameras, but so what? Any one of three dozen brands on the market will take professional quality photos. Providing your camera functions properly, don't blame the camera for lousy pictures. Blame yourself.

Photos have two qualities—technical and artistic. Before a picture can have artistic value, it must be technically good, which means it must be sharp and properly exposed.

Sharpness. Blurred photographs infest most hunting-photo albums, and two things yield fuzzy photos. Most obvious is poor focusing. Double check your focus on every shot, and when a photo contains a person or animal, always focus on the eye of the subject, because that's the center of attention. If the subject's eye is sharp, the whole photograph will appear sharp.

Camera movement may be a more common cause of blurred photos. If possible always shoot at a shutter speed of 1/125 of a second or faster. With care you can hand-hold a camera at 1/60, but if the light is so poor you must go to 1/30 or slower, either use a tripod or brace the camera against a tree, rock, or other steady object. And always squeeze the shutter release gently. Don't try to smash it through the camera.

Those shutter speeds apply to wide-angle and normal-length lenses—28mm to 50mm. With longer lenses, shutter speed becomes more critical. A 200mm (or 4X) lens, for example, magnifies everything, including camera movement, four times. You probably can hand hold a 200mm lens at 1/250 of a second, but at slower speeds either use a tripod or a shoulder mount. The longer the lens, the more critical movement becomes.

335

Exposure. This is the other half of technical quality. With modern automatic cameras, exposure shouldn't be a major problem, but washed-out or black photos still seem to plague many hunters. As I mentioned above, the wrong ASA setting or weak batteries could be the culprit. Always double check these.

Then, use the automatic-exposure setting on your camera. Before you take any pictures, first check to make sure the camera is set on auto. In situations where the light is fairly even, with no great contrast between sunlight and shadows, you will get a good exposure on auto.

However, if lighting is uneven, the automatic

In uneven lighting situations, you may have to override the automatic exposure setting on your camera. In this case the camera is pointed toward a bright sky, which will "tell" the lens to stop down. The subject is shaded, however, and the lens must be opened up to get a good exposure of the subject. So in this case you take a light reading on the subject and base your exposure on that. To make sure you get a good one, bracket at least one full stop each way from your meter reading.

setting may produce a bum exposure. Let's say, for example, your hunting buddy is wearing a white T-shirt. The light meter in your camera reads "bright light" off that shirt and stops down the shutter on your camera to a small opening (f-stop). The T-shirt will come out properly exposed, but the rest of the picture will appear dark. A bright, cloudy sky can produce the same effect. On cloudy days eliminate the sky from your photos so you get a true light reading.

To get proper exposures in uneven light situations, move in close and take an exposure reading on your subject. Normally I read on the subject's face. Then take your camera off auto-exposure and manually set the proper exposure and take your picture. The rule of thumb is to expose for the subject. Other areas in the photo may be too dark or light, but at least the subject will look right.

On priceless photos, an even better solution is to "bracket." That's what most professionals do to assure perfect exposures. Take a light reading on your subject. Let's say the exposure meter indicates f/8. First take a picture at that setting, and then bracket it by shooting a second exposure at f/11, and a third at f/5.6. With that range, you're assured of getting one that's just right.

Under some light conditions (for example, forest that contains bright sunlight and deep shadow) getting perfect exposures is impossible. There's such great contrast between the shadows and sunny spots that you can't reconcile them on film. Either move your subject fully into sunlight or fully into shadows to reduce contrast, or use a flash unit. To use fill-in flash, set your camera to expose the bright areas properly, but take the picture with a flash unit on your camera. The flash will "fill in" black, shadowed areas, which in essence reduces contrast to produce an acceptable exposure.

Composition

These procedures will produce technically good photos, but that still leaves artistic quality. An outstanding example of bad art ap-

Before taking pictures, clean up your animal and get the body as well as the head in your photo. Get close enough to fill the frame. And for Pete's sake, smile!

Get close enough to fill the frame with your subject. If you're too tired, or don't have time, to take photos during the heat of action, set them up later. At least you show what the trip was like.

peared in a regional hunting publication. It showed only a deer's head, cut off just behind the ears, lying on a snow bank. That was it. No body on the deer, no person in the photo. And the head was so far from the camera it looked about the size of a pine cone; 90 percent of the picture showed a dirty snowbank.

That photo points out a few elements involved in the artistry of photography. First, take pictures of decent-looking animals that have bodies and aren't covered with blood. Second, have someone in the picture. Most of your friends are more concerned about you than they are the animal itself. And smile. Are you having a good time or not?

Get Close. Without question, the major sin among amateur photographers is standing too far from the subject. For Pete's sake, get close! My rule of thumb is to fill the frame with the subject. If the subject is a hunter kneeling by a deer, the photo should show nothing but hunter and deer. If you want scenics, don't try to get them along with the deer. First take the deer, and shoot some separate scenics later.

The smaller the subject, the tougher this rule becomes. If you stand the same distance from a hunter posing with a bull elk as you do from a person holding a rabbit, the elk may look okay, but the rabbit will look like a fly speck. For small subjects you simply must move in close so your subject fills the picture.

Get Variety. Try shooting from different angles. If you stand up to shoot down on a deer, the deer looks small. If you get down on your belly and shoot at eye level or from below the deer, you get a dramatic effect and the deer looks bigger.

Different angles also give you varied lighting effects. If you shoot with the sun at your back, the subject will be lighted from the front and there will be few shadows. That's called flat lighting. If you move to the side, you'll get distinct shadows. If you step to the opposite side and shoot toward the sun, back lighting will create a partial or total silhouette. Shoot a few shots from each angle, bracketing each for perfect exposures, and you'll come up with some pleasing effects.

Here's one other point about composition: Place the subject slightly to one side so it looks

337

Always look for unusual lighting that might make a striking picture. Early morning and late evening are the best times to shoot photos. This silhouette was taken just before the sun set.

Take pictures of different aspects of your trip. Most people want to see pictures of other people, their friends and relatives, so take pictures of your partners doing something, even if it's only trying to catch a drink from a splattering waterfall.

like he's moving into the picture, not falling off the edge.

Self-Photography

How do you take pictures of yourself? Self-photography is no easy assignment, but it can be done. I frequently hunt alone, and many of the photos I submit with articles are self-portraits. To get these, you must carry a tripod or other device to hold the camera. Around camp, of course, you can use a large tripod, but in the field you'll want something more convenient. Bushnell makes a small, adjustable tripod, and an even smaller and lighter gadget is the Ultrapod made by Early Winters of Seattle, Washington.

To take pictures of yourself, set up the camera securely on the tripod and look through the viewfinder to determine where you'll be. Use branches or rocks to mark your position, trip the shutter release, and run to pose in the picture. Most delay timers give you about ten seconds, so don't try this if you have far to go. I've taken a number of unique shots of my leg or arm just entering the picture.

Remember one thing in self-photography: the light meter on a camera reads light coming in from the viewfinder (the hole you look into) as well as through the lens. When you're looking into the camera, that's no problem because your head blocks out light from the viewfinder. But when you set the camera on a tripod and take a delay-timer photo of yourself, light can shine directly into the viewfinder to throw off the exposure if the camera is set on auto exposure. To get a proper exposure, either set the lens manually or cover the viewfinder with a piece of tape or your hanky to block out light.

Camera Gear

The kinds of photos you take will depend on your goals. Maybe you're interested only in getting some snapshots of yourself with a deer or elk. In that case a small, light, range-finder camera is more than adequate. When traveling light, I carry a Konica S-3 camera and the Early Winters Ultrapod, and I've got some good shots of myself posing with game.

If your goal is to record your entire trip, you'll probably want a single lens reflex (SLR) camera with interchangeable lenses. For all-around photography, I carry three lenses: a 28mm wide angle, a 50mm "normal" lens, and a 135mm telephoto. My favorite lens for dramatic effects is the 135mm. This 2½X lens

A small camera like this doesn't weigh much so you can carry it all the time. With the lightweight tripod you can either set up the camera on a rock or strap it to a limb with the Velcro strap to take pictures of yourself.

Photography can be a major part of any hunting trip, but you must work at it. Keep your camera available at all times. Try to take photos that capture the mood and essence of the hunt. You could caption this one "Are we having fun yet?"

pulls the subject in close and eliminates distracting detail. However, if I were to choose only one lens for all-around photography, I'd go with the 50mm.

Perhaps an even better one-lens alternative is a zoom lens. I have a 28–135mm zoom lens that covers virtually any hunting situation. It's fantastic for composition, because I can zoom in and out until the subject is perfectly framed. Unfortunately, it's bulky and heavy so I don't carry it into the backcountry with me. Smaller zoom lenses, say a 35–70mm, are better suited to carrying with you as you hunt. Unfortunately, many zooms are relatively slow (that is, the largest aperture may be only f/3.5 or so), so they're not ideal in poor light conditions.

Recording a hunting trip on film isn't a snap. You have to plan photographic gear in advance just as you do hunting equipment, and you have to take time out from hunting long enough to shoot some pictures. But if you'll make the effort, you can show your photos with pride.

PHYSICAL CONDITION   A few years ago I shot a bull elk in Montana. I suppose killing the elk took a certain amount of knowledge or

skill, and I was proud. In all honesty, though, bugling in that bull wasn't real tough.

It was getting *to* him that took some doing. I'd hunted the easier fringes of the area and had found no elk, so I continued to penetrate farther and farther over a week's time until I reached a hidden stronghold several miles from—and 3,000 feet higher than—the road. And that's where I found the eager bull. He was easy to kill once I found him.

Without question, physical condition played a far bigger part in my success than hunting skill or knowledge, and I think that's the case in much Western hunting. Long miles, long hours, steep grades, and high elevation combine to make western hunting tough, and if you're not prepared for the grind, you'll fold.

I've talked to a number of outfitters about the reasons their clients fail to take game. Rarely is it because the clients can't shoot well enough, don't have good enough equipment, don't have the needed enthusiasm or knowledge. Invariably it's because they're out of shape. They simply can't get to the game, or once they do, they're too bushed to hunt well or shoot accurately.

Granted, great physical endurance isn't needed to walk 100 yards and climb into a tree

Hunting Western mountains can demand miles of hiking in steep terrain. To hunt well, day after day, you must be in shape.

stand, but that's not the average picture of mountain hunting. In much of the West, particularly for elk, high-country mule deer, sheep, or goats, you can expect to hike at least five to ten miles a day and climb vertically — up and down — 2,500 feet or more. Add to that the draining effects of high altitude, short nights, skimpy meals, and heavy packs, and you've got the recipe for fatigue. Hunting knowledge, shooting ability, quality of your gear, all these will have little bearing on the outcome of your hunt. Physical condition will determine your success — or failure.

Even though major endurance may not be needed for sedentary hunting, I think you'll hunt better under any conditions if you're in shape. Tournament archery would hardly be viewed as strenuous, but top-level archery teams have adopted endurance and weight-lifting programs, and their performances under pressure have improved greatly. General strength and endurance training can make you a better all-around archer.

Endurance Training

Endurance training is most commonly called aerobic exercise. Dr. Kenneth Cooper popularized the wood *aerobic* with his classic book, *Aerobics*, in the late 1960s. Put simply, aerobic means "with oxygen." In other words, during aerobic training you maintain a level of activity over a long period of time without building up an oxygen debt. Walking, jogging, swimming, and bicycling are common aerobic exercises. In anaerobic (without oxygen) activity, such as sprinting or weight lifting, you quickly build up an oxygen debt, which forces you to stop and rest before you can continue. Anaerobic training may build strength, but not endurance.

Value of Aerobics. Aerobic training is the foundation for mountain hunting because it builds strong internal systems. Aerobic exercises enlarge and strengthen your heart; with each contraction, a strong heart pumps more blood than a weak heart, so it makes fewer contractions. That's why well-conditioned people have a slower pulse rate than out-of-shape

Aerobic exercise for the heart and lungs can take many different forms. Riding a bicycle, or a stationary cycle like this, is one good way to train aerobically.

people. The average American man has a resting pulse rate of about 72, but with training that generally drops to 60, and in many well-conditioned people it drops to 50 or lower.

A strong heart also recovers more quickly than a weak one. If you're in poor shape, your pulse rate after exertion may drop from 160 to 120 within 5 minutes; if you're in good shape, it probably will drop to 90 or slower within 5 minutes. That kind of recovery, coupled with an overall slower resting pulse rate, will save you a lot of heartbeats over a tough two-week hunt.

In addition, aerobic training increases the amount of blood in your body, expands lung capacity, increases the number of capillaries to the muscles, and yields other benefits. In short, it makes your body a lean, efficient machine, which means you'll be able to hunt longer and farther with less fatigue than you can when you're out of shape.

You'll also be bothered less by altitude. In essence, high elevation reduces your overall aerobic capacity. Up to 5,000 feet elevation, you'll notice little effect, but altitudes higher than that will take a toll. Exercise physiologists say that from 7,000 to 10,000 feet elevation, you lose from 10 to 15 percent of your aerobic capacity. That's true whether you're in shape or not, but obviously the better your shape to start with, the higher your aerobic capacity will remain at altitude.

Aerobic training also burns up fat. As you've probably noticed, overweight runners are a rare breed. Being lean in itself is a benefit in hunting, because it reduces the amount of weight you have to pack up and down the hills. Fat serves no more value in hiking than a backpack full of rocks; it's dead weight that does no work. Physiologist Covert Bailey, best known for his book *Fit or Fat?,* said a person needs about 2 percent body fat to function normally, but any fat over that level is excess baggage.

Evaluating Your Condition. Fat is not only useless baggage; it's a fairly accurate gauge of your overall fitness. It's possible to have some excess weight and still be in good shape. I know one man who has run several marathons (26.2-mile races), and yet he appears to be at least 50 pounds overweight. But that's the exception. If you're sagging on the outside, you're probably pretty flabby inside, too, and need some conditioning before a hard hunt. Most physiologists agree that to be considered in good shape, men should have less than 15 percent body fat and women less than 22 percent (the American average is about 23 percent for men and 36 for women).

The most accurate way to determine body fat is underwater weighing. Fat floats, so by weighing you first in water and then out, physiologists can determine the exact percent of body fat.

That's a specialized process, though, so most of us won't go to that trouble. A doctor or physical therapist can gauge body-fat content by measuring skinfold thickness with cali-

pers at various points on your body. At home you can roughly gauge your fitness with the pinch test. If you can "pinch an inch" on the back of your arm between the elbow and shoulder, you're probably overweight.

Doctors also have charts that list recommended weights for given heights. At his Aerobics Center, Dr. Cooper has modified this formula so people can calculate their own ideal weight. It's simple. A man multiplies his height in inches by 4 and subtracts 128. For example, I'm 74 inches tall. Four times 74 equals 296. Subtracting 128, I come up with an ideal weight of 168. To my satisfaction, I weigh exactly 168. Women should multiply 3.5 times their height in inches and subtract 108. Dr. Cooper recommends that heavy-boned persons add 10 percent to the computed weight to determine their own ideal weight. (For more on this, see *The Aerobics Program for Total Well-Being* by Kenneth Cooper.)

Maintaining an ideal weight gets you started right, but weight isn't the only criterion for gauging fitness. You could be skinny and still be in poor shape, so you need to go beyond that. Step tests have been devised to determine physical condition, but the simplest methods I've seen have been perfected by Dr. Cooper at his Aerobics Center. In one test, you walk or run for 12 minutes as fast as you can. The distance you cover indicates your fitness level. In another, you measure a course of 1½ miles (six laps around a quarter-mile track), and run it as fast as possible. The length of time required indicates your fitness level (see accompanying charts). If you fall anywhere below the "good" category, you need some work before a tough mountain hunt.

Getting in Shape. Physiologists recommend a physical exam before beginning any exercise program, particularly if you're over 35 and have not been training, or regardless of age if you have a family history of heart disease. The exam should include a stress electrocardiogram (your heart is monitored as you walk or run on a treadmill), because heart problems that might go unnoticed at rest will show up under stress.

12-Minute Walking/Running Test
Distance (Miles) Covered in 12 Minutes

Fitness Category		13-19	20-29	30-39	40-49	50-59	60+
				Age (years)			
I. Very Poor	(men)	<1.30*	<1.22	<1.18	<1.14	<1.03	<.87
	(women)	<1.0	<.96	<.94	<.88	<.84	<.78
II. Poor	(men)	1.30-1.37	1.22-1.31	1.18-1.30	1.14-1.24	1.03-1.16	.87-1.02
	(women)	1.00-1.18	.96-1.11	.95-1.05	.88-.98	.84-.93	.78-.86
III. Fair	(men)	1.38-1.56	1.32-1.49	1.31-1.45	1.25-1.39	1.17-1.30	1.03-1.20
	(women)	1.19-1.29	1.12-1.22	1.06-1.18	.99-1.11	.94-1.05	.87-.98
IV. Good	(men)	1.57-1.72	1.50-1.64	1.46-1.56	1.40-1.53	1.31-1.44	1.21-1.32
	(women)	1.30-1.43	1.23-1.34	1.19-1.29	1.12-1.24	1.06-1.18	.99-1.09
V. Excellent	(men)	1.73-1.86	1.65-1.76	1.57-1.69	1.54-1.65	1.45-1.58	1.33-1.55
	(women)	1.44-1.51	1.35-1.45	1.30-1.39	1.25-1.34	1.19-1.30	1.10-1.18
VI. Superior	(men)	>1.87	>1.77	>1.70	>1.66	>1.59	>1.56
	(women)	>1.52	>1.46	>1.40	>1.35	>1.31	>1.19

* <Means "less than"; >means "more than."

1.5-Mile Run Test
Time (Minutes)

Fitness Category		13-19	20-29	30-39	40-49	50-59	60+
				Age (years)			
I. Very poor	(men)	>15:31*	>16:01	>16:31	>17:31	>19:01	>20:01
	(women)	>18:31	>19:01	>19:31	>20:01	>20:31	>21:01
II. Poor	(men)	12:11-15:30	14:01-16:00	14:44-16:30	15:36-17:30	17:01-19:00	19:01-20:00
	(women)	16:55-18:30	18:31-19:00	19:01-19:30	19:31-20:00	20:01-20:30	21:00-21:31
III. Fair	(men)	10:49-12:10	12:01-14:00	12:31-14:45	13:01-15:35	14:31-17:00	16:16-19:00
	(women)	14:31-16:54	15:55-18:30	16:31-19:00	17:31-19:30	19:01-20:00	19:31-20:30
IV. Good	(men)	9:41-10:48	10:46-12:00	11:01-12:30	11:31-13:00	12:31-14:30	14:00-16:15
	(women)	12:30-14:30	13:31-15:54	14:31-16:30	15:56-17:30	16:31-19:00	17:31-19:30
V. Excellent	(men)	8:37- 9:40	9:45-10:45	10:00-11:00	10:30-11:30	11:00-12:30	11:15-13:59
	(women)	11:50-12:29	12:30-13:30	13:00-14:30	13:45-15:55	14:30-16:30	16:30-17:30
VI. Superior	(men)	< 8:37	< 9:45	<10:00	<10:30	<11:00	<11:15
	(women)	<11:50	<12:30	<13:00	<13:45	<14:30	<16:30

* <Means "less than"; >means "more than."

Credit: *The Aerobics Program for Total Well Being*, by Dr. Kenneth Cooper; M. Evans and Company, Inc., New York

Running may be the fastest way to get in shape. It conditions the heart, lungs, and legs. Many dedicated hunters train year-round so they're fine-tuned and tough when the time comes to take to the mountains.

A number of exercises qualify as aerobic, so choosing the right one is partly a matter of personal choice. Running has become popular and that's my personal choice, but you might prefer swimming, bicycling, jumping rope, walking, playing raquetball, or whatever. The exercise you choose doesn't matter as long as you can sustain it for long periods without creating an oxygen debt. Nonstop activities like running, swimming, or cycling yield quicker benefits than stop-and-go sports like basketball and handball. A mix of sports might be best, because each one works your muscles differently.

From that point on, four variables govern aerobic workouts—intensity, duration, frequency, and progression.

Intensity. Most physiologists use a set formula to define maximum heart rate: 220 minus age. Thus if you're 20 years old, your maximum heart rate is 200 ($220 - 20 = 200$). If you're 40 years old, your maximum heart rate is 180. To improve physical fitness, you must train at a given heart rate. If you're in very poor condition, you should start at 70 percent of your maximum heart rate, and if you're in good shape, you should train at about 80 percent. Let's say you're 40 years old and keep yourself in good condition. Then $220 - 40 = 180$ (maximum heart rate) x .80 = 144. Your training pulse rate should be about 144 beats per minute.

To determine pulse rate, exercise long enough to raise your heart rate, and then stop and take your pulse for 6 seconds and multiply by 10 to determine beats per minute. If it's slower than the prescribed training rate, work harder; if it's higher, slow down. If you're in poor shape you may raise your heart to the prescribed training rate simply by walking slowly; if you're in good shape, you may have to run hard to bring it up to the training rate.

Duration. Physiologists have found that activity must be sustained for a given length of time to be of benefit. Few agree on the exact duration, but virtually all say you should exercise for at least 12 minutes; some say 20. Fifteen minutes seems to be a reasonable minimum. In a report prescribing a physical fitness program for top archers, Rick McKinney, a world champion and Olympic silver medalist, said that training for 15 minutes increases physical condition by 8.5 percent; 30 minutes by 16.1 percent; and 45 minutes by 16.85 percent. "Since there is a major difference between 15 and 30 minutes and a minor difference between 30 and 45 minutes, your best bet would be 30 minutes," McKinney writes.

With that in mind, 30 minutes for each session would be a good goal to shoot for. When you first start out, though, you may not be able to sustain activity for that long, so shoot for a minimum of 15 and plan to work up. For greatest benefit, you must maintain your training rate the entire workout. That's why stop-and-go sports like handball and tennis, which allow your heart to rest, don't improve fitness as fast as continuous sports like running and swimming.

Frequency. Most trainers agree that you must work out at least three nonconsecutive days each week to maintain a given level of fitness, and you must train four or more days a week to improve. If you lay off more than two days in a row, you begin to lose some of your conditioning. So plan to work out a minimum of three days each week; four or five days if time permits and you feel comfortable with greater frequency.

Progress Gradually. It doesn't matter what kind of exercise you choose as long as it meets the above criteria—maintains your heart rate at a minimum training level for at least 15 to 30 minutes and is done at least three times a week. Walking is the most highly recommended exercise, particularly if you're in poor condition. However, once you start getting in shape you won't be able to raise your heart rate to the prescribed training level by walking, unless you're climbing a steep hill. Then you can switch to running, swimming, bicycling, rope jumping, calisthenics, or any other exercise that meets the criteria for aerobic training.

One good addition to any training program for hunting is what physiologists call "specificity training"; you train by doing the same thing you'll be doing in the field. In hunting you'll be hiking, and probably carrying heavy loads, so that's a good way to train. Locate a hill near home; if there aren't any, find a tall building with long stairways. Start out hiking for 20 minutes, carrying little or no weight. Gradually increase that until you can hike steadily with a 50-pound pack for 45 minutes to an hour. That kind of conditioning will get you in shape for just about any Western bowhunting. And it conditions the same muscles you'll be using in the mountains.

Assessing Your Condition. A few years back I wrote an article containing much of this same information for *Outdoor Life* magazine, and the editors titled the article, "Make Your Big Game Hunting Easy." I appreciate the intent of the title, but it is misleading—nothing can make tough mountain hunting easy. Conditioning can only make it eas*ier*, saving you from undue fatigue, exhaustion, and soreness.

There's no accurate way to quantify the level of fitness needed for mountain hunting or to equate a home conditioning program to field conditions. You certainly don't have to be a serious distance runner to hunt well. Besides, I've found that after a certain point the law of diminishing returns applies to aerobic training. Some years when time and energy permitted I've run 40 to 50 miles per week, including individual runs as long as 19 miles. Other years I've run only 12 to 15 miles a week with long runs of 5 miles. In terms of my mountain endurance, I can't see that I performed significantly better on the high-mileage years.

I would say—and this is subjective, based on my own experience of trying to correlate my performance in the field with preseason training—that you must run at least 12 to 15 miles a week (or the equivalent with other exercises). I would also say that if you can't run 5 miles at will, and do it without serious aftereffects such as extreme muscle soreness or fatigue, then you're not in shape for tough mountain hunting. Dr. Cooper's 12-minute and 1½-mile-run tests offer a good gauge of fitness. If you can't perform in the "good" category, you'll hunt less than "good" in the mountains.

(As a general training guide, I strongly recommend *The Aerobics Program for Total Well-Being* by Kenneth Cooper. It contains a variety of training programs for persons at all levels of fitness and all ages.)

Strength Training

Endurance training plays by far the biggest part in mountain hunting, but strength is involved, too. The stronger your muscles, the less they must work to accomplish a given task. As you know, climbing stairs requires more strength than walking a flat sidewalk, and carrying a load up those stair demands more power than climbing without a load.

And so it is in mountain hunting. The average stairway has a 70 percent slope, and many Western mountains are equally steep. Imagine wearing a 50-pound backpack and climbing

Squats. These work the thighs and buttocks. They can be done with barbells or on a Universal Gym or other machines such as a hip sled. Stand straight with your feet about shoulder width, bar balanced on your shoulders. Squat until your thighs are nearly parallel with the floor, and then stand back up. It's very important to keep your back straight and head up. Don't bounce.

Leg Extensions. These build the thighs. They can be done with a Universal Gym or with some benches and barbell weights. Sit on the edge of the bench with your feet under the rollers. Hold onto the side of the bench to steady yourself. Extend your legs fully and then slowly let them back down. This can also be done one leg at a time.

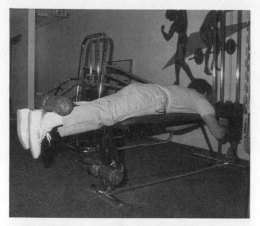

Leg Curls. These strengthen the hamstrings, calves, and buttocks. Lie face down on the same bench used for the extensions. Place your heels under the rollers and slowly curl your legs to your buttocks and then straighten them out.

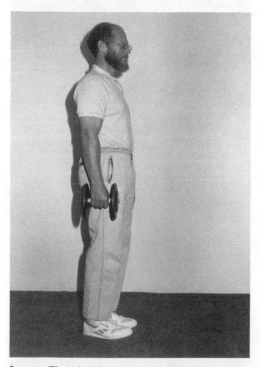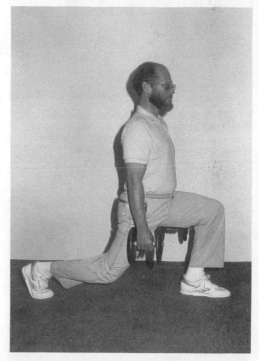

Lunges. These build strength and flexibility in the hamstrings and buttocks. They can be done with a barbell or dumbbells (as shown here). To start, stand straight, and then lunge straight ahead with the left foot as far as possible and bend the left knee, keeping the right leg as straight as possible. Then thrust hard with the left leg to push yourself back to standing position. Repeat, lunging forward with the right leg. As in the squats, it's mandatory to keep your back straight and head up.

Calf Raises. As the name implies, these strengthen the calves. They're most easily done on a machine like the Universal Gym. Stand with your heels on the floor and toes raised three to four inches on a block of wood. Rise onto your tiptoes and then lower your heels back to the floor. Do one set with your toes pointed in, one with toes straight, and one with toes pointed out.

Situps. These strengthen the stomach muscles. They also help the back, because a strong abdomen supports the back. Lie on your back, hands locked behind your head. Slowly curl to a sitting position and let yourself back down slowly. Don't jerk yourself up. On subsequent situps, twist first to one side, then the other, to strengthen side muscles.

If you're in poor shape or have a bad back, you can do "stomach crunches" in place of situps. They strengthen the stomach just as well. Lie on your back, hands behind your head, and legs supported over a chair or bench. Sit up as far as possible and lower yourself back down. As in regular situps, twist to the sides on alternate crunches.

Shoulder (Military) Press. This strengthens the shoulders, upper back, and chest muscles. Grasp the barbell with your hands about six inches wider than your shoulders, thumbs turned in. Start by standing straight up, bar held at shoulder level. Push the bar up until your elbows lock. Lower the bar behind your head onto your shoulders, push it back up, and lower it to your chest. With each repetition, alternate lowering it to your chest and back. Keep your back straight.

Bench Press. This builds the chest, triceps (backs of arms), and shoulders. It can be done with a barbell or on the Universal Gym. Lie on your back on the bench. Hold your hands at about shoulder width, thumbs in. Start with the weight at your chest. Straighten your arms to lift weight and then slowly lower it to your chest. Keep your rear end flat on the bench.

stairs all day. You can see the value of added strength.

But strength and endurance contribute to more than just your ability to climb. They add to general muscle control, and that can come down to the most critical moment of all—making the shot.

Earlier I mentioned Rick McKinney, a world-class tournament archer. Along with Shari Rhoades, McKinney helped write a general training program for serious archers. One component of that program is endurance training as described above, but another is strength training, primarily through weight lifting. The U.S. Archery Team now uses the program, as well as the Arizona State University team, the best college team in the country.

McKinney said the program is designed to strengthen specific muscles used in shooting,

Lat Pulldowns. This exercise strengthens the back (latissimus dorsi), biceps, forearms, and shoulders. A machine like the Universal Gym is required. Kneel at the machine and hold the bar at the ends, thumbs in. Start with your arms fully extended and pull the bar down to the back of your neck. Slowly straighten your arms to the starting position.

Shoulder Shrugs. These as well as the following two exercises strengthen the shoulders and the upper back. For these use dumbbells or similar weights. Hold a weight in each hand and stand straight with your arms hanging at your sides. Shrug your shoulders as high as possible, and then relax them to the starting position.

but it's also well balanced to promote all-around conditioning.

"When I first started training this way, I found right off I could hold my bow longer and remain steady," McKinney said. "There's no question it improved my stability. My scores jumped up almost 20 points, and I set a world record about four months after I started this training program."

Granted, you can't directly correlate hunting and tournament archery, but the bottom line is identical—putting the arrow in the spot. For that reason such a training program can benefit hunters as much or more than target archers. After all, in hunting you'll get only one shot at that animal (in most cases). You've got to be ready, and training is the only way to ensure that.

You also need strength and endurance to

practice well, and conditioning can prevent injuries. I speak from experience along these lines. I've had shoulder problems for more than a decade, and they started because I tried shooting heavy bows before doing anything to get in shape for it. I know very few hunters who shoot heavy-weight bows, especially recurves, who don't have some problems with shoulders or elbows. I suspect a good training program could prevent most injuries.

The following program comes largely from the training program outlined by Rick McKinney. I've also added a few exercises recommended by athletic trainers Luke Klaja and Harris Hinden.

Most of the following exercises can be done either with barbells or on machines such as the Universal Gym. Start out with just enough weight so you can complete 10 repetitions with-

Lateral Arm Raises. Use dumbbells or similar weights. Hold a weight in each hand and stand with your arms hanging at your sides, palms in. Lift your hands above shoulder level and return them to your sides.

Forward Arm Raises. Start in same position as lateral arm raises, but lift one arm straight out to shoulder level and lower it to the starting position, and then lift other arm.

out excessive strain. McKinney recommends this rule of thumb (this can vary greatly among individuals): Men try half their body weight for leg exercises and one fourth for arms and shoulders; women two fifths of body weight for legs and one fifth for arms and shoulders.

The two important terms involved in lifting are "repetitions" and "sets." Repetition applies to the number of times you consecutively lift a weight, and a set is given number of repetitions. For example, if you lift a weight 10 times and then stop to rest, that's one set of 10 repetitions.

Luke Klaja recommends that you start with one set of 10 to 15 repetitions. After the third workout, do two sets of 10 to 15 repetitions, and after the eighth workout, increase to three sets of 10 to 15 repetitions. When you can do three sets and feel like you could do several more, increase the weight.

Before any workout, you should warm up first to prevent injury. Do some shoulder shrugs, shoulder rotations, hip rotations, squats, lunges, jumping jacks, toe touches, and similar movements without weight to loosen and warm up your muscles. Then do the exercises shown in the photos.

352

PIGS *(Sus scrofa)* Two kinds of wild pigs live in the United States: the European wild boar, originally introduced into North Carolina from Germany in 1912, and the feral pig. Domestic hogs readily take to the wilds when given the opportunity, and many feral hogs in the United States today have descended from hogs that escaped from homesteaders' farmyards more than a century ago. European boars, which have been stocked in many locations, and feral hogs interbreed freely, so blood lines are mixed throughout most of the range in North America.

The Nature of Pigs

Range. Hogs are abundant throughout the coastal plain zone from North Carolina across the entire South to east Texas. Their range extends up the Mississippi Valley into the Ozarks, and also into the Great Smokey Mountains. In California, pigs are abundant in the Sierra foothills as well as the Coast Range from Humboldt County to Santa Barbara. They're also numerous on several islands in the Santa Barbara Channel, and special feral goat and pig hunts are popular with bowhunters there. In California, pigs are the number two big-game

animal, second only to deer. Pigs also thrive in Hawaii.

In terms of harvest, Florida is the number one pig state. In 1977, Florida hunters killed 77,500 wild pigs. California ranked second that year with a harvest of 32,000, and Hawaii was third at about 10,000. Some are taken in Tennessee, North Carolina, and other Southern states, but the harvest is small.

Color. Feral hogs come in many colors, just as their domestic relatives do, but after a few generations in the wild, black becomes the predominant color. Baby European boars have brown and black stripes, but adults have a characteristic agouti coloration—grizzled reddish-brown to gray-black.

Size. You hear stories about the huge size of wild hogs, but many are exaggerated. Dye Creek Ranch in California became famous for its pig hunting, and many thousands of hogs were killed there over a 15-year span. In 1985 I killed a sow there that hog-dressed 240 pounds, and the hunt manager said that was the biggest sow ever taken at Dye Creek. The rare boar at Dye Creek hog-dresses over 300 pounds, but the average is closer to 200.

A friend of mine hunting on his own land in

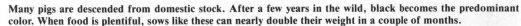

Many pigs are descended from domestic stock. After a few years in the wild, black becomes the predominant color. When food is plentiful, sows like these can nearly double their weight in a couple of months.

California said he killed a sow that dressed 800 pounds. It was weighed on scales. That seems too incredible to believe (that's heavier than the average bull elk), but he showed me pictures of it, and indeed it appears that big, and friends support his story. That's one big pig.

It's hard to give averages, because pigs can vary in weight rapidly. During dry, poor-feed years, they get as skinny as jackrabbits. Then when acorns or other rich crops are available they put on weight fast. A sow that weighs 100 pounds one year could weigh 200 the next.

When they're healthy, pigs breed like flies, and they can virtually overrun a ranch unless they're strictly controlled. They compete heavily with native wildlife for valuable forage, particularly mast crops. They also root up pastures and croplands and foul waterholes, so some landowners hate them and try to wipe them out. In contrast, other landowners have promoted the idea of pig hunting and have turned their pigs into a cash crop.

Hunting Wild Pigs

In the thick bottomlands and flats of the South, hunters run and bay pigs with dogs. In California, hunting on foot by spotting and stalking, or still-hunting, has become more popular. On private lands where they're protected to some extent by limited access, pigs normally become abundant and they're not tough to stalk. On public lands, or on ranches where the landowner goes out of his way to destroy them, the animals are wary.

A majority of the best pig hunting takes place on private lands, so commonly you either have to know a landowner who'll give you permission to hunt, or you pay. (See also Javelina.)

Pigs don't sweat or pant as other animals do to keep cool, so in hot weather they congregate around water sources. On the central coast of California, Pat Miller and I found all the pigs on one ranch congregated in several little tule marshes, and to hunt them we had to wade right in and kick them out. The pigs were making lots of noise so they didn't pay a lot of attention to our thrashing around, and we often walked within four or five feet of feeding or resting hogs. It seemed they all suddenly caught onto our presence at once, because about 30 pigs erupted in a squealing, snorting mass as they stampeded out of the marsh, tails waving in the air.

In fall and winter with cooler weather, pigs disperse into the uplands to feed on acorns,

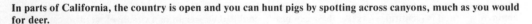

In parts of California, the country is open and you can hunt pigs by spotting across canyons, much as you would for deer.

Any boar with tusks three inches long or longer would have to be considered a good trophy.

grass, roots, and whatever else they can find. In the foothills in California, you can spot them much as you would deer, and then stalk them. Pigs have good noses and hearing, but their eyesight is poor, so they make ideal bow animals because you generally can stalk within close bow range; 10- to 15-yard shots are average.

You hear a lot about the ferocity of wild pigs. Some of the stories are probably true; certainly pigs don't have sweet temperaments. Nevertheless, they don't pose any great threat to human life. About the only time they get vicious is when cornered by dogs, or when wounded and cornered.

Most mature boars have tusks longer than two inches, and really big boars have tusks of three inches or slightly longer. Pigs are hard to judge on the hoof, but if you can see teeth at all the animal probably has two-inch tusks,

and if you can see an inch exposed, the tusks are probably three inches. You can best judge body condition by looking at a pig from end to end. If it's round-looking, it's probably in pretty good shape. A skinny pig will have a ridged back, and the hip bones will be sticking out noticeably.

For pig hunting you need a bow with some punch. All pigs have tough hides, and mature boars have an armor plate of gristle an inch or more thick over the chest and front shoulders. A bow suitable for elk, something in the 60-pound class or heavier, is none too heavy for pigs.

Also, broadheads with sharp cutting tips are far better for slicing through the hide than are the pencil-pointed broadheads. Using a modular broadhead with a pointed round tip, I hit a sow at a diagonal angle. Rather than poking through the hide, the tip of the broadhead slid along the tough skin for about eight inches and then ricocheted off, and the arrow landed 70 yards beyond the pig. With a sharp-tipped broadhead, such as the Zwickey or Bear, I'm sure the point would have sliced through the hide and killed the pig.

Hogs have a small kill zone and a lot of nonvital body area, so you've got to hit them on the money to kill them cleanly. A poorly hit pig can go forever, so get close and slip that arrow in right behind the front leg.

Rich LaRocco, right, killed this boar on the Dye Creek Ranch in northern California. It has nearly three-inch tusks, which would be considered large anywhere.

In southern California, I shot this small boar as it fed in a boggy, cool creek bottom in hot weather. Sows and immature boars like this make for fine eating.

Old boars can get pretty raunchy and are generally not considered great table fare. Most hunters who kill boars have the meat ground and seasoned for breakfast sausage. If you want a meat pig, shoot a sow or immature boar. They're excellent eating, much like domestic pork although generally not as fat.

PLANNING A HUNT   This section tells how to plan your own self-guided hunt, one that you plan and execute on your own. (For details on planning a guided hunt, see Outfitters and Guides.)

That might mean you'll travel from the East to hunt a Western state, but the same principles apply for hunting close to home. For many of us, home ground becomes jaded, but with a fresh look we could find some great hunting.

As one example, Jim Martin from Kansas City had killed many deer, but never a really big one, so in 1984 he set out to kill a trophy white-tail close to home. His regular hunting spots had plenty of deer but no big bucks, so he started a systematic planning process and late that year he killed a buck that scored 197⅛, the biggest nontypical ever killed by a bow-hunter in Missouri. All this took place within 30 miles of his home.

Prerequisites

You can hunt new country for new game on your own and expect success from the start, but it requires two qualities: experience and the right personality.

The need for experience should be obvious. If you've never bowhunted, you have a lot to learn about basics. Planning a hunt to a distant state isn't the way to start. Get a few deer or other animals under your belt at home first. Then you can set out with confidence, knowing what to expect from bowhunting, knowing your own capabilities and weaknesses.

The personality requirement might not be so clear. Some people have the insight and initiative to do things for themselves, others don't. If you're aggressive and bold about plowing new ground, then you can plan any kind of hunt and pull it off. If you're timid, you may not be able to cope with the unknowns of hunting new territory. It takes a certain toughness and craving for adventure. If you're lacking in these qualities, then hire a guide the first time around, or team up with an experienced, aggressive hunter who can lead the way.

Hunt planning is by no means an exact science. A lot of feel goes into it, but a few general guidelines can be useful. I break it down into two categories: Questions to Answer, and Information Sources.

Questions to Answer

The purpose of planning is to compile a mental picture of the country you want to hunt, before you ever see it. The following list of questions offers guidelines for building a mental picture. Not every question pertains to every hunt, but these serve as a good starting point.

1. What are the hunting options? To plan, you must know what's available. Some states offer early seasons in July, August, and September; others hold late seasons in November, December, and January; some have both. In some states you can hunt only one species, but in others you can hunt a combination, say for mule deer and elk, whitetails and elk, mule deer and antelope, Coues deer and javelina, and so forth. Many hunters just pick a given state (commonly Colorado out West) and accept whatever that state has to offer. That's not necessarily bad, but with some investigation, you might find better options in other states. If you're serious about bowhunting, make a habit of ordering hunting regulations from several states each year so you can pick out the best hunting opportunities.

2. Are animals sparse or numerous? Biologists often speak of deer (or elk or bear) densities. By that they mean the number of animals per square mile. Whitetails, for example, may number 5 to 10 per square mile in some regions, and 50 per square mile in others. It's not always that simple, but you can get a feel for the number of animals. Ask biologists whether densities are low, medium, or high. Unless you've got lots of scouting time, you're wise to stay away from low-density areas because you might spend your entire hunt just trying to locate a buck or two. As a general rule, bowhunters need fairly high densities for good hunting.

Densities also can be expressed in terms of what you could expect to see. That might not mean much in Eastern whitetail hunting where you might only see one or two bucks a day even in high-density areas, but it works well in much of the West. To research Western country, I often ask, "How many bucks could I expect to see in a day?" If the answer is "Two or three," I figure deer numbers are too low for good hunting; if the answer is 10 or 12, I'm interested; if the answer is 30 or 40, I'm eager.

Of course, you have to put numbers into context. If you're planning an elk hunt, you might ask, "How many elk could I expect to hear bugling in a hard day's hunting?" If you averaged hearing one or two a day, you'd be in a good area. And if you're planning a Western bear hunt and someone says you might spot two or three bears a day, you know it's a good area.

3. What is the hunter success rate? In a way this is redundant, because it tells you something about densities. Generally, the higher the game densities, the higher the hunter success, and if your only concern is killing a deer, regardless of size or competition from other hunters, then you might choose an area based strictly on high hunter success. That tells you the odds are in your favor.

But don't take harvest stats as law, because they could be misleading. Hart Mountain National Antelope Refuge in Oregon presents a good example. There the average bowhunting success on mule deer averages less than 5 percent, which looks poor, but it's not because there aren't any deer. Deer numbers are high, and trophy bucks are plentiful, and some hunters who've figured out how to hunt there take big bucks year after year. Hunting the open sagebrush just takes special techniques. You have to interpret harvest rates in light of terrain, vegetation and hunting pressure. For a clear picture, ask locals why hunter success is high or low.

4. What is the buck/doe ratio? Density refers to the number of animals available, and the buck/doe (or bull/cow) ratio says something about the quality of animals. Biologists rarely count absolute numbers of bucks, but rather the number of bucks in relation to the number of does. Generally, the higher the ratio, the higher the number of mature bucks. (I don't say "trophy" bucks because the area might not have the heredity or minerals to grow huge bucks.)

For example, biologists count deer in winter, following general hunting seasons; if they count only 10 bucks/100 does, you know a

Through planning you can find out the densities of deer in a given area, and you can also assess the buck/doe ratio, which indicates the number of mature bucks available.

high percentage of bucks were killed during the season and few mature bucks remain for next year. Most of the bucks available next fall will be yearlings, this year's fawns. On the other hand, a ratio of 30 bucks/100 does tells you quite a few bucks escaped the season and they'll be available as 2½-year-old or older bucks next fall.

If you're interested in taking a big buck, then, you want to hunt places with high buck/doe ratios. For trophy hunting, I'd say you want to hunt where the ratio is at least 20 bucks/100 does, and 30/100 is better. For trophy elk hunting, look for areas with at least 20 bulls/100 cows.

5. *Where will animals be concentrated during the season?* In any given range, deer, elk, and other animals congregate in specific terrain or vegetation. So even if densities are high, some parts of an area may hold little or no game, and other spots will be crawling with animals. Western hunters and biologists often refer to "buck pastures," and I've seen this term in action. In some mountain ranges I've looked over many miles of country that held either no deer, or only does and fawns. Then suddenly

I've found one or two basins filled with herds of bucks.

The same is true for elk. A biologist told me about a "bull pasture" in Montana. I hiked in to investigate. Indeed most of the surrounding country was devoid of elk, but this one basin, which apparently had just the right combination of huckleberries, mountain ash, alders, and other forage to appeal to elk, contained at least a dozen good bulls. For best hunting, you want to find concentration points like that.

From region to region, food preferences of animals vary greatly. During your planning, quiz locals about preferred forage for animals, and ask on what slopes and at what elevations deer, elk, and other animals will live at a given time.

In some places, mule deer and elk, even whitetails and blacktails, respond quickly to weather. Heavy winter weather forces them to migrate long distances, and you must know migration routes and the location of winter ranges to hunt successfully during late seasons. And even during summer and early fall, game will shift location quickly in response to weather. An early frost could burn grasses in

358

open meadows and animals may move to lower, more protected slopes to find green feed. During the planning process, ask locals about the habits of game in a particular area.

6. *When are animals in rut?* The rut gives you a great advantage in hunting most big game, so you're wise to hunt during that period whenever possible. The bugling season for elk may vary from one latitude to another, so ask locals when the bulls start bugling and when the peak of the rut occurs.

Rut timing for deer can vary considerably. Blacktails on the California coast rut during September. Most whitetails in northern latitudes start rutting in mid-October and peak in mid-November, but in Texas the rut falls in December, and in Arizona for Coues whitetails in January. In most regions, mule deer rut in late November, but in Southwestern deserts, the rut occurs in late December and January. To plan your hunt around the rut, you must know the precise timing.

7. *What are the terrain and vegetation like?* One time a hunter from Florida called me to get information about hunting areas in Colorado. I suggested a couple of mountain ranges, but I warned, "They're rough. You'd better be in good shape or you won't make it."

"No problem," he assured me. "We work hard to keep in shape."

I thought no more about it until mid-September, when the phone rang, and it was the same Florida hunter. "We're down here in Colorado," he said. "We tried that mountain range you suggested, but it's just too rough. Do you know any easier places that would suit some Florida flatlanders?"

To plan, you must know what the terrain looks like. You can get the idea from photos in books and magazines, but locals can give you a better description of the elevations, steepness of the mountains, and so forth. You must know this in order to prepare physically (for more details, see Physical Condition). And believe what you hear.

Also find out about vegetation. I often hear hunters talk about hunting "Montana." Well, what is Montana? In the southwest corner near Yellowstone National Park and in most mountains east of the Continental Divide, you'll find open lodgepole pine forests where you can see elk at considerable distances and can get clean shots out to 50 yards. In the northwest corner, rain forests with a dense undergrowth of alder and willows are the rule, and there you can call a bull within 10 yards and still not get a clear

To plan any hunt, you must know what the terrain and vegetation look like.

shot. In planning, piece together a picture of the terrain and vegetation, because it could affect your choice of areas.

8. What kind of access will I find? Your idea of good access may be lots of roads so you can cover an entire area by vehicle; or it may be few roads so you can hike a few miles to get away from other hunters. Whatever your personal preference, research access thoroughly.

That must be emphasized, because you can't gauge access just by looking at maps. First, many, particularly the U.S. Geological Survey maps, are out of date. Second, many states now enforce road closures during hunting seasons, so even if your map accurately shows roads, you may not be able to drive them. Third, not all symbols on maps are accurate. I've trusted my Forest Service maps, which showed hiking trails in a given area, and to my frustration have found these "trails" to be jeep roads, with four-wheel-drive rigs and all-terrain vehicles (ATVs) grinding everywhere. Talk to public agencies or landowners in the area to update your maps.

On the subject of ATVs, ask about them. In some areas you can't legally take a motor vehicle off established roads. Also, in some regions, so-called three-wheelers have proliferated, and you may not be able to escape them, which can

To fill in the planning picture, you must get an idea of weather conditions, and you must know how animals react in response to weather.

be frustrating if you like to hike and want to get away from machines.

9. How heavy is the hunting pressure? Hunting success depends as much on competition with other hunters as it does on herd quality, so finding low-competition units rates high priority with me. Of course, that could depend on your hunting style. If you hunt strictly from a tree stand, you might prefer having other hunters around to keep deer moving past your stand. For other styles of hunting, you might want to find an area that's either overlooked or is too rough and remote for most hunters.

10. How is access onto private lands? If you plan to hunt public lands, access might not be a major concern, but even then you should inquire. In some Western states, ranchers own and control the access onto public lands. In Colorado, one ranch owned a strip only 100 yards wide, but with it they could control access to thousands of acres of national forest land, and they charged hunters a hefty fee just to drive across their land to hunt public property. Find out the location of best access points before you leave home. And if you plan to hunt private lands, find out if landowners are receptive to hunters. In some states you can get permission by asking; in other states, private clubs lease virtually all private lands and you can't get on unless you pay.

11. What are the camping conditions? In Arizona I found the land so flat I could pitch a tent or park a motor home anywhere, but there was no water. In other states, I've found plenty of pure, running water, but the country was so steep I could scarcely find a flat place big enough for a tent. The camping options are limitless, so inquire about campgrounds, water, proximity of camping to hunting areas, and so forth before you set out. (For more details, see Camping.)

You might also ask about livestock. Some areas are grazed heavily during the summer by sheep and cattle. You could be disappointed if you expect pristine, quiet high country and find yourself amid 2,000 bawling sheep. Not that livestock necessarily hurt the hunting, but they can influence game distribution, and they might take up residence in the best camping areas and foul water sources you'd planned to use for drinking water.

12. What is the weather like? Can you expect 100-degree days, thunderstorms every afternoon, zero temperatures, possible blizzards? Obviously you can't plan clothing and camp gear without insight into these matters. Weather could also affect your preparations in terms of meat care in the field. If hot weather will be the rule, you must arrange for locker space. In short, get a general weather picture before your trip, and prepare for the worst. (For more details, see Clothing; Meat Care.)

You can't plan well unless you've visualized all conditions ahead of time. Get an accurate picture of the country and the weather so you can plan ahead for meat care and other aspects of the hunt.

Information Sources

The above questions aren't intended as absolute, only as a guideline of subjects I've found apropos in planning. It should serve as a good takeoff point for you. The following information sources will help you answer your questions.

Books and Magazines. So many writers have suggested reading as a source of information I hate to say it again. Nevertheless, it's true. You've got to read to keep up with trends in big game populations. Harold Boyack, one of the finest bowhunters in the United States, told me his planning starts with reading. "I read every outdoors magazine that comes out," Boyack said. "That's how I keep track of the best trophy areas from year to year." You can get a virtual college course on big-game hunting from books and magazines today.

Record Books. The Boone and Crockett Club, and its bowhunting equivalent, the Pope and Young Club, each publish record books with listings of trophy animals, the areas where they were taken, and the date of kill. Analysis of these records gives excellent clues toward current big-game trends. If you're serious about killing a larger-than-average animal, you must study the record books. (For more details, see Boone and Crockett Club; Pope and Young club; and Trophy Scoring.)

Tape Recordings. Dozens of companies sell audio tapes on elk calling, turkey hunting, rattling for whitetails, predator calling—all aspects of hunting; many more produce excellent video hunting tapes. You can sit right in your living room and get a full course on hunting techniques as well as a fair idea of hunting conditions in your chosen state. Take advantage of the many audio and video recordings available.

Maps. Maps fascinate me, and I can trace many of my best hunts to that fascination. I order maps of prospective hunting areas and pore over them, vicariously hunting this ridge, that drainage. Through such dreaming, ideas and trends emerge, and soon one particular canyon or mountain begins to catch my eye, and I have to investigate further.

For best results, start with small-scale maps to get an overview. The smaller the scale, the larger the area covered. The U.S. Geological Survey prints state topographic maps, and from these you can get an overview of the terrain in an entire state. Once you've chosen a specific area, you'll want to order quadrangle topographic maps. These large-scale maps show much detail, and you can fine-tune your planning and scouting on these.

U.S. Forest Service and Bureau of Land Management maps don't show topography as well, but they're more current and they show roads and trails, wilderness areas, public-land boundaries, and other mandatory information, so they're a must for planning. Plat maps from local counties show private-land ownership, state maps detail wildlife management areas and public hunting grounds, and so forth. Get as many different kinds as possible and study them diligently, because each will contribute a piece to the hunting puzzle. (For more details, see Map Sources.)

Biological Data. Every state gathers harvest statistics and biological data from big-game surveys. In some it's very detailed, in others skimpy, but whatever the case, biological data can help you plan. Write to state game departments to ask for a summary of this data; if that doesn't work, call and ask one of the big-game biologists what's available. Some states compile statistics and sell them. Biological data aren't magic, and you have to interpret them in the light of other information, but they form another essential piece in the planning puzzle. (See individual state listings for game department addresses.)

Local Hunters and Biologists. Perhaps your most valuable asset will be locals who work and hunt in an area. They've seen the country and know the animals there. The biggest step you can take toward a good hunt is tapping into their knowledge and experience. I commonly start out by calling and chatting with local wildlife biologists who manage the game herds in a given area. I also call any hunters, foresters, ranchers, taxidermists, and so forth who might know something about a particular piece of country.

Always prepare specific questions before calling anybody. Study your maps and harvest statistics, and read articles and record books. With sound background knowledge, you can ask precise questions, and then you'll get precise information. If you ask only general questions, you'll get only general answers. One time two friends and I asked the manager of a wildlife management area in Colorado where we'd find the good deer country. He waved his arm at the surrounding mountains and said, "You're looking at it." End of conversation. We'd got a stupid answer, but only because

we'd asked a stupid question. We should have got out maps and grilled him about specifics.

Second, a local source will open up far quicker if he thinks you already know something, because he'll see he can't hide anything and might as well be frank. Besides, people like sharing mutual secrets. My friend Cliff Dewell was sitting in a backcountry camp when a local guide dropped by. The guide was friendly, but he obviously was avoiding spilling any secrets. Cliff didn't push him, just chatted; but Cliff also shared his knowledge of the area so the guide knew he'd already done his homework. After an hour of talking, the guide could see they were on common ground and began to open up, and pretty soon he'd revealed several good spots Cliff hadn't even thought of.

Long-distance research can severely damage your phone bill, but it's still cheaper than hiring an outfitter, and probably a lot more satisfying. Budget phone expenses into your hunting trip, and start calling.

Bringing It All Together

Bob Hernbrode, head of Colorado's Game Division, one time critiqued an article I'd written on planning. He said he agreed with me in principle, but he questioned whether the average hunter could gather harvest data and the other information I'd suggested and interpret it meaningfully.

As I've suggested above, planning a hunt resembles putting together a puzzle. You gather a pile of pieces, and then by guess and by golly you start fitting them together. I'll admit it's no exact science and involves a lot of feel and intuition, but if you work at it long enough, you'll see a picture emerging. It could be the picture of a great hunt.

PLUCK To pluck the bowstring means you snap open your fingers quickly and jerk your hand back or to the side. Plucking the string generally produces erratic arrow flight, and because it can increase draw length slightly as you jerk on the string, it can cause arrows to hit high. In good shooting form, your hand will move straight back slightly after you release the bowstring, but in plucking, your hand will move out to the side of your face. (For details on correct release, see Release, and Shooting Basics.)

POINT-OF-AIM   See Aiming Methods.

POINT-ON   Point-on distance is the distance at which, when the arrow is point-on the target, the arrow will hit the target. Point-on distance varies greatly with shooting styles, arrow speed, trajectory, and anchor method. The lower your anchor, the longer the point-on distance. With a conventional corner of the mouth anchor, point-on distance might be 60 yards. With an under-chin anchor, it will increase to 80 yards or greater. With a high anchor or Apache draw (three fingers under the arrow), point-on distance will decrease to 40 yards or less.

Knowing point-on distance can be useful, especially for instinctive shooters, because it can be used as a gauge for maximum effective range (although few bowhunters can shoot well out to point-on distance). Beyond point-on distance, the arrow covers the target and makes aiming difficult.

POPE AND YOUNG CLUB   This official records-keeping organization for archery-killed animals is named after Dr. Saxton Pope and Art Young, archers of the early 1900s considered by many as the fathers of modern bowhunting.

The club was founded in 1961, primarily under the guidance of Glenn St. Charles of Seattle, Washington, and it was patterned after the Boone and Crockett Club. The Pope and Young Club holds an awards program and banquet every two years. Top trophies measured during the biennium for entry in the Pope and Young Club's official record book, *Bowhunting Big Game Records of North America*, are measured by a panel of judges, and awards are presented for the largest trophies. These top trophies are displayed at the banquet, and first-place, second-place, and honorable mention plaques are awarded to the three top heads in each big-game category. The club also may present the Ishi Award for a truly outstanding trophy taken during the scoring period.

Anyone can join the Pope and Young Club as an associate member. The number of associate members isn't limited, but to qualify you must have taken at least one big-game animal by bow and arrow. The animal must be taken under the rules of fair chase, as defined on official score charts. (See Trophy Scoring.)

Regular members, limited to 100 persons, move up through the associate ranks. To qualify as a regular member, you must have taken with bow and arrow at least three species of North American big game, and at least one of these must be listed in the record book.

The next step is senior membership. There is no limit to the number, but to qualify as a senior member, you must have five years' seniority as a regular member, you must have taken at least four species of North American big game, and three of the animals must be listed in the Pope and Young records.

Contact. Pope and Young Club, 1804 Borah, Moscow, ID 83843.

PORPOISE   This term describes undesirable up-and-down wobble of an arrow when it is shot from a bow, opposed to fishtailing, which describes side-to-side wobble. (See Fishtail.) In virtually all cases, porpoising is caused by improper nocking-point height. Raising or lowering the nocking point will eliminate porpoising. (For more details, see Bow Tuning.)

POTENTIAL ENERGY   See Energy.

POWDER POUCH   A small bag filled with baby talcum or similar fine powder. Target shooters commonly use powder as a dry lubricant to dust their shooting tabs or gloves, which ensures a clean, smooth release. For hunting, you can also use powder to check wind direction; just shake a little out. A powder pouch can be a handy addition to your gear list. Some hunters wouldn't be caught without one.

POWER RELEASE   See Release.

PRAIRIE DOG   See Squirrel.

PREDATOR CALLING   The most commonly hunted predators are coyotes, foxes, and bobcats, but virtually any predatory animal, including bears and mountain lions, can be pulled within range by calling.

Many hunters prefer calling in winter, because that's when pelts are in best condition, and some predator calling helps fill in the gaps between big-game seasons. For sheer action, though, you can't beat summer. That's when young predators start foraging on their own, and they're not yet call-wise. One summer I saw two coyotes trotting through the open ponderosa forest, maybe 100 yards from me. They were nearly grown, but from their actions it was obvious they were pups. I ducked behind a log and squawled on a call. Without hesitation the coyotes charged toward me. One stopped

Coyotes are thriving throughout much of North America, and they're popular with predator callers.

just across the log from me and the other ran around the end of the log and came up behind. They were within mere feet by the time I could draw my bow. I shot at the one out front—shot over him—and they both scrambled. That reaction was typical of young, naive animals. Older ones aren't always so eager.

Larry D. Jones has devoted much of his hunting life to predator hunting and has called in hundreds of coyotes, along with bobcats, bears, and other predators. Many of the following ideas have been passed on to me by Larry. For simplicity, I'll talk primarily about calling coyotes here, but the same principles apply to all predator calling.

The Setup

Most important may be the setup—where and how you blind in. The normal routine is to move and call, move and call. You walk a ways and blind in and call for a certain amount of time; if nothing comes in, you move, blind in, and call again. The more broken and enclosed the country, the less distance you'll cover between setups because sound won't travel as far as it will in open or flat terrain.

As in any big-game hunting, wind gets first play. You've got to hunt into the wind so you're always downwind of the animals you're calling. Incidentally, while we're on that subject, windy days make for tough calling. Larry figures if the wind is blowing 15 miles an hour or harder, you might as well stay home and weed the garden; you'll kill just as many coyotes. Calm, warm days, when rodents frolic in the sun are best, because that's when predators will frolic, too, and on quiet days, the sound of your call will carry well. The first nice day after a storm or hard wind could be the best time of all to call.

You can expect a third or more of the coyotes you call to circle downwind of you. After all, they live by their noses, so a downwind approach is only predictable. For that reason, do everything possible to reduce your own smell. (For details, see Scents.) Also, try to set up so you can shoot at a circling animal, and if you're hunting with a partner, put the shooter

Bobcats also respond well to a predator call. Larry
D. Jones called in this cat one soggy day in western
Oregon. *Photo courtesy Larry D. Jones.*

larly on your hands, face, and equipment, the
parts that will be seen first by an incoming
predator. (For details, see Camouflage.)

When you've located a good blind site, slip
into position quietly and stay low, below the
skyline. Choose a blind in front of a rock or
big bush so you're not silhouetted. It's okay to
have sparse cover in front to prevent being
seen, but make sure you've got clearance for
shooting. To further aid in hiding, Larry cuts a
branch from the cover he's hiding in and hooks
it between the arrows in his quiver (special
branch holders are also made for this purpose).
When he holds his bow at shooting level, the
branch hides his face and any hand movement
while calling.

To relieve his arm of bow weight, he fits the
lower bow tip into a small pocket sewn on his

downwind of the caller so a circling animal will
unknowingly blunder into the shooter.

Larry likes to call from places where, first,
the sound of his call will carry well, and, second, he can see animals coming for some distance. In the open desert, that's not hard because visibility often is unlimited, but in timber
it takes more thought. He calls at the edges of
natural openings or clearcuts, and at the intersection of several skid trails.

If possible, he'll set up on a steep hill at least
50 yards from the bottom so animals must
come up to him. Larry's theory is that on flat
ground a coyote can spot movement even when
he's running hard. But on a steep hill he must
stop to look up, and that gives the shooter a
little more latitude for drawing and getting the
shot.

Finally, in a good setup you're well hidden.
That starts with complete camouflage, particu-

In a good setup, you'll have cover behind so you're
not silhouetted, and a branch attached to your bow
can help hide your fact. The call should be cupped in
the V between your thumb and index finger.

This hunter has made a blind of camouflaged burlap supported by stakes and chicken wire. He sits on a stool so he can wait comfortably. *Photo courtesy Larry D. Jones.*

pants leg. When he's ready to shoot he only has to raise the bow enough to clear the pocket and he's ready to draw. In forest you probably can stand in your blind, but in low sage or other desert scrub you'll probably have to kneel.

Some callers also make blinds of camouflage cloth set on stakes. In such a blind you can sit on a low stool, which can be more comfortable over a long calling session. Whatever method you choose, make sure you have the wind in your favor, can see well, are well hidden, and can shoot with little movement.

Making the Sounds

Larry Jones uses a mix of soft and loud sounds to call in predators. At any new setup, an animal could be lurking close by, and a sudden screech on a loud call could startle the

animal into running. That's why Larry commonly starts out with his quiet sounds to attract animals that could be close. He sucks on a wet finger or on the palm of his hand to create a raspy squeak, the kind of sound a hurt bird or small mammal might make. In some areas, predators have heard enough calling that they're getting wise to the common sound of a screaming rabbit call, and "off-brand" calling like this will fool them.

I've used a commercially made squeaker call (it could imitate a mouse or other small rodent) with good results. One day I saw a coyote sitting on a sagebrush point, looking out over a valley. I'd scared off a couple of other coyotes with the screams of my regular rabbit call, so as I hid I just squeaked a couple of times on that mouse call. The coyote jumped up and ran toward me. I was hunting only with a camera, so I started taking pictures. But soon he came too close for my long lens, and he just kept coming. I finally yelled to head him off. He'd come within five feet.

Larry uses his soft sounds for five minutes or so. If nothing comes in by then, he switches to more conventional calls with longer range, such as the wounded jackrabbit or cottontail call. To use one of these, hold the barrel of the call in the notch between your thumb and index finger so you can open and close your hand to regulate the sound.

Here's how Larry recommends blowing these calls. Start with your index finger pinched over the front of the call and blow "to" into the call. Now open your hand and blow "wah." To-wah, to-wah. As Larry points out, these calls are meant to imitate a hurt rabbit, and rabbits have small lungs, so their cries come in short bursts, not a drawn-out tooo-wahhhhhhh.

To vary the cry, switch to an "ow" sound. On this one start with your hand open and blow "ow" into the call and as you do, close your hand and drop the pressure. OOWWwww. Again, these should be abbreviated bursts, not long moans. As you produce these calls, quiver your diaphragm to impart despair and excitement. Remember, you're trying to imitate a rabbit in agony, so you want to sound agonized. Picture a rabbit screaming as he's being shaken in the jaws of a coyote.

You can create similar sounds with a mouth diaphragm, the kind of call used by turkey and elk callers. The diaphragm offers a couple of advantages. First, you can vary the pitch greatly, from tiny squeals to voluminous screams. Second, you don't need your hands to operate the call. That's particularly important for a bowhunter, because it allows you to continue calling without hand movement even as a predator approaches, and you can call and hold your bow ready to shoot at the same time.

The Calling Sequence

Using the sounds described above, call for 45 seconds or so and then stop and catch your breath for 15 seconds. Then call another 45 seconds, quiet 15; call 45, quiet 15; and so

A variety of calls will fool most predators. Pat Miller squeaked on his hand to imitate a hurt mouse, and it was enough to fool this young coyote.

forth. After several series of calls, begin to taper off in volume as a wounded rabbit might do when it runs out of energy.

If you see an animal coming your way, continue to call, but soften your calling a little and hold your bow at the ready. Some hunters prefer a recurve bow for this kind of hunting because they can draw smoothly and shoot quickly when a predator presents a close, open shot. Other hunters advocate shooting a fairly light compound bow, which they can predraw and hold until an incoming animal presents a close shot. I personally advocate the second method, but either one will work as long as you practice it.

In any kind of calling, a decoy can help divert an animal's attention to help you get a shot. Turkey hunters use decoys with good success (for details, see Turkey Hunting), and you can do the same in predator hunting with a stuffed jackrabbit or other small animal. Some hunters dangle a duck wing or dried rabbit hide on a string in a prominent bush where it will flutter in the breeze to catch a predator's eye. Some even use one of those wind-up toys that waves its arms or moves its head so the movement will distract the predator while they shoot. The Skotch predator call is operated by a bellows, so you can tie this call in a tree and operate it remotely with a string. With the sound coming from a point away from your blind, you're better able to draw and shoot without being seen.

Duration

The amount of time you spend at each setup depends on the animal you're hunting. For coyotes and foxes, Larry recommends 15 to 20 minutes. These animals may sneak in slowly, but they'll often come on the run. Many times I've seen coyotes in the distance come running full bore as soon as I've blown a call. (In places where they're hunted hard, I've seen them run full bore the other way, too.) If, after 20 minutes, you've got no response, move into the wind a few hundred yards, pick a new blind, and start a new calling sequence.

Bobcats tend to come in slower, sneaking in

quietly, so for these animals Larry suggests calling from one spot for at least a half hour. If you feel you have a good location, an hour would be none too long.

Calling doesn't fool only the small predators—coyotes, bobcats, foxes—it works on bigger animals as well, if you've got the patience. Arizona hunter Reed Peterson has called in three mountain lions and nearly 50 black bears. He uses the same calling techniques (much like those described above) he'd use for any predator. He believes the agonized sounds of a predator call produce a universal distress sound that could fool any predatory animal anywhere.

He does only one thing differently for larger predators, and that's to call for a longer time from one setup. He's watched bears come in, and they often move very slowly and casually; lions also approach slowly, silently and cautiously. For bears and lions, he advises calling for at least an hour from each setup.

Many states have spring bear seasons, and during this time, the sounds of a fawn deer can attract bears. I know hunters in Montana who've called in several bears by mimicking the frightened bleat of a fawn. You can make the sound with any predator call, except you draw the bleat out longer, more like the baaa of a lamb than the short, frantic screams of a hurt rabbit. Several instructional tapes on deer calling have good recordings of the fawn bleat.

PRINCE EDWARD ISLAND   This island off the coast of New Brunswick is the smallest Canadian province. It has some small-game and bird-hunting opportunities but no big game.

Contact. Fish and Wildlife Division, Community and Cultural Affairs, P.O. Box 2000, Charlottetown, Prince Edward Island, Canada C1A-7N8.

PRONGHORN   See Antelope.

Q

QUEBEC Quebec has a total area of 594,860 square miles. North of the 52nd parallel (roughly the southern end of James Bay), nonresidents are required to hunt with an outfitter.

Big Game

Whitetail Deer. An estimated 70,000 whitetail deer live on less than 7 percent of the area. Bowhunters killed 240 deer in 1983. The archery season throughout whitetail range runs for two weeks in October. The limit is one deer of either sex. Nonresidents aren't required to hire a guide for deer hunting.

Boreal forests north of the St. Lawrence River support relatively low numbers of deer. Lawrence lowlands produce most of the deer taken on the mainland of Quebec. Hunting clubs are common on private land along the U.S. border. Anticosti Island has a very high deer population, although the forests there are not productive and deer are smaller than on the mainland. The limit is two deer on Anticosti.

Moose. These animals are abundant throughout Quebec from the southern border north to tree line, except in heavily farmed southern regions. Some special archery moose seasons are held prior to general gun seasons. Moose seasons take place in September and October.

Caribou. Quebec has built a fine reputation in recent years, particularly among bowhunters, for its Quebec-Labrador caribou hunting. The season runs from late August through September. Many archers hunt the George River south of Ungava Bay. Success generally is very high, although it depends on timing of annual migrations.

Black Bear. The spring season is open all of May and June, and hunting also is allowed in the fall. Most animals are taken by baiting. Bears are most abundant in heavy forests of the southern province, but they range north to tundra areas.

Contact. Wildlife Management Division, Fish and Game Branch, Place de la Capitale 150 East, St. Cyrille Blvd., Quebec City, Quebec, Canada G1R-4Y1.

QUIVER Any device that holds arrows in a convenient, ready-to-use position while you're shooting or hunting could be called a quiver. In general there are three types of quivers: bow, back, and belt.

Bow Quivers

Bow quivers have been around since the 1950s, and they've become almost universally popular today. The major reason probably is convenience. A bow quiver molds bow and arrows into one easy-to-handle unit, and it holds arrows in a convenient position for reasonably quick usage.

I think a bow quiver offers a couple of other advantages. Many archers put stabilizers on their bows to add weight; the extra weight makes the bow steadier and prevents torque. To some extent a bow quiver does the same thing. The added weight adds stability. The quiver also absorbs some of the energy that vibrates through a bow, and helps to quieten the bow. In essence, a solid, tight bow quiver performs some of the functions of a stabilizer.

On the other hand, because a bow quiver fits on the side of the bow, it throws the bow out of balance, which could affect accuracy to some degree. I doubt, however, that the average bow-hunter could notice a difference in accuracy between a bow with a quiver and one without. A quiver full of arrows also can make a bow uncomfortably heavy and a little bulky. The pop-

Before all other considerations, a bow quiver must be safe, by holding broadheads securely and fully covered.

ularity of bow quivers, however, indicates that most hunters feel the advantages outweigh the disadvantages. I'm among those who do.

Safety. First thought goes to safety. Any quiver must have a hood that fully covers the broadheads. Whenever I see a picture of the old clip-on quiver with broadheads exposed, I picture myself stumbling and falling on the bow and driving the broadheads into my leg. Not only must a hood cover the tips to prevent such disasters, but it should cover the full length of the heads to prevent your cutting your fingers. The foam or rubber in the hood should be solid enough to hold the heads securely, and the shaft grippers must hold the arrows tightly so arrows won't get yanked out as you're moving through brush.

Strength and Silence. For some time, plastic quivers with single-point, quick-detach mounts captured the market. Those quivers are convenient, but they've lost favor because they pop like a drumhead when you shoot, and many of them rattle. If you use a quiver just to carry your arrows to a stand and then remove the quiver before shooting, this style is okay. But if you plan to shoot with the quiver on your bow, I don't recommend a plastic, quick-off quiver. Incidentally, always tune and practice with your gear setup the way you plan to hunt. Don't practice shooting with a quiver on the bow and then take it off for hunting.

To be of any value, a quiver must be strong, which means it's made of steel (except the broadhead hood, which is made of plastic on most bow quivers), and it must mount solidly. That, in my opinion, means it should have two mounting points. The Sagittarius Pegasus may employ the most foolproof concept. This two-piece quiver attaches under the limb bolts on your bow. There are no moving parts, so the thing can't rattle, and unless your bow limbs are falling off, the quiver can't get loose. The standard Pegasus holds 8 arrows, and the Pegasus Magnum holds 16. The one drawback is that these quivers can't be easily removed.

Other styles screw directly to the side of the bow, some attach with a dovetail bracket that

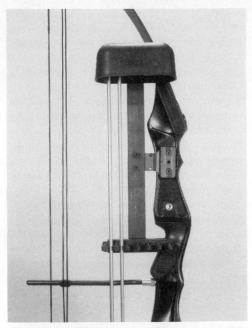

To be of value, a bow quiver must mount solidly. This PSE Q-D Quiver screws onto the riser handle so it will not rattle.

other components screw on. Check accessories before you buy to make sure they'll work together.

Size. Quiver size depends on usage. Many hunters who spend only a couple of hours each evening in a tree stand near home prefer relatively lightweight 4- or 6-arrow quivers. They don't need a warehouse full of arrows to get through an evening's hunt. In the West, where a day's hunting could take you far from a road, most hunters prefer 8-arrow quivers. That way they can carry 6 or 7 big-game arrows and a practice arrow or two for shooting throughout the day. Some even go with 12- or 16-arrow quivers so they can carry several "woods" for grouse as well as a generous supply of broadhead-tipped arrows.

screws to the bow, and others attach to the stabilizer hole. Some quivers are mounted semipermanently, but other solid quivers can be removed easily. Browning's Twist-Lock Quiver is as solid as a rock, yet it swivels to detach quickly. The Fred Bear quiver, made of steel rods, hasn't changed since the year one, and it continues to be one of the most solid and indestructible quivers on the market. It's held on by two easily removed screws.

On any quiver, the broadhead hood must be far enough from the shaft grippers to prevent the arrows from rattling. On most good quivers these are at least 15 inches apart, and on some they're 20 or more. They should fan out the ends of the arrows to separate the fletching.

In selecting a quiver and other components, make sure everything is compatible. You may not be able to mount a quiver, sight, and cable guard all on the same holes, especially if one has a dovetail mount, for example, and the

These Sagittarius Pegasus quivers attach under the limb bolts so they can't come loose or rattle. The model at left holds 8 arrows and the Magnum model at right carries 16.

Some hunters like hip quivers. This quality leather model has sheepskin lining to hold the arrows solidly and to prevent rattling.

Belt Quivers

Some hunters don't like shooting a bow with a quiver attached, so they look for alternatives, and one of these is a belt quiver. Most belt quivers ride on the hip with the fletching pointing back, but some ride in the middle of your back. Most belt quivers are made of leather or synthetic materials similar to leather.

The same criteria that apply to bow quivers apply to belt quivers. The broadheads must be fully protected, and for the sake of safety and quietness, the arrows must be held securely in individual grippers. The arrows also must be convenient and easy to remove when the time comes to shoot. Some hunters swear by hip quivers, but I don't like the arrows flopping around at my side, particularly in heavy cover.

Many target shooters use cylindrical hip quivers to hold several arrows loosely. These are great for the target range (as a hunter you need something like this to carry a bunch of target-tip arrows) but they're not for hunting.

Back Quivers

Back quivers and shoulder quivers shouldn't be confused. Several decades ago, most archers used shoulder quivers, and some traditional archers still use them today. These quivers have shortcomings that disqualify them for most serious hunting. They're basically open tubes, so the arrows can rattle together, which can be noisy and can dull broadheads.

And they can be dangerous. Recently in Colorado, a longbowman killed an elk and got a packer with horses to come in to retrieve his animal. As they were riding out, the archer's horse jumped a log and some arrows from the hunter's quiver fell to the ground, points up. The horse lurched again and the hunter fell off.

The shoulder quiver has been used by traditional archers for years. It's okay for carrying a bunch of spare arrows, but it has limitations for hunting.

Quiver

Quiver

A back quiver like this fully protects arrows, and it can double as a daypack. If you shoot long arrows, a back quiver can be excessively long, protruding below your rump and above your head.

Some modern back quivers are made to double as backpacks. Rancho Safari's Catquiver IV holds enough gear to serve as a bivouac pack as well as a quiver.

Right onto his own arrows. He died shortly afterward.

Again, to be safe and quiet, a quiver must hold arrows securely. Most modern back quivers fit like backpacks with two shoulder straps, and many also have a waist belt. The St. Charles back quiver has been around for years, and the Cat Quiver is a newer version of the back quiver.

Modern back quivers have foam-padded plates at each end. The broadheads are stuck into one plate and the nocks into the other. The ends of the quiver are just far enough apart to hold the arrows securely.

Back quivers have their strong points. They protect fletching from the elements, so if you shoot feathers, you don't have to worry about keeping them dry during wet weather. The back quiver holds the arrows in the middle of

your back where they're out of the way for hiking and crawling through brush. And many modern back quivers, such as the Cat Quivers III and IV, have a built-in pack so the quiver doubles as a hunting pack.

On the debit side, if you shoot real long arrows (like my 33-inchers), you might find the quiver longer than you prefer. That is, it could protrude above your head or down well below your beltline. That's not a problem with shorter arrows. Also, if it holds the arrows in place by pressure on both ends, then all your arrows must be near the same length. If you carry a blunt-tipped practice arrow that's shorter than the broadhead arrows, the quiver won't hold it tightly. With a back quiver, you may not be as fast on the draw as with a bow quiver.

373

R

RABBIT Hares and rabbits are commonly lumped together as "rabbits" by most hunters, but there are differences. Hares—jackrabbits, snowshoe hares, and European hares—are precocial (for details, see Hares); rabbits are born naked and with closed eyes. In contrast to the long ears and long legs of the hares, rabbits have relatively short ears and legs, and they scurry short distances into cover to hide from danger rather than running high speed into the open, as most hares do. Rabbits live in burrows or in nests enclosed in rocks, tree roots, or brush piles, opposed to the open forms of hares. Jackrabbits and cottontails often share the same desert country, but the jacks stay out on the open flats, while the cottontails hide in broken rims and rock slides above the flats.

Cottontail rabbits are found in just about every corner of the United States. The eastern cottontail has the widest distribution, ranging from the eastern seaboard west through the Plains states, and from Canada into Mexico. The mountain cottontail inhabits the entire intermountain West; the desert cottontail lives throughout all arid environments of the West; and the New England cottontail ranges from Maine south through the Appalachians. Several other rabbit species overlap with the cot-

tontails: the tiny pigmy rabbit lives in the arid Great Basin; brush rabbits reside in the rain forests along the Pacific Coast; and swamp and marsh rabbits live in the mid- and Deep South. These rabbits all have a similar appearance, with short ears, brown or grayish coats, and fluffy white tails. Many hunters lump them all together as "cottontails."

It's often said that cottontails are the most popular game animal in the United States. I can't verify or disprove that, but indeed they're fun to hunt with a bow and they're good eating. Rabbits are easiest to spot and hunt early and late in the day while they're feeding. During midday they brush up and hide, and you have to do some brush busting to kick them out. You'll rarely get good shots as they run, but they won't go far before they hide, and more often than not you can sneak on them and get a close shot. Learn to look for the shining brown eye, because that's the most visible part of a rabbit as it hides, peering from the brush.

In dense brambles and brush, Judo heads work well because they won't slip through the brush to be lost. In rocky, desert cottontail country, breaking arrows is more of a problem than losing them, so there I prefer rubber

Rabbits of one species or another live throughout the United States. This cottontail was taken in the oak forests of northern Missouri.

blunts, which will bounce off rocks and reduce bending and breaking of shafts. (For more details, see Small-Game Hunting.)

RANGE FINDER   See Trajectory.

RATTLING   Antler rattling, or horn rattling as I'll call it for simplicity, is one form of calling deer. It apparently originated in south Texas, or at least that's where it first gained popularity, and for years many hunters thought it would work only on Texas whitetails. Now hunters know that's not true. Rattling has proved deadly for whitetails from Montana to New Jersey to Alabama. A friend of mine in Idaho rattled in seven bucks during two days of hunting, five one day and two the next.

And rattling doesn't work just for whitetails. In Oregon, the only Pacific state with a black-

tail deer season during the November rut, bow-hunters have done very well rattling in black-tails. In western Oregon, the deer live in low-elevation brushy country where they stick to small territories, much as whitetails do. That probably explains why the same techniques work for both species.

Some hunters have rattled in mule deer, but this has never really caught on, probably because few states hold mule-deer seasons during the rut. Also, mule deer have different breeding habits from whitetails. Whitetail bucks establish small home ranges and will challenge invading bucks, but mule deer are migratory, and even during the rut they could be here today, gone tomorrow. They have no specific territory to defend.

Horns for Rattling

Choice of rattling horns is a favorite topic of disagreement. Some hunters say the antlers should be large, some say small; some say you should cut the tines off to prevent stabbing yourself, others say never do that because the horns won't sound natural; some say you should use antlers off the same side, and others say you should use opposing antlers. Frankly, I doubt that any of that makes a lot of difference. I'd say use average-size antlers, and smooth down the bases so they're comfortable to grip tightly. Drill a hole in each base and connect the antlers with a leather thong or cord.

Virtually all rattlers do agree on one thing—antlers should be unweathered. Shed antlers, bleached and weathered, don't make good rattling horns because they're porous and create a tinny sound. Use fresh, solid antlers. One company in Texas produces synthetic Rattlin' Horns that sound good and have been proven in the field.

Rattling Technique

When you rattle, grip the horns tightly to dampen the clinky sound. Real antlers are attached solidly to a buck's skull, and you want your phonies to sound like they are too.

In rattling, the idea is to simulate a fight between two bucks, and you can just about imagine what that would sound like. If you want some instruction, you can get good audio tapes with recorded sounds of bucks actually fighting. Bob McGuire of Tennessee, and Loren Butler at Mountain Scent and Bugle Manufacturing in Stevensville, Montana, produce good tapes on this subject.

Clash the antlers together forcibly and then grind and twist them and rattle them together for 30 seconds or so. That's about as long as two bucks would fight before breaking. During the rattling sequence, pound the butts of the antlers on the ground and rake brush around you. Bucks pushing each other around make lots of noise with their hooves as well as their antlers. Wait 5 to 10 minutes and repeat this sequence, and then wait another 10 minutes or more and repeat. Stay in one place at least 30 minutes. As in any calling, you can't predict how an animal will come in. Some bucks will come charging and nearly run you down, but more commonly they'll approach cautiously and may take 20 minutes sneaking in.

Don't be intimidated if you've never done this before and aren't sure you're making exactly the right sounds. You don't have to be a Ph.D. in deer behavior to rattle in bucks. In all calling circles, whether for elk, turkeys, predators, or whatever, a few hotshots would have you believe you can't call game if you're not a world-champion caller. That's hogwash.

One time I spotted a whitetail buck trotting across a weed field. This looked like a perfect chance to rattle in a buck, but I was turkey hunting at the time and had left my horns back in the car. So I grabbed the nearest antler at hand—an arrow from my quiver—and started "rattling" on the nearest object of resistance—my bow.

With the first clackety-clack, the buck stopped short and stared. I rattled again and he headed my way. At 60 yards he disappeared from sight into a shallow ravine, and at 30 he reappeared, bearing straight toward me. If I'd had an unused tag, that buck could have been in a world of hurt.

Conditions for Rattling

I don't suggest you can rattle in bucks consistently with such sloppy technique. I just want to make a point: calling ability isn't the whole answer. I consider other qualities far more important.

One is the confidence to believe it will work. Just like any other hunting method, rattling doesn't work every time you try it. Some hunters get discouraged and quit if they don't have instant success. Rest assured, it does work, so give it a fair trial.

And remember, circumstances must be right. Rattling works only during the rut. That's not to say it won't attract bucks, possibly out of curiosity, at other times, but you can't depend on it. That's because rattling simulates the sounds of two bucks fighting, and about the only time they really fight is during the rut, or more specifically, the breeding season when does are in estrus. Bucks do spar as soon as they shed the velvet from their antlers, but these sparring sessions are only to establish a heirarchy and they're not prompted by a doe in heat. During the breeding season, fights involve particular hot does, and that's probably why the sounds of fighting then attracts other bucks. In short, for rattling to work consistently, you've got to rattle during the breeding season, which lasts only about two weeks in most regions. (For details, see Whitetail Deer.)

Then, competition among bucks for does must be high, and that means a high ratio of bucks to does. (For details, see Question Number 4 in Planning a Hunt.) Among other reasons, bucks come to the sound of a fight to look for a receptive doe. In heavily hunted regions where does far outnumber bucks—say, where the buck/doe ratio is 10 bucks per 100 does—most bucks already have more does than they can service, so they have little reason to come to sounds of fighting bucks. For good rattling, the buck/doe ratio should be at least 20 bucks per 100 does, and 30/100 would be better. Bucks in areas of heavy competition will be aggressive and come in eagerly.

And, of course, you must scout to understand the territory of the dominant buck. I suppose you can walk through the woods, rattling randomly, hoping you're close to a buck, but you'll succeed only by luck in that case. Your chances are far higher if you scout to find the rubs and scrape line of a dominant buck. Then when you start rattling, you can feel confident a buck roams within hearing distance of your horns.

Choosing the Blind

Again, choosing a good location ranks above actual calling technique, and you must have a good blind where you can move and shoot without being detected. At the same time you must have visibility so you can see animals coming in. Remember that in many cases, suspicious bucks will circle downwind to get your scent, so pick a blind with an opening downwind so you can shoot at these sneaking critters.

Some hunters rattle from ground blinds. This hunter is using synthetic antlers called Rattlin' Horns.

Ground Blinds. One approach to rattling is to roam through the woods (always working into the wind, of course) much as you would in coyote hunting. You find a good blind location (for more details, see Predator Calling) where you're well hidden and have good visibility and shooting clearance. Wait a few minutes for things to settle down, and go through your rattling sequence. Stay in place at least 20 to 30 minutes before moving on to try a new location.

This method might be best suited to areas you don't know intimately. If you know the country contains good bucks but you don't know bucks' specific core areas, you could hunt this way to cover some ground until you make contact with deer. It also works in some Western mountains where storms can influence deer movements. In Oregon, for example, heavy snow during the rut could force deer to move a mile or more to lower elevations, so you might have to roam to relocate bucks from one trip to the next.

For hunting Oregon's blacktails, Rob Dunson modifies the technique a little. In the open oak forests of some winter ranges, deer are reasonably visible, so Dunson sneaks through the woods quietly, looking for bucks he thinks will respond to rattling. That's usually a lone buck traveling in search of does, and Dunson figures at least 70 percent of these will come to his rattling.

Dunson claimed his first good blacktail this way. He saw the buck at 80 yards so he hid and started rattling, and the buck came in so fast that Dunson was the one who got rattled and shot 6 inches over the deer's back. The animal ran off but stopped at 80 yards, and when Dunson rattled a second time, the buck came back and Dunson nailed him at 30 yards.

Never rattle until you're in a good position and ready to shoot. One buck may come in slowly but another might charge in recklessly, and you've got to be ready. That's another lesson Rob Dunson learned by experience. He saw a three-point buck, but the deer seemed so far away that Dunson figured he'd have time to get ready if the buck responded. So Dunson rat-

The problem with rattling on the ground is that a buck coming in can spot you at eye level. It's harder to get a shot in this situation than it would be if you were off the ground.

tled his horns without blinding in. The three-point paid no attention, but a four-point, unseen up to that point, came on the run and stopped at 15 yards broadside. Dunson's bow hung impotently at his side. Be ready when you rattle.

Tree Stands. The other method involves taking a stand in one place and rattling right there over a long period of time. Most hunters who do this use tree stands for the same reason they'd use tree stands in any other situation: the stand puts you up where you're less visible, and where you have a better view.

Charles Allen, doing research for his synthetic Rattlin' Horns, found the value of this. While Allen rattled from a ground blind, his cameraman sat in a tree stand to videotape the action. In eight days of filming, Allen saw 23 bucks he'd rattled up, but the cameraman, from his higher viewpoint, saw 36. Allen simply didn't see the other bucks that came in and detected him.

That same thing undoubtedly happens in many calling situations. A hunter on the ground can't get a broad perspective, and he's at eye level with game where they can see him. You can probably rattle in as many bucks if

From a tree stand, your view of incoming bucks is much better than from a ground blind, and up there you're less likely to be seen.

you're on the ground, but rattling them in and shooting them are far different. A tree stand provides by far your best opportunity for getting a good shot while rattling.

To rattle from a stand, plan to stay in one place for several hours. Get into the stand well before daylight if you're hunting in the morning, or early in the afternoon for an evening hunt. Wait awhile for the woods to settle down, and then begin your rattling sequence. Continue to repeat it every half hour or so for several hours. Don't get down; rattle from that one spot. This method works best if you know your country and the habits of bucks there. If you've scouted well and know you're in the territory of a good buck, you can feel confident he'll eventually hear your rattling and come to investigate.

RECOVERING GAME   See Trailing.

RELEASE   The term "release" refers to the process of letting go of a bowstring. Formally this is called the loose, but that term is rarely used among American bowhunters.

The moment of release is one of the major elements in shooting form. A clean release assures that the bowstring, and thus the arrow, gets off to a good start. A sloppy release virtually guarantees a bad-flying arrow. (For details, see Shooting Basics.)

Release Methods

Generally, there are two methods of release: live and dead. Some archers refer to a live release as a power release. With this method, you come to full draw and firmly anchor in as you would with any shooting technique. Then you continue to pull with the back, increasing tension on the bowstring until the string slips from your fingers. When the string slips away, your hand moves back sharply. That is, you have a "live" string hand. It should come back straight along your face and stop by your neck, although some shooters exaggerate this power movement and jerk their hands well behind their heads.

With a dead release, you anchor your hand firmly against the side of your face, and then you let the string slip away with little or no back tension. After the release, your hand stays firmly planted against your face. It doesn't move; it's "dead."

Most archery instructors teach a live release, because it potentially yields a smoother release and greater arrow speed. With your hand actually moving back before the string leaves your fingers, the string is released even with the anchor point. That is, it does not creep forward before clearing your fingers. With the dead release, in contrast, your hand doesn't move back, and in order for the string to slip away, your fingers must straighten. That allows the string to creep forward before clearing your fingers, which, in essence, shortens your draw length slightly.

Using a chronograph, I've tried to gauge the effects of a live versus a dead release. Granted, I don't normally shoot with a dead release, so I may not have perfected the technique, but I do think my testing at least hints at the facts. These tests were done with an overdraw-equipped PSE Mach II. Using a live release my arrow speed averaged 216 feet per second. Using a dead release, average arrow speed dropped to 214.3 fps. The variation in arrow speed reflects the fact that with the dead release, my fingers followed the string just enough to shorten draw length slightly.

RELEASE AID   Most hunters refer to methods for drawing and holding a bowstring as a "release." In a general sense, any device used for that purpose could be called a release aid, but strictly speaking, most bowhunters use this term to apply to mechanical release aids. A person who doesn't use a release aid "shoots with fingers."

Shooting with Fingers

Shooting Glove. Years ago, most American bowhunters shot with leather shooting gloves that have individual stalls for the three shooting fingers and a wrist strap to hold the glove snugly on the hand. A leather shooting glove is durable and is always in place, ready for

Traditionally hunters used shooting gloves with three finger stalls and a wrist strap to hold the glove in place. This Sagittarius Pony Hide glove assures as smooth a release as you'll get with a glove.

action, so it's fast and convenient. Many traditional archers still prefer shooting gloves to other types of finger protection.

Shooting gloves do have drawbacks, however. After repeated shooting, the stalls tend to groove and the string can't slip smoothly off your fingers. Also, because your fingers sit in individual stalls they can operate independently of each other, and it's tough to get them to slip off the string identically shot after shot.

Because gloves are made of leather, they get soggy and change consistency in wet weather, and in hot weather they make your fingers sweat, which can cause problems. I remember drawing on the first deer I ever killed. It was a blistering day and I'd hiked several miles. When the time to shoot finally arrived, I was sweating hard, and the finger stalls of my shooting glove had got soggy, and slippery, with sweat. As I started to draw my bow, the string pulled the shooting glove right off my fingers. I had to let up and slip the glove back onto my fingers. Somehow the buck stood still for all this nonsense and I finally got off a shot and killed the buck.

Finger Tab. Nevertheless, that incident soured me on shooting gloves and since then I've far preferred a tab. The growing popularity of tabs and their extensive use among competitive archers attests to their accuracy and reliability.

Most finger tabs are held in place only by a ring of plastic, rubber, or leather around the middle finger so your fingers can breathe, which eliminates the problem of sweat slippage. You can rotate a tab to the back of your finger so it's out of the way for other tasks, and in cold weather you can slip a tab on over gloves and shoot with no major adjustment (with a shooting glove, you have to cut out the fingers of your warm gloves). And some of the stiffer tabs tend to unify the fingers into a single unit so you don't have the problem of getting all three of your string fingers to do the same thing at the same time.

Tabs are made from a variety of materials. Pony-hide or calf-hair tabs are super-slick and assure a good release. The only problem is that the hair eventually wears off and you end up with bare leather. You can continue shooting that way, but I don't think it's smart. By shooting through a chronograph, I've compared the performance of tabs at various stages of wear, and worn hair tabs consistently deliver arrows two to three feet per second slower than new, unworn tabs.

For that reason, I prefer smooth leather tabs. They might not be quite as slick to start with, but at least they maintain a consistent surface. Any leather tab will develop a groove

Today, many hunters prefer finger tabs to shooting gloves. The Saunders Super Slick tab shown here is made of plastic so it's impervious to weather and doesn't groove as badly as leather. Most tabs will fit over tight-fitting wool gloves.

after long use, and the groove can affect the quality of your release.

Some tabs are made of plastic, and I think these show great promise. The Saunders Fab Tab, for example, consists of two layers of slick plastic sandwiched around a felt pad. The plastic doesn't change when it gets wet, it doesn't groove as badly as leather, and surface doesn't change with use. The plastic assures good arrow speed and consistency from one shot to the next.

One good feature on any tab is a finger spacer that reduces arrow pinching. Some shooters pinch the arrow so hard at full draw they put a noticeable bend in the arrow shaft. The instant they release, the arrow recoils to straighten out and it's oscillating before it even passes the rest, which almost guarantees bad arrow flight. It can even affect arrow speed. Again, chronograph testing revealed some

A finger spacer as shown here can prevent your pinching the nock.

interesting facts. Shooting with a Sagittarius pony-hide tab, I found that my arrows averaged 195.7 feet per second. With an identical tab minus the finger spreader, they averaged 194 fps. Apparently, without the spreader I pinch my arrows hard enough to affect arrow flight.

It's important to draw so you don't torque the shaft at full draw. That's why some hunters prefer shooting with three fingers under the arrow (for details, see Apache Draw) and why others prefer a release aid to fingers (see below). If you choose to shoot with a conventional split-finger hold and a finger tab, try a tab with a spacer that fits between your index and middle fingers.

You can condition a tab to keep it slick. For this purpose, many shooters carry a small powder pouch and occasionally dust their tabs. Saunders makes a silicone-based Friction Fighter that makes the plastic tab slicker than ever, and it can be used on any kind of tab or glove.

Pros and Cons of Finger Shooting. Shooting with fingers offers some advantages over shooting with a mechanical release, primarily simplicity and reliability. With fingers, you can feel the string, and you can nock and shoot an arrow quickly. I've talked to many release-aid shooters who've blown good opportunities because they couldn't get the release on the string fast enough or because they accidentally triggered the release before they were ready to shoot. These problems are unlikely when shooting with your fingers.

Conceivably, you could lose your finger tab or glove, but that's not likely since it's attached to your hand in some way, and even if you do lose it you can, in a pinch, shoot with bare fingers. If you lose a release aid—and I've talked to more than one hunter who has— you're in a bind.

Shooting with a Mechanical Release Aid
Styles of Release Aids. It seems like almost as many companies make release aids as make buck scents, and you can choose from hundreds of models.

The concho-style release aid has a long stem that you grasp in your hand while shooting. This Jim Dougherty Fail Safe release has a trigger guard and safety mechanism much like those on guns.

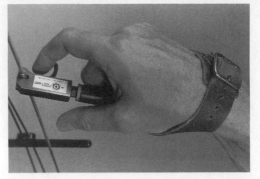

The wrist-strap release has a strap that wraps around the wrist; you hold the weight of the bow with that strap rather than with your fingers. The Barner release aid shown here has a very smooth trigger pull, but it has no safety mechanism.

First comes basic form. In the concho style, the release head is attached to a long stem you grip in the palm of your hand. The wrist-strap release, as the name implies, attaches to your wrist with a strap; as you pull, your hand can be wide open and all pulling pressure comes at the wrist.

Most concho and wrist-strap release aids have a trigger very similar to a rifle trigger, and you can squeeze off a shot just as you would with a gun. Some have an exposed trigger with no guard around it. These scare me a little because the trigger conceivably could be bumped and released at the wrong moment. Others, such as the Dougherty Fail Safe, have a full trigger guard, and the Fail Safe also has a safety mechanism much like the safety on a gun. Even with the bow at full draw, you can't pull the trigger until you release the safety, and that feature puts me a little more at ease.

A third style of release has a basic "T" configuration; releases are held in the fingers with no strap or grip handle. Some T-style release aids are held vertically, others horizontally, and some have a rotating head so they can be held either way. Triggering method also varies, and some are made to be triggered with the thumb, others with the little finger. Some models can be triggered either way. Triggering method is strictly a matter of personal choice. For horizontally held releases (which place your thumb against your cheek) I personally prefer the finger trigger. With vertically held models, I prefer a thumb release mechanism.

Release aids attach to the bowstring by one of two methods. Rope releases have a loop of nylon cord that hooks around the string. These are used almost universally by target archers. Most bowhunters prefer release aids that attach to the bowstring with a solid pin because they're faster to use.

Most release aids have fine adjustments for trigger tension. If possible, try various release aids before buying one because they vary

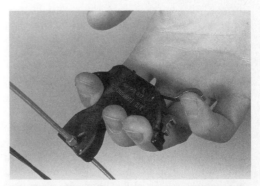

The Golden Eagle Bowhunter is one example of the T-shaped finger-held release aid. This model is triggered with the little finger.

Some release aids are held horizontally, as Gale Cavallin demonstrates here.

greatly in terms of trigger pull. Some are rough and others are ultra-smooth, and a rough trigger release can definitely affect your accuracy.

Pros and Cons of Release Aids. The less contact you have with the bowstring, the easier it is to release the string without throwing it off. For that reason, the release aid comes close to perfection, because it grips the string at only one point, and it also eliminates string pinch and torquing of the arrow at full draw. For these reasons, a mechanical release virtually guarantees a smooth release of the bowstring.

A mechanical release lets the bowstring go virtually straight toward the bow, and arrow paradox is somewhat less than it is when releasing with your fingers, which push the bowstring to the side. As a result, off any bow at a given poundage, you can shoot lighter-spined arrows with a release aid than with fingers. That's why many speed-conscious bowhunters, who want to shoot the lightest possible arrows at maximum poundage, shoot with release aids.

Release aids aren't foolproof, however. You still must use good form with a steady bow arm and good follow through (for details, see Shooting Basics), and you must release smoothly. It is possible to get a rough release with a mechanical aid, especially if you flinch—and you will flinch if your release aid has a rough trigger pull. That's why it's important to get one that works smoothly.

Compared to fingers, they're relatively slow

to use, and like any other mechanical device, they can break, get misplaced or otherwise give you problems. A release aid does allow you to shoot a short bow at a long draw length without string pinch (a problem you'd experience with fingers), but at the same time it wears bowstrings faster at the point of attachment. Release aids also produce more bow noise than do fingers, and you'll notice a definite slapping sound when shooting with a release.

Setting Up for Release Shooting. A mechanical release places great upward pressure on the arrow nock at full draw, so the nocking point on your bowstring must be very secure. To hold a clamp-on nock, simply place another nock directly above it and clamp it down tight. Or you can wrap dental floss or serving thread on the string above the nock point to keep it from sliding up. You also might want to place another clamp-on nock point below the release

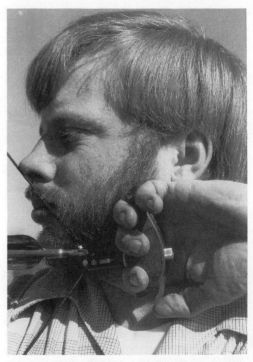

Others are held vertically, or they have rotating heads so they can be used in any position.

This is one way of setting up a bowstring for use with a release aid. Double nock locators above the release prevent slippage, and with a nock locator below the string, you can lock the release onto the string and it won't slide down.

aid. That way you can hook the release onto the string and carry it in that position, and it won't slide down the string.

Incidentally, if you've never shot with a release aid before, I'd suggest that before proceeding further you equip your bow with a wrist strap. Until you get used to it, the release will go off unexpectedly, and you'll drop your bow. I've bounced more than one bow across my basement floor that way.

RHODE ISLAND This tiny state contains 1,214 square miles. Basically, the topography is flat. Oak and beech forests cover nearly 80 percent of the state, with maple forests in scattered wet lowlands. In the south end, potatoes and turf grass are major crops. In a state 30 miles wide and 50 long, with a human population of 1 million, hunting opportunity is necessarily limited. However, Rhode Island does have public hunting on 38,000 acres of state-owned lands, and the Division of Fish and Wildlife plans to buy additional lands for hunting. Little private land in Rhode Island is leased for hunting, but law requires written permission from the owner.

Big Game
Whitetail Deer. Rhode Island has an estimated 2,400 whitetail deer. Average density is 10 to 20 deer per square mile, but on Prudence Island, it may be as high as 70 per square mile.

An average of 1,073 bowhunters kill an average of 97 deer annually, with a high in 1982 of 104, about half bucks, half does. The archery season runs from October 1 until the end of January with a limit of one deer, either sex. In addition, there are shotgun and muzzleloader seasons, and a hunter can take one deer by each method, so the legal yearly bag limit could be as high as three.

Contact. Department of Environmental Management, 83 Park Street, Providence, RI 02903.

RISER This center section of a bow consists of handle and attachment positions for the limbs. Most bowhunters call it the handle or handle riser.

ROCKCHUCK See Marmot.

ROYAL This term refers to a cuplike formation, or crown, formed by three or more points at the end of an elk's antlers. Royal formations are fairly common among Roosevelt elk, but they're uncommon on the antlers of Rocky Mountain elk.

Some hunters also refer to a six-point bull elk as a royal. Along the same lines, they call a seven-point bull an imperial and an eight-point a monarch. These terms aren't common among elk hunters. Most hunters simply refer to a bull with six points to the side as a six-point, seven to the side as a seven-point, and so forth.

RUT This term comes from a Latin word meaning "to roar," referring, I suppose, to the roaring of red deer stags during the breeding period. The term *rut* generally applies to the estrus period of deer, elk, and other mammals. It's when females are in heat.

Most hunters expand the term to encompass all rut-related activities. Whitetail deer bucks, for example, start making scrapes, a breeding-related activity, about a month before does actually come into heat, and most archers who hunt these scrapes would say they're "hunting the rut." The same goes for elk hunting. In preparation for the rut, bulls start bugling in late August, even though cows won't actually come into heat until mid-September, and hunters can use bugling to their advantage well before actual breeding starts.

For many big-game species, the actual breeding period, when females come into heat, lasts about two weeks. Most hunters refer to this as the peak of the rut. In most latitudes, that period for whitetail and mule deer takes place the last two weeks in November, and for elk the last two weeks in September. Many hunters consider the peak of the rut the ideal time to hunt, although any rut-related activity before or after the actual estrus period can make trophy animals abnormally vulnerable.

Some hunters think weather conditions affect rut timing, but that's not true. Weather may affect the amount of daytime activity, but it doesn't advance or retard the breeding season. The rut is triggered by what scientists call photoperiod, a $10 word for daylight length. Shortening days trigger a hormonal response in animals, and this triggers the rut. Since the days shorten at the same rate every year, the rut occurs, in any given latitude, at the same time every year. (For more details, see species listings such as Elk, Whitetail Deer, etc.)

S

SAFETY Reading about safety is a little like listening to preaching—it may be good for us but it's not real exciting. Nevertheless, thrilled or not, we should all give safety much thought. It can be a life-and-death matter.

Equipment Safety

Consider, for example, what happened to a bowhunter in the mountains of Colorado. He was a longbow specialist and, true to tradition, he carried his arrows loose in a shoulder quiver. As his horse jumped a log, the arrows in his quiver fell to the ground, points up, and with the horse's next jump the archer fell off directly onto his own arrows. He died there before medical help could arrive.

A quiver must hold arrows securely. Shoulder quivers filled with arrows might look romantic and all that, but old-time archers used them only because they hadn't thought of anything better. Then along came Fred Bear with his bow quiver and Glenn St. Charles with a reliable back quiver. With these ideas and the many improvements of recent years, the need for open quivers has vanished. Whether you use a back, hip, or bow quiver, it must hold arrows tight. If you can jerk arrows out easily, the quiver isn't doing its job. In going through heavy timber, I've had branches jerk arrows from my quiver. I've never got hurt as a result,

but the possibility exists, so I always keep fresh rubber grippers on my quiver to hold arrows solidly.

It should go without saying that any quiver should have a hood large enough to cover the broadheads completely. Quivers that leave broadheads exposed have just about passed from the scene, but you still see one occasionally. The only suitable place for a quiver like that is the trash can. One fall on those broadheads could end a hunt—and a life—in a hurry.

Equally dangerous is carrying a bow with an arrow nocked on the string. An arrow should be nocked only when you're ready to shoot or when you're on stand and can use a bracket to hold your bow at the ready. In the West, I've seen hunters hike for miles with arrows nocked, hoping for a quick shot. That's insane. One acquaintance of mine drove a broadhead deep into his thigh as a result of that practice. You can't predict when you might stumble or fall, so *never* nock an arrow until you're ready to shoot.

Check your arrows regularly, particularly during practice. A slight crease in an aluminum arrow isn't dangerous (for details, see Arrow Care), but any crack is. Never shoot a cracked arrow, whether it's made of glass, wood, or aluminum. Throw it away.

If you shoot a compound bow, check regularly to make sure all screws are tight. In particular, check the axle keepers before every shooting session. One hunter had a compound bow fly apart in his face because a keeper had come off and the axle slipped from its hole upon release. Repair badly frayed strings or damaged cables immediately.

Look Before You Shoot

Surrounding an animal might be a good way to get game, but it's also a good way to get killed. Several hunters surrounded a herd of Roosevelt elk in the junglelike vegetation of western Oregon, and when one of them shot, he accidentally hit another hunter on the far side and killed him. In another similar incident, two men were hunting a bugling bull elk. They decided to split up and work the bull from separate directions. They got totally separated and the one hunter didn't see his partner for more than three hours, so when the bull came within range the hunter didn't give his partner much thought. He overshot the bull and hit his partner, who was standing 100 yards downhill. The partner died shortly after.

Always keep track of your partners, and if you're in doubt about their location, don't shoot. The potential for accidents is especially great in calling situations like elk bugling, where two or more hunters, possibly unbeknown to each other, are working the same animal. If you suspect at all that another hunter is moving toward the animal you're after, back off. That's better than getting shot. Or shooting someone else.

Other Thoughts on Safety

Knife Safety. One evening I'd killed a bull elk. Five miles of ungodly terrain separated me from camp, where my hunting partner was sleeping at the moment, and another five miles separated camp from the road. To put it another way, I was alone and help was a long way away. For taking care of game, I was carrying a folding fillet knife, which works great for skinning and boning an animal. But as I reached far up inside that elk to cut guts and lungs free, working strictly by feel, I suddenly realized

how easy it would be to slash myself with that knife, and how quickly I could bleed to death with no one to help me. To say the least, I proceeded with caution.

And that's the point. One slip of a knife could be your end. A friend of mine was gutting a deer when he glanced down and saw his wrist coated with blood. At first he thought it was the deer's blood, but then he could see it was spurting out and that it was his own blood. He had felt no pain, but he'd somehow cut his wrist to the bone. He grabbed the wound with his other hand to close off the artery and ran to a nearby farmhouse for help. He was rushed to a hospital and survived the incident, but what if he'd been far from help, as I was on that elk hunt? The outcome might have been different.

Before gutting, open up an animal as far as possible so you have room to work comfortably, not awkwardly. And always, always cut away from yourself, especially if you're trying to sever tough tendons. When you're applying pressure, one slight slip could plant a knife in your own anatomy. I also recommend using a fairly small blade, especially for internal work like gutting where you can't see what you're doing. That fillet knife I carried was great for taking care of an animal in a hurry, but it was dangerous. A three- to four-inch blade is plenty big enough to take care of any kind of game.

Tree Stand Safety. Without question, some of the most severe bowhunting injuries result from careless tree-stand use. Every year many hunters are either killed or paralyzed as a result of falls from tree stands. Always use a safety belt, and pull gear up to your stand with a rope once you're securely in the stand. Never try to carry up gear as you climb. (For more details on stand safety, see Stand Hunting.)

SASKATCHEWAN This province, with about 250,000 square miles, can be broken into four zones, working south to north: grasslands and prairies along the U.S. border; farmlands, where vast grainfields and potholes breed waterfowl by the millions; then the parklands, which consist of rolling hills, vast aspen and conifer forests, intermixed with ranch and farmlands and numerous lakes; and the northern half of the province, a land of endless forest wilderness. The terrain throughout Saskatchewan can be described as flat to rolling hills. Nonresidents must hire guides to hunt most big game, although there are exceptions.

Big Game

Deer. An estimated 300,000 to 400,000 whitetails live throughout 60 percent of the province, and 50,000 to 60,000 mule deer occupy the southern end. About 2,000 bowhunters pursue deer in Saskatchewan each fall. Few data are kept on archery harvest, but it appears archers have about 10 percent success. Special archery seasons are held in September and rifle seasons in early October, but these are open to Saskatchewan residents only. Additional general seasons in November allow residents from other Canadian provinces to hunt in the southern zones. Nonresident aliens (outside Canada) may hunt deer only in the northern forest zones during November and December seasons.

The overall record whitetail, taken in 1983, scored 204⁶/₈ points, and the record nontypical, also killed in 1983, scored 254. The province record mule deer scored 199²/₈, and the record nontypical mule deer, 282²/₈. Without question, Saskatchewan leads the way for trophy whitetails with nearly 12 percent of the total listings in the Boone and Crockett record book. Unfortunately, nonresident alien hunters are not allowed to hunt agricultural zones where most of the whoppers live. They can hunt deer in the forest zone, and no guide is required.

Black Bears. Saskatchewan has gained a reputation for big whitetail deer, but its reputation for big bears isn't far behind. In some areas bears have become overabundant and the limit is two, and a number of bears large enough to make the Boone and Crockett record book have been taken in recent years. The province holds both spring and fall seasons.

Moose. These animals are abundant throughout all the forest fringe region and northern forests covering roughly the northern half of the province. Nonresident aliens must hire a guide to hunt moose legally. Seasons range from September into December, depending on area.

Caribou. Barren-ground caribou inhabit the extreme northeastern corner, but these may be hunted only by residents of that region. Woodland caribou live throughout the forested northern region; nonresidents must hunt with a guide.

Other Game. The province also has small populations of elk and antelope, but these animals are reserved for residents only.

Contact. Saskatchewan Parks and Renewable Resources, 3211 Albert Street, Regina, SK S4S-5W6.

SCENTS The use of scents in hunting may generate more disagreement among bowhunters than any other topic. Some hunters say scents are a joke, and others swear vehemently that scents work wonders.

The truth probably lies somewhere between. For those who have no faith in them, scent products will never work because those hunters won't give them a fair trial. Scents probably do work for those hunters who believe in them because they select conditions and make the preparations required to make the scents work.

The fact is, scents and odors must be taken seriously by hunters. To humans, who are virtually odor-blind, it's hard to conceive, but smell is a major form of communication among big-game animals, and they can attract or repel each other with their odors. And it's no secret that most big-game animals instantly recognize the smell of man and flee from it. For these reasons it's important to use scents wisely to attract game, and to do everything possible to keep animals from smelling you.

Scents come in three general categories: coverup or masking scents, sex attractors, and food scents.

Masking Scents

Undoubtedly the chief hunting bugaboo is human scent. In most cases when a deer hears or sees you, it will investigate until it confirms your presence through one of its other senses. But if it smells you, it doesn't wait for secondary confirmation; it takes off immediately. As Loren Butler, one authority on the use of scents, put it, "Sense of smell is an animal's only independent means of alarm. That's why odor is such a headache for hunters." (That's true for most big game, but maybe not for all. Antelope and bighorn sheep, for example, rely heavily on their eyes for defense, and even when they do smell you, they'll often stare until their eyes confirm what their noses have suggested.)

Sweat causes the major problem for hunters. Sweat itself is odorless, but as soon as it surfaces on the skin, bacteria go to work on it, and bacterial action creates odor. As Butler explained, odor is physical substance, made up of free-floating molecules; it has mass and can be measured. Picture it as invisible smoke. That image clarifies why you want to stay downwind of animals. If wind blows from game animals toward you, they simply can't smell you. The idea that a deer or elk has a nose keen enough to smell you from the upwind side is a myth. If they smell you from upwind, it's because an eddy of wind has carried your scent to them.

Obviously, then, the first and most important step in preventing an animal's smelling you is to understand wind currents and to use them to your advantage. You can learn a lot about wind by watching smoke. You'll see that natural features dissipate smoke, and they do the same to scents. A ledge may throw it straight into the air, and the smoke will scatter more quickly over trees and broken topography than over open ground. In open sagebrush, I've had mule deer smell me nearly three quarters of a mile away. If you're hunting in a tree stand, you may find that your tree creates a vortex on the off-wind side that sucks your scent right to the ground.

Using the Wind. Hunters often ask whether I use coverup scents, and my general answer is "No." That's because I hunt most often from a backpacking camp. When rain or snow are falling every day and the air temperature is 30 degrees and the biggest thing I've got to heat water in is a tin cup and the nearby creek is running at 40 degrees and I've got only one set

The wind offers the only true guarantee that you won't be smelled—provided you can keep it in your favor. The Nirk Wind Tester, which shoots out a small puff of powder, is just one of many ways to gauge wind direction.

of clothing, I find it a little tough to keep my clothes and body clean and pretty soon I smell worse than a barnyard bull.

Under those conditions, no masking scent is powerful enough to cover my BO, so I don't bother. I just try to keep downwind of the animals I'm hunting. My beard makes a good wind detector, but I also use a butane lighter occasionally to check faint air currents. The Nirk Wind Tester and similar products shoot out a small puff of powder that indicates the slightest breeze, and some hunters tie a duck feather onto their bows as a wind indicator. Monitoring the breeze like this, you can position yourself to stay downwind and in most cases can get within good bow range without being smelled.

If that were always possible, of course, human scent would be no problem. Unfortunately, winds are fickle and can swirl and blow in all directions at once, it sometimes seems. If that's the case on a backcountry hunt, where I can do little to reduce my own smell, I just back off and leave the animals alone until conditions improve.

In other situations, however, it's possible to deodorize yourself significantly, and you can use masking scents to your advantage. When I'm hunting from a big camp or hunting where I can bathe and wash my clothes, then I do use

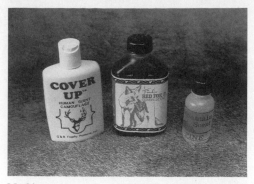

Masking scents come in three general types: non-natural scents that "confuse" an animal's sense of smell; natural animal scents such as red fox urine; and natural plant extracts such as pine scent.

masking scents. The idea behind a masking scent is to flood an area with an odor that will disguise human scent, and the possibilities fall into three categories.

Plant Aromas. Plant extracts such as pine, juniper, sage, cedar, and hemlock are supposed to make you smell like the native flora. Along with these, or in place of commercial extracts, many hunters use plants from their hunting areas to perfume their clothes. They seal the clothes in a plastic bag along with crushed sage or juniper leaves, or they grind fir needles into their clothing.

Animal Odors. Hunters have used skunk musk for years and many companies sell it commercially. Skunk odor gets mixed reviews, however, because some hunters say deer avoid it, not necessarily because deer are afraid of skunks but because they instinctively know a skunk puts up a smoke screen when it's threatened, and that could signal danger for the deer as well as the skunk. Red fox urine is now more commonly used among whitetail deer hunters, and many swear by it.

Some hunters use pure deer urine as a coverup scent, and as an attractor (attractor scents are discussed below). Jim Martin takes every opportunity to collect urine from deer. When he or someone in his party kills a deer, Martin sucks all the urine from the deer's bladder with

a hypodermic needle and stores the urine in a plastic bottle for later use as a coverup.

For elk hunting, you can buy straight elk urine for the same purpose, or you can use natural elk scents. Many hunters look for spots where elk have urinated, and then they rub the urine mud on their clothes, or they scoop it into a sock and tie the sock to their belt or pack. Also, many elk hunters, when they kill a rutting bull, cut the ripe-smelling belly patch from the bull and wear it around their waist to mask their scent. It looks like a cummerbund, but it probably wouldn't win any favors at a black-tie party.

Nonnatural Odors. Some hunters swear by coverup scents that imitate nothing native to their hunting areas. Examples are Jim Martin's Deer Insurance and Russell Hull's Cover Up. Most of these have a vanilla base along with other "secret" ingredients. I know some hunters who simply douse themselves with straight vanilla extract. These masking scents aren't formulated to represent any natural plant or animal. Rather they "confuse" a deer's sense of smell so the animal can't distinguish the human odor.

The principle seems fallacious because the foreign smell of the coverup itself seemingly would spook deer, but apparently it doesn't. Jim Martin said, "I used it extensively before

Some coverup scents consist of pure plant extracts. These from Mountain Scent and Bugle are made from trees that grow in various kinds of big-game country. Choose plant scents to match the area you're hunting.

These masking scents represent no natural odors. Their aroma covers up your human smell but does not alarm deer.

In the late 1960s, Butler experimented with 122 hounds and retrievers. He found that these dogs could recognize their owners by smell at ranges of 225 to 310 yards. He said the noses of dogs and most big game are comparable, a point he's tested hundreds of times in the field. In one standard test, he puts 10 to 15 drops of sweat in a sealed container and conceals it on the west side of a field where wind is blowing from the west. He waits until a herd of animals comes into the field. Then he opens the container by remote radio control as he watches from a distance. That amount of sweat, a fraction of what would build up on your clothes during a day of hunting, consistently spooks deer and elk out to 300 yards.

Animals' noses not only pick up minute odors at long range, but they can sort out odors as well. "With the right apparatus, you can block several frequencies of radio waves," Butler said. "But there are channels within that range you can't block. It's the same with scents. Animals can smell through strong scents, because some smells have different chemistry ranges. Skunk scent, for example, can block odors within its chemistry range, but it can't block all odors. These are the smells a deer notices, even when you're covered with skunk scent."

This doesn't mean that masking scents won't work. It simply points out that they're not a panacea and that they must be used right. Remember first that body odor is cumulative. The longer you go without a bath, the stronger you smell, and at some point you begin to smell bad enough that no kind of scent will mask your odor.

That point varies, depending on how much you're sweating and how often you can wash your clothes and body. In his testing with dogs, Butler had hound owners get as clean as possible, and then apply a good masking scent. For the first two or three hours, during which the owners didn't exercise to work up a sweat, hounds had to get within 20 to 30 feet to smell their owners. After four hours, the distance increased to 50 to 70 feet. From that time on, distance increased rapidly until dogs could smell their owners out to 300 yards.

putting it on the market, and several instances convinced me it works. One time while hunting mule deer in Colorado I'd put Deer Insurance on my clothes. Some deer walked within mere feet of me, straight downwind. They had to be getting my wind but they never spooked, so apparently the coverup was doing the job."

Making Masking Scents Work. There's no question that masking scents can help, if they are used under the right conditions, but, as Loren Butler said, it's possible to overrate their value because we judge scents from a human point of view. Skunk smell, for example, is so noxious that it would seemingly drown out all other smells.

"That's not necessarily true," Butler said. "Compared to animals, humans are odor-blind. Our noses have about 10 million olfactory receptors; most big-game animals' noses have several hundred million."

"No masking scent in the world will cover up a 24-hour accumulation of BO," Butler said.

Keeping Clean. Obviously the bottom line is cleanliness. Use a nonscented soap to wash yourself and your clothes. You can get nonperfumed, nonallergenic soap from drugstores that works well for this purpose. And some companies make soaps especially for hunters, such as Tink's Non-Scent Soap, and another called Earth Soap.

Baking soda also serves as a good deodorant. In camp I commonly wash my clothes with baking soda and it really takes out the odor. You can also sprinkle some baking soda under your arms as a body deodorant. Cornstarch mixed with the soda makes the soda a little less abrasive.

If you're hunting from a camp, keep your hunting clothes outside the tents so they don't pick up the smells of frying bacon, gasoline, and other human odors. After each day of hunting, wash them or at least hang them out to air. After they've aired, crush native vegetation into the clothes or sprinkle some coverup scent on them and seal them in a plastic bag so scent fumes will pervade the clothing. Cloth fibers retain scent well, and scent applied this way will last the better part of a day.

You can also get scent dispensers that clip onto your clothing and scent pads that strap onto your boots. The boot pads are useful for covering up a scent trail when walking to and from a tree stand.

Wherever possible, wear clothing that will reduce human scent. While working with scrapes, pruning, or climbing into tree stands, most experienced whitetail hunters wear rubber gloves to seal in odor from their hands, and they wear rubber boots to minimize foot odor in the hunting area.

As I said earlier, sweat is the chief source of human odor, so obviously the best line of defense is to avoid sweating. In mountain hunting that's impossible, and for that reason I'd say masking scents are of marginal value. In stand hunting, however, sweating presents no major problem, so I'd say without question that masking scents have greatest value in hunting from stands, or in still-hunting where you never move fast enough to work up a sweat.

Sexual Attractor Scents

Many hunters question the value of buck lures and so-called doe-in-heat scents, and I suspect that's because they question the contents. Companies that sell buck lures say the lures are made of deer urine taken from estrus does. That's probably true—I've never analyzed any scents to prove it one way or the other—but actually the point is irrelevant. The

In order for masking scents to work, you and your clothes must be relatively odor-free. Washing your clothes and body in nonperfumed soap like Tink's Non-Scent Camo Soap and in baking soda is a good starting point.

Attractor scents have long been sold for deer hunting, but they're now used in hunting many kinds of animals. Buck Stop is one company that sells attractors for elk, bear, and moose.

question is, do they work? If they do, who cares what they're made of?

And I'd say unequivocally that they do. But just as with masking scents, they must be used correctly. First, that means during the rut. Most attractors are made to attract rutting bucks, and they have marginal value at other times. Then they must be used in the right place. You can't just sprinkle some buck lure on the ground and expect it to attract bucks from all around. You have to put it where bucks are looking for hot does.

And, finally, you can't expect great results under wrong conditions. If you try buck lures once or twice on cold, dry, calm days when scent dissipates rapidly, or during heavy rain that washes scent from the air, chances are you won't see much response. Animals can't smell

You can buy many commercial deer attractors, but you can also collect your own. With a hypodermic needle, you can extract urine directly from the bladder of a deer; it works well as a coverup and attractor.

well under those conditions. The best conditions are warm and reasonably humid, along with a breeze that wafts the scent some distance through the woods. The fact is, scents will work better some days than others, simply because animals can smell them better.

The proliferation of scent companies alone says something about the value of deer lures. Selling scents has become big business, as you can see from glancing through any outdoors magazine, and all these companies couldn't survive if lures were a total sham.

But more important, many successful white-tail hunters use buck lures as a regular part of their hunting scheme. Jim Dougherty, a famed bowhunter who has taken game all over North America, is one among many who verifies the value of attractor scents. "I've used them all, and at least two brands absolutely work," Dougherty said. "I used to wear this stuff in pads on the bottoms of my boots as I walked to my tree stand, but I've quit that because I've had deer that were following my trail run up to my tree so fast I didn't have time to shoot. And I don't like to shoot straight down at them."

Jim Martin has had similar experiences with commercial buck lures, as well as urine he's collected himself. As mentioned earlier, he uses a hypodermic needle to extract urine from freshly killed deer, either bucks or does. Once he got eight ounces of urine from a buck killed by one member of his party. The next morning Martin coated his rubber boots with the urine before walking to his stand, and then he sprinkled more urine around below his tree stand. Pretty soon a little buck came sniffing along Martin's trail and followed it right to the tree. Martin didn't want to shoot the forked horn so he just watched, and for 45 minutes this buck circled the tree. Several times he started to walk away, but then he'd trot back to sniff the ground under Martin's stand.

Using Buck Lures. Wearing scent-saturated boot pads is one way to use buck lures. As you walk, the lure serves not only as an attractor but as a coverup scent, too. By doing this you lay down a scent trail that can lead deer right to your tree stand. Dougherty said one of the best

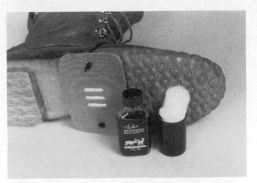

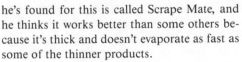

There are two ways to use attractors in the field. You can lay down a scent trail to your stand with the use of boot pads, and you can create a scent station by saturating cotton in a plastic film cannister.

This buck lure comes with a golf tee topped with foam rubber. You poke the tee into the ground where you want the buck to come, and saturate the foam with the buck lure.

he's found for this is called Scrape Mate, and he thinks it works better than some others because it's thick and doesn't evaporate as fast as some of the thinner products.

When you get to your stand, don't wear the pads up the tree. Deposit them out front where you want a buck to stop to present a shot.

One value of scents is not only to bring bucks into your vicinity, but to pull them to a specific spot where you can get an open shot. One common method is to put cotton in a 35mm plastic film canister and to saturate the cotton with buck lure. Keep the canister sealed until you arrive at your stand. Then take off the top to release the alluring aroma, and set the canister out front where you want the buck to stop for a shot.

As I've said, smells don't travel well in cold weather, so you might be able to help your cause by heating up the buck lure a little. Mountain Scent and Bugle Manufacturing makes a product called a Hot Scent Station. It's powered by batteries, and it keeps liquid scents warm even in cold weather so the smell dissipates well. I haven't used one for deer hunting, but I suspect it could help. In warm weather it's not needed.

You can also dispense buck lures with a drip bag. As discussed under Whitetail Deer, Jim Martin fills a hospital IV bag with Indian Buck Lure or Tink's #69 and hangs this over a white-

tail scrape or a mock scrape. (For details, see Whitetail Deer.) He regulates the nozzle so it will drip slowly for two to three days, and it keeps the scrape fresh with the smell of a hot doe.

Food Lures

Some scents are extracts of good-smelling foods like grapes, apples, corn, and so forth. I don't know any hunters who've used these as successfully, at least not to the extent of sex lures.

Loren Butler has tested food lures extensively, and he's never found any he felt were

Food attractors do not work well for hoofed animals, but for scavengers, which locate food by smell, scents like Nirk's Bear Grenade can help pull animals to your stand.

worth marketing. Butler works extensively with public agencies as a consultant on reducing animal depredation and on trapping animals. Over a period of years, Butler has conducted 487 tests that involved 11,452 deer in an attempt to develop an effective scent for live-trapping deer. He's found that from January through April, when deer have depleted body fat and were nearly starving, animals indeed would come to food scents. During that period, anywhere from 17 to 28 percent of deer in an area came to scent stations. But from May through December less than 2 percent came in. Butler believes a small number of animals will wander in to investigate smell just out of curiosity.

Why don't food lures work during summer and fall, when they'd be of value to hunters? According to Butler, deer and elk use their noses primarily for social interaction and defense, but not to find food. During this time of year, food is abundant and deer and other hoofed animals feed by sight.

That's not to say that all food scents are useless. Bears, for example, readily come to scent stations, and trappers have long used rabbit scents and other powerful odors to attract coyotes and other animals. Butler has developed a rotten-meat extract for use in live-trapping bears, and it has worked well during tests in Canada, Idaho, and Colorado. Other products, such as Nirk's Bear Grenade and Buck Stop's Bear Bait, also emit aromas of rotten meat that will draw bears and other scavengers from some distance. Used in conjunction with a bait station, these attractor scents can work very well. (For details, see Black Bear.)

"Scavengers are easy to attract because they make their living with their noses," Butler said.

SCOUTING The first step in making a hunt work is planning, locating a good hunting area. (For details, see Planning a Hunt.) The second step is scouting, the process during which you analyze the area on the ground and locate concentrations of game.

Time-management consultants say that time devoted to planning in an office or business is

never wasted because it eliminates confusion and assures direction and purpose. Scouting does the same. You might think you're wasting time, especially if you take time out to scout during the season, but you're not. Scouting time will contribute a lot more to your eventual success than will most of your hunting time, because it will tell you not only where to hunt, but where not to hunt.

Time of Year for Scouting
Off-Season Scouting. When and how much you scout depends a lot on how close you live to your hunting area. Eastern hunters who plan to hunt the West often combine a family summer vacation with scouting, and that preview of their hunting area, even if it entails no more than driving through and getting a look at the land, helps once the hunting starts.

Many hard-core hunters who hunt near home scout all year. As soon as the season closes they're out there looking around for sign. In winter, deciduous trees have dropped their leaves so you can see well and actually get a better feel for the land than you can when foliage is lush. Sign will linger clearly into the winter, so you can discern trails, rub trees, scrapes, wallows, and other signs of rut (discussed in detail below) that indicate what animals were doing during the season.

Barring major changes in land use, deer traditionally rut in the same places year after year, so any sign you find in winter could mean hot hunting there next fall. The same holds for other animals. In the spring, I've observed concentrations of elk rub trees and wallows, and I've returned there in September and had good bugling. If bulls rut in a particular basin one year, chances are good they'll be there again the next.

During winter and spring, you also can find shed antlers. Some hunters make a study of "sheds" and base much of their trophy scouting around this sign.

Winter scouting for sign, of course, assumes your fall hunting areas aren't covered by deep snow. Even if they are, you still can scout by observing animals themselves on winter ranges

Winter scouting can pay off because in many regions, deep snow forces game animals onto open winter ranges where they are most visible. This might not tell you exactly where to find game the following season, but it gives you an indication of the quality of animals present.

and deer yards. At this time animals are concentrated and on a snowy background they're easy to observe, so winter scouting with high-power optics is an ideal way to locate trophy animals. Obviously, if you're watching migratory animals, you won't find them in the same spot next fall, but at least you can find out whether big bucks or bulls are present in that region. And if you know migration patterns of the animals there, you can just about guess where you'll find the big ones next fall.

Midsummer, from July into early September, also presents an ideal time to scout with your eyes because deer are most visible then, and that's true around cornfields and woodlots of the East as well as alpine mountains of the West. The antlers of deer and elk are covered with soft velvet then, so the animals stay in fairly open country where they won't bang up their tender racks. Maybe even more significant, the metabolism of deer peaks during July and August, so that's when deer are most active and most visible. (For details, see Weather.)

Jim Martin, a Missouri bowhunter, used that fact to his advantage when he set out to kill a trophy buck in his home state. He started scouting in early August, two months before the season opened, because he knew deer would be easiest to see then. He scouted strictly by watching corn and soybean fields each evening.

"Late in the afternoon, deer would come frolicking out into the open fields in broad daylight," he said. "We located at least eight trophy bucks just by watching, and we saw them time after time. By mid-September, they seemed to vanish because they quit moving in the open during the day, but they were still in the same areas when the season opened in October. They just stayed back in the woods until dark."

Martin passed up many average bucks in October and November, and finally on December 19, he killed a nontypical whitetail that scored 197⅛, a Missouri bowhunting record. He'd located the area where that buck lived by scouting with his eyes in August.

Of course, if you scout in the off-season, you have to interpret what you see. If you spot whitetail bucks feeding near cornfields, as Martin did, you can assume you'll find those

Even for wary whitetails, you can scout effectively with your eyes during the off-season. In late summer you'll see bucks coming out to feed in fields you'd never see later in the year.

Jim Martin killed the Missouri record nontypical whitetail (for archery) as a result of summer scouting.

animals in the same general area throughout the season, because they're residents there. The same could be said for blacktail deer in many parts of the Pacific states.

But for mule deer, elk, and other mountain game, that's not necessarily the case. As Dave Snyder, a well-known trophy hunter, said, it's not good enough to locate a trophy mule deer buck before the season; you've got to anticipate where he'll go as soon as hunters invade the woods. Locating potential refuge areas plays a big part in preseason scouting. And, of course, you've got to know migration routes and anticipate how animals will react when snow or other hard weather hits.

Near-Season and In-Season Scouting. If you can't scout during the off-season, at least try to arrive a few days before the season to look around. Two or three days of concerted scouting just before the season will prove invaluable later. Even if you arrive after the season has opened, leave your bow cased and spend your first day or two scouting rather than hunting. If you take your bow and try to hunt as you scout, you might be tempted to start hunting as soon as you find hopeful sign. Don't do it. Mentally note your findings (or better yet, mark them on your map) but don't quit looking until you've got the complete picture.

When Cliff Dewell and I arrived to hunt mule deer in Idaho, we found lots of tracks in the snow in a series of rolling juniper foothills. We were tempted to start hunting right there, but instead we decided to split up the first day and cover some ground in different directions to get a broader picture. It's a good thing we did.

Cliff headed west to look over the hills with all the sign, and I went east to climb a long, high ridge where the snow was much deeper. During a long day of hiking, Cliff saw more than 200 deer but only a dozen bucks, and they were all small, not the kind we'd driven 800 miles to hunt. "I was ready to pack up camp and head somewhere else," he said that night.

But we didn't. Although I'd seen only 18 deer, 4 of them were good bucks. We decided to investigate that high country further, and we found many big bucks there. If we'd automatically started hunting the obvious country with hordes of deer, we'd have overlooked some great hunting.

Here's the point one final time—if your country isn't producing, get out of there and look around. Even during the hunt, continue to scout, scout, scout.

Learn the Country

If you're hunting close to home, you probably know your area intimately and aren't concerned with this, but if you're traveling to new territory, you must learn your way around before you start hunting.

Use Maps. First, study your maps. It should go without saying that you have them. (See Map Sources.) See which way the rivers and creeks run, the general direction of ridges and canyons, the location of high peaks, waterholes, fencelines, and so forth. You can get a general picture of the country from maps. With some knowledge of map reading and the habits of animals you're after, you can scout more intensely and plan your daily hunting by reading maps too.

Drive. Then drive every road within the area

you plan to hunt. That's the only way to learn the road systems, and knowing every road will help you find the easiest access for hunting and for retrieving game. Obviously, at the same time you'll be looking for tracks, feeding areas, crossings, and other game sign to help you key in on good game areas later.

Just as important, driving will tell you where other hunters are camped and where they'll most likely be hunting. In this era, you can't expect to have all the country to yourself, and other hunters can affect your success as much as the presence (or absence) of game. In some cases you might want to avoid all other hunters, and in others you might want to use other hunters to push game by your stand. Whatever the case, you must know the whereabouts of other hunters in your area.

Aerial View. If you've got a few extra dollars (or own an airplane), fly over your country. In an hour of flying you can get a better overview than you can in a week on the ground. One friend of mine planned a first-rate elk hunt as a result of a brief plane ride over a mountain range in Oregon. Flying during the middle of the day, he didn't see any animals, but he did see some large meadows he'd never noticed before. He figured they might attract elk, so he drove there to investigate further, and he had some tremendous bugling success.

If you don't have access to a plane, you can accomplish nearly as much from the ground. In mountain regions, fire towers sit atop many of the higher peaks. Your first move in any country should be to spend a couple of hours at every fire tower you can find, analyzing the country. If there aren't any fire towers, climb high ridges and other vantage points that offer a good view and study the land. Use your binoculars.

Talk. As you're scouting, never pass up the chance to talk to someone. Be friendly. One time my friend Larry Jones was bowhunting and stopped on the road to talk to a man sitting in his truck. It turned out the man was scouting for elk to hunt during the rifle season. Larry didn't ask what he'd seen, but during the conversation the rifle hunter mentioned seeing

Before you start hunting, drive all the roads in your hunting territory and use your binoculars to study the terrain. You can learn nearly as much this way as you can from flying.

a nice seven-point bull on a certain peak. Larry played it cool, but as soon as the guy was out of sight, he streaked for his car and drove 200 miles to the spot the hunter had mentioned. He found the big bull right there. When you're scouting, it pays to be friendly.

Walk. The same principles apply even if you plan to hunt roadless country on foot. Get out and walk hard to learn the trails and the lay of the country. At first don't waste time sneaking around, hoping to get a shot. Hoof it hard the first day or two to get an overview, and then you'll be able to hunt intelligently.

All these steps aren't part of a single-purpose mission, of course, and as you learn the country you're also watching for spots where animals will congregate. Watch for likely feeding areas with good browse, grass, shrubs, acorns, and other forage, and take note of potential bedding areas.

Keep an eye open for mineral licks. In some places ranchers put out mineral blocks for livestock, and deer and elk will use them heavily; in other areas, natural minerals in the soil attract game animals. Most mineral licks are fairly obvious. If they're heavily used, they'll consist of a hole in the ground where animals

have dug for salt, surrounded by ground trampled bare of all vegetation.

Look for water sources too. In wet country, animals can find water about anywhere, but in dry country they're tied to specific waterholes. Knowing the location of water could lead you to excellent stand locations.

Anytime you're scouting, observe one final phenomenon—air currents. Obviously wind direction will affect your hunting, so the more you know about wind patterns in an area, the more effectively you can hunt. In many regions, prevailing winds blow constantly, and breezes also follow ground contours. With close observation, you can just about map these out to use as a hunting guide later.

Locating Animals

Look for Animals. Many hunters think scouting means just looking for tracks, droppings, and so forth, but that's only part of it. Wherever feasible, I start out looking, or listening, for animals themselves. I find the best vantage points available and spend hours not only analyzing the country as discussed above, but looking for animals. In any mountain country, you can scout many miles at one sitting (for

Whenever you enter new country, take time to get an overview before you settle on any one spot to hunt. If the country is roadless, hike the highest ridges and look things over.

details, see Spotting), and you can do it a lot faster than you can by walking around looking for tracks or other sign. Duwane Adams, a proficient trophy hunter from Arizona, scouts almost exclusively by spotting. He sets up his 15X60 Zeiss binoculars on a tripod and glasses for hours.

"Scouting is the most important step in hunting," Adams said. "In any new area, I get on the highest point with good visibility and start looking. I frequently spot animals three to four miles away. I can scout a lot of country that way. When I've located a concentration of deer, I move my camp close enough so I can get to the deer quickly each day."

To scout visually, get out right at daybreak when animals are feeding in the open—on top of ridges, in meadows, fields, burns, or clearcuts. They're easiest to see then, and you'll see more animals in an hour of looking than you could in a week of walking.

Don't be satisfied only with spotting high numbers, but study the animals long enough to identify movement patterns. If you see a buck walking deliberately, note what he does. Most animals make habitual movements from bed to feed to water, and you might figure them out

Mineral licks often attract animals regularly. Deer have nearly dug an open-pit mine to get at minerals here.

just by watching, and you can use that knowledge to plan a hunt. This knowledge is the basis for choosing good stand sites.

You can scout with your ears too. If your elk hunting goes stale, drive back roads or walk the tops of ridges, bugling to locate bull elk. That's especially effective at night. If you can hear one then, you can feel confident he'll be nearby the next day. On one recent hunt when elk had become scarce, I drove out at night and bugled for a couple of hours. I got two responses from bulls way out on a juniper flat, a place I would never have expected to find elk, and I returned the next morning and killed a bull there. It may not have been one of the ones I'd heard the night before, but the fact is, scouting by calling at night put me in a productive area.

Tracks. Looking for sign—tracks, droppings, and so forth—could be called "intuitive"

In scouting, look not only for tracks, but for trails that indicate something about the habitual movements of deer. In particular look for a convergence of trails.

scouting, because you must work with circumstantial evidence. You're not only an observer but a detective, trying to piece together a picture of animal movements only from what you see on the ground. Sign reading proves most valuable in enclosed, flat country where you can't scout by glassing.

Tracks are the most obvious sign. They can tell you roughly how many animals inhabit an area, which directions they move, and which routes they use to get from point A to point B. In some cases tracks reveal time of travel. And in the form of trails, they can reveal constriction points, ideal places for stands.

If you're just hunting for any deer, finding lots of tracks may be all that interests you, but if you want a big buck, don't stop with that. Evaluate size. Most authorities agree you can't distinguish buck and doe tracks by shape, but you often can by size. If you find tiny tracks mixed in with adult deer tracks, you can assume most of the tracks were made by does and fawns and probably a few yearling bucks that still hang around family groups. On the other hand, if you find solitary tracks much larger than average, you can bet a larger-than-average buck made that track. Outsized tracks are always worth investigating.

At times it's easy to tell how old tracks are; at other times it's not. By checking periodically, say at a waterhole or trail, you can tell whether new tracks have appeared since your last check. To make this even more reliable, brush out a section of trail.

In mud, tracks may appear fresh for days, but in dust or snow, they'll age instantly, so there's no absolute guide for aging tracks. You have to compare sign of a known age with surrounding tracks. If you see a deer, compare its tracks with others around it, or press your fingers into the soil as a basis for comparison. If the impressions of your fingers and nearby tracks look nearly the same, the tracks are probably no more than a few hours old. If the sides of the tracks are rounded or dull-looking, or debris has blown into them, you know they're older. Of course, rain or snow helps you age tracks. If the last rain shower took place

You can't tell the sex of a deer from the shape of its tracks, but you can get a good idea from size. Oversized tracks indicate the presence of a buck.

three hours ago, tracks with no rain in them are less than three hours old.

In scouting for tracks, or any sign for that matter, never jump to conclusions; scour an area thoroughly before you give up. I hunted whitetails in the Arkansas Ozarks at the end of October, when five to six inches of freshly fallen oak leaves covered the ground. After a day of scouting I'd have sworn there weren't two deer in the whole place, because I couldn't see any tracks. But I sat in a ridgetop tree stand anyway, and to my amazement seven deer walked by. That made a believer out of me and I scouted even harder, and I learned to spot depressions in the leaves that indicated deer tracks. If I'd based my hunt strictly on cursory scouting for tracks, I'd have left the first day.

In Western mountains, animals can be scattered far and wide. That's particularly true for elk. You can walk for miles and scarcely see an elk track and you'll swear the country is barren, and then suddenly you'll hit a basin or pocket that's torn up like a stockyard. For that reason, I don't worry much about *not* finding tracks, but I take it seriously when I *do* find them.

Trails. A trail is nothing more than an accumulation of tracks, but they're tracks with a pattern, and that should rev up your motor. Never ignore a trail, because it was formed by habitual usage. That means it will be used again. In areas with high numbers of deer,

finding tracks is no problem. They'll be everywhere. That was the case where I hunted the farm country of northern Missouri. You could hardly take a step without stepping on a deer track, so the scouting mandate there wasn't in finding tracks, but in making some sense of them, discerning a pattern. In other words, finding trails.

In particular, look for places where trails converge. Animals being somewhat like people, they'll follow the path of least resistance and their trails will lead them around tough spots — dense vegetation, rock slides, bluffs. That's where you'll find two, three, or more trails coming together, and that's the kind of place you're looking for, particularly if you want to hunt from a stand. Explore any trail fully, and watch for converging trails and other constriction points.

You don't necessarily need to walk to scout for tracks and trails. In canyon country with good visibility, you can use a scope to spot tracks a mile or more away, and you can scout a lot faster that way than you can by walking. Mountain-lion hunters commonly use the same approach to locate cat tracks in snow across open canyons.

Droppings. I wouldn't consider droppings as primary sign, but more as confirmation sign. If you see tracks, you already know the animals are there and roughly what they're doing. Droppings normally confirm what you already know, although they can add to your knowledge.

You can get some idea of an animal's size from them, and it's generally agreed that a big buck's droppings will be bigger around than those of does and fawns. If you're finding piles of pellets around a feed area and some are noticeably bigger than others, you can assume a buck is hanging around there.

With animals like bears that don't always leave distinct tracks, scat can help you pinpoint prime areas. In spring right after hibernation, a bear will spend a lot of time in one small location. If you find a place with lots of dung piles, you know that bear is right there close. The same holds in the fall when bears start feeding on berries. You may not see any tracks, but you'll know the instant you get into a hot bear area, because you'll see berry-filled piles of scat all over.

You can age droppings with some accuracy, although it varies greatly with the weather. In dry weather, droppings age fast. I killed an elk in Arizona, and while gutting it I noticed a couple of pellets fall from its intestine onto the ground. They were olive green at first, but within a half hour they'd turned black. They looked like they could have been there a couple of days, although they were still moist and green inside. In wet weather, they'll stay green on the outside for several hours or days, so you always have to judge age in relation to conditions.

Rub Trees. In deer and elk hunting, particularly during the rut, you'll find trees with the bark skinned off and branches broken and scattered. Rubs are always exciting finds because there's no question about whether the sign was made by a buck or doe, bull or cow.

Everyone has his own theory about the reason for rubs. Some hunters say they're the result of rubbing velvet off antlers. Others say bucks deposit scent off their foreheads as they rub, and that rub trees mark a certain territory. Still others say bucks and bulls fight trees to condition their necks for the real thing—fighting with each other. All these may have some element of truth, but in many cases I think animals just feel feisty and want to beat up on something.

Animals don't return to the same rub trees over and over, so the rubs don't have much value in telling you where to place a stand. Nevertheless, they are significant, because they tell you without question that male animals are present, and they can tell you something about those animals.

First, they roughly indicate the number of bucks or bulls in the vicinity. One or two rub trees might not mean much because a single buck could have made those, but lots of rub trees do mean something—lots of animals. I've never seen a place with lots of rubs where I haven't later seen several good bucks or bulls.

Second, rubs indicate size of animals. Small

bucks normally rub trees one to two inches in diameter and not much larger. Big bucks will tear up small trees and bushes, but they'll attack bigger stuff too. If you're hunting whitetails and find rub trees five to six inches in diameter, you'd better get serious because you know a big buck roams that country.

The same holds for elk. You can roughly gauge the size of a bull by the size of his rubs, not necessarily in diameter but height. If he's broken off branches ten feet off the ground, you know he's a pretty good bull. Don't be misled on small trees, though, because a bull will bend over trees three inches or larger in diameter and strip them clear to the top. The height gauge works only on big trees that can't be tipped over.

Don't ignore old rub trees made in previous years. Deer and elk have traditional rutting grounds, and if they rutted there one year, they'll most likely be back the next.

Scrapes. Scrapes have probably become the hottest topic among whitetail hunters, much like bugling has to elk hunters. Most trophy whitetail hunting in recent years has revolved around knowledge of scrapes. Scrapes are most often associated with whitetail hunting, although blacktail deer of the Pacific Coast also make scrapes during the rut.

In simple terms, a scrape is a place where a buck scrapes away leaves and other debris as a signpost of his presence. In essence it's his calling card, but it's also a place for does to leave their calling cards. Scrapes are strictly rut-related. Bucks start making scrapes roughly a month before the peak of the rut, and they check these scrapes continually to see whether an estrus doe has visited. If she has, the buck bird-dogs her until she's receptive, when he breeds her. Then he continues to check his scrapes for signs of other hot does.

You'll find scrapes along natural travel lines used by whitetails. They're commonly placed along abandoned trails or roads, along the tops of ridges, saddles, or other flat spots, at the edges of corn and soybean fields, and other common travel routes. (For more details, see Stand Hunting and Whitetail Deer.)

Wallows. As scrapes are to whitetails, wallows are to elk. During the rut, bull elk wallow regularly to cover themselves with mud and take on a rough-and-tumble appearance — and smell. Animal behaviorists say bulls wallow to make themselves look and smell more intimidating to other bulls. Here again, the reasons don't really matter. What does matter is that where you find wallows, you'll probably find bulls.

Wallows are bathtub-size depressions full of water, or they might just be muddy spots torn to shreds. You'll commonly find wallows in wet meadows where springs seep from the ground, but bulls will wallow anywhere they can find moisture, and I've discovered hidden wallows in heavy timber where seep springs created only a few square feet of damp soil.

Elk aren't necessarily tied to any home territory; if they're harassed, they'll move out to set up housekeeping elsewhere, so it's important that you find fresh wallows. Muddy water in a wallow tells you a bull has used it recently. You often can see impressions of hair and antlers where the bull has rolled, and fresh mud will be splattered all over nearby trees. If the water has cleared and mud is dry and hard, you know the bull hasn't been around for a while and you'd better search elsewhere.

Beds. Any sign that helps you piece together the hunting puzzle is valuable, and beds can do that. You probably won't put up your tree stand over a deer bed, but finding that bed can tell you something about the animal's habits that could help your cause. Fresh beds tell you where animals hide out during the day, and they can give you a good idea of where to look for game. In desert country, I've found many mule deer beds under rimrocks, so those are the places I first look for animals, and many times I've spotted deer in the same beds I'd seen empty on other days. Any time I find an animal's bed I analyze why he lay there, and this knowledge has helped in finding other animals and in planning hunting strategy.

Other Signs. The sign discussed above applies to most common hoofed animals, but other game have specialized sign you must learn to recognize. Bears commonly rip up logs and stumps, and they dig deep holes in rotten

logs to search for ants and insects. They also flip over rocks to look for insects and other tidbits. Any serious bear hunter learns to spot these signs instantly.

In turkey hunting you look not only for tracks, but for places where birds have scratched for acorns and nuts, and you look for concentrated droppings under roost trees. To scout for pigs, you look for wallows and torn-up ground where the animals have been rooting. You have to know the habits of each species to scout intelligently. (For more details, see species listings such as Bear, Elk, Whitetail Deer, and so forth.)

Pulling It All Together

Tread Softly. Any time you're scouting (or hunting, for that matter) conduct yourself so that you don't destroy what you're trying to find. Some animals in particular, like elk and bears, will abandon ship and look for new territory if you stumble into their home grounds. Then you've got to start all over to find them. You might not spook a wise old buck out of his home range, but with every human encounter, he'll just become that much more furtive and harder to fool.

If you're scouting on foot and plan to enter an area several times, come and go on different routes each time. Try not to form a pattern that deer can discern. If you habitually follow the same course, concentrating scent and other signs of your presence, you could force deer into unnatural movements. I especially favor scouting from a distance with my eyes and ears, because I can spot or hear animals at long range and don't have to disturb them at home.

Map Your Findings. One final tip might help turn good scouting into successful hunting. Mark all your observations on a map. That might seem senseless since you've got a good brain, but memory is notoriously fallible. You tend to forget some details and remember others, so even if your scouting has produced the needed facts, you end up with a distorted view.

There's something about a graphic presentation on paper that makes things clearer. If you put Xs where you saw rubs, scrapes or wallows, mark in all trails, shade in feeding areas, draw in herds you've observed, and so forth, you'll suddenly find yourself with a precise picture of your area, and your hunting strategy will simply fall into place. Shari Fraker, the Colorado elk hunter, does just that. She scouts year-round and carefully marks every significant finding on topographic maps. By the time hunting season arrives, she's got the searching out of the way. Then she can concentrate strictly on the hunting, and that's how she's killed elk for eight straight hunting seasons.

SCRAPE During the rut, whitetail bucks paw out small clearings that serve as signposts for does in heat. These pawed-out places are called scrapes. (For details, see Whitetail Deer.)

SELF-BOW The word "self," used as an adjective, means "being of the same color, substance, etc., throughout; uniform; unmixed." Thus a self-bow is a bow made of one material, such as yew wood, osage orange, or pure fiberglass. That's opposed to the laminated bow, which contains multiple layers of wood commonly backed with layers of fiberglass.

SERVING See Bowstring.

SHED In hunter's parlance this means an antler or set of antlers shed by a member of the deer family.

Many hunters scout for deer and elk, especially trophy animals, in the spring by looking for "sheds." If animals in a given area migrate to winter ranges, shed antlers will be found there. If that's the case, they won't tell you exactly where to find your dream animal next fall, but they do indicate the quality of animals in a given region, and you often can interpret where deer or elk from a given winter range will summer. Looking for sheds in winter and spring is a valuable means of assessing an area's trophy potential. (For more details, see Scouting.)

SHEEP Mountain sheep span the extremes of North America from the Arctic mountains of Alaska to the furnacelike mountains of Mexico. Sheep are classified into two species: thinhorn *(Ovis dalli)* and bighorn *(Ovis canadensis)*. Undoubtedly more money has been spent on sheep per animal taken than on virtually any other game in North America. For years the goal of many hunters has been to score a "grand slam," to take the four major varieties of North American sheep. Many rifle hunters, of course, have accomplished that feat, but at this writing, only three archers have taken grand slams.

Varieties of Sheep

Thinhorns. Most hunters and record books recognize two kinds of thinhorn sheep, the Dall and the Stone. (Sticklers for accuracy will tell you these sheep were named after men— Dall and Stone—so the common names of the sheep should include an apostrophe "s." Thus, they're Dall's sheep and Stone's sheep. Common usage, however, has eliminated the possessive, so for convention, I'll do likewise.) Dall sheep live throughout the major mountain ranges of Alaska, the Yukon Territory, eastern Northwest Territories, and extreme northeastern British Columbia. Dalls are pure white except for black tails in some parts of their range.

Some Stone sheep inhabit the mountains of the southcentral Yukon Territory, but by far the greatest numbers are found in British Columbia north of the Peace River. Most Stone sheep are dark brown or black with lighter heads and whitish muzzles, but coloration can vary greatly from nearly pure black to white. Average height for both Dall and Stone rams is about 36 inches at the shoulder and average weight is 180 to 220 pounds for Dall sheep, 220 to 230 for Stones. Nowhere can a nonresident pursue these sheep legally without a guide.

Bighorns. According to most scientists and hunters, there are three races of bighorn sheep: the Rocky Mountain bighorn, California bighorn, and desert bighorn. Rocky Mountain bighorns, as their name implies, live primarily in the Rocky Mountains from the Peace River

Dall sheep live in the higher mountains of Alaska, the Yukon, Northwest Territories, and British Columbia. The horns are thinner and more flared than the horns of bighorn sheep. Using a homemade longbow, Jay Massey killed this Dall sheep in Alaska's Brooks Range. *Photo courtesy Jay Massey.*

in Alberta and British Columbia south into New Mexico. Alberta has by far the most bighorns, but good numbers live throughout all the rugged mountains of Montana, Idaho, Wyoming, and Colorado. Small herds also exist in New Mexico, Utah, Nevada, Oregon, and South Dakota.

California bighorns are most abundant in central British Columbia north along the Fraser River. Historically they occurred in several Western states but were eliminated in the early 1900s. Now they've been restored, and are hunted, in Washington, Idaho, Oregon, and Nevada. Even though Rocky Mountain and California bighorns are distinct subspecies, record books lump them together. California bighorns rarely attain the massive size of their larger cousins, so you see few listed in the record books.

Desert bighorns are most abundant in Arizona, California, Nevada, and Mexico. Unfortunately, California allows no hunting for these animals, hunts in Mexico carry a high price tag, and tags are in short supply in the other states, so hunting opportunity is even more severely limited than for other kinds of

sheep. New Mexico, Utah, Colorado, and Texas also have some desert bighorns.

Sheep Seasons

You have two options for sheep hunting. You either hire an outfitter to take you in Canada, Alaska, or Mexico, or you go for the luck of the draw in the states. Unquestionably, the toughest part of sheep hunting in the Lower 48 is getting a tag. Nine Western states have sheep seasons.

For bowhunters, Colorado offers by far the best opportunity because that state holds a number of archery-only bighorn hunts. For some years these were undersubscribed and some archers hunted sheep for eight or ten consecutive years. That's not likely now, but still the odds for drawing are better than they are in other states where bow and rifle hunters apply for the same hunts.

Montana has good numbers of sheep and even offers unlimited sheep hunting in some districts, the only unrestricted sheep hunting in the Lower 48. The unlimited hunts take place in the rough Absaroka country near Yellowstone and sheep are scattered, so the unlimited

Rocky Mountain bighorns are the largest sheep in North America. The toughest part of hunting these animals is getting a tag. *Photo courtesy Steve Gorr.*

hunt isn't as good a deal as it sounds. To get the picture, compare it to the limited-entry hunts. In 1983, Montana issued 350 licenses for limited-entry districts and 316 hunters killed sheep for 90 percent success. That same year Montana issued 538 licenses for its unlimited districts, and hunters there killed 33 sheep for 6 percent success (remember, those were virtually all rifle hunters). I talked to one rifle hunter, a hard hunter, who backpacked in an unlimited sheep area for 43 days and never saw a sheep. About 10 percent of Montana's sheep tags are reserved for nonresidents.

Wyoming has some good bighorn sheep hunting concentrated mostly around Yellowstone National Park and in the Wind River Range. Unfortunately, much of the sheep hunting takes place in designated wilderness, where nonresidents are required to hunt with a guide, so the nonresident doesn't have many options for hunting on his own.

Idaho issues between 150 and 200 sheep tags each year. Most of these are for Rocky Mountain bighorns in the remote central part of the state, but a few are for California bighorns in the Owyhee River drainage, stark desert country in the southwest corner. Nonresidents receive about 10 percent of the tags.

Oregon also issues several dozen tags for California bighorns in some of its desert ranges, as well as a few tags for Rocky Mountain sheep in the Snake River country in the northeast. Unfortunately only residents may apply. Just to the north, Washington has some very limited hunting for California bighorns, and a few of the licenses are issued for archery hunting only. Nonresidents may apply.

Nevada is the only state with three varieties of sheep. Desert bighorns, which live in many arid ranges across the south half of the state, are the most plentiful. Roughly 10 percent of the desert sheep tags are allotted for nonresidents. A few tags are issued for Rocky Mountain bighorns in the Snake Range on the Utah border and for California bighorns on the Sheldon Antelope Range in the northwest corner, but these are reserved for residents.

Arizona has major herds of desert bighorn sheep in most of the mountain ranges from Phoenix west to the Colorado River and north along the Colorado to Lake Mead. Nonresidents are allowed to apply for these tags.

California bighorns were eliminated from most of the Pacific states, but transplanting projects have restored these animals to many of their former ranges. This young ram was living on Hart Mountain in eastern Oregon.

Utah offers a few tags for desert bighorns, and one of these tags is allotted for a nonresident. New Mexico has some desert bighorns, too, but these sheep have been hit hard by disease and predation, and the season has been closed for some time. New Mexico does offer about a dozen Rocky Mountain bighorn tags for the mountains near Santa Fe.

Two universal principles apply to stateside sheep tags—they're expensive, and the odds for drawing range from bad to zero. Nevertheless, these seasons offer the potential for sheep hunting on your own if you get lucky enough to draw a tag.

Sheep Hunting

Sheep are known primarily as high, open-country animals so they're visible and easily spotted in many situations. Virtually all sheep hunting involves spotting at long distances, and for that reason good binoculars and a spotting scope are mandatory sheep-hunting gear. (For details, see Optics and Spotting.)

That doesn't mean sheep are always easy to locate. In some situations they live in timber as much as in the open. In Montana one year,

Desert bighorns are limited to the rugged, barren mountain ranges of the Southwest. Bowhunters have taken very few desert bighorns. *Photo by Charles G. Hansen, courtesy U.S. Fish and Wildlife Service.*

Steve Gorr hunted for more than three weeks before he located a single ram, and when he finally did find one it was in timber. Lee Kline, who has killed sheep in Colorado, said you see sheep in the timber more and more frequently.

"In some parts of Colorado, you might spot them very early and late feeding along the edges of timberline, but you'll find them lower in the timber during the day," Kline said. "Many of them stay in timber all the time. I doubt that it's from hunting pressure as much as general human contact with backpackers and climbers. We get a lot of foot traffic in the Colorado backcountry."

Even where visible, spotting the *right* sheep can take some doing. Most states and provinces define legal sheep according to age or horn size. In British Columbia, Oregon bowhunter Don Rajnus said he glassed more than 50 Stone rams in several days of hunting, but only 2 were of legal size. Hunting desert sheep in Arizona, Brad Siefarth scouted for 11 days before he saw a ram of the quality he wanted. Siefarth said that was the toughest part of his hunt—finding trophy rams.

The rut can be an aid in locating rams. Paul Schafer, the third archer ever to take a grand slam on sheep, waited until November to hunt bighorns in Montana because that's when the animals are in rut, and he felt the sound of fighting might help him locate rams. Indeed it did. When he heard the rifle-shot crack of butting heads he stalked toward the sound, and he eventually killed one of the fighting rams, a fine sheep that scored 185.

Sheep are generally creatures of habit, and that can work in your favor. In Colorado, Steve Gorr located two rams in midsummer, and during many scouting trips before the season, he saw these sheep use the same beds day after day. When the season finally opened, he found one of the rams bedded right there as usual, and he killed it the first day of the season.

After his 11 days of scouting, Siefarth finally found two large rams, and he watched them in the same spot on his next nine consecutive scouting trips.

"Those big rams looked a little lazy to me," Siefarth said. "They often bedded under rock ledges or in holes in the lava, and instead of walking downhill to water at a tank as the ewes did, they'd just beat saguaro cactus with their horns and lick up the oozing juice. They seemed content to browse and rest in an area no more than 200 yards square."

Don Rajnus has taken three sheep—Dall in the Yukon Territory, Stone in British Columbia, and California bighorn in Oregon—and he believes you can use the predictable habits of sheep in your favor.

"If you just use your head you can figure them out," Rajnus said. "We spotted many sheep from long distances, and then looked above them for trails to determine where they'd go. Then I'd get out of sight and circle the sheep and wait on a trail above them and the guide would walk in view below to push the animals my way. I got several good shots that way."

Rajnus also stalked a number of sheep successfully. In British Columbia he missed a 40-yard shot as several sheep trotted past him on a trail, so he watched the animals and eventually saw them bed under an overhanging cliff. He climbed for two hours to get around them and from above he was in perfect position with the wind in his favor. He couldn't see the sheep from there, however, because they were too far back under the cliff. So he sat down and waited, and after several hours a large ram walked out to feed and Rajnus got him.

On his first Dall sheep hunt, which took place in Alaska, Rajnus faced one of the hazards of sheep hunting—bad weather. Heavy snow fell 19 of the 21 days he was there, and he and his party virtually never hunted. In the Yukon, however, he enjoyed 10 days of warm weather, and he successfully stalked several sheep.

In most cases, he has found the terrain in sheep country conducive to stalking, and as long as he could stay out of sight he hasn't had trouble getting close. "Sheep don't seem to have great noses," he said. "And they don't pay much attention to noise at all. I guess they're used to the sounds of rolling rocks. I think you could just about bounce a rock off their heads and they wouldn't get too excited."

In eastern Oregon, Rajnus stalked several California bighorn rams and missed a shot, and on the third day, after spotting a small herd from a distance, he climbed down to them and snuck onto a rock pinnacle just above the sheep. He could see one ram 15 yards away, straight down. He wasn't sure it was the biggest one, but he figured a "bird in the hand. . . ." So he shot the ram, and as the animal bounded out of sight, a much larger ram casually walked from under the cliff and stood there, watching the other depart. The stalk had worked perfectly, and Rajnus' only regret was that he hadn't been a little more patient. Rajnus's ram was the first ever taken by a bow-hunter in Oregon.

San Stiver may be the only person to hunt both desert and California bighorns in Nevada. He was only the second bowhunter ever to kill a desert ram. He said the main difference in his two hunts was the density of sheep. He was hunting a high-density area for desert sheep and saw and stalked many rams every day and finally killed one at 30 yards. In hunting California bighorns, he saw few sheep. He watched the same ram for 10 straight days, waiting for him to lie in a vulnerable position. But the sheep never did, and in those 10 days, Stiver never got closer than 100 yards.

Stiver generally found that he could get close to sheep. It involved a lot of crawling and patience, so it couldn't be called easy. But it could be done consistently. "I've got within 35 yards of at least 85 percent of rams I've tried sneaking on," Stiver said.

From his experiences, Don Rajnus concludes that sheep aren't overly hard to hunt if you've got the needed stamina. "I don't think they're near as hard as a big mule deer or bull elk. Don't get me wrong. They're a lot of fun and I've enjoyed sheep hunting as much as anything I've ever done.

"But a lot of people view sheep as impossible to hunt with a bow. That isn't the case. The problem is that some people just don't have the ambition to get into position. To stalk sheep, you've got to be determined to get around and above the animals, and that can mean several hours of hard climbing once you've spotted the sheep you want. But if you can do that, you can kill sheep with a bow."

Brad Siefarth offered a similar view. "After studying and hunting these animals, I wouldn't stack a desert ram — in terms of hunting difficulty — against a good mule deer. The hard part of sheep hunting is, first, getting the tag, then finding the right animal and getting to him."

Trophy Hunting

Average horn length for both Dall and Stone sheep is 35 to 36 inches, with the maximum about 48 inches, and circumferences around the base average about 14 inches. Most Boone and Crockett–size bighorns have horns of 40 inches or more, with basal circumferences greater than 15 inches.

To get these kind of curls the bottom of the horn must curve down below the bottom of the jaw and then come back up to the nose or higher. You just about have to have a front-on view to judge length and a side view to judge mass. Of course, the criteria for judgment depends largely on which sheep you're after, because horn formation varies greatly between the thinhorns and the bighorns.

With a good spotting scope, and assuming you've got time to study an undisturbed animal, you can count annual growth rings on the horns. In some states, rams must be at least seven years old to be legal. The largest rams normally are at least 10 years old, and few sheep live longer than 13 years.

SHOOTING BASICS No one can dictate an absolute style for good shooting, because every archer will adopt his own pet methods. Still, certain principles apply to all bow shooting, and a good foundation will produce good shooting habits under any conditions. Many of the principles here come from champion target archers.

You might ask: What does target archery have to do with bowhunting? The answer is: Everything. Target shooters have studied human physiology and anatomy, and they've learned the technical side of tackle. They've then brought this knowledge together to develop a reliable shooting style and to eliminate variables that lead to inconsistency. Since the same physical principles govern both target and hunting tackle and all human bodies function similarly, the principles that work for target archers work for hunters.

Building a Foundation

Many articles stress that you should shoot from different angles, awkward positions, and varied distances to prepare yourself for hunting. That's sound advice, and I advocate this kind of practice. (For details, see Shooting Practice.) But the ability to hit game doesn't start there; it starts with a good foundation. Unless you've developed good form, varied practice does nothing but ingrain bad habits. If you learn good habits in the first place, they carry over into all situations.

I've heard many bowhunters say, "I can't stand there and hit a target, but I can hit game in the field." My response to that is, "Baloney!" If you can't regularly hit a paper plate at 30 yards on an inanimate target butt, you certainly can't guarantee clean hits on deer. You're just hoping to get lucky.

Relaxation versus Tension

Most archery instructors agree that muscle tension is the enemy of good form, and relaxation is the ally. For best shooting, develop a *natural* style that will let your body do what it wants to do. The more one group of muscles has to fight another, the harder it becomes to duplicate one good shot with another. A relaxed, natural form eliminates many of the variables created by tense muscles. It's difficult or impossible to duplicate the same amount of muscle tension shot after shot, but if you relax so your body assumes a natural alignment in stance, bow arm, shooting arm, neck, and so forth, it will assume the same natural position each shot—if you'll relax and let it.

That's why photos of archers skewed one way, bent another, leaning back or forward are

so misleading. These guys may appear to be with the program, but chances are they're poor shooters. In contrast, look at pictures of top archers like Terry Ragsdale, one of the top tournament archers and bowhunters in North America. A photo of Ragsdale at full draw commonly runs with a bow ad, and in that picture he looks like he's about to fall asleep. He's totally relaxed, as if carrying on a casual conversation rather than shooting for the gold. That's championship form for hunters as well as target shooters. If you learn a relaxed, natural shooting style from the start, it will carry over into all areas of shooting.

Al Henderson, 1976 Olympic archery coach and an avid bowhunter, emphasizes that good hunting starts with good form.

"Hunters say they don't need the technical stuff, but I say you can't help but be a better hunter if you know your equipment and form. Shooting basics are just as important for hunters as for Olympic archers, because a hunter is a competitor in every sense of the word.

"It may be even more important for hunters to practice form than for target shooters, because in the field you're shooting under totally uncontrollable conditions—fatigue, weather, hunger, bad shooting positions. You have to concentrate 100 percent on aiming and holding on that animal, and you have to entrust your physical form to practice."

Professional archery instructor Lonnie Jones points out that a natural, relaxed style eliminates fatigue and soreness because one muscle doesn't have to fight another, and it promises greatest accuracy because it ensures proper body alignment. Your body will align itself naturally if you allow it to. You've probably seen archers jerk their bow to the right, left, or down after a shot. This quick, unavoidable movement is the result of forced alignment. If you're relaxed, your bow will scarcely move after a shot because your body is aligned naturally.

The steps outlined here aren't haphazard suggestions that might work; they're proven principles perfected by some of the nation's best archers, and they're designed to produce the most relaxed, natural style possible, a style that will bring results in the field.

Here are a couple of final tips before you start shooting. First, warm up. Professional archery coaches say they advocate a thorough warmup—arm circles, shoulder stretching exercises, light isometrics—before shooting to enhance flexibility and to prevent injury. I personally have had a shoulder injury for years, and a doctor that specializes in sports medicine said it was probably caused by muscle strain as a result of pulling my bow without warming up. (For details, see Physical Condition.)

Second, during the learning stages, and when you practice strictly for form, shoot a lightweight bow. Under the pressure of a heavy hunting bow, you can't concentrate on shooting form. Either buy two bows, one light and one heavier for hunting, or initially turn down the weight on your hunting bow so you can hold it for several seconds without strain.

Checkpoints

Stance. Good shooting starts with a solid foundation. Place your feet shoulder width apart at a 90-degree angle to the target. Step forward a few inches with the rear foot and pivot slightly toward the target. This gives you a mildly open stance, which offers better balance than a 90-degree stance. Your weight should be centered evenly on both feet. That is, you should be standing straight up, not leaning one way or the other. Foot position dictates body alignment, and if, as you shoot, you find yourself jerking after a shot, you might want to open or close your stance to adjust alignment.

Bow Hand. When you've assumed a solid stance, nock an arrow, and before raising your bow to draw, deliberately set your hand position on the bow handle and string. The bow hand and arm may be the most critical link in consistent shooting, so follow these steps carefully. A slight variation can throw an arrow well off target.

As you place your hand on the bow, major pressure should be on the meaty part of your thumb about an inch below the big thumb

In these photos, archery champion and bowhunter Jim Pickering demonstrates aspects of good form. It begins with a slightly open stance, which gives you better balance than if you're facing 90 degrees to the target. Feet should be about shoulder width, and weight should be evenly distributed on both feet. You should not be leaning forward or back.

Before each shot, take time to line up your hands and to think about your form before you draw the bow. Get everything set correctly now so you don't have to make adjustments at full draw.

413

Your bow hand should be set so maximum pressure falls on the meaty part of your thumb about an inch below the big joint. In essence this produces a "low wrist" shooting style.

knuckle. In essence, this will produce a low or straight wrist, depending on the shape of your bow handle. Some shooters swear by the high wrist, which places greatest pressure on the web between the index finger and thumb, and inherently it's as accurate as a low or straight wrist. However, with a high wrist you must use muscle tension to hold your wrist up, and also the wrist can swing from side to side like a hinge. For that reason, the high wrist is less stable, and can lead to muscle fatigue and inconsistent shooting faster than a natural, low-wrist position.

Al Henderson said, "The high wrist might be ideal because it puts the pressure higher, closer to the center of the bow. But with a relaxed, natural wrist, you don't have to control the wrist and the bow. It naturally falls into the same position every time. That's why I teach the natural wrist position."

With the wrist bent downward, be sure not to palm the bow. By palming the handle, you create two pressure points—one on the thumb, one on the heel of the hand—and you'll have a hard time getting equal alignment each time. It's vital that you have only one pressure point, and that's on the meaty part of the thumb.

To ensure only one pressure point, your bow hand should be rotated one eighth turn off vertical. To see why, hold your hand up and naturally point at a distant object. You'll see that

your hand turns to the side. You want to grip the bow with your hand in that natural position. Holding your bow correctly, your little finger should not come in front of the handle. This natural alignment not only swings your palm to the side away from the bow hand, but it also eliminates torque on the handle that could twist the bow and throw an arrow off target.

This natural position, with your hand rotated one eighth turn off vertical, also is the most stable position. If your hand is vertical, your wrist acts as a hinge and allows sideways movement of the bow.

Finally, the bow hand must be relaxed. You often see hunters with bow fingers extended as stiff as spokes on a wheel, or they grip the bow handle like they're choking a chicken. That kind of tension torques the bow and ruins accuracy. At full draw your fingers should droop, totally relaxed.

As you set your hand on the bow, keep one other point in mind: your arm bone should run directly into the bow handle. Again, this is the most stable position. If your hand is too far outside or inside the handle, you'll twist the bow.

String Hand. The string hand acts as a hook to connect the string to your drawing arm. Like

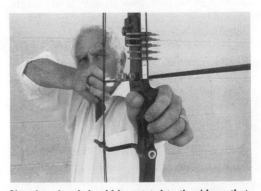

Your bow hand should be rotated to the side so that only the thumb rests on the handle. If you turn your bow hand vertically, you'll palm the bow, which can torque the bow during a shot. Notice that the fingers are totally relaxed. They'll remain that way throughout the shot. They should never be stiff or tense.

The string fingers merely form a hook between your drawing arm and the bowstring. The wrist on the string hand should be straight and the anchor should be solid.

The wrist on your drawing hand should remain straight, acting only as a connection between the string hook (fingers) and the elbow of your drawing arm. That's because if you try to release with a crooked arm and hand, you must relax your entire arm before you can get rid of the string. If your arm is straight, it's relaxed from the beginning and does not affect your release.

Raise the Bow-and-Arm Unit. With your hands set in the correct positions, raise your bow into shooting position until your bow arm is horizontal. It's important to have your hands set first, so that you don't have to make any adjustments later while you're shooting. Now aim at the target. Don't worry about holding dead on, because you're more concerned here with your form than with hitting the bull's eye. (For details, see Aiming Methods.)

The Bow Arm. Before going further with the shot, analyze the position of your bow arm. This may be the most important step in accurate, consistent shooting. Here again, relaxation is the key.

Al Henderson said: "You have to learn to relax that bow arm. That's the most important part of shooting, because the bow arm puts the arrow in there. You can have an imperfect release and if your bow arm is solid the arrow will go in; but if your bow arm is off, the most perfect release won't put the arrow on target.

the bow hand, the string hand should be rotated one eighth turn off vertical in a natural position. If you place your fingers vertically on the string, your hand will try to rotate back into a natural position as you draw, and you'll twist the string. On a light bow, you actually can see some shooters put a big bend in the string as they torque it with their fingers. It's impossible to release smoothly with this kind of off-line pressure.

To start out, hook the string on your fingers right to the first joint. As you draw you may keep even pressure on all three fingers, but most likely one finger will receive greater pressure than the others. Jim Pickering suggests that greatest pressure should transfer to the middle finger, and the other two fingers should serve primarily as support.

When your hands are set, raise the entire bow/arm unit, ready to draw. The drawing arm should be held high for maximum leverage, and the wrist on the drawing arm should be straight.

It's absolutely critical to have a good bow arm. And that means it's absolutely relaxed, but controlled. You relax every bit of tension you don't need to hold that bow up there."

According to Jim Pickering, the only tension occurs in the tricep. "You must relax the forearm from the elbow down," Pickering said. "The only acceptable tension occurs in the tricep, which supports the bow arm. The tricep on my bow arm is nearly 5/8-inch bigger than on my drawing arm."

Lonnie Jones said: "Many shooters tense up here because they think they must hold the bow up, but the bow arm is just a brace. Once you get the arm up and pull on the string, the arm locks into place. It can relax."

To form that brace, you must position the arm correctly. Don Rabska, a top tournament archer and a consultant for the U.S. Olympic Archery Committee, said your bow arm shoulder should be held low.

"Pull down with the muscles along your side below the shoulder to pull the shoulder down. This locks the shoulder into a solid position so the arm bone is pushing directly into the shoulder socket, bone into bone. That's solid.

"If your shoulder is high, you have to control it strictly by muscle tension, which offers little control and will tire you quickly. It's im-

At full draw you should remain relaxed. Run through the checkpoints to see that your bow hand and arm, your neck, and your drawing arm are all relaxed. Notice that Pickering's bow shoulder is pulled down in a straight line with his arm. This shoulder should not be "hunched."

portant not to lean back as you shoot because that only raises the bow shoulder. Stand straight up and pull down with the side muscles to keep that shoulder low. With the shoulder in the correct position, you can feel a little V where the arm and shoulder meet."

Also, rotate your bow arm so the inside of the elbow is vertical. This gives more string clearance. If you allow the elbow to face upward, the bowstring is more likely to slap your arm when you release.

The Drawing Arm. With the bow held up in a shooting position, the drawing elbow should be held high, above shoulder level. In this high position, you can get plenty of leverage to pull with your back. With the elbow low, you pull with your bicep.

Jim Pickering said: "Keep the elbow high. If you draw low you must pull with the bicep and chest. With a high elbow you get a rotating movement that brings the back into play, and that's where you get your power. Visualize a wall just behind your draw elbow. Push your elbow against the wall. As you draw, the only tension you feel occurs in your back."

Don Rabska made one other suggestion for bringing your back into play. "Before you draw, bring your shoulder back first. That preloads your back for action. If you leave your shoulder forward, you pull primarily with your arm and biceps. Doing this you can stretch the tendons in your shoulder and end up with bad tendinitis. Pull with your back."

The Anchor Point. At full draw you must take a solid anchor. Probably the most common anchor point among bowhunters is the index finger at the corner of the mouth. (For alternatives, see Anchor Point.) The point at which you anchor isn't as important as consistency. Anchor exactly the same way each time, and anchor solidly. As Jim Pickering said, the anchor point is the rear sight of your bow shooting machine. If the rear sight changes position from shot to shot, you'll shoot no more accurately than a rifle shooter with a wobbly rear sight. Work to develop a solid, consistent anchor point.

For hunting, Pickering anchors with the index finger at the corner of his mouth. He then locks his thumb under his chin, which braces his hand solidly, and he lays the string lightly against the side of his nose. This gives him three anchor checkpoints—finger to mouth, thumb to chin, string to nose—to assure exact alignment every shot.

Alignment. At full draw, you probably won't pause for several minutes to check alignment, but it's something you must think about, for full draw is the time your alignment must be right.

This possibly could be called "extension." At least extension is one aspect of alignment. Theoretically, your body should fall in a straight line from your bow hand up through your bow arm and shoulders through your string hand and right out to the elbow of your drawing arm, and the bowstring should run right down through your bow arm. That would be perfect alignment.

Obviously that's impossible, but you want to come as close to that ideal as possible. That calls for complete extension. In other words, you don't want to underdraw your bow. Some archers suggest modifying your shooting style so you can shoot a shorter arrow for greater arrow speed. That sounds great in theory, but it means you have to compromise your shooting style, and you may lose more than you gain.

Don Rabska said he encourages all archers to shoot the absolute maximum-length arrow they can shoot without forcing or overstretching. That's because the longer the draw length, the closer you come to getting the bow, string, and arrow into the same line. (For more details, see Draw Length.)

As part of alignment, check your head position and stance. In essence, your stance should not change when you draw. At full draw, your head should be straight up, not cocked to the side, forward, or back. Your weight should be distributed evenly on both feet, and your hips should be straight, not cocked to the side like a belly dancer's. In other words, if you took photos of yourself before and after drawing your bow, the only thing that should have

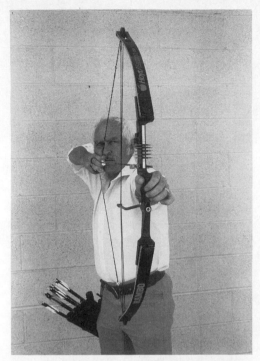

Even under the tension of a hunting bow at full draw, you should remain relaxed. Shooting should be a process of relaxation, not tension. For best shooting, shoot the maximum draw length comfortable for you to ensure good alignment. Notice that Pickering's bow hand, aiming eye, string hand, wrist, and elbow fall into virtually a straight line. That's good alignment that ensures consistent shooting.

changed is your arm position. Your body position and alignment should be identical.

The Release. A good release ranks just behind a solid bow arm for accuracy. This is the one point when your body moves during a shot, so you must practice over and over to get that movement consistent. If you release differently from shot to shot, you'll spray arrows all over the target.

Again, the release is an act of relaxation, not tension. To release the string, you simply relax your fingers and the string will slip away. Lonnie Jones suggests that to achieve the perfect release, you forget about your fingers. If you concentrate on them, you'll deliberately open your fingers to let go of the string. And that will produce a terrible release.

Instead, concentrate on lifting the draw-arm elbow *up and back*, and allow the fingers to relax. As pressure on the string increases, the string will slip away smoothly.

"You release by allowing the string to go," Jones said. "You just quit holding onto it. To put it another way, Don't let go of the string; let the string go."

Jim Pickering said you should "drop" the string. "You don't let go of the string," he said. "Instead, you drop it. To practice this movement, pick up a bucket of sand by the bail like you'd hold a bowstring and lift it a couple of inches off the floor. Now let your fingers relax and drop the bucket. You drop the bowstring in a similar fashion."

The problem with deliberately opening your fingers is that your fingers will follow the string. It's hard to develop consistency doing that, and in effect you also shorten your draw length, which will decrease arrow speed.

If you release correctly, your hand will move back sharply when the string slips away, but it will stay close to your face. The fingers will be limp and relaxed. Several checkpoints indicate a bad release. One, if your fingers are stiff, you opened your hand deliberately to get rid of the string. Two, if your string hand has moved out from your face, you plucked or twanged the string, which will throw an arrow well off target. Three, if your hand has moved forward, you've followed the string. Again, after a perfect release your hand will move back along your face, and your fingers will be limp. (For details, see Release.)

Follow Through. After the release, you should continue to aim until the arrow hits the target. Your bow may move slightly after the shot, but it should move very little, and it should move the same way after every shot. If the bow jerks violently after the release, you've developed tension somewhere. Adjust your body alignment. Try opening or closing your stance, and as you practice concentrate on each of the checkpoints to eliminate all muscle tension.

As you follow through, mentally run through these checkpoints to see if you've maintained good form. Are you still aiming at the target? Is your bow arm relaxed? Where is your string hand? Is it right beside your face, and are the string fingers limp? Is your body still in a relaxed, comfortable stance, or have you contorted or twisted, trying to force the arrow into the target?

Practicing the Basics

"Relaxed shooting is a learned condition," Jones said. "You can't just say, 'I'll relax today.' You have to learn to relax. You have to practice it over and over."

And the same goes for all aspects of good form. You have to practice them deliberately until they become second nature. To do that, practice under controlled conditions in your yard or at an archery range. Don't take on tough field conditions until you've learned the fundamentals. And even when you do start field practice, regularly return to the target butt to work on the basics. You don't need much room to practice form. If you can shoot no more than five or ten yards in your basement or garage, that's enough; all you're concerned with at this stage is what your body is doing, not where the arrows are going.

Avoid the tendency to shoot masses of arrows, because volume shooting will only ingrain bad habits. It's better to shoot 10 careful arrows than 100 careless ones. With each arrow, run the checkpoints of form. And after each release, analyze your form and try to improve on it the next shot. Shoot each arrow deliberately, as close to perfect as you can get.

Lonnie Jones suggests practicing with your eyes closed, and I've found this a valuable tool. You stand close to the target, ten feet or so to make sure you don't miss, and you go through all the steps until you come to full draw and aim. Then you close your eyes, and as you stand at full draw, you mentally check your bow hand, bow arm, string hand, back tension, and so forth. When all feels right, you release and follow through—eyes still closed—and then hold your position and check your hands and stance to see that you're still relaxed. Don't worry about hitting the target. If your form is right, you'll hit right where you were aiming, and you should be able to shoot tight arrow groups even with your eyes closed.

The value of such practice should be obvious—you forget about where your arrows are going and concentrate solely on form. Shoot a few arrows this way each day to fine-tune your form.

For your quick reference, I'll list the basics of shooting form here to serve as a convenient checklist during practice:

1. Stance. Slightly open, weight even on both feet, body straight.

2. Bow hand. One eighth turn to side, fingers limp, hand pressure only on meaty part of thumb.

3. String hand. One eighth turn to side, greatest pressure on middle finger, wrist straight.

When you're satisfied with your hand, arm and body position, raise your bow into shooting position.

4. Bow arm. Shoulder low, arm straight and relaxed, elbow turned vertical.

5. Drawing arm. Elbow high, fingers and wrist straight.

6. Solid anchor. Finger at corner of mouth, hand solid against face.

7. Drawing the string. Push elbow against "wall," pull with back, not arm.

8. Alignment. Extend fully to create small "triangle." Body still erect, neck straight, hips straight, weight still even on both feet.

9. Release. Relax fingers. Don't let go of the string; let the string go.

10. Follow through. Alignment unchanged. Fingers on bow hand limp, string hand behind face and fingers limp. Still aiming at target.

If you follow these basics for good shooting, you'll develop a natural, easy shooting style that will serve you well in the field. (For tips on putting this style to work in the field, see Shooting Practice.)

SHOOTING GLOVE See Release Aids.

SHOOTING PRACTICE Shooting ability in the field starts with good form. (For details, see Shooting Basics.) But it doesn't stop there. You have to adapt your form to field conditions, and that's where field practice comes in. The most obvious function is to make you a good shot, but that's not the only value. Practice under field conditions also serves as a gear shakedown to eliminate bugs before the hunt, it allows you to test yourself to find your own limitations, and it prepares you mentally for close encounters with game. Don't take it lightly.

Amount of Practice

The number of arrows you shoot during a practice session and the number of days you practice each week depend on your physical condition, the weight of your bow, how you feel on a given day, and whatever. Some writers prescribe a set number of arrows, so many days a week, but that seems too arbitrary to me.

You practice to improve, and to do that you have to concentrate and shoot each arrow well. Even under field conditions, follow the same advice given under Shooting Basics. Concentrate on each shot, trying to make it as perfect as possible. Don't start mass shooting. As Jim Pickering said, "Shoot each arrow individually and analyze each shot. If you're just shooting arrows to build muscles, you might as well lift weights. If you don't analyze each shot, you won't accomplish what you set out to do."

How much should you practice? As much as you can while shooting your best. I know some hunters who shoot 10 or 12 arrows a day and others who practice 2 to 3 hours a day. They're all good shooters. If you feel good after 30 arrows and can improve, keep shooting. When you get tired or sore, lose your concentration, get angry because you're missing, or notice other negative signs, quit.

Varied Practice

When you practice strictly for form, you assume the best possible stance, but that's not always possible in hunting. Kneeling, bending to shoot from a tree stand, twisting to shoot

Shooting at awkward angles from a tree stand requires different muscles from shooting on level ground at a target butt. Practice these shots before the season.

Any hunting could involve shooting at sharp uphill and downhill angles, which not only affects how you pull a bow but trajectory, too. Work on this so you'll have no surprises during the season.

around a rock—any variation in position brings new muscles into play, and it also affects alignment and aiming. Even if 90 percent of your practice takes place on a target butt at home, you can work on these positions. Shoot some arrows while kneeling, squatting, sitting on a stool, or leaning on one knee. Turn your back to the target and twist around to shoot.

Most experienced archers agree that most hunters miss because they fail to pick a small spot on an animal to shoot at. To work on that, practice regularly on animal targets that have no aiming spot. If you don't want to spend money on them, make cardboard silhouettes.

Shoot Up and Down. If you hunt from a tree stand or in steep country, you must practice shooting up and downhill. For one thing, you have to learn how to aim, because from a sharp

angle, either up or down, you must hold low. (For details, see Trajectory.) It's also important to maintain good body alignment, and to do that you should draw your bow and then bend at the waist, rather than raising or lowering your bow arm. You'll find it's particularly hard to pull your bow while aiming up, so work on coming to maximum draw at this angle.

If you have hills in your area, put up some targets there and shoot up and downhill from various yardages. If that's not possible, put a portable stand in one of the trees in your yard and shoot down from it. If you don't have suitable trees, shoot from the roof of your house or garage. That's what I do.

Vary the Speed. During any practice session, vary the tempo of your shooting. Try a slow 10-second draw followed by a hold on target for 30 seconds before you release, as you might if a deer or elk catches you off guard. And then practice shooting fast, coming to full draw, aiming, and releasing within 3 seconds, as you might when a buck flits through one small hole in the brush.

Try Bad Conditions. To simulate field conditions, practice in bad weather. That's what Harold Boyack, one of this country's most successful trophy hunters, does. "My wife thinks I'm a masochist," Boyack said. "Guys come by on nice days and say, 'Let's go shoot our bows,' but I say, 'No, let's go when the wind is blowing or when it's raining.' That's when you really learn something."

Not only do you learn about yourself, but you learn about your clothing and gear. In cold weather you've got to bundle up, so practice in the cold to find out if bulky clothing restricts your shooting, and how it feels to shoot while wearing gloves and a face mask. Also, use this as a final shakedown of tackle. You might discover your cushion plunger freezes up in bitter cold or that the cable slide squeaks when the cable guard gets rained on (these are things I've learned). If you wait to learn things like this during a hunt, it could cost you an animal.

If you carry a pack while hunting, wear the pack during practice. It might affect your shooting, and you want to know that now. I've hunted with guys who always take off their daypacks to shoot at game, and that's nonsense. Use practice sessions to work the bugs out of your equipment system.

Shoot at Long Range. To work on followthrough, try shooting from ranges of 60 to 80 yards. That's not good deer-shooting range, but it helps your form. As the arrow flies through the air—it seems to take forever to reach a target 80 yards away—stand motionless, continuing to aim, with perfect followthrough, until the arrow hits. Long-range practice makes close shots seem easy.

Stump Shoot. Some hunters call this roving. Equip yourself with a quiver full of arrows tipped with blunts or Judo heads and wander through the woods, shooting stumps, pine cones, rotten logs. Shoot from various positions, distances, and angles. You'll develop the

Shoot from your knees and other possible hunting postures. And wear your hunting gear as a shakedown before the season.

instinct to judge range quickly. Along that line, if you plan to use a range finder in hunting, use it while stump shooting. It takes practice to get good with a range finder, just as it does with a bow.

To carry that a step further, shoot in the field as you're hunting. My quiver always contains a practice arrow tipped with a Judo head, and any time I'm walking a trail or relaxing around camp, I shoot some practice shots. Continual shooting during a hunt keeps your eye and mind sharp and your muscles loose, so you'll be ready when the real thing comes along.

Hunt Small Game. During the off-season, hunt rabbits, squirrels, and other small game. Shooting live animals, no matter what the size, differs from shooting targets and stumps. Ground squirrels, considered pests by farmers, are common near my home. Some years I've spent many days shooting ground squirrels, and other years time has been tight and I've hunted squirrels very little. Invariably I've had more confidence and have fared better on big game during years when I've shot lots of squirrels. It's the final tuneup, the closest you can come to the real thing.

Small-game hunting can sharpen your skills for hunting big game. If you can consistently pick off chucks like this, you can shoot deer.

Shooting practice involves taking game in the field. This hunter's doe may not be a trophy animal, but taking a few animals like this will give him the experience needed when the trophy buck comes along.

You might not consider big-game hunting in itself as practice, but in a sense it is. I've talked to a number of guys who've bowhunted for several years and have yet to kill a big-game animal. "I'm holding out for a big one, strictly trophy hunting," they say. In my opinion, that's a mistake. If you've never "practiced" shooting big game, you may not have the cool needed to collect Mr. Big.

Jim Martin has killed some huge whitetails in Missouri, and through his archery shop and seminars he talks to many hunters. "When beginners ask for my advice on trophy hunting," Martin said, "I tell them to shoot the first deer that comes along. You can't learn to shoot deer by thinking about it." I agree. Fill a few tags first; that's valuable practice for trophy hunting.

Shoot in Competition. You may not have any desire to become a champion archer, but competitive shooting can help your hunting. In hunting, you're under pressure, and you must learn to cope with that. As I mentioned above, shooting animals, even if they're not huge, helps immeasurably. So does shooting in competition during the off-season.

Harold Boyack attributes much of his success to competitive shooting. "It puts you under pressure. The eyes of your peers are upon you. If you learn to handle that, you can handle the tension of hunting. I shoot a lot of tournaments for that reason."

Join a night league, compete in trail shoots, shoot in field tournaments, instigate friendly competition with your friends—do anything you can to create pressure on yourself as a shooter. It will improve your hunting.

Some Final Thoughts on Practice

During any practice session, concentrate on good form. Are your bow and drawing hands relaxed? Is your bow arm stable? How is your release? Are you following through until the arrow strikes home? No matter what your practice conditions, work on these basics.

As former Olympic archery coach Al Henderson said, that's the very reason for practice. "Good shooting is 80 percent mind, 20 percent tackle and form. In fact, hitting an animal may be 100 percent mental," Henderson said. "In the field you're under stress, you're fatigued, the weather is bad, the animal is alert, you have to deal with all these things, and that doesn't give you time to think about shooting. That's why it's so important to practice, so you can forget the physical and concentrate totally on the mental plane when it comes time to shoot." (See also Shooting Basics.)

SHOOTING PROBLEMS Many shooting problems are the result of fatigue. Try to restrict practice to short sessions so you're alert and enthusiastic. Shooting dozens of arrows at a time might seem like the way to get good quickly, but if it tires you out, it will just ingrain bad habits. Practice form when your body and mind are fresh so you feel good and can concentrate on building good habits.

Also, don't mistake off-target arrows for bad shooting problems. If you're shooting tight groups that simply aren't hitting the bull's eye, your tackle and form are probably okay. You simply need to adjust your sights. It's when your arrows spray all over the target or fly erratically, dipping and swerving, that you need to troubleshoot your tackle and form. Here are some possible solutions to common shooting problems.

Erratic Arrow Flight

First, suspect tackle problems. If your arrows are matched to your bow and you're getting good arrow clearance, your arrows will fly reasonably straight, even if your shooting form is lousy. Before indicting yourself, inspect your tackle.

Tuned Tackle. First, make sure your arrows and bow are compatible. The nock locator must be set at the proper height to prevent porpoising, and arrows must be spined properly for your bow at a given weight to prevent fishtailing. Second, check for clearance. If the vanes on your arrows hit the side of your bow or the arrow rest, you'll get crazy, inconsistent arrow flight. You'll detect bad flight as the arrows fly through the air, and after a few shots, you'll see streaks on the bow or rest where the vanes hit. (For more details, see Bow Tuning.)

Bowstring Clearance. Your bowstring also could be hitting your clothing or arm to cause erratic flight. Bulky vests or jackets will interfere with the bowstring, and so will any bulky sleeve. Solving the problem may be only a matter of wearing snugger clothing or readjusting your arm guard so it will hold your sleeve tight.

Changing shooting stance could solve the problem. If you're standing 90 degrees, or nearly so, to the target, try opening your stance. That will bring your bow shoulder back and increase clearance between your bow arm and the bowstring. Also, make sure you hold your bow arm in direct line with your shoulder. Particularly if you're shooting a heavy bow that makes you strain, you'll tend to rotate your shoulder up and in toward your neck, which forces your bow arm into the string's path.

Also, rotate your bow arm so the broader axis of the elbow is vertical. If you hold your bow arm with the wide part of the elbow horizontal, the bowstring commonly will hit your elbow or forearm.

Arrows Off Target

Arrows Hitting Low. If you're following the bowstring with your hand before you release, you essentially shorten your draw length and the result could be low-hitting arrows. When you come to full draw, anchor solidly and continue to pull with your back muscles as you release to ensure that you maintain your full draw.

You also could be dropping your bow arm as you shoot. That's a common fault, because you want to see where your arrow hits. Some archers call this "caving in." When you release the string, your bow arm should move very little. Forget about watching the arrow in flight and concentrate on continuing to aim after the shot.

Arrows Hitting High. You could be plucking the string (jerking it as you release), which effectively lengthens your draw slightly. In plucking, your string hand often will end up well out to the side of your face after the release. A grooved shooting tab or glove can aggravate this problem, because the grooving makes it hard to get rid of the string. In response, you jerk your hand back. Get a new tab or glove, or try lubricating the one you have with talcum powder or silicone treatments such as Saunders Friction Fighter. Concentrate on relaxing your fingers and letting the bowstring slip away smoothly. You can also switch to a release aid, which can help eliminate plucking.

Arrows Hitting to the Side. An inconsistent anchor could be at fault here, too. Work on anchoring solidly and exactly the same way every time. Remember, your anchor point is the rear sight of your aiming system, and if the rear sight is loose, your shots will spray all over the target.

Again, plucking the string could be a problem. Work on the solutions described above under "Arrows Hitting High."

Tension in your bow arm could be forcing your arrows to one side or the other. If you're gripping the bow too tightly, it indicates tension, and so does violent movement of your bow arm to one side or the other after the shot. Again, your bow arm should remain relaxed even at full draw, and it should scarcely move upon release. You should continue to aim right at the target until the arrow strikes. Your bow hand should be totally relaxed, never gripping the bow tightly. A tight grip can torque the bow and throw arrows off target. If you're afraid you'll drop the bow when you shoot, use a wrist sling. (For details, see Wrist Sling.)

Other Shooting Problems

Arrow Falls Off Rest. If the arrow continually flops off the rest as you draw, take a slightly deeper grip on the string, and let the string roll in your fingers as you draw. As the string twists, it will pull the arrow in tight against the arrow rest. With practice this will become automatic and the problem will disappear on its own. Also, inspect your rest. It could be bent slightly down so that the arrow

slides off. Some arrow rests actually have little hooks to hold the arrow on. If you have a severe problem, this style of rest could help you. Even with a Flipper Rest or similar rest with a straight arm, the arm should be tilted up slightly so the arrow will slide toward the bow, not away. If your rest has a wire arm, bend it up just enough to hold the arrow in place.

Blisters on String Fingers. This occurs most commonly on the index finger where that finger presses into the nock. If you have this problem, you're probably pinching the nock forcibly. As you come to full draw, transfer most of the string weight to your middle finger and let your index finger "float" on the string. This should reduce the pressure of your finger on the nock. Also, if you have a long draw length and shoot a short bow, the acute angle of the string at full draw could be pinching your fingers against the nock. Shooting a longer bow, which produces a gentler string angle, or shooting with a release aid, can solve the problem.

If you develop a blister or heavy callus on one finger where the string crosses it, you're probably pulling too hard with that finger. I have a tendency to pull too hard with my fourth finger and sometimes get a painful blister on the ball of that fingertip. At full draw, try to distribute weight more evenly across all three fingers, with greatest pressure on the center finger.

Work on Form

I hesitate to list shooting "problems" because it's easy to become problem-oriented rather than "doing it right"–oriented. These suggestions might help you analyze and solve some of your problems, but don't try to improve accuracy simply by looking for things you're doing wrong. Instead, concentrate on doing everything right in the first place and building a base of good form. (For complete details, see Shooting Basics. See also Target Panic.)

SHOOTING UP AND DOWN See Trajectory.

SHOT SELECTION Shot selection involves two elements: distance and placement. Few bowhunters agree on the definition of "maximum shooting distance," or on exactly where you should place an arrow. Here are some of my opinions on shot selection and placement.

Shooting Distance

A friend of mine is adamant about shooting distance. "No one should ever shoot farther than 40 yards," he says. "That's a long shot on game, and if you can't get closer than that, you shouldn't shoot."

He's not alone in that view. In one of my articles, I suggested that shooting out to 50 yards was okay if you could shoot accurately at that distance. A respected bowhunter quickly took me to task for that; people in my position, he said, should not encourage such long-range shooting.

Assigning an absolute maximum shooting distance has two problems. One, it assumes that everyone shoots the same kind of equipment and has equal skill. Two, it assumes that the closer you are, the better your chances for making a clean hit. I think both premises are dead wrong.

Tackle. It's no secret that some bows shoot arrows faster and with flatter trajectory than other bows. By virtue of speed alone, effective shooting range varies. Many of the short-range-only advocates shoot longbows or recurves, and many such bows cast an arrow no faster than 160 to 180 feet per second. How can you equate the effective distance of such a bow with that of a compound bow that shoots an arrow at 240 fps? This isn't to say one is better than the other, only that they aren't comparable.

Not all tackle is equally well tuned, either. Some shooters spend hours fine-tuning their tackle so their arrows fly perfectly straight and group well, even with broadheads, out to 50 yards and farther, while other hunters slap on a rubber rest, buy a half dozen arrows across the counter, and go hunting. Even if the arrow speed is identical, arrows shot from well-tuned

Shot selection can't be gauged in terms of absolute yardages. Effective range depends on a shooter's skill, the amount he practices, his experience, and the speed and quality of his tackle.

tackle will fly accurately to much greater distances than arrows from ill-tuned tackle. (For details, see Bow Tuning.) Again, prescribing a maximum shooting distance for all hunters is invalid.

Shooting Ability. Some hunters simply shoot more accurately than others. Partly that has to do with tackle, as described above, but it also involves physical ability and practice. Steve Gorr, who outfits antelope hunts in Wyoming, has opportunity to associate with dozens of hunters from across the United States each year, and he sees great variations in shooting ability.

"You'd better get the guys from Wisconsin and Michigan within 15 yards or they won't kill antelope," Gorr said. "The California guys are another story. They're far better shots, and there's no question that many Western hunters can kill animals cleanly at 40 yards and farther. They practice at long range, they shoot field tournaments with long-range targets, and they shoot hot bows. Some of them are deadly.

"I came from the Midwest myself, and I never practiced at long distances. My first years in Colorado, I got within 45 yards of bighorn sheep more than once and I didn't shoot. Looking back now, I still can't believe I didn't shoot at those sheep."

Personal Ability. This doesn't mean I advocate long-range shooting, only that no one can impose a set standard on all hunters. Some archers can shoot more accurately at 60 yards than others can at 20, so who's to say maximum effective range is 40 yards? For some hunters it's much farther, and for others it's much shorter. (And some hunters have no business hunting with a bow at all.) You must determine your own effective range. Cliff Dewell suggests putting a pie plate (about the size of a deer's vital area) on a target butt and then roving and shooting the plate from various distances. As long as you can keep arrows within the plate, you're within effective range; when

you start spraying arrows outside the plate, you're too far. Use that as a gauge in hunting.

The same things that can be said about shooting distance can be said about running shots. Some hunters advocate running shots (even some who decry long-range shooting) and others say no, no, no. I'd say if you've practiced on running shots and can make them consistently, then you're qualified to take such shots within your range of competency. I would add, however, that few hunters—maybe one in a thousand—are qualified to shoot at running game. Today's compound bows with sights are far more suited to deliberate, precision shooting than to impulsive shooting at moving game, and I'd say that for most hunters, a 50-yard shot at a standing, calm deer is far better than a 10-yard shot at a running animal.

Size of Animal. Much of the controversy over shooting distance relates to the potential for wounding an animal. Everyone agrees—or at least they should—that the object is to make a clean kill. The worst thing any hunter can do is to wound an animal.

But shooting distance isn't the only variable

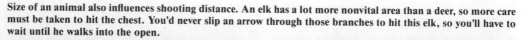

Size of an animal also influences shooting distance. An elk has a lot more nonvital area than a deer, so more care must be taken to hit the chest. You'd never slip an arrow through those branches to hit this elk, so you'll have to wait until he walks into the open.

in governing that. Size of the animal enters in, too. To see why, consider an extreme example. A squirrel has a high ratio of vital to nonvital area, so virtually any kind of hit, except in the tail, will kill a squirrel cleanly. So if you want to shoot at squirrels at 70 or 80 yards, why not? You might not hit many, but if you do you'll kill them cleanly.

The bigger the animal, the smaller the ratio of vital to nonvital area, so the closer your shots should be for a clean kill. Sure, an elk has a bigger kill zone (heart and lungs) than a deer, but an elk also has a lot more guts, neck, legs, and other nonvital tissue. A poorly placed shot on an elk is a lot more likely to produce a crippling wound than it is on a deer. Given my personal ability, I would shoot at a deer in the open at 50 yards, but under most conditions I would hold out on an elk until it was closer than 30 yards.

Cover. Decisions like that have a lot to do with circumstances, too. You'll encounter virtually all elk in heavy cover, and the longer the shot in timber or brush, the less reliably you can judge obstructions between you and the animal. I shot at one bull elk at 30 yards and hit a limb, and my arrow deflected into the dirt. As soon as the elk ran, I bugled and he came back in. I picked what appeared to be an open lane and shot as he entered that lane. Again my arrow hit a limb, and this time it bounced off the elk's rump. He wasn't hurt, but the arrow could just as easily have hit him in the paunch, which would have produced an ugly wound and little chance for recovery. (For details, see Trailing.)

In contrast to that situation, most mule deer and antelope live in wide-open terrain where nothing but pure air separates you and the animal. Under those circumstances, a long shot is far more feasible than in timber.

Animal Reaction. "Jumping the string" means an animal reacts to the sound of a bow quickly enough to get out of the way of an arrow. There's some debate as to whether an animal reacts to the sound or to the sudden movement of the bow's limbs, but I think it can be either or both, depending on the situation.

Terrain and cover also influence shooting distance. A 50-yard shot in this country differs greatly from a 50-yard shot in dense forest.

One way or the other, such reaction isn't uncommon.

String jumping has commonly been used as an argument against longer-range shooting. The logic goes that the farther an animal, the more time it has to move before the arrow gets there. For a couple of reasons, I think that reasoning is wrong. First, it assumes that big game animals need the time provided by long arrow flight to evade an arrow, and that's not true. One time I shot at a bull elk, 700 to 800 pounds worth of animal, facing me at 18 yards. When I released, the arrow was on target, but the bull whirled and the arrow missed him completely. In that case, the elk reacted by sight.

Steve Gorr said one of his hunters, shooting a 70-pound compound bow, shot at an antelope 10 yards away as it drank from a waterhole. When the bow went off, the antelope instantaneously dug in to run, and as its back dropped several inches, the arrow went over it and killed a buck standing beyond. In this case, the reaction probably was to sound.

Maybe the average deer can't match an antelope for quickness, but the reaction speed of any big-game animal is astonishing. Even if a deer or other animal can't completely dodge an

This deer is certainly within good range, but does he present a good shot? Maybe not, because he's alert and knows you're there. "Close range" isn't necessarily the same as "good shot."

arrow at 15 to 20 yards, it can, without question, move far enough to turn a well-aimed arrow into a messy hit.

At least two things contribute to string jumping. One is alertness of the animal. If a deer, for example, senses your presence and stands tense and poised to bolt, your chances of hitting it cleanly are poor. It will react instantly to the slightest movement or sound.

The other is proximity. The nature of an animal's reaction is proportional to distance: the closer, the more violent the reaction; the farther, the milder the reaction. When an animal perceives the slightest unnatural movement or sound at close range, say 20 yards or less, it explodes like a stick of dynamite. In contrast, an animal often reacts with mild curiosity to unidentified sounds or movements at longer distances, say 30 to 40 yards on out. I personally consider a 50-yard shot at a feeding, undisturbed buck a far better bowhunting opportunity than a 20-yard shot at a tense, alert buck.

Human Reaction. I also generally consider shots at the long end of your effective shooting range better than shots at the short end for another reason—human reaction. The one thing that distinguishes bowhunting from firearms hunting is proximity. In bowhunting you

get close, and that's what makes the whole thing exciting.

At the same time, that can be a serious obstacle, because it's an intense, supercharged experience. Shooting at a big buck 10 yards away is not like shooting at a bale of hay at the same distance. I personally feel charged with electricity, and I'm overcome with an unrelenting urge to hurry and shoot. I've missed a number of shots at 10 and 15 yards, not because I can't shoot well at those yardages, but because I can't keep my cool when shooting at animals at such close quarters. In contrast, shooting at a deer feeding calmly 50 yards away is little different for me from shooting at a target at that range. I can draw, aim, hold, and release with cool deliberation, and I've got a very high clean-kill ratio on deer shot at 40 to 50 yards.

This trait isn't unique to me. Again, Steve Gorr offers observations from his guiding experiences. "I've seen guys who shoot release aids and sights—these guys are deadly shots—miss 10 and 15 shots at antelope less than 20 yards away, and then they'll turn around and make clean kills at 50 to 70 yards. One guy had over 200 antelope come within close range of his blind over a two-day period, and he never killed one."

This buck presents the kind of shot you're looking for. He's unaware of your presence and he's relaxed and most likely won't jump the string. The hole through the bushes may be slightly too far back. An arrow through there would catch him in the liver.

"Killing game under 20 yards has nothing to do with shooting ability. It's all between your ears."

The effect an animal has on you may depend on circumstances. If you're hunting from a tree stand and can see a deer coming for some time and can wait until he's in just the right place, then maybe you can keep calm. But if you're at eye level with an animal and so close you can feel his breath, your reaction might be different.

Shot Placement

Nonvital Shots. One book shows a bedded deer, and the author advises "punching" an arrow through the neck. The implication is that that's the only alternative, which, of course, is hogwash. You always have another alternative: not shooting. The neck is 90 percent bone and muscle, and the only vital part is the carotid artery, which feeds the brain. If you hit that, the deer is obviously dead. Possibly you could hit the spinal cord and drop a deer in its tracks, but on heavy deer and bigger animals such as elk, you're not likely to get the spinal cord. With most neck hits, you'll generally just plant a broadhead ineffectually in a vertebra, or you'll poke a hole through the windpipe or esophagus and leave the deer with a painful but nonvital wound. Shoot at the neck on a rabbit or grouse if you want, but for Pete's sake, don't shoot at the neck, or head, on any big-game animal.

Some hunters advise shooting deer in the rump. Possibly if you shoot with pinpoint accuracy and have a close shot at a calm deer, that's okay. The femoral artery runs down the inside of the back leg, and if you cut that artery or the many vessels branching off it, the deer will die quickly. Also, if you put the arrow through the hole in the pelvis, it will go the full length of the body to hit the lungs and other vital organs. Unfortunately, if you miss the mark even slightly, you can stick an arrow in the pelvis or heavy leg bone, and you've done nothing but cripple the deer. And on bigger animals like elk, your arrow might not go full length even if it goes dead center through the

Some hunters advise shooting animals in the rump. On a deer the arrow will penetrate the full length of the animal to hit lungs. And an arrow along the inside of the back legs will get the femoral artery. However, those shots must be exact, and any miscue in accuracy could produce a messy hit. I advise not shooting. That's especially true on a buck like this. He's calm and will feed into a better position to give you a chest shot.

pelvis, and then you've got a gut-shot animal. On animals bigger than deer, I'd say never take a rear-end shot. On deer, rear-end shots must be taken with discretion, and in most cases you're wise to bide your time and let the animal turn to give you a direct chest shot.

Hitting the Vitals. You often read that a broadhead kills by hemorrhage (bleeding). That's true in some cases, but that's not how it kills with a well-placed hit. If an arrow goes through an animal's lungs or heart, the animal dies of organ failure within seconds, well before it bleeds to death. For that reason, I consider the chest, and more specifically the lungs and the heart, the only legitimate aiming point. The chest also houses the liver just behind (posterior to) the lungs, and a shot slightly far back will hit this blood-rich organ and cause an animal to bleed to death within a few minutes.

Broadside presents a good aiming shot, but to be sure of a lung hit, you must shoot close to the front leg. An animal quartering slightly away presents the ideal angle, because any ar-

With a broadside shot, you must keep your arrow fairly close to the front shoulder to hit the lungs. If you aim for the hairline where the front leg meets the chest, and about one third of the way up the chest, you'll kill this buck cleanly. If you hit two thirds of the way up the chest, you'll hit the shoulder blade and an "air space" above the lungs, and you won't get the buck.

This buck presents a nearly ideal shooting angle. An arrow behind the near front leg, just below the midline of the chest, will pass through the chest diagonally to get both lungs.

row hitting the mid- to rear chest will angle diagonally forward through the lungs, or if a little low, into the heart.

Aim Low. Perhaps the most serious mistake on these shots is shooting too high. If you're at eye level with an animal, aim slightly below the center line of the chest. That way if you shoot high, you'll still hit lungs, and if you shoot low you'll get the heart or miss the deer completely. If, on the other hand, you aim above the mid-

line of the chest and accidentally hit a little high, you could hit above the lungs. Between the lungs and the backbone is a nonvital "air space," and I'll guarantee you won't recover a deer hit high in the chest. The animal will leave fair blood sign for a while, but soon the blood will stop but the animal won't. I followed one buck hit high in the chest for six miles (this was on snow, which helped in trailing) and he was still going strong when I last saw him topping out on a distant ridge.

Of course, if you're shooting sharply down, say from a cliff or tree stand, you must adjust your shooting angle. The steeper the angle, the higher your arrow must hit on the chest to pass through the lungs.

If a deer is quartered sharply toward you, don't shoot behind the front legs as you'd do on a broadside or quartering-away animal because the arrow could completely bypass the lungs and liver and end up in the guts. Instead aim just in front of the front leg fairly low. The arrow will cut through ribs there to hit the heart. I shot a bull elk just in front of the leg, and he ran only 75 yards before dropping. The arrow had cut an X right through his heart.

If the animal is facing straight on, shoot for the base of the neck, where the windpipe enters

This buck presents a good shot. His leg is pulled well forward to expose his heart and lungs. Aim directly above his "elbow," one third to halfway up the chest. To ensure a well-placed arrow, pick an aiming spot on the deer's chest.

the chest. If the arrow is a little high it will get lungs, and a little low it will get heart. For either a quartering-toward-you or head-on shot, I recommend waiting if the animal has you spotted and has tensed. Odds are against hitting him cleanly, because he'll jump the string the instant you let go.

Making the Shot

The points mentioned and shown in the accompanying photos not only tell you where to hit, they tell you where to *aim*. There is a difference. You can learn right now where you must hit a deer to kill it, but putting the arrow in that spot during the heat of action isn't so easy.

Most experienced hunters agree that to kill animals consistently you must pick a specific spot on an animal and aim for that, just as you would to hit a spot on a target. Failure to pick that spot probably rates as the number one reason for missed animals in the field. Before you draw to shoot, consciously make yourself pick out a hair or a fold of skin, and concentrate only on that as you proceed with the shot. (For more details, see Shooting Practice.)

On a deer facing toward you, aim right where the windpipe passes between the front legs to enter the chest. You'll get heart or lungs. A front-on shot, however, is not well advised if a buck is tense or alert, as this one is. He'll very likely jump the string and you'll get a bad hit, or no hit at all.

SIGHTS   See Bowsight and Peep Sight.

SITKA DEER (Odocoileus hemionus sitkensis)   These animals are classified as a subspecies of mule deer, and they're commonly called Sitka blacktails. No distinct line can be drawn between the ranges of Sitka deer and Columbian blacktail deer, so generally Sitka deer are defined as deer living in Alaska and the Queen Charlotte Islands of British Columbia.

The Nature of Sitka Deer

Range. These deer generally live in a band along the coast and coastal islands of southwestern Alaska that corresponds to old-growth spruce and hemlock forests. They require the shelter of these forests in winter. The exception occurs on Kodiak Island, where Sitka deer have done well in the absence of old-growth timber. Hard winters present the major limitation on numbers; following severe winters, deer populations diminish drastically. Before planning a hunt, investigate to find out where the deer are doing best at the moment. Most

When shooting down, you must adjust your aiming spot to hit a little higher so the arrow will pass down through the lungs.

areas in Alaska have multiple-deer limits. (For more details, see Alaska.)

Size. Sitka deer have a reputation for being tiny, but they're no smaller than blacktails and whitetails from many regions. The average yearling Sitka buck weighs somewhere around 100 pounds live weight, and mature bucks will weigh close to 150 pounds. The biggest Sitka deer on record field dressed 209 pounds, which would give it a live weight around 250 pounds.

Hunting Sitka Deer

During early seasons in August and September, Sitka deer live at relatively high elevations in alpine terrain, and here you hunt them much as you would mule deer in any other timberline country. The weather in August can be a little warmer than later in the year (although it can be nearly intolerable at any time) but to get to the deer, you may have to backpack uphill from the beach as much as 3,000 feet. And in the process, you'll have to force your way

Bob Long killed this Sitka buck on Kodiak Island in early November. Temperature was about −15 degrees F. This buck scored 90 Pope and Young points.

through heavy forests and alder jungles. Early-season hunting can be a rugged proposition.

Deepening snows in fall force deer to lower elevations to winter in old-growth forests where snow doesn't accumulate as heavily. In severe winters, many Sitka deer congregate right along the ocean beaches, and many hunters wait until this time to hunt them where they're easier to get to.

Bob Long, a California archer, hunted Sitka deer on Kodiak Island the first week in November. At this time the deer were concentrated about 1,000 feet above sea level, an elevation at which alder trees form a fairly continuous band. That late in the year all the leaves had fallen from the trees and brush, and Long had no trouble spotting deer; he saw a dozen or more bucks each day. He killed bucks scoring 90 and 102 Pope and Young points, and one of his companions killed a buck measuring 107.

"I consider them the dumbest deer in the world," Long said. "They don't have any enemies there except bears, and bears are half blind so the deer probably don't run from them at long range. They were also in rut during that time, which undoubtedly reduced their caution. For trophy hunting, I would definitely recommend hunting when they're in rut in November.

"A lot of the deer would just stand there and look at me, and I had little trouble getting within range. I shot at the smaller of my two bucks three times. The first two arrows rattled off alder branches and the buck never moved, and I got him with the third arrow."

Long thinks late November might be even better because then deep snow normally has pushed the deer right down onto the beach where they're most accessible. The only problem then is the short daylight. During the first week in November there was no surplus of daylight—first light about 9:30 A.M., dark at 4:00 P.M.—and it would be even scarcer later in the year.

Long and his companions hunted on their own without an outfitter, but even at that it wasn't an easy or cheap hunt. They flew by commercial airline to Kodiak and then by bush

432

plane to their hunting area. They also rented a raft to cruise the coast so they could camp in various locations. They found plenty of deer wherever they hit the coast.

Anyone going after Sitka deer has to consider a couple of potential problems. One is bears. "We had bears in camp about half the nights we were there," Long said. "That got a little spooky. We were up half the night a couple of times, shooting guns in the air, trying to scare them off."

It's fairly common for bears to claim a deer carcass, and brown bears normally win disputes over deer. Have some means for hanging meat high off the ground, and always approach a kill cautiously. Most hunters I know who hunt Alaska regularly agree hunters should carry an open-choke shotgun loaded with buckshot as defense against bears.

Another problem Long encountered was cold. "The temperature was 15 below zero and the wind brought the chill factor down somewhere around 30 below," Long said. "It was so cold the ocean water was freezing out several feet from shore. I slept in three sleeping bags and still got cold. With the right clothes you can tolerate the cold, but one problem we had was finding fresh drinking water. Everything was frozen."

Long hunted primarily by spotting deer in the leafless alders and stalking, but he thinks the deer also could be called or rattled in. Frequently he heard bucks fighting, and he said they regularly made a grunting sound similar to that of rutting whitetails.

Deer calling has been a proven method for Sitka deer for years. Hunters use a small call made with a rubber band clamped between two blocks of wood so the rubber band vibrates when you blow on it. It works the same as clamping a blade of grass between your thumbs and blowing on it to produce a squawling sound. The deer call makes a bleating sound that attracts Sitka deer.

Trophy Hunting

The typical antler formation consists of two points on the main beams plus brow tines, but to score really well a rack must have at least three points plus brow tines on each side. Like other deer antlers, Sitka antlers must have relatively long main beams and a good spread. Inside spread should be at least 16 inches or greater, which means you should see some daylight between the ears and the main beams. The largest racks will score close to 130, but anything over 90 has to be considered good.

At this writing, too few Sitka deer have been recorded for the record books to serve as a reliable guide to the best trophy areas. Kodiak and Afognak islands have been fairly popular with bowhunters (by Alaskan standards — which means archers are scarce), but undoubtedly any part of the Sitka's range can produce record-book animals. Most of it is so remote, and the deer kill is so light, that plenty of bucks live to old age. Buck/doe ratios are generally high.

SMALL-GAME HUNTING Some archers hunt small game as seriously as they hunt big game, others shoot an occasional small-game animal incidental to big-game hunting, and many hunt small game during the off-season as practice for big-game hunting. Whatever your motive, small game can add to your hunting time and efficiency.

Small animals most commonly shot for food are rabbits, tree squirrels, and various birds such as grouse and ptarmigan. Other animals that are unprotected and are generally considered pests are hunted primarily for shooting practice. Among these are ground squirrels, prairie dogs, jackrabbits, woodchucks, and marmots. (For details and hunting methods on each small-game animal, see Hares; Marmot; Rabbit; and Squirrel.)

Arrow Heads for Small Game

When you shoot big game, you use a sharp broadhead to ensure good penetration and bleeding. Arrows don't deliver enough shock, as a bullet might, to do much damage. On small game, that isn't the case. Arrows kill primarily by shock, so you want to use a head that delivers the maximum wallop. The biggest con-

Some archers, Bill Bechen among them, take small-game hunting seriously. A cottontail and rockchuck make up part of Bechen's morning bag of game.

cern in small-game hunting, I think, is pass-through shots, so you want to use heads that hit hard and won't go through an animal.

Never use straight field points on small game, and avoid using steel blunts. These will simply poke a hole through most animals, and the animals will run off. You'll lose your arrow and the animal will die a slow, ugly death. I'd recommend steel blunts only for ground squirrels. These animals are small, and the blunt delivers enough shock to kill them outright, even if it passes through.

For most squirrels, rabbits, marmots, grouse, and other small game, something with more surface area is needed. Two kinds of heads work well: the rubber blunt and the Zwickey Judo. In brushy country or where thick leaves cover the ground, the Judo works better because its little spring arms snag on leaves and twigs and keep it from sliding under cover. John Zwickey promotes the Judo as the "unlosable" head, and that's almost an accurate statement (although I've lost a couple under thick oak leaves). For hunting rabbits in briar patches or grass, squirrels on the ground in thick leaves, grouse in conifer forests, and

Many archers regularly kill grouse and other game birds incidental to big-game hunting. A big old blue grouse like this can really sweeten the pot around a hunting camp.

The HMT rubber blunt at left works well for general small-game hunting, and it's especially good for shooting up into trees because it won't stick in the bark. The steel blunt is ideal for stump shooting, but it will pass through small game unless backed by a stopper of some kind. Saunders' Roverine small-game head can be placed behind a field point or steel blunt. The Judo head at far right is one of the best all-around stump-shooting and small-game heads.

For shooting snowshoe rabbits like this and other small game on the ground, use a Judo head that won't slide under grass and leaves.

Chances are pretty good you might hit something besides squirrel when you shoot at this guy. For shooting into trees, use rubber blunts or bludgeons that won't stick in bark.

similar situations, the Judo point is hard to beat.

The rubber blunt delivers instant knock-down shocking power, so for shooting ground squirrels, prairie dogs, jackrabbits or other open-field animals where arrows won't get lost easily, I prefer rubber blunts like the HMT rubber blunt that slips over the shaft or the Saunders screw-in Bludgeon. Rubber heads are better for chuck hunting in rocks because they'll bounce off rocks and save you an occasional shaft, and they're better for shooting up into trees, say for grouse or tree squirrels. A Judo head will stick in bark and you'll find yourself climbing to save your arrows, but a rubber blunt will bounce off and fall to the ground.

Other devices also work well on small game. Saunders' Roverine can be screwed onto a shaft behind a broadhead or field point to prevent pass-throughs. If you're shooting a light draw-weight bow for bigger animals — jackrabbits and chucks — a head that kills by impact might not hit with enough power to kill cleanly. In that case, broadheads are superior, but you should use a "stopper" of some kind to prevent pass-throughs. The Zwickey Scorpio and Saunders' Penetration Limiter are spring devices that slip on the shaft. They slide down the shaft on impact to allow adequate penetra-

tion, but they keep the arrow from going on through.

For field hunting in soft dirt, you might shoot your regular hunting shafts, but in rocks or limby cover, you'll destroy a lot of expensive arrows that way. To save money, shoot cedar shafts. Production-grade "woods" might be slightly less accurate than your good arrows because they're not matched precisely for spine

For prairie dogs and ground squirrels, you can use your regular hunting arrows because you won't destroy many in the soft dirt where these animals live. Colonial animals like these sometimes host plague and other diseases.

and mass weight, but they shoot acceptably, and you won't fret over destroying a few of them. For hunting on the ground, use normal fletching, but for shooting into trees, use flu-flu arrows. (For more details, see Flu-Flu Arrow.) These fly well out to 30 yards or so, but then they slow quickly and fall to the ground within easy-to-find range.

How to Clean Small Game

If weather is cold, you can get away with carrying small game uncleaned in a game pouch for a while, but the animals will keep better, particularly in hot weather, if you gut and skin them immediately in the field. The following method works on most small game such as rabbits and squirrels, and it takes only a couple of minutes for each animal.

1. Cut off the feet, head, and tail. A knife will do, but heavy shears make the job quick and neat.
2. Slit the hide across the middle of the back. You don't need a big slit, just enough to slip your fingers into.
3. With one hand on each side of the slit, grasp the hide and pull in opposite directions. The skin will tear all the way around the animal and slip off each end.
4. Slit the stomach and split the pelvic bone.
5. Holding the animal by the front shoulders, sling it hard toward the ground (don't let go!). The guts should fly out. Pull out the lungs and liver to complete the job.

Disease in Small Game

Hunters traditionally eat some small mammals and shun others. They say tree squirrels and cottontails are okay, for example, but jackrabbits are anathema because they've got diseases.

The fact is, most rodents could have diseases, and jackrabbits are no more lethal than any other small game. Most biologists who regularly work with rabbits and hares give disease little thought. They don't deny its existence. They simply know that if they use caution, animal diseases pose no threat.

Jackrabbits often have been maligned as disease-ridden, but they're no greater offenders than most other small-game animals. To kill big jacks, use tackle that packs a wallop.

Tularemia is the disease most commonly associated with jackrabbits, but the fact is, jackrabbits aren't the only animals affected. Dave Brown, a biologist with the Arizona Game and Fish Department, said far more cases of tularemia in his state result from handling cottontails than jackrabbits.

Chris Maser, a biologist with the Bureau of Land Management in Oregon, has worked with small mammals for more than 20 years. He doesn't give tularemia much thought. He simply advises hunters to use some caution by avoiding animals that are obviously sick. If they move slowly, have poor posture or rough hair, or have lots of ticks and fleas, they're probably infected. If an animal looks or acts less than healthy, he said, don't handle it.

A definite indication of tularemia is yellow spots on an animal's liver. Of course, by the time you've seen that, you may have it too. Tularemia is transmitted when an infected animal's blood comes directly into contact with yours. That happens as you dress an animal, and then only if you have a cut or open sore, or cut yourself on a broken bone. Rubber gloves ensure protection against infection, so as a precaution, always wear rubber gloves while skinning and cleaning rabbits. Then you can pretty well forget about tularemia. You can't get it from cooked meat.

Tularemia is easily cured by prompt treatment with antibiotics. Symptoms are fever, headache, and general bad feeling, two to ten days after infection. If you feel that way, see a doctor and make sure you tell him you've been handling small mammals (actually not just small game; a friend of mine contracted tularemia while skinning a bear). Doctors don't see a lot of this disease, so they might misdiagnose your problem without the proper background.

Plague also inspires fear among some hunters, probably because of the grisly history of this disease. That's not to make light of plague and other diseases, because they do occur and can be serious. In 1983, Arizona reported at least ten cases of plague, and three were fatal. In most cases, the plague was contracted from cottontail rabbits, and all were in a certain area where the disease had apparently built to an explosive level. That's very unusual. Plague is normally rare among solitary animals such as rabbits and hares. It's more common among colonial animals like ground squirrels.

Plague is transmitted to man primarily by fleas. Again, if you kill a weak or sick-looking animal, leave it alone. One biologist warned that plague commonly is spread by fleas that ride home with family dogs and cats.

Symptoms of plague are nausea, high fever, and severe muscle ache, one to six days after infection. Again, prompt treatment with antibiotics will cure plague.

SNOWSHOE HARE   See Hares.

SOUTH CAROLINA   South Carolina has an area of 31,055 square miles. The state can be broken into three major regions: the coastal plain, which covers the eastern half of the state; the Piedmont just inland; and the foothills region along the western boundary. State-wide, 1.6 million acres of state-managed lands are open to public hunting.

Big Game

Whitetail Deer. The whitetail population is estimated at 300,000. No data are available on the number of bowhunters or harvest. Seasons vary by management zone. The most generous run from mid-August through December in the coastal plain. In the Piedmont and foothills regions, seasons run from October 1 through January 1. These ranges of dates include archery, muzzleloader, and regular gun seasons. Multiple-deer bag limits are in effect throughout the state. Regulations for public game management areas vary by area, but most have bow seasons in October and December with a three-deer limit.

The coastal plain has about half croplands and half forest. Major farm crops are corn and soybeans, and much of the forestland consists of small commercial plots of loblolly pine. This zone has the highest deer densities in South Carolina, but the average size of deer here is smaller. A high percentage of private land here is leased by hunting clubs. The Piedmont has nearly as many deer per square mile as the coastal plain, but they generally are bigger. The Piedmont offers good public hunting on nearly 1 million acres of public lands. The scenic mountain country of the foothills region

Deer along the coastal plain of South Carolina are numerous but not large in body size. Hunting clubs have leased much of the land here.

along the fringe of the Blue Ridge Mountains has extensive hardwood forests and relatively low deer numbers.

Bear. South Carolina has very limited bear hunting in the foothills region.

Other Game

South Carolina has good hunting for turkeys, squirrels, rabbits and other small game and predators.

Contact. Wildlife and Marine Resources Department, Rembert C. Dennis Building, P.O. Box 167, Columbia, SC 29202.

SOUTH DAKOTA South Dakota covers 77,047 square miles, roughly divided into two even halves by the Missouri River. For management purposes, biologists break the state into three segments: East River, West River, and Black Hills. Country east of the Missouri is farmed intensively, so game is restricted primarily to bottomlands and stream courses. West of the river, habitat varies greatly, and both whitetails and mule deer live throughout. Upland prairie, consisting of grasslands and cultivated crops, covers 80 percent of this region. The Black Hills form a forested island about 100 miles long and 40 miles wide on the western border. Eighty percent of the Black Hills is national forestland open to public hunting, but most of the remainder of South Dakota is privately owned. Some farmers charge a trespass fee, and others allow hunting by permission.

Big Game

Deer. Whitetail deer numbers are estimated at 150,000, and mule deer at 80,000. An average of 3,500 archers kill about 1,500 deer a year, two thirds does. The bow season generally opens in early October and runs until the opening of gun seasons in mid-November. It's closed during gun seasons, but then it reopens and runs through December. It's open statewide to residents and nonresidents, and the number of permits is not limited.

Small woodlots and belts of hardwood trees, dry marshes, and brushy cover along stream

and river bottoms support most of the deer in eastern South Dakota. Throughout prairie country of the West River region, scattered islands of woody cover and brushy stream courses provide cover for moderate numbers of deer. The most densely populated areas are high bluffs and creek drainages adjacent to major rivers. In the Black Hills, both mule deer and whitetails are abundant. The vegetation consists largely of ponderosa pine. The Black Hills have the highest deer densities in South Dakota. South Dakota offers reasonable potential for taking a trophy buck. The largest typical whitetail scored 192 and the largest nontypical 249⅛. Boone and Crockett lists nearly two dozen South Dakota whitetails. Pope and Young bucks aren't uncommon.

Antelope. South Dakota offers good potential for bowhunters. Pronghorns are plentiful throughout West River and even in a couple of counties east of the Missouri. The archery season opens in August and extends into October, and licenses are unlimited.

Elk. These animals are hunted in the Black Hills and Custer State Park. Tags are limited and are reserved for residents only.

Sheep and Goats. A few tags are issued to residents for bighorn sheep. Some goats live in the Black Hills but they're not hunted.

Other Game

Turkeys. Seasons are held spring and fall. Nonresidents are allowed to hunt only in the Black Hills.

Small Game. As in most prairie and Western states, predators such as coyotes are abundant. So is small game in the form of squirrels, cottontails, jackrabbits, and prairie dogs.

Contact. Division of Wildlife, Sigurd Anderson Building, 445 East Capitol, Pierre, SD 57501-3185.

SPINE This term refers to the stiffness of an arrow shaft.

Two Kinds of Spine

Static Spine. This is a measurement of the stiffness of a given shaft material. For example,

Easton measures the spine value of an aluminum arrow shaft by supporting the shaft on two points 27 inches apart and hanging a 2-pound weight on the shaft halfway between the two points. The amount of deflection determines the spine value.

This value indicates only the stiffness of the material. Shafts of different dimensions—diameter, wall thickness, head weight, and length—could have the same static spine value.

Dynamic Spine. This refers to the bending characteristics of a shaft when it's shot from a bow. One of the major influences is static spine, as discussed above, but many other factors influence dynamic spine.

One is arrow length. The longer an arrow of a given spine value, the more it will bend as it leaves a bow. As you can see from an Easton shaft selection chart (see Arrow Shaft Selection), every 1-inch variation in shaft length equals a 5-pound difference in dynamic spine.

Head weight also affects dynamic spine. The heavier the head the more the arrow flexes. Easton's Don Rabska said every 20 grains of head weight equals 2 pounds in bow weight. In other words, if you set your bow up to shoot certain arrows well at a given draw weight and you increase arrowhead weight by 20 grains, you must decrease bow weight by 2 pounds to achieve similar dynamic spine effects.

Mass weight of the shaft itself can affect dynamic spine. For example, 2117 and 2020 aluminum shafts have similar static spine values, but they may not bend the same as they leave a bow because they don't weigh the same. The 2020s are somewhat heavier, so they have greater inertia (resistance to change). To use one of Rabska's terms, the "column load" is greater for the heavier shafts, and the resistance to movement (the force of the arrow string) causes the shaft to bend more before it takes flight. Column loading is less on the lighter-weight 2117, so it may bend less during a shot, even though static spine is similar.

Method of release (mechanical aid versus fingers) can affect dynamic spine, too. A mechanical release aid reduces paradox, so you can shoot weaker-spined arrows with a release than with your fingers. That's because a mechanical release lets the string go almost straight toward the bow, but fingers force the string to the side and this sideways movement enhances arrow paradox. Most hunters buy arrows spined for peak bow weight. That is, if peak weight of a compound bow is 60 pounds, they buy arrows, according to the arrow charts, spined for 60 pounds. Some good release-aid shooters shoot arrows spined for the holding weight of their bows, say 30 pounds for a 60-pound compound with 50 percent letoff. For hunting that would be too light, but you could get away with arrows spined about halfway between peak and holding weights.

Shooting form also can affect dynamic spine. As Don Rabska said, the better your alignment during a shot, the less paradox you impart to the arrow because you let the arrow go in line with the forces of the bow. Even the way you grip a bow can affect dynamic spine. The more lightly you hold the bow, the less severe the effects of paradox. If, for example, you clamp a bow tightly in a shooting machine, you must increase spine weight of the arrows drastically to get even reasonably good arrow flight because the bow does not move out of the arrow's path at all. That's an extreme example, but gripping a bow tightly has a similar effect, although to a much smaller degree.

SPLIT-FINGER DRAW or RELEASE Also called the Mediterranean draw, this is the most commonly used method of drawing and releasing a bowstring. With this method, the index finger rides above the arrow nock and the third and fourth fingers ride below the nock.

This method evenly distributes pressure across the three fingers and allows for a fairly clean release. It's also a fairly fast method, and with fingers on both sides of the arrow, you have good control to hold the arrow on the string and on the arrow rest.

Some problems can creep into the system, however, to produce a rough release and poor arrow flight. One is arrow pinch. If you stand behind a shooter who pinches the nock badly at full draw, you'll see a distinct bend in the arrow. Starting from that bent position, the arrow is almost assured of flying poorly.

To evaluate your own draw and release, have someone stand behind you and watch you at full draw. They can tell whether you're pinching too hard and torquing the arrow. If you do pinch the arrow hard, you'll also develop a painful blister or callus at the edge of the fingernail on your index finger where it presses into the nock. Another common problem is pulling too heavily with the fourth finger. If that's the case, you'll see a definite blister or callus building up where the string creases the finger.

To solve these problems, transfer most of the string weight to your middle finger, and let your index and fourth fingers "float" lightly on the string. Weight should be centered on the middle finger. (See also Apache Draw or Release.)

If you can't use a tripod with your binoculars, at least support your elbows on your knees and brace your hands against your forehead to steady the glasses.

SPOTTING This may rank as the most important part of big-game hunting, because you hunt primarily with your eyes. Sure, you use your ears to listen for movement or certain kinds of calling, and you may use your nose to smell some kinds of game. But for the most part you locate game animals with your eyes, so you have to perfect your ability to see game.

Here I emphasize the technique of hunting by spotting, which commonly involves open-country hunting for mule deer, sheep, antelope, bears, elk, and other Western game. Nevertheless, the same principles apply in still-hunting through timber and spotting game from a tree stand. The differences are only a matter of degree.

Good game spotting starts with good eyes. You might have 20-20 vision, but you're still relatively blind compared to what you could be with good optical equipment. Good binoculars make your vision seven to eight times better than normal, so choosing the right binoculars and other optical gear is the starting point for effective game spotting. (For details, see Optics.)

Using Your Eyes

Whatever I say here about binoculars applies also to the use of a scope, only to a greater degree in most cases.

Stability. Binoculars magnify hand movement just as much as they magnify what you're looking at. In other words, 7X binoculars magnify hand movement seven times. Of course, the greater the power, the greater the need for stability. I consider a tripod or comparable support mandatory for using binoculars greater than 10X. Ultrahigh-power binoculars will magnify even your own heartbeat so greatly you can't spot effectively without solid support.

Nowadays, very few binoculars under 10X come equipped with a tripod mount, so they must be hand-held, but there are right and wrong ways to do that. For quick detail checking, you can stand up and take a quick offhand look. If you don't wear eyeglasses, press the eye cups directly against your "eyebrow" bone to

With a spotting scope you must use a tripod to see anything, and you must be able to sit up comfortably as you spot or you won't spend much time at it. This Bushnell tripod is lightweight, but it extends high enough to bring the scope right to your eye.

steady the binoculars. If you do wear glasses, try hooking your thumbs under your cheekbones for stability.

For serious spotting, you need better support than you can get standing up. Wherever possible, lean across a rock or the hood of your truck or against a tree for a solid rest. If that's not possible or comfortable, glass from a sitting position. Sit with your knees bent and rest your elbows on your knees. Then wrap your hands around your binoculars and as you look through the glasses, press your fingers against your forehead. With your elbows stabilized on your knees and your hands tight against your forehead, the binoculars will be plenty steady for long-term glassing.

With a spotting scope, you must use a tripod. For best results, you have to be comfort-

able, so use a tripod that's high enough so you can sit up comfortably as you look through the scope. If you're glassing from your truck, a window mount works very well.

Many hunters say a spotting scope gives them a headache because of eye strain. I think a lot of the strain comes from squinting the off eye (the one not looking through the scope). To prevent strain, keep both eyes open and simply cover the off eye with your hand. You'll find your face stays a lot more relaxed that way.

Commonly you'll spot game with your bare eyes but then you can't find it with your binoculars, or you see a deer through the binoculars, but when you lower the glasses and put them up again, you can't relocate the animal. To

Some hunters complain that a scope gives them eye strain, and much of that comes from squinting the off eye. To prevent that strain, leave both eyes wide open but cover the eye not looking through the scope.

441

If you can spot from a road, a window mount works ideally with a spotting scope.

prevent that, first look around the animal for landmarks like a tree, big rock, patch of snow—any little clue you can refer back to later.

Second, if you're looking with your bare eyes, keep your eyes fixed on the animal and bring the glasses to your eyes without looking away. When the binoculars are aligned with your eyes, you'll be looking right at the animal. That takes a little practice, but it works.

Finally, for binoculars to be of value, they must be used. That might seem obviously trite, but I'm always amazed at how many hunters carry their binoculars in a pack or pouch, I suppose to keep them clean. When they want to glass they have to stop and take off the pack and dig out the binoculars. Good grief. By the time they've done all that, the game has all bedded for the day. Some huge, specialized binoculars like the 15X60s or 15X80s are for long-range spotting, and these can be carried in a pack, but the only place for normal hunting binoculars is around your neck.

You can swing them to the side out of the way under your arm, which works okay, but then you have to lift them over your arm every time you want to glass. I prefer to keep the binoculars ready for instant use. To do that I tie an elastic band to them. With the binoculars hanging around my neck, the elastic goes around my back. It's just snug enough to hold the glasses tight against my chest so they don't

swing out as I bend over, but it stretches enough so I can pull the binoculars directly to my eyes.

To keep them ready all the time, I don't put covers over the lenses or put them in a case. The only time they really need protection is during rain or snow, and then I tuck them inside my shirt.

Method to Your Madness. A few years ago I wrote an article about Jerry Walters, a very successful trophy hunter from Arizona. Of all his photos, he seemed most proud of one showing his backside and a big hole worn in the bottom of his pants. "That's from many hours of glassing," he said.

He made a valid point. To see game you have to spend time looking. Lots of time. Some hunters think "hard hunting" means walking until you're too tired to walk any farther, but in my book it means hunting efficiently. The guy who has sat in one place for 3 hours and spotted 20 deer, all of them undisturbed, has hunted a lot harder than the guy who has hiked 10 miles and seen a half dozen deer, most of them spooked and running.

The amount of time you spend in any one location depends on how much area you can see. In open country with a wide view, I'd say 2 to 3 hours glassing from each position is none too long. If you're still-hunting in timber and

To be of value, binoculars must be handy and ready for use. An elastic band holds my binoculars tight against my chest out of the way, but the band stretches enough so the glasses can be pulled directly to eye level.

For best spotting, find vantage points that command a wide view, and where the sun and wind are in your favor.

can see only 50 yards, you obviously won't spend that long at each stop, but you still want to look more than you move. The amount of time spent glassing under any given conditions probably would be best stated as a ratio, and I'd say you should spend at least four times as much time looking as moving.

Try to look systematically. Start at one side of your field of view and methodically work across to the other so you don't overlook any detail. Then go over it again. Again. And again. You might not see a partially hidden animal the first time or two, but if you look enough times you'll eventually see him as he moves into a more visible position or flicks his ear at just the right moment. Never quit looking until you're positive you've seen every possible detail. Then go over the area a couple more times just to make sure.

Where to Look

Vantage Points. While scouting I always keep my eye open for points that command a relatively large view. I say "relatively" because the view will be related to the country you're hunting. In the desert or alpine mountains you can spot animals as far as three to four miles away, so your vantage points may overlook sev-

eral square miles. In dense or broken country that won't be possible, but you can still find viewpoints from which you can spot plenty of game. In dense forest country, I've spotted many whitetail and blacktail deer by sitting on strategic high points overlooking brushy draws and breaks where only a few acres were visible.

In choosing spotting points, consider the wind and sun. Know the prevailing wind direction in your hunting area, and take it into consideration. In open country, deer and elk can smell you from a half mile or more, so distance is no barrier. As in actual hunting, you want the wind in your face, or at least from the side.

Never try to glass with the sun in your face. In heavy forest that might not be a concern, but in open country it is. You might climb to a high point early in the morning to eagerly glass a ridge to the east. That's great until the sun comes up, and then it's shining right in your face and you can't see a thing. Pick vantages so that in the morning you're roughly facing west, and in the evening east.

Also pick points where you can come and go unseen. If you have to walk across a mile of open country to reach your glassing point, you won't see much game when you get there. You have to get into position secretly.

Where to Look. In most cases, animals hang out in pockets, and you have to know those pockets to spot game. Dan Eastman, a game biologist who spent hours in the field surveying deer, said he could spot more deer more quickly than the average person primarily because he'd learned where to look.

"You can't have wide-angle vision," he said. "You have to focus on the key spots."

It would take an entire book to catalog these prime areas for every region of the country. You have to learn these places through your hunt planning and scouting, but with experience you'll learn which areas to skim over quickly and where to focus your attention.

A few general guidelines will give you the idea. In hot, dry country, I concentrate most of my spotting, particularly during midday, on north and east slopes. These slopes retain moisture longer than those facing south and west, so vegetation is lusher and air temperatures are cooler.

Conversely, in winter you're more likely to spot animals on southern and western exposures, or where wind has blown ridges bare. On one late mule-deer hunt, I was surprised to find most of the bucks at very high elevations where the wind and cold seemed unbearable (at least to me) but high winds had swept the ridges free of snow and deer were able to feed on exposed grasses and low sage. I guess deer chose the good feed and bitter weather up high to the milder weather and deeper snow down lower.

Whenever you notice deer or other animals in a particular spot, mentally mark that down for later reference. Game animals gravitate toward traditional areas, and conditions that drew them there one time will attract them another. That holds for bedding as well as feeding sites. In open country where shade is scarce, I've found mule-deer beds dug out three to four feet deep under juniper and mahogany trees and cliffs.

When to Look

When you look for game ranks equal in importance to *where* you look. Some people get the impression you've got great eyes if you con-

The secret to spotting lots of game is looking at the right time, when animals are easiest to see. Look early and late in the day, and focus your hunting on times of year, such as during the rut, when animals are most active.

stantly spot lots of deer, but the fact is, anyone can spot them if they look in the right place at the right time.

Obviously a deer walking across an open field will be easier to see than one lying motionless in an alder tangle, so a major principle of game spotting is to look when animals are moving in the open. In an article about game spotting, one writer wrote: "Don't waste time looking at terrain such as clearings, bare sidehills and open ridge tops." His point was that whitetails will stick to cover most of the time, so that's where you've got to search for them. I agree to some extent, but I think his statement misses the point a little. If you look early or late enough in the day, you'll see them in those openings. Granted, some country doesn't lend itself to spotting from a distance, but even in flat, wooded whitetail country you can spot deer in the open—the edges of fields, meadows, brushy clearcuts—if you look at the right times.

Morning. His idea certainly doesn't apply to Western mountain hunting. You'll find mule deer in alpine meadows and open sage flats, far from cover, if you're watching at sunup. I've also had good luck spotting elk and bears, basically secretive timber animals, at dawn because they feed into meadows at night and they often linger there in the open until sunrise or after. For this reason, I think the first hour of daylight in the morning is the best time for spotting, especially in open country where you'll hunt by stalking. Not only will you see the most animals then, but if you spot the animal you want, you'll have all day to stalk him.

In some situations, particularly where hunting pressure is heavy or daytime temperatures get very hot, I've seen deer feed actively until sunrise and then just disappear, as if they evaporated. That's why it's important to be in position by first light, and that's why you should locate vantage points ahead of time, so you can find your way there in the dark. That gives you the most time to spot game, and under cover of darkness you can get into position undetected.

On the other hand, don't quit looking just because the sun comes up. If animals are undisturbed they'll feed very slowly back toward cover, and they'll linger in the open for an hour or more after sunrise. In backcountry where hunters are few, I've often watched deer feed placidly in the open until 10:00 A.M. or later.

Evening. Late afternoon and evening runs a close second to morning, and you can see lots of deer then. But at that time animals are just emerging from cover, and they often won't venture into the open until it's too dark for you to see. Besides, if you do spot an animal late in the day, you might not have time to stalk him before dark. Most stand hunters far prefer evening over morning, but that's because they're back in the woods where the animals hang out until dusk. If you're hunting back in the timber, evening can be as good or better than morning. But for open-country spotting, I'll take morning.

All Day. Now, to contradict myself, I'll confess that one reason I prefer hunting by spotting over other methods is that I can see game all day long. That's not really true in forestland where animals bed in heavy brush, but it is where cover is sparse. If you don't see the buck you want early, you can continue to spot all day, and chances are you'll eventually spot him bedded. Many times in sage and rimrock desert, badlands of the Great Plains, and above-timberline mountain country, I've spotted bedded bucks and stalked successful at midday.

The secret goes back to knowing where to look. In the section on Scouting I talked about

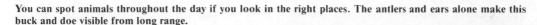

You can spot animals throughout the day if you look in the right places. The antlers and ears alone make this buck and doe visible from long range.

locating specific "buck pastures," and if you can spot these, you'll most likely locate bedded deer. In the desert I've spotted lots of bedded bucks by glassing the shade under juniper and mahogany trees and by studying high sage, looking for antlers. I've seen just as many by glassing from one side of a canyon to the other, inspecting every shady spot under rimrocks and cliffs.

Under the right conditions, you can spot game all day. Animals with heavy fur—elk, bears, deer with winter coats—avoid direct sunlight. In many cases, I think they seek cover more for shade than to hide from hunters. In Oregon's Wallowa Mountains, I've rarely spotted elk after sunrise or before sundown on sunny days, but on cloudy, cool days I've watched them feed in open alder patches and meadows all day long.

Time of Year. Season could affect your game spotting. Here again, the time when animals are most active presents the best time for spotting. Deer have the highest metabolism rate in summer, so that's when they're most active and easiest to spot. Also, until early September their antlers are in velvet and are tender, so they tend to stay out of heavy cover. For these reasons, August and early September are by far the best times to spot lots of deer. Many studies show that as metabolism rate decreases in September and October, deer sightings decrease markedly.

Those same studies also show that activity, and sightings, pick up again briefly during the rut, so the breeding season is always a good time to spot animals. That's true for all animals, not just deer.

During late seasons, animals are less active than earlier because their metabolic rate has slowed markedly, but by December, leaves have fallen from the trees, and in northern latitudes snow forces animals onto small winter ranges where they're relatively visible, so late seasons again offer ideal spotting conditions. If you have a choice, try to plan your hunt for a season when game will be easiest to see. (For more details, see Weather.)

What to Look For

Many writers advise that you look for parts of deer—a flicking ear, antler tine, horizontal line of back, and so forth—and I suppose that's good advice, but I've never thought it was the essence of game spotting. If you follow the steps described above—use good optics, look for long periods of time, look at the right spots at the right time—animals will be so obvious you can't miss them.

Besides, learning what to look for can't be described in writing. You can study photos of deer, elk, or antelope in a magazine and get an idea, but only experience can make you good at game spotting.

A few years back I learned some lessons in a speed-reading class that apply to game spotting. Most important, I learned how fast detail registers on the human eye and brain. The instant your eye sees a word or number, the meaning registers in your brain. As an example, the instructor would flash an eight-digit number on a screen for one tenth of a second or faster, and then we were supposed to write down the numbers. In that span, less than a finger snap, it seemed that I'd scarcely even seen the numbers, let alone recognized them, yet I invariably wrote down the right numbers in the right sequence. My eye and brain were seeing and recognizing the numbers much faster than I could consciously think them.

That principle works in game spotting. Hunters who spend a lot of time in the woods, seeing deer all the time, can spot one animal after another, while a less experienced person will stare for hours and scarcely see an animal. That's because the experienced guy has built up a catalog of images. He's seen deer in all sorts of poses, and, when he sees any of these poses a second time, his brain (much as a computer matches up corresponding digits) instantly pairs the image in his eye with one in his memory and screams "Deer!" even before the hunter can consciously think it. That's why practice is so important; you must build up a catalog of images, such as the white on the inside of a leg, the shape of antlers, shades of

Sitting in one spot for hours might seem like the lazy man's way to hunt, but if that's how you find — and kill — game, it could be considered hard hunting in any sense of the term. But as in anything, getting good takes practice.

hair on various parts of a deer's body, the patterns of white and black on its nose, and so forth.

I've seen this work both ways. One day while glassing a distant hillside a good mile away, I saw a small yellow spot. It seemed insignificant, yet it caught my eye and I couldn't quit checking it out. After nearly an hour, an elk stood up and walked into the open. I'd been seeing only a small patch of hair through tree limbs, but I'd looked at so many elk over the years that that particular tawny yellow registered in my mind instantly.

In just the opposite way, my first whitetail hunt gave me fits. The fellow I was hunting with would say, "There's one!" and I'd stare and see nothing until the animal moved. The deer were much browner than the mule deer I was used to, they had whiter racks, and they lacked the white rump and black-tipped tail. They just wouldn't register in my mind. Finally, after a couple of days of spotting, I caught onto the whitetail shadings and was spotting them quickly.

To spot effectively, train your eye and your mind. Any time you see a deer as you're hunting, study its features to imbed those images in your mind. To keep in practice, scout and look for game year-round; if that's not possible, go to the local zoo or park and study the animals there. The more familiar you are with each species you plan to hunt, the faster you'll spot them in the field. And that's the essence of successful hunting.

SQUIRREL A great variety of squirrels are popular with bowhunters, some for eating, some for shooting practice. The squirrel family (*Sciuridae*) includes marmots and woodchucks, prairie dogs, ground squirrels, chipmunks, and tree squirrels. From a hunter's point of view, these break down neatly into two categories: ground squirrels and tree squirrels. (For details on chucks and marmots, see Marmot.)

Ground Squirrels

About a dozen varieties of ground squirrels live throughout the Western states, western Canada, and Mexico. Prairie dogs are closely

Prairie dogs are common ground-dwelling squirrels found throughout the Great Plains and Rocky Mountain states.

Ground squirrels and prairie dogs live in colonies, and they dig burrows and make their nests underground. These animals hibernate in winter, and they begin to emerge with the first warm weather of spring, normally in March. About May the young animals start leaving the nests, and May and June, when the animals are most abundant and young squirrels haven't yet learned the ways of the world, present the best time to hunt. The animals come out best on warm sunny days; shooting will be slow on windy, cold days.

Hunting ground squirrels doesn't take any particular talent. By far the best way is to walk into a colony and stand or kneel there. As you approach, the animals will go underground, of course, but if it's a nice day, they'll soon be popping back up, and many will stand on their hind legs to look around. That habit has given rise to the name "picket pin gophers," because they look somewhat like picket pins (stakes driven into the ground for tethering horses) when they stand erect.

I've killed several dozen squirrels in a morning and know die-hard squirrel shooters who've killed more than 200 in a day. It's great shooting practice for big game. Rubber blunts and Judo heads work best on ground squirrels and

related to ground squirrels and have similar habits, so I'll lump them together here. The blacktail prairie dog inhabits the short-grass prairies of the Plains states, and whitetail prairie dogs live at higher elevations in the Rocky Mountain states.

Hunting ground squirrels is a shooter's game, demanding patience, a sharp eye, and plenty of arrows. Farmers welcome hunters who'll eliminate a few squirrels from their pastures.

prairie dogs. (For details, see Small-Game Hunting.)

Tree Squirrels

The red squirrel and chicaree live throughout the coniferous forests of North America. They're well known, but not particularly loved, by most big-game hunters. These feisty little squirrels fight constantly, and they make a terrible racket when they spot a hunter sneaking through the woods. It's probably a rare deer or elk hunter who hasn't vowed to make war on chicarees just to shut them up. Chicarees (commonly called pine squirrels in the West) and red squirrels live primarily in higher-elevation fir and spruce forests. A few may be shot incidental to big-game hunting, but I don't know any archers who specifically hunt these animals.

Most other tree squirrels are highly prized game animals for both sport and food. The eastern gray squirrel and the fox squirrel, the largest of the tree squirrels, live throughout the eastern United States. The western gray squirrel, or silver-gray as most Westerners call it, is also a large squirrel that lives in the oak and pine lands of the Pacific states. The tassel-eared squirrel (also called Abert squirrel) is a common resident of northern Arizona and New Mexico. Other varieties of gray and fox squirrels inhabit specific localities. Generally, all the larger tree squirrels live in lower-elevation hardwood and pine forests.

Tree squirrels build nests that look like big round balls of leaves high in the trees (spotting nests is one way of locating squirrels) or they make dens in hollow tree cavities, most commonly in hardwoods. Unlike ground squirrels, tree squirrels aren't colonial and they don't hibernate.

Squirrels are most active when temperatures are comfortable. During hot weather in summer, they'll be most active and visible during the cool of morning and evening, and they'll loaf unseen during the heat of midday. During fall and winter, you'll see the most squirrels at midday during warm, calm weather.

During periods of activity, you can scout efficiently by looking for squirrels scurrying

Tree squirrels are wary animals that can test the skill of the best hunter.

around in search of food. With snow on the ground, you'll see their bounding tracks and find places where they've dug through the snow to uncover nuts stored earlier in the year. You can also scout by looking for cuttings (nut shells gnawed open by squirrels) or in pine

The silver-gray squirrel is a popular game animal in many Western states.

country for the scales of cones squirrels have chewed off to get at the pine nuts.

Tree squirrels can truly be considered game animals, in the sense that they're challenging to hunt and you've got to hunt carefully to fool their senses. They probably don't use their noses much in detecting enemies, but they've got sharp eyes and ears, and they react instantly to any signs of danger.

Seasons vary greatly, depending on region, so you may have the option of hunting from summer well into winter. Tree squirrels aren't necessarily tied to specific locations as ground squirrels are, so they'll move around to take advantage of good feed. In summer or early fall when food crops are abundant, they may be scattered, so that's a good time to sneak through the woods, just as you would still-hunt for deer.

And you have to be every bit as sharp as you would for deer. Many times I've seen squirrels in the distance and tried sneaking in on them, only to find them noticeably absent when I got there. Disturbed tree squirrels aren't like the proverbial mule deer that stops for one last look before disappearing. They scamper for all they're worth until they're out of sight, so sneaking on squirrels demands stealth. Binoculars can be invaluable for spotting squirrels at a distance on the ground or lying hidden on limbs in the trees. You also can hear squirrels scampering through the leaves or gnawing nuts, so hunt with your ears as much as your eyes.

You might find late fall an easier time to hunt than summer, because then the leaves have fallen from trees, improving visibility, and squirrels are very active, gathering and storing nuts for winter. They'll concentrate around trees that have produced lots of mast (acorns and nuts). At this time, you'll probably do best if you find a concentration of squirrels and take a stand there, waiting for them to show themselves. If you've got the patience for it, stand hunting presents by far the best way to bag squirrels with a bow.

For shooting at squirrels on the ground, use arrows with regular fletching and Judo heads.

The Judo heads prevent arrows from skipping long distances or slipping under leaves where you can't find them. For shooting into trees, use arrows with flu-flu fletching and rubber blunts. The flu-flus won't fly dangerously far, and the rubber blunts will bounce off limbs and fall back to the ground so you can retrieve your arrows. If you shoot Judos or steel blunts into trees, you'll either lose a lot of arrows or you'll do a lot of climbing to retrieve them. (For more details, see Small-Game Hunting.)

STABILIZER   A stabilizer is a metal rod that attaches to the riser of a bow. Some stabilizers are made of solid aluminum or steel, while others are partitioned and have rubber shock absorbers between the sections.

Functions of a Stabilizer

Reduce Torque. Stabilizers basically come in two sizes: long and short. The long ones, the ones you see on target bows, are primarily torque stabilizers. To understand their function, pick up a broom by the end of the handle and try to move it quickly. As you'll see, you can't twist (torque) your hand quickly while you're holding that broom. A long stabilizer serves the same function. It prevents torque, or twisting, of the bow when the string is released.

Hunting stabilizers come in many shapes, sizes, and weights. Pictured here are the Easton Gamegetter, the Saunders Torque Tamer, and the Jones Ez-It-Out, which doubles as a broadhead puller.

Under tournament conditions the value of a long stabilizer can be measured in fractions of an inch in arrow grouping, which can make the difference between winning and placing second. Under field conditions, a long torque stabilizer would not be practical.

Add Weight. For that reason most hunters use short stabilizers, 6 to 12 inches long. Hunting stabilizers may help to reduce torque, but because of their short length, they're not as efficient for that purpose as long stabilizers. A primary function of a hunting stabilizer is to add mass weight to a bow so you can hold the bow steadier at full draw. That's particularly helpful in wind or when you're tired and shaky and your bow wants to bounce around. Added weight will stabilize it. Added stability also smooths out shooting errors. If you get a sloppy string release, a heavy bow will react less violently than a lighter bow.

Improve Balance. Some bows have reasonably good balance, but others—particularly if they're equipped with a cable guard in the high position, a heavy bowsight, or a long overdraw unit—will tip back sharply when you shoot. Ideally, the bow should tilt forward. A hunting stabilizer screwed into the handle below the hand grip will balance the bow so it tilts forward after the release.

Reduces Vibration. A stabilizer also absorbs unused energy that vibrates through the limbs and riser of a bow after each shot. That's an especially hazardous problem if you shoot ultralight arrows that absorb little of a bow's energy. (For details, see Bow Efficiency.) The stabilizer soaks up some of the excess energy, which not only adds to the life of a bow but helps to quieten it, too.

Choosing a Stabilizer

Hunting stabilizers vary greatly in length and weight. Some are adjustable so you can add or remove weights to get the perfect balance. Some hunting models are nearly 15 inches long, and the longer the stabilizer, the more it will reduce torque. But longer models also are more cumbersome and may not be practical in brushy country. Short stabilizers,

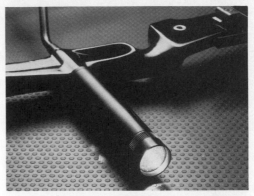

Some stabilizers serve double duty. Hoyt/Easton's nine-ounce Flashlight Stabilizer can be screwed off the bow for use as an emergency light.

six to eight inches, add plenty of weight and they're easier to maneuver.

Some stabilizers are hollow for storage of extra tackle or survival gear. Others, such as Saunders' Torque Tamer, have a screw hole for attachment of a string tracker, and others, such as the Jones Ez-It-Out, can be used as a broadhead puller.

Is a stabilizer absolutely necessary? That probably depends on your setup. Added weight of any kind will serve a similar function. When you add a bow quiver and eight arrows, plus whatever other accessories you deem necessary, you add nearly two pounds of weight to your bow. This might not be quite as efficient as the weight of a stabilizer, but it helps. The weight of accessories alone stabilizes the bow to some extent, and if the quiver is solidly attached, it absorbs some of the excess energy.

For hairline accuracy, you probably should remove the quiver from your bow and replace the lost weight with a stabilizer. That's because the quiver adds weight to the side of the bow, which throws it slightly off balance, whereas a stabilizer adds weight to the center line of the bow, which directs all pressure forward in line with arrow flight. Many hunters, however, will sacrifice that tiny edge in accuracy offered by a stabilizer for the convenience of a bow quiver (I'm one of those).

Of course, you can equip your bow with a stabilizer as well as a quiver. It's just a question of how much weight you're willing to carry. I personally don't like to pack around much more than 6 pounds in bow weight. If your bow with quiver, arrows, and all accessories weighs more than 5½ to 6 pounds, I doubt that you gain a lot from using a stabilizer. If you shoot an ultralight or short bow, an inherently unstable setup, then a stabilizer probably will help your accuracy. And it might add life to your bow if you shoot a heavy draw weight with ultralight arrows.

STALKING Stalking may provide the ultimate form of hunting challenge and thrill; it puts you at eye level with an animal and matches your physical and mental discipline against his senses. Your only advantage over an animal is self-control. You don't hide unseen as the stand hunter does, and you can't rely on an animal's fright or confusion as driving hunters do. Stalking tests all your hunting skills.

But challenge isn't the only reason for stalking. In many settings, particularly the wide-open West, it's also the surest way to bowhunt for deer and other big game. I say that for one reason: in stalking you know the exact location of your quarry before you make a move. In a common stalking sequence you'd spot a deer or bear, for example, across a canyon, plan an approach route, and sneak within bow range. Opposed to still-hunting, in which you sneak along looking for animals as you go, in stalking you first locate an animal from a distance and then you sneak up on him. Knowing an animal's location before you make a move is the thing that makes stalking deadly.

Planning a Stalk
Locating an Animal. To find stalkable animals, seek open country with good visibility and study the country with high-power optics to spot game. (For details, see Optics, and Spotting.) Spotting and stalking obviously works best on animals of the high, wide, and open (mountain sheep and goats, mule deer, antelope, spring bear) but it can be used for cover animals as well. I've put the method to use on whitetail and blacktail deer, both of which are known for living in dense country. It's a matter of finding broken terrain and small opening where you can spot the animals.

The important first step in stalking is spotting. You must locate an animal before you begin your sneak. And when you do see the animal you want, take plenty of time to study the country and map out your stalking route.

In the case of elk, a call sometimes replaces binoculars for locating game. (For details, see Elk.) Once you've located an elk by bugling, you can stalk him. You actually might not lay eyes on the bull until you're within bow range, but as long as you can keep track of him by sound, you can, in the strictest sense of the word, stalk him.

Take Your Time. Once you've located an animal, think before you move; first decide whether to stalk immediately or to wait. In many cases, you'll first spot a deer feeding early in the morning out in the open, and you'll watch him patiently until midmorning when he finally beds down for the day. That's when you stalk him bedded. Stalking a bedded animal offers advantages, and a major one is time. Once an animal beds for the day, he'll stay put for hours, which gives you lots of time to sneak within range. Also, if you wait until late morning before stalking, thermal currents will have stabilized for the day and you can count on them better than you could earlier.

In some cases, this approach won't work. If deer head toward heavy timber to bed, chances are you'll never see where they lie up. And in some cases, you can get a better shot at a moving deer than a bedded one. Harold Boyack has stalked and killed many trophy mule deer, and he prefers to stalk moving deer because he believes they're less alert than bedded animals, and he can plan right where he wants to get his shot.

Don't try to overtake a moving animal from the rear; ambush him. Once you've spotted an animal, watch him awhile to predict where he's going, and then circle ahead quickly to position yourself in his path. Boyack has killed several Pope and Young mule deer this way, including an incredible 40-incher. I've used the same approach successfully on elk that were traveling from nighttime feeding grounds to daytime bedding ridges.

Plan Your Route. Whether you plan to stalk a moving deer or wait until he's bedded, plan your approach carefully. First consider the wind. In some cases, masking scents (for details, see Scents) may help, but don't count on

A bedded buck presents the ideal stalking situation, because he'll give you plenty of time to sneak in. Even in open, sparse country like this you can find enough terrain features to provide ample cover if you plan your stalking route carefully.

them. The only sure way to prevent an animal's smelling you is to keep the wind in your favor, so plan for the wind. With a strong prevailing wind, you can assume the wind will be blowing the same way at the animal's location as at yours. If you're not sure, use your binoculars to watch grass or moss on trees near the animal. Usually these will indicate what the wind is doing over there.

Remember that the wind could change. In calm weather, cool early-morning thermals will drift downhill. By 9:00 or 10:00 A.M., warming

453

air will begin rising to produce an uphill breeze. If you spot an animal at midmorning and can't get to him right away, you're wise to bide your time, keep an eye on him, and wait until the thermals begin a steady uphill flow. Otherwise, you could get caught just as they're changing. In the afternoon, the same thing could happen but the thermals will be shifting from an up-canyon to a down-canyon direction.

Second, look for other animals. Often in stalking, your biggest concern isn't the animal you're after but animals around him. Take time to look for "spoilers," and plan your route around them.

Third, map out landmarks before you begin a stalk. As soon as you change viewpoints, everything will look different. You'll get over there where the buck was feeding, and you'll scratch your head. "Now, was he under this tree or the one down the hill?" Before you move from your spotting location, memorize landmarks and terrain features near the deer, and picture just how you'll approach. Most likely you'll mentally map your route, but often, if the situation looks complicated, you'll do well to get out a notebook and draw a simple map for reference later.

Relocating an Animal

With your stalk mapped out, you're ready to go, and you should have little trouble getting near the animal, but that doesn't mean you'll walk right to him. In most cases you'll have to circle out of sight at some point and you'll lose track of his position. That brings up the next, and often the most difficult, step in stalking — relocating the animal.

Deer and other game have a knack for lying in places where they're concealed. From your spotting position out front, a buck lying down may be obvious; from behind he may be invisible. If you've spotted a buck far away, you probably can hurry at first to close the distance quickly, but as you get close, say within 100 to 200 yards, you have to slow down and really start looking.

Close-Range Spotting. Some hunters use binoculars at long range, but they forget them up close. That's a mistake. If ever you used binoculars, use them now. Take one or two slow steps and study the brush ahead with your binoculars, and take another step and study. If you take enough time you'll spot that animal before he sees you.

If the deer is up feeding, he may be fairly easy to see as you notice his back or rump or

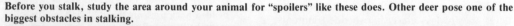

Before you stalk, study the area around your animal for "spoilers" like these does. Other deer pose one of the biggest obstacles in stalking.

antlers, but if he's bedded, he could be all but invisible. In open sage, mule deer often lie in brush high enough to conceal their bodies and eyes, but their antlers will show above the brush and you can see them quite easily. In heavier brush or forest, you may be able to see only a tiny patch of hair, a flicking ear, a nose. But you know the animal is there, so keep looking until you've relocated him.

If you still can't see him, you might try one of Cliff Dewell's tricks. When he can't relocate a sagebrush buck, he hides behind a rock or bush and blows his predator call, quiet at first, then louder until the deer stands up. Then he shuts up, and if the deer is out of range, he stays hidden. Eventually the deer will forget the racket and lie down again. Then Cliff knows right where he is and can continue the stalk.

Have Confidence. Here's an important point I've learned the hard way: have faith an animal remains where you last saw him. When you can't find him right away, it's easy to think, "Aw, shucks, he must have wandered off. Or maybe he smelled me and snuck away."

Don't you believe it. Unless you actually saw him run off, he's there. You just can't see him. Many times I've convinced myself a deer had given me the slip, only to stand up and have him explode at my feet.

Wide-Angle Vision. As you move in, always watch for other animals. If you took your time while spotting, you probably already know where most of them are, but you could still run into unseen critters. You'll be tempted to focus just on the buck you're after and to forget everything else, but one false step and you could have deer running everywhere. Maintain wide-angle vision so you know everything that's going on around you.

The Stalk

You'll normally relocate a buck at 100 yards or farther, so you've got to move in. Now comes the real stalking challenge. You've got to close that gap down to 40, 30, even 20 yards. It might sound impossible. But you can do it 80 percent of the time if you do it right.

Smell. That's the one unmistakable human characteristic. A deer could see you moving or hear you and still not recognize you as human, but if he smells you, he knows. And he's gone. That's why it's so critical to keep the wind in your favor.

As you enter the final stages of a stalk, monitor the wind continuously. Here again, masking scents might help, but I doubt whether any coverup can mask your scent fully when you're within bow range of a deer. Wind in your face offers the only guarantee, so do whatever is necessary to keep it that way. If the wind shifts, back off quickly and change your direction of approach.

Sight. Camouflage clothing in itself won't prevent your being seen, because animals detect movement regardless of color. But, camouflage probably helps soften sharp outlines that could brand you as human. More important than a strict leaf or tiger-stripe pattern are subdued colors and soft, quiet material.

I consider camouflage on the face and hands far more critical than clothing. Your body may be hidden, but to shoot at an animal, your face and hands must be in his view, so do everything possible to camouflage them. Either cover them with cream, or wear a headnet and gloves. (For details, see Camouflage.)

How and where you move probably means a lot more than the color of your clothing. As most hunters know, quick movement is the thing that catches an animal's eye. My friend Pat Miller had the rare thrill of watching a cougar stalk and kill a deer. The cat had very little cover, but it moved so slowly that the deer never noticed it until, from a distance of 20 yards, the cat shot forward like a rocket off a launching pad and nabbed one of the fawns for dinner. That's the kind of slow movement you must duplicate, and with it, you can cross ground in open view of deer without being detected.

Any game animal will recognize the human form instantly, so go to extremes to avoid crossing skylines, open meadows, or bare hillsides where you'll stand out. Stick to the shadows; move with trees, shrubs, or cliffs behind you to prevent being silhouetted; and crouch or crawl to stay below the shrub line and to hide your human form. (For details, see Camouflage.)

Hearing. On a recent deer hunt I wore camouflage pants made of fairly heavy cotton, a popular style. They'd been worn and washed several times and felt soft, but as I walked along, I kept hearing a whistling sound. At first I thought it was Pat Miller whistling to get my attention, and I was about to tell him to knock it off when I discovered it was created by my pants cuffs slapping together as I walked.

That's typical of heavy cotton and denim. Wear wool, knit synthetics, fiber pile—anything but coarse cotton. It's terrible for stalking. (For details, see Clothing.)

You might not eliminate all other sounds, but you can eliminate most that brand you as human. Talking, whispering, coughing, change

You can stalk a lot quieter in socks than in boots or shoes.

clinking in your pocket, binoculars tapping on a belt buckle, arrows rattling in your quiver— those are human. Test your gear before you hunt; tape buckles so they don't click, cover your nylon pack with soft cloth, put fresh rubber in your quiver so the arrows don't rattle, and so forth.

Finally, take off your boots. Stalk in sock feet. When I get to close to an animal, say within 200 yards, I slip off my boots and pull on an extra pair of wool socks to protect my feet and to save my good socks. Wool socks absorb ground noises, and they allow you to feel the ground, in essence giving you a second pair of hands to feel your way along. In rank of importance, this step falls second only behind keeping the wind in your favor.

Invariably when I suggest this, hunters say they can do as well in tennis shoes or moccasins. My response is "No way." A rigid sole can't absorb noise like wool, and even the thinnest sole ruins your sense of feel.

To stalk silently, you have to keep your balance. Slow movement helps, but so does body position. As you know, a tripod is much more stable than a two-legged structure, so make yourself into a tripod. Try to keep both feet and one hand on the ground, or crawl to keep both knees and one hand on the ground. On a steep hillside, I often sit down and essentially crabwalk downhill to keep my rear end plus my feet and a hand in contact with the ground at all times. If you keep three or more points on the ground, you can maintain good balance in any kind of terrain.

In some kinds of hunting, certain noises are no problem, but try to sound natural. That's true, for example, in elk hunting. Bull elk aren't quiet, and during normal activity they clomp, break branches, plow their way through brush, clatter their antlers on trees, and so forth. As you stalk a bull, you can get away with these kinds of sounds. It's better to sound like another bull than to let an elk hear you sneaking around like a predator. Just be sure the noise you make sounds natural in an elk's environment; you still have to avoid humanlike sounds.

Don't Give Up. Even with the greatest care you'll slip up occasionally and get caught in the act. If a deer sees or hears you and tries to stare you down, freeze. You might be tempted to shoot quickly before he bolts, but don't do it. Wait him out. If he's tense, he'll likely jump the string when you shoot. (For details, see Shot Selection.) If you're camouflaged well he won't see you, and if you're motionless he won't hear you, and it becomes a contest of your patience against his. If you hold out long enough, he'll return to feeding or bed back down, and then you can stalk closer or wait for him to present the ideal angle for your shot.

The Shot

With these techniques, you can get close shots time after time. How close should you get? That depends, of course, on how well you shoot. To answer in a general way, you should get close enough to make a clean hit. If you're competent out to 50 yards, then that's close enough; if your range is 30 yards and under, then get within your range. (For details, see Shot Selection.)

And you can do it. I've successfully stalked elk, bear, whitetail, blacktail, and mule deer. Eighty percent of the time, regardless of terrain or cover, I can get within 50 yards, and 50 percent of the time I can get within 30 yards or less. You can do as well or better.

On the other hand, you can try to get too close. I've talked to dozens of hunters about stalking and hunters commonly say, "He came boiling out of his bed and I had to take a running shot."

That's no kind of shot at all. That just means you blew the stalk. Once you've got within your range, stop and wait. Don't keep pressing forward. Within bow range, movement becomes so critical a deer can almost sense your breathing, and the more you fiddle around, the more likely he is to sense you and bolt. Of course, if you're stalking a feeding or moving deer you probably can shoot as soon as you're within range.

But if you've stalked a bedded animal, it might not be that easy. Animals normally lie in

When you've snuck within range of an animal, take your time and don't force the animal to jump and run. Wait for him to present a standing shot.

protected positions, and you must make them stand up to get a clear shot. If conditions are right—meaning the wind is stable—I think you're wise to settle in and wait for a deer to stand up on his own to feed or stretch. Then you have plenty of time to shoot at a calm animal.

If the wind seems unstable, you might not be able to wait. Then you have to force him up. To do that, hide well and try flipping pebbles off to the side. A rock hitting the ground nearby usually will get a deer to stand up, and it will divert his attention. I've done that a number of times with great success.

Another alternative is to blow a call to sound like a bleating fawn. The sound will get the deer up, but it won't spook him. I've done this successfully on a number of occasions. Then it's just a matter of putting the arrow where it

These two blacktail bucks were taken by stalking.

belongs. (For details, see Shooting Basics, and Shooting Practice.)

STAND HUNTING Some hunters confuse still-hunting with stand hunting. Still-hunting means you sneak through the woods quietly, looking for game. Stand hunting means you wait in one spot for animals to come to you. Without question, where conditions are right, stand hunting is the deadliest way to bowhunt. The two major bowhunting challenges are, first, staying undetected, and second, seeing animals before they see you. A stand presents the best way to do these things. You remain motionless so animals won't see or hear you, and because you're sitting still and watching continuously, you'll almost always spot animals before they see you.

Stands also allow anticipation of a shot. In movement hunting, you never know just when or how you'll get a shot, or what the range will be. From a stand, you can gauge how an animal will approach, and you can anticipate the range. Many hunters even mark off various ranges so they know exactly how far a deer is at any given point. That's an immeasurable advantage.

Variables for Stand Placement

Water. Stand placement has to capitalize on the weaknesses of game. In many cases, that could be water. By far the most deadly method for antelope hunting is the waterhole stand. The same can be said for other game in desert country. In Arizona, the only water sources for elk are stock tanks, and virtually every waterhole in northern Arizona has either a tree stand or ground blind on it. In parts of the Great Basin or the Sonoran desert of southern Arizona, mule deer are extremely vulnerable to waterholes stands. Of course, the value of waterhole stands relates directly to the weather—it must be dry. During wet periods, you're not likely to do well on stand at a waterhole.

Mineral licks or food sources serve a similar function of pulling animals to specific points. Bear baiting, of course, is the most obvious example, but in many areas you can find natural areas that perform a similar function. I've seen spots where mule deer have literally dug pits to get at minerals, and I know elk hunters who have killed elk by taking stands near salt licks.

Escape Routes. In sweeping sagebrush desert country, hardly the kind of place you'd expect to take a stand, Clark Unruh found a trail sandwiched between a rock slide on one side and a tangle of aspens on the other. It was the only logical escape route for bucks pressured by hunters from below, so Unruh took a stand there. He killed bucks in that spot three out of four years.

In the rain forests of Oregon's Coast Range, George Shurtleff discovered a big camp of hunters. He figured in the morning they'd fan out and stir up the deer above their camp so he scouted around to find the most logical escape trail through the briar tangles and alders, and

Escape routes are good places for stands. Mule deer often will use saddles or breaks through rims to get away from other hunters, and if you can locate those places, you've found a good place for a stand.

the next morning he killed a huge blacktail buck coming up that trail.

Any point of constriction that forces animals to take a certain route, such as a notch through an otherwise impassable rim; any point of easiest travel, such as a saddle in a high ridge; or thick cover that offers concealment between more open terrain, holds promise as a stand site.

Natural Travel Routes. Deer and most other big-game animals do the same thing day after day, week after week, unless changing conditions—weather, foliage, food, hunting pressure—force them to change. If you can figure out that pattern and place yourself in it unnoticed, you can take animals from a stand.

Most hunters realize that whitetails (blacktails too) have small home ranges. Once you learn this range for a given buck, you can just about figure he's there somewhere and you can plan a stand-hunting strategy accordingly. Figuring out the patterns of woodland deer often becomes intuitive, based on sign. You must scout intensively to learn where deer feed, where they bed, and how they get from one spot to the other. The most obvious stand sites

The key to any stand hunting is locating points at which animals are most vulnerable. Heavily used trails like this show promise as stand sites.

To place a stand effectively, you must know where deer feed and bed, and you must know their routes in between.

are trails. Even better than a single, well-used trail is a confluence, where two or more trails merge.

It could be important to determine which way deer travel a trail at a given time of day. For a morning stand, you probably would choose a different trail, or a different location along a given trail, than you would for an evening stand.

Circumstances may be different, but the same principle holds for mule deer. Sure, mule deer may migrate long distances between winter and summer ranges, but within any given range they'll adopt small home territories and use those in a habitual manner. During a late bow season in Idaho, deer descended each evening from a high ridge to feed on a windblown south slope. They stayed there all night, and then early in the morning they paraded back up the top of the ridge, where snow was shallowest, to bed high. It took me awhile to catch onto that pattern, but it was obvious once I opened my eyes. In this same spot I saw a huge buck, and even after that buck had been spooked badly twice, and apparently run out of the entire country, he returned to the exact

same hillside. These observations led to some excellent stand locations.

Jay Verzuh has one of the most successful bowhunting operations in Colorado. He uses tree stands in aspen groves with great success. Rather than the on-the-ground scouting for sign required in most timbered country, Verzuh patterns deer on his ranch by watching them through binoculars. After hours and days of observation, he discerns habitual movements, and he can very closely predict where the deer will go each morning and evening. The method differs from dense country scouting, but the results are the same—the deer follow specific routes from bed to feed in the evening and from feed to bed in the morning, and stands placed along those routes produce deer.

Fences sometimes serve as excellent places for blinds. Elk don't jump fences as readily as deer do, and they'll often travel fencelines so these can be good places for stands. Antelope rarely jump fences; they crawl under, generally at specific points with the best clearance. I know archers who've taken several antelope at such crossings.

Rutting Areas. For some species, the rut

460

may be the surest guide for stand placement. The most obvious example is scrape hunting for whitetails. Rutting bucks make scrapes— calling cards for does. Primary scrapes serve as excellent stand locations. Just keep in mind that bucks can check scrapes from 50 yards or more downwind with their noses, so in many cases the best place for a stand is not directly over the scrape but overlooking heavy cover 50 yards or more downwind of the scrape. (For more details, see Whitetail Deer.)

Rutting activity can serve as a guide for stand hunting other animals, too. Bull elk wallow during the rut, and unless they're disturbed they'll return to the same wallows. Some bowhunters have killed numerous bulls by taking stands near fresh wallows. (For more details, see Elk.)

Universal Stand-Hunting Principles

Wind. Without question, this is number one. Always place your stand downwind of the game you plan to hunt and of the travel routes used by game. If you don't do anything else right, do this. That requires some knowledge of the country so you know what the wind will be doing at certain times. It also could require

several stand sites, so that if wind is wrong at one, you can hunt at another.

Visibility and Shooting Clearance. The whole idea of stand hunting is to see animals before they see you, and to get a clear shot. Doing anything less defeats the purpose, so look over an area well before placing your stand to make sure you can see or hear animals approaching before they catch you off guard. If necessary, do some clearing or pruning to assure clear shots, and make sure your blind is positioned so you can shoot in various directions without having to do gymnastics moves.

Along the lines of visibility, consider the sun. If the sun shines in your face and at an animal's back, you're essentially blinded and the animal can make you out in detail. In heavy timber or a shadowed canyon, the problem may be insignificant, but in open country it's critical. You want the sun at your back so your eyes are shaded, and so an animal looking your way must look toward the blinding sun.

Undetected Entrance and Exit. Again, you defeat your purpose if animals know you're in a blind. You have to be able to get in and out undetected. Darkness presents one solution. Hunting antelope in flat grasslands, for exam-

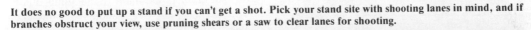

It does no good to put up a stand if you can't get a shot. Pick your stand site with shooting lanes in mind, and if branches obstruct your view, use pruning shears or a saw to clear lanes for shooting.

ple, about the only way you'll get to a blind unseen is to get there before daylight.

In a whitetail woodlot, that's not necessarily true, but you still must get to your blind without disturbing the deer you plan to hunt. Analyze their travel routes, and figure out how to approach your stand without being seen and without contaminating the deer's trails with your scent.

Comfort. Possibly the toughest part of stand hunting is persevering long enough to make it work. That starts with comfort. A stand or blind must be built so you can relax. If you're bent or crouched or forced into unnatural positions, you won't last long. Some tree-stand hunters insist on standing; they will not sit down because they can't shoot from a sitting

In many cases, stand hunting success equates to time, and you'll never spend the requisite time in your stand if you're uncomfortable. Work on your gear until you can stay comfortable for motionless hours. The Carlton Bow Stand holds my bow ready for action.

position. I personally can't hack standing for long periods and must sit to be comfortable. You can do whatever works best for you; just don't be satisfied with your stand until it's comfortable for you.

Clothing contributes to comfort as well. In warm weather, that could mean keeping bugs away. You can't stand still for long with mosquitoes and black flies chewing on you, so for reasonable comfort wear net clothing and bug dope. In cold weather, warmth, or lack of it, becomes the major problem. A cool breeze that feels good to the foot hunter can turn a stand hunter into an ice cube in an hour. You've got to wear layers so you can shed clothing to prevent sweating on the way to the stand. But on stand you need insulation that no foot hunter could tolerate. (For details, see Clothing.)

Ground Blinds

Advantages and Drawbacks. A ground blind is a lot safer than a tree stand. At least I've never read about anyone's falling from a ground blind, but I can document plenty of injuries resulting from falls from tree stands. I have read about rattlesnakes in ground blinds, however, so it pays to look before you leap into your blind.

Some hunters maintain that ground blinds work better than tree stands for whitetails. They say that some heavily hunted public woodlots contain so many tree stands that deer are more alert to danger in the trees than on the ground. In those situations, pit blinds or other ground stands can be more effective. I've never hunted areas with that many hunters, so I can't confirm or deny that.

In some places, ground blinds may be the only choice. Obviously, if there aren't any trees around (a common situation in the West for antelope and mule deer) you're stuck with a ground blind. And in predator or turkey hunting, where you're moving regularly, a ground blind is the only practical choice.

A ground-level position also gives you an optimum shooting angle, because you see the maximum kill zone. The higher you go in a tree, the more precise your shot must be to make a clean hit.

Ground blinds do have shortcomings. They put you at eye level with game, where the slightest movement on your part will give you away, and it's harder to draw and get a shot than it is from a tree stand. You also have limited visibility. From a tree stand you command a fairly wide view, but from a ground blind — at least in brush country — your view can be severely limited. A ground blind also puts your scent at ground level, so unless wind is ideal, animals will smell you.

Posting. The simplest form of ground stand involves no blind at all. Many hunters would call this "posting." You simply find a deer crossing or other likely place for a stand and post yourself downwind there. The requisites are camouflage and the ability to stand still.

Portable Blinds. Some hunters build portable blinds with stakes at the corners and a camouflage-cloth covering. These are commonly used in predator and turkey hunting where you move from one calling site to another and can't quickly find natural blinds or the materials to build a blind. You can make a similar blind of chicken wire and cover it with natural materials like sagebrush or juniper.

Permanent Blinds. For permanent blinds, some hunters drive metal fence posts into the ground at the corners and tie wire and natural materials to these.

Where cover plants are scant, a pit blind serves best. Antelope guide Judd Cooney digs big pits with a seat carved right into the back of the blind so his hunters can sit for long hours in comfort. He also builds up the back of the blind with sage and other native plants so the hunter sits in shade and isn't silhouetted. Any pit must be deep and wide enough to assure room to draw and shoot.

Tree Stands

Advantages and Drawbacks. In writing an article about increased bowhunting success (from 1974 until 1983 average success in the United States rose from about 5 percent to 11 percent) I interviewed a number of authorities

Ground blinds with natural cover can be just as good as tree stands in some cases. I killed a small buck from this "tree stump" stand.

about the reasons. Most of them gave major credit to the tree stand. Studies in the East have shown that about 80 percent of the bow-killed deer are taken by hunters using tree stands. Obviously tree stands have something going for them.

For one thing, they help you to see well. The higher your viewpoint, the larger your perspective. Ten feet off the ground, you can see much farther than you can from ground level. You'll spot whitetails sneaking through the brush 100 yards away you'd never know existed if you were on the ground.

At the same time, you're less likely to be seen. Sure, a deer will look up if you make wild movements or noise, but with reasonable caution, you're much less likely to be seen up in a tree than you are at ground level. And with a deer at close range, you have a much better chance of drawing your bow and getting off a clean shot from a tree stand than from a ground blind.

The higher you are off the ground, the more your human smell can dissipate before it descends to ground level. If you watch smoke coming from a chimney you get the idea. With any kind of breeze blowing, the smoke may travel several hundred yards before it fans out to reach the ground. If that were your scent, it could drift well beyond the critical deer runways you're watching before it drops low enough for animals to smell you. Climbing a tree doesn't cure all your scent problems, but it does help. (For more details, see Scents.)

One chief drawback is danger. Tree-stand accidents aren't uncommon, and they're often serious. The North American Association of Hunter Safety Coordinators reported that from 1981 to 1983, 62 hunters in the United States fell from trees. That might not sound like a lot, but when you consider that 32 of those hunters died from their injuries, more than 50 percent, and that some were paralyzed for life, you can see that falling from a tree is no joke.

Safety should be the first priority in tree-stand hunting. Always use a safety belt. In shooting downhill as you do from a stand, bend at the waist. Don't drop your bow arm because it alters your shooting alignment.

Safety. Those statistics bring up another interesting point. In all other injury categories listed by the Hunter Safety Coordinators, at least some of the accidents involved two people. But in the "fell from tree" category, 100 percent of the accidents were self-inflicted. In other words, the victims had no one else to blame.

Safety rule number one is to use a safety belt. It seems inconceivable to me that anyone would stand on a platform high above the ground without wearing a safety belt, yet I know hunters who do. They're suicidal.

Before using any tree stand, check screws, bolts, and other structural points. If you use tree steps, use good ones, and practice using a climbing tree stand before you go too high. And then be careful which trees you climb. Some oaks and other trees have slick bark, especially when they're wet, and you could find yourself coming down like a runaway elevator, leaving parts of your anatomy on the tree as you descend. On such trees, many hunters prefer screw-in steps and semipermanent stands that lock on with rope or chain.

To keep both hands free for climbing, and to prevent falling on your bow, always climb into your stand first and then pull up your bow and other gear with a rope.

Portable versus Permanent. On your own property, or private property where you have permission to build stands, permanent stands may be the way to go. You can build them large enough for comfort, and you can move around safely, especially if you build them with railings. Lugging the needed lumber and getting it up into the trees to build a stand can be hard work, but the convenience later can be worth it. I know hunters who've used the same permanent stands for 20 years. They figure the time and effort to build the stands have paid off.

On the other hand, laws may dictate whether you use portable or permanent stands. In some states it's illegal to construct permanent tree stands on public property, and if that's the case you go portable. Besides, on accessible land, you're liable either to find someone using your stand, or to find your stand missing, and conflicts over stand sites have serious potential. In Arizona, during one bow season, hunters filed five assault charges as a result of conflicts over waterhole stands. In heavily hunted areas, the portable is the only way to go.

And with portables you can move around to catch deer off guard. In whitetail hunting — and for other species, I suppose — where you hunt the same country over and over, you've got to move around. It's a matter of conditioning. When you go to and from a stand location, you leave sign of your passing. Deer aren't oblivious to that. They may ignore it once or twice. After all, in many areas they're used to human contact, so a little man smell or other human sign is nothing out of the ordinary. But if that human sign becomes a pattern, then deer learn to head the other way. That's why many hunters prefer portable stands.

Also, if you want to hunt a particular spot but the wind is wrong from one side, you can put your stand up on the other side to get the wind right. Portable stands just offer a lot more flexibility than permanent stands. If you do go with permanent stands, put up several so you can alternate to avoid conditioning animals and to take advantage of different winds.

On private land where you'll be hunting the same locations over and over, permanent stands may be the best way to go.

On public lands where you must compete with others, portable stands are preferable because they eliminate most conflicts among hunters. They also allow greater hunting flexibility.

Missouri bowhunter Jim Martin likes the TSS portable stand with a steel band that goes around the tree. This stand climbs with the "bear hug" method.

Portable Stand Styles. You can get several styles of portable stands. Climbing stands have been around a long time, and their longevity speaks for their value. You can quickly hunt anywhere you want with little or no preparation, provided you can find trees with straight trunks and no big limbs. Some climbing tree stands are noisy, so you can't climb a tree right next to the deer cover you plan to hunt. Using a climbing stand also requires a fair amount of strength on your part, and it can be tiring, especially if you climb by "bear hugging" the tree and pulling yourself up. Some stands have hand climbers that double as seats, which make climbing easier, and with some climbing stands, like Amacker Products' Lil' Joe, you just sit on a seat and alternatively stand up and sit down to walk yourself up the tree.

Nonclimbing portable stands cinch up tight to the tree with either chain or rope. To get them up there, you have to first climb the tree yourself and then pull the stand up to you. On limby trees, you can climb up on the limbs, or you can use tree steps, which come in a couple of styles: screw-in or rope-on blocks. Many hunters leave these in place for short periods so they can climb into and out of the stands silently.

Ladder-type portables are perhaps the simplest, and require the least physical effort. You simply lean a ladder stand against a tree and climb up and chain it to the tree to hold it in place. Then you sit on the top platform. Some have a safety railing around them to hold you in. Ladder portables are relatively heavy and bulky, so you wouldn't be carrying them too far from the road.

Another style of portable could be called a hanging stand. One example is the Anderson Tree Sling. It consists of a harness made of heavy nylon straps. You slip the harness around your rear end, and then you climb a tree you want to hunt from and tie the harness to the tree. Then you hang in the harness with your feet braced against the tree. With the Ultimate tree sling made by Hunter's Products, Inc., you throw a rope over a limb and climb and pull yourself up with the rope. A ratchet-type lock keeps you from slipping back down and holds you at the desired level.

The simplest form of portable is no stand at all. Many trees, particularly old oaks, have huge limbs that form great natural blinds, but you can make a blind with materials at hand in about any tree. My friend Pat Miller has made many a makeshift blind. He climbs a suitable tree and uses his bow saw to cut a couple of limbs, and with nylon cord he ties these across a couple of other limbs on the tree to make a small platform. One year he killed an elk in Oregon, and a couple of days later he discovered a bear was eating the guts. He'd brought no tree stand, so he threw together a quick stand in a tree near the "bait" and killed a nice bear there the first afternoon.

Again, regardless of what style of stand you choose, always wear a safety belt.

With portables that are not self-climbing, you must either climb up on limbs or use tree steps like this EZY Climb screw-in model.

The Anderson Tree Sling is an alternative to the conventional platform tree stand. With this sling, you first climb the tree and then tie yourself in and relax. It's portable enough to be carried into the backcountry.

Tree-Stand Height. Hunters commonly disagree over stand height. If your stand is too low, of course, you essentially defeat the purpose of using a tree stand because a deer can see and smell you about as well as he could if you were on the ground. Ten feet is probably a practical minimum.

At the same time, going too high creates its own problems. Fear could be one. If you're like me, you'll get queasy much above 15 feet. Incidentally, to overcome this fear, I put on my safety belt and lean out from the platform so the belt is holding me. It gives me confidence to know I really am strapped in.

Another problem is the acute shooting angle. When shooting down, you pull with different muscles than when shooting on flat ground, and the steeper the angle the tougher it could be to pull your bow. Make sure you practice from all potential shooting angles.

Also, the higher you are the greater the disparity between actual distance to an animal and the "aiming" distance. To prevent shooting over an animal, measure the distance (a range finder works well here) to various points around your tree. Don't measure from your stand, however, but from the base of the tree. Regardless of how high you climb, the trajectory of the arrow is equal to the trajectory for the horizontal distance. (For more details, see Trajectory.)

The higher you go the more limbs you'll find obstructing your shooting lanes and, even more serious, the smaller your view of a deer's vital area. You have to put shots on the money or you could completely miss the lungs. You also must learn to adjust shot placement. From ground level you should shoot a deer mid- to low chest, but from high in a tree, you must hit high on the chest to angle the arrow down

Arkansas bowhunter Bob Coffey incorporated a seat into his safety harness, so he can sit down comfortably without fear of falling. At the same time, he can swing far out from his stand to shoot in virtually any direction.

A bow holder is an added convenience for any tree stand. Wayne Carlton designed this stand to hold a bow upright and ready to shoot. It screws or bolts right onto the stand platform.

This Saunders Double Duty Device serves as both a bow holder for stand hunting and as a broadhead puller.

through the lungs. Practice these shooting nuances from a tree stand before you start hunting.

In *Battling Bucks*, an excellent book on rattling, Noel Feather says he likes his stand 10 to 12 feet above the ground. Arkansas hunter Bob Coffey likes his stands as high as he can get them, often up around 20 feet. Jim Martin, a very successful whitetail hunter from Missouri, favors 15 feet off the ground, and he thinks you should always put your stand at the same height to eliminate shooting guesswork. Martin gauges the height of his stand with his pull-up cord. He ties the cord to his belt and to his bow the same way each time so the length never varies, and then he starts climbing. When he feels the cord tugging he knows he's at the right height.

Final Thoughts on Tree Stands. To be of any value a tree stand must be silent. Check all

screws and bolts to make sure they're tight, and cover the platform of your stand with carpet to prevent scraping or squeaking of boots on wood or metal. If you leave a stand out in late season, cover it with plastic (slip a plastic garbage bag over it) or take it down to prevent ice and snow from building up on it.

Always check your shooting lanes and clear away any branches that might deflect an arrow. Nippers and a folding limb saw should be standard equipment in your stand-hunting gear. Carry away cut branches so deer—and other hunters—won't notice the disturbance.

Make sure you can shoot in the desired directions. If you're right-handed you can't swing far to the right, so you must set up with shooting lanes straight ahead or to the left (and opposite if you shoot left-handed). And rig your safety belt so you can swing out to shoot to the side or behind your tree. Bob Coffey has built a safety belt that incorporates a seat like an old-style tractor seat. This rig hangs from a strong nylon strap, and while seated Coffey can swing out from his stand and shoot in nearly any direction. It's more or less a hanging tree stand in itself, but Coffey uses it with a climbing portable so he also has a platform to stand on.

If you plan to spend many hours in the stand, you'll have to relieve yourself. Take a plastic jug up to your stand so you don't have to climb down.

Include in your gear a hanger for your bow—not all trees have limbs in convenient places—or use a bow stand. Wayne Carlton's Hunting Accessories makes a bow holder that fits on the front of the stand and holds your bow in a ready position.

It should go without saying your stand and accessories should be camouflaged.

STATIC SPINE   See Spine.

STILL-HUNTING   The term "still-hunting" creates a lot of confusion. Some hunters think it means hunting from a stand, because one definition of "still" is "without movement; motionless." That's not the meaning implied in still-hunting. The first two dictionary definitions for "still" are: (1) making no sound; silent, and (2) free from disturbance or agitation; peaceful; tranquil. These are the implied meanings in still-hunting. You hunt on foot, continually moving, but you make no sound and leave the area free from disturbance.

Some hunters also confuse still-hunting with stalking. Many of the same principles apply, but in a strict sense, stalking involves sneaking up on a known animal, one you've spotted (or heard, as in the case of bugling for elk) from a distance. In still-hunting you don't know the exact location of an animal. You move through the woods, looking for animals as you go. In essence, you're stalking blind.

That puts you at a handicap, and wherever possible, I'd opt for spotting and stalking over still-hunting because then you start out with your quarry located. On the other hand, you can't spot animals in every situation, and in some cases stalking simply isn't the best way to hunt. Under the right conditions, still-hunting can be deadly.

Conditions for Still-Hunting

Scouting. Before you ever set out to still-hunt, scout first; find plenty of fresh tracks, beds, feeding areas, and other concentration points for game. (For details, see Scouting.) That's a prerequisite. Placing one foot after another quietly on the ground, straining to see the slightest part of a deer before the deer sees you, forcing yourself to inch along when you feel compelled to hustle—these require discipline, and if you're in doubt about the presence of animals, you'll never muster the discipline to maintain control. You must have confidence, knowing you'll see game, or you'll lose concentration and end up just strolling along. And that's not hunting.

Scouting also reveals movement patterns and habits of the animals you're hunting. You may find an area with ample fresh sign, but if you don't know the habits of the animals there, you might never cross paths with them, despite your best efforts.

Rich LaRocco has observed that deer in the mountains of central Utah move uphill in the evenings to feed high at night. Then in the morning, just after daybreak, they slip back downhill to bed in heavy cover low in the canyons. With that knowledge, Rich knows that in the early morning, he must start at the bottom of a canyon and slowly still-hunt up through the oak brush, and chances are good he'll meet deer moving down to their bedding areas head on. During midday, he'll still-hunt slowly in bedding cover at the lower ends of the canyons. And in the evening he'll begin his hunt at the top of a ridge and slowly work downhill to meet deer coming up for the evening feeding period.

The specifics might differ, depending on the area. In fact, more commonly deer in Western mountains feed low in creek bottoms and meadows at night, and move high to bed during the day. Whatever the case, you must scout and observe enough to understand these movements so you're hunting where the animals are at a given moment.

The Right Country. Some places just aren't made for still-hunting. In open sage country, where animals can see you long before you get within bow range, I'd suggest you spot game from a distance, and then stalk. In places where slide rock or crusty leaves and dry grass make silent movement virtually impossible, I'd try driving or stand hunting in preference to still-hunting. But in flat or rolling country, or heavily timbered regions where you can't see animals from a distance and where you can move silently, still-hunting works.

It also works where deer are too numerous for good stalking. In Idaho, for example, I had no trouble spotting whitetail bucks feeding in little canyons and breaks, and if it had been just me and those bucks I'd have pulled off a number of successful stalks. Without fail, though, I ran into unseen deer between me and my quarry, and they scattered like quail to stampede deer every which way.

With so many deer there, stalking wasn't working but still-hunting might, so one morning I set out from camp an hour before daylight, and under the cover of darkness slipped quietly into a grove of pine trees where a lot of deer were hanging out. By first light I was still-hunting slowly, taking a half step and then standing still for a minute or more to look. The important thing was that I'd got into their territory unseen.

In the first 10 minutes I'd moved no more than a few feet when I noticed a white line darting erratically near the ground about 15 yards ahead. In the dim morning light, I couldn't identify it, so I studied the moving line with my binoculars. As I watched it rose above the bushes, and I could see the deer's entire head, a big 10-point buck. I'd been watching the white line across his nose as he nibbled grass. The buck had no idea I was there, and he returned to feeding and eventually presented a 20-yard shot. That situation—hordes of deer and fairly dense brush—presented ideal conditions for still-hunting.

Early and Late. As I've said under Spotting,

the way to see game is to look when animals are visible. That's why the first and last hours of daylight, when they're feeding and active, present by far the best times for still-hunting. Your chances for spotting an undisturbed animal are far better when you're quietly watchful and the animal is moving than when you're moving and the animal lies motionless.

Good Weather. On the other hand, in the right weather you can still-hunt successfully all day. Following a heavy storm at night, deer and other animals will feed actively throughout the day (for details, see Weather), and under any heavy overcast or drizzling rain, you might catch animals feeding. Still-hunting for elk is never easy, but I've taken two cows by still-hunting during drizzling rain.

On one I'd found a north-sloping ridge torn up with elk sign. It was too early in the year for bugling, so one afternoon during a steady rain I started at one end of the ridge and slowly crept through the spruce trees and sopping wet huckleberry bushes. About 2:00 P.M. I heard a faint swish, swish, and as I waited to see what made the noise a herd of six elk fed into view, no more than 50 yards away. I slowly crept to the side to get in their path and eventually shot a cow at 15 yards as the animals fed toward me. Often during soft rain, game will be active and visible, and in the damp woods you can drift along silently. Dank weather, the kind that

I killed this cow elk while still-hunting one rainy afternoon.

If you know the habits of game well enough, you may be able to still-hunt effectively for bedded animals during midday.

makes you want to stay in camp by the wood-stove, promises good still-hunting.

Bedded Bucks. In some cases, if you know the habits of the animals you're after, you can still-hunt for and spot bedded animals, as Paul Mustain does on blacktails in California. Early in the fall, bucks have put on winter coats, but the weather remains warm, so Mustain figures the deer will bed on the tips of points where they're shaded by heavy timber and cooled by thermal currents blowing uphill during the day. In good blacktail country Mustain doesn't scout so much for deer as for good bedding points. He has confidence that the bucks will be there. Then during midday he sneaks onto a chosen point and starts still-hunting down. He may cover only 100 yards in 4 hours, but that's enough. He's taken a number of bedded bucks this way.

Wind and Sun. Finally, in choosing conditions keep the wind at your face and sun at your back. It should go without saying that your own scent will be your biggest obstacle and that the wind must favor you. Coverup scents (for details, see Scents) may help, but don't count strictly on them. Hunt into the wind, or at least crosswind.

And try to keep the sun behind you. Sometimes these exclude each other; that is, to hunt with the wind right, you might have to move toward the sun. But whenever possible move away from the sun. That way the animals you're hunting must look toward the sun, which partially blinds them, and you're looking at well-lighted details, which helps you see better.

Still-Hunting Technique

In a nutshell, these are the mechanics of still-hunting: you take a step or two and then stand quietly, looking for animals. Then you take another step and look, step and look.

Clothing. Obviously, your tasks are to see deer before they see you, and to keep from being seen. Camouflage and quiet clothing (for details, see Camouflage, and Clothing) should be taken for granted in all bowhunting, and that's especially true in still-hunting because you're on the ground and moving, on equal footing with the game you're hunting. In a sense you're the hunted as much as the hunter. Clothing must be whisper quiet, and you must make yourself as invisible as possible. In most cases that means camouflage, but Shari Fraker,

472

Silent movement requires the right clothes. The lightweight wool pants, knit acrylic sweater, and wool gloves I'm wearing are ideal for silent still-hunting.

a master still-hunter for elk, wears brown and tan clothing. She figures if elk spot her, they'll mistake her for another elk.

Footwear. Running shoes, moccasins, or soft rubber-bottom boots like L. L. Bean's Maine Hunting shoes are ideal because they give and allow you to feel the ground. Heavy, stiff soles, so well suited to packing heavy loads, are anathema to still-hunting. As you step, set your heel down first and then roll your foot to the ground.

Under the section headed Stalking I advocate shedding your boots to cover the last critical yards of a stalk in sock feet. I don't suggest you still-hunt that way for long distances, but for short, known routes, sock feet can produce some miracles. In California I found a small patch of brush where a dozen or more blacktail bucks fed every morning and evening, but the

gravelly ground among the shrubs crunched under my shoes. Socks seemed to be the answer. The patch was small and didn't require any long walking, so for each hunt I'd deposit my shoes at the bottom and make my 200-yard loop through the brush in sock feet. I spent 2 to 3 hours covering that short distance. Over a period of 5 days I made that loop a half dozen times, and not once did I fail to sneak within 25 yards or less of a buck.

Go Slow. The right clothes and shoes help a lot, but the way you move may be more significant. "Slow" sums up still-hunting movement. Remember, you're not out there to cover ground but to spot game, so you have no reason to stride out. Take only half steps to avoid clomping and to maintain balance.

And take no more than two or three steps before you stop to look. Every step you take

The secret in all hunting is to spend more time looking than moving. You take one step and stop and look, then take another step and look.

473

Still-hunting isn't just a fancy name for walking through the woods. To hunt effectively, you must take your time, and squat or kneel frequently to look under branches.

gives you a new viewpoint, so you walk only far enough to get a fresh perspective, where you stop and look until you've identified every detail there. Then you move another step or two and look, look, look.

If you have to blow your nose, raise your binoculars, or wipe the sweat off your face, move your hands methodically. Fast movement will catch a deer's eye, but he won't notice slow-motion hands. Even turn your head slowly as you look for deer, and if you catch movement to the side or hear a sound, resist snapping your head around to see what's there. Even if you feel like a bear is breathing down your neck, turn your head with marked precision.

But at times you must cross downfalls, dry leaves, rock slides, or other problem areas where you'll make some kind of noise. All is not lost. Animals themselves make noise, so they're not alarmed at the sound of rustling leaves or a cracking branch. One time I watched three bucks on steep hillside as a rock broke loose near them and created a small rockslide. The deer stared curiously, but when they failed to see any cause for alarm, they settled down as if nothing had happened. I suspect they were used to the sounds of falling rocks and slides in that country.

Natural Sounds. If you can't move silently, try to make natural sounds that won't attract attention. You rarely hear animals clomping steadily or moving continuously. Undisturbed deer will take a couple of steps, nibble a branch or twig, take another step, and so forth. They make desultory, sporadic sounds. You can do the same, and your noises will attract little attention.

Even with the greatest care, you'll blunder once in a while and crash to the ground or jump a deer and send it bounding away. Naturally you'll assume you've just spooked every animal out of the country and will want to hurry on since there's little sense in sneaking any more. Avoid that temptation and keep hunting, because you can't be sure nearby animals have even heard you, and even if they have, they may pay no attention. One time I was sneaking up on a whitetail buck when a herd of does scattered in front of me and streamed past the buck in a frenzied getaway. "That's the end of that," I sighed. But to my amazement, the buck froze and watched the does race past. He stood motionless for five minutes, watching for danger. When he saw none, he returned to feeding. I've seen many other similar responses.

Sneakers. Not all deer will run even if they do see, hear, or smell you. They may very well hide or sneak away, and you have to use special strategies to spot them. Anyone who's hunted whitetails much can relate stories about watching bucks sneak away from other hunters, but don't think whitetails alone will pull that stunt; mule deer will too. I once watched a big buck stand frozen below a rim as two bowhunters walked within 30 yards. When the hunters had got about 100 yards past, the buck ducked low and sneaked the opposite way. I suspect those hunters would have called me a liar if I'd told them what had happened.

Kirt Darner, a well-known trophy hunter, plans much of his hunting strategy around the assumption that wizened mule deer will hide and sneak. In his book *How to Find Giant Bucks*, he says: "Thousands of today's smart muleys allow hunters to pass nearby. . . ." To counteract that, he's devised what he calls the fishhook pattern. He still-hunts straight through heavy brush or timber for a quarter mile or so. Then he turns right or left, walks 100 yards or so, and hooks again to hunt back parallel with his original path. Many times he's caught big bucks sneaking out behind him.

The Art of Seeing

Slow motion not only helps you keep from being seen or heard, but it helps you to see. I view still-hunting as roving stand hunting. You move a tiny bit; then you go on stand. You should spend far more time on stand than moving. If forced to express it in terms of numbers, I'd say move one quarter of the time and stand motionless at least three quarters. You have to look long enough to make out every detail in view, and your chances of spotting an animal's movement are far better when you're standing still.

Binoculars help in still-hunting as much as in long-range spotting. In a welter of forest branches, your naked eye might never pick up an antler tine or tip of a tail, but binoculars will isolate and magnify that detail so it stands out clearly. Use binoculars even in the densest brush. (For details, see Optics, and Spotting.)

Frequently get down to look under branches and brush lines. A deer's body may be totally obscured by tree limbs, but his legs could be very obvious underneath. I recall the last deer my dad ever shot. He was hunting with a rifle, but the facts apply just as well to bowhunting. My dad liked to still-hunt, and he frequently crouched or knelt to get a low viewpoint. On this particular day, he'd got down to look under low-hanging fir bows when he saw a deer's legs 20 yards ahead. The deer may have sensed my dad's presence because he stood motionless for nearly 5 minutes, but my dad was patient and waited the deer out. Finally the buck turned his head and my dad caught a flicker of antlers through the brush and slowly raised his rifle and dropped the buck right there. He'd never have got a shot if he hadn't knelt and seen the animal's legs.

Matching Patience. You've talked about matching wits with an animal, but in the case of still-hunting (and most hunting methods, for that matter) matching wits with game animals may not be as critical as matching patience. Animals live in the woods, and they're in no hurry to go anywhere. A deer might feed in one spot for ten minutes, it might lie nearly motionless in its bed for two hours, it might

In still-hunting you must spot the tiniest part of a deer or the slightest movement. You'd have to be sharp to spot the antler tines and back of this buck before the deer spotted you.

stare toward an unidentified sound for five minutes without moving.

To still-hunt well, you have to apply equal patience and control. You have to develop the same sense of "at homeness" in the forest as the deer have. When you can become a part of the woods, moving with the same quiet pace as the woods creatures do, you'll be a good still-hunter.

STRINGING A BOW   See Bow Stringer.

STRING PEEP   See Peep Sight.

STRING PINCH   If the angle of a bowstring is too acute at full draw, the result is pinched fingers. String pinch can cause sore fingers and severe blisters, particularly where your fingers are pressed against the arrow nock. Pinching the nock also contributes to a poor release and erratic arrow flight.

Causes of String Pinch

String pinch is most severe if you have a long draw length and shoot a short bow. When recurve bows were the rage in the 1960s, very short bows, 50 and 52 inches, swept the market, but their popularity was short-lived because, I suspect, they caused finger-pinching problems. With short bows and heavy full-draw weights, the effects of string pinch can be severe.

The lower holding weight of a compound bow mitigates the problem somewhat, but it can still affect your shooting. If your draw length is 30 inches or longer and you shoot a short compound bow, say with an axle-to-axle length of 44 inches or shorter, you'll probably have problems with pinched fingers.

Solving String Pinch

You can't do much to shorten your draw length, so the most logical solution is to buy a longer bow. If you have an especially long draw length, your compound bow should be at least 45 inches or longer, axle to axle. Most recurve shooters prefer bows of 60 inches or longer.

If you insist on shooting a short bow, you can solve the problem by shooting with a mechanical release aid. The release aid grips the string at one point only, so acute string angle isn't a problem. You can also shoot with three fingers under the arrow. That doesn't eliminate finger pinch, but it does prevent your pinching the nock, a primary cause of poor arrow flight.

STRING TRACKER   See Game Tracker.

STUMP SHOOTING   In this form of hunting practice, you wander randomly through the woods or fields, shooting at rotten stumps, logs, pine cones, or other suitable targets at various distances. The best heads for stump shooting are steel blunts or Judo heads. (For details, see Arrowhead.) This is one of the best forms of shooting practice for hunting. It's also called roving. (For more details, see Shooting Practice.)

SURVIVAL   Hunters often suffer catastrophe because they blame conditions for their problems rather than themselves. In virtually all cases, the victim is at fault. I suppose if you get bit by a snake or attacked by an enraged bear, you are blameless, the victim of unavoidable circumstances, but can the hypothermia victim blame cold weather for his plight? Can the person lost and freezing in fog blame the fog? Can the person stranded by a sudden blizzard sue the weatherman?

The answers should be obvious. The weather or other "acts of God," as the insurance companies would say, aren't at fault. Sure, they can test your ability as a woodsman, alter your original plans, and make you miserable, but they don't kill you. It's your reaction to natural phenomena that dictates the outcome, that governs your survival. If you're ill prepared and react stupidly, you die; if you're well prepared and react wisely, you live.

For that reason, I think the real survival secret, if "secret" is the right word, lies in prevention. Once you're snowed in or injured in the backcountry, it's too late to prepare. You begin survival at home while planning your hunting trip. The gear you assemble then, and the mental attitude you take to the field, govern your survival.

A Near Disaster

One September Gale Cavallin, a national archery champion and marketing director for Golden Eagle Archery, and two companions set out for elk in northern Idaho, a land of endless mountains and forests, typical Western hunting country. Weather had been warm, so one morning as they hiked out a timbered ridge, they wore only light clothing. Not far from the car they heard elk in different directions, so Cavallin went one way and his friends went the other. It would be a quick hunt; they'd meet back at the car about noon.

As Cavallin followed a bull, rain started falling and the temperature dropped radically. The hunter gave it little thought, though, because this was only September and just the day before he'd had to shed his shirt to cool down. The bull steadily herded his cows away, and Cavallin continued to follow for 3 hours, when the animal finally came within 20 yards before winding the hunter. Cavallin had been at full draw but thick brush prevented a clear shot. Still, he was excited and craved more action. He wrung out his sopping clothes, ate a granola bar, and started bugling again.

Two bulls responded, and the chase was on. It lasted until 2:00 P.M., when Cavallin suddenly realized he was well overdue at the car and reluctantly started back. Black clouds blotted out the sun, and in the junglelike forest, visibility was nil. Cavallin soon found himself in jackstraw blowdown. He followed a creek drainage but soon realized it led him not out, but deeper into the mountains. With nightfall, he was lost.

Just before dark he found a level spot for a fire and gathered kindling, but then he discovered his butane lighter was broken. He resorted to his backup matches, but the striker for them had got wet, and they wouldn't light either. So much for a fire.

The weather and other "acts of God" aren't to blame for emergency conditions. The hunter who doesn't think ahead and plan for the worst is to blame for his own predicaments.

By now it was dark. Cavallin figured his best hope lay in climbing high to watch for headlights on any nearby roads, so he climbed upward, lighting the way with a new flashlight. But before long the light dimmed and then died. So much for light.

He now had only one choice—to stay right where he stood. Throughout the night he alternated huddling under a fallen tree with standing up and moving his arms, legs, toes, and fingers to generate warmth. By dawn he'd lost coordination and was so weak he threw up when he tried drinking from his canteen and then he started dry heaving. He knew he was freezing and had to get warm before long.

In the faint morning light he began hiking on wobbly legs. Then he heard the growl of heavy equipment in the distance. This tenuous contact with civilization renewed his strength, and he headed toward the sound eagerly and eventually hit a logging road. Snow was falling, his clothes were frozen stiff, and he had to keep walking.

Fortunately, the ordeal ended quickly after that. When Cavallin had failed to show up the previous day, his friends had called authorities. A helicopter was sent out to search for the lost hunter, and the chopper crew found Cavallin walking along the road.

Gale Cavallin's story isn't the exception. Rather, his predicament typifies a common hunting ordeal. It's the epitome, the perfect example, of the situation that most commonly spells trouble for bowhunters. Many hunters, including myself, have lived through similar ex-

The groundwork for survival is preparation. Put together a hunting pack containing survival gear, and carry that pack whenever you leave the car. The "let's just take a quick look-see" syndrome that lulls you into leaving your pack in the car could be the most dangerous attitude in hunting.

periences; others have died. An analysis of this scenario reveals survival basics that guarantee your safety in all hunting situations.

Anticipate the Worst

Cavallin and his party first erred by expecting good weather, and that brings up the number one survival lesson: anticipate and prepare for the worst. Even modern meteorologists, with all their satellites and maps and knowledge, can't correctly predict the weather more than 80 percent of the time. How can you guess it in the field? You can't, so the only smart alternative is to expect terrible weather. That way, you can't go wrong.

That's not to say you shouldn't keep tabs on weather conditions. A series of very high frequency (VHF) weather stations provides the most accurate weather information available, and nearly 400 stations across the United States now reach an estimated 90 percent of the American people. You can get a complete list of stations at your local Weather Service office, or by writing to the National Weather Service, National Oceanic and Atmospheric Administration, Silver Spring, MD 20910. You can buy a battery-powered VHF weather radio from most radio and stereo shops for the price of a dozen arrows. From these stations, you can get daily weather forecasts that might help you escape disaster, such as a coming blizzard.

But I wouldn't plan my day-to-day hunting around any forecasts, particularly in the mountains, where weather can change instantly and drastically. During my first 15 years of elk hunting in September from Montana to Arizona, I saw sunny weather through an entire hunt only twice, in 1974 and 1979, both in Oregon. Every other year has been marked by terrible weather. In Colorado, it was violent thunderstorms with rain and hail. In Montana one year it was drenching rains day after day, and another year it was heavy snow and fog. In central Idaho, a virtual blizzard swept the mountains and dumped a foot of snow. Even in Arizona, rain fell constantly to keep us wet and cold. This has all occurred in September, which would be considered summer in many regions.

A small, lightweight pack with essential survival items could save your life. It should be your constant companion in the field.

If you accept bad weather as reality, you'll take adequate gear to camp, but will you have it when you need it? As Cavallin discovered, the weather can change instantly, and then it's too late to prepare. The "let's just take a quick look-see" syndrome may be the most dangerous philosophy you can take to a hunting camp. It nearly got Gale Cavallin, and it did get two bowhunters near LaGrande, Oregon. They walked a short ridge late one afternoon, apparently just to "take a quick look," and rescue workers found their bodies four days later. Sadly, they had survival gear; it lay in their vehicle while they froze to death in the field. How do you know when you'll hear a bull elk bugling, or spot the buck of a lifetime? And when you do, will you head back to camp to get your gear? Not likely. You'll go after the animal because that's why you're out there.

So any time you take so much as one step away from your car or camp, take your survival gear. That's the number one survival rule. You might just stuff the needed items in your pockets, but it's more reliable to assemble a survival kit in a pack, such as a fanny pack or small rucksack. (For details, see Hunting Pack.) It doesn't matter what kind of system you choose as long as it's light, comfortable, and convenient so you'll always take it with you. Carrying survival gear should become second nature. Then you'll never get caught without.

Gear for the Pack

Pathfinding Gear. In my opinion, gear to help you find your way ranks number one. That includes flashlight, map, and compass. Again, analyzing Gale Cavallin's predicament, the fact that he was cold seems the most serious threat, but the question is: Why was he cold? The answer is obvious: He got lost. If he'd had a map of the area and a compass to direct him, he'd have got back to camp the first day and wouldn't have needed fire or shelter.

If you're hunting a woodlot on the back 40 where you know every tree and rock, this might not apply, but any time you head into new territory, have maps. A map provides your only means of getting an overview and perspective of the area. Without it, you're lost.

Regardless of your circumstances, always carry a reliable compass. It can serve many survival functions.

Without a map you're essentially lost. A map goes hand in hand with a compass as basic survival gear.

Your hunting pack should never be without a flashlight, along with spare batteries and bulb. An elastic headband that frees your hands can be handy.

Same goes for a compass. I'm continually amazed at how few hunters carry a compass. You might think, "I would use it so little, it's not worth the bother." Indeed, I've gone through two complete hunting seasons without ever taking my compass out of my pack, but does that mean it's excess baggage? If my life depends on it only one time, that's justification enough for carrying it.

And don't think you can get along without it. Under a heavy overcast, for example, you can't tell which direction you're headed. In the bottomlands of northern Missouri, I was hunting along a small creek that flowed south. Heavy clouds blacked out any hint of the sun, so I was making my way by feel. Somehow I got turned around and walked the wrong way, but I was so sure my direction was right that I convinced myself the stream actually flowed north. Not until I found myself returned to my starting point would I admit to my mistake. In fog, darkness, blinding snow, heavy timber, and so forth, you often can't tell direction. A compass offers your only recourse, so have one with you.

The need for a flashlight should be obvious. Any time you get caught out after dark, you need light. Gale Cavallin had one, sure enough, but it went dead, which brings up another lesson. First, don't rely on a rechargeable light; there aren't any outlets in the woods. Second, always carry a spare bulb and spare batteries.

Shelter and Warmth. Even with these preparations, you could find yourself spending a night or two in the woods. It has happened to me more than once.

On one occasion, I shot an elk just before dark and by the time I'd dressed the animal and headed for camp, it was 11:00 P.M. In the black forest under heavy clouds, I could see no landmarks to keep me on course. I knew I had to follow a ridgetop due north for at least a mile, and using my compass I was able to do that. But many small finger ridges angled off the main ridge, and after an hour's hiking, I couldn't tell whether I was on the main ridge or a side ridge, and country was getting treacherous. I was worn out, slipping and stumbling, so I decided to stop before I got hurt. I built a big fire and settled in for the night, and the next morning I easily found my way back to camp.

Many circumstances could prevent your returning to camp, so you must be prepared to stay out, and that means you need warmth and shelter. I place highest priority on fire. Not only can you dry your wet clothes and keep warm, but a cheerful dancing orange blaze provides mental comfort, a sense of home. That's why a reliable fire starter deserves high priority in your hunting pack.

A butane lighter works great for general fire starting and could be considered standard gear, but don't rest your life on one. As Cavallin painfully discovered, lighters can break. Besides, butane burns poorly in cold weather.

As a backup, carry wooden matches, and make sure they're the strike-anywhere kind. Safety matches require a special striker, and if that striker gets wet, you're sunk. Dip the matches in melted paraffin to waterproof them, and as added insurance seal them in a plastic bottle.

In addition, carry a supplemental starter that will burn long enough to dry and ignite damp kindling. A number of companies make good firestarters. One called Lightning Nuggets consists of compressed, pitchy wood shavings. Mountain Products, Inc. of Libby, Montana, packages small blocks of pitch wood in its Fast Fire Starter Pack. A small can of Sterno works well as a fire starter.

An emergency road flare, or fusee, is hard to beat as a fire starter in wet weather. These flares have a striker on one end and will light under the soggiest conditions. A full flare will burn for 20 minutes, but it's heavy so you might want to cut one in half. You can reseal the cut end with the plastic cap off the original end.

A guaranteed fire begins with a no-fail starter, but it ends with your preparations in the field. First gather a big pile of twigs and other kindling. Many spruce and fir trees have a shag of fine twigs next to the trunk, and often you can find an old log or blowdown from

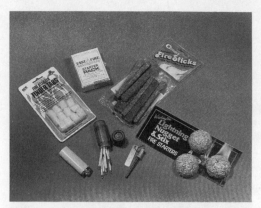

Fire starters come in many shapes and forms. The important point is that you choose one that's reliable, and see that it's always in your pack.

which you can whittle dry shavings. Along with this kindling, stockpile plenty of bigger branches.

When you have enough wood for a bonfire, loosely stack kindling over your fire starter, and make a teepee of bigger branches over that. Light your fire starter on the upwind side so the flame will blow into the kindling, and before long you'll have a cheerful—and live-saving—blaze.

Shelter goes hand in hand with fire. In high-mountain hunting, particularly for elk and other animals that can draw me a long way from camp, I generally carry a 9 x 12, 1 mil painter's tarp. It's very light, yet it can serve as good emergency shelter. Some hunters carry a Space Blanket or similar product. With these you can construct quick shelter against pouring rain or snow.

Obviously, you first look for natural shelter—an overhanging cliff, cave, downed tree—you can crawl under. If those aren't available, you can throw together a lean-to simply by leaning a long pole over a low tree limb or log, and then draping your plastic over that and anchoring it with rocks. If you don't have plastic you can thatch this with tree boughs or slabs of bark.

Or you can make a simple A-frame. Start with three poles, two about six feet long, one at

A smart hunter is one who goes prepared for the worst. Emergency shelter, fire starter, adequate clothing, and other essentials should accompany you on every hunt.

least ten. Lay the two short poles together and tie them together near one end. A shear lashing, made by wrapping cord around both poles several times and then wrapping it around itself between the poles and tying it off, works well for this. Separate the bottom ends to form a V, set them on the ground as legs, and place the long pole in the crotch of the two shorter poles to form a tripod. Now drape your plastic over this and anchor it, or thatch the roof with natural materials.

Clothing also can be considered part of shelter. During warm weather, nobody will carry a pile of heavy clothes, "just in case," but certainly dressing properly with wool or comparable clothing can contribute to your survival. And no matter how promising the weather, carry a wool shirt or sweater. While hiking I tie this around my waist, but during rest breaks I slip it on, and the warmth of that extra garment has saved me from many a miserable day.

A rain parka can also be a wise addition to your hunting pack. (For details, see Clothing.)

Other Survival-Pack Items. Additional items round out your survival pack. A good knife obviously serves many purposes, and a small sharpening stone or steel helps keep the knife sharp. Sometimes I add a small folding saw, particularly in elk hunting where I might have to saw bones or antlers, or where I might end up miles from a road and want to cut poles for shelter. As a compromise between carrying a saw and knife, I often carry Browning's Big Game knife, which includes a small saw blade.

Injuries are always a possibility in the field, so a first-aid kit is a must. It should contain, at the very minimum, Band-Aids, a gauze roll, sterile pads, aspirin, moleskin, and a small bar of soap for cleaning wounds.

My pack also contains a whistle for emergency signaling, and plastic flagging for marking a trail, which might be necessary in many circumstances. As one example, an experienced woodsman in Maine shot a huge buck late one evening. He gutted the deer and then headed to the road. On the way a blizzard hit. The man had to spend the night in the woods, and the next morning, deep snow covered his trail—and his deer. He eventually found the road and safety, but he never did find the deer. If he'd flagged the trail, he'd have recovered that deer. I've often marked trails at night to help me retrace my steps the next day.

Food helps you keep up your strength, so you'll want to carry high-energy foods in your hunting pack. Still, you can survive for days, even weeks without food, so don't get carried away. Map, compass, and fire starter are more crucial to your survival.

Fifty feet of nylon cord proves useful, too. If you're alone and kill an animal, you can use the cord to tie the animal's legs back during the gutting and skinning process. And you can use the cord to tie together an emergency shelter and to lash meat onto your pack.

Contaminated water has caused many hunters problems in recent years, even in the backcountry, so unless you know positively you can get pure water, carry a water bottle and purification tablets. You also might find three feet of surgical tubing useful. With it you can siphon pure water directly from a ground source. An aluminum cup can be handy for siphoning into and for boiling water.

Rescue Gear. Regardless of your caution, you can get hurt or stranded, so you need some way to signal for help. Many search-and-rescue workers suggest a shrill whistle like a police whistle, because it's foreign to the woods and will attract attention, and blowing a whistle takes less energy than yelling for help. A signal mirror can be seen for miles on sunny days and can be used to catch the eye of a distant hunter or passing airplane. A compass mirror can double as a signal mirror. You can also signal with smoky fires during the day and bright, flickering fires at night. Three of anything—three whistle blasts, three fires, three mirror flashes—is a universal distress signal.

Miscellaneous Gear. At times, depending on conditions, survival gear might also include extra eyeglasses (if you can't see without glasses), sun protection and sunglasses (particularly on snow), and a snakebite kit.

Here's a concise list of survival-pack items. Some gear should go with you regardless of conditions, whereas other gear might be contingent. If you don't wear eyeglasses, for example, there's not much reason to carry a spare pair.

Flashlight (spare bulb and batteries)
Map
Compass
Fire starters
Knife
Sharpening stone or steel for knife
First-aid kit (Band-aids, sterile 3 x 3-inch gauze pads, adhesive tape, gauze roll, aspirin, moleskin, small bar of soap)
50 feet of nylon cord
Whistle for signaling
Signal mirror (could be built into compass)
Fluorescent plastic flagging
Aluminum cup
3 feet of surgical tubing for water siphon
Water-purification tablets
Pen
Snakebite kit (in known snake country)
Sunburn protection (on bright snow)
Sunglasses (on bright snow)
Plastic for emergency shelter

The Survival Mind

With the above items always at hand, you can survive any sudden emergency. That's the first step toward survival. The second involves your mind, and that may be more critical than your gear.

File a Trip Plan. To begin with, admit that you're fallible, and tell others where you'll be, in case you don't return. Many times I've talked to wives who hadn't the slightest idea where their husbands were hunting. Not even which state they were in. What are they going to do if the husbands don't return? Nobody will know where to look. Before you leave home, tell your wife (or husband if you're a woman) or other relative where you'll be and when you plan to return. Leave phone numbers to call (Forest Service, Fish and Game, sheriff, and such) in case of an emergency. If you're in camp, tell your buddies where you plan to hunt each day, and agree among yourselves how long you'll wait before starting to search. I tell my friends, "Don't worry about me if I'm gone one night. If I'm gone two, start looking."

Use Your Head, Not Your Legs. Veterans of search and rescue tell me most people they rescue have got into predicaments simply because they've lost their heads and done stupid things.

I could go into a mystical discussion about how you have to flow with the land and become a part of nature rather than fighting it, the kind of thing primitive-survival writers talk about, and that would be valid, but I doubt that it would mean much to most modern hunters. Many of us sit in an office eleven months of the year and then we hunt for a week or two each fall. We barely start feeling comfortable outdoors when it's time to come home. For that reason, it does little good to wax eloquent about becoming part of nature. We just don't have time.

Nevertheless, you can develop a survival

mind at home that will serve you well in a crisis: When you can see you're in a predicament, don't push on. Before it ever happens, vow that you'll stop while you still have the faculties to help yourself, and to get the shelter and warmth you need to survive. If necessary — you're hurt badly or lost hopelessly — sit tight. Signal with your whistle, mirror, or fires until someone finds you.

One search-and-rescue worker in Wyoming said his crews have spent many days looking for hunters who've got lost in the fog and then have wandered, desperately trying to find their way out.

"If they'd just stop and build a fire to get comfortable and wait until the fog lifts, they'd have no problem," he said. "But they just keep wandering, and it only makes things worse."

Point of No Return. If you push on long enough, you reach a point where you can't help yourself, and then pushing on can become a fatal survival error. Hypothermia has been well publicized as an outdoor killer, and well it should be, because it's one of the major causes of death among outdoorsmen.

But in many cases it's not actually lowered body temperature, but irrational thinking, that leads to disaster. Dr. John Hayward, who has studied hypothermia extensively at the University of Victoria in British Columbia, said that during the early stages of hypothermia, your body remains quite healthy. You may be shivering and think you're freezing, but the vital core temperature remains nearly normal. Hayward said severe chilling affects motor performance and the will to survive.

"After prolonged cold we estimated a 40 percent decrease in mental performance and physical ability," Hayward said. "That brings about strange behavior, but it doesn't indicate a cold heart, which is life-threatening. When a person becomes exhausted and runs out of the energy required to shiver and exercise, that's when deep hypothermia sets in."

"A 40 percent decrease in mental and physical ability" seems to be the key to developing a survival attitude. Admit beforehand, right now even as you read this, that even though prolonged cold may not be threatening your life with hypothermia, it will insidiously rob you mentally and physically until you're not able to function. If you push on to that point, you may be unable to help yourself. Your hands will shake so badly you can't strike a match, and your thinking will become so blurred you can't build shelter. Here's the point: realize beforehand that this can happen, and stop before you reach a point of mental and physical no return.

Nothing in the woods — bears or darkness or loneliness or strange sounds or cold or rain — can harm you. Only you can harm you, and if you accept that now and resign yourself to taking care of yourself with shelter and warmth before it's too late, you'll survive the worst of situations.

SWORD POINT   See Dagger Point.

T

TAB See Finger Tab, and Release Aids.

TACKLE BASICS Getting started in bow-hunting requires a minimum selection of gear. Some hunters would call a bow and arrows the essentials and they would classify all other gadgets, such as sights or release aids, as accessories. One person's necessities might be another's accessories, so it's up to you to decide what you must have and what you can do without. Nevertheless, bowhunting requires a minimum battery of gear, and the list that follows outlines equipment items used regularly by bowhunters. Some you might find essential, some nonessential.

Bows and Shooting Gear

Bow. You first choose among bow styles: longbow, recurve, or compound. If you choose a compound you must decide whether it should have wheels or cams, and whether you should equip it with an overdraw. Then come draw weight and draw length. Handle material, bow length, mass weight of the bow, and many other variables also must be considered. (For details, see Bow Selection.)

Bow Case. For protecting the bow and accessories during transport, you need either a hard bow box or a padded bow case. (For details, see Bow Care.)

Arrows. First considerations are length, spine weight and mass weight. Then you choose shaft material, most likely aluminum or cedar; fletching material and configuration; nocks; and inserts. (For details, see Arrow Selection.)

Arrow straightener. You can straighten arrows by hand, but a straightening device can speed up the process and allow greater precision. These come in several models. (For details, see Arrow Care.)

Arrowheads. Many styles of heads are needed to accommodate all hunting situations. Weight, shape, size, and other aspects must be considered. (For details, see Arrowhead, and Broadhead.)

Fletching jig. Many hunters make their own arrows. It's a way to save money and to build custom arrows best suited to your particular equipment and shooting style. (For details, see Arrow Making.)

Quiver. The general choices are bow, back, or hip quiver, and then size: 4, 8, 16-arrow? Whatever the style and size, a quiver must hold your arrows securely and protect the broadheads, and it must be durable, convenient, and quiet. (For details, see Quiver.)

Arrow rest. For good arrow flight, the arrow rest may be the most significant accessory, yet it's probably the most commonly overlooked.

Most bows come equipped with solid, one-piece plastic rests. These are okay for casual shooting, but if you're serious about perfecting your shooting, consider a flipper/plunger setup, or one of various shoot-through rests. (For details, see Arrow Rest.)

Bowsight. Some hunters prefer shooting barebow, but sights have become standard equipment with many hunters in recent years. You can choose between pin or crosshair sights, and a number of different materials and mounting methods. Some hunters also use a peep sight mounted in the bowstring, and others use a kisser button to assure consistent aiming. (For details, see Bowsight, and Peep Sight.)

Bowstring and accessories. The main concern is getting the right length, and selecting the right strength. You can choose various silencing devices to reduce string noise, and a nock locator is critical for consistent arrow placement. Wax will keep the string in good shape, and knowledge of serving will help you repair a string in the field. (For details, see Bowstring.)

Armguard. As a beginner, you'll need an armguard to protect your arm from bowstring slap. Most experienced shooters rarely hit their arms with the string, but they still wear an armguard to assure that a shirtsleeve doesn't interfere with the bowstring. Many styles are available. (For details, see Armguard.)

Release aids. Here I've lumped together all devices that help you hold and release the string: tabs, gloves, and mechanical string releases. Release aids protect your string fingers and assure a better release than you can get with bare fingers. Each type has its strong and weak points. Powder and other lubricants can improve the efficiency of some tabs and gloves. (For details, see Release Aid.)

Stabilizer. Stabilizers are heavy rods that screw into the bow to add weight, reduce torque, and dampen noise. They come in various weights and lengths. A stabilizer might improve your accuracy, although it's not mandatory. (For details, see Stabilizer.)

Wrist sling. This leather strap loops around your wrist to prevent your dropping the bow when you release the string. It can help improve your shooting form. (For details, see Wrist Sling.)

Target butts. Straw bales or stacked cardboard offer a good shooting backstop, but many commercial butts made of foam, woven grass, and nylon prove more convenient in many cases. Some targets are made for field points only, while others will stop broadheads as well. (For details, see Target Butt.)

Arrow puller. For target shooting, you might want a rubber gripper to help pull arrows from tight target butts. And for hunting, a broadhead puller can be useful. (For details, see Arrow Puller.)

Range finder. Probably the single major reason for missed shots is misestimation of range. Some hunters can instinctively estimate range accurately, but an optical range finder can be invaluable in certain situations. (For details, see Range Finder, and Trajectory.)

Game tracker. Many hunters equip their bows with a string tracker, especially for turkeys, which may fly when hit, and bears, which often leave a poor blood trail. (For details, see Game Tracker.)

Tree stand and accessories. Tree-stand hunting has become a universal method, especially for whitetail deer, but it's equally adaptable to other species. Most serious bowhunters have a tree stand and the needed accessories, such as safety belt, tree steps, folding seat, and so forth. (For details, see Stand Hunting.)

Camouflage. "Bowhunting" and "camouflage" have become nearly synonymous. Most hunters think in terms of camouflage clothing, but camouflage must extend to any exposed skin and to gear as well. (For details, see Camouflage.)

Clothing. Some hunters view camo pattern as the only basis for choosing clothing, but quietness, comfort, warmth, durability, and other criteria come into play. Proper clothing contributes not only to comfort but to success. (For details, see Clothing.)

Bow slings. For hunting, you might find a bow sling useful for packing your bow over your back, rather than in your hand. And some hunters use a "spare arm" hook to hold their bows while glassing. (For details, see Bow Sling.)

Tackle box. For all practice and hunting situations, you need a general array of gear for working on bows and arrows. A small, well-equipped tackle box should be part of your normal equipment. (For details, see Tackle Box.)

Bow-Testing Gear

Bow and grain scale. To work with tackle and fine-tune your setup, you must know the draw weight. You can take your bow to a pro shop for weighing, but serious hunters often make their own scales. A grain scale for weighing heads, fletching, arrows, and other components can also prove useful. (For details, see Arrow Shaft Selection, and Bow Scale.)

Chronograph. For serious bow testing, you must be able to measure arrow speed. A simple chronograph makes this possible. (For details, see Bow Tuning, and Chronograph.)

TACKLE BOX Archery tackle requires little maintenance, but small repairs are a routine aspect of all bowhunting. A tackle box with an assortment of tools and spare gear helps you solve a lot of problems in the field. Put together a standard tackle box and carry it along on every trip. The following list is the standard items found in my tackle box. You might want more or less, depending on the kind of bow you shoot and your hunting conditions.

Tools: pliers, Allen wrenches, screwdrivers
Various screws for sights, quiver, and other accessories
Inserts, broadhead adaptors, arrowheads
Hot-melt glue, contact cement, epoxy
Bowstrings
Boxstring wax
Serving string and serving jig
Nocks and nock pliers

A small tackle box like this filled with spare parts and tools should be part of your standard hunting gear.

Axle keepers
Fletching and fletching jig
Fletching glue
Tape: duct tape, electrician's tape
Arrow rests
Bow square
Tape measure
Light oil or other lube for bow
Sharpening stone, steel, oil

TARGET BUTT Several target butt styles are suitable for a home shooting range. One of the cheapest and most dependable is three straw bales stacked on top of one another. Set the bales on 2 x 4s to keep them from soaking up water and rotting underneath, and cover them to keep off the rain, and they'll last for many months, even years. To improve on this backstop, you can band them all together and pull them tight so arrows won't slip between the cracks. Bales of cedar shavings cost more than straw, but they stop arrows better and generally last longer.

You can make an equally good target butt by stacking corrugated cardboard until you get a butt the size you need. Band the cardboard together tightly as you would cedar bales. Make the butt so you're shooting into the cut sides of the cardboard, because the arrows will be much easier to pull than if you shoot into

Straw or compressed cedar bales, as this archer is using, strapped tightly together, make ideal backstops.

same company makes a butt out of excelsior impregnated with foam. No perfect solution has ever been found for broadheads, but this one does a good job. I've shot several hundred broadhead arrows into mine, and it still has plenty of life left in it.

Some ethafoam targets are suitable for both field points and broadheads. The Stanley Hips target has been around for some time. It will take a lot of shooting from field points, but broadheads will chew it up fairly quick. It does come with a replaceable core, however, so you can just replace that rather than the whole target. A thinner version of the ethafoam target made by Foam Experts in Redding, California, is made of denser foam and is much thinner. It's very light and compact and makes an ideal target butt for use in camp. Again, it will take

the finished side of the cardboard. Some archery clubs use baled cardboard boxes—the big bales you see stacked out behind variety stores—as target butts on their ranges.

The Saunders Indian rope grass mats are ideal for shooting in your back yard or basement. These are made of tightly twisted grass covered with burlap. These are the target mats used at many major archery tournaments. They'll stop fast-flying arrows and will hold up under a lot of shooting, and you can get various sizes.

Another good butt for the home target range is made by Impact Industries, Inc., Wausau, WI. This style of butt has a foam face, and a foot or so behind it a very tough nylon backstop. The arrows pass through the foam and stop when they hit the nylon. I've shot thousands of arrows into mine and it seems to be holding up well. For broadhead practice, this

Saunders Indian rope grass mats are tough and will take thousands of shots. They come in various sizes. This 30-inch model is ideal for a backyard shooting range.

broadheads, but they'll eat it up fairly quickly; however, it also has a replaceable core.

A friend of mine had the best broadhead backstop I've seen. To make it he simply had an insulation company fill a big cardboard box full of the injection-style foam insulation. When the foam had hardened, he peeled off the cardboard and had a target. It was a good 20 inches thick, and even after taking several thousand broadheads, the butt was still stopping arrows well.

One other kind of target makes a good portable butt for home or camp use. It's a burlap bag stuffed with some kind of tough webbing. You can't shoot broadheads into one of these "stuffed" targets, but you can shoot field points into one forever without hurting it. Several companies make these.

TARGET PANIC　　In one form, this is the inability to bring your sight (or sight picture, in the case of instinctive shooting) onto the target. In other forms, it results in snap shooting the instant the sight passes the target, or in freezing on the target to the point that you can't let the string go. Target panic is also called freezing.

Causes of Target Panic

All experienced archers have their own theories on target panic, many of them conflicting, but a few principles seem universal. Generally target panic is considered a psychological or mental problem. It comes from fear of missing. As archery champion Jim Pickering said, "Archers try to become machines, and when a guy becomes afraid to make a mistake, he freezes and can't release the string."

Even though the end product might be mental, the cause can be physical. Again, most experienced archers agree that shooting a heavy draw-weight bow is a major cause of target panic. A friend of mine, at one time an excellent shot, shoots a 70-pound recurve bow, and he's developed target panic so bad he can hardly release an arrow at a target or a game animal.

This thin ethafoam target by Foam Experts is compact and lightweight, and it's an excellent target butt for use around camp.

From left to right, Saunders Indian rope grass mat, Impact Industries' foam target with a nylon arrow backstop, and an ethafoam target all have their place in practice for hunting.

Popular writer and expert bowhunter Chuck Adams said, "Target panic occurs when muscles knot up and joints lock in, and then it becomes psychological. I've never met anyone who could hold more than 50 pounds and really shoot well. It's largely a function of holding weight on your fingers. The heavier the bow, the less time you have to bring the pin up to the bull and let go."

Jim Pickering said, "To shoot well you have to learn to relax even under the tension of holding your bow at full draw. With a heavy bow you can't relax. Shooting a bow should be a process of total relaxation, but target panic is a process of total tension, and heavy draw weight only aggravates the problem." (For more details, see Shooting Basics.)

Cures for Target Panic

Since heavy bow poundage causes target panic, reducing poundage can be a major first step toward curing it. As Pickering said, "As you hold heavy poundage at full draw, you're not able to *think* about your shooting system. You just worry about hitting the target, and you can't concentrate on form at all."

Reduce Bow Weight. Obviously, then, shooting a light-poundage bow serves as a good starting point. For severe cases, Pickering suggests going even further by putting an elastic band on your bow and "shooting" with that for a while instead of the bowstring. You can draw, aim, hold, and release the elastic without strain, which allows you to concentrate on form, and you can do these things without worrying about shooting a good arrow or hitting the target.

Clicker. Gale Cavallin, also an archery champion and hunter, said, "Your mind gives you the command to shoot, but because you don't want to miss, and at the same time are afraid you will, your mind won't make that command. You've got to trick your mind into letting you shoot." One method is a clicker, a device that attaches to the bow and clicks when you reach full draw. As Cavallin said, "A clicker relieves your mind from making the de-

cision about when to shoot. When you hear that click, you release automatically. All the top shooters use a clicker, and mostly it has to do with target panic."

Silent clickers for use with broadheads are also available. Most experienced shooters say that if you practice with a clicker, you should hunt with one, because your mind is waiting for that signal to release.

Release Aid. Cavallin strongly recommends a mechanical release aid as a cure for target panic, because, just as the clicker does, the release aid relieves your mind from the duty of deciding when to release. "The trick is to not know when the bow is going off," Cavallin said. "With a release aid you get on target and slowly start squeezing, and you're surprised when the bow goes off."

No Aiming. Shooting with your eyes closed, or shooting with no target on the butt at all, can help, too. These methods allow you to concentrate strictly on shooting form. To cure target panic, you must take control of your body to release the string at your command, and these methods help. All these methods, of course, assume you've reduced bow poundage so you can draw, aim, hold, and release comfortably. If you continue to shoot the same heavy tackle that caused you to strain and develop the problem in the first place, you don't have much hope for curing it.

TENNESSEE Tennessee covers an area of 42,187 square miles, about 5 percent of it federal or state-owned; these lands provide public hunting. In the past it has been fairly easy to get permission to hunt private lands, but the trend toward hunting leases has grown in recent years.

Big Game

Whitetail Deer. The deer population is estimated at 325,000 animals. Bowhunters number about 44,000, and they have harvested as many as 6,700 deer (3,000 bucks and 3,700 does) in one year. Highest archery success on record has been 13 percent and the lowest about 5 percent. The bow season opens the last Saturday in September and closes October 31, although archers can hunt during gun seasons in November and December. Bag limits have been generous, ranging from one to four deer per hunter, depending on area.

In general, deer are sparse in the east and become more plentiful as you move west. In the steep, timbered Smokey Mountains at the far eastern end, deer numbers are low. In the central part of the state, which includes the Cumberland Plateau and Nashville Basin, deer densities run from moderate to high, depending on the exact locality. In the far western portion, from the Tennessee River basin to the Mississippi River, deer numbers generally are very high.

Deer herds virtually exploded in Tennessee during the 1970s, and annual harvest increased every year from the 1960s through the early 1980s. With growing interest in deer hunting, more and more private land is being leased by clubs or posted against hunting. The state record typical whitetail scored 186⅛, and the record nontypical 196⁶⁄₈.

Pigs. Pigs are hunted in three general areas: the Smokey Mountains, the Cumberland Plateau in the central state, and the Mississippi bottomlands at the far western end. Pig hunting is open in several counties concurrent with the deer archery season, and some hunting is allowed at other times throughout the fall.

Black Bears. Some limited hunting for black bears is allowed in the mountain region at the eastern end of the state in counties bordering North Carolina.

Other Game

Turkeys. These birds have done exceptionally well and most counties have a spring season. Annual bag limit could be as high as four birds if you take advantage of all options.

Small Game. Squirrels, rabbits, and various other small game provide wide hunting opportunity throughout the state.

Contact. Tennessee Wildlife Resources Agency, Ellington Agricultural Center, P.O. Box 40747, Nashville, TN 37204.

TEXAS   Along with its huge expanse of land, the Lone Star State has more deer, wild turkeys, and javelina than any other state, so it could be counted as a hunter's heaven. Only trouble is that virtually all land in Texas is privately owned, and the hunting-lease tradition runs strong. You might get a personal invite to hunt a ranch, and you can find some very limited public hunting, but for the most part, if you plan to hunt in Texas, you plan to pay.

Big Game

Deer. About 50 percent of Texas's 267,338 square miles supports 3.4 million whitetails. In addition, mule deer occupy about 12 percent of the state, primarily in the far western Trans-Pecos region. There is some overlap in range.

Total deer harvest in Texas averages nearly 300,000 animals, but the average archery harvest has been only about 3,000 deer, evenly divided between bucks and does, although the kill will continue to rise as bowhunting interest increases in Texas. Archery license sales have risen rapidly the past few years. Average bowhunter success has remained fairly stable at about 10 percent. The archery-only season runs for about one month, starting in early October. The limit is three deer in many regions.

The quality of hunting in Texas varies from outstanding to poor, depending on how landowners manage their deer herds. Most states have traditional "deer factories," and in Texas, it's the Edwards Plateau, which roughly covers the west-central portion of the state, primarily hill-country rangeland. Many mature bucks are killed here, but competition with livestock, and too many deer in some areas, have resulted in small average size and poor trophy quality.

Texas has gained a reputation for producing trophy whitetails. The state record typical whitetail scores 164⁴⁄₈, and the record nontypical, which held the Boone and Crockett world-record position for many years, scored 286.

Texas ranks third in Boone and Crockett trophy production, and virtually all those bucks have come from the south Texas brush country south of San Antonio. Many ranches are managed strictly for trophy animals, so deer harvest is relatively light and herds contain a high percentage of older bucks.

All other regions of Texas have fair to good deer numbers as well. All deer are whitetails except in the Trans-Pecos in the extreme western corner south of New Mexico. Whitetails are scattered throughout this arid region but desert mule deer predominate.

Antelope. Limited antelope hunting takes place, primarily in the Trans-Pecos country of west Texas.

Javelina. These animals live throughout south Texas, and they're so numerous in some places that landowners consider them pests. They're sometimes hunted with dogs. The season and bag limits are generous.

Exotics. A number of ranches have imported a variety of exotic animals from Africa and other parts of the world. Regulations for hunting these animals are set by the landowners, and generally you pay for what you kill.

Other Game

Turkeys. As in many states, turkeys have responded well to modern management, and they're now hunted both spring and fall in more than 60 counties.

Small Game. Squirrels are heavily hunted in the Pineywoods region on the eastern side of the state. Rabbits are abundant throughout suitable habitat.

Predators. Texas may be the predator hunting capital of the world, and coyotes, bobcats, and foxes can be hunted day or night with either hand-held or electronic calling devices. Most hunters focus on the animals in winter when pelts are prime.

Contact. Texas Parks and Wildlife Department, 4200 Smith School Road, Austin, TX 78744.

THREE FINGERS UNDER THE ARROW
See Apache Draw.

TILLER This term originally meant the stock of a crossbow. The term also refers to a notched bar used by a bowyer to study the bend of the limbs. Tillering is the process of removing material from a bow's limbs until the limbs bend equally at full draw.

Tiller, then, generally describes the bending relationship between the top and bottom limbs. On a properly tillered bow, the limbs at full draw will bend equally so that when the string is released, the tips of the bow (or the wheels in the case of a compound) will return to brace height at the same time. Tiller becomes necessary because the bow handle is set below the center of the bow, which places more pressure on the bottom limb than on the top.

Most bowhunters loosely use *tiller* to de-

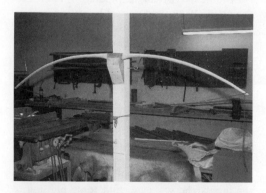

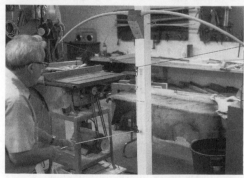

Tiller describes the bending relationships between top and bottom limbs. Traditional bowmakers used a tiller to visually gauge the bend in the limbs, and if one limb bent more than another, the limbs were reworked until they both bent equally.

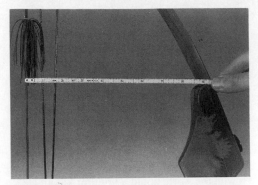

On a compound bow you can gauge tiller by measuring from the bowstring to the bow limb where the limb meets the handle. In this case, tiller on the top limb is nine inches. The bottom limb should also be close to nine inches although it doesn't have to be exact on a compound bow.

scribe the distance from the bow limbs to the string. You can use a bow square, ruler, or one of your arrows to measure tiller. If you use an arrow, place the tip of the arrow against the upper limb just above the handle and set your thumbnail against the bowstring. Now, keeping your thumb at the same spot on the arrow, move the arrow down and place the tip against the lower limb just below the handle. You should see a space between the string and your thumbnail. In other words, the lower limb should be closer to the bowstring than the upper limb.

On a recurve bow, tiller should measure about ¼ to ½ inch. Of course, you can't do much about it if it doesn't, except to buy a different brand of bow. For compound bows, most bow manufacturers recommend a tiller measurement of ⅛ inch, and you can vary tiller greatly by tightening or loosening one or both limb weight-adjustment bolts. Most bow tuners agree, however, that tiller measurement is insignificant on a two-wheel compound bow; that it can vary from zero to ¼ inch and the bow will still shoot well.

Even though actual measurement doesn't matter, changing the measurement does because it affects nocking point height. Some archers actually change nocking point height,

not by moving the nock locator, but by changing tiller. If you want the height of your nocking point to remain constant, always turn both top and bottom limbs bolts the same amount when you turn the bolts to change draw weight of your bow.

TRAILING The final step in successful bowhunting is recovering an animal you've hit. Many hunters stress the need for trailing skill in recovering arrow-shot animals, and that skill is indeed necessary.

But I think it's important to emphasize first that 100 percent recovery starts with well-placed shots. If your arrow hits an animal's heart or lungs, trailing skills are nearly academic. It's often said that an arrow kills by hemorrhage, and that's indeed true in some cases, but an arrow through the lungs or heart

All bowhunters must assume they'll have to trail a deer, even if they make a vital hit. Larry Jones has perfected his trailing skills.

causes massive organ failure well before the animal bleeds to death. Virtually no trailing skills are needed to recover well-hit animals. It's rare that an animal hit in the heart or lungs will travel more than 100 yards before piling up. (The same, of course, can be said for an animal hit in the spinal cord because it will drop in its tracks, but most spine shots are accidents.) In short, the best way to ensure recovery of an animal is to shoot it in the right spot. (For more details, see Shot Selection.)

Unfortunately, that doesn't always happen, even for the most conscientious bowhunter. Not every arrow hits dead center in the chest, and even a lung-shot deer can travel some distance. As a result, trailing ability plays a big part in all bowhunting, and learning trailing and other recovery techniques is just as important as any other hunting skill.

Snow can aid in trailing a deer, but you must learn to recognize signs of a deer's passing under all conditions. In open country like this, you should do everything possible to keep a deer in sight until it goes down.

After the Shot
Follow Up Every Shot. Frequently you can't judge the nature of a hit from an animal's reaction or blood sign. Your only option is to follow up on every hit. Never assume that an animal will be okay just because you didn't hit it in the heart. You're obligated to investigate every hit thoroughly. One friend of mine shot at an elk, and his arrow deflected off a branch and hit the elk in the hoof. Most hunters wouldn't consider searching for that animal. How in the world could a hoof hit kill an elk?

But my friend found a speck of blood, so he started trailing and kept at it for several hours until he could find no more sign. It seemed hopeless, but not one to give up, this fellow returned the next morning and searched systematically. And he found the elk dead. The arrow had cut an artery just behind the hoof and the animal had bled to death.

The lesson should be clear enough. Don't give up hope until all hope is gone. Armed with nothing other than that philosophy, you'll recover 90 percent of the game you ever hit, because if you have a strong enough desire to succeed, you'll find ways to do it.

Keep Quiet. Many animals hit with an arrow don't even know what's happened. They suddenly feel pain, but they don't know the source of the pain and they don't know any human beings are in the area. In many cases, I'm sure, animals run not so much because of their wounds but because the hunter reveals himself too soon and the animal runs from the person.

After you've hit an animal, stay absolutely quiet and hidden. Don't run into view or yell to your buddy or generally go berserk as many of us are inclined to do. Watch and listen quietly until you're sure the animal is either down or is out of sight and hearing. Elk hunters have found that if they bugle immediately after the shot, a bull, even if it's mortally wounded, will stop and respond and will often fall dead within sight rather than running off. Whatever you do, keep the surroundings as natural and peaceful as possible.

Keep Him in Sight. In open country, you often can see an animal for miles. In guiding

494

for antelope, Judd Cooney tells his hunters to get out of their blinds and run to the top of the nearest hill or do whatever is necessary to keep a hit animal in sight. Watching a wounded animal in open country can save you hours of slow tracking.

In any desert country you can watch animals for a long way. One January Mike Cupell shot a desert buck in Arizona at 8:30 A.M. The deer sprinted for 150 yards, and then it stopped and bedded. Cupell sat down to watch. The deer moved several times, but Cupell could always see it, and finally, at 1:30, when the deer hadn't moved for some time, Cupell walked over and found his deer dead. If he'd pushed that deer, the animal could have traveled a long way. Always get to the nearest vantage and watch a wounded animal either until it goes out of sight or, as in Cupell's case, until you're sure it's dead.

To Wait or Not to Wait. Standard advice says you should wait at least a half hour before following up on any hit. Some hunters insist that if you wait less than an hour, you're committing a sin. I think your response depends a lot on the nature of a hit and on weather conditions.

In some cases you'll see the arrow hit an animal and you can gauge what to do from that. In other cases, you won't see the hit. As Norm Jolliffe, a deer and bear guide in Maine, said, "In our country, vegetation is dense, so you see a deer through a hole in the brush, you shoot, and the deer is out of sight. You can't tell where you hit a deer from that.

"But signs on the ground can give you a good idea. A broadhead will cut hair, so look for that. Belly hair is white and curly, leg hair is short, spine hair is long and dark. That's hard to remember, of course, so I recommend hunters carry a small card describing various types of hair on a deer. Blood sign also indicates position of a hit. Bright red blood means a cut artery. Frothy blood indicates a lung hit. Dark blood mixed with green juices means an animal is hit in the stomach or intestines."

Gut hits require the longest waiting period because they rarely bleed much and the blood trail will be skimpy. And to heighten the problem, an animal hit in the stomach can run many miles. It also will be alert and watching its back trail and it will run or sneak off before you have time for a followup shot. You're almost assured of losing a gut-hit animal if you push it, so your only hope is to let it bed and die before it goes far. That means a long wait. If you hit it in the morning, go on back to camp and try to relax for four or five hours at least and return late in the afternoon to search. If you hit it late in the afternoon, leave it alone that night and return at daylight the following morning to search.

You should give most other body-cavity hits a half hour or so. An animal hit in the liver will die before long, but it could travel some distance first and leave a medium to sparse blood trail. This hit deserves some time, and any other chest hit you're not sure of does too. You can't go wrong by waiting but you can by hurrying, so always err on the conservative side.

If you know positively you've hit an animal in the heart or lungs, waiting really isn't necessary. The animal will hit the ground within 100 yards. I've heard two of my elk go down with a thunderous crash followed by a couple of moans and then silence. And I've watched several deer go down. I usually give them 10 to 15 minutes, just in case, but I don't think that's necessary. This assumes, of course, you're positive of the hit. If you're not, wait.

Most hunters advise following leg-hit animals immediately and pushing them hard. I think that's right in most cases. The philosophy is that pushing the animal will keep the wound open and bleeding and will tire the animal. Indeed, once an animal lies down, it often stops bleeding, and that's particularly true with muscle wounds. Once bleeding has stopped, trailing becomes next to impossible. One time a friend and I followed a deer, which had been hit in the back leg, nearly ten miles across the open desert. We pushed it hard and finally got the animal, but I suspect we'd have lost it if we'd backed off and given that animal time to rest and stop bleeding.

During rain or snow, you gain nothing by

waiting. Your only link with an animal is its tracks and blood trail, and if you lose those you have little hope. You've got to get on him fast. In heavily hunted country, I'd follow up fast, too. I've never had an animal taken away from me, but I personally know two hunters who have. If there's a chance someone else will find and tag your animal before you do, don't linger too long.

This doesn't mean I'd ever rush, even in rain. To trail well you must work methodically and observantly, and when you get in a dither to find your animal, you'll get careless and lose the trail. Take the time required to do it right.

Following the Sign

Blood Sign. Obviously you're first looking for blood. On a lung- or heart-shot animal you won't have to look hard to find it, and you probably won't have to look far for the animal. But in many cases mortally wounded animals will bleed internally, leaving a sparse trail. That's especially true if you're shooting downhill and your arrow hits high, or if it passes through the paunch on the way to the lungs. One time I hit a deer perfectly, yet I couldn't find a single speck of blood. I followed tracks and found the deer dead within 50 yards. The arrow had passed forward through the paunch before taking out both lungs.

Even when there's a decent blood trail, never assume blood will be easy to see. It may be, but often you have to look closely. If you just walk along, crouched over, you'll miss all but the most obvious sign. Often I've done that and would swear the bleeding had stopped. Then I'll get down on my hands and knees and really look close, and the trail will be obvious. My reaction is, "How could I miss that in the first place?"

If you have to crawl to follow the trail, then humble yourself and crawl. Late one evening, I shot an elk and the animal covered a lot of ground in a hurry. Before long, darkness set in, and I had to trail with a small flashlight. In the dim beam I could scarcely see the ground, let alone blood, so I crawled and was amazed at how easily I could detect spots of blood the

size of a pinhead. It was only because my face was right next to the ground, close enough to see. The same intense approach often is needed during the day.

Getting close to the ground like that not only gives a closeup view, but it gives you a better angle to spot some kinds of blood. Frequently blood running down an animal's leg or side won't drip onto the ground, but it will smear onto bushes and grass. Looking down from a standing position, you'll never see blood on the undersides of grass or leaves, but from a low angle looking up, you'll quickly notice dark smears on vegetation. Bare dry soil, typical of desert country, soaks up blood fast, so inspect rocks and vegetation where the blood won't dissipate.

Also inspect blood for direction of travel. Sometimes an animal will circle, and you can end up following the wrong way. I've done it. When blood hits the ground it makes a big splotch and then sprays out in several tiny drops. The deer is heading toward the side with the little drops. If drops are round, the deer obviously is standing still.

Other Signs. Always look for signs other than blood. Here again, you may have to get down on your knees and look close to find them, but if you really fine-tune your senses, you'll notice all kinds of things you'd normally overlook. You'll see an overturned pebble, a broken twig, or a smear of mud on a rock. You might see flecks of saliva from a deer's mouth or nose, and if an animal was hit in the abdomen, you'll find specks of stomach matter.

In hardwood forests, look especially for overturned leaves. In the morning or on a misty day, leaves will be damp, so a dry leaf tells you an animal has passed. In the afternoon, when the leaves have all dried, a moist-looking leaf indicates the same thing.

Tracks. Above all, inspect an animal's tracks and learn their exact appearance. All animal tracks are distinct, and a wounded animal in particular may leave a clearly recognizable track. One time I hit an elk that traveled a long way after the shot. Fat sealed the arrow hole and stopped external bleeding, so I had only the tracks to follow. At first I hadn't thought about how those tracks looked until they got mixed in with a maze of other elk tracks. It appeared I'd lost the trail, but in circling, hoping to hit definite sign, I noticed an elk track that stood out from all the rest. There was a slight drag mark in the pine needles just before each hoof mark on the right side. "That's his track," I said to myself. "He's dragging a leg." I followed and eventually found a speck of blood to confirm I was on the right track, and I finally recovered the animal.

Larry Jones and I tracked a Coues deer in Arizona similarly. The deer wasn't leaving drag marks or other obvious indicators, but we got so tuned into the specific size and freshness of its track that we could recognize it at a glance, and even on hard ground we unwaveringly followed that deer.

Stay with the Trail. One lesson Larry has taught me is to stick with the trail. That might seem obvious, but when a trail gets sparse, it's easy to get impatient and course out ahead like a bird dog, hoping to stumble onto the animal or luck onto obvious blood sign. Often while hunting with Larry, I've given up on the blood trail and searched out ahead in places where I've thought a wounded animal most likely would go. At the same time, Larry has patiently snooped around looking for the trail, and time after time he has picked up the trail again, heading in the opposite direction I'd been searching. Any more I don't put much credence in the theories that wounded animals will head downhill, seek heavy cover, go to water, or whatever. Predicting an animal's movement involves too many variables. Sleuth out his trail instead.

But as you follow the trail, always be watching ahead, trying to anticipate where an animal will bed and looking for the animal itself. It's critical to get him in that first bed. If you spook him up, you'll rarely find any blood to follow after that, and the adrenalin-charged animal will cover a lot of ground in short order. So keep watching ahead and use your binoculars to inspect any possible bedding cover. This is where two hunters can work effectively to-

gether, one following the trail, the other looking for the animal.

The Last Resort

Flagging. In some cases, you'll simply run out of sign, and then you may have to search for the animal or make educated guesses about where he might go. Flagging your trail with bright plastic tape can help the process, because you can quickly return to your trail after circling ahead. And the flagging gives you a line to predict where an animal might go. Mike Cupell shot a desert mule deer that disappeared over a hill. Flagging as he went, Cupell followed the scant trail as far as possible. When the trail played out, he climbed back up the hill to sight along his flag line.

"That buck is bedded right there," he thought as he noticed a small patch of cover in line with the flags. He circled to get the wind in his favor and found the buck within ten yards of where he'd predicted.

In searching for an animal, watch for what one hunter called "refuge" sites: places with good cover where an animal could be well concealed and comfortable, and where it could watch its back trail. And search systematically. Block off a small section and comb it thoroughly. When you're positive the animal isn't there, block off another small area. Keep up this systematic process of elimination until you either find your animal or convince yourself that all hope is gone.

Trailing at Night

Some hunters advise not shooting an animal in late afternoon because you might not recover it before dark. That sounds great, but we all know the last hour before dusk holds some of the best hunting of the day, and few hunters are going to pass up a shot then.

And I see little reason for passing up evening shots, because you can trail efficiently after dark. In fact you can trail better in total darkness than you can on gloomy, dark days. You have to be equipped right, however. Never get caught without a flashlight—that should be part of your standard hunting gear anyway—

and spare batteries. Leaving a deer in the field overnight, even if it's dead, probably won't ruin any meat, but leaving an elk can. Unless an elk (or other equally big, thick-skinned animal) is gut-shot, in which case you should purposely back off, you must recover it the night you shot it or you'll lose most or all the meat. One butcher told me hunters had brought in several soured elk to his shop, and in most cases spoilage was caused by letting the animals lie in the field overnight.

A flashlight will do the job, and I've recovered several animals by trailing with a flashlight, but a lantern works even better. Norm Jolliffe uses a Coleman gas lantern with an aluminum reflector on one side to keep the light out of his eyes. On an animal hit in late afternoon, Jolliffe prefers to wait the required period of time, and then to track in total darkness. "If you push the trailing job, trying to take advantage of the last light of day, you'll make mistakes. I've done about 75 percent of my trailing at night, and I find it fairly easy, because lantern light is brighter than natural light at dusk or in deep woods during the day."

Don't take trailing for granted. It takes just as much training as any other aspect of hunting. Mike Cupell said he considers trailing a sixth sense type of skill, built on experience, knowledge, and common sense. "As I'm walking along, say back to camp, I try to read tracks along the way," Cupell said. "I practice tracking all the time so when the time comes to recover an animal, the trailing is second nature. In bowhunting, trailing can be just as much a part of the hunt as the shooting and the eating, so you'd better learn to do it right."

TRAJECTORY You hear a lot about modern, "flat-shooting" bows, and it is indeed true that some of the new compound bows shoot arrows in a flatter trajectory than traditional longbows that lobbed heavy cedar arrows. But the implication of "flat shooting" is misleading, because even the fastest bows have grossly curved trajectories compared to firearms. For that reason, every bowhunter has to understand trajectory.

Obviously gravity is the primary influence that makes an arrow drop (rather than rise) when it's shot. But other influences—air density, size and weight of the arrow, amount of drag caused by feathers or vanes, and initial velocity—affect the rate of drop. Ranging, Inc. a company that makes archery rangefinders, has studied trajectory extensively. According to that company's findings, "Initial velocity is by far the most significant factor in arrow drop. If the velocity increases by 10 percent, the drop will decrease by approximately 20 percent."

Thus, the interest in shooting heavier bows and lighter arrows to achieve greater arrow speed isn't total folly. Even a slight increase in arrow speed cuts inches from a bulging trajectory, and the end result can be cleaner kills. Of course, tradeoffs enter the picture, and at some point in the speed-seeking game, you may lose more in terms of accuracy than you gain. (For more details, see Bow Efficiency, and Bow Selection.)

Even with a high-speed bow, however, range estimation and knowledge of trajectory can be critical. For example, as Ranging's figures show, a 2117 arrow from a 70-pound compound aimed at a 20-yard target will hit 3.8 inches high at 10 yards. It's then on at 20, but at 25 yards the arrow has dropped 4.9 inches low, which would produce a wounding shot or a miss, and at 30 yards the arrow has dropped 11.8 inches below target, a guaranteed miss. To carry that on out, at 35 yards the arrow has dropped 20.8 inches below target, and at 40 yards more than 36 inches. So even for this relatively powerful bow shooting arrows well faster than 200 fps, the trajectory is greater than 36 inches at 40 yards. That allows plenty of room for missing.

And it points out the need for accurate estimation of range. From zero to 25 yards, you probably would have hit a deer, although not perfectly, by aiming with your 20-yard pin. But past 25 yards, the error in estimation becomes critical, and from 30 yards on out, if you misjudge range by more than a couple of yards, you'll either make a poor hit high or low, or you'll miss altogether.

IMPACT POINT OF AN ARROW

When using the 20 yard aiming pin and shooting at various distances. Figures given assume a perfect shot.

Bow & Arrow Combination (50% let off)	10 yds.	15 yds.	20 yds.	25 yds.	30 yds.	35 yds.	40 yds.
50 lb. Compound/2016 Arrow 28″ Draw	5.6″ High	4.2″ High	◎	7.0″ Low	16.9″ Low	29.8″ Low	45.6″ Low
50 lb. Compound/2016 Arrow 30″ Draw	4.6″ High	3.4″ High	◎	5.8″ Low	13.9″ Low	24.6″ Low	37.6″ Low
55 lb. Compound/2016 Arrow 28″ Draw	5.0″ High	3.8″ High	◎	6.3″ Low	15.4″ Low	27.0″ Low	41.4″ Low
55 lb. Compound/2117 Arrow 28″ Draw	4.3″ High	3.2″ High	◎	5.4″ Low	13.0″ Low	23.2″ Low	35.5″ Low
60 lb. Compound/2018 Arrow 30″ Draw	4.9″ High	3.7″ High	◎	6.2″ Low	15.0″ Low	26.3″ Low	40.3″ Low
60 lb. Compound/2117 Arrow 30″ Draw	4.3″ High	3.3″ High	◎	5.5″ Low	13.3″ Low	23.4″ Low	35.8″ Low
65 lb. Compound/2117 Arrow 28″ Draw	4.5″ High	3.4″ High	◎	5.7″ Low	13.8″ Low	24.2″ Low	37.2″ Low
65 lb. Compound/2117 Arrow 30″ Draw	4.1″ High	3.1″ High	◎	5.2″ Low	12.4″ Low	22.0″ Low	33.5″ Low
70 lb. Compound/2117 Arrow 28″ Draw	4.0″ High	3.0″ High	◎	5.1″ Low	12.2″ Low	21.4″ Low	32.7″ Low
70 lb. Compound/2117 Arrow 30″ Draw	3.8″ High	2.9″ High	◎	4.9″ Low	11.8″ Low	20.8″ Low	36.4″ Low

This simple chart shows the differences in trajectory made by arrow speed and weight. It gives you an idea of how critical range estimation can be in making a clean hit. *Chart courtesy Ranging, Inc.*

Estimating Range

If you shoot instinctively, of course, the question of range estimation is moot. Most instinctive shooters want no part of guessing yardages. They purposely ignore yardages to let their aiming instinct, developed through long hours of practice, take over.

For sight shooters, on the other hand, accurate range estimation is the very essence of shooting accuracy. Some hunters develop a proficient eye for estimating distance, but it requires a lot of practice. You can practice anywhere as you're walking along, even on the city street. Glance at a telephone pole or mailbox, guess the yardage, and then pace it off. (You have to learn how long your paces are. If I take long strides, my steps are an even yard long.) With practice like this, you'll build a quick, accurate eye.

Stump shooting and other forms of field practice also help. My friend Pat Miller has an exceptional ability to gauge range, and he developed it primarily by stump shooting. He'd pick a target, estimate the range, shoot, and then pace it off. He can guess the range within a yard or two out to nearly 50 yards.

I've found it helps, particularly on longer ranges, to break the distance down into smaller segments. You can more accurately judge 5 yards than 35 yards, for example. So if a deer stands about 35 yards away, don't try to guess the range in one big lump; do it in 5-yard increments. Say to yourself, "It's 5 yards to that green bush, and it's another 5 to the brown rock. That's 10. Then the big tree is another 5 . . ." and so forth. With practice you can click off 5-yard increments like a computer to judge range quickly and accurately.

With experience, range estimation becomes instinctive, just as learning to aim a bow without sights becomes instinctive. In that sense, shooting with sights requires just as much "instinct" as does shooting bare bow.

Range Finders

Purpose of Range Finder. In the absence of that ability—you either don't have time to develop it or you just never get the hang of it—

you can use a range finder. Some hunters question the ethical aspect of using a range finder, because it turns bowhunting into a fairly mechanical process. At one time, I felt that way, but my thinking has changed. No hunter would pass up an open 30-yard shot, yet by relying on instinct alone, either to form a sight picture or to estimate range, you could be off a fraction and make a bad hit on the deer. On the other hand, if circumstances allow, you could use an optical range finder, determine the exact distance to the deer, say 32 yards rather than 30, and put an arrow on the money to make a clean, killing shot. Is there anything unethical about using all legal methods to ensure a good hit?

Incidentally, I don't advocate using a range finder to extend shooting ranges. With a range finder, you might accurately determine the distance out to 80 yards or farther, but can you shoot well out to that distance? Not likely. A range finder should be used only to gauge distances within your effective shooting range. (For more details, see Shooting Practice, and Shot Selection.)

Styles of Range Fingers. There are two kinds of range finders: stadimetric and optical. A stadia is a rod with graduated markings used by surveyors for measuring distance. Thus, a stadimetric range finder is one that employs graduated marks to indicate various distances.

The lines in these range finders are calibrated to correspond to objects of a given size, in most cases the chest of a deer. To use the range finder, you frame a deer's chest between the stadia lines of corresponding width. If the chest fits perfectly between the most widely spaced lines on your range finder, for example, he's 20 yards away. If his chest fits between closer spaced lines, he might be 40, and so forth. Most such range finders are built into sights and are marketed as "range finder bowsights."

This system has some inherent problems. For instance, the lines can be calibrated only for animals of a given size, so if you're hunting elk or antelope, your "deer" range finder isn't much good. It's not valid for all deer either, because the chest on a big buck could be several inches deeper than that of a yearling. The deer also must be nearly broadside and in full view, and it must be at your same level. If you're above or below the animal, you can't get a full chest view, which skews your reading. For these reasons, I think range-finder sights have marginal value.

Bushnell has come out with a range finder that improves on the stadia principle. The basic unit is a five-power monocular, and when you look through it you see three sets of stadia, one each for deer, elk, and antelope. With the magnification and the accurately calibrated lines, I believe this range finder has much greater potential than bow-mounted range-finder sights.

Optical Range Finders. These work on a triangulation principle. They have two windows, and a combination of lenses and prisms inside produces two images of the object you're viewing. As you look through the viewfinder, you turn a distance indicator dial, which pulls the two images together. To put it another way, turning the dial makes the images coincide. Thus, this is called the coincidence style of range finder. When the two images merge into one, you've hit on the range from you to the object and you read the distance in yards on the dial. The principle is sound, and even the simplest range finders, like the Ranging 50/2 and 80/2, prove accurate out to 50 yards and farther.

Using an Optical Range Finder. That doesn't mean range finders are foolproof. For one thing, you have to be a good hunter to use one, because you have to remain totally undetected. To use the range finder, obviously, you must move your hands, and if a buck is the slightest bit alert, he'll catch you in the act. In several cases, using a range finder has cost me a good shot rather than helping me make the shot.

To minimize movement, learn to use your range finder with one hand. Unfortunately, most range finders are built to be used with two hands, and one-handed use is particularly

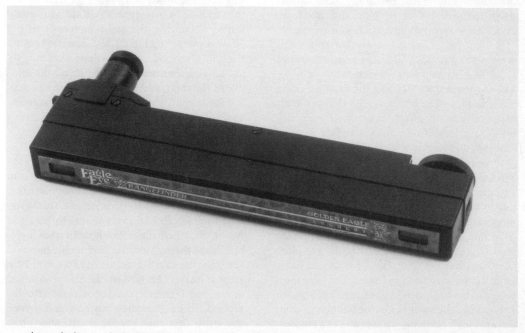

An optical range finder like the Eagle Eye 3X can help you estimate yardages accurately for clean kills.

To minimize movement, learn to use a range finder with one hand. That way you can hold your bow ready to shoot as you slowly raise the finder to your eye and take a reading.

tough if you're right-handed. That's because, as you prepare to shoot, you hold your bow in your left hand. That leaves your right hand free, but the dial is on the left end. To solve that problem, I turn the range finder upside down so the dial is on the right, and then I can operate it with my right hand only.

Optical range finders have other shortcomings. A solid knock will bang the prisms out of alignment so the range finder must be readjusted (it's easy to do, and instructions come with the range finder), and gross changes in air temperature will affect accuracy. If you calibrate your range finder for warm, late-summer hunting, double check it before setting out on a cold winter hunt. You may have to readjust it for the colder temperatures. The range finders I've used also aren't watertight, and any slight moisture has fogged them up and made them inoperable. You must keep a range finder dry.

In dim light, you'll have a hard time seeing the images, and in cluttered woods you often can't sort out the image you're trying to judge from all the surrounding clutter. The view must be clear for both windows of the range finder. If anything covers either of the windows—your finger, a leaf, clothing—you can't get a reading.

For quickest ranging, pick out an object with very sharp lines, such as a deer's antlers or white tail. Then you'll have no doubt about when the images merge in the range finder. If you can't get a clear view of the animal you want to shoot, take readings on objects around him, and if you're set up in a blind or stand, use your range finder to judge distance to various nearby trees and other objects. That way when an animal approaches, you have distance checkpoints already in mind.

For best range-finding results, start with the dial at the shortest setting and dial out until the images merge. Stop there instantly and read the distance off the dial. If you have plenty of time, you can take several readings, first starting with the dial set at 20 yards and working up, and then starting at 70 yards and turning down. Then compare readings as crosschecks against each other.

One time I spotted a buck lying on top of a knoll. He lay there for more than an hour, giving me plenty of time, and his antlers were silhouetted against the blue sky, which gave me a good sharp line for ranging. First I dialed one way, then the other, and always the reading was the same—27 yards. I rehearsed the shot many times, visualizing the sight picture with my 30-yard pin at the top of his chest. When the buck finally stood up, everything went exactly as pictured. The arrow hit just below the midline of the chest, and the deer piled up less than 100 yards away. Under the right circumstances, a range finder and accurate shooting are a deadly combination.

Gauging Trajectory

Knowing the trajectory for your bow can help you make shots you might otherwise miss, or pass up altogether because you think you might not be able to make them. In his *Field Notes*, Fred Bear describes how he shot a record Stone sheep. Looking over a rise, he could see only the ram's head 35 yards away. Bear knew if he drew his bow to full draw and aimed at the ram's chest, he'd shoot right into the ground, so he underdrew his bow and lobbed the arrow over the rise. He hit the sheep perfectly.

I don't recommend that practice for us mortals, and with a compound, shooting from a half-draw position is virtually impossible anyway, but that illustration does show the value of understanding arrow trajectory. You can develop similar knowledge to help you make shots.

For example, if your closest sight pin is set for 20 yards, you'll want to know how much to hold under for closer shots. You can actually plot the trajectory of your arrow between zero and 20 yards by shooting into a target at 5-yard increments. Always aiming with your 20-yard pin dead on the target, shoot at 5 yards, 10, and 15. At each distance, measure how high your arrow hits. With that knowledge you'll know how low to aim on a deer closer than 20 yards. For example, if your arrow hits 5 inches high at 10 yards, then you know you must hold your 20-yard pin 5 inches below your aiming spot to make a perfect hit on a deer 10 yards away.

Don't kid yourself into thinking it's not critical at short ranges. A couple of the worst shots I've made on game occurred at ranges of 10 and 15 yards, simply because I didn't compensate for trajectory. A few inches high or low make a lot of difference.

Some hunters prefer a one-sight-pin system to a multi-pin sight. For example, if you put one pin on your bow, set dead on at 30 yards, you can use that for aiming from zero out to 40 yards or farther. But you can't aim dead on over that entire range. You must know your arrow's trajectory so you know how much to hold under at distances shorter than 30 yards and how much to hold over for longer yardages. You can plot the trajectory as described above for a 20-yard sight pin.

Understanding the nature of your trajectory can help greatly in shooting over and under limbs, too. Perform the same test described above using your 30- and 40-yard pins to see how high your arrows will fly at given intermediate yardages. Then, if you see a buck standing at 30 yards, but a limb hangs down between you and the buck, you can gauge whether your arrow will clear the limb. But to make a judgment like that, you must understand your arrow's trajectory.

Also, remember that if your sight is on an object at the same distance the sight is set for, you'll hit that object. For example, if you're aiming at that deer 30 yards away, and your 20-yard sight pin covers a limb hanging down 20 yards away, rest assured your arrow will hit that limb. On the other hand, if your 20-yard pin is on a limb only 15 yards away, then you know your arrow will clear it.

Shooting Up and Down Hill

Shooting at sharp angles up and down can be a major cause for missing. I'll never forget making three clean misses on a cow elk. I was on a cliff as the elk fed in an alder patch below me. The angle down to the elk was steep, probably 30 to 40 degrees, and the animal was about 50 yards away on my first shot. My arrow hissed about a foot over the elk's back and hit the ground beyond, and she ran up toward me. Now I had a 40-yard shot and felt confident, but again I shot about a foot high and the arrow hit downhill of the animal. Again she ran my way and stopped at 30 yards, looking downhill for the source of those strange noises. "She's in the bag this time," I thought, holding plenty low to guarantee a good hit. To my astonishment the third arrow also flew about a foot over the elk's back, and she fled for good.

With mathematical formulas you can judge exactly how much to hold under for sharply angled shots. That's all well and good, but how will you apply those in the field when you can't measure the exact angle and distance? Here again, as in learning to hold under on fish underwater, I think experience is the best teacher. You must shoot up and downhill to perfect this ability. And in hunting steep Western country, or in shooting down from high tree stands, the ability will serve you well.

Some hunters think you must aim low for downhill shots and high for uphill shots. That's not true. You must hold low for both, because gravity affects the arrow the same whether you're shooting up or down (there are minor differences, but for practical purposes they're insignificant over moderate bow ranges).

To put this in very simple terms, the amount an arrow drops is equal to the horizontal distance to the target, not the actual distance. Let's say, for example, you're on a vertical cliff 20 yards high, and you see a buck below you at a 45-degree angle. Your range finder shows the buck is slightly farther than 28 yards away. A little basic geometry (the Pythagorean Theorem says that A squared + B squared = C squared) shows, however, that the horizontal distance from you to the buck is only 20 yards. To put it another way, if you measured from the base of your cliff to the buck, the distance would be 20 yards. To hit that deer squarely, you must aim with your 20-yard sight pin. If you aim for 28 yards—actual distance to the deer—you'll shoot over him. The same would apply if you were shooting uphill at a comparable angle and distance.

Again, if you're in a tree stand 18 feet (6 yards) above the ground, and a deer walks by 3 yards out from the tree, he'll actually be about 7 yards from you. If you aim for 7 yards, you'll shoot high, maybe over his back. You must aim for 3 yards. In measuring distances as a guide for shooting from your tree stand, don't measure from your stand but from the base of the tree your stand is in.

Keep Good Form. Misjudged range isn't the only reason for missed shots at steep angles. Poor form is responsible, too. To maintain proper bow and arm alignment, you must bend at the waist when shooting up or down. That is, to shoot down from a tree stand, you shouldn't just lower your bow arm. Rather you should draw as if shooting horizontally and then bend at the waist so that your bow arm, head, and drawing arm maintain the same positions relative to the bow. With a safety belt around your waist, that's fairly easy to do.

Unfortunately, human beings weren't made to bend backward, so bending at the waist on uphill shots isn't so easy. I suspect that's why many bowhunters think they must aim high on uphill shots. They try to aim up simply by rais-

ing the bow arm, a difficult way to pull a bow, and as a result they underdraw and the arrow goes low. As in shooting down, you must draw as if shooting on the level, and then bend backward at the waist so you maintain good alignment and a full draw.

TREE STAND   See Stand Hunting.

TREZ TINE   The third antler tine. In North America, the term most commonly refers only to elk antlers. Classified as G-3 on record-book scoring charts. Also called tres or trey tine.

TROPHY SCORING   Whether you're trying for a Pope and Young (P&Y) or a Boone and Crockett (B&C) buck, you must learn to judge a rack in the field. For simplicity, I'll discuss only deer and elk here, although the principle is the same for all antlered game. General ideas for judging horned game—antelope, sheep, goats—as well as bears and cats are given under the individual species sections (for example, Antelope, Black Bear, etc.).

You can read about field judging and get the idea, but without actual practice, you'll never perfect the art of judging trophy racks. First learn the dimensions of deer antlers by measuring several, then take that knowledge to the field and apply it to deer on the hoof. Practice is the only way to develop a good trophy eye.

Field Judging a Trophy

Primary measurements are length of main beams, length and number of tines, inside spread, and mass. These are discussed individually below.

Main Beams. Length of main beams may be the single most important figure in judging antler score because the main beams comprise a high percentage of the total score. For whitetails and elk, main-beam measurement alone equals, on the average, nearly 28 percent of the score, for mule deer about 25. Essentially, beam length is a function of width and curve. To have long beams, the rack must be reasonably wide, and it must curve far forward. For that reason, you must see the rack in profile

Main beam length contributes heavily to overall score, and to judge beam length you need a profile of the antlers. On whitetails and mule deer, the antler tips should curve forward nearly to a line drawn vertically from the tip of the nose.

to judge beam length accurately. Exceptional main beams on both whitetails and mule deer extend forward as far as a line drawn vertically from the tip of a buck's nose. On big elk, they sweep back past the middle of the body.

Tines. The number and length of points also contribute heavily to a good score. Cumulative length of the tines equals more than 40 percent of the score on most trophies, so you can see the importance of having the maximum number of tines and good long tines.

To score well an animal must have the maximum number of tines allowed by the scoring charts. On whitetails the average is five points to the side, and a buck just about has to have that many to score high in the book, although large 4 x 4 bucks will make the lower end of the P&Y book fairly easily. You don't find many 4 x 4 whitetails in the B&C book. Whitetail scoring charts allow for up to seven tines on each side, and obviously the more points a buck has, up to that maximum, the better the score. Out of 440 typical whitetails listed in *Records of North American Big Game*, eighth edition, only 10 had as few as four points on

one side, and the highest scoring 4 x 4 was listed number 211.

For mule deer, the typical configuration is four points off the main beams plus brow tines. Westerners would call such a buck a four-point or a 4 x 4, although it would be listed in the book as a 5 x 5, because the record book counts brow tines as points. Unlike whitetails, which virtually always have brow tines, many mule deer don't, and a buck can score fairly well without brow tines. It just about has to have four points on the main beams, though. An occasional buck with only three main-beam points will make the Pope and Young book, but he has to be huge. You won't find many toward the top end.

To score well, elk must have six points on each side (that includes the tip of the main beam as a point). Most hunters would classify such an animal as a 6 x 6. Scoring charts allow up to eight points, including the main beam, so the more normal points a bull has up to the maximum, the better he'll score. Some 5 x 5 bulls will score well enough to make Pope and Young, but they have to be exceptional ani-

Most bowhunters would consider this a fine buck, but he won't make the record book. To score well, a trophy must have the maximum allowable number of tines. This buck has only three on the right side.

Most high-scoring elk racks have six points or more to the side. The fourth, or sword, point is the long point that rises straight up, so to count points quickly, you start counting there with number four. Thus you know instantly this is a five-point bull. A bull this size would fall far short of the Pope and Young record book.

mals. You can quickly figure the number of points on a bull because the fourth, or sword, point is normally the longest. Start counting there at number four.

Tines also must be long to score well. Brow tines on most Boone and Crockett bucks measure 4 to 6 inches long, and most other tines are no shorter than 6 to 8 inches. Of course, the fewer in number, the longer each individual tine must be. That is, a 4 x 4 buck must have significantly longer tines than a 5 x 5 to score equally well. The ears on a mature whitetail measure about 7 inches long, and the distance from the tip of the nose to the antler base measures about 10 inches, so you can use these dimensions to gauge tine length.

On mule deer, look for deep forks off the main beam. The closer the bottom of the fork is to the main beam, the longer the tines are and the more inches they'll add to the score. Tines should be 10 inches or longer. Use the ears, which measure 9 to 10 inches long on a big buck, as a ruler. The back fork (G-2 on the score charts), must be 16 to 18 inches long for the buck to score well. The chest on mature buck measures about 20 inches deep, so that gives you another ruler. You often hear mule deer hunters talk about bucks with tall racks. In general, the higher the rack, the better the buck will score because height equates to long tines and long main beams. A wide, flat rack generally won't score nearly as well as a tall, narrow rack.

On elk, the brow tines should curve well out nearly as far as the tip of the nose. The brow tines should be 16 to 18 inches or longer, and other tines up to the sword point should be equally long. The distance from the tip of the nose to the base of the antlers is 15 to 16 inches. The third and fifth points are commonly major weaknesses, so if you really want a high-scoring bull, look at these carefully.

If you look at score charts carefully, you'll see that symmetry plays a big part in score. That's because any difference (in inches) between one side of a rack and the other is subtracted from the total score. You can gauge symmetry fairly quickly in the field. Rather than looking at all tines and trying to add them up in your head, look only at the poorer side and double it. That's a valid way to judge, because, in essence, total score is equal to the poorer side doubled. For example, if a buck has three points on one side and four on the other, he'll actually be scored like a symmetri-

On mule deer, look for deep forks off the main beam. The closer the bottom of the fork is to the main beam, the longer the tines are and the better they'll score. This rack has fairly deep forks, and all the tines are ten inches or longer. Total score is about 190.

On high-scoring elk, the brow tines curve out at least as far as the tip of the nose, and all other tines up the main beams are equally as long or longer. These are the number one, three, and four Boone Crockett bulls.

cal three-point. As another example, I killed a bull elk that actually had grown 6 x 6 antlers. He'd broken off one brow tine, however, which made him a 5 x 6. Since the remaining brow tine had to be subtracted from the score, the bull, for scoring purposes, was an even 5 x 5.

Spread. This is the antler dimension that awes most hunters. For mule deer, 30 inches seems to be the magic number. Everybody wants a 30-incher. That's all well and good, but in terms of scoring systems, width doesn't necessarily mean much. An analysis of record heads shows that width is a small percentage of the score. For whitetails it's about 11 percent, elk 11 percent, and mule deer 12 percent. In other words a buck or bull elk can have a rela-

Nontypical antlers are measured the same way as typicals. They must have long main beams, good spread, long points, and mass. The only difference is that all odd tines are added to the score rather than subtracted. This nontypical buck from Missouri scores 197.

tively narrow rack and score high, and it can have a wide rack and score poorly. Of course, if a buck has a wide rack, along with all the other qualities that contribute to score, then so much the better. Remember that in terms of scoring, "width" means inside spread of the main beams, not outside width.

Most high-scoring whitetails have a spread of 20 inches or greater. Tip-to-tip spread of the ears on a mature buck is about 16 inches, so you should see at least a couple of inches of daylight between the ear tips and the main beams. On mule deer, inside spread on most high-scoring bucks will be 20 to 25 inches. Tip-to-tip ear spread is about 20 inches, so again, you must be able to see some daylight between the ears and the inside of the main beams. Be careful about gauging width from the rear on any deer, especially if his ears are laid back, because the rack will appear much wider than it actually is. A bull elk measures 20 to 24 inches through the chest, and to score well, the rack should be at least twice as wide as the chest is thick.

Mass. Heavy, thick-beamed antlers inspire awe among hunters, and few would pass up any buck with a massive rack. In terms of scoring, however, circumference measurements, or mass, comprise a relatively small percentage of the overall score. Length and height add much more to the score. If you compare a massive rack with relatively short main beams and tines to a thinner rack with long beams and tines, the thinner rack will score better every time. Mass is good, of course, because it contributes valuable inches to the overall score, but it's secondary to length.

Nontypical Antlers. In essence, nontypical antlers are measured exactly as typical except that abnormal points are added to the total score. To gauge a nontypical, then, you start with a strong typical base, which consists of long main beams, long tines, wide spread, and mass, and then you start adding on all the extra points. It's hard to judge absolute score of a nontypical in the field, and few hunters would care anyway. When they see a grotesque rack coming, they know they're going to shoot.

Measuring a Trophy

The only equipment you need for measuring antlers and horns is a quarter-inch-wide steel tape measure. One tape with a hook on the end is adequate, but a tape with a ring on the end helps in making circumference measurements. In addition you need a copy of the appropriate scoring chart. All charts appear later in this section.

Steps for measuring a rack are outlined on the scoring charts, but differences in technique can yield substantial variations in score, so it's important to conform to standard methods. Sixty days must elapse from the time of kill before a trophy can be measured officially.

Also, notice that all fractions are measured to the nearest ⅛ inch, and to simplify addition, these fractions are recorded in ⅛-inch increments. They are not reduced to the lowest common denominator. For animals on which the skull is measured—bears and cats—measurements are recorded in ¹⁄₁₆-inch increments.

The score charts explain the measuring procedures, and space doesn't allow a complete explanation for all species. For a complete and detailed explanation of measuring procedures for all species, get a copy of *Measuring and Scoring North American Big Game Trophies*, published by the Boone and Crockett Club. For the ordering address, see Boone and Crockett Club.

Entering Your Trophy. If you think your animal will qualify for the record book, contact an official measurer, who will run through the process again (records-keeping clubs won't accept your measurements). If you don't know any scorers, write to the Pope and Young Club, or Boone and Crockett if your animal is *that* big, and these clubs will send you a list of official measurers in your state.

Call the nearest one and make an appointment. Remember, most measurers are busy and they donate their time for measuring, so don't bother them to measure green antlers that will have to be rescored later. Wait the 60 days before submitting your trophy.

If your animal qualifies for either record book, you then must sign a fair-chase affidavit

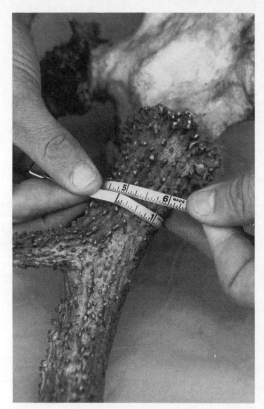

The only equipment you need for measuring antlers is a ¼-inch-wide steel tape measure.

and have it notarized, which verifies that you took the animal by legal means. You send the score chart and the affidavit to the appropriate club. Along with this package, you must submit a processing fee (the scorer can tell you how much it is) and three photos of the trophy rack: right, left, and front views.

Incidentally, any rack is eligible for entry into the Boone and Crockett book, and if you come across antlers from a deer killed many years ago, or find a record-class animal dead in the field, you can enter that rack in the book. However, only animals killed by means of bow and arrow can be entered into the Pope and Young Club's *Bowhunting Big Game Records of North America*. Animals killed by crossbow will not be accepted.

Official scoring charts from Boone and Crockett, showing both the fronts and backs.

Records of North American
Big Game

BOONE AND CROCKETT CLUB

205 South Patrick Street
Alexandria, Virginia 22314

OFFICIAL SCORING SYSTEM FOR NORTH AMERICAN BIG GAME TROPHIES

BEAR

Kind of Bear _____

Sex _____

Minimum Score:
Alaska brown   28
black   21
grizzly   24
polar   27

SEE OTHER SIDE FOR INSTRUCTIONS	Measurements
A. Greatest Length without Lower Jaw	
B. Greatest Width	
TOTAL AND FINAL SCORE	

Exact locality where killed _____

Date killed _____ By whom killed _____

Present owner _____

Address _____

Guide's Name and Address _____

Remarks: (Mention any abnormalities or unique qualities)
_____

I certify that I have measured the above trophy on _____ 19___
at (address) _____ City _____ State
and that these measurements and data are, to the best of my knowledge and belief, made in
accordance with the instructions given.

Witness: _____   Signature: _____   Official Measurer

INSTRUCTIONS FOR MEASURING BEAR

Measurements are taken with calipers or by using parallel perpendiculars, to the nearest
one-sixteenth of an inch, without reduction of fractions. Official measurements cannot
be taken for at least sixty days after the animal was killed. All adhering flesh, mem-
brane and cartilage must be completely removed before official measurements are taken.

A. Greatest Length is measured between perpendiculars parallel to the long axis of the
    skull, without the lower jaw and excluding malformations.

B. Greatest Width is measured between perpendiculars at right angles to the long axis.

* * * * * * * * * * * * *

FAIR CHASE STATEMENT FOR ALL HUNTER-TAKEN TROPHIES

To make use of the following methods shall be deemed as UNFAIR CHASE and unsportsmanlike,
and any trophy obtained by use of such means is disqualified from entry for Awards.
    I.   Spotting or herding game from the air, followed by landing in its vicinity for
          pursuit;
    II.   Herding or pursuing game with motor-powered vehicles;
    III. Use of electronic communications for attracting, locating or observing game, or
          guiding the hunter to such game;
    IV.   Hunting game confined by artificial barriers, including escape-proof fencing;
          or hunting game transplanted solely for the purpose of commercial shooting.

I certify that the trophy scored on this chart was not taken in UNFAIR CHASE as defined
above by the Boone and Crockett Club. I further certify that it was taken in full compliance with local game laws of the state, province, or territory. _____
Date _____   Signature of Hunter
(Have signature notarized by a Notary Public)

OFFICIAL SCORING SYSTEM FOR NORTH AMERICAN BIG GAME TROPHIES

Records of North American   BOONE AND CROCKETT CLUB   205 South Patrick Street
Big Game   Alexandria, Virginia 22314

Minimum Score: COUGAR and JAGUAR   Kind of Cat _____
cougar 15
jaguar 14½   Sex _____

SEE OTHER SIDE FOR INSTRUCTIONS	Measurements
A. Greatest Length without Lower Jaw	
B. Greatest Width	
TOTAL AND FINAL SCORE	

Exact locality where killed _____

Date killed _____ By whom killed _____

Present owner _____

Address _____

Guide's Name and Address _____

Remarks: (Mention any abnormalities or unique qualities) _____

I certify that I have measured the above trophy on _____ City _____ 19 __ State _____
at (address) _____
and that these measurements and data are, to the best of my knowledge and belief, made in
accordance with the instructions given.

Witness: _____   Signature: _____   Official Measurer   ☐☐☐

INSTRUCTIONS FOR MEASURING COUGAR AND JAGUAR

Measurements are taken with calipers or by using parallel perpendiculars, to the nearest
one-sixteenth of an inch, without reduction of fractions. Official measurements cannot
be taken for at least sixty days after the animal was killed. All adhering flesh, mem-
brane and cartilage must be completely removed before official measurements are taken.

A. Greatest Length is measured between perpendiculars parallel to the long axis of the
   skull, without the lower jaw and excluding malformations.

B. Greatest Width is measured between perpendiculars at a right angle to the long axis.

* * * * * * * * * * * * *

FAIR CHASE STATEMENT FOR ALL HUNTER-TAKEN TROPHIES

To make use of the following methods shall be deemed as UNFAIR CHASE and unsportmanlike,
and any trophy obtained by use of such means is disqualified from entry for Awards.
   I. Spotting or herding game from the air, followed by landing in its vicinity for
       pursuit;
  II. Herding or pursuing game with motor-powered vehicles;
 III. Use of electronic communications for attracting, locating or observing game, or
       guiding the hunter to such game;
  IV. Hunting game confined by artificial barriers, including escape-proof fencing;
       or hunting game transplanted solely for the purpose of commercial shooting.

I certify that the trophy scored on this chart was not taken in UNFAIR CHASE as defined
above by the Boone and Crockett Club. I further certify that it was taken in full compliance with local game laws of the state, province, or territory.
Date _____   Signature of Hunter _____
(Have signature notarized by a Notary Public)

INSTRUCTIONS FOR MEASURING WALRUS

All measurements must be made with a ¼-inch flexible steel tape to the nearest one-eighth of an inch. Enter fractional figures in eighths, without reduction. Tusks must be removed from mounted specimens for measuring. Official measurements cannot be taken for at least sixty days after the animal was killed.

A. Greatest Spread is measured between perpendiculars at a right angle to the center line of the skull.

B. Tip to Tip Spread is measured between tips of tusks.

C. Entire Length of Loose Tusk is measured over outer curve from base to a point in line with tip.

D-1. Circumference of Base is measured at a right angle to axis of tusk. Do not follow edge of contact between tusk and skull.

D-2-3-4. Divide measurement C of LONGER tusk by four. Starting at base, mark both tusks at these quarters (even though other tusk is shorter) and measure circumferences at these marks.

* * * * * * * * * * * *

FAIR CHASE STATEMENT FOR ALL HUNTER-TAKEN TROPHIES

To make use of the following methods shall be deemed as UNFAIR CHASE and unsportsmanlike, and any trophy obtained by use of such means is disqualified from entry for Awards.

I.   Spotting or herding game from the air, followed by landing in its vicinity for pursuit;
     Herding or pursuing game with motor-powered vehicles;
II. Use of electronic communications for attracting, locating or observing game, or guiding the hunter to such game;
III. Hunting game confined by artificial barriers, including escape-proof fencing;
IV. or hunting game transplanted solely for the purpose of commercial shooting.

I certify that the trophy scored on this chart was not taken in UNFAIR CHASE as defined above by the Boone and Crockett Club. I further certify that it was taken in full compliance with local game laws of the state, province, or territory.

Date _____ Signature of Hunter _____

(Have signature notarized by a Notary Public)

OFFICIAL SCORING SYSTEM FOR NORTH AMERICAN BIG GAME TROPHIES

Records of North American Big Game

BOONE AND CROCKETT CLUB
205 South Patrick Street
Alexandria, Virginia 22314

Minimum Score:
Atlantic 95
Pacific 100

Kind of Walrus _____ Sex _____

WALRUS

SEE OTHER SIDE FOR INSTRUCTIONS		Column 1	Column 2	Column 3
		Right Tusk	Left Tusk	Difference
A.	Greatest Spread			
B.	Tip to Tip Spread			
C.	Entire Length of Loose Tusk			
D-1.	Circumference of Base			
D-2.	Circumference at First Quarter			
D-3.	Circumference at Second Quarter			
D-4.	Circumference at Third Quarter			
	TOTALS			

ADD	Column 1	
	Column 2	
	Total	
SUBTRACT Column 3		
FINAL SCORE		

Exact locality where killed	
Date killed	By whom killed
Present owner	
Address	
Guide's Name and Address	
Remarks: (Mention any abnormalities or unique qualities)	

I certify that I have measured the above trophy on _____ 19___ at (address) _____ City _____ State _____ and that these measurements and data are, to the best of my knowledge and belief, made in accordance with the instructions given.

Witness: _____   Signature: _____ Official Measurer

Copyright © 1981 by Boone and Crockett Club
(Reproduction strictly forbidden without express, written consent)

OFFICIAL SCORING SYSTEM FOR NORTH AMERICAN BIG GAME TROPHIES

Records of North American   BOONE AND CROCKETT CLUB   205 South Patrick Street
Big Game   Alexandria, Virginia 22314

Minimum Score:
Roosevelt 290
American 375

WAPITI   Kind of Wapiti _____

Abnormal Points
	Right	Left

		Column 1	Column 2	Column 3	Column 4
SEE OTHER SIDE FOR INSTRUCTIONS		Spread Credit	Right Antler	Left Antler	Difference
A.	Number of Points on Each Antler R. L.				
B.	Tip to Tip Spread				
C.	Greatest Spread				
D.	Inside Spread of Main Beams Credit may equal but not exceed length of longer antler				
	IF Spread exceeds longer antler- enter difference.				
E.	Total of Lengths of all Abnormal Points				
F.	Length of Main Beam				
G-1.	Length of First Point				
G-2.	Length of Second Point				
G-3.	Length of Third Point				
G-4.	Length of Fourth (Royal) Point				
G-5.	Length of Fifth Point				
G-6.	Length of Sixth Point, if present				
G-7.	Length of Seventh Point, if present				
H-1.	Circumference at Smallest Place Between First and Second Points				
H-2.	Circumference at Smallest Place Between Second and Third Points				
H-3.	Circumference at Smallest Place Between Third and Fourth Points				
H-4.	Circumference at Smallest Place Between Fourth and Fifth Points				
	TOTALS				

ADD	Column 1	
	Column 2	
	Column 3	
	Total	
SUBTRACT Column 4		
FINAL SCORE		

Exact locality where killed	
Date killed	By whom killed
Present owner	
Address	
Guide's Name and Address	
Remarks: (Mention any abnormalities or unique qualities)	

I certify that I have measured the above trophy on _____ City _____ State _____ 19 ___
at (address) _____
and that these measurements and data are, to the best of my knowledge and belief, made in accordance
with the instructions given.

Witness: _____   Signature: _____   OFFICIAL MEASURER

INSTRUCTIONS FOR MEASURING WAPITI

All measurements must be made with a ¼-inch flexible steel tape to the nearest one-eighth of an inch. Wherever it is necessary to change direction of measurement, mark a control point and swing tape at this point. Enter fractional figures in eighths, without reduction. Official measurements cannot be taken for at least sixty days after the animal was killed.

A. Number of Points on Each Antler. To be counted a point, a projection must be at least one inch long and its length must exceed the width of its base. All points are measured from tip of point to nearest edge of beam as illustrated. Beam tip is counted as a point but not measured as a point.

B. Tip to Tip Spread is measured between tips of main beams.

C. Greatest Spread is measured between perpendiculars at a right angle to the center line of the skull at widest part whether across main beams or points.

D. Inside Spread of Main Beams is measured at a right angle to the center line of the skull at widest point between main beams. Enter this measurement again in Spread Credit column if it is less than or equal to the length of longer antler; if longer, enter longer antler length for Spread Credit.

E. Total of Lengths of all Abnormal Points. Abnormal points are those nontypical in location (such as points originating from a point or from bottom or sides of main beam) or pattern (extra points, not generally paired.) Measure in usual manner and enter in appropriate blanks.

F. Length of Main Beam is measured from lowest outside edge of burr over outer curve to the most distant point of what is, or appears to be, the main beam. The point of beginning is that point on the burr where the center line along the outer curve of the beam intersects the burr, then following generally the line of the illustration.

G-1-2-3-4-5-6-7. Length of Normal Points. Normal points project from the top or front of the main beam in the general pattern illustrated. They are measured from nearest edge of main beam over outer curve to tip. Lay the tape along the outer curve of the beam so that the top edge of the tape coincides with the top edge of the beam on both sides of the point to determine the baseline for point measurement. Record point length in appropriate blanks.

H-1-2-3-4. Circumferences are taken as detailed for each measurement.
* * * * * * * * * *

FAIR CHASE STATEMENT FOR ALL HUNTER-TAKEN TROPHIES

To make use of the following methods shall be deemed as UNFAIR CHASE and unsportsmanlike, and any trophy obtained by use of such means is disqualified from entry for Awards.

I.   Spotting or herding game from the air, followed by landing in its vicinity
     for pursuit;
II. Herding or pursuing game with motor-powered vehicles;
III. Use of electronic communications for attracting, locating or observing
     game, or guiding the hunter to such game;
IV. Hunting game confined by artificial barriers, including escape-proof fencing;
     or hunting game transplanted solely for the purpose of commercial shooting.

I certify that the trophy scored on this chart was not taken in UNFAIR CHASE as defined above by the Boone and Crockett Club. I further certify that it was taken in full compliance with local game laws of the state, province, or territory.

Date _____   Signature of Hunter _____
(Have signature notarized by a Notary Public)

OFFICIAL SCORING SYSTEM FOR NORTH AMERICAN BIG GAME TROPHIES

Records of North American
Big Game

BOONE AND CROCKETT CLUB

205 South Patrick Street
Alexandria, Virginia 22314

Minimum Score:
mule   195
blacktail   130

TYPICAL
MULE AND BLACKTAIL DEER

Kind of Deer _____

DETAIL OF POINT
MEASUREMENT

Abnormal Points	
Right	Left

SEE OTHER SIDE FOR INSTRUCTIONS	Column 1	Column 2	Column 3	Column 4
	Spread Credit	Right Antler	Left Antler	Difference
A. Number of points on Each Antler R. L.				
B. Tip to Tip Spread				
C. Greatest Spread				
D. Inside Spread of Main Beams Credit may equal but not exceed length of longer antler				
IF Spread exceeds longer antler, enter difference				
E. Total of Lengths of Abnormal Points				
F. Length of Main Beam				
G-1. Length of First Point, if present				
G-2. Length of Second Point				
G-3. Length of Third Point, if present				
G-4. Length of Fourth Point, if present				
H-1. Circumference at Smallest Place Between Burr and First Point				
H-2. Circumference at Smallest Place Between First and Second Points				
H-3. Circumference at Smallest Place Between Main Beam and Third Point				
H-4. Circumference at Smallest Place Between Second and Fourth Points				
TOTALS				

		Total to E	
ADD	Column 1		
	Column 2		
	Column 3		
	TOTAL		
SUBTRACT Column 4			
FINAL SCORE			

Exact locality where killed _____
Date killed _____ By whom killed _____
Present owner _____
Address _____
Guide's Name and Address _____
Remarks: (Mention any abnormalities or unique qualities)

I certify that I have measured the above trophy on _____ 19____
at (address) _____ City _____ State _____
and that these measurements and data are, to the best of my knowledge and belief, made in accordance
with the instructions given.

Witness: _____   Signature: _____
                                        OFFICIAL MEASURER

INSTRUCTIONS FOR MEASURING MULE AND BLACKTAIL DEER

All measurements must be made with a ¼-inch flexible steel tape to the nearest one-eighth of an inch.
Wherever it is necessary to change direction of measurement, mark a control point and swing tape at
this point. Enter fractional figures in eighths, without reduction. Official measurements cannot
be taken for at least sixty days after the animal was killed.

A. Number of Points on Each Antler: To be counted a point, a projection must be at least one inch
long and its length must exceed the width of its base. All points are measured from tip of point to
nearest edge of beam as illustrated. Beam tip is counted as a point but not measured as a point.

B. Tip to Tip Spread is measured between tips of main beams.

C. Greatest Spread is measured between perpendiculars at a right angle to the center line of the
skull at widest part whether across main beams or points.

D. Inside Spread of Main Beams is measured at a right angle to the center line of the skull at widest point between main beams. Enter this measurement again in Spread Credit column if it is less
than or equal to the length of longer antler; if longer, enter longer antler length for Spread Credit.

E. Total Lengths of all Abnormal Points. Abnormal points are those nontypical in location such as
points originating from a point (exception: G-3 originates from G-2 in perfectly normal fashion) or
from sides or bottom of main beam or any points beyond the normal pattern of five (including beam
tip) per antler. Measure each abnormal point in usual manner and enter in appropriate blanks.

F. Length of Main Beam is measured from lowest outside edge of burr over outer curve to the tip of
the main beam. The point of beginning is that point on the burr where the center line along the
outer curve of the beam intersects the burr, then following generally the line of the illustration.

G-1-2-3-4. Length of Normal Points. Normal points are the brow and the upper and lower forks as
shown in the illustration. They are measured from nearest edge of beam over outer curve to tip.
Lay the tape along the outer curve of the beam so that the top edge of the tape coincides with the
top edge of the beam on both sides of the point to determine baseline for point measurement. Record
point lengths in appropriate blanks.

H-1-2-3-4. Circumferences are taken as detailed for each measurement. If brow point is missing,
take H-1 and H-2 at smallest place between burr and G-2. If G-3 is missing, take H-3 halfway between
the base and tip of second point. If G-4 is missing, take H-4 halfway between the second point and
tip of main beam.

* * * * * * * * * * * * *

FAIR CHASE STATEMENT FOR ALL HUNTER-TAKEN TROPHIES
To make use of the following methods shall be deemed as UNFAIR CHASE and unsportsmanlike, and any
trophy obtained by use of such means is disqualified from entry for Awards.

   I. Spotting or herding game from the air, followed by landing in its vicinity
      for pursuit;
  II. Herding or pursuing game with motor-powered vehicles;
 III. Use of electronic communications for attracting, locating or observing
      game, or guiding the hunter to such game;
  IV. Hunting game confined by artificial barriers, including escape-proof fencing;
      or hunting game transplanted solely for the purpose of commercial shooting.

* * * * * * * * * * * * *

I certify that the trophy scored on this chart was not taken in UNFAIR CHASE as defined above by the
Boone and Crockett Club. I further certify that it was taken in full compliance with local game laws
of the state, province, or territory.

Date _____   _____
                              Signature of Hunter
(Have signature notarized by a Notary Public)

OFFICIAL SCORING SYSTEM FOR NORTH AMERICAN BIG GAME TROPHIES

Records of North American
Big Game

BOONE AND CROCKETT CLUB

205 South Patrick Street
Alexandria, Virginia 22314

NON-TYPICAL
MULE DEER

Minimum Score: 240

DETAIL OF POINT MEASUREMENT

		Abnormal Points	
		Right	Left

SEE OTHER SIDE FOR INSTRUCTIONS			Column 1 Spread Credit	Column 2 Right Antler	Column 3 Left Antler	Column 4 Difference
A.	Number of Points on Each Antler	R.	L.				
B.	Tip to Tip Spread						
C.	Greatest Spread						
	Inside Spread Credit may equal but not exceed length of longer antler						
	of Main Beams						
	IF Spread exceeds longer antler, enter difference						
E.	Total of Lengths of Abnormal Points						
F.	Length of Main Beams						
G-1.	Length of First Point, if present						
G-2.	Length of Second Point						
G-3.	Length of Third Point, if present						
G-4.	Length of Fourth Point, if present						
H-1.	Circumference at Smallest Place Between Burr and First Point						
H-2.	Circumference at Smallest Place Between First and Second Points						
H-3.	Circumference at Smallest Place Between Main Beam and Third Point						
H-4.	Circumference at Smallest Place Between Second and Fourth Points						
	TOTALS						

ADD	Column 1	
	Column 2	
	Column 3	
	TOTAL	
SUBTRACT Column 4		
	Result	
Add Line E Total		
FINAL SCORE		

Exact locality where killed	
Date killed	By whom killed
Present Owner	
Address	
Guide's Name and Address	
Remarks: (Mention any abnormalities or unique qualities)	

I certify that I have measured the above trophy on _____ 19___
at (address) _____ City _____ State _____
and that these measurements and data are, to the best of my knowledge and belief, made in accordance
with the instructions given.

Witness: _____ Signature: _____ OFFICIAL MEASURER

INSTRUCTIONS FOR MEASURING NON-TYPICAL MULE DEER

All measurements must be made with a ¼-inch flexible steel tape to the nearest one-eighth of an inch.
Wherever it is necessary to change direction of measurement, mark a control point and swing tape at
this point. Enter fractional figures in eighths, without reduction. Official measurements cannot
be taken for at least sixty days after the animal was killed.

A. Number of Points on Each Antler. To be counted a point, a projection must be at least one inch
long and its length must exceed the width of its base. All points are measured from tip of point to
nearest edge of beam as illustrated. Beam tip is counted as a point; but not measured as a point.

B. Tip to Tip Spread is measured between tips of main beams.

C. Greatest Spread is measured between perpendiculars at a right angle to the center line of the
skull at widest part whether across main beams or points.

D. Inside Spread of Main Beams is measured at a right angle to the center line of the skull at widest point between main beams. Enter this measurement again in Spread Credit column if it is less
than or equal to the length of longer antler; if longer, enter longer antler length for Spread Credit.

E. Total of Lengths of all Abnormal Points. Abnormal points are those nontypical in location or
points beyond the normal pattern of five (including beam tip) per antler. Mark the points that are
normal, as defined below. All other points are considered abnormal and are entered in appropriate
blanks, after measurement in usual manner.

F. Length of Main Beam is measured from lowest outside edge of burr over outer curve to the tip of
the main beam. The point of beginning is that point on the burr where the center line along the outer
curve of the beam intersects the burr.

G-1-2-3-4. Length of Normal Points. Normal points are the brow and the upper and lower forks, as
shown in the illustration. They are measured from nearest edge of beam over outer curve to tip. Lay
the tape along the outer curve of the beam so that the top edge of the tape coincides with the top
edge of the beam on both sides of the point to determine baseline for point measurement. Record
point lengths in appropriate blanks.

H-1-2-3-4. Circumferences are taken as detailed for each measurement. If brow point is missing,
take H-1 and H-2 at smallest place between burr and G-2. If G-3 is missing, take H-3 halfway between
the base and tip of second point. If G-4 is missing, take H-4 halfway between the second point and
tip of main beam.

* * * * * * * * * * * * * * * *

FAIR CHASE STATEMENT FOR ALL HUNTER-TAKEN TROPHIES

To make use of the following methods shall be deemed as UNFAIR CHASE and unsportsmanlike and any
trophy obtained by use of such means is disqualified from entry for Awards.

I. Spotting or herding game from the air, followed by landing in its vicinity
for pursuit;
II. Herding or pursuing game with motor-powered vehicles;
III. Use of electronic communications for attracting, locating or observing
game, or guiding the hunter to such game;
IV. Hunting game confined by artificial barriers, including escape-proof fencing;
or hunting game transplanted solely for the purpose of commercial shooting.

* *

I certify that the trophy scored on this chart was not taken in UNFAIR CHASE as defined above by the
Boone and Crockett Club. I further certify that it was taken in full compliance with local game laws
of the state, province, or territory.

Date _____ Signature of Hunter _____
(Have signature notarized by a Notary Public)

Copyright © 1981 by Boone and Crockett Club
(Reproduction strictly forbidden without express, written consent)

OFFICIAL SCORING SYSTEM FOR NORTH AMERICAN BIG GAME TROPHIES

Records of North American
Big Game

BOONE AND CROCKETT CLUB

205 South Patrick Street
Alexandria, Virginia 22314

TYPICAL
WHITETAIL AND COUES' DEER

Kind of Deer _____

Minimum Score:
Whitetail 170
Coues 110

DETAIL OF POINT
MEASUREMENT

			Abnormal Points	
			Right	Left

		Column 1	Column 2	Column 3	Column 4	
SEE OTHER SIDE FOR INSTRUCTIONS	R.	L.	Spread Credit	Right Antler	Left Antler	Difference
A.	Number of Points on Each Antler					
B.	Tip to Tip Spread					
C.	Greatest Spread					
D.	Inside Spread of Main Beams	Credit may equal but not exceed length of longer antler				
IF Spread exceeds longer antler, enter difference.						
E.	Total of Lengths of all Abnormal Points					
F.	Length of Main Beam					
G-1.	Length of First Point, if present					
G-2.	Length of Second Point					
G-3.	Length of Third Point					
G-4.	Length of Fourth Point, if present					
G-5.	Length of Fifth Point, if present					
G-6.	Length of Sixth Point, if present					
G-7.	Length of Seventh Point, if present					
H-1.	Circumference at Smallest Place Between Burr and First Point					
H-2.	Circumference at Smallest Place Between First and Second Points					
H-3.	Circumference at Smallest Place Between Second and Third Points					
H-4.	Circumference at Smallest Place between Third and Fourth Points (see back if G-4 is missing)					
TOTALS						

ADD	Column 1		Exact locality where killed	
	Column 2		Date killed	By whom killed
	Column 3		Present owner	
	Total		Address	
SUBTRACT Column 4			Guide's Name and Address	
FINAL SCORE			Remarks: (Mention any abnormalities or unique qualities)	

I certify that I have measured the above trophy on _____ 19___
at (address) _____ City _____ State _____
and that these measurements and data are, to the best of my knowledge and belief, made in accordance
with the instructions given.

Witness: _____   Signature: _____ OFFICIAL MEASURER

INSTRUCTIONS FOR MEASURING WHITETAIL AND COUES' DEER

All measurements must be made with a ¼-inch flexible steel tape to the nearest one-eighth of an inch.
Wherever it is necessary to change direction of measurement, mark a control point and swing tape at
this point. Enter fractional figures in eighths, without reduction. Official measurements cannot
be taken for at least sixty days after the animal was killed.

A. Number of Points on Each Antler. To be counted a point, a projection must be at least one inch
long and its length must exceed the width of its base. All points are measured from tip of point to
nearest edge of beam as illustrated. Beam tip is counted as a point but not measured as a point.

B. Tip to Tip Spread is measured between tips of main beams.

C. Greatest Spread is measured between perpendiculars at a right angle to the center line of the
skull at widest part whether across main beams or points.

D. Inside Spread of Main Beams is measured between perpendiculars at a right angle to the center line of the skull at widest point between main beams. Enter this measurement again in Spread Credit column if it is less
than or equal to the length of longer antler; if longer, enter longer antler length for Spread Credit.

E. Total of lengths of all Abnormal Points. Abnormal points are those nontypical in location (points
originating from points or from sides or bottom of main beam) or extra points beyond the normal pattern
of up to eight normal points, including beam tip, per antler. Measure in usual manner and enter in
appropriate blanks.

F. Length of Main Beam is measured from lowest outside edge of burr over outer curve to the most
distant point of what is, or appears to be, the main beam. The point of beginning is that point on
the burr where the center line along the outer curve of the beam intersects the burr, then following
generally the line of the illustration.

G-1-2-3-4-5-6-7. Length of Normal Points. Normal points project from the top of the main beam. They
are measured from nearest edge of main beam over outer curve to tip. Lay the tape along the outer
curve of the beam so that the top edge of the tape coincides with the top edge of the beam on both
sides of the point to determine baseline for point measurements. Record point lengths in appropriate
blanks.

H-1-2-3-4. Circumferences are taken as detailed for each measurement. If brow point is missing, take
H-1 and H-2 at smallest place between burr and G-2. If G-4 is missing, take H-4 halfway between G-3
and tip of main beam.

OFFICIAL SCORING SYSTEM FOR NORTH AMERICAN BIG GAME TROPHIES

Records of North American
Big Game

BOONE AND CROCKETT CLUB

205 South Patrick Street
Alexandria, Virginia 22314

NON-TYPICAL
WHITETAIL AND COUES' DEER

Minimum Scores:
Whitetail 195
Coues'   120

Kind of Deer

	SEE OTHER SIDE FOR INSTRUCTIONS			Column 1	Column 2	Column 3	Column 4		Abnormal Points
					Total to E				Right / Left
		R.	L.	Spread Credit	Right Antler	Left Antler	Difference		Right | Left
A.	Number of Points on Each Antler								
B.	Tip to Tip Spread								
	Greatest Spread								
D.	Inside Spread Credit may equal but not ex-								
	of Main Beams ceed length of longer antler								
	IF Spread exceeds longer antler, enter difference								
E.	Total of Lengths of Abnormal Points								
F.	Length of Main Beam								
G-1.	Length of First Point, if present								
G-2.	Length of Second Point								
G-3.	Length of Third Point								
G-4.	Length of Fourth Point, if present								
G-5.	Length of Fifth Point, if present								
G-6.	Length of Sixth Point, if present								
G-7.	Length of Seventh Point, if present								
H-1.	Circumference at Smallest Place Between Burr and First Point								
H-2.	Circumference at Smallest Place Between First and Second Points								
H-3.	Circumference at Smallest Place Between Second and Third Points								
H-4.	Circumference at Smallest Place Between Third and Fourth Points								

	Column 1	
ADD	Column 2	
	Column 3	
	Total	
SUBTRACT	Column 4	
	Result	
Add Line E Total		
FINAL SCORE		

TOTALS		
Exact locality where killed		
Date killed	By whom killed	
Present owner		
Address		
Guide's Name and Address		
Remarks: (Mention any abnormalities or unique qualities)		

I certify that I have measured the above trophy on _____ 19___
at (Address) _____ City _____ State _____
and that these measurements and data are, to the best of my knowledge and belief, made in accordance
with the instructions given.

Witness: _____   Signature: _____ OFFICIAL MEASURER

INSTRUCTIONS FOR MEASURING NON-TYPICAL WHITETAIL AND COUES' DEER

All measurements must be made with a ¼-inch flexible steel tape to the nearest one-eighth of an inch. Wherever it is necessary to change direction of measurement, mark a control point and swing tape at this point. Enter fractional figures in eighths, without reduction. Official measurements cannot be taken for at least sixty days after the animal was killed.

A. **Number of Points on Each Antler.** To be counted a point, a projection must be at least one inch long and its length must exceed the width of its base. All points are measured from tip of point to nearest edge of beam as illustrated. Beam tip is counted as a point but not measured as a point.

B. **Tip to Tip Spread** is measured between tips of main beams.

C. **Greatest Spread** is measured between perpendiculars at a right angle to the center line of the skull at widest part whether across main beams or points.

D. **Inside Spread of Main Beams** is measured at a right angle to the center line of the skull at widest point between main beams. Enter this measurement again in Spread Credit column if it is less than or equal to the length of longer antler; if longer, enter longer antler length for Spread Credit.

E. **Total of Lengths of all Abnormal Points.** Abnormal points are those nontypical in location (points originating from points or from sides or bottom of main beam) or extra points beyond the normal pattern of up to eight normal points, including beam tip, per antler. Measure in usual manner and enter in appropriate blanks.

F. **Length of Main Beam** is measured from lowest outside edge of burr over outer curve to the most distant point of what is, or appears to be, the main beam. The point of beginning is that point on the burr where the center line along the outer curve of the beam intersects the burr, then following generally the line of the illustration.

G-1-2-3-4-5-6-7. **Length of Normal Points.** Normal points project from the top of the main beam. They are measured from nearest edge of main beam over outer curve to tip. Lay the tape along the outer curve of the beam so that the top edge of the tape coincides with the beam on both sides of the point to determine baseline for point measurement. Record point lengths in appropriate blanks.

H-1-2-3-4. **Circumferences** are taken as detailed for each measurement. If brow point is missing, take H-1 and H-2 at smallest place between burr and G-2. If G-4 is missing, take H-4 halfway between G-3 and tip of main beam.

****
FAIR CHASE STATEMENT FOR ALL HUNTER-TAKEN TROPHIES

To make use of the following methods shall be deemed as UNFAIR CHASE and unsportsmanlike, and any trophy obtained by use of such means is disqualified from entry for Awards.

I. Spotting or herding game from the air, followed by landing in its vicinity for pursuit;
II. Herding or pursuing game with motor-powered vehicles;
III. Use of electronic communications for attracting, locating or observing game, or guiding the hunter to such game;
IV. Hunting game confined by artificial barriers, including escape-proof fencing; or hunting game transplanted solely for the purpose of commercial shooting.
****

I certify that the trophy scored on this chart was not taken in UNFAIR CHASE as defined above by the Boone and Crockett Club. I further certify that it was taken in full compliance with local game laws of the state, province, or territory.

Date _____ Signature of Hunter _____
(Have signature notarized by a Notary Public)

All measurements must be made with a ¼-inch flexible steel tape to the nearest one-eighth of an inch. Wherever it is necessary to change direction of measurement, mark a control point and swing tape at this point. Enter fractional figures in eighths, without reduction. Official measurements cannot be taken for at least sixty days after the animal was killed.

A. Greatest Spread is measured between perpendiculars in a straight line at a right angle to the center line of the skull.

B. Number of Abnormal Points on Both Antlers - Abnormal points are those originating from normal points or from the upper or lower palm surface, or from the inner edge of palm (see illustration). Abnormal points must be at least one inch long, with length exceeding width at one inch or more of length.

C. Number of Normal Points - Normal points originate from the outer edge of palm. To be counted a point, a projection must be at least one inch long, with the length exceeding width at one inch or more of length.

D. Width of Palm is taken in contact with the under surface of palm, at a right angle to the length of palm measurement line. The line of measurement should begin and end at the midpoint of the palm edge, which gives credit for the desirable character of palm thickness.

E. Length of Palm including Brow Palm is taken in contact with the surface along the under side of the palm, parallel to the inner edge, from dips between points at the top to dips between points (if present) at the bottom. If a bay is present, measure across the open bay measurement. The top line of measurement is parallel to inner edge, follows this path. The one measurement should begin and end at the midpoint of the palm edge, which gives credit for the desirable character of palm thickness.

F. Circumference of Beam at Smallest Place is taken as illustrated.
* * * * * * *

FAIR CHASE STATEMENT FOR ALL HUNTER-TAKEN TROPHIES

To make use of the following methods shall be deemed as UNFAIR CHASE and unsportsmanlike, and any trophy obtained by use of such means is disqualified from entry for Awards.
I. Spotting or herding game from the air, followed by landing in its vicinity for pursuit;
II. Herding or pursuing game with motor-powered vehicles;
III. Use of electronic communications for attracting, locating or observing game, or guiding the hunter to such game;
IV. Hunting game confined by artificial barriers, including escape-proof fencing; or hunting game transplanted solely for the purpose of commercial shooting.

I certify that the trophy scored on this chart was not taken in UNFAIR CHASE as defined above by the Boone and Crockett Club. I further certify that it was taken in full compliance with local game laws of the state, province, or territory.
Date _____ Signature of Hunter _____
(Have signature notarized by a Notary Public)

OFFICIAL SCORING SYSTEM FOR NORTH AMERICAN BIG GAME TROPHIES

Records of North American Big Game

BOONE AND CROCKETT CLUB

205 South Patrick Street
Alexandria, Virginia 22314

MOOSE

Kind of Moose _____

Minimum Score:
Alaska-Yukon 224
Canada 195
Wyoming 155

DETAIL OF POINT MEASUREMENT

SEE OTHER SIDE FOR INSTRUCTIONS		Column 1	Column 2 Right Antler	Column 3 Left Antler	Column 4 Difference
A.	Greatest Spread				
B.	Number of Abnormal Points on Both Antlers				
C.	Number of Normal Points				
D.	Width of Palm				
E.	Length of Palm Including Brow Palm				
F.	Circumference of Beam at Smallest Place				
	TOTALS				

ADD	Column 1	Exact locality where killed	
	Column 2	Date killed	By whom killed
	Column 3	Present owner	
	Total	Address	
SUBTRACT Column 4		Guide's Name and Address	
FINAL SCORE		Remarks: (Mention any abnormalities or unique qualities)	

I certify that I have measured the above trophy on _____ 19___
at (address) _____ City _____ State _____
and that these measurements and data are, to the best of my knowledge and belief, made in accordance with the instructions given.

_____ Signature: _____ Official Measurer

Witness: _____

OFFICIAL SCORING SYSTEM FOR NORTH AMERICAN BIG GAME TROPHIES

Records of North American Big Game

BOONE AND CROCKETT CLUB
205 South Patrick Street
Alexandria, Virginia 22314

CARIBOU

Kind of Caribou _____

Minimum Score:
barren ground mountain 400
Quebec-Labrador 390
woodland 375
295

DETAIL OF POINT MEASUREMENT

SEE OTHER SIDE FOR INSTRUCTIONS		Column 1	Column 2	Column 3	Column 4
		Spread Credit	Right Antler	Left Antler	Difference
A.	Tip to Tip Spread				
B.	Greatest Spread				
C.	Inside Spread of Main Beams	Credit may equal but not exceed length of longer antler.			
	IF Spread exceeds longer antler, enter difference.				
D.	Number of Points on Each Antler excluding brows				
	Number of Points on Each Brow				
E.	Length of Main Beam				
F-1.	Length of Brow Palm or First Point				
F-2.	Length of Bez or Second Point				
F-3.	Length of Rear Point, if present				
F-4.	Length of Second Longest Top Point				
F-5.	Length of Longest Top Point				
G-1.	Width of Brow Palm				
G-2.	Width of Top Palm				
H-1.	Circumference at Smallest Place Between Brow and Bez Points				
H-2.	Circumference at Smallest Place Between Bez and Rear Point, if present				
H-3.	Circumference at Smallest Place Before First Top Point				
H-4.	Circumference at Smallest Place Between Two Longest Top Palm Points				
	TOTALS				

ADD	Column 1	
	Column 2	
	Column 3	
	TOTAL	
SUBTRACT Column 4		
FINAL SCORE		

Exact locality where killed		
Date killed	By whom killed	
Present owner		
Address		
Guide's Name and Address		
Remarks:	(Mention any abnormalities or unique qualities)	

I certify that I have measured the above trophy on _____ 19__ at (address) _____ City _____ State _____
and that these measurements and data are, to the best of my knowledge and belief, made in accordance with the instructions given.

Witness: _____   Signature: _____ OFFICIAL MEASURER [ ]

INSTRUCTIONS FOR MEASURING CARIBOU

All measurements must be made with a ¼-inch flexible steel tape to the nearest one-eighth of an inch. Wherever it is necessary to change direction of measurement, mark a control point and swing tape at this point. Enter fractional figures in eighths, without reduction. Official measurements cannot be taken for at least sixty days after the animal was killed.

A. Tip to Tip Spread is measured between tips of main beams.

B. Greatest Spread is measured between perpendiculars at a right angle to the center line of the skull at widest part, whether across main beams or points.

C. Inside Spread of Main Beams is measured at a right angle to the center line of the skull at widest point between main beams. Enter this measurement again in Spread Credit colum if it is less than or equal to the length of longer antler; if longer, enter longer antler length for Spread Credit.

D. Number of points on each antler. To be counted a point, a projection must be at least one-half inch long, with length exceeding width at the point of measurement. Beam tip is counted as a point but not measured as a point. There are no "abnormal" points in caribou.

E. Length of Main Beam is measured from lowest outside edge of burr over outer curve to the most distant point of what is, or appears to be, the main beam. The point of beginning is that point on the burr where the center line along the outer curve of the beam intersects the burr.

F-1-2-3. Length of Points are measured from nearest edge of beam on the shortest line over outer curve to tip. Lay the tape along the outer curve of the beam so that the top edge of the tape coincides with the top edge of the beam on both sides of the points to determine baseline for point measurement. Record point lengths in appropriate blanks.

F-4-5. Length of points are measured from the tip of the point to the top of the beam, then at a right angle to the lower edge of beam. The Second Longest Top Point cannot be a point branch of the Longest Top Point.

G-1. Width of Brow is measured in a straight line from top edge to lower edge, as illustrated, with measurement line at a right angle to main axis of brow.

G-2. Width of Top Palm is measured from midpoint of lower rear edge of main beam to midpoint of a dip between widest part of palm. The line of measurement begins and ends at mid-points of palm edges, at widest point, which gives credit for palm thickness.

H-1-2-3-4. Circumferences are taken as described for measurements. If rear point is missing, take H-2 and H-3 measurements at smallest place between bez and first top point.

* * * * * * * * * * * * * *

FAIR CHASE STATEMENT FOR ALL HUNTER-TAKEN TROPHIES

To make use of the following methods shall be deemed as UNFAIR CHASE and unsportsmanlike, and any trophy obtained by use of such means is disqualified from entry for Awards.

    I. Spotting or herding game from the air, followed by landing in its vicinity for pursuit;
   II. Herding or pursuing game with motor-powered vehicles;
  III. Use of electronic communications for attracting, locating or observing game or guiding the hunter to such game;
   IV. Hunting game confined by artificial barriers, including escape-proof fencing; or hunting game transplanted solely for the purpose of commercial shooting.

* * * * * * * * * * * * * *

I certify that the trophy scored on this chart was not taken in UNFAIR CHASE as defined above by the Boone and Crockett Club. I further certify that it was taken in full compliance with local game laws of the state, province, or territory.

Date _____   Signature of Hunter _____
(Have signature notarized by a Notary Public)

INSTRUCTIONS FOR MEASURING PRONGHORN

All measurements must be made with a ¼-inch flexible steel tape to the nearest one-eighth of an inch. Wherever it is necessary to change direction of measurement, make a control point and swing tape at this point. Enter fractional figures in eighths, without reduction. Official measurements cannot be taken for at least sixty days after the animal was killed.

A. Tip to Tip Spread is measured between tips of horns.

B. Inside Spread of Main Beams is measured at a right angle to the center line of the skull, at widest point between main beams.

C. Length of horn is measured on the outside curve on the general line illustrated. The line taken will vary with different heads, depending on the direction of their curvature. Measure along the center of the outer curve from tip of horn to a point in line with the lowest edge of the base, using a straight edge to establish the line end.

D-1. Measure around base of horn at a right angle to long axis. Tape must be in contact with the lowest circumference of the horn in which there are no serrations.

D-2-3-4. Divide measurement of longer horn by four. Starting at base, mark both horns at these quarters (even though other horn is shorter) and measure circumferences at these marks. If the prong interferes with D-2, move the measurement down to just below the swelling of the prong. If the prong interferes with D-3, move the measurement up to just above the swelling of the prong.

E. Length of Prong- Measure from the tip of the prong along the upper edge of the outer curve to the horn; then continue around the base from a point at the rear of the horn where a straight edge across the back of both horns touches the horn, with the latter part being at a right angle to the long axis of horn.

* * * * * * * * * * * *

FAIR CHASE STATEMENT FOR ALL HUNTER-TAKEN TROPHIES

To make use of the following methods shall be deemed as UNFAIR CHASE and unsportsmanlike, and any trophy obtained by use of such means is disqualified from entry for Awards.
I.   Spotting or herding game from the air, followed by landing in its vicinity for pursuit;
II.   Herding or pursuing game with motor-powered vehicles;
III. Use of electronic communications for attracting, locating or observing game, or guiding the hunter to such game;
IV.   Hunting game confined by artificial barriers, including escape-proof fencing; or hunting game transplanted solely for the purpose of commercial shooting.

I certify that the trophy scored on this chart was not taken in UNFAIR CHASE as defined above by the Boone and Crockett Club. I further certify that it was taken in full compliance with local game laws of the state, province, or territory.
Date _____ Signature of Hunter _____
(Have signature notarized by a Notary Public)

OFFICIAL SCORING SYSTEM FOR NORTH AMERICAN BIG GAME TROPHIES

Records of North American Big Game

BOONE AND CROCKETT CLUB

205 South Patrick Street
Alexandria, Virginia 22314

Minimum Score: 82

PRONGHORN

SEE OTHER SIDE FOR INSTRUCTIONS	Column 1	Column 2 Left Horn	Column 3 Difference
	Right Horn		
A. Tip to Tip Spread			
B. Inside Spread of Main Beams			
IF Inside Spread exceeds longer horn, enter difference.			
C. Length of Horn			
D-1. Circumference of Base			
D-2. Circumference at First Quarter			
D-3. Circumference at Second Quarter			
D-4. Circumference at Third Quarter			
E. Length of Prong			
TOTALS			

ADD	Column 1	
	Column 2	
	Total	
SUBTRACT Column 3		
FINAL SCORE		

Exact locality where killed	
Date killed	By whom killed
Present Owner	
Address	
Guide's Name and Address	
Remarks: (Mention any abnormalities or unique qualities)	

I certify that I have measured the above trophy on _____ 19___
at (address) _____ City _____ State _____
and that these measurements and data are, to the best of my knowledge and belief, made in accordance with the instructions given.

_____ Signature: _____ Official Measurer

Witness: _____

OFFICIAL SCORING SYSTEM FOR NORTH AMERICAN BIG GAME TROPHIES

Records of North American Big Game

BOONE AND CROCKETT CLUB

205 South Patrick Street
Alexandria, Virginia 22314

Minimum Score: 115

BISON

Sex _____

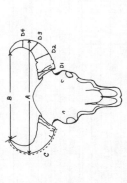

SEE OTHER SIDE FOR INSTRUCTIONS		Column 1	Column 2	Column 3
		Right Horn	Left Horn	Difference
A. Greatest Spread				
B. Tip to Tip Spread				
C. Length of Horn				
D-1. Circumference of Base				
D-2. Circumference at First Quarter				
D-3. Circumference at Second Quarter				
D-4. Circumference at Third Quarter				
TOTALS				
ADD	Column 1	Exact locality where killed		
	Column 2	Date killed	By whom killed	
	Total	Present owner		
SUBTRACT Column 3		Address		
FINAL SCORE		Guide's Name and Address		
		Remarks: (Mention any abnormalities or unique qualities)		

I certify that I have measured the above trophy on _____ 19____
at (address) _____ City _____ State
and that these measurements and data are, to the best of my knowledge and belief, made in
accordance with the instructions given.

Witness: _____   Signature: _____ Official Measurer

INSTRUCTIONS FOR MEASURING BISON

All measurements must be made with a ¼-inch flexible steel tape to the nearest one-eighth of an inch. Wherever it is necessary to change direction of measurement, mark a control point and swing tape at this point. Enter fractional figures in eighths, without reduction. Official measurements cannot be taken for at least sixty days after the animal was killed.

A. Greatest Spread is measured between perpendiculars at a right angle to the center line of the skull.

B. Tip to Tip Spread is measured between tips of horns.

C. Length of Horn is measured from lowest point on under side over outer curve to a point in line with tip. Use a straight edge, perpendicular to horn axis, to end the measurement, if necessary.

D-1. Circumference of Base is measured at a right angle to axis of horn. Do not follow the irregular edge of horn; the line of measurement must be entirely on horn material, not the jagged edge often noted.

D-2-3-4. Divide measurement C of longer horn by four. Starting at base, mark both horns at these quarters (even though the other horn is shorter) and measure circumferences at these marks, with measurements taken at right angles to horn axis.

* * * * * * * * * * * * *

FAIR CHASE STATEMENT FOR ALL HUNTER-TAKEN TROPHIES

To make use of the following methods shall be deemed as UNFAIR CHASE and unsportsmanlike, and any trophy obtained by use of such means is disqualified from entry for Awards.

I. Spotting or herding game from the air, followed by landing in its vicinity for pursuit;

II. Herding or pursuing game with motor-powered vehicles;

III. Use of electronic communications for attracting, locating or observing game, or guiding the hunter to such game;

IV. Hunting game confined by artificial barriers, including escape-proof fencing; or hunting game transplanted solely for the purpose of commercial shooting.

I certify that the trophy scored on this chart was not taken in UNFAIR CHASE as defined above by the Boone and Crockett Club. I further certify that it was taken in full compliance with local game laws of the state, province, or territory.

Date _____   Signature of Hunter _____

(Have signature notarized by a Notary Public)

INSTRUCTIONS FOR MEASURING ROCKY MOUNTAIN GOAT

All measurements must be made with a ¼-inch flexible steel tape to the nearest one-eighth of an inch. Wherever it is necessary to change direction of measurement, mark a control point and swing tape at this point. Enter fractional figures in eighths, without reductions. Measurements are most accurately taken before mounting of the trophy. Official measurements cannot be taken for at least sixty days after the animal was killed.

A. Greatest Spread is measured between perpendiculars at a right angle to the center line of the skull.

B. Tip to Tip Spread is measured between tips of horns.

C. Length of Horn is measured from lowest point in front over outer curve to a point in line with tip.

D-1. Circumference of Base is measured at a right angle to axis of horn. DO NOT follow irregular edge of horn.

D-2-3-4. Divide measurement C of longer horn by four. Starting at base, mark both horns at these quarters (even though other horn is shorter) and measure circumferences at these marks.

* * * * * * * * * * * * * *

FAIR CHASE STATEMENT FOR ALL HUNTER-TAKEN TROPHIES

To make use of the following methods shall be deemed as UNFAIR CHASE and unsportsmanlike, and any trophy obtained by use of such means is disqualified from entry for Awards.
I.   Spotting or herding game from the air, followed by landing in its vicinity for pursuit;
II. Herding or pursuing game with motor-powered vehicles;
III. Use of electronic communications for attracting, locating or observing game, or guiding the hunter to such game;
IV. Hunting game confined by artificial barriers, including escape-proof fencing; or hunting game transplanted solely for the purpose of commercial shooting.

I certify that the trophy scored on this chart was not taken in UNFAIR CHASE as defined above by the Boone and Crockett Club. I further certify that it was taken in full compliance with local game laws of the state, province, or territory.

Date _____ Signature of Hunter _____
(Have signature notarized by a Notary Public)

OFFICIAL SCORING SYSTEM FOR NORTH AMERICAN BIG GAME TROPHIES

Records of North American Big Game

BOONE AND CROCKETT CLUB
205 South Patrick Street
Alexandria, Virginia 22314

ROCKY MOUNTAIN GOAT

Minimum Score: 50   Sex _____

SEE OTHER SIDE FOR INSTRUCTIONS	Column 1	Column 2	Column 3
	Right Horn	Left Horn	Difference
A. Greatest Spread			
B. Tip to Tip Spread			
C. Length of Horn			
D-1. Circumference of Base			
D-2. Circumference at First Quarter			
D-3. Circumference at Second Quarter			
D-4. Circumference at Third Quarter			
TOTALS			

ADD	Column 1	
	Column 2	
	Total	
SUBTRACT	Column 3	
FINAL SCORE		

Exact locality where killed	
Date killed	By whom killed
Present owner	
Address	
Guide's Name and Address	
Remarks: (Mention any abnormalities or unique qualities)	

I certify that I have measured the above trophy on _____ 19 ____
at (address) _____ City _____ State _____
and that these measurements and data are, to the best of my knowledge and belief, made in accordance with the instructions given.

Witness: _____   Signature: _____   Official Measurer

OFFICIAL SCORING SYSTEM FOR NORTH AMERICAN BIG GAME TROPHIES

Records of North American
Big Game

BOONE AND CROCKETT CLUB
205 South Patrick Street
Alexandria, Virginia 22314

Minimum Score: 90   MUSKOX   Sex _____

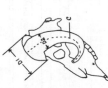

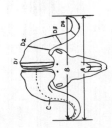

SEE OTHER SIDE FOR INSTRUCTIONS	Column 1	Column 2	Column 3
	Right Horn	Left Horn	Difference
A. Greatest Spread			
B. Tip to Tip Spread			
C. Length of Horn			
D-1. Width of Boss			
D-2. Width at First Quarter			
D-3. Circumference at Second Quarter			
D-4. Circumference at Third Quarter			
TOTALS			
ADD Column 1			
Column 2			
Total			
SUBTRACT Column 3			
FINAL SCORE			

Exact locality where killed _____
Date killed _____ By whom killed _____
Present owner _____
Address _____
Guide's Name and Address _____
Remarks: (Mention any abnormalities or unique qualities)

I certify that I have measured the above trophy on _____ 19____
at _____ _____ State _____
   (address)   City
and that these measurements and data are, to the best of my knowledge and belief, made in
accordance with the instructions given.

Witness: _____   Signature: _____   Official Measurer

INSTRUCTIONS FOR MEASURING MUSKOX

All measurements must be made with a ¼-inch flexible steel tape and adjustable calipers to the nearest one-eighth of an inch. Whenever it is necessary to change direction of measurement, mark a control point and swing tape at this point. Enter fractional figures in eighths, without reduction. Official measurements cannot be taken for at least sixty days after the animal was killed.

A. Greatest Spread is measured between perpendiculars at a right angle to the center line of the skull.

B. Tip to Tip Spread is measured between tips of horns by using large calipers, which are then read against a yardstick.

C. Length of Horn is measured along center of upper horn surface, staying within curve of horn as illustrated, to a point in line with tip. Attempt to free the connective tissue between the horns at the center of the boss to determine the lowest point of horn material on each side, near the top center of the skull. Hook the tape under the lowest point of the horn and measure the length of horn, with the measurement line maintained in the center of the upper surface of horn following the converging lines to the horn tip.

D-1. Width of Boss is measured with calipers at greatest width of base, with measurement line forming a right angle with horn axis. It is often helpful to measure D-1 before C, marking the midpoint of the boss as the correct path of C.

D-2-3-4. Divide measurement C of longer horn by four. Starting at base, mark both horns at these quarters (even though other horn is shorter). Then, using calipers, measure width of boss at D-2, making sure the measurement is at a right angle to horn axis and in line with the D-2 mark. Circumferences are then measured at D-3 and D-4, with measurements being taken at right angles to horn axis.

* * * * * * * * * * * * * *

FAIR CHASE STATEMENT FOR ALL HUNTER-TAKEN TROPHIES

To make use of the following methods shall be deemed as UNFAIR CHASE and unsportsmanlike, and any trophy obtained by use of such means is disqualified from entry for Awards.

I.   Spotting or herding game from the air, followed by landing in its vicinity for pursuit;
II. Herding or pursuing game with motor-powered vehicles;
III. Use of electronic communications for attracting, locating or observing game, or guiding the hunter to such game;
IV. Hunting game confined by artificial barriers, including escape-proof fencing; or hunting game transplanted solely for the purpose of commercial shooting.

I certify that the trophy scored on this chart was not taken in UNFAIR CHASE as defined above by the Boone and Crockett Club. I further certify that it was taken in full compliance with local game laws of the state, province, or territory.
Date _____ Signature of Hunter _____
(Have signature notarized by a Notary Public)

OFFICIAL SCORING SYSTEM FOR NORTH AMERICAN BIG GAME TROPHIES

Records of North American Big Game

BOONE AND CROCKETT CLUB
205 South Patrick Street
Alexandria, Virginia 22314

SHEEP Kind of Sheep _____

Minimum Score:
bighorn   180
desert   168
Stone   170
white or Dall 170

MEASURE TO A POINT IN LINE WITH HORN TIP

SEE OTHER SIDE FOR INSTRUCTIONS		Column 1	Column 2	Column 3
		Right Horn	Left Horn	Difference
A. Greatest Spread (Is often Tip to Tip Spread)				
B. Tip to Tip Spread				
C. Length of Horn				
D-1. Circumference of Base				
D-2. Circumference at First Quarter				
D-3. Circumference at Second Quarter				
D-4. Circumference at Third Quarter				
TOTALS				

	Column 1	
ADD	Column 2	
	TOTAL	
SUBTRACT Column 3		
FINAL SCORE		

Exact locality where killed	
Date killed	By whom killed
Present owner	
Address	
Guide's Name and Address	
Remarks: (Mention any abnormalities or unique qualities)	

I certify that I have measured the above trophy on _____ 19____
at (address) _____ City _____ State _____
and that these measurements and data are, to the best of my knowledge and belief, made in
accordance with the instructions given.

Witness: _____   Signature: _____   Official Measurer

INSTRUCTIONS FOR MEASURING SHEEP

All measurements must be made with a ¼-inch flexible steel tape to the nearest one-eighth of an inch. Wherever it is necessary to change direction of measurement, mark a control point and swing tape at this point. Enter fractional figures in eighths, without reduction. Official measurements cannot be taken for at least sixty days after the animal was killed.

A. Greatest Spread is measured between perpendiculars at a right angle to the center line of the skull.

B. Tip to Tip Spread is measured between tips of horns.

C. Length of Horn is measured from the lowest point in front on outer curve to a point in line with tip. Do not press tape into depressions. The low point of the outer curve of the horn is considered to be the low point of the frontal portion of the horn, situated above and slightly medial to the eye socket (not the outside edge). Use a straight edge, perpendicular to horn axis, to end measurement on "broomed" horns.

D-1. Circumference of Base is measured at a right angle to axis of horn. Do not follow irregular edge of horn; the line of measurement must be entirely on horn material, not the jagged edge often noted.

D-2-3-4. Divide measurement C of longer horn by four. Starting at base, mark both horns at these quarters (even though the other horn is shorter) and measure circumferences at these marks, with measurements taken at right angles to horn axis.

* * * * * * * * * * * * * *

FAIR CHASE STATEMENT FOR ALL HUNTER-TAKEN TROPHIES

To make use of the following methods shall be deemed as UNFAIR CHASE and unsportsmanlike, and any trophy obtained by use of such means is disqualified from entry for Awards.

  I.   Spotting or herding game from the air, followed by landing in its vicinity for pursuit;
  II. Herding or pursuing game with motor-powered vehicles;
  III. Use of electronic communications for attracting, locating or observing game, or guiding the hunter to such game;
  IV. Hunting game confined by artificial barriers, including escape-proof fencing; or hunting game transplanted solely for the purpose of commercial shooting.

I certify that the trophy scored on this chart was not taken in UNFAIR CHASE as defined above by the Boone and Crockett Club. I further certify that it was taken in full compliance with local game laws of the state, province, or territory.

Date _____   Signature of Hunter _____
(Have signature notarized by a Notary Public)

TURKEY *(Meleagris gallopavo)* Four subspecies of wild turkeys live in the United States. The Eastern wild turkey thrives in most Eastern states and into the Midwest; the Florida subspecies lives primarily in Florida; the Rio Grande turkey is a native of Texas and other southern Plains states; and the Merriam's turkey is a bird of the Southwest. In recent years, Rio Grande and Merriam's turkeys have been transplanted throughout the West (Rio Grandes at lower elevations in oak forests, Merriam's higher primarily in pine forests), and now all Western states except Nevada have thriving turkey populations and open seasons.

At one time, hunting turkeys with a bow was viewed as a gimmick, a far-out venture strictly for fanatics. That view has changed in recent years. Sure, it's tougher to kill a turkey with a bow than with a shotgun, but many avid archers have proved they can take turkeys consistently, and turkey hunting has become a popular bowhunting challenge.

Turkey hunting may gain its appeal by combining the best of two worlds. Technically, turkeys are upland game and multiple-bird limits (in some states) give them an upland quality. But any turkey hunter will tell you turkeys are big game, pure and simple. Size may have something to do with it. A mature tom, the bird most hunters seek, may weigh more than 20 pounds.

But more significant is the challenge. You don't just go out one day and bust up a flock of turkeys and kill your limit as you might on quail. Most hunters pursue turkeys by calling, much as elk hunters do, and they work as hard to kill one turkey as they would to take any other big game.

"Of all the game I've killed, the turkey is by far the toughest," said Cliff Dewell, an archery shop owner and rabid turkey hunter from California. "The challenge of turkey hunting, watching that old tom strutting and gobbling out front, or sensing him sneaking in like a ghost, cautious and wary, that's what makes turkey hunting exciting. I've taken a number of elk, but I've got more thrill out of killing one turkey than all those elk."

Calls and Decoys

You don't have to be a world-champion caller to call in turkeys. With a few basic calls you can fool birds consistently. The yelp is by far the most commonly used sound for both spring and fall hunting, and some hunters add a purr and cluck for spring hunting and the kee-kee call for fall hunting. I can't describe these on paper, so get three or four tapes from call makers and practice. That's the only practical way to learn calling on your own. Of course, if you've got an experienced friend to help you, that's even better.

Most bowhunters prefer mouth diaphragm calls over other types of calls because it leaves their hands totally free for shooting. Unfortunately, not everyone can use a mouth diaphragm. If you have trouble with it, consider a slate call. With this call you can set the slate in your lap and operate the scratcher with the

California archer Cliff Dewell figures turkey hunting provides more thrills than virtually any kind of bowhunting. Dewell has taken several gobblers with his bow.

If you can't perfect a mouth diaphragm, use a slate call or one of the many variations.

other hand, which still leaves you one free hand with which to hold your bow. Calls such as box calls that require two hands for operation aren't well suited to bowhunting.

Most bowhunters also like to use a decoy. The decoy gives incoming turkeys something to focus on—other than you—and as a gobbler spots the decoys and struts around, it gives you added time to make a clean shot. Some hunters use only one decoy; others place two about 15 feet apart in front of their blinds. Decoys are used most commonly in spring during the breeding season. Gobblers are looking for receptive hens then, and the sight of a hen decoy will stir them up pretty well. Even in fall, however, a decoy can help distract the turkeys' attention from you. If nothing else it gives you a positive reference point for estimating range. Several companies make durable plastic turkey decoys.

Spring Hunting

The mating season for turkeys begins in late March, peaks about mid-April, and continues on into May, and this is the time for traditional gobbler hunting. The idea at this time is to imitate the sounds of a hen turkey in order to call gobblers within range. Actually this system goes a little against nature, because under natural conditions, the tom struts and gobbles and hens come to him. Still, you can bring gobblers to you if you sound enticing enough and have patience.

Locating a Gobbler. Chuck Graves, who studies turkeys year-round as a hunter and biologist, considers locating a bird the toughest part of the hunt.

"Turkey hunting takes a lot of prescouting," Graves said. "I've spent five days in a row in a spot I know contained turkeys without seeing

Many bowhunters like to use a decoy for turkeys. The decoy gives you a positive range marker, and it distracts the incoming bird so he's got his eye on something besides you.

Spring hunting is probably the most popular time for turkey hunting because big gobblers are most vulnerable then. Watching a tom strut and prance in response to your alluring yelp-yelp is a thrilling experience. *Photo courtesy John Higley.*

or hearing a bird. Then the sixth day birds appear everywhere. The person who just wants to go out one day during the season and shoot a turkey . . . well, let's just say his chances aren't good."

Initial scouting means looking for sign. In some places, especially the mountainous West, snow could still cover the ground during turkey season. That makes spotting tracks easy. Hen tracks are about 4 inches long, those of toms 4½ inches or longer. Also look for tracks around water sources, streams and stock tanks. You'll also find distinct scratchings in pine duff or leaves where turkeys have scratched for acorns, seeds, and other food. In these areas you'll find droppings, too. Commonly hen droppings are small, coiled piles, but tom droppings are bigger around and virtually straight except for a hook on the end. You also might locate roosts where droppings and feath-

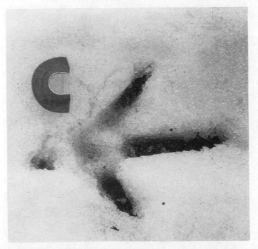

Looking for tracks is one way of scouting. In some country, snow could still cover the ground during spring season and that simplifies scouting. A tom's track could be 4½ inches long.

ers have accumulated under big trees, and you'll find feathers in places where toms have been fanning and strutting.

You can also scout with your ears. Toms start gobbling before dawn while they're on the roost. You get out during this prime early period and cover ground, listening for birds. Some hunters call to stimulate a response, and once they've heard a gobbler they mentally mark the location. That's where they'll be when the season opens. If you hear turkeys before the season, don't play around, trying to call them in. Just leave them alone. You know their territory, and that's good enough for now.

If, once the seasons opens, you don't kill the particular bird or birds you located by scouting, you'll have to locate new birds during the season. Most hunters like to "roost" a bird in the evening and return the next morning to

You can also scout with your ears. Hike to high vantage points, then call and listen. You frequently can get a turkey to respond by gobbling.

hunt him. Turkeys fly into tall trees for safety at night, so late in the evening, you listen for turkeys flying into their roosts. Turkeys' huge wings make a lot of racket, especially as they bang through branches, so you can hear the birds flying up, and the toms often gobble as they settle in, which can be heard from some distance.

If you don't hear any birds, try calling to make them sound off. If it's still light, imitate the sound of a hawk, crow, or owl, and toms will often respond by gobbling. Even after dark they'll gobble. At that time hoot like an owl, or in the West (or anywhere coyotes live, I suppose) howl like a coyote. One night my friend Larry Jones and I had listened until dark and had heard nothing. I headed toward camp, but Larry, a total diehard, insisted we push on. Every five minutes or so he'd howl like a coyote, and a full hour after dark we heard a turkey gobble at the very top of a ridge. We returned there the next morning and called that gobbler within bow range.

What if you can't roost a turkey the night before your hunt, and don't hear any on the roost before daylight? Are you done for the day? Not at all. Start at first light and hunt along a high point or ridge, calling to both sides. The predator sounds—coyote, owl, and so forth—may work at this time, and gobbling also will make a gobbler talk, but the sounds of a hen work best during the day.

"Occasionally I gobble, but mostly I make loud, excited hen yelps," Cliff Dewell said. "I keep moving and calling, just as I would for elk. Turkeys move around a lot, especially in the West where they have lots of country to roam, so in one day they could end up a mile or more from where you found them the first time. Sometimes you have to cover a lot of ground to find turkeys."

Don't give up just because you don't hear a turkey the first hour of daylight. They'll be active all morning, and it might take you two or three hours to get within ear shot of a receptive tom. Keep at it until at least 10:00 A.M. I've had great action late in the morning.

The Setup. Whether you've roosted a bird

To blind in, you want good cover behind so you're not silhouetted. Camouflage plays an important role in turkey hunting. You're also wise to use a bow you can pull and hold for a while, because you may have to wait for a turkey to come within range.

Camouflage plays a big part in hiding. No turkey hunter will deny the value of camouflage, and your hands, face, bow, arrows, every tiny detail, must be camouflaged. And as a turkey starts your way, stay absolutely motionless. If you're still, he won't see you; if you so much as blink, he'll be gone like a streak.

Don't expect a gobbler to come running in. Some may, but more often they'll take their time.

"The thing to remember is that you're going against nature," Cliff Dewell said. "That old tom is used to having hens come to him. When he has to go to the hen, he's suspicious. He may take three hours to come in. Even if he quits gobbling, I'll give him another half hour or 45 minutes. And often that hasn't been long enough. I've spooked birds that were sneaking in on me."

Making the Shot Count. To bring a turkey down fast, you must use a wide, very sharp

the night before or located one during the day, try to get within 100 to 200 yards of them before setting up. Setting up means you take a stand, usually with your back against a tree and with some concealment out front. You want to be fairly well hidden, but you have to maintain good visibility. A turkey may charge straight in, but just as often he'll circle and approach from the side or rear.

Turkeys don't like moving through thick brush, so set up on an opening where the turkey will come in readily and where you can get an open shot. Place your decoy or decoys (if you use two) 15 yards or so from your blind, and start calling. Even if you can make no sound but the hen yelp, you can call in a turkey (here's where you need the instructional tapes to learn the technique).

In choosing a setup, make sure you have some openings. Turkeys won't plow through brush to get to you, and you can't get a clear shot through heavy brush. *Photo courtesy John Higley.*

For turkeys you need a wide broadhead that will kill cleanly. A penetration restrictor like the Zwickey Scorpio prevents the arrow from passing through the bird.

broadhead like you'd use for any big game. A string tracker also can prove valuable. Your shots on turkeys should be close, under 20 yards, so the tracker doesn't seriously affect arrow trajectory, and it can help you follow a bird, especially if he flies. Also consider using a "turkey stopper" on your shaft. As one example, the Zwickey Scorpio is a spring device that slips on the shaft just behind the broadhead. When the arrow hits a turkey, the Scorpio slips up the shaft ten inches or so to allow good penetration, but it keeps the arrow from going on through.

You also have to shoot a bow you can handle without strain. The hardest part of killing a turkey with a bow is drawing once the bird comes within range. Try to select a blind where the turkey must walk behind a tree or bush on the way in, so you can draw while his view is blocked.

Some hunters advocate using a recurve bow, which they can draw slowly and smoothly and shoot quickly; others recommend using a light compound bow, which you can hold at full draw for some time. As Cliff Dewell said, "Predrawing means I may have to hold at full draw

for many seconds while the turkey approaches close enough. That's why I shoot a lightweight bow. My standard turkey bow is a 39-pound Dynabo. I can hold it a minute or longer if necessary. A turkey's eyesight is tremendous. If you move, the bird is gone. It's just that simple. You may make mistakes and kill a young jake, but you won't kill a mature bird by accident. You have to do everything right to get that old bird. It's an altogether different battle, going after jakes and old birds."

Gun hunters usually refrain from shooting at a strutting gobbler because the bird's drawn-back head presents a poor shot, but for bow-hunters a strutting bird presents a good shot, because you're shooting for the body. Aim for the vitals as you'd do on any other game. If the bird is sideways to you, shoot for the base of the wing, and if it's head on, aim for the top of the beard. If it's facing away, aim for the center of the back.

Turkey Identification. In the spring, you have to be able to tell hens from toms. Obviously if a bird comes in gobbling and strutting, it's a tom. But it's not always that simple. One time Cliff Dewell and I were hunting together, and as Cliff called, three turkeys, two gobblers

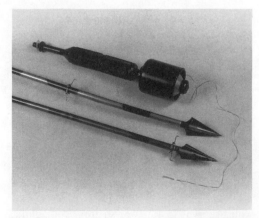

The arrow on top here was shot into a turkey, and you can see how far it penetrated, about ten inches. It killed the turkey almost instantly. A string tracker like Saunders' Trail Tracker is a good addition to your turkey hunting tackle.

and a hen, came right in. The hen walked right to me as I waited at full draw, and because she had a small beard, I wasn't positive she wasn't a young gobbler. Fortunately, one of the gobblers started strutting right behind her, which removed any doubt about his sex, and I popped him.

In general, the heads on hens are darker and are covered with hairlike feathers. The top of a gobbler's head is almost white and the rest of his head and the naked part of his neck is very red. Gobblers also have a snood, a long wormlike affair that hangs over the bill.

If you're "trophy" hunting, you have to distinguish between mature gobblers and young birds (jakes, as most hunters call them). Mature birds have long spurs, jakes have only stubs. A jake's beard, a hairy projection hanging from the chest, will be only 2 to 4 inches long, but on a mature gobbler it will be 6 to 12 inches long. Also, on a jake the central tail feathers are an inch or two longer than the outside tail feathers. On a mature tom, all the tail feathers are the same length, forming a smooth-edged fan.

Fall Hunting

Many states have fall as well as spring seasons. Fall is a good time to hunt because you're not restricted to gobblers (or bearded turkeys) only. Also, birds are generally more numerous in the fall, and you'll sometimes see huge flocks. While hunting in Missouri, I saw flocks of 100 and more turkeys. Generally in the fall, mature toms hang out in bachelor groups separate from the large flocks of hens, poults, and jakes.

The idea in the fall is to break up these flocks. You can locate them essentially as you do in the spring, although they generally aren't as vocal in the fall. Do a lot of listening in the fall for the little clucks and yelps made by a contented flock of feeding turkeys. Toms don't gobble a lot in fall, but I've heard them gobbling on occasion.

When you've found a flock, you run into it and scatter turkeys in as many directions as possible. Then you blind in right there, just as

On a young gobbler—a jake—the central tail feathers are an inch or two longer than the outside feathers. On a mature bird, tail feathers are all the same length.

you would in spring. Wait a half hour or so and start calling. You can use the same general yelping technique you'd use in spring, and I've called in fall turkeys by using only the hen yelp. Another common call used in fall, however, is the kee-kee, a high-pitched whistle sound. You can use an ordinary diaphragm to imitate the kee-kee, or you can do it with a police-type whistle.

If everything works right, you'll soon hear the turkeys calling back and forth to each other as they reassemble. Stay right there in that one spot and continue to call until you bring a bird within range. It could take an hour or more, so be patient.

Safety

Most bowhunting takes place during special archery seasons, so most bowhunters aren't particularly concerned about getting shot. Remember, though, that most turkey seasons are simply general seasons when gun hunters will be hunting, too.

Set up so you can see some distance and so you can spot any hunter who might be slipping in on you. Obviously you should never purposely try to call in another hunter, because he might be one of those guys who takes "sound shots," and you might be his target. At the least he might shoot your decoy, and if you're in the path, he could get you at the same time.

U

UTAH The total area of Utah is 84,916 square miles. From Salt Lake City north to the Idaho border and in the northeast corner along the Wyoming state line, most of the best big-game land is privately owned, and it's leased by outfitters or hunting clubs. In general, you pay to hunt here. Throughout the rest of the state, public lands are extensive and access is good. The Bureau of Land Management administers vast acreages throughout the arid western one third of Utah, and the U.S. Forest Service manages most of the land in the mountainous central, southern, and eastern sections. Much of the public land is heavily hunted, but there are many roadless canyons and ridges where an ambitious hunter can find solitude and quality game.

Big Game

Mule Deer. These are the only deer hunted in Utah and the population is estimated at 500,000 animals. About 20,000 archers hunt deer in Utah each fall, and average archery harvest has been 2,477 bucks each year. Archers enjoyed their best season in 1973 when they killed 3,825 bucks. The average bowhunting success rate has been 15 percent, with the highest in 1961 at 22 percent and the lowest in 1975 at 7.5 percent. The archery season generally opens the third Saturday in August and continues through Labor Day. Traditionally archers have been allowed to take one buck on the general deer license and a second on a special archery tag, for a limit of two bucks.

Utah has produced more than its share of huge bucks. A sampling of the Boone and Crockett records shows typical mule deer with scores of $212\frac{1}{8}$, 210, 208, $205\frac{6}{8}$, $205\frac{5}{8}$. Nontypicals have been equally impressive: $330\frac{1}{8}$, $284\frac{3}{8}$, 284, 283, $276\frac{5}{8}$. Unfortunately many of these were taken years ago, and Utah has fallen off as a trophy producer. However, in some units permit numbers have been limited, and many bucks are surviving to maturity. As a result, I expect archers, particularly those lucky enough to draw tags for the limited-entry hunts, to haul monster bucks out of Utah. The southern and southeastern sections have the best potential for huge bucks.

Elk. Utah isn't known for elk hunting, but elk herds are expanding there, putting elk within reach of more bowhunters. Also, the archery elk season has been moved back so it falls in early September (rather than late August as it did for many years), and that should offer better opportunity for bugling. The Uinta Mountains and the Book Cliffs offer the best potential for bigger bulls. Some fair elk herds are scattered throughout the mountains near Richfield and Beaver in the southcentral part of the state.

Antelope. Utah has a special archery antelope season in September, but permits are restricted in number. Most antelope live in the desert country in the western third of the state.

Black Bears. Utah isn't noted for high numbers of bears, but it does produce some big ones. At this writing, the number one and two bears listed by Boone and Crockett come from San Pete County, Utah. Utah has spring and fall seasons, and dogs and baiting (for archers only) are allowed.

Cougar. Utah perennially has been one of the top lion-producing states, with an average annual harvest of 200 or more. The season runs from November into April in some regions, and it's year-round in others. Virtually all cats taken are run with hounds.

Moose. Good numbers of Shiras moose live throughout the northeast corner and the Uinta Mountains. A limited number of permits are issued each year. At this writing, nonresident permits cost $1,000, but that's not bad compared to the price of a Canadian or Alaskan moose hunt.

Buffalo. Wild, free-roaming buffalo live in the Henry Mountains of southern Utah, and limited permits are issued for hunting them each year.

Desert Bighorn Sheep. A dozen or so permits are issued for desert bighorns each year, but generally no more than one permit goes to a nonresident.

Mountain Goat. A small herd of goats live in the Wasatch Mountains near Salt Lake City. Very few permits are issued, none to nonresidents.

Other Game

The extreme southern end of the state has fair numbers of turkeys, and these are hunted in spring and fall. Rabbits are abundant throughout the state, and coyote hunting is good.

Contact. Utah Division of Wildlife Resources, 1596 North Temple, Salt Lake City, UT 84116.

V

VALLEY As you draw a compound bow, you reach peak weight about midway through the draw. Draw weight then drops off and reaches a low point at your maximum draw length. This lowest draw-weight point is called the valley. If you continue beyond the valley, draw weight again increases. The valley can vary from one to three inches or longer, depending on bow style. It's generally longer on round-wheel compounds than on cam bows. That's one reason, some archers would say, the round wheel is a little more forgiving. Most archers agree that for best accuracy you should shoot from the valley, rather than in front or back where poundage is higher.

VANE Plastic fletching. For details, see Fletching.

VERMONT The Green Mountain State covers a total area of 9,609 square miles. About 90 percent of it is privately owned, but access is fairly good. The Green Mountain National Forest and some state lands assure extensive public access, and in Vermont, tradition has it that unposted private land is open to hunting. Posting has spread in recent years, but much private land can still be hunted. The tradition of hunting clubs hasn't spread into Vermont.

Big Game

Deer. Vermont supports an estimated 80,000 to 90,000 whitetail deer. An average of 12,000 residents and 5,000 nonresidents hunt during bow seasons each year. Average bow harvest, including bucks and does, has been about 1,300 deer, and in 1977 archers killed a record high of 2,094. Average archery success has been 5.1 percent, with a high in 1977 of 7.8 percent. The archery season traditionally has been open for 16 days, starting the second Saturday in October.

The northern hardwood forests of the western foothills along the New York border have the highest deer densities in Vermont, although deer are relatively small in size here. The Green Mountains, which extend north and south the full length of the state, contain rugged terrain up to 4,000 feet elevation. Northern hardwoods and spruce-fir combinations make up most of the forests here, and harsh winters and restricted winter range limit the number of deer in this region, although some large bucks are taken. Much of the land is public so hunting pressure is heavy, although some roadless backcountry offers potential for escaping the crowds.

The southeastern corner consists of forested rolling hills intermixed with croplands and abandoned farms and orchards. Deer numbers are high here. In the northeast, winters are severe with cold temperatures and deep snow. Spruce-fir forests cover most of the rolling hills here. Deer are sparse, but some of the largest bucks killed in Vermont come from this region.

Bear. Vermont produces a harvest of 400

or more bears annually. The northeast corner, which has the lowest human population and extensive forests, produces the most bears. The season opens in September and runs for three months. No baiting is allowed, but hunting with hounds is legal.

Other Game

Vermont also has turkeys, gray squirrels, cottontails, snowshoe rabbits, and foxes and other predators.

Contact. Agency of Environmental Conservation, Fish and Game Department, Montpelier, VT 05602.

VIRGINIA The Old Dominion State has a total area of 40,817 square miles. The Blue Ridge divides Virginia into two general hunting regions. In general, country west of the Blue Ridge consists of mountains and ridge-and-valley terrain. The valleys are farmed, but most of the uplands remain in hardwoods, interspersed with some pine and other conifers. The George Washington and Jefferson national forests, plus a few state areas, hold more than 1.5 million acres of public land open to hunting west of the Blue Ridge.

East of the Blue Ridge, the Piedmont with its rolling farmlands mixed with extensive timberlands, covers most of central Virginia. Along the eastern fringe, the coastal plain, locally called the Tidewater, has many commercial pine plantations along with farming for soybeans, small grains, and other crops. Except for a few heavily hunted public areas, all of eastern Virginia is privately owned, and hunting clubs lease large tracts. Unless you know the right person, getting permission to hunt east of the Blue Ridge could be tough.

Big Game

Whitetail Deer. Virginia has an estimated population of 500,000 deer. No figures are available on the number of bowhunters, but annual archery harvest runs somewhere between 2,500 and 3,000 deer. Special archery

seasons also are held in October in most counties, and again in November into January in a few counties. In most areas the limit is two deer per license year.

In the hardwood forests west of the Blue Ridge, carrying capacity for deer is relatively low. Some remote areas offer the potential for uncrowded hunting. In the Piedmont of central Virginia, deer numbers are moderate to high. The southern Tidewater zone supports the highest deer densities in Virginia, but the deer are relatively small in size here.

The state record typical whitetail from Virginia scored 177^2/$_8$, and the record nontypical 219^7/$_8$. Boone and Crockett lists only a half dozen or so bucks from Virginia.

The history of deer in Virginia parallels that of other Southeastern states. Deer were nearly extinct in the early 1900s, but with improved habitat, extensive stocking, and law enforcement, deer herds grew rapidly after the 1930s, and biologists predict the total harvest will stabilize around 100,000 deer.

Black Bear. These animals are hunted in the mountains west of the Blue Ridge and in the Dismal Swamp area of the southeast corner. Seasons run from November into January, with variations depending on region. Dogs are allowed. No special bow seasons are held for bears.

Other Game

Turkeys. Turkeys are available throughout the state, but highest numbers live in the mountains along the western border. Spring and fall seasons are held in most counties, and the limit is one bird per day (in spring it must be bearded) and two per calendar year.

Small Game. Fox and gray squirrels are abundant throughout the state wherever hardwoods provide good feed and cover. Rabbits are also common in areas with good brush cover.

Contact. Commission of Game and Inland Fisheries, P.O. Box 11104, Richmond, VA 23230-1104.

W

WALLOW This is a muddy or water-filled depression the size of a bathtub or bigger made by bull elk during the rut. You'll find most wallows in damp meadows or oozing springs back in dark timber; in some cases just one wallow, in others a series of wallows covering hundreds of square feet. Wallowing is rut-related. Mature bulls wallow most frequently, and abandoned sites with no fresh wallows probably indicate a decline in the number of mature bulls in an area.

Bulls commonly urinate in the mud and then roll over and over to coat themselves with a thick, crusty layer of smelly mud. Animal behaviorists say they do this to increase their apparent size and raunchy smell as another means—along with big antlers, lots of bugling, and aggressive postures—to intimidate other bulls (and maybe to impress cows). Unless disturbed, bulls will return to the same wallows time after time, so stand hunting near a fresh wallow can work pretty well. Also, elk have traditional rutting grounds, so if you locate old wallows during the off-season, you can assume the area will be good for rutting bulls another season.

WAPITI This term, a Shawnee Indian word meaning "white deer," is another name for the elk of North America. Elk, strictly speaking, refers to European moose, but when early settlers came to North America, they saw large deerlike animals and mistakenly called them elk, and the name has stuck. Sticklers for correct usage maintain that the *Cervus elaphus* of North America should be called wapiti, but virtually no hunters use that name. To American hunters, wapiti are elk. So be it. (For details, see Elk.)

WASHINGTON With 66,570 square miles, Washington is the smallest of the 11 Western states, yet it has the second highest population (behind California), so hunting pressure is fairly intense. Nevertheless, the state has some excellent hunting, perhaps better than any other in two categories—black bears and mountain goats.

The Cascade Range, which runs north and south from Canada to the Oregon border, divides Washington into two sections. The west side receives some of the highest rainfall in North America, and as a result the forests are dense and wet. East of the Cascades, rainfall is scant, and the country consists of relatively open forests in the mountains to rolling grasslands and many miles of grainfields. National forestland assures good access throughout the

Cascades and in the northeast and southeast corners, but some of the best hunting on the west side occurs on private lands.

Big Game

Deer. Many states have good hunting for two kinds of deer, but Washington may offer the best hunting for three. Estimated populations in Washington are 69,000 whitetails, 138,000 mule deer, and 210,000 blacktails. Hunters must choose their weapon—firearm or bow—but they can't hunt during both seasons. West of the Cascades, general deer and elk bow seasons run for about two weeks in September, and late seasons in a number of units offer deer and elk hunting in December. East of the Cascades the general archery season for deer and elk is open for about two weeks in October, and late seasons offer deer and elk hunting in late November and early December.

Rain forests of the west side are the province of blacktail deer. This country is heavily logged and many clearcut patches are interspersed with pockets of old-growth timber. Blacktails feed along the edges of clearcuts or natural openings and bed in heavy timber. Nearly a quarter of the blacktails listed in Boone and Crockett come from the southwest corner of Washington, roughly from King County (where Seattle is located) southwest to the Columbia River. The B&C world record, with an incredible score of 182⅜, was killed in Lewis County near Forks in 1953. Pope and Young–size blacktails are fairly common.

Mule deer live in the drier half of the state east of the Cascades. The Okanogan country in northcentral Washington is generally considered Washington's "deer factory." Herds here are managed for maximum production, so densities are high, but most deer killed are yearlings. However, the Cascade Range contains rugged country that provides good refuge, and when heavy snow falls and pushes bucks from the remote mountains, opportunities are good. Archers have taken some huge bucks from this country during late bow seasons.

Between the forested Cascades and the Idaho border, much of the land consists of rolling grainfields and open prairies and supports few deer, but the southeast corner in the Snake River drainage has deep canyons with timbered breaks, and this country holds high numbers of mule deer and some whitetails. Much of this country is heavily hunted during rifle season, so trophy bucks are scarce.

Some mule deer live in the northeast corner in the higher mountains north of Spokane, but whitetails predominate in the heavily forested mountains of this region, and several special archery seasons in December offer good prospects for taking a quality whitetail buck.

Elk. The coastal region including the Olympic Peninsula has high numbers of Roosevelt elk. Some of the best hunting takes place around Olympic National Park. To be considered Roosevelt elk for scoring purposes, the elk must be taken west of Interstate 5. The Cascade Range east of I-5 has good elk herds and some huge bulls are taken, especially around Rainier National Park and in the Mt. St. Helens region. These are considered Rocky Mountain elk. The southeast corner near the Snake and Wenaha rivers has good numbers of Rocky Mountain elk.

Bear. Washington consistently has the highest bear kill in the United States. At one time it was as high as 8,000 annually, but many of those bears were killed on depredation permits by private timber companies. In recent years, the harvest has been about 2,000 a year. Bears may be hunted by baiting or with hounds. In eastern Washington bear season is open in September and October. In the northeast corner, many hunt by spotting bears in huckleberry patches in early September. The west side bear season opens August 1 and extends through October. Among bowhunters, baiting is the common method. Depredation hunts are also held each spring in specific units, and there's no bag limit at this time.

Mountain Goat. In the Lower 48, Washington ranks number one for goats, particularly for archers. Tag numbers are limited, but a number of units have archery-only seasons and the drawing odds are much better than they are in rifle units. The goat season is open throughout October.

Bighorn Sheep. Washington has limited hunting for California bighorns. Several archery-only permits are issued, and nonresidents may apply.

Moose. Occasionally Washington issues a very limited number of moose tags for the Selkirk Mountains in the northeast corner, four, for example, in 1985.

Cougar. Tags for cougars are not limited, and Washington has excellent cougar hunting. General late seasons are open throughout the state in December and January, and some areas are open to cougar hunting from September through November.

Contact. Washington Department of Game, 600 North Capitol Way, Olympia, WA 98504.

WEATHER: ITS EFFECTS ON HUNTING

Weather is probably the most talked about and least understood subject ever to plague mankind. Who can change the weather? Who can even predict it accurately? The answers are obvious.

But even if we can't predict just what the weather will do, we can make some educated guesses about what deer and other animals will do in reaction to the weather, and that can help us to hunt more efficiently. Most of the discussion here centers on deer because the greatest amount of research has involved deer, but the same principles apply to most big-game animals to varying degrees.

Season

Many hunters falsely picture summer as a lazy time for deer and winter as a time when cold weather increases deer's energy needs and forces them to feed more actively for long periods of time.

In fact, just the opposite is true. Deer are most active in the pleasant weather of summer, and they're least active during bitter winter weather. Actually, the change in activity may

not have so much to do with weather as it does with length of daylight, or photoperiod. Scientists say that changing length of daylight affects the production of a hormone called thyroxin, which influences the basic metabolism of deer.

To put it simply, with shortening daylight in fall, metabolic rate decreases and, with the exception of a flurry of activity during the rut, metabolism reaches a low point during the shortest, coldest days in winter. In essence, deer go into semihibernation in winter. Their metabolism slows down greatly so their food needs are least at this time of year. If winter weather makes them more visible it's not because they move around more at that time, but because they concentrate in large groups, commonly (in the case of mule deer, at least) on open winter ranges where they're easy to see.

In contrast, during summer, does are nursing fawns and bucks are growing new antlers and putting on fat for the coming fall and winter. As a result, food needs are greatest during the summer, and deer are most active and visible at that time.

Many studies bear this out, including one by Dr. Don Behrend in the Adirondack Mountains of New York. Behrend progressively observed more and more deer from June through a peak of activity in August, and then he observed fewer and fewer deer through September to reach a low point in October. Activity picked up briefly in November during the rut and then dropped off into the winter "dormant" period.

Observations by a group called the Stump Sitters bears out this trend. Al Hofacker, records keeper for the nationwide organization, said that members recorded more than 7,500 hours of deer observations during the 1977 and 1978 hunting seasons (summer months are excluded because no one was hunting then). The Stump Sitters' data show the greatest deer movement during September and the least in October. Deer activity then increased during the rut in November.

My observations on mule deer parallel these findings for whitetails. Many Western bow sea-

sons open in August, and I've found this an excellent time to hunt because deer are extremely visible. Undoubtedly many influences enter in. Bucks are in velvet then and avoid heavy cover that could tear up their tender antlers, and prior to heavy frosts they feed in open alpine country where they're easy to see.

But they're also active for long periods in the summer. They commonly feed in the open until 10:00 A.M., and they'll start feeding an hour or two before sunset in the evening. And they'll often feed for extended periods during the day. In areas where they weren't disturbed, I've watched many bucks feed for two to three hours during the heat of day.

Daily Activity

Daily movements can be gauged only within the framework of these seasonal patterns. At the same time, you have to remember that deer and other animals also have fairly set daily patterns, or circadian rhythms as scientists would say. Deer and elk, for example, are crepuscular animals, which means they're most active during twilight periods, primarily dusk and dawn.

Research has shown that the peak activity takes place in the evening right at dark, and a lesser peak occurs about dawn. Unless thrown

Hunters have traditionally believed that deer are least active during hot summer weather and most active in winter, but research indicates just the opposite is true. In summer, the metabolism of deer reaches a peak, and that's when deer are most active.

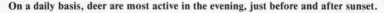

On a daily basis, deer are most active in the evening, just before and after sunset.

off by unusual circumstances, most deer will adhere to this general pattern from day to day.

Within this seasonal and daily framework, movement patterns can vary greatly depending on external influences, such as weather. Like people, animals seek specific comfort zones, but it's dangerous to make generalizations based on the comfort zones of human beings. Studies have shown that as long as whitetail deer have adequate food, such as a rich corn diet, they can survive very well with little or no protection in all but the most savage weather.

One morning I saw three elk lying in a high alpine meadow, far from any trees. To me the weather seemed cold, and to make it more miserable, a storm was brewing. As black clouds opened up and hail blotted out the surrounding mountains and hid the elk from me, I figured that was the last I'd see of those animals. Surely they'd head for the tall timber in this barrage of falling ice. But when the storm passed ten minutes later, the elk lay right where they'd been, and over the next hour they stayed right there through a deluge of rain and another hailstorm. Unquestionably elk and other animals continually seek the most comfortable places, but obviously an elk's definition of comfort differs from mine.

Temperature and Humidity

Numerous studies show that temperature and humidity affect the activities of deer, and most observers relate this general pattern: deer are most active when temperatures are warmest and when humidity is lowest.

That observation is consistent with climatological facts. Relative humidity and air temperature are so closely interrelated you can't discuss one independent of the other. Relative humidity is a measurement of moisture in the air. In general, the warmer the air the lower the humidity, and the cooler the air the higher the humidity. That's because warm, expanded air can hold more moisture than cool, dense air, so relatively, there's less moisture in the warm air.

Under average conditions, humidity drops to a low level in late afternoon when air temperature is highest. I live in a dry climate where the humidity drops to about 30 percent in the afternoon. At sunset the air temperature drops and humidity begins to rise, and it peaks in early morning just before sunrise when daily temperature is lowest. In my area it rises to 75 percent or higher. Of course, cloud cover or storms, which bring moisture and lower daytime temperatures, can raise humidity at any time of day. Weatherman Jim Rawles said that for all practical purposes, relative humidity measures 100 percent during rain or snowstorms.

Now, the question is, which affects deer movements more—temperature or humidity? Although the two are inseparable, some studies indicate a stronger correlation between deer activity and humidity than between temperature and activity. Some biologists speculate that this has to do with body cooling, while others think it's associated with the deer's ability to smell. Deers' noses are most sensitive during high humidity.

Whatever the reasons, the following relationship seems to exist: high humidity, less deer activity; low humidity, more deer activity. In other words, deer seem to move more freely under drier conditions. For that reason, you're more likely to see more deer moving on an evening of low relative humidity than one with high humidity, and you should see more deer moving on a warm, clear day than on a cloudy, cool, or stormy day.

That would seem to fly in the face of tradition, because any hunter knows that cool, cloudy days are better for hunting. Indeed cool, damp weather may present better conditions for hunting, because you can move more quietly then and may simply be more comfortable yourself, but that doesn't mean more deer are moving, and the sizable data indicate deer are more active on clear days than on cloudy.

"I always thought deer moved more on cloudy days," Al Hofacker said. "But input from hunters across the country has proved me wrong."

During 5,000 hours of observation from stands over two hunting seasons, Hofacker said, hunters averaged seeing 41 deer per 100

Tradition again says that deer will move and feed most on cloudy, damp days, but research shows that stand hunters see the most bucks on clear, warm days.

hours of observation on partly cloudy days; 45 deer per 100 hours on overcast days; and 59 deer per 100 hours on clear days.

"In other words, we're seeing 40 percent more deer on clear days than on cloudy," Hofacker said. "This is a good example of how gut reactions don't always hold up. A wise hunter keeps accurate records."

Hofacker said he personally thinks the most important factor is temperature. "Deer seem to have their comfort zones," Hofacker said. "Basically here's what we've found: if it's abnormally cold, deer become inactive; if it's abnormally hot, they seem to become less active during the day and become more nocturnal."

Of course, different animals have different comfort zones. Based strictly on my personal observation, I'd say mule deer and whitetails have similar comfort levels, but for elk it's probably 20 degrees cooler.

Even though animals may be more active on warm, dry days, I think they generally avoid direct, intense sunlight. Without question that's true of elk. Studies on Roosevelt elk in western Oregon showed that on hot, sunny days with low relative humidity, elk fed in early

mornings and late evenings in the open, but during the day they retreated into heavy timber. On rainy or cool days with high relative humidity, they were active all day, spending little time in timber.

My observations are similar. During hot, dry weather I've spent days searching for elk, in country I know contained lots of animals, and have scarcely seen an elk. In that same country on cool, blustery days and during steady rain, I've seen elk in the open all day long. One drizzly afternoon I watched a herd remain bedded or feeding in an open meadow on a south slope all afternoon. That leads me to think elk seek cover more to escape direct sunlight than they do to hide from hunters.

I think the same generally holds for deer. One afternoon I sat on a ridge overlooking a deep canyon under an intense sun, and try as I might through a spotting scope, I couldn't see one deer on the far side of the canyon. Suddenly at 3:00 P.M., a small cloud drifted in front of the sun to send a cool shadow over the canyon. Instantly, deer began to emerge and within five minutes I could see two dozen deer, including several bucks, feeding in the open. About 4:00 P.M. the cloud dissipated, and as direct sunlight hit the hillside, the deer disappeared as fast as they'd appeared.

Storms and Wind

One writer said that whitetails retreat to cover during heavy storms only because wind and falling rain dull their senses and make them nervous, but the animals don't need protection from severe weather. "Physically it doesn't bother them," he said.

During early seasons, that might be true. At that time, air chill isn't severe, yet deer do hole up during heavy wind. Hofacker said the Stump Sitters' figures show that as wind velocity increases, deer activity decreases. Under the category "light wind," members recorded an average of 70 deer sightings per 100 hours of observation. Under the "moderate" and "gusty" categories, sightings decreased, and for "continual strong wind," deer sightings averaged only 22 per 100 hours of observation.

Weather affects the movements of game, but during the rut, deer may remain active regardless of conditions. A near blizzard didn't slow this mule deer buck at all.

Wind affects elk hunting, too. In the Wind River Range of Wyoming, the wind blew hard for three days. During that time my companions and I hunted some fine country with lots of sign, yet we saw no elk and heard none bugling. The fourth day the wind finally died down, and immediately we got into some great action. Maybe we just weren't hearing them during that wind, but I suspect the elk were just kegged up and not moving, and that has been my general experience. Hard wind makes for hard hunting.

Once cold sets in, wind chill probably does bother deer, and they seek protection from severe weather. Biologist Don Behrend reports that the "trend toward concentration in evergreen shelter is most closely associated with increasing frequency . . . of severe windchill in November and December."

Thomas Allen, studying whitetails in Maine, found that deer sought shelter when the air chill, a combination of air temperature and wind speed, dropped below 9 degrees F. (For details, see the wind-chill chart under Hypothermia.)

"You may not be able to put it into exact degrees, especially from region to region," Allen said. "But any time the air-chill equivalent drops below 20 degrees, I think it affects the animals."

During severe weather, whitetails and other animals move into dense evergreens, which moderate the effects of bitter weather. In Michigan, the temperature of softwood swamps can be 20 to 30 degrees warmer than in surrounding uplands. In any conifer cover, temperature fluctuates less than in the open, and conifers can reduce wind velocity by 50 to 75 percent. Obviously, these are the places to focus your efforts during periods of severe wind chill.

Precipitation

Light rain or snow doesn't bother animals much, but heavy precipitation can. Most researchers agree that heavy rain or snow forces deer into shelter. That could be the result of chilling, but most observers think it's because the noise of falling precipitation limits a deer's ability to hear and smell, and the animals feel more secure in quiet cover.

The fact that you observe fewer deer during rain or snow doesn't necessarily mean animals

A sudden storm with violent winds and heavy snow can shut down the hunting for a while. Even at that, any serious hunter knows that the best time to hunt is when you have time to hunt, and some diehards just won't give up.

are less active. Stormy conditions simply make spotting game and hunting tougher. Arthur Tubbs, studying deer in Pennsylvania, said without question he saw fewer deer during heavy precipitation, but deer could have been moving far back in cover where he couldn't see them. At any rate, deer do seek cover that offers umbrella protection from falling rain and snow, so that's where you should look for them during storms.

That was the case when I hunted a late mule-deer season in Idaho. The wind blew furiously and heavy snow fell at times. To say the least, it made spotting tough, but when I kept with it and looked in protected pockets, I found deer feeding and active.

Snow Depth

Deep snow can force deer to change locations. In snow up to six inches deep, according to Hofacker, deer can still feed on ground foods such as fallen acorns by pawing the snow away. In deeper snow, the animals switch to woody browse and may change location to find

it, and you have to keep up with these movements to hunt successfully.

Thomas Allen observed that even when snow of 18 inches and deeper forced deer into wintering areas, the animals would return to upland locations to feed as soon as conditions permitted. After strong winds had swept hillsides bare or had compacted snow into a strong crust that would bear their weight, whitetails would travel up the slopes to feed and return to softwood shelter only during storms and periods of cold. I found that true for mule deer during that winter season in Idaho. During heavy storms they would disappear into juniper cover, but as soon as the storms let up, the deer, especially the bigger bucks, appeared right at the tops of the highest ridges. The severe wind up there swept the hillsides bare, and that's where the deer fed.

Barometric Pressure

No biologists I've talked with have correlated barometric pressure with deer activity. However, a falling barometer (low air pressure) pre-

544

FAHRENHEIT WIND CHILL EQUIVALENT TEMPERATURE

TEMPERATURE FAHRENHEIT

Wind Speed MPH	50	45	40	35	30	25	20	15	10	5	0	-5	-10	-15	-20	-25	-30	-35	-40	-45	-50	-55	-60
Calm	50	45	40	35	30	25	20	15	10	5	0	-5	-10	-15	-20	-25	-30	-35	-40	-45	-50	-55	-60
5	48	44	37	33	27	21	16	12	6	1	-5	-11	-15	-20	-26	-31	-36	-41	-47	-52	-57	-65	-70
10	40	34	28	21	16	9	4	-2	-9	-15	-24	-27	-33	-38	-46	-52	-58	-64	-70	-75	-83	-90	-95
15	36	29	22	16	9	1	-5	-11	-18	-25	-32	-40	-45	-51	-58	-65	-72	-77	-85	-90	-99	-105	-110
20	32	25	18	12	4	-4	-10	-17	-25	-32	-39	-46	-53	-60	-67	-75	-82	-89	-96	-102	-110	-115	-120
25	30	23	16	7	0	-7	-15	-22	-29	-37	-44	-52	-59	-67	-74	-83	-88	-96	-104	-111	-118	-125	-135
30	28	21	13	5	-2	-11	-18	-26	-33	-41	-48	-56	-63	-70	-79	-87	-94	-101	-109	-115	-125	-130	-140
35	27	19	11	3	-4	-13	-20	-27	-35	-43	-51	-60	-67	-72	-82	-90	-98	-105	-113	-120	-129	-135	-146
40	26	18	10	1	-6	-15	-21	-29	-37	-45	-53	-62	-69	-76	-85	-94	-100	-107	-115	-125	-132	-140	-150

Exposed Flesh Can Freeze in 60 Seconds

Exposed Flesh Can Freeze in 30 Seconds

NOTE 1. The above chart has been based upon the Siple Equation and reflects Wind Chill Equivalent temperatures in Fahrenheit.

NOTE 2. At low wind speeds, relative humidity and radiant heat are more important than wind speed in determining equivalent temperature comfort.

NOTE 3. Most charts indicate that at wind speeds over 40 mph there is little additional wind chill effect. This is a reflection of an error in the basic equation at these higher wind speeds and is not correct. Heat loss IS magnified by these higher wind speeds, but the chart is an accurate indicator of equivalent temperature at speeds lower than 40 mph.

From *Hypothermia* by William W. Forgey, M.D. Copyright © 1985 by William W. Forgey, M.D. Reprinted by permission of ICS Books.

cedes most major fall storms, and as most hunters know, deer activity often increases just prior to storms. So the evidence suggests that a dropping barometer does spur increased deer activity.

Hofacker personally has observed an increase in activity just before storms, particularly prior to big snowstorms during the December bow season in Wisconsin. And Thomas Allen observed that deer in Maine became unusually active prior to and during the early stages of snowstorms. But when as little as three inches of snow had fallen, they congregated in softwood cover. This indicates that the time preceding a heavy storm, when the barometer is dropping, presents a good time to hunt, and that during the storm hunting could be tough.

My experience bears that out, and that's true for elk as well as deer. During most September elk seasons I've hunted through at least one heavy snowstorm. The bugling will go great until the storm settles in. Then everything shuts down, and for a couple of days during and after the storm, the elk will clam up. The weather in itself is not cold enough to send elk into hiding, so I'm inclined to think it's related to low barometric pressure. As the barometer starts back up and the weather improves, bulls come out of the woodwork. Many other hunters have related similar experiences.

Of course, as the saying goes, the best time to hunt is when you've got the time, and few of us will plan a hunt based strictly on the weather. Nevertheless, understanding weather and the animals' response to it can help shape your hunting plans and improve your all-around success.

WEST VIRGINIA　West Virginia has an area of 24,292 square miles. Average elevation of the Mountain State is 1,500 feet, the highest of any state east of the Mississippi. West Virginia lies totally within the Appalachian Mountain region. More than 90 percent of West Virginia is privately owned. However, three national forests provide more than 1 million acres of public hunting, and state management areas offer another 250,000 acres. Except in the northeast corner and some of the western counties, clubs and leases have not become prevalent, and a person can still get permission by asking.

Big Game

Whitetail. An estimated 600,000 whitetail deer occupy about 94 percent of the land area. West Virginia, even though not a large state, is popular with bowhunters and attracts about 80,000 resident and 15,000 nonresident archers annually. Average bow harvest has been just under 10,000. Bowhunters average about 10 percent success. The bow season runs from mid-October through December, and hunters can take a deer of either sex (except during bucks-only gun seasons). In some cases, by participating in various seasons hunters have been able to take from three to five deer per year.

The mountains along the Virginia border at one time yielded the heaviest harvest, although it has dropped off somewhat in recent years. The highest mountains in West Virginia lie south of the panhandle along the eastern border. The U.S. Forest Service administers much of this rugged, forested region. Deer herds have grown dramatically in the rolling country of central and western West Virginia. Many abandoned farms have grown up into brush, and the ideal deer habitat supports high numbers of deer. Some of the largest bucks taken in West Virginia also come from this region. The south end of the state has the poorest deer herds. Coal mining has been the major industry in this steep, rough country. Free-roaming dogs and poaching take a heavy toll on deer here. Average field-dressed weight for all deer taken in West Virginia is 114 pounds.

Bears. Black bears live throughout the mountains on the eastern side of the state, and a number of counties are open to hunting. An archery season runs from October through December.

Pigs. Very limited pig hunting takes place in the several southern counties in November.

Other Game

Turkeys. A fall season is held in the eastern counties, and a statewide spring season runs for about a month in April and May.

Small Game. Gray and fox squirrels live wherever hardwoods provide suitable feed and cover. Cottontails are found around farmlands and brush cover, and snowshoe hares live in mountain country.

Contact. Department of Natural Resources, 1800 Washington Street East, Charleston, WV 25305.

WHIP FINISH   See Bowstring.

WHITETAIL DEER *(Odocoileus virgin-ianus* Scientists recognize about 30 sub-species of whitetail deer, 17 of which live in the United States and Canada. Since the early 1900s, whitetails have been transplanted from one region to another to rebuild depleted pop-ulations, so isolating distinct subspecies would be difficult, and except from a scientist's point of view, splitting hairs on whitetail subspecies is probably irrelevant anyway. As far as most hunters are concerned, a whitetail is a white-tail.

The record books take that same view and lump all whitetails together, with one excep-tion—the Coues deer, or Arizona whitetail, of the Southwest. These deer uniformly are smaller in body and antler size than most other whitetail subspecies, and they inhabit a discrete region, which limits the potential for cross-breeding with larger subspecies. (For details, see Coues Deer.)

The Nature of Whitetails

Whitetail deer are the most widespread big-game animals in North America and that fact, along with their beauty, challenge to hunters, and fine table value, accounts for their ranking as the number one game animal in the United States. Some reference books say whitetail deer live in all the contiguous 48 states. That may be true, but for all practical purposes, Utah, Ne-vada, and California do not have whitetails, at least not in huntable numbers. Whitetails abound in all other states of the Lower 48 as well as the eight Canadian provinces bordering the United States.

No average size can be given for whitetails because they're basically a product of their food supply. Among the corn and soybean

This may be one of the most familiar scenes in North American hunting. Is there any question about where the whitetail deer gets its name?

There is no "average"-sized whitetail, because these deer are products of their food supply. Corn-fed whitetails get big in a hurry. In rich farmland, 200-pound bucks aren't uncommon.

although south Texas has grown some of the largest racks ever recorded, and other Southern states are producing a few outsize bucks.

Whitetail Behavior

Scouting. Whitetails generally don't live in open country where you can spot them as you would mule deer. At some times of year, however, primarily in late summer when they're most active and visible, whitetails can be seen easily. Watch for them very early and late in the day at the edges of fields, and if your area doesn't have open fields, watch openings through the woods—power lines, fencerows, old roads—where you can see deer crossing. You can't determine exactly where and how to hunt from this kind of observation, but you can get a good feel for the number and quality of deer in an area. (For details, see Scouting, and Weather).

That's because whitetails stick to a relatively small home range. In some mountainous country whitetails do migrate long distances to winter ranges, and in northern regions with deep snow they'll shift location in winter to protected yards. But as a general rule, whitetails have well-defined home ranges where they spend the better part of their lives. Studies have shown that for bucks, home ranges vary from 200 acres up to 800 or 900 acres. That

fields of northern Missouri I shot a yearling buck with antlers scarcely as wide as his ears, and he hog-dressed 135 pounds. His body looked much too large for his antlers. In northern Idaho, a land of endless forests and no croplands whatsoever, I shot a mature 10-point buck with a 20-inch spread. This buck's rack dwarfed that of the Missouri buck, and he was at least a couple of years older, yet he didn't weigh as much. He needed some Missouri corn.

In rich farmland, whitetails weighing more than 200 pounds hog dressed aren't uncommon, and an occasional bruiser tops 300. As a general rule, northern whitetails average larger in body size than southern races. Most of the largest antlers come from northern states, too,

Whitetails are considered brush-country deer, but you can scout them visually if you watch openings at the right time of day and right time of year.

means a buck's home range could be less than a mile square, although you can't simply block out a section and say that's where a buck lives. His home territory might be long and narrow or oval-shaped or round, depending on the nature of plants and terrain. Generally the higher the deer densities or the thicker the cover, the smaller the home ranges. Where deer numbers are low or the country is sparse, as in the Plains states, home ranges tend to be larger.

Within any given home range, deer have specific key areas where they eat, bed, breed, and find security. It would be impossible to describe them all here. In wooded, hilly country whitetails often bed on higher ridges with thick, cool timber, but where uplands are farmed they'll bed in thick draws and bottomlands, and where corn and other tall crops remain standing, they'll often stay all day in the fields.

Scouting in the summer by observing deer will tell you the quality of bucks in an area and roughly the home ranges, but it doesn't tell you much about the movements of individual deer within those ranges. That's where on-the-ground scouting comes in. Scouting should start well before the season, but it must be a continuing process on through the season as you're hunting. Whenever you enter the woods, become a detective and look for clues—tracks, trails, rubs, scrapes, and other sign—that indicate where a buck eats, sleeps, fights, and mates, and what routes he takes between each key location. That's the knowledge that will get you a deer.

The Rut

No one can question the popularity of bowhunting for whitetails, but it's not just whitetail hunting in general that has set the hunting world on fire but hunting *rutting* whitetails. Undoubtedly many things about rut hunting fascinate hunters, but the bottom line is productivity. During rut, bucks are active and visible, they leave definitive sign, they respond to calling, they lose some of their inherent caution, and so forth. The rut presents not only the best time for killing a buck, but more

To hunt whitetails effectively, you must find not only tracks but trails, and you must interpret the sign to determine what the deer are doing and when they're doing it. This trail leads from a soybean field where deer feed at night to a daytime bedding ground in a hardwood bottom.

importantly (to many hunters) for killing a *big* buck.

Bow seasons further sweeten the pot for archers, because many states have long bow seasons that take in part or all of the rut. That fact gives bowhunters great opportunity to kill super-bucks, putting archers almost on equal footing with rifle hunters.

Some hunters would say the rut begins as soon as bucks rub the velvet off their antlers and ends when the last doe is bred some four to five months later. Others would say "rut" means only the period when bucks make scrapes and breed does, a span of roughly 1½ months. Some might even say the rut includes only the peak breeding period, about two weeks.

549

Regardless of your definition, the activities of whitetails follow a predictable pattern and occur at a predictable time each year in any given location. You often hear hunters complain that the rut was delayed by hot weather or whatever, but that's not true. The actual trigger for the rut is what scientists call photoperiod. In simple terms, daylight reaches a certain length each fall, hormonal changes take place in deer, and they go into rut regardless of weather. Weather could affect the amount of daytime activity or in the distribution of animals, but the fact is if whitetails are in rut one year on a specific date, they're in rut in that locality every year on that date.

If you hunt one area regularly, keep records based on your observations from hunting and scouting, and you should be able to determine when certain phases of the rut take place. If that's not possible, ask local biologists. If they

can't tell you exact rut timing, they may be able to tell you when the fawn drop takes place. From that time count backward 200 days (or just under seven months, the gestation period of whitetail deer), to determine the peak of the rut, and from that you can fill in the blanks on deer activity throughout the fall.

The blanks consist of various phases of the rut. Marchinton and Hirth, in *White-Tailed Deer, Ecology and Management*, call these the sparring, courtship, and estrus periods; they are followed by a secondary breeding, or post-rut period. For simplicity I'll follow their lead. Many hunters have different names for these periods, but it doesn't matter what you call them as long as you understand the general progression.

Sparring Period. This phase begins when velvet is shed from bucks' antlers. As soon as their antlers are polished, bucks start shoving

Rubs aren't good stand locations, but they can be exciting finds because they indicate the size of bucks present. Virtually any buck could have made the smaller rub, but you can bet a big buck made the big rub. This tree is nearly six inches in diameter (the hunter is on his knees).

each other around, apparently to establish a heirarchy of dominance, but they don't engage in serious fights as they might later during the actual breeding period. They frequently spar with trees and shrubs, too, and create what hunters call rubs.

Rub trees are important in scouting because they assure you of the presence of bucks, and they indicate size. Most hunters agree that the bigger the rub trees, the bigger the buck. That doesn't mean a big buck won't rub small trees, but small bucks generally won't take on big trees. If you find rubs only on trees no larger than one to two inches in diameter, there may or may not be a big buck around. But if you find rubs on trees over four inches in diameter, you've located a hummer. Rubs aren't good indicators for stand placement, but they're important sign for locating the territories of big bucks.

Courtship Period. The sparring period lasts four to six weeks, and then the courtship phase begins. Many hunters consider this the start of actual rut, because at this time bucks start making scrapes, the first purely rut-related activity.

A scrape is a buck's signpost. To make a scrape he paws the ground to clear a small area, and during this process he urinates on glands on the insides of his back legs and rubs the glands together. Urine dripping from the glands leaves the buck's scent on the scrape. Among whitetails, does come looking for bucks when they're ready for mating, and the scrape gives them both visual and olfactory means for locating a suitable Romeo.

As a buck makes a scrape, he also reaches up and pulls at a twig above the scrape with his mouth. Most observers believe he does this to leave scent on the branch from glands at the corners of his eyes and on his forehead. In most cases, you'll find the broken twig hanging down, but it may be broken off completely and you see just the broken stub. Rarely will you find scrapes that don't have a branch overhead.

With experience you learn to spot potential scrape sites from a distance. In hilly terrain, bucks make scrapes on trails, abandoned

Buck scrapes are commonly made along trails and other frequently traveled deer routes. This fresh scrape indicates the presence of a buck, although it's not necessarily a good place for a stand because it's not a primary scrape.

roads, flat points off ridgetops or at the edges of fields — likely travel for does. As soon as you see a characteristic flat spot with a branch four to five feet above it, you instinctively recognize it as a probable scrape site, and you check it out. There may be none, but in many cases you'll be right.

During the courtship period, does will urinate in these scrapes, and as a buck scent-checks his scrape line, he'll smell the doe and start trailing her. The doe isn't yet ready to breed so she generally runs from the buck, and a courtship chase ensues as he follows a hundred yards or so behind, nose to the ground, tail in the air like a bird dog hot on a pheasant track. When they're hot after does, bucks often make a low but clearly audible piglike grunt.

During these chases bucks become more visible than normal and they lose some of their caution. One day a friend and I saw a doe bounding across a soybean field. This was mid-morning, so she obviously wasn't just feeding out there. Pretty soon another deer appeared behind her, and even though we couldn't see his antlers (they weren't very big) we knew instantly it was a buck by his "birdy" actions.

The doe passed by us some 300 yards away, and we knew the buck would follow, so we ran pell-mell up a creek bottom and took makeshift stands where the doe had crossed. Not two minutes later we heard the buck's distinctive "oink, oink," and soon he bounded from a brushy fencerow and trotted along an open path where the doe had gone. He stopped 10 yards from me to sniff the ground and that's where he met his Waterloo. When my arrow hit him, he ran 50 yards and piled up.

Breeding Period. Following about a month of scraping and courting, the actual breeding period begins. That's when does come into estrus and are receptive for mating. When a doe comes into heat, she no longer runs from courting bucks and she'll pair off with the buck of her choice. The actual estrus period lasts less than 24 hours, but a buck and doe will stay together, possibly several days, until the doe is ready and mating takes place. Then the buck returns to his scrapes, looking for another doe. All bucks will court does, but in areas with a good supply of mature bucks, does will reject smaller bucks and dominant bucks will do a majority of the tending and breeding. Most of the does come into heat and are bred within a two-week period.

Fall Calendar. As a general rule throughout the United States and Canada, bucks shed the velvet off their antlers the first week or so in September, and the sparring phase lasts from then until about October 15. Then bucks start scraping and chasing does, and the courtship phase continues for about a month until November 15. That's when does start coming into estrus, and the primary breeding period lasts roughly from November 15 through 30. Secondary estrus cycles occur through December or longer.

This calendar holds true for the majority of whitetail range, although timing in certain regions diverges for various reasons. In south Texas, for example, the rut peaks about a month later, and in Alabama, where deer have

A friend and I saw this buck coming in hot pursuit of a doe, so we ran to intercept him. The rut obviously can work in your favor.

In their thick-cover homes, whitetails have the advantage over hunters moving on foot. Chances of spotting a buck in this jungle before he spots you, and then making a clean shot, are slim. That's why the stand hunter, waiting for the buck to come to him, has an immeasurable advantage.

been stocked from various regions around the country, the timing varies by a month or more from one section of the state to another.

Stand Hunting

Without question, tree stands offer the surest way to kill whitetails. Surveys in the East show that 80 percent of the deer are taken by tree-stand hunters, and the bow-and-arrow shooting distance averages just under 20 yards. On foot, hunters simply can't consistently see deer before the deer see them. In the Arkansas Ozarks, for example, friends and I were hunting a wooded ridge. We found several scrapes there on an abandoned trail, and even in the deep oak leaves on the ground I could see pock marks that indicated the passing of many deer hooves.

But after three days of still-hunting there, I'd have sworn not a single deer lived on that ridge. I never saw an animal. Then I put up a tree stand, and the first night I saw seven deer, including three bucks.

This isn't to say tree stands are the only way to hunt whitetails, because other methods might work better under some circumstances.

Nevertheless, they generally are most effective, and serious whitetail hunters use tree stands, or other elevated stands, almost universally. (For details, see Stand Hunting.)

Stand Hunting Before and After the Rut. In early fall, during the sparring period (before scrapes are made), and again after the rut when deer return to a normal lifestyle, stands are placed along trails leading to and from bedding areas.

As you scout, don't just look for sign but analyze your country to determine where deer feed and bed. They'll make regular daily movements between these locations, moving in the evening from dense-cover, daytime beds to fields or other feeding grounds where they'll stay all night. Then in the morning they'll move from open feeding areas back to daytime beds. Your assignment as a hunter is to waylay them somewhere along these routes.

If you've seen deer feeding in certain fields in late summer, you might be tempted to place your stands there. In September when deer remain fairly active, that might work. (For details on seasonal activity, see Weather.) But by late September and into October, whitetail activity diminishes and your chances for catching bucks on feeding grounds in daylight are slim. Jim Martin, a successful whitetail hunter in Missouri, said, "I want to be back on trails at least 200 yards in the woods. Deer will meander along in the woods until dark. I've seen them do it lots of times. If you're on the edge of a field, you'll never see the big bucks. It's not that they aren't moving early enough. They are. They just hang back in the woods, piddling around until dark."

Most whitetail hunters prefer evenings to mornings for stand hunting. Surveys by a group of avid hunters called the Stump Sitters showed that deer sightings from evening stands far outnumbered those from morning stands. Regardless of whether you hunt mornings or evenings, you might have to adjust stand location to catch moving deer. The later they come out in the evening or the earlier they return to beds in the morning, the closer your stand must be to bedding areas. You can dust out trails and study tracks to gauge when animals are passing. Some hunters set electronic timing devices on trails to analyze the timing of animals' movements.

Remember, also, that big bucks are creatures unto themselves, and they won't necessarily follow the well-used trails of does and young bucks. While you're watching like a hawk over a well-beat trail, a big buck could be sneaking by 50 yards behind you. If tracks and rubs indicate the presence of a big buck, but you never see him, analyze to see if he's furtively bypassing you, taking a less obvious route in heavy cover, as you watch a parade of does come down the thoroughfare.

Stand Hunting Over Scrapes. About October 15 bucks start making scrapes, and many hunters consider that the time to hunt big whitetails. Not only do bucks become more active then, which makes them more visible, but the scrapes they make serve as a guide to stand location.

That doesn't mean a stand overlooking just any scrape will produce a deer. You must distinguish productive scrapes from nonproduc-

tive. At first, bucks scrape the ground randomly wherever they may be when they're feeling "horny," and they'll rarely, if ever, return to most of these scrapes. Hunters give these scrapes various names—secondary, tertiary, boundary, transient, hoof, and so forth. Like rubs, they indicate the presence of bucks, but they probably aren't good places for stands.

Eventually the mature bucks in an area will establish scrape lines, and bucks—and does—will return to particular scrapes over and over. Many hunters call these primary scrapes. You'll recognize primary scrapes by their heavily used appearance and possibly by their "deery" smell. Well-beat trails will lead to them. More than one buck could be using this site, and primary scrapes become the local hangout for bucks and does looking for some action. Some hunting parties have killed several bucks in one season off one primary scrape. The number of bucks using one primary scrape probably depends a great deal on deer densities.

If you're new to whitetail hunting, you might be tempted to put a stand over the first hot scrape you find and sit right there. That could work great, but give stand location some thought first. You must be downwind from the scrape, and you should plan your approach so you come in from a downwind direction and don't have to cross the deers' approach trails on the way to your stand.

If you take a stand there several days and never see the bucks you know are present, analyze the situation. Make sure deer are using the scrape. If you kick leaves onto it when you leave and the leaves are cleaned out when you return, you know a buck has been there. That means he's coming in when you're not there. If he's checking it at night, you might have to move your stand out along one of his trails to intercept him during daylight hours.

Also, remember a buck doesn't have to walk right up to a scrape to tell if a doe has been there. He can smell her sign from some distance, and he might scent-check the scrape from downwind and walk right on by. If you hear deer go by but never see them, move your stand 50 yards or more downwind of the scrape to ambush these unseen animals.

Scents. Scents are covered under another section (for details, see Scents), but they deserve special mention here, because doe in heat–type lures are most commonly used in relation to scrape hunting. Some hunters swear by them.

Jim Martin, the Missouri bowhunter mentioned earlier, is one who does. Martin wears rubber boots going to and from his stand and he showers regularly and washes his clothes with nonscented soap to reduce his own odor to a minimum. With that precaution (so human odor doesn't negate the buck scent), he believes buck lures work very well. One morning Martin put some Indian Buck Lure on his boots and pants cuffs and walked to his stand. Not long after he got situated, a doe came trotting along and an eight-point buck followed hot on her trail. When the buck hit Martin's trail, the deer stopped instantly and turned off the doe's trail to follow Martin's footsteps right to the hunter's stand. That turned out to be a fatal mistake.

As many hunters do, Martin commonly puts deer lure on cotton and seals it in a 35mm film canister. When he goes to his stand he opens the canister and sets it near the scrape just to enhance the buck-attracting aroma of the scrape a little.

In areas where he plans to hunt one scrape regularly, Martin employs a more refined technique, using a hospital IV (intravenous) unit, which consists of a plastic bag and a drip tube. He pours a bottle of doe-in-heat scent into the bag and dilutes it two to one with water to make it last longer. Then he hangs the bag on a limb over the scrape and turns on the nozzle so it drips very slowly. The constant dripping keeps the scrape fresh with hot scent. Units similar to the IV, such as Tink's Sky Skrape, are available commercially.

Mock Scrapes. Martin also uses the drip bag to help create new scrapes. These are commonly called mock scrapes, and they're used if

Jim Martin uses a hospital IV unit to slowly drip doe-in-heat lure onto a scrape. Here he regulates the valve to get just the right drip rate.

you can't find a scrape in a good place for a stand. For example, in one case Martin found a line of scrapes, but they were surrounded by small trees, nothing big enough for a tree stand. There were some big trees not far away, so Martin created a mock scrape within bow range of a big tree where he could place his stand. A couple of evenings later, Martin had three bucks come into that mock scrape at one time, and bucks continually pawed it up and refreshened it. Martin has had similar results at other mock scrapes.

To make a scrape he uses a stick to "paw" the ground clear as a buck might do. He always creates the scrape under an overhanging limb, or if he can't find a site with a suitable limb, he cuts the overhanging limb from a buck's scrape and tapes it over his mock scrape. Then he hangs an IV unit full of buck lure above the

Mock scrapes can be effective medicine for white-tails. If a buck won't make a scrape where you want one, then you make one for him.

scrape, turns on the nozzle and he's got an instant primary scrape. He also may destroy the buck's other scrapes by cutting off the branches above them. Without the branches, the bucks will abandon the scrapes.

Other Methods

Rattling. During the courting and breeding phases of the rut, bucks often fight, and sounds of buck fights often attract other bucks. Bucks most likely come to these fights either to defend their territories, or to claim hot does the other bucks are fighting over. Whatever the reasons, bucks do come to rattled antlers. Used at the right time, rattling can be a deadly way to fool big whitetail bucks. (For details, see Rattling.)

Calling. Whitetails make a number of sounds that can be used to your advantage in hunting, and calling can be an effective way to

hunt whitetails under the right conditions. (For details, see Deer Calling.)

Still-Hunting. Tommy Mills, from Rogers, Arkansas, killed 23 whitetails in his first ten years of bowhunting, all by still-hunting in the oak-hickory forests of the Ozarks. I've used still-hunting successfully in hunting whitetails of the Western conifer forests. (For details, see Still-Hunting.)

Stalking. Hunting primarily in the West, I've also successfully spotted whitetails from a distance and stalked them. Rarely is spotting associated with whitetail hunting, and some hunters infer from that that whitetails are too sneaky and can't be seen from a distance. That's not true. It does hold in many places because whitetails, as a general rule, live in flat country or bottomlands where you simply can't get a good vantage to see into their homes.

But hunting in Idaho and Montana, where steep hillsides allow spotting from one side of

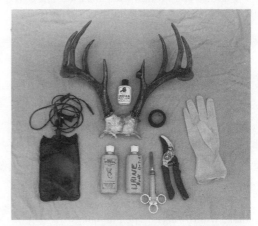

Here are a few tools of the whitetail-deer hunting trade. The IV unit at left is used to freshen a scrape, either one made by a buck or a mock scrape. The Deer Insurance is used as a coverup scent, and the Indian Buck Lure and deer urine are used as attractors. The hypodermic needle is used to extract urine from a deer's bladder. Nippers are used to prune limbs for use above mock scrapes, and the tape is used to tape the limbs in place above the scrapes. The rubber gloves are worn to retard human scent while working on a scrape.

a canyon or ravine to the other, I've spotted dozens of whitetails and have stalked them just as I would mule deer, and I've talked to hunters who've done the same thing in Wyoming's Black Hills. In hardwood forests of the Midwest and East, spotting during the early season can be tough, but from November on, after leaves have fallen from the trees, I believe spotting could work in any hilly to mountainous terrain. (For details, see Spotting, and Stalking.)

Driving. Particularly during times when deer are brushed up and not moving, driving may be the only method that will stir up some action. Generally this method hasn't been as popular with archers as rifle hunters, because driven deer may be moving and present tough bow shots. Nevertheless, done in the right way, driving can be deadly for whitetails. (For details, see Driving.)

WILD BOAR   See Pig.

WISCONSIN   Wisconsin has a total area of 56,154 square miles. The hilly northern forest region, covering the northern one third of the state, has vast forests with lakes and streams. The central forest region is much flatter, and vegetation consists of jack pine, scrub oak, and aspens. Throughout these regions, which collectively cover the northern two thirds of the state, federal, state, and county forests provide vast public hunting. Most of the land in the southern third of Wisconsin is privately owned.

Big Game

Whitetail Deer. Wisconsin has about 850,000 whitetail deer. It's one of the major bowhunting states, and nearly 200,000 archers hunt deer in the state each year. The average bow kill has been 25,000 deer (10,000 bucks, 15,000 does) but it has soared well over 30,000 some years. Bowhunters have an average success rate of 10 percent, with a high of 17 percent. The bow season is open statewide from mid-September until mid-November. It closes

during the gun season, but then it opens again during December.

Throughout the northern forest zone, deer densities vary according to local habitat types. Severe winters can take a heavy toll on deer in this northern region, so deer numbers fluctuate more than they do farther south. Large roadless blocks of land offer backcountry hunting along the Minnesota border and near Lake Superior. Some big bucks come from this region. The central region supports high numbers of deer, and this region does not suffer the severe winters that plague the northern forests, so deer numbers are more stable. Given good numbers of deer and good public access, this region is popular with hunters.

The southwest corner consists of breaks and deep valleys associated with the Mississippi River. A mix of farms and woodlands supports very high densities of deer. The southeast corner is the most intensively farmed section of Wisconsin. Deer numbers are moderate, and high human population is high, so hunting is more restricted here than elsewhere in the state.

Wisconsin traditionally has ranked among the top three trophy whitetail states and provinces. Many of the bigger bucks come from the northern forest region, where hunting pressure is lightest, and from the productive southwest corner. The Boone and Crockett world-record whitetail of 206⅛ was killed in northwest Wisconsin close to the Minnesota border in 1914. The state record nontypical buck scored 245. Bowhunters have taken many record-book bucks, and many big bucks have been taken in recent years.

Bears. Wisconsin has some of the best bear hunting east of the Mississippi River. Baiting is allowed, although some restrictions are in effect. Wisconsin has produced some very large bears, including a 700-pounder killed by Bob Faufau in 1981, which scored 21¹⁴/₁₆. The bow season for bears runs from mid-September into November.

Other Game

Turkey hunting is limited, and most turkeys live in the southwest along the Mississippi

River. Abundant small game includes squirrels, cottontail rabbits, and snowshoe hares.

Contact. Department of Natural Resources, Bureau of Wildlife Management, Box 7921, Madison, WI 53707.

WOODCHUCK See Marmot.

WRIST SLING To shoot accurately, you must maintain a relaxed bow hand (see Shooting Basics), but in doing that you may develop the habit of grabbing your bow as you release the string, which can throw off a shot, or you may drop the bow occasionally. In practicing with a sensitive mechanical release, I've dropped my bow more than once when the release aid went off unexpectedly.

A wrist sling allows you to keep your bow hand relaxed without fear of dropping the bow. This simple strap attaches to the bow handle and loops around your wrist as you shoot. The purpose is strictly to prevent your dropping the bow. The sling should remain loose; it should not bind your hand as you shoot.

You might consider a wrist sling superfluous baggage for the one or two shots you'll take at

A wrist sling can be an invaluable aid in shooting practice. It allows you to relax your bow hand without fear of dropping the bow. The sling should not be tight on your wrist. Its only purpose is to catch an accidentally dropped bow.

deer each fall, but it can help immeasurably as you practice form on the target range. And the form you develop there dictates how you'll shoot in the field. For that reason, a wrist sling can be a valuable aid for the hunting archer.

WYOMING Wyoming covers an area of 97,914 square miles. In the Black Hills region, and throughout the major mountain chains at the western end of the state, national forestland provides several million acres of public hunting. The Bureau of Land Management administers lands throughout the state, and these hold some good hunting, but much of the eastern half of the state is privately owned, and many landowners charge trespass fees. The land situation is particularly tight in the northeast corner. Wyoming has a law that says nonresidents can't hunt in designated wilderness areas unless they're accompanied by a guide. So if you plan to hunt on your own, make sure it's not in designated wilderness.

Big Game

Deer. An estimated 60,000 whitetail deer live in the northeastern quarter of the state, and roughly 400,000 mule deer live throughout the state. About 5,500 bowhunters kill an average of 800 deer each year for a success rate of about 15 percent. Bow seasons in many units are open the two weeks preceding general rifle seasons. That puts them primarily in September, although in some units, the bow season is open the entire month of September.

Wyoming has excellent whitetail hunting, particularly in the Black Hills in the northeast corner. The foothills of the Bighorn Mountains have lots of whitetails, but most of the land is private there, and getting permission to hunt can be tough.

Mule-deer hunting is good throughout the state. The prairies and breaks have lots of deer, but they're not particularly famous for huge bucks. The Bighorn Mountains are one of Wyoming's "deer factories," but the Wind River Range, once famous for big bucks, now has few deer.

Wyoming ranks among the top elk states. Thousands of elk winter at the National Elk Refuge near Jackson, Wyoming.

The Wyoming Range and Salt River Range south of Afton probably have the best mule-deer hunting today. Several Boone and Crockett bucks have been taken here. The Gros Ventre Range just to the north offers good hunting for record-class bucks, too. The number 2 Boone and Crockett typical mule deer with a score of 217 came from Hoback Canyon near Jackson. The largest nontypical from Wyoming scored 292⅝. Most record-book heads have come from mountains along the western border.

Elk. Wyoming ranks among the best elk states. Total annual harvest runs about 15,000 (a very small part of that is taken by bowhunters). The wilderness regions around Jackson and west of Cody have high numbers of elk and trophy bulls. The Wyoming and Salt River ranges also have good all-around hunting. The mountains of the southeast have plenty of elk, but they're fairly heavily hunted, so trophy potential is lower than in the remote western mountains. Virtually all the best elk hunting takes place on public lands, and bugling seasons are held in most ranges.

Antelope. Antelope have contributed heavily to Wyoming's reputation for big-game hunting. These animals are abundant everywhere except in the forested mountains. During good years, a hunter could shoot up to five antelope. Generous bow seasons take place primarily in September.

Bears. Hunting for black bears is good in most of the forest ranges. Some very large bears are taken in the Bighorn Mountains. Baiting is legal, but hunting with hounds is not. Both spring and fall seasons are held.

Moose. Wyoming offers a generous number of permits each year for Shiras moose, and most of the Shiras moose in the record books have come from Wyoming. (For more details, see Moose.)

Sheep. Bighorns are fairly abundant in most of the rugged western mountain ranges. Drawing a tag is the hard part. Also, most sheep live in wilderness areas, so you must hire a guide to hunt them legally.

Goats. A limited number of tags are issued, but Wyoming isn't one of the better goat states.

Mountain Lions. The harvest on these animals has been very restricted, but where hunting is allowed, some very large cats have been taken. The Bighorn Mountains is one of the best regions.

Other Game

Turkey hunting has become outstanding, particularly in the northeast. Much of the better hunting takes place on private land. Like all Western states, Wyoming has endless hunting opportunities for coyotes and other predators, and for small game like jackrabbits, cottontails, and prairie dogs.

Contact. Wyoming Game and Fish Department, 5400 Bishop Boulevard, Cheyenne, WY 82002.

Y

YUKON This province bordering Alaska covers more than 207,000 square miles.

Big Game

Moose. Record books consider moose from the Yukon as Alaska-Yukon moose, the largest members of the deer family on earth. Most moose in this category listed by Boone and Crockett come from Alaska, but the Yukon makes a fair showing, too. Moose live throughout the territory.

Caribou. North of the Yukon River, caribou are classified as barren ground caribou, and south they're considered mountain caribou. Barren ground generally have larger antlers. Caribou live throughout the Yukon in tundra areas, either above timberline in the many mountain ranges, or north of the tree line on the Arctic Coast. The famous Porcupine caribou herd migrates into the Yukon.

Sheep. Dall sheep predominate in this province, and the record books list a number of Dalls taken in Yukon. Stone sheep live in the mountains in the southern end near the British Columbia border, but far more Stone sheep are taken in B.C. Boone and Crockett lists very few Stone sheep from the Yukon.

Mountain Goats. These animals live in mountains of the southern province, commonly in the same general areas as Stone sheep, but the Yukon isn't a major goat-producing province.

Bears. The Yukon has good grizzly and black-bear hunting, although it's not noted for record-book animals.

Other Game. Wolves and wolverines are also common. This province has virtually no deer.

Contact. Department of Renewable Resources, Box 2703, Whitehorse, Yukon, Canada Y1A-2C6.

Archery Manufacturers

Accra 300
805 South 11th Street
Broken Arrow, OK 74012
(918) 251-7471

Acme Wood Products Company
P.O. Box 636
Myrtle Point, OR 97458
(503) 572-2353

Amacker Products, Inc.
602 Kimbrough Drive
P.O. Box 1432
Tallulah, LA 71282
(800) 228-4846

American Archery
American Archery Lane
P.O. Box 200
Florence, WI 54121
(715) 528-3000

Anderson Designs, Inc.
P.O. Box 605
Gladstone, NJ 07934
(201) 234-0123

Arizona Archery Enterprises
P.O. Box 25387
Prescott Valley, AZ 86312
(602) 772-9887

Barner Release Company
Timeless Archery Products
216 S. Alma School Road, #14
Mesa, AZ 85202
(602) 844-2138

Barnett International, Inc.
P.O. Box 934
Odessa, FL 33556
(813) 920-2241

Bear Archery
Rural Route 4
4600 Southwest 41st Blvd.
Gainesville, FL 32601
(904) 376-2327

Bighorn Bowhunting Company
1340 Factory Circle
Ft. Lupton, CO 80621
(303) 659-0077

Bob Kirschner Deer Lure Company
5050 Mamont Road
Murrysville, PA 15668
(412) 325-2496

Bohning Company, Ltd.
7361 North Seven Mile Road
Lake City, MI 49651-9379
(616) 229-4247

Browning
Route One
Morgan, UT 84050
(801) 876-2711

Brunton/Lakota
620 E. Monroe
Riverton, WY 82501
(307) 856-6559

Buck Stop Lure Company
P.O. Box 636
Stanton, MI 48888
(517) 762-5091

Bushnell/Bausch & Lomb
300 North Lone Hill Avenue
San Dimas, CA 91773
(714) 592-8000

Camo Clan Corporation
3011 Main Street
Dallas, TX 75226
(214) 742-9260
(800) 344-7716

Cavalier Equipment Company
1849 West 3rd Place
Mesa, AZ 85201
(602) 898-1424

Century/Primus
P.O. Box 188
Cherry Valley, IL 61016
(815) 332-4951

Coleman Company, Inc.
250 North St. Francis
Wichita, KS 67202
(316) 261-3316

Columbia Sportswear Company
P.O. Box 03239
6600 N. Baltimore
Portland, OR 97203
(503) 286-3676
(800) 547-8066

Coverup Products
G&R Trophy Products, Inc.
Rt.1, Box 66
Hill City, KS 67642
(913) 674-5503

Custom Chronograph, Inc.
Route 1, Box 98-T
Brewster, WA 98812
(509) 689-2004

Darton Archery
3261 Flushing Road
P.O. Box 4340
Flint, MI 48504
(313) 239-7361

Deer Insurance Coverup
920 E. Lexington
Independence, MO 64050
(816) 461-8351

Dyna Vane Inc.
P.O. Box 3369
Des Moines, IA 50316
(515) 243-2904

Early Winters, Ltd.
110 Prefontaine Place South
Seattle, WA 98104
(206) 624-5599

Easton Aluminum, Inc.
7800 Haskell Avenue
Van Nuys, CA 91406
(818) 782-6445

Fine-Line, Inc.
1220 164th Street E.
Puyallup, WA 98374
(206) 848-4222

Flex-Fletch Products
1340 Chandler Avenue
St. Paul, MN 55113
(612) 488-4948

Foam Experts
696 ½ Grove Street
Redding, CA 96002
(916) 221-0311

Frontier Archery Company, Inc.
9777 Business Park Drive
Sacramento, CA 95827
(916) 362-1332

The Game Tracker
3476 Eastman Drive
Flushing, MI 48433
(800) 241-4833

Golden Eagle Archery
104 South Mill Street
P.O. Box 310
Creswell, OR 97426
(503) 895-3371

Golden Key Futura, Inc.
14090-6100 Road
Montrose, CO 81401
(303) 249-6700

Hoyt/Easton Archery Co., Inc.
605 N. Donald Doublas Road
Salt Lake City, UT 84116-2881
(801) 537-1389

Indian Buck Lure
Pete Rickard, Inc.
Cobleskill, NY 12043
(518) 234-2731

Indian Industries, Inc.
817 Maxwell Avenue
Evansville, IN 47717
(812) 426-2281

Jennings by Bear
P.O. Box 1750
Gainesville, FL 32601
(904) 376-2327

Jim Dougherty Archery
Bowhunting Equipment Distributors
4304 East Pine Place
Tulsa, OK 74115
(918) 622-9516

JVA Astro
Highway 16 & N. Kinney Road
Onalaska, WI 54650
(608) 783-2889

Kelty Pack, Inc.
P.O. Box 7048-A
St. Louis, MO 63177
(314) 576-3476

Lightning Nuggets
Washington Lightning Stixs
403 Main, Box 928
Davenport, WA 99122
(509) 725-6211

L.L. Bean, Inc.
Freeport, ME 04033-0001
(800) 341-4341

Martin Archery, Inc.
Route 5, Box 127
Walla Walla, WA 99362
(509) 529-2554

Mountain House
Oregon Freeze Dried Foods
P.O. Box 1048
Albany, OR 97321
(503) 926-6001

Mountain Safety Research
P.O. Box 3978, Terminal Station
Seattle, WA 98124
(206) 624-7048

Mountain Scent and Bugle Manufacturing
P.O. Box 545
Stevensville, MT 59870
(406) 777-3920

Muzzy Products, Corp.
3705 S.W. 42nd Place
Gainesville, FL 32608
(904) 372-5943

New Archery Products, Inc.
6415 Stanley Avenue
Berwyn, IL 60402
(312) 795-6160

Nirk Archery Company
Potlatch, ID 83855
(208) 875-0808

The North Face
999 Harrison Street
Berkeley, CA 94710
(415) 548-1371

Pearson
P.O. Box 7465
Pine Bluff, AR 71611
(501) 534-6411

Posi-Nok
3505 E. 39th Avenue
Denver, CO 80205

Precision Shooting Equipment, Inc.
P.O. Box 5487
Tucson, AZ 85703
(602) 884-9065

Pro Line Company
1675 Gun Lake Road
Hastings, MI 49058
(616) 948-8026

Rancho Safari (Cat Quiver)
P.O. Box 691
Ramona, CA 92065
(619) 789-2094

Ranging, Inc.
Routes 5 & 20
East Bloomfield, NY 14443
(716) 657-6161

Rattlin' Horns
P.O. Box 1035
Lufkin, TX 75901
(409) 875-4676

Richmoor Corp.
Box 2728
Van Nuys, CA 91494
(818) 787-2510

Sagittarius, Inc.
9030 Carroll Way #5
San Diego, CA 92121
(619) 566-6290

St. Charles Quiver
Northwest Archery Company
19807 First Avenue South
Seattle, WA 98148-2493
(206) 878-7300

Saunders Archery Co.
P.O. Box 476
Columbus, NE 68601
(402) 564-7176
(800) 228-1408

Scotch Game Call Co.
60 Main Street
Oakfield, NY 14125
(716) 757-9958

Stanley Hips Targets
17499 Blanco Road
San Antonio, TX 78232
(512) 492-4675

Stemmler Archery, Inc.
984 Southford Road
Middlebury, CT 06762
(203) 758-2727

Sure-Stop Manufacturing
1233 Junction Street
Wausau, WI 54401
(715) 848-3320

Sweetland Products
1010 Arrowsmith Street
Eugene, OR 97402
(503) 345-0928

Therm-A-Rest
Cascade Designs, Inc.
4000 1st Avenue South
Seattle, WA 98134
(206) 583-0583

Tink's Safariland Hunting Corp.
P.O. Box NN
McLean, VA 22101
(703) 356-1997

Total Shooting Systems, Inc.
390 Rolling Meadows Drive
Fond du Lac, WI 54935
(414) 922-3890

TruAngle Hones
R.R. 3
Wabash, IN 46992
(219) 563-8160

Tru-Fire Corporation
732 State Street
North Fond Du Lac, WI 54935
(414) 923-6866

Vector (Lowe Alpine Systems, Inc.)
P.O. Box 444
Lafayette, CO 80026
(303) 665-9220

Wayne Carlton's Hunting Accessories
P.O. Box 1746
Montrose, CO 81402
(303) 249-8456

Wilderness Sound Productions
1105 Main
Springfield, OR 97477
(503) 741-0263

Winona Camo System
827 E. 5th Street
Winona, MN 55987
(507) 452-3966

York Archery
P.O. Box 110
Independence, MO 64051
(816) 252-9612

Zeiss Optical Inc.
P.O. Box 2010
Petersburg, VA 23804
(804) 861-0033
(800) 446-1807

Zwickey Archery, Inc.
2571 E. 12th Avenue
North St. Paul, MN 55109
(612) 777-1965

Index

569